T0235352

Communications
in Computer and Information Science 538

Commenced Publication in 2007
Founding and Former Series Editors:
Alfredo Cuzzocrea, Dominik Ślęzak, and Xiaokang Yang

More information about this series at http://www.springer.com/series/7899

Giedre Dregvaite · Robertas Damasevicius (Eds.)

Information and Software Technologies

21st International Conference, ICIST 2015
Druskininkai, Lithuania, October 15–16, 2015
Proceedings

 Springer

Editors
Giedre Dregvaite
Kaunas University of Technology
Kaunas
Lithuania

Robertas Damasevicius
Kaunas University of Technology
Kaunas
Lithuania

ISSN 1865-0929   ISSN 1865-0937 (electronic)
Communications in Computer and Information Science
ISBN 978-3-319-24769-4   ISBN 978-3-319-24770-0 (eBook)
DOI 10.1007/978-3-319-24770-0

Printed on acid-free paper

Springer International Publishing AG Switzerland is part of Springer Science+Business Media (www.springer.com)

Preface

We are pleased to introduce to scholars and researchers the selection of papers presented during the International Conference, on Information and Software Technologies – ICIST 2015. This year the ICIST conference, formerly known as the IT Conference, welcomed scholars from all over the world for the 21st time.

In 2012 the proceedings of the conference were published by Springer for the first time, marking a new qualitative step. This volume of the *Communications in Computer and Information Science* series signifies our continuing cooperation, which we are proud of.

The change of the venue of the conference from the second largest city Kaunas to one of the resorts of Lithuania, Druskininkai, resulted in making the event even more attractive to scholars from Western Europe. Moreover, the scope and topics of the conference were also reconsidered to rely on developing fields of information technology the most. Therefore, the topics this year were modified to encourage the submission of papers in the fields of information systems, business intelligence for information and software systems, software engineering, and IT applications. These themes have definitely become indistinguishable objects of discussion in society encouraging researchers to develop interdisciplinary approaches and employ multivariate ways of thinking and analysis. On the other hand, scientific innovation is no longer an issue of academia only, hence the attempt to integrate science into business is also of importance. The organizers of the conference also aimed to promote a link between researchers and industry representatives to foster the development and application of new supporting information technology means. As a result, participants of the conference were also encouraged to take part in both the research sessions and the industrial tutorials on sophisticated technologies that influence to business development as well as consumers' impact on the mentioned development discussed by well-known practitioners. The event was co-located with the conference for the fifth year in a row.

There were 125 submissions this year, and 51 paper were selected for this publication. The number of Program Committee members also increased this year, which reflects the growing attention aimed at improving the quality of submissions and of those accepted for publication afterwards. The papers were reviewed and selected by the Program Committee consisting of 89 reviewers (supported by 62 additional reviewers) representing more than 50 academic institutions. Each submission was reviewed following the double-blind process by at least two reviewers, while borderline papers were evaluated by three or more reviewers. We believe the selection of 51 accepted papers presented in this book is a good reflection of the latest research on the selected topics.

Finally, we would like to express our gratitude to the Lithuanian State Science and Studies Foundation and the Faculty of Informatics of Kaunas University of Technology, whose support made this event and this book possible.

July 2014

Giedre Dregvaite
Robertas Damasevicius

Organization

The 21st International Conference on Information and Software Technologies (ICIST 2015) was organized by Kaunas University of Technology and took place in Druskininkai, Lithuania (October 15–16, 2015).

General Chair

Eduardas Bareisa   Kaunas University of Technology, Lithuania

Local Organizing Committee

Giedre Dregvaite (Chair)	Kaunas University of Technology, Lithuania
Gintare Dzindzeletaite	Kaunas University of Technology, Lithuania
Romas Slezevicius	Kaunas University of Technology, Lithuania
Lina Repsiene	Kaunas University of Technology, Lithuania
Mindaugas Vasiljevas	Kaunas University of Technology, Lithuania
Kestutis Valincius	Kaunas University of Technology, Lithuania

Special Section Chairs

Irene Krebs	University of Technology Cottbus, Germany
Marcin Woznak	Silesian University of Technology, Poland
Danguole Rutkauskiene	Kaunas University of Technology, Lithuania
Ondrej Krejcar	University of Hradec Kralove, Czech Republic
Marek Krasinski	Wroclaw University of Economics, Poland
Rolf Engelbrecht	ProRec Germany, Germany
Justyna Patalas-Maliszewska	University of Zielona Gora, Poland
Emiliano Tramontana	University of Catania, Italy
Grzegorz Borowik	Warsaw University of Technology, Poland
Radu Adrian Vasiu	Politechnica University of Timisoara, Romania
Hana Mohelska	University of Hradec Kralove, Czech Republic
Pavel Bachmann	University of Hradec Kralove, Czech Republic
Vytenis Punys	Kaunas University of Technology, Lithuania
Giedrius Vanagas	Lithuanian University of Health Sciences, Lithuania

Program Committee

Lina Nemuraite	Kaunas University of Technology, Lithuania
Olga Kurasova	Vilnius University, Lithuania
Jurgita Kapociute-Dzikiene	Vytautas Magnus University, Lithuania
Yuh-Min Tseng	National Changhua University of Education, Taiwan
Irene Krebs	University of Technology Cottbus, Germany

Constantine Filote	Stefan cel Mare University of Suceava, Romania
Jose Luis Herrero Agustin	University of Extremadura, Spain
Massimo Tivoli	University of L'Aquila, Italy
Vladimir Hahanov	Kharkov National University of Radio Electronics, Ukraine
Yuko Murayama	Iwate Prefectural University, Japan
Ivana Podnar Žarko	University of Zagreb, Croatia
Graziano Pravadelli	University of Verona, Italy
Sevinc Gulsecen	Istanbul University, Turkey
Marisa Gil	Polytechnic University of Catalonia, Spain
Achim Schmidtmann	Dortmund University of Applied Sciences and Arts, Germany
Mehmet Aksit	University of Twente, The Netherlands
Saulius Gudas	Vilnius University, Lithuania
Sanda Martinčić-Ipšić	University of Rijeka, Croatia
José Raúl Romero	University of Córdoba, Spain
Milena Krumova	Technical University of Sofia, Bulgaria
Marite Kirikova	Riga Technical University, Latvia
Mirjana Ivanovic	University of Novi Sad, Serbia
Alvydas Jaliniauskas	SubscriberMail, A Harland Clarke Company, USA
Raimundas Jasinevicius	Kaunas University of Technology, Lithuania
Damjan Vavpotič	University of Ljubljana, Slovenia
Sandro Leuchter	Rhine-Waal University of Applied Sciences, Germany
Martin Gaedke	Technical University of Chemnitz, Germany
John Gammack	College of Technological Innovation, United Arab Emirates
Paulo Rupino Cunha	University of Coimbra, Portugal
Jyrki Nummenmaa	University of Tampere, Finland
Björn W. Schuller	University of Passau, Germany
Nuno Castela	Polytechnic Institute of Castelo Branco, Portugal
Algirdas Pakstas	London Metropolitan University, UK
Marcin Paprzycki	Systems Research Institute, Polish Academy of Science, Poland
Stefano Squartini	Polytechnic University of Marche, Italy
Henrikas Pranevicius	Kaunas University of Technology, Lithuania
Janis Grabis	Riga Technical University, Latvia
Marite Kirikova	Riga Technical University, Latvia
Ana Paula Neves Ferreira da Silva	University of Coimbra, Portugal
Tor-Morten Grønli	Brunel University, Norway
Christophoros Nikou	University of Ioannina, Greece
Elena Sánchez Nielsen	University of San Fernando de la Laguna, Spain
Vira Shendryk	Sumy State University, Ukraine
André Schekelmann	Niederrhein University of Applied Science, Germany
Oleg Zabolotnyi	Lutsk National Technical University, Ukraine
Harri Oinas-Kukkonen	University of Oulu, Finland

Virgilijus Sakalauskas	Vilnius University, Lithuania
Dalia Kriksciuniene	Vilnius University, Lithuania
Audrius Lopata	Vilnius University, Lithuania
Aleksandras Targamadze	Kaunas University of Technology, Lithuania
Laimutis Telksnys	Vilnius University, Lithuania
Peter Thanisch	University of Tampere, Finland
Lovro Šubelj	University of Ljubljana, Slovenia
Karin Harbusch	University of Koblenz-Landau, Germany
Joao Manuel R.S. Tavares	University of Porto, Portugal
Winfried Lamersdorf	University of Hamburg, Germany
Ernest Teniente	Polytechnic University of Catalonia, Spain
Marco Bajec	University of Ljubljana, Slovenia
Zakaria Maamar	Zayed University, United Arab Emirates
Juan Manuel Vara Mesa	University of Rey Juan Carlos, Spain
Kari Smolander	Lappeenranta University of Technology, Finland
Alexander Maedche	University of Mannheim, Germany
Ljupcho Antovski	University of Ss. Cyril and Methodius, Macedonia
Pavel Kordik	Czech Technical University, Czech Republic
Olegas Vasilecas	Vilnius Gediminas Technical University, Lithuania
Radu Adrian Vasiu	Politehnica University of Timisoara, Romania
Rimantas Butleris	Kaunas University of Technology, Lithuania
Tomas Krilavicius	Vytautas Magnus University, Lithuania
Lucio Tommaso de Paolis	University of Salento, Italy
Eduard Babkin	National Research University, Russia
Jorg Becker	University of Münster, Germany
Albertas Caplinskas	Vilnius University, Lithuania
Tommi Mikkonen	Tampere University of Technology, Finland
Hana Skalska	University of Hradec Králové, Czech Republic
Linas Laibinis	Abo Akademi University, Finland
Benkt Wangler	Stockholm University, Sweden
Valentina Dagienė	Vilnius University, Lithuania
Andras Javor	Budapest University of Technology and Economics, Hungary
Kuldar Taveter	Tallinn University of Technology, Estonia
Grzegorz Borowik	Warsaw University of Technology, Poland
Kaspars Sudars	Institute of Electronics and Computer Science, Latvia
Cahit Gungor	Middle East Technical University, Turkey
Kristina Sutiene	Kaunas University of Technology, Lithuania
Raimundas Matulevicius	University of Tartu, Estonia
Janis Stirna	Stockholm University, Sweden
Hana Mohelska	University of Hradec Králové, Czech Republic
Justyna Patalas-Maliszewska	University of Zelona Gora, Poland
Pavel Bachmann	University of Hradec Králové, Czech Republic
Miloslava Cerna	University of Hradec Králové, Czech Republic

Additional Reviewers

Robertas Damasevicius	Kaunas University of Technology, Lithuania
Giedre Dregvaite	Kaunas University of Technology, Lithuania
Marcin Woznak	Silesian University of Technology, Poland
Tomas Blazauskas	Kaunas University of Technology, Lithuania
Prima Gustiene	Karlstad University, Sweden
Vita Speckauskiene	Lithuanian University of Health Sciences, Lithuania
Petra Poulova	University of Hradec Králové, Czech Republic
Darius Birvinskas	Kaunas University of Technology, Lithuania
Wojciech Mitkowski	AGH university of Science and Technology, Poland
Christian Napoli	University of Catania, Italy
Irina Kliziene	Kaunas University of Technology, Lithuania
Renata Burbaite	Kaunas University of Technology, Lithuania
Virginija Limanauskiene	Kaunas University of Technology, Lithuania
Daina Gudoniene	Kaunas University of Technology, Lithuania
Jordan Hristov	University of Chemical Technology and Metallurgy, Bulgaria
Kristina Bespalova	Kaunas University of Technology, Lithuania
Jorge Garcia	University of Porto, Portugal
Tomas Skersys	Kaunas University of Technology, Lithuania
Kestutis Kapocius	Kaunas University of Technology, Lithuania
Peter Jelinek	Hogeschool van Amsterdam, The Netherlands
Martynas Patasius	Kaunas University of Technology, Lithuania
Vytautas Stuikys	Kaunas University of Technology, Lithuania
Jurij Novickij	Vilnius Gediminas Technical University, Lithuania
Robert Nowicki	Czestochowa University of Technology, Poland
Sarka Hyblerova	Technical University of Liberec, Czech Republic
Rytis Maskeliunas	Kaunas University of Technology, Lithuania
Vacius Jusas	Kaunas University of Technology, Lithuania
Grzegorz Chmaj	University of Nevada, USA
Jonas Valantinas	Kaunas University of Technology, Lithuania
Lina Ceponiene	Kaunas University of Technology, Lithuania
Raimundas Matulevicius	University of Tartu, Estonia
Damian Mazur	Rzeszów University of Technology, Poland
Rimantas Barauskas	Kaunas University of Technology, Lithuania
Rita Butkiene	Kaunas University of Technology, Lithuania
Leslaw Golebiowski	Rzeszów University of Technology, Poland
Maciej Laskowski	Lublin University of Technology, Poland
Bronius Paradauskas	Kaunas University of Technology, Lithuania
Katarzyna Wasielewska	The State University of Applied Sciences in Elblag, Poland
Agnius Liutkevicius	Kaunas University of Technology, Lithuania
Ana Mestrovic	University of Rijeka, Croatia
Antanas Lenkevicius	Kaunas University of Technology, Lithuania

Andrzej Jardzioch	West Pomeranian University of Technology Szczecin, Poland
Germanas Budnikas	Kaunas University of Technology, Lithuania
Juozapas Virbalis	Kaunas University of Technology, Lithuania
Miloslav Hub	University of Pardubice, Czech Republic
Tomas Danikauskas	Kaunas University of Technology, Lithuania
Emiliano Tramontana	University of Catania, Italy
Antonino Laudani	Roma Tre University, Italy
Beata Gavurova	Technical University of Košice, Slovakia
Zdenek Mlcoch	University of Hradec Králové, Czech Republic
Armantas Ostreika	Kaunas University of Technology, Lithuania
Tomas Rasymas	Vilnius University, Lithuania
Ka Lok Man	Xi'an Jiaotong-Liverpool University, China
Grazia Lo Sciuto	University of Catania, Italy
Dominykas Barisas	Kaunas University of Technology, Lithuania
Pavel Jirava	University of Pardubice, Czech Republic
Alius Noreika	Kaunas University of Technology, Lithuania
Eva Rakovska	University of Economics Bratislava, Slovakia
Gabriel Svejda	University of West Bohemia, Czech Republic
Vytenis Punys	Kaunas University of Technology, Lithuania
Josef Basl	University of West Bohemia, Czech Republic
Ali Isik	Mehmet Akif Ersoy University, Turkey

Co-editors

| Giedre Dregvaite | Kaunas University of Technology, Lithuania |
| Robertas Damasevicius | Kaunas University of Technology, Lithuania |

Contents

Business Intelligence for Information and Software Systems

Special Session on Innovative Applications for Knowledge Transfer Support

Special Session on Impact of Business Intelligence on the Economy
and Society

Software Engineering

Special Session on Intelligent Systems and Software Engineering Advances

Information Technology Applications

Special Session on Language Technologies

Regular Session on Information Technology Applications

Information Systems

A System for Uncovering Latent Connectivity of Health Care Providers in Online Reviews

Frederik S. Bäumer$^{(\boxtimes)}$, Michaela Geierhos, and Sabine Schulze

Heinz Nixdorf Institute, University of Paderborn, Fürstenallee 11, 33102 Paderborn, Germany
{fbaeumer,geierhos,sabine.schulze}@hni.upb.de

Abstract. The contacts a health care provider (HCP), like a physician, has to other HCPs is perceived as a quality characteristic by patients. So far, only the German physician rating website jameda.de gives information about the inter-connectedness of HCPs in business networks. However, this network has to be maintained manually and is thus incomplete. We therefore developed a system for uncovering latent connectivity of HCPs in online reviews to provide users with more valuable information about their HCPs. The overall goal of this approach is to extend already existing business networks of HCPs by integrating connections that are newly discovered by our system. Our most recent evaluation results are promising: 70.8 % of the connections extracted from the reviews texts were correctly identified and in total 3,788 relations were recognized that have not been displayed in jameda.de's network before.

Keywords: Latent connectivity · Person named entity recognition and disambiguation · Health care provider reviews

1 Introduction

When patients are seeking for a suitable physician or other health care providers (HCPs), they are usually influenced by recommendations given by family and friends as well as by the distance to travel for health care services [12]. Besides, contacts to and recommendations given by other doctors are seen as quality characteristics of physicians [15]. Germany's most frequently used physician rating website (PRW) jameda.de [10] already considers the latter criterion, i.e. the embedding of a HCP in a network of physicians – a so-called business network. Such connectivity can result from long-term professional collaboration, as it is usually the case for joint practices.

Although jameda.de provides information about the contacts that a physician has to others in the network (cf. Fig. 1, translated from German), this network information is only visible for users if HCPs voluntarily add this information to their own accounts. This again has two serious drawbacks: first, these provided individual networks (see right part of Fig. 1) are incomplete because not all profiles are currently maintained. Secondly, unwanted connections may intentionally be omitted by HCPs. Consequently, there are several HCPs on jameda.de that do not display any information about their contacts to other HCPs in the network.

G. Dregvaite and R. Damasevicius (Eds.): ICIST 2015, CCIS 538, pp. 3–15, 2015.
DOI: 10.1007/978-3-319-24770-0_1

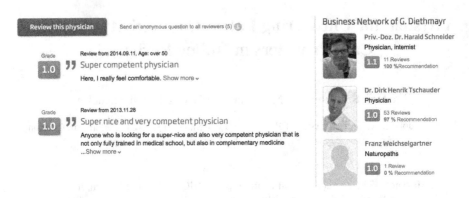

Fig. 1. HCP's jameda profile with reviews (left) and connections to other HCPs (right)

Hence, we developed a system for the detection of latent connectivity information hidden in patients' reviews (see left part of Fig. 2). These can be divided into a qualitative (i.e. review text) and a quantitative (i.e. numerical ratings) part, whereby only the qualitative part is considered by our system because we cannot identify latent connections between HCPs with the help of numerical ratings. Additionally, HCPs can respond to the reviews and leave comments as well as reviewers can provide metadata (e.g. age, insurance). In particular, our algorithm automatically extracts connections between HCPs from patients' review texts. Since their relationship is not explicitly mentioned in the reviews, we call them latent connections. Therefore, the overall goal of our approach is to extend already existing business networks by integrating the newly discovered connections. We also intend to prospectively score and classify them by a search engine that we are currently developing (cf. Fig. 3, translated from German).

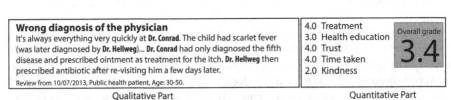

Fig. 2. Sample physician review on jameda.de (translated from German)

The structure of the paper is as follows: in Sect. 2, we provide an overview of the related work. Then, we present our system for uncovering latent connectivity in online reviews (cf. Sect. 3), which we evaluate in Sect. 4. Finally, we draw a conclusion and give an outlook on future work in Sect. 5.

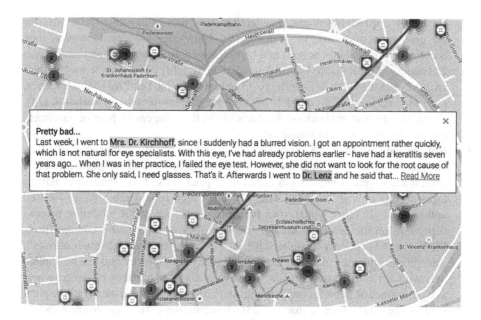

Pretty bad...
Last week, I went to **Mrs. Dr. Kirchhoff**, since I suddenly had a blurred vision. I got an appointment rather quickly, which is not natural for eye specialists. With this eye, I've had already problems earlier - have had a keratitis seven years ago... When I was in her practice, I failed the eye test. However, she did not want to look for the root cause of that problem. She only said, I need glasses. That's it. Afterwards I went to **Dr. Lenz** and he said that... Read More

Fig. 3. Localization of a recognized latent connection between two HCPs

2 Related Work

2.1 Recognition of Named Entities

In order to reliably uncover (latent) connections, it is necessary to recognize the occurrence of paired person names by applying *Named Entity Recognition (NER)* methods [8]. Although we concentrate on the identification of person named entities, NER "is concerned with identifying names of entities such as people, locations, organizations and products" [8]. During the last decades, the NER task "has been studied extensively" [19] and can be done by means of (1) **statistical models** on the one hand, which usually involves machine-learning techniques for the named entity classification. On the other hand, NER is performed by means of (2) **gazetteers**. Thereby, the classification is done by comparing tokens with predefined entity lists [20]. Furthermore, there is another possibility to conduct NER by means of (3) **local rules**. Rule-based systems use pattern-matching techniques and heuristics derived from the morpho-syntactic structure and/or the semantics of the input sequence in order to identify and classify named entities [16]. These methodologies can be combined, too: for instance, rule-based systems are used in combination with machine learning techniques [1, 9, 20].

(1) **Statistical models** perform better across domains and can make predictions about named entities that are not included in gazetteers. These systems use statistical models [5, 22, 30] and feature identification [20]. But they require annotated training data [28]. Another disadvantage of this method is the danger of overfitting because they do not apply non-local models for entity resolution.

(2) **Gazetteer approaches** require handcrafted seed lists or dynamic techniques for the generation of gazetteers from external knowledge sources. However, they become very large and complex and hence cause considerable maintenance costs. The quality of NER results highly depends on the quality of the gazetteers. But their greatest weakness is their inability to disambiguate named entities [24]. Moreover, gazetteers can never be complete, as they are subject to constant variation [24]. Therefore, most of research on this topic shifts from the enrichment of gazetteers to more dynamic lexicon formats [18, 27].

(3) **Rule-based systems** have the significant advantage of little computational effort, but lack in recall. Our approach therefore implements domain-specific rules in combination with gazetteers (so-called local grammars [17]). Their main advantages are the almost unlimited extensibility, a high reproducibility and focused optimization. In other words, own priorities can be set in the modeling process depending on the use case and the characteristics of a particular domain (here: PRWs) can be explicitly considered [6]. However, these advantages also come with some disadvantages: rules lead to a high degree of complexity and can be applied only with difficulty across domains. These rules are often based on evidence, where a basic distinction between implicit (e.g. unambiguous parts of a name) and explicit evidence (e.g. titles) can be made [7, 23]. However, since we concentrate on PRWs, domain dependency is no problem.

2.2 Disambiguation of Named Entities

Besides NER, *Named Entity Disambiguation (NED)* has to be conducted, which "refers to the task of mapping different named entity mentions in running text to their correct interpretations in a specific knowledge base (KB)" [4]. This is necessary because "references to entities in the real world are often ambiguous" [4]. For example, "Schlangen" may refer to the person "Albert Schlangen" – an internist registered on jameda.de – or to the name of the German village. However, in our context we rather have to deal with *Named Entity Linking (NEL)*, which "is a similar but broader task than NED" [3]. "NED is concerned with disambiguating a textual NE mention where the correct entity is known to be one of the KB entries, while EL also requires systems to deal with the case where there is no entry for the NE in the reference KB" [3]. Here, we have to deal with both tasks (i.e. NEL and NED) simultaneously. On the one hand, we have to conduct NEL because names oftentimes refer to persons that have no entries in any knowledge base like a neighbor, for example, which are just mentioned in the reviews because he recommended the physician to the person who has written the review. On the other hand, we have to face the NED task because we also have to identify person named entities (i.e. the HCPs) that are included in the knowledge base (i.e. jameda.de's HCP repository). Anyway, the state of research in NEL and NER is not considered separately here, since both tasks are quite intertwined [25, 29] as they "both involve the disambiguation of textual fragments according to a reference inventory" [25]. In addition, NED is one of the main subtasks of NEL [2, 3] rather than a separate research area.

Nobody in the literature about NEL or about NED has already solved the task of named entity disambiguation on German physician reviews by considering geographical information. Thus – to the best of our knowledge – our entity disambiguation approach presented in Sect. 3.4 is unique.

3   Discovering Latent Connections

Our system is based on different processing steps, which are illustrated in Sect. 3.1. In the following section, we describe how data is acquired and the preprocessing is done (cf. Sect. 3.2) before we explain the named entity recognition (cf. Sect. 3.3) as well as the disambiguation process (cf. Sect. 3.4).

3.1   System Design

Every day, users add new reviews for particular physicians to the PRW databases. For this reason, our system is designed to iteratively acquire new reviews (cf. Sect. 3.2). The subsequent 'Data Preprocessing' (cf. Fig. 4) has access to this 'Cache' and performs quality-improving operations such as duplicate removal. After that, the new records are transferred to the existing text collections.

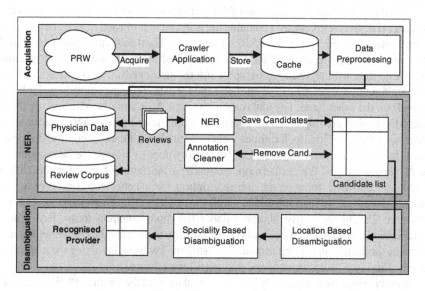

Fig. 4. System overview

In order to discover latent connections between HCPs, 'NER' is performed on all 'Reviews' (cf. Sect. 3.3). Here, a list of entity candidates per HCP is generated respectively, which contains all recognized person named entities. In the next step, the 'Annotation Cleaner' processes these candidates in order to remove duplicates. The resulting new 'Candidate list' contains only validated candidate pairs, where a latent connection between two HCPs is assumed. However, the new lists of candidates still contain all the recognized person named entities, regardless of the role the person plays in the particular review (cf. Sect. 3.3). For this reason, a disambiguation of the person name candidates is performed (cf. Sect. 3.4). The goal of this disambiguation step is to link the HCPs (mentioned in the reviews) to their corresponding profile on the PRW. This is challenging because many HCPs might have the same (common) name, practice in the same specialist field or work in a large medical center together. For that reason, we developed a multi-stage disambiguation approach, which is able to differentiate person names by the HCP's location, gender and specialty.

3.2 Data Acquisition and Preprocessing

Our text collection was created by crawling data from the most popular German PRW jameda.de between October 2013 and January 2015. More than 213,000 HCP data records and 860,000 individual reviews cover the time period from January 2009 to January 2015 and are cached for preprocessing. The HCP repository (i.e. 'Physician Data' in Fig. 4) contains personal information such as name, address and specialty. It consists of various types of HCPs, especially physicians (67.6 %), health practitioners (7.9 %), psychotherapists (6.8 %), pharmacies (5.5 %) and physical therapists (5.3 %). A total of 243,000 already known connections are gathered, where 10.5 % are derived from jameda.de's business network and 89.5 % from known joint practices. The review repository (i.e. 'Review Corpus') contains the title and text of each review. In total, the corpus contains 327,625 types and 45,023,119 tokens. The data preprocessing is divided in two steps: first, the gathered data must be enriched to enable the handling of more complex queries with regard to geographic information needs, which is necessary for the disambiguation approach on the one hand and for data cleansing (especially duplicate removal) on the other hand. For that reason, external APIs from Google and the Open Street Map project are implemented in order to gather missing geographic information such as coordinates (latitude, longitude) and to normalize all data. Secondly, duplicate records have to be removed from the HCP repository in order to improve the recognition rate of person names. We furthermore normalized the female forms for the HCP's specialty to the male form of the job description for a better comparability across genders. Moreover, we also subsumed similar specialties like "Nervenarzt" ('neurologist') and "Psychiater" ('psychiatrist') under the more common term "Psychiater" ('psychiatrist'). In addition, we classified the specialty to increase the comparability and determine the affiliation to a department (e.g. 'surgery') without involving the respective specialization (e.g. 'surgery, esp. oral and maxillofacial surgery').

Recently, a representative study has shown that users of the German PRW jameda.de are mostly satisfied with their HCPs [11]. We can substantiate these results when comparing them with our data. However, we had to remove potential distorting reviews (because of cognitive bias) [14] from the corpus.

3.3 Named Entity Recognition

The recognition of person identities is challenging because of the fact that they can occur in different roles within a text. On PRWs, a reviewer r is able to share reviews containing his or her experiences with the health care system or with a particular HCP p_0. This is usually a physician, but can also be, for example, a pharmacist or a midwife. r can be the object of treatment (object o), but may also report a third person experience. Next to the HCP p_0, other person named entities (p_{1-n}) may occur which are also treating in this medical field (e.g. another HCP than p_0) and are of high importance for uncovering latent connectivity. Other person named entities mentioned in the review (e.g. a neighbor of the patient or a taxi driver) should be removed during the disambiguation step because they do not belong to the health care domain and have no effect on latent connections between HCPs.

When selecting the right NER application, some requirements must be met, which may vary depending on the particular task: first, German must be supported. Second, batch processing must be possible in order to handle large amounts of data. Third, it is fundamental that the software can be adapted to domain-specific terminology and rules. Fourth, it is necessary to identify titles such as "Dr. med. dent." which are an important evidence for NER in the health care domain. Fifth, it should be noted that the software licenses allow the free and unrestricted use of the software component. The corpus processing system UNITEX [26] matches all these requirements and allows us to work with electronic lexicons and gazetteers in order to implement our rule-based approach.

Local grammars are well suited for our purpose because they achieve promising results in information extraction [17] on short texts like online reviews. The average review length is about 48 tokens, whereas the longest review in the data set consists of 348 tokens. The problems that arise when automatically processing short texts are due the lack of context. Context information is needed for the identification and disambiguation of named entities. The advantage of local grammars thus is that they describe the context relevant for the disambiguation [17]. That is, they enable the description of a local context and restrict the occurrence of certain lexical or morpho-syntactic features to a window of predefined size. In this regard, they perfectly fit in the extraction process of named entities performed on the reviews mentioned above. Local grammars are represented by directed acyclic graphs and implemented as finite state transducers [13]. An example of a local grammar for person name candidates recognition is given in Fig. 5 showing three main paths through this graph. We will select the second path in the middle in order to explain its functionality in general. This regular expression recognizes person named entities when a `<Title>` occurs in the text, which – denoted by `<PRE>` – is followed by "any sequence of letters that begins with an upper case letter" [26]. Hence, by means of this path, person named entities in the form of "Dr. Meier" or "Prof Dr. Schahler" can be recognized. The classification of words as titles is enabled by the automatic look-up in the underlying lexical resources, which include entries such as "Prof.", "Dr.", "Mrs.", etc. Furthermore, "#-#" denotes that also double names can be detected like "Dr. Schmidt-Schaller". Then the 'Annotation Cleaner' (cf. Fig. 4) removes duplicates as well as the HCP p_0 from the 'Candidate list' (based on unique HCP IDs), before the disambiguation starts.

3.4 Disambiguation

The disambiguation module gets the 'Candidate list' as input and tries to link the recognized HCPs to existing person named entities from the HCP repository. For this purpose,

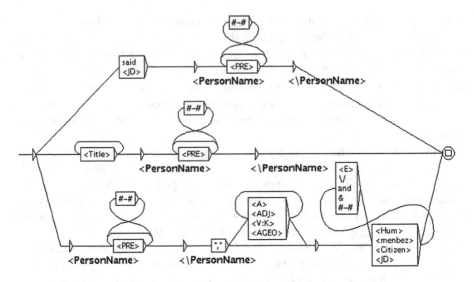

Fig. 5. Local grammar for the recognition person name candidates

(1) **practice location**, (2) **specialty** and (3) **gender** of all HCPs serve as disambiguation criteria.

(1) **Practice location.** When we disambiguate by using locative information, we assume that reviews are written by patients who have their HCPs in their place of residence or within a radius of maximal 50 km (cf. Fig. 6). This assumption is based on the fact that patients prefer to visit the nearest HCP [12]. For that reason, we have defined two radii as shown in Fig. 6. First, the system searches in a radius of 25 km (r_1) around the practice of HCP p_0 for HCPs whose names are identical or similar to one of the candidates (A).

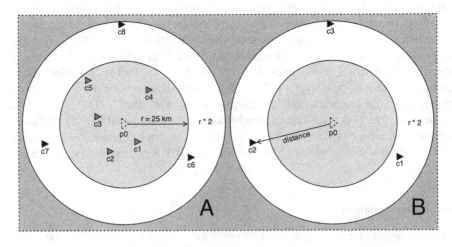

Fig. 6. Candidates within the disambiguation radius r_1 and r_2 of HCP p_0

If no HCP is found within r_1, the radius will be set to r_2, which is the doubled value of r_1 (B). These values cover both family physicians (who have a smaller catchment area) and specialists (who have a larger catchment area) [12]. If we apply this to the example in Fig. 2, we get a list of possible disambiguation candidates (cf. Table 1). In this case, we receive three candidates whose last name is at least similar to the person named entity "Dr. Hellwig". Moreover, similarity retrieval is applied in order to find misspelled entities in the database (e.g. "Dr. Hellwig" instead of "Dr. Hellweg"). Furthermore, we calculate the distance of the individual HCP candidate to the practice of the pediatrician "Dr. Conrad" p_0 and compare their corresponding specialties.

Table 1. Disambiguation of possible network candidates of HCP p_0

HCP p_0	Candidate	Disambiguation Cand.	Distance	Specialty
Dr. Conrad	Dr. Hellweg	Dr. Heribert Pütz-Hellweg	5.9 km	Internist
		Dr. Jan Hellwig	0 km	Pediatrician
		Dr. Hans-Joachim Hellwig	0.9 km	Psychotherapist

Obviously, "Dr. med. Jan Hellwig" is meant in the review text because the distance to the practice of "Dr. Conrad" is zero kilometer – both therefore share an office or at least work together in the same house. This is not obvious because physicians in the surrounding area can be meant.

(2) **Specialty.** For this reason, we consider the specialty as additional criterion. In this case, "Dr. med. Jan. Hellwig" works – just like his assumed colleague "Dr. Conrad" – as pediatrician. So we have a simple match here. But since physicians not only interact with faculty colleagues, the probability that two departments work together has to be analyzed. For this reason, we have calculated for the entire HCP repository, which specialties often cooperate and take this as further evidence (cf. Table 2). The disambiguation can show clearly that "Dr. med. Jan Hellwig" is meant based on the location as well as on the specialty information.

Table 2. Selected probabilities of specialty constellations

Specialty of p_0	Specialty of Cand.	%	Candidates
Pediatrician	Pediatrician	94.5 %	Dr. Jan Hellwig
	Internist	2.80 %	Dr. Heribert Pütz-Hellweg
	Psychiatrist	0.07 %	Dr. Hans-Joachim Hellwig

(3) **Gender.** Since the review in Fig. 2 does not contain further evidence (e.g. titles) about the gender of the recognized entities like "Herr" ('Mr.') or "Frau" ('Mrs.',

'Ms.'), this disambiguation criterion cannot be applied in this case. First attempts to determine a person's gender based on the first name and the nationality (via https://genderize.io/), were promising. So we can take the gender of the HCP into account, even in cases where no explicit evidence is given. This feature will be implemented in the next version of our system.

4 Evaluation

In the following, we are going to describe the evaluation of our system. Therefore, first of all, we explain the evaluation methodology (cf. Sect. 4.1) and afterward we describe the results of the evaluation (cf. Sect. 4.2).

4.1 Methodology

We manually evaluated our system with respect to both, (1) the **NER** as well as (2) the **disambiguation task** (cf. Fig. 4). For this reason, we randomly selected 600 connections as test set.

(1) **Named Entity Recognition.** The quality of our NER is measured in terms of *precision*. Thereby, we identified two different error types: tokens were mistaken for names (error type 1) or not recognized as such even if they should have been annotated as names (error type 2). While error type 1 is resolved automatically when no corresponding person named entities are found, error type 2 leads to the fact that existing latent connections were not found and consequently reduces the recall of our system.

(2) **Disambiguation.** Evaluating the disambiguation of latent connections is a time consuming task because it has to be validated for each recognized connection if it really exists on the PRW in order to calculate the *precision*. Therefore, it has to be checked if the system has detected a link between physician A and B even though A and B are one and the same person. This is particularly the case when persons are named differently in reviews because of name change after marriage. Moreover, there were other cases when a practice was taken over by another physician while keeping the former practice's name. Hence, in such cases it has to be verified if the system recognized that there is a new physician in a practice even though the practice's name did not change.

4.2 Results

In total, we identified 6,636 connections in 6,407 reviews. We could verify 40.1 % of the connections because of already-known joint practices and another 14 relations (2.3 %) according to jameda.de's business network. In addition, these results seem to be representative, since the distribution of the known contacts from the whole review corpora is almost identical to the distribution of the detected connections from the test set: compared to the whole review corpus, 2,682 (40.4 %) of the identified connections existed indeed due to joint practices and 166 (2.5 %) of the recognized contacts were already included in jameda.de's business network. Furthermore, we could discover 3,788 connections between HCPs that were unknown before. In brief, 70.8 % of these connections were correctly recognized and disambiguated in our HCP repository.

In 12.6 % of the 600 connections in our test set, there was at least one capitalized word sequence mistaken for a person name (e.g. "Mal Kontakt"). This means that 87.3 % of the recognized person named entities are correct, which is a satisfying value for the error type 1 (precision) but still needs improvement. We pass on the calculation of recall, since it is not a suitable measure for web retrieval systems because of the unknown total number of relevant hits [21].

5   Conclusion and Outlook

The choice of HCPs is partly influenced by a number of highly subjective factors that are only partially covered by the existing PRWs [15]. In this paper, the role of business networks and relations between health care providers was discussed as influencing factor. Current PRWs provide basic business networks, which can be explored by users. But since these networks are maintained by the HCPs themselves, they can be incomplete or consciously manipulated. Our system is able to overcome these weaknesses by automatically discovering latent connections between HCPs in reviews on PRWs.

Anyway, even though the recognition rate of 70.8 % is promising, there is still left room for improvement: (1) First of all, we will skip HCPs that are mentioned even though they do not practice anymore and therefore left their former business network. (2) A second issue for future research is the person name disambiguation in the case of name changes. Until now, various person named entities as well as connections between them are recognized, even though it is the same person identity mentioned in the text. (3) Third, it would be interesting to vary the radii for person name disambiguation instead of using predefined ones because – in some cases – smaller towns and cities (too large radius) and larger cities (too small radius) are not adequately covered. (4), a further intriguing task for future work would be to make our approach multilingual. Hence, we intend to adapt our rules to further languages and generate dictionaries for other languages than German. (5) In addition, we have to consider more features than practice location, specialty and gender for differentiating high frequent person names like "Michael Müller" in metropolitan areas.

Acknowledgments. Special thanks go to our student assistant Markus Dollmann who contributed to this project. Funding has been granted in part by the University of Paderborn and by the Ministry of Innovation, Higher Education and Research of North Rhine-Westphalia, Germany.

References

1. Abdallah, S., Shaalan, K., Shoaib, M.: Integrating rule-based system with classification for Arabic named entity recognition. In: Gelbukh, A. (ed.) CICLing 2012, Part I. LNCS, vol. 7181, pp. 311–322. Springer, Heidelberg (2012)
2. Alhelbawy, A., Gaizauskas, R.: Named entity disambiguation using HMMs. In: 2013 IEEE/WIC/ACM International Joint Conferences on Web Intelligence (WI) and Intelligent Agent Technologies (IAT), vol. 3, pp. 159–162 (November 2013)
3. Alhelbawy, A., Gaizauskas, R.: Collective named entity disambiguation using graph ranking and clique partitioning approaches. In: Proceedings of the 25th International Conference on Computational Linguistics, pp. 1544–1555 (2014)
4. Alhelbawy, A., Gaizauskas, R.: Graph ranking for collective named entity disambiguation. In: Proceedings of the 52nd Annual Meeting of the Association for Computational Linguistics, pp. 75–80. ACL (June 2014)
5. Chieu, H., Ng, H.: Named entity recognition: a maximum entropy approach using global information. In: COLING 2002: The 19th International Conference on Computational Linguistics, vol. 1, pp. 190–196. ACL (2002)
6. Chiticariu, L., Krishnamurthy, R., Li, Y., Reiss, F., Vaithyanathan, S.: Domain adaptation of rule-based annotators for named-entity recognition tasks. In: Proceedings of the 2010 Conference on EMNLP, pp. 1002–1012. ACL (2010)
7. Cucerzan, S., Yarowsky, D.: Language independent named entity recognition combining morphological and contextual evidence. In: Proceedings of the 1999 Joint SIGDAT Conference on EMNLP and VLC, pp. 90–99 (1999)
8. Derczynski, L., Maynard, D., Rizzo, G., van Erp, M., Gorrell, G., Troncy, R., Petrak, J., Bontcheva, K.: Analysis of named entity recognition and linking for Tweets. Inf. Process. Manage. **51**(2), 32–49 (2015)
9. Drozdzynski, W., Krieger, H., Piskorski, J., Schäfer, U., Xu, F.: Shallow processing with unification and typed feature structures – foundations and applications. Künstliche Intelligenz (KI) **18**(1), 17–23 (2004)
10. Emmert, M., Meier, F.: An analysis of online evaluations on a physician rating website: evidence from a German public reporting instrument. J. Med. Internet Res. **15**(8), 161–167 (2013)
11. Emmert, M., Meier, F., Heider, A.K., Dürr, C., Sander, U.: What do patients say about their physicians? An analysis of 3000 narrative comments posted on a German physician rating website. Health Policy **118**(1), 66–73 (2014)
12. Fülöp, G., Kopetsch, T., Schöpe, P.: Einzugsbereiche von Arztpraxen und die Rolle der räumlichen Distanz für die Arztwahl der Patienten. In: Strobl, J., Blaschke, T., Griesebner, G. (eds.) Angewandte Geoinformatik 2009: Beiträge zum 21. AGIT- Symposium Salzburg, pp. 218–227. Wichmann, Heidelberg (2009)
13. Geierhos, M.: Grammatik der Menschenbezeichner in biographischen Kontexten, Arbeiten zur Informations- und Sprachverarbeitung, vol. 2. Centrum für Informations- und Sprachverarbeitung, Munich (2007)
14. Geierhos, M., Bäumer, F.S., Schulze, S., Stuß, V.: Filtering reviews by random individual error. In: Ali, M., Kwon, Y.S., Lee, C.-H., Kim, J., Kim, Y. (eds.) IEA/AIE 2015. LNCS, vol. 9101, pp. 305–315. Springer, Heidelberg (2015)
15. Geraedts, M.: Informationsbedarf und Informationssuchverhalten bei der Arztsuche. In: Böcken, J., Braun, B., Amhof, R. (eds.) Gesundheitsmonitor 2008: Gesundheitsversorgung und Gestaltungsoptionen aus der Perspektive der Bevölkerung, pp. 29–47. Bertelsmann Stiftung, Gütersloh (2008)

16. Grishman, R.: Information extraction. In: Clark, A., Fox, C., Lappin, S. (eds.) The Handbook of Computational Linguistics and Natural Language Processing, pp. 517–530. Wiley, New York, NY (2013)

17. Gross, M.: Local grammars. In: Roche, E., Schabes, Y. (eds.) Finite-State Language Processing, pp. 330–354. MIT Press, Cambridge (1997)

18. Kazama, J., Torisawa, K.: Exploiting Wikipedia as external knowledge for named entity recognition. In: Proceedings of the 2007 Joint Conference on EMNLP- CoNLL, pp. 698–707. ACL (June 2007)

19. Khalid, M.A., Jijkoun, V., de Rijke, M.: The impact of named entity normalization on information retrieval for question answering. In: Macdonald, C., Ounis, I., Plachouras, V., Ruthven, I., White, R.W. (eds.) ECIR 2008. LNCS, vol. 4956, pp. 705–710. Springer, Heidelberg (2008)

20. Klahold, A.: Empfehlungssysteme: Recommender Systems - Grundlagen. Konzepte und Lösungen. Vieweg + Teubner in GWV Fachverlage, Wiesbaden (2009)

21. Manning, C.D., Raghavan, P., Schütze, H.: Introduction to Information Retrieval, vol. 1. Cambridge University Press, Cambridge (2008)

22. McCallum, A., Li, W.: Early results for named entity recognition with conditional random fields, feature induction and web-enhanced lexicons. In: Proceedings of the 7th CoNLL at HLT-NAACL, vol. 4, pp. 188–191. ACL (2003)

23. McDonald, D.D.: Internal and external evidence in the identification and semantic categorization of proper names. In: Boguraev, B., Pustejovsky, J. (eds.) Corpus Processing for Lexical Acquisition, pp. 21–39. MIT Press, Cambridge (1996)

24. Mikheev, A., Moens, M., Grover, C.: Named entity recognition without gazetteers. In: Proceedings of the 9th Conference of the European ACL, pp. 1–8. ACL (1999)

25. Moro, A., Raganato, A., Navigli, R.: Entity linking meets word sense disambiguation: a unified approach. TACL **2**, 231–244 (2014)

26. Paumier, S.: UNITEX 3.1. BETA USER MANUAL (2015). http://igm.univ-mlv.fr/~unitex/UnitexManual3.1.pdf. Accessed 18 May 2015

27. Ritter, A., Clark, S., Etzioni, M., Etzioni, O.: Named entity recognition in Tweets: an experimental study. In: Proceedings of the Conference on EMNLP, pp. 1524–1534. ACL, Edinburgh, UK (2011)

28. Scherfer, K., Pieplow, B.: Methoden der Webwissenschaft. Teil 1, Schriftenreihe Webwissenschaft, vol. 2. LIT Verlag Münster (2013)

29. Sil, A., Yates, A.: Re-ranking for joint named-entity recognition and linking. In: Proceedings of the 22nd ACM International Conference on Information & Knowledge Management, pp. 2369–2374. ACM (2013)

30. Zhou, G., Su, J.: Named entity recognition using an hmm-based chunk tagger. In: Proceedings of the 40th Annual Meeting of the Association for Computational Linguistics, pp. 473–480. ACL (2002)

Business Intelligence Application for Analyses of Stress Potential Zones in the Population Doing Sports

Věra Strnadová$^{(\boxtimes)}$ and Petr Voborník

University of Hradec Králové, Rokitanského 62, 500 03
Hradec Králové, Czech Republic
{vera.strnadova,petr.vobornik}@uhk.cz

Abstract. The article presents the results of the research focused on stress factors followed in two groups – top-level athletes and recreational sportsmen. With regard to the methods used in the research the answers obtained in subjective questioning were statistically processed and then the respondents were classified into the zones of stress potential. In the field of frustration tolerance half of the top-level sportsmen group have low to average value of stress factors. The situation is similar in the recreational sportsmen group where 50 % of them also show low to average value of stress factors. As far as coping with stress is concerned it has been revealed that about two thirds of the surveyed top-level athletes and three quarters of the recreational sportsmen group are included into the optimal stress zone. The electronic online application which enabled subjective questioning and classification into stress factors was set up and placed on the web.

Keywords: Frustration tolerance · Handling stress · Psychosomatic symptoms · Web application · Database

1 Introduction

An important element in reducing stress factors is physical fitness. People who regularly do *aerobic exercises*, that is any kind of endurance activity which increases heart rate and oxygen consumption – e.g. running, swimming, cycling or cross-country skiing – have significantly lower heart rate and blood pressure in a stress situation than other untrained people.

Physically fit individuals tend to fall ill as a result of stress events less often than people who are not in a good condition. In relation to these facts the programmes for coping with increased stress load are currently focused on *physical fitness*. The study on patients suffering from chronic chest pain has revealed that the combination of stress management techniques and regular exercise resulted in less frequent occurrence of angina pectoris than the actual stress management training [1].

© Springer International Publishing Switzerland 2015
G. Dregvaite and R. Damasevicius (Eds.): ICIST 2015, CCIS 538, pp. 16–28, 2015.
DOI: 10.1007/978-3-319-24770-0_2

2 Theoretical Basis

2.1 Mental and Physical Heath

The belief of connection between physical exercise and mental health is known from the history of ancient times. It is reflected in the message *mens sana in corpore sano – there is a healthy mind in a healthy body*. The science started to be interested in this relation much later and it has not brought a closer understanding of the relation between physical exercise and mental health until the recent years [2, 3]. In 2004 the representative of the British Ministry of Health came up with the thought that *it is necessary to think about physical activities not only with respect to their therapeutic effect on mental illnesses but also due to their impact on mental health*. (Ministry of Health, DH, 2004: 58–59).

With the growth of intensity of physical activity the positive mood decreases and the negative mood increases even though the reaction to the load is not the same with all people. After finishing exercise the *back-reflection effect* occurs during which the mood improves. Although further research needs to be conducted, it is possible to say that people doing regular exercises are less likely to be depressed. Moreover, exercises are recommended as a suitable therapy of mild to medium depression, in combination with other interventions (pharmacotherapy or psychotherapy) and under the control of a qualified mental health specialist. Research confirms the British Ministry of Health statement that active people have fewer symptoms of anxiety than inactive people. After all, physical activity significantly affects people with bad physical condition and high level of anxiety. It turned out that exercise is a feasible intervention for cancer patients, even those who are undergoing chemotherapy and suffering from an acute stage of the disease – here a number of benefits were recorded, such as the quality of life improvement and a depression decline [4].

2.2 Frustration Tolerance

Frustration is defined as a state threatening the integrity of organism when a person must engage all abilities to protect himself/herself. The effort based on the natural necessity of satisfying a person's needs is blocked. In a narrower sense, frustration is the result of dissatisfying biologically primary, instinctive claims or the failure in achieving a goal, which is accompanied by feelings of destruction. As one of the determinants of human behaviour frustration is sometimes incorrectly mistaken for deprivation or the phenomenon of unfinished activity, which has similar symptoms as frustration.

Manifestations of frustration fall into the area of perception and behaviour disorders and often acquire the character of neurovegetative or psychosomatic symptoms. They depend not only on the intensity and length of duration of frustration but also on *a person's resistance to frustration – so called frustration tolerance.*

The ability of frustration tolerance is connected with inborn properties of an individual (temperament, emotional stability versus instability) and further with influences of social environment (family influence and acquired experience) [5].

Although frustration can cause aggression, anxiety as well as neurovegetative disorders [6], it is an inseparable part of human life. Gradual and bearable frustration loading of organism even leads to increased psycho-physiological resistance of an individual.

2.3   Dealing with Stress

Stress is generally understood as exertion, load, as an adaptation stimulus, as a demanding situation that must be managed by an athlete – physical load (training) and mental load (competition). The following degrees of load can be distinguished: extreme, excess, boundary, increased, adequate, optimal, negligible. In fact, load is any energetic demand on the organism. Reference [7] There is a known concept of organism as a balanced system (homeostasis) which is deflected by a load and tends to regain the balance again. According to the adaptation theory [8] every other analogous load causes a smaller deflection, the organism gradually adapts to loads. The essence of training programmes for athletes is based on this fact.

In the 20th century the *theory of stress* brought a new approach to the issue of load. Its author is Hans Selye [9] who found out through experiments that all loading stimuli (stressors) from a certain intensity lead to triggering a unspecific reaction in the organism (i.e. always the same regardless of the initiator of stress), called general adaptation syndrome (GAS). It progresses in three phases: 1st – alarm (alarm reaction), typical for mobilization, inefficiency, 2nd – resistance, defence by drawing from energy storage, 3rd – exhaustion, spreading the reaction onto the whole organism, collapse. The criterion of GAS progress is production of hormones preparing the organism for physical exertion.

In fact stress is intensive emotion with all the activating consequences. The asthenic emotion is called distress, the sthenic emotion is eustress. Depending on the place affected by a stressor we speak about physical stress when it affects periphery (most often pain), and mental stress which is cerebral, brain, mental. For example, the ankle distortion means the physical stress for an athlete and the disqualification from the race is the mental stress. The response of the organism to both stress types is the same, unspecific, global. It differs only in intensity. The main criterion is the amount and kind of hormones identifiable in blood, saliva etc. (corticoids, adrenalin, noradrenalin, cortisol, hydrocortisol) [10].

The most frequent stressors in sport are expectation based tension (see pre-start condition, fear when taking a risk), demands of the programme, defeat, injury, loss of physical condition or disqualification.

Intensive and long-term distresses mean quality of life worsening and they can have an unpleasant impact on health – today this issue is dealt with by a modern field of *psychosomatic medicine*.

2.4   Psychosomatic Symptoms

Psychosomatic symptoms in a stress situation during sport activities can be classified into three groups:

Organic – palpitation (the heart beat is too strong, fast and irregular in relation to the current exertion), losing breath and sweating without an exertion cause, chest pain, cramps and pain in the bottom part of stomach, metabolic disorders – loss of appetite, enormous muscle tension, especially in the area of cervical and lumbar spine, migraines that spread from the neck to the top of the head and forehead.

Emotional – sharp mood fluctuation, hypochondria, dreaming, autistic thinking, lack of concentration, neurotic symptoms, inadequate tiredness, fear from social contact, loss of empathy, impulsiveness.

Behavioural – decline in performance, loss of physical condition, worsened quality of training preparation, taking anaesthetics, disorders of life rhythm (insufficient sleep, chronic tiredness), excesses in behaviour, tendency towards isolation [11].

As it can be concluded from the previous enumeration, the difficulty in diagnostics results from variety and also contradiction of symptoms which are sovereignly individual. Unlike a physical illness, which manifests itself e.g. by a fever, the situation in psychosomatic symptoms is unclear and the affected person often refuses to admit the seriousness of his/her condition. A frequent danger in sport is overtraining, which has stress effects. Psychological dangerousness lays in the fact that it is the result of good intentions, increased motivation and big effort to assert oneself. The cause are big training dozes and underestimating the regeneration of performance disposition. A lot of coaches of top-level athletes still see regeneration as a luxury. It results in protracted stress conditions. Therefore it is absolutely essential not to underestimate psychosomatic symptoms in a stress situation, regard them as a warning signal and adopt routine measures to eliminate them.

3 Methodology

3.1 Method of Research and a Group of Respondents

The method of a questionnaire survey was used in the research on the basis of subjective evaluation according to the questionnaire by Micková [12, 13].

The research was focused on finding out stress factors in three sectors:

1. frustration tolerance – the form of YES/NO questions was used here
2. handling stress, i.e. behaviour in a stress situation – the form of questioning by means of assessing scale was used and two aspects of the research were followed here – the amount of emotional reaction to stress and the amount of using malcoping (harming) strategies
3. psychosomatic symptoms - the form of questioning by means of assessing scale was used here

3.2 Group of Respondents

50 athletes in total were included in the research set. Most of the athletes were secondary school or university students.

Top-level athletes – cross-country skiers, 25 men; age 19–25 (Ø 21) years. The athletes were selected into this set according to the criterion of sport performance efficiency. At the time of the survey they belonged to the 1st class of performance efficiency and they regularly took part in the races of Czech Cup or a higher category (at least 5 races). At the same time 15 athletes from this set were or still are the members of the representation team. However this was not the condition for inclusion into the research. For none of the athletes sport was the source of livelihood. With regard to various training methods it can be assumed that at the time of racing period, during which the research was carried out, the average weekly sport activity occupied between 10 and 15 h. It should be noted that the athletes of this group belonged mostly to the Czech performance top level.

Common population doing sport as a leisure activity, 25 men; age 21–25 (Ø 22.5). The athletes selected into this set do a sport regularly in various sport activities, maximum of 8 h a week (the average of a weekly sport activity was 5 h in this set), at the same time they were not included in any representation team and currently did not have their performance efficiency certified in any sport. On the basis of the collected data it can be said that this group represents common population doing sport as a leisure activity which mostly does not interfere with the life of the athletes.

3.3   Procedure of Conducting the Research

Modern technologies were used for doing the research. It was carried out with the help of the company Google Inc., thanks to which the questionnaire was converted into electronic form and the company Facebook Inc. enabled direct communication with the respondents – each of them was approached individually on the basis of pre-prepared list of names. Thus obtaining proper answers only from the selected people was guaranteed. The research was conducted and gradually statistically processed in the years 2013–2014. 88 questionnaires in total were sent off, out of these 64 (73 %) completed questionnaires were used.

Set 1 – Top-level athletes – cross-country skiers: Sent off 40 questionnaires, returned completed 30 (75 %).
Set 2 – Common population doing sport as a leisure activity: Sent off 48 questionnaires, returned completed 34 (71 %).

Consequently the number of respondents was reduced to 50 (25 in each of the two sets) due to meeting assigned criteria. Individual components of the questionnaire were evaluated in points. The statistical significance of differences was owing to a small number of subsets (n = 25) calculated by means of Mann-Whiteny U-test. For statistical processing a complement for Excel, trial version of the program SigmaXL was used.

3.4   Characteristics of Stress Potential Zones

Zone 1: The stress level is *very low*. The personality needs to be encouraged and motivated in his/her life so that they could use their abilities better. Here it is necessary to realize the existence of so called positive stress – eustress which enables to manage the demands of modern life, strengthens and develops a human personality (Fig. 1).

Zone 2: The stress level is *low*. It can be connected with introvert orientation of the personality and a stabilized way of life progressing without changes and excitement. The personality is in a rather balanced life situation and does not have to be afraid of stress-related diseases.

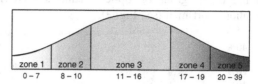

Fig. 1. Zones of stress potential

However he/she does not use all their abilities. It is necessary to place bigger demands on themselves, set more ambitious goals and overcome passivity.

Zone 3: The stress level is *average*. It is an optimal zone of stress potential. Most of the population find themselves in this zone. In the personality's life the periods of increased load alternate with the periods of peace and relaxation. For achieving goals the certain stress level is necessary but it must not be permanent and long-term. Increased load-peaceful condition rhythm enables a person to live a balanced and satisfying life.

Zone 4: The stress level is *high* and it means a warning signal. The personality should explore individual areas of his/her life and consequently decide which problems need a quick solution. This way mental problems as well as threatening physical problems can be turned away. It is time to change the lifestyle and prevent complications. It is necessary to seek advice from close friends and relatives or ask for a professional help. It is also advisable to get to know strategies of coping with excessive stress.

Zone 5: The stress level is *dangerously high*. The personality is currently experiencing abnormally high stress. He/she has serious problems requiring an urgent solution. The personality is no longer capable of helping himself/herself a so it is necessary to seek professional help of a psychologist or a psychiatrist.

4   Results

4.1   Zones of Stress Potential

The limit values of individual stress potential zones were converted into their percentage in the scale 0 (0 %) up to 39 (100 %; see Fig. 2). Also the point results of each respondent from individual questionnaires were converted into percentage.

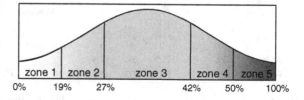

Fig. 2. Zones of stress potential converted into percentage

4.2 Frustration Tolerance

First of all numbers of inclusion in stress potential zones were compared for frustration tolerance of the group of top-level athletes – cross-country skiers and of common population sportsmen (see Fig. 3).

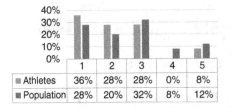

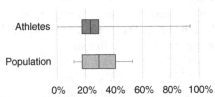

Fig. 3. Comparison of numbers of inclusion in zones for frustration tolerance of groups of athletes and common population sportsmen

Fig. 4. Boxplot representation of amount of frustration tolerance in top-level athletes and common population sportsmen

Half of the group of **athletes** (approx. 12 people) range on the border of zones 2 and 3 (18–29 %). Other members (other approx. 12 people) diverge from the average of the group by their inclusion in zones – they are more divergent.

Half of the **population** group (approx. 12 people) is included in zones 2 and 3 (18–41 %). The group does not contain too different/divergent individuals. Other members (approx. Other 12 people) do not diverge from the group average by their inclusion in zones as in the athletes group. Further a boxplot representation of the amount of frustration tolerance in athletes and population groups was created for a more detailed comparison (Fig. 4).

4.3 Handling Stress

First of all we compared numbers of inclusions in zones for optimal handling stress of the top-level athletes group and the group of common population sportsmen (Fig. 5) a then for a more detailed comparison a boxplot representation of the amount of stress handling by top-level athletes and common population sportsmen was created (Fig. 6).

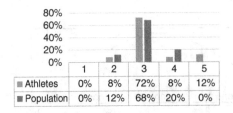

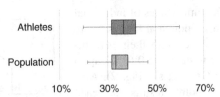

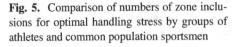

Fig. 5. Comparison of numbers of zone inclusions for optimal handling stress by groups of athletes and common population sportsmen

Fig. 6. Boxplot representation of amount of stress handling by top-level athletes and common population sportsmen

68 % of group members of **athletes** fall into stress zone 3 which is the healthiest one with respect to handling stress. 72 % of group members of **population** again fall into stress zone 3 which is the healthiest one with respect to handling stress (Fig. 7).

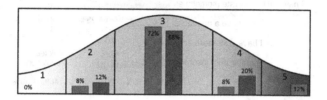

Fig. 7. Number of psychosomatic symptoms in groups of top-level athletes and common population sportsmen

4.4 Psychosomatic Symptoms

Further the research focused on the comparison of the numbers of inclusions in stress potential zones for psychosomatic symptoms in the groups of top-level athletes – cross-country skiers and common population sportsmen (Fig. 8).

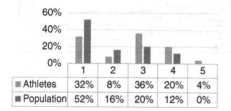

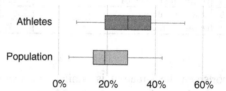

Fig. 8. Comparison of numbers of inclusions in zones for psychosomatic symptoms in groups of top-level athletes and common population sportsmen

Fig. 9. Boxplot representation of amount of psychosomatic symptoms occurrence in top-level athletes and common population sportsmen

Approximately the same number – one third – of group members of **athletes** occur both in stress zone 1 and zone 3. More than a half of group members of **population** are from the point of view of psychosomatic symptoms included in stress zone 1.

Consequently, for a more detailed comparison a boxplot representation of amount of psychosomatic symptoms occurrence in top-level athletes and common population sportsmen was created (Fig. 9).

Further we focused on the comparison of amount of individual psychosomatic symptoms in the groups of top-level athletes and common population sportsmen (Fig. 10).

Consequently, the number of psychosomatic symptoms was found out in the groups of top-level athletes and common population sportsmen (Table 1).

From the above mentioned symptoms the group of top-level athletes show feelings of tiredness and lack of energy most often (47 %). In the group of common population

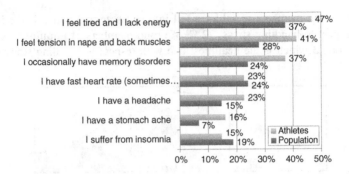

Fig. 10. Comparison of amount of individual psychosomatic symptoms in groups of top-level athletes and common population sportsmen

Table 1. Number of psychosomatic symptoms in groups of top-level athletes and common population sportsmen

	Population		Athletes	
1	I feel tired and I lack energy	37%	I feel tired and I lack energy	47%
2	I feel tension in nape and back muscles	28%	I feel tension in nape and back muscles	41%
3	I have fast heart rate	24%	I occasionally have memory disorders	37%
4	I occasionally have memory disorders	24%	I have a headache	23%
5	I suffer from insomnia	19%	I have fast heart rate	23%
6	I have a headache	15%	I have a stomach ache	16%
7	I have a stomach ache	7%	I suffer from insomnia	15%

sportsmen the situation is similar, the feelings of tiredness and lack of energy are shown also in the highest rate (37 %).

The second position in the table is held by feelings of tension in nape and back muscles in the group of athletes (41 %) and also in the group of common population sportsmen (28 %).

In the third place top-level athletes show memory disorders (37 %) and common population sportsmen fast heart rate sometimes connected with excessive heart beat (24 %).

5   Application for Independent Testing

The data for this research was obtained by individual respondents filling in printed paper questionnaires. That brought a few difficulties such as the distribution of questionnaires, time and space limitation for filling them in, insufficient anonymity, collection of completed questionnaires, conversion of data into a digital form and its statistical processing.

In order to eliminate these problems in future or at least reduce them considerably, an on-line business intelligence application was created which facilitates the whole process significantly. Users then do not fill the data in the paper forms but on-line in web forms, which is more preferred [14]. Thanks to that it is also possible to reach far larger sample of respondents because apart from those directly involved in the project other "anonymous" volunteers can participate in the research. All the recorded data is available immediately after it is entered and thus it can be automatically continuously evaluated.

This application is freely available on the address http://qol.alltest.eu/stress. Here we can find a signpost to all three questionnaires relating to stress: Frustration tolerance, handling stress and Symptoms of stress. The first one includes yes/no question type and for better user comfort the answer is selected only by clicking (with a mouse or a finger on the touch device) on the icon which gradually switches over from the original state of a question mark ❓ (answer not selected) to the option yes ✅ (for the approval of a statement on a given line) and consequently no ❌ (for the disapproval of the appropriate statement; see Fig. 11).

In other two forms answers are given on a scale 0–3, which was simplified here by the selection of number of stars. It expresses a degree of agreement with a given item (1 star – total disagreement, 4 stars – total agreement; see Fig. 12).

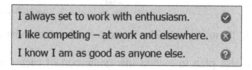

Fig. 11. Illustration of filling answers in Frustration tolerance questionnaire

After filling in all the items in the questionnaire the user clicks on the push button *Evaluate* and immediately a graphic evaluation is displayed and in percentage put in the appropriate stress zone (see Fig. 13).

I feel tension in nape and back muscles	⭐⭐⭐⭐
I suffer from headache	⭐☆☆☆
I suffer from stomach ache	⭐⭐⭐☆

Fig. 12. Illustration of filling answers in questionnaire Symptoms of stress

A constituent part of the questionnaire is also the data for categorization of respondents (see Fig. 14): year of birth (for putting in the age group), sex, occupation (student of secondary school, university student, worker, senior) and determination of intensity of doing sport activities (regularly, sometimes, never). Name and e-mail are optional but in case of filling them in they can serve for the evaluation of the development of individual stress level in time.

The complete data of the questionnaire is during the evaluation simultaneously saved in a database on the server for later anonymous, collective, statistical processing. This gives us a possibility to continue in the research all the time with the growing sample of respondents and thus with more relevant results.

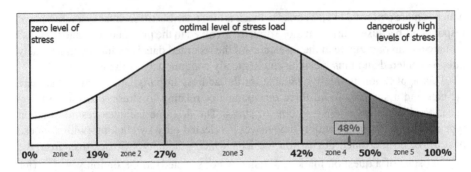

Fig. 13. Illustration of questionnaire evaluation – putting user in stress zone

Fig. 14. Illustration of filling in categorization data about user

For the future we also plan to extend the evaluation of each questionnaire by the comparison of individual figures with average results of the other respondents. This way users will also get information on what their figures are in relation to the whole population, the same age group, the same sex etc.

6   Conclusion

Physical activities can represent an effective prevention of the development of both physical and mental illnesses.

Our research was comparing two groups, the group of top-level athletes and the group of common population doing sport on a recreational basis. In the area of *frustration tolerance* it has been found out that a half of the top-level athletes group (approx. 12 people) ranges on the border of the second and third zone of stress potential (18–29 %), where the third zone is understood as an optimal zone, the healthiest one. The other members (the other 12 people) diverge more from the average of the group as far as the inclusion in the zones is concerned. They are more divergent. A half of the common population group (approx. 12 people) is included in the second and third zone (18–41 %). The individuals in this group are not as different as in other group. The other members (the other 12 people) do not diverge from the group average as much as top-level athletes do when the inclusion in the zones is concerned.

In the area of *handling stress* it was revealed that 68 % of members of the top-level athletes group fall into the 3rd stress zone, which is the healthiest one concerning handling stress. In the population group 72 % of its members fall again into the healthiest third stress zone.

In the area of *psychosomatic symptoms* the group of top-level athletes show in the first place feelings of tiredness and energy shortage (47 %). The similar situation is in the group of common population doing sport for pleasure where the feelings of tiredness and energy shortage are also shown in the highest rate (37 %). The second position in the table is held by the feelings of tension in nape and back muscles in the athletes group (41 %) and also in the common population group (28 %). In the third place the top-level athletes show memory disorders (37 %) and the common population sportsmen state fast heart rate sometimes connected with excessive heart beat (24 %).

On the address http://qol.alltest.eu/stress the original electronic application was created in the Czech and English version thanks to which it is possible to reach much larger sample of respondents because apart from those directly involved in the project other "anonymous" volunteers can participate in the research. All the recorded data is available immediately after it is entered and thus it can be automatically continuously evaluated.

Physical activities, exercise and sport can thus represent an effective *prevention* of physical and mental illness development. However the fear of self-presentation may be one of the factors which prevent people from doing exercises and thus make them deprived of these preventive effects. When introducing exercise interventions specialists must take into consideration *individual routine of exercise* in order to ensure the possibility of achieving optimal benefits for a particular individual.

References

1. Kuo, C.T.: The effect of recreational sport involvement on work stress and quality of life in central Taiwan. Soc. Behav. Pers. Int. J. **41**(10), 1705–1715 (2013)
2. Bidle, S.J., Mutrie, N.: Psychology of Physical Activity: Determinant, Well-Being and Interventions, vol. 2. Routledge, London (2008)
3. Strnadová, V.: Interpersonální komunikace, Reviewed monograph, vol. 1, 542 p. Gaudeamus, Hradec Králové (2011). ISBN 978-80-7435-157-0
4. Tod, D., Thatcher, J., Rahman, R.: Psychologie Sportu, vol. 1, 200 p. Grada Publishing, Prague (2012). ISBN 978-80-247-3923-6
5. Strnadová, V., Vašina, L.: Psychologie Osobnosti I, vol. 3, 299 p. Hradec Králové, Gaudeamus (2009). ISBN 978-80-7041-491-0
6. Ciairano, S.: Sport, stress, self-efficacy and aggression towards peers: unravelling the role of the coach. Cognitie Creier Comportament/Cogn. Brain Behav. **11**(1), 175–194 (2007)
7. Arnold, R.: Psychometric issues in organizational stressor research: a review and implications for sport psychology. Meas. Phys. Educ. Exerc. Sci. **16**(2), 81–100 (2012)
8. Strnadová, V.: Kurz Psychologie, vol. 3, 309 p. Gaudeamus, Hradec Králové (2009). ISBN 978-807-0415-993
9. Selye, H.: The Stress of Life. McGraw-Hill, New York (1978)
10. Gerber, M.: Concerns regarding hair cortisol as a biomarker of chronic stress in exercise and sport science. J. Sports Sci. Med. **11**(4), 571–581 (2012)
11. Slepička, P., Hošek, V., Hátlová B.: Psychologie Sportu, 232 p. Karolinum, Praha (2006). ISBN 80-246-1290-9
12. Micková, E., et al.: Nepodléhejte stresu, Manuál poradce pro práci s videoprogramem. Regionální zaměstnanecká agentura, Ostrava (2004)

13. Vozka, P.: Stresové faktory a jejich vliv na organismus ve vrcholovém sportu. Bc. thesis, Faculty of Informatics and Management, University of Hradec Králové, Hradec Králové, Czech Republic (2013)
14. Šedivý, J., Chromý, J., Hubálovský Š., Šedivá K.: Research of web tools and mobile devices in education. Recent Adv. Comput. Eng. Commun. Inf. Technol. 231–235 (2014). ISBN 978-960-474-361-2

Application of ISO 13606 Archetypes for an Integration of Hospital and Laboratory Information Systems

Georgy Kopanitsa[1,2(✉)] and Maxim Taranik[1]

[1] Tomsk Polytechnic University, Lenina 30, Tomsk, Russia
georgy.kopanitsa@gmail.com
[2] Tomsk State University for Architecture and Building, Tomsk, Russia

Abstract. The paper presents a study of the application of ISO 13606 archetypes for HIS – LIS data exchange purposes. The archetypes defined a structure of laboratory tests. The archetype tests definitions were processed by a HIS to build a user interface for entering data that was required to correctly run the tests. The archetypes also contained LOINC codes in the ontology sections to provide semantic interoperability between a HIS and a LIS. The evaluation of the approach in the pilot project setting showed the feasibility of the approach.

Keywords: ISO 13606 · Archetypes · LOINC · LIS

1 Introduction

In order to achieve semantic interoperability between healthcare institutes data must be transmitted in a standardized format. The archetype model of the international standard ISO 13606 provides a means for modelling medical content and for defining knowledge for the electronic exchange of health records [1–3].

Efficient data exchange between a laboratory information system (LIS) and a hospital information system (HIS) requires that both information systems understand the semantic of the data and support its structure [4]. So ISO 13606 archetypes can serve a good basis to define laboratory tests and transfer them to a hospital information system [5]. Archetypes provide structure for a data exchange along with the semantics of the data. The semantics of the data can be defined using the ontology section of an archetype by linking an archetype data element to an international nomenclature for example LOINC [6].

The basic process of communication between a HIS and a LIS can be divided into the basic steps [7] that are presented in the Fig. 1. The steps 2 and 3 are performed to ensure that all the required data is added to the order and all the required samples are taken correctly.

When a hospital information system generates an order to perform lab tests it has to follow the tests' rules. This requires that a HIS can analyze the selected tests and conclude how many specimens of which type must be taken and which additional required fields must be filled [8–10]. Normally this requires implementation of an extra module for a HIS that works with external dictionaries. Not all the HIS developer are

G. Dregvaite and R. Damasevicius (Eds.): ICIST 2015, CCIS 538, pp. 29–36, 2015.
DOI: 10.1007/978-3-319-24770-0_3

Fig. 1. Basic data exchange process

eager to do this work. Several hospital information systems are capable of building user interface based on the structure of an archetype. So the idea was to employ an archetype approach for a semantic data exchange between a HIS and a LIS. This also provides opportunities to build efficient user interfaces [20].

If a HIS is able to build interfaces and to store data according to the ADL definition of an archetype a developer can skip the analytical routine and concentrate only on the import-export functionality.

Wide acceptance of medical data exchange standards archetype based standards (ISO 13606, openEHR) [3, 7, 11] allows implementation of integration solution between archetype based HISes. The standards employ a dual model approach to express medical knowledge [12, 13]. The reference model captures the global characteristics of medical records. It defines generic building blocks for aggregating health record components and for collecting the context information required to meet ethical and legal requirements. A hierarchical structure accommodates the separate parts reflecting the organization of medical records. The single building blocks are specified as follows. EHR_EXTRACT is the top-level container for the complete patient EHR or parts thereof. FOLDER is an optional organization element that divides content into compartments. COMPOSITION represents an encounter or document that may contain SECTIONs that provide clinical headings. The ENTRY represents a clinical statement that has ELEMENTs, i.e. the concrete data values that may be contained within CLUSTERs for organizing data structures like tables. All the building blocks within an EHR_EXTRACT have common attributes including a persistent unique identifier, a clinical name labeling each part, a standardized coded concept and the identifier of an archetype node.

The archetype model provides meta-data used to define patterns for the specific characteristics of the clinical data. Archetypes are formal definitions of combinations of the building blocks defined by the reference model for particular clinical organizations or settings. They express distinct clinical concepts by specifying a particular hierarchy of record components and define or constrain names and other relevant attribute values, data types and value ranges. The Archetype Definition Language (ADL) is a formal syntax for the definition of archetypes. It provides a general description of the concept specified and includes terminologies and translations. Archetypes deliver meta-data that consistently define the diverse, complex and frequently changing concepts in clinical practice and, thus, facilitate semantic interoperable EHRs. Based on this principle any part of a medical record can be interpreted faithfully even if the structure and nature of the clinical content had not been agreed in advance.

The complexity of the approach can be hidden from the user. Appropriate archetype editors assist in the creation of archetypes and give support through a user-friendly graphical editor. The main issue of archetype based visualization methods is that the structure of an archetype does not provide (and in fact it should not) the information necessary to build an optimal presentation layer [14, 15]. The modeling functionality provided by archetype model allows building a medical document of any complexity.

So the goal of the paper is to present a study of an archetype based HIS – LIS data exchange.

2 Methods

Helix laboratory is a clinical laboratory service located in Saint-Petersburg, Russia. The laboratory uses a self-developed LIS, with a unified LOINC based dictionary. The laboratory receives orders and biomaterial from multiple clinics and sends back results using a proprietary protocol.

For the project we employed a partner clinic that uses a HIS that could natively process ADL definitions of archetypes. The HIS is capable of creating both static and dynamic interface forms to support the data entry and validation [2, 14, 15].

Laboratory tests were modelled as ISO 13606 in LinkEHR modelling tool [16]. After the archetype repository with laboratory test archetype was created we have connected the HIS to the repository to download and process the archetype definitions.

To secure medical data we have organized a transfer of the medical data through a proprietary https based protocol. To enable the data exchange we developed an additional module to our LIS that could import archetyped data. The archetype repository with laboratory tests definitions was organized on the laboratory site. A web service approach was used to enable communication between a HIS and a LIS.

Archetypes can be linked to medical terminologies (in its ontology section), which is the way to give them semantic meaning. As the laboratory service uses LOINC codes for the lab tests we used the ontology section of archetypes to associate laboratory test components with LOINC codes. The approach was evaluated within an integration project of a Helix laboratory service in Saint-Petersburg, Russia. To evaluate the approach we calculated the number of erroneous electronic orders that could not be accepted by the LIS.

We have also evaluated the ability of the HIS to correctly define the orders when the archetypes' definitions change. This is very important case for the laboratory service as it happens when the test method is changed and this requires a change of obligatory parameters. To evaluate this we have performed the following steps:

- changing the obligatory fields
- removing fields from archetypes
- adding new fields to archetypes
- changing LOINC codes

On each step we have checked the ability of the HIS to process the archetypes correctly and to correctly define lab test orders. To check this we analyzed the user interface forms generated by the HIS and calculated the rate of errors on the stage of orders' validation. We organized a transfer of the medical data through a proprietary https based protocol.

Laboratory tests were modeled as ISO 13606 in LinkEHR modeling tool [16]. To enable the data exchange we developed an additional module to our LIS that could import archetyped data. The archetype repository with laboratory tests definitions was organized on the laboratory site. A web service approach was used to enable communication between a HIS and a LIS.

We used the ontology section of archetypes to associate laboratory test components with LOINC codes [17]. The approach was evaluated within an integration project of a Helix laboratory service in Saint-Petersburg, Russia. To evaluate the approach we calculated the percentage of erroneous electronic orders that were generated by the HIS that were correctly accepted by the LIS. We have compared the result with the average error rate of the same systems before the introduction of archetypes.

3 Results

Laboratory tests were modeled as ISO 13606 archetypes using a LinkEHR tool. As the participating LIS and HIS supported LOINC as a nomenclature coding system, LOINC codes were added to the ontology section of each archetype to provide an unambiguous interpretation of the archetypes by information systems.

The archetype serialization mechanisms were used to preserve the common structure for all the archetypes. A generic archetype for each dataset section was developed and then used as a basis for others. After the two levels were ready finding a proper structure to organize the medical results appeared to be a problem. This is due to ISO 13606 specification it, however, does not influence re-usability and flexibility of the archetyped data set, but makes modeling itself a little more challenging.

A serialization of the generic archetype for laboratory tests is presented in Fig. 2. The other laboratory test archetypes were implemented based on this generic archetype keeping its structure with only the names of the fields and the units being changed. We found the current standard archetype specialization method not very convenient. To serialize an archetype a developer needs to rename and redefine the generic archetype instead of defining the necessary structure and then generating the specific archetypes based on this structure (Fig. 2). If for example, the generic archetype is changed at a later point of time there is no mechanism to consider these changings in the specialized archetypes.

The specialized archetypes were combined into a composition (Fig. 3) that contains all the laboratory test results. This method has also a weak point – if one of the archetypes is changed the corresponding section in the composition will not automatically be adapted.

We employed an ADL capable HIS system to test the approach. The HIS was enabled to send the list of analysis to an archetype repository using a web service and receiving a set of archetypes that correspond to the order list. After the HIS has received the set of archetypes it processed them to build an interface for with additional data that a laboratory doctor had to enter (i.e. week of pregnancy). After all the required data has been entered the HIS submitted the order to the LIS.

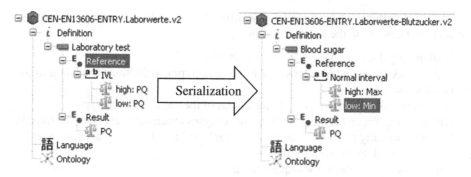

Fig. 2. Archetype serialization

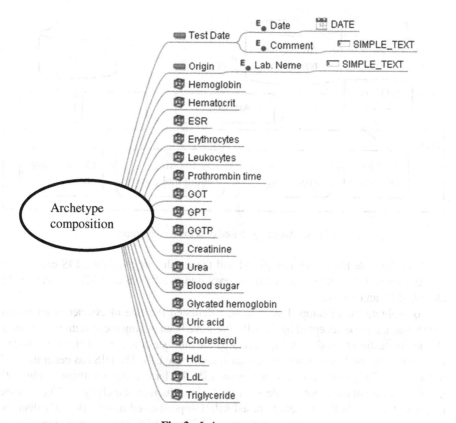

Fig. 3. Laboratory test

Two web services were developed to enable a communication between a HIS and a LIS. One web service was installed on the LIS site another on the HIS site. The LIS web service provided a method "send order" that could be called by a HIS to send electronic orders. The HIS web service provided a method "send results" that could be called by a LIS to send laboratory test results to a HIS.

Figure 4 presents the process of the electronic lab test order generation. The process can be decomposed to the following steps:

A laboratory doctors makes a list of tests in a HIS
HIS queries the archetype repository to get archetypes' definitions according to the list of tests
Archetype repository returns ADL definitions of the requested archetypes
HIS processes the archetype definitions and analyses which data fields must be filled in
HIS automatically fill in the data that is available and builds an interface form to enter the additional data required for the tests
Laboratory doctor fills in the required data
HIS generates electronic orders as an XML file and exports it to a LIS.

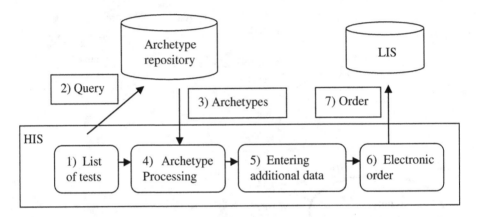

Fig. 4. Archetype based data exchange process

After the tests have been completed and the results are available, LIS exports the results back to HIS. The results are being exported to a LIS as an XML file that can be identified by an order id.

To evaluate the developed system we calculated the rate of erroneous electronic orders that could be accepted by the LIS. We have been testing the system for 1 month. During the testing period we have calculated the number of generated electronic orders and the number of orders that were not accepted by the LIS. The HIS has generate 1576 orders, 43 (2.73 %) were not accepted by the LIS. We have compared these results with the average rate of unaccepted orders before the introduction of archetypes. The average rate was 4.17 %. So the archetype based solution performed more efficiently than the non-archetype based integration solution with 2.73 to 4.17 % of not accepted orders. On the next step we have evaluated the ability of the HIS to correctly define the orders when the archetypes' definitions change. None of the scenarios (described in the methods section) have caused the misinterpretation of archetypes by the HIS. User interface forms have been generating correctly and the lab test orders have been generated without errors.

4   Conclusion

The study showed that archetype based architecture provides an efficient solution for laboratory data exchange. Application of LOINC as a canonical coding method also supported semantic interoperability for the data exchange process.

5   Discussion

The presented approach showed a high efficiency in the pilot project settings. The next step of the project will be implementation of the archetype based process of exporting results form a LIS to a HIS.

As this was a pilot project we have not defined all the laboratory tests as ISO 13606 archetypes. However, the archetype set was sufficient for a data exchange with a partner clinic. We have archetyped 72 laboratory tests.

Due to the ability of the HIS to build user interface forms dynamically based on the archetype structure the effort of maintenance of the archetype repository along with the LOINC mapping is relatively low [18, 19]. This has been proved by the evaluation. This provides the opportunity to avoid a cumbersome and complicated task of mapping clinical terms to the laboratory coding schema during the integration projects.

We have used LOINC codes in the ontology section of archetypes to preserve the semantic of the laboratory tests. This allowed avoiding extra effort to map clinical terms from a HIS nomenclature to LIS.

The archetype based approach requires a very high quality of archetypes' definition and a timely and correct updates of a repository that plays a major role in a data exchange process. This solution can be reused and applied to other environments that need to record this type of information, providing the necessary logic to work with these archetypes.

References

1. Garde, S., et al.: Expressing clinical data sets with openEHR archetypes: a solid basis for ubiquitous computing. Int. J. Med. Inform. **76**(Suppl 3), S334–S341 (2007)
2. Kopanitsa, G., Veseli, H., Yampolsky, V.: Development, implementation and evaluation of an information model for archetype based user responsive medical data visualization. J. Biomed. Inform. **55**, 196–205 (2015)
3. Veseli, H., Kopanitsa, G., Demski, H.: Standardized EHR interoperability - preliminary results of a German pilot project using the archetype methodology. Stud. Health Technol. Inform. **180**, 646–650 (2012)
4. High, S., Rowe, J.: When LIS meets HIS: refining the design of an order entry process. Healthc. Inform. **11**(8), 46–48, 50 (1994)
5. Huebner-Bloder, G., et al.: An EHR prototype using structured ISO/EN 13606 documents to respond to identified clinical information needs of diabetes specialists: a controlled study on feasibility and impact. AMIA Annu. Symp. Proc. **2012**, 380–389 (2012)
6. McDonald, C.J., et al.: LOINC, a universal standard for identifying laboratory observations: a 5-year update. Clin. Chem. **49**(4), 624–633 (2003)

7. Kopanitsa, G., Yampolsky, V.: Application of ISO 13606 archetypes for a HIS-LIS integration. Stud. Health Technol. Inform. **210**, 1018 (2015)
8. Visinoni, F.: Towards the lean lab: the industry challenge. Recent Results Cancer Res. **199**, 119–133 (2015)
9. MacMillan, D.: Calculating cost savings in utilization management. Clin. Chim. Acta **427**, 123–126 (2014)
10. Yavas, S., et al.: Influence of blood collection systems on coagulation tests. Turk. J. Haematol. **29**(4), 367–375 (2012)
11. Kopanitsa, G.: Standard based multiclient medical data visualization. Stud. Health Technol. Inform. **180**, 199–203 (2012)
12. Kopanitsa, G.: Arranging ISO 13606 archetypes into a knowledge base. Stud. Health Technol. Inform. **205**, 33–37 (2014)
13. Martinez-Costa, C., Menarguez-Tortosa, M., Fernandez-Breis, J.T.: Towards ISO 13606 and openEHR archetype-based semantic interoperability. Stud. Health Technol. Inform. **150**, 260–264 (2009)
14. Kopanitsa, G.: Evaluation study for a multi-user oriented medical data visualization method. Stud. Health Technol. Inform. **200**, 158–160 (2014)
15. Kopanitsa, G., et al.: Visualization of medical data based on EHR standards. Methods Inf. Med. **52**(1), 43–50 (2013)
16. Maldonado, J.A., et al.: LinkEHR-Ed: a multi-reference model archetype editor based on formal semantics. Int. J. Med. Inform. **78**(8), 559–570 (2009)
17. Kopanitsa, G.: Mapping Russian Laboratory Terms to LOINC. Stud. Health Technol. Inform. **210**, 379–383 (2015)
18. Kopanitsa, G., Tsvetkova, Z., Veseli, H.: Analysis of metrics for the usability evaluation of electronic health record systems. Stud. Health Technol. Inform. **174**, 129–133 (2012)
19. Kopanitsa, G., Tsvetkova, Z., Veseli, H.: Analysis of metrics for the usability evaluation of EHR management systems. Stud. Health Technol. Inform. **180**, 358–362 (2012)
20. Kopanitsa, G.: Evaluation Study for an ISO 13606 Archetype Based Medical Data Visualization Method. J Med Syst, 2015. **39**(8), 82

Using Semi-automated Approach for Mapping Local Russian Laboratory Terms to LOINC

Georgy Kopanitsa[1,2(✉)] and Maxim Taranik[1]

[1] Tomsk Polytechnic University, Lenina 30, Tomsk, Russia
georgy.kopanitsa@gmail.com
[2] Tomsk State University for Architecture and Building, Tomsk, Russia

Abstract. Manual mapping of laboratory data to Logical Observation Identifiers Names and Codes (LOINC) requires a major effort. Application of the LOINC mapping assistant RELMA V.6.6 can reduce the effort required for mapping. The goal of the paper s to study the potential of semi-automated mapping of Russian laboratory terms to LOINC.

We performed semi-automated mapping of the 2563 terms from two clinics in Russia. The first step was automatic mapping using RELMA V.6.6 and LOINC V.2.48 Russian translation by Yaroslavl state medical academy. The second step was a manual expert mapping.

To evaluate the correctness of mapping we randomly selected 50 of the most commonly (from the first 20 %) and 50 of the most rarely (from the last 20 %) used terms from each clinic (in total 200 terms from each clinic). This sample of 200 terms was reviewed by two experts. The paper presents the results of semi-automatic mapping of Russian laboratory terms to LOINC. Two clinics (A and B) and a laboratory service participated in the project. We were able to map 86 % (Clinic A) and 87 % (Clinic B) of laboratory terms and 99 % of terms used in 2014. In total 2372 out of 2563 were mapped.

The required effort was reasonable and the price of mapping and maintenance was considered as relatively low in comparison to manual methods.

RELMA V.6.6 and LOINC V.2.48 offer the opportunity of a low effort LOINC mapping even for non-English languages. The study proved that the mapping effort is acceptable and mapping results are on the same level as the manual mapping.

Keywords: LOINC · Laboratory information system · Hospital information system · Mapping

1 Introduction

The integration of laboratory information systems (LIS) and hospital information systems (HIS) is growing fast [1]. The data exchange process usually consists of the following steps: HIS defines a task for lab tests, the task is exported to a LIS, a LIS exports the results back to a HIS [2–4]. Laboratory analysis results are typically well-structured and well-defined data elements, often generated in an automated, quality-controlled fashion. As EHRs become more widespread, clinical laboratories

© Springer International Publishing Switzerland 2015
G. Dregvaite and R. Damasevicius (Eds.): ICIST 2015, CCIS 538, pp. 37–44, 2015.
DOI: 10.1007/978-3-319-24770-0_4

are increasingly delivering reports electronically in a form that can be directly stored in the client's EHR. However, the content of electronic health records (EHR), is often coded using locally developed schemes [5]. Integration with each HIS requires that individual interface terminologies are carefully inspected and mapped to a common set of concepts that are in use in the laboratory. As a laboratory service introduces new tests almost every month and excludes other tests the mapping should be maintained and the mapping schema should be kept up to date, which is resource consuming work. The choice of a coding system is left to the communicants. Usually local idiosyncratic codes are used and no universal coding scheme has yet gained a widespread acceptance. This situation is particularly of current interest in Russia, where international identifiers and coding schemes face a problem of translation. The Logical Observation Identifiers Names and Codes (LOINC) terminology [6–8] has been reported to be a promising tool for being a basis for definition and exchange of laboratory data. It provides a large, structured and multiaxial coding system for clinical observations with a major focus on laboratory data. LOINC terminology covers at least 98 % of the average laboratory's tests [9]. During its development, researchers already used the logical structure of LOINC terms as a way to translate local terms into LOINC for the purpose of sharing patient data.

Since LOINC was introduced in 1996, it has been cited in more than 140 peer-reviewed publications addressing its use for coding EHR data, mapping between terminologies and other topics. However, the application of LOINC for routine use in clinical laboratories has been limited. Published LOINC mapping projects indicate that the availability of efficient tools and the effort to define and maintain full coverage of laboratory observations are important factors influencing the decision to employ LOINC as a coding system [6, 8, 11–15].

LOINC has been widely adopted internationally. The worldwide LOINC community presently has more than 14 000 users in 143 countries. In the USA LOINC has been widely adopted by large laboratories, healthcare providers, insurance companies and research applications. LOINC is commonly used in data analysis and decision support systems. LOINC was adopted as the standard for laboratory orders and results as part of the Centers for Medicare and Medicaid Services Electronic Health Record Meaningful Use incentive program. LOINC gained an international adoption as a national standard in Brazil, Canada, Germany, the Netherlands, Mexico and Rwanda.

As LOINC's international adoption has grown there appeared translations to non-English languages. The "Centre Suisse de Contrôle de Qualité" released the first set of LOINC term name translations along with the LOINC version 2.00 release in January 2001. Currently, there are LOINC translations into 12 different languages.

In addition to the LOINC database, Regenstrief has also developed a free software program called RELMA (the REgenstrief LOINC Mapping Assistant). RELMA facilitates searching the LOINC database, viewing detailed information about the terms, and facilitates mapping local terminology to LOINC terms. RELMA also provides multilingual searching capabilities using language indexes. As an automatic mapping tool RELMA processes local terms files and creates mapping to LOINC indexes. RELMA desktop mapping and searching program is available free for download from the LOINC website (loinc.org) [10].

Despite all the advantages that the LOINC coding system provides its application in the routine work of the health care providers I limited especially in non-English environments. One of the factor that users indicate is that mapping of local terms is a difficult and a time consuming task with a lack of proper mapping tools and local language indexes.

In this paper, we present our experience with a semi-automated approach to mapping Russian local laboratory terms to LOINC with the Regenstrief LOINC Mapping Assistant (RELMA) [10] and discuss its advantages and disadvantages in comparison with previously reported approaches. Our project focused on the following aspects:

1. Semantic integration between a LIS that uses LOINC a coding system and hospital information systems by mapping the interface terminologies of HIS to LOINC.
2. Evaluation of the semi-automated mapping approach and comparing it with the methods and results of previously reported LOINC mapping projects.
3. Study of the conditions and effort for application and maintenance of LOINC as a coding system.

2 Methods

Helix laboratory is a clinical laboratory located in Saint-Petersburg, Russia. The laboratory uses a self-developed LIS, with a unified LOINC based dictionary. The laboratory receives orders and biomaterial from multiple clinics and sends back results using a proprietary protocol. The necessity to work with different clinics that use different coding systems makes each integration cumbersome and time consuming. At the moment the laboratory is working with more than 100 health care providers and health care providers' chains. Most of them use the coding schema of the laboratory (about 70 %) other 20 % use another 3 different coding schemes of 3 HIS vendors. About ten health care providers use their own coding schemas. Each of them should be mapped and maintained.

The goal was to establish LOINC as a canonical coding system for data exchange purposes, without replacing the existing interface terms of the routine HIS systems.

We employed 2 of our partner clinics (clinic A and clinic B) to participate in the pilot mapping project.

To run semi-automated LOINC mapping, we exported two datasets, each from one HIS containing all Russian language interface terms, including available additional information such as specimen type, rules (e.g., 5 blood samples each after 30 min) and specimen volume where applicable.

Two RELMA local term files were created as Excel sheets from these two HIS datasets. The local terms files were exported to RELMA using "Import local terms from delimited file or Excel spread sheet" functions to start the concept extraction. RELMA V.6.6 and LOINC V.2.48 were used for the project. A linguistic index for the Russian language (Russian translation by Yaroslavl State Medical Academy) was added by the "Set preferred language" function to correctly process the Russian terms. The index contains official LOINC Russian translation of more than 11000 terms. Our data set contained 92 % of Russian terms other terms were in English.

We performed semi-automated mapping of the 2563 terms from Clinic A (1358 terms) and Clinic B (1205 terms). The first step was automatic mapping using RELMA. This was done using "Lab auto mapper" tool from RELMA followed by the "Choose From" screen. The RELMA Lab auto mapper takes the available local test information and returns the best matches in LOINC. After the mapping has been completed the mapping file was exported to excel.

The second step was a manual expert mapping using RELMA manual search tool.

After the automated terms processing by RELMA the results were sorted to the following categories:

1. Fail: No appropriate LOINC code were found
2. Success: Exactly one matching LOINC code were found
3. Several possible codes found

In the second and the third cases a semi-automated mapping process required an additional task when an expert analysed the English LOINC V.2.48 for matching codes (second case) and an expert reviewed all 1:N results to select the right LOINC code (third case).

To evaluate the correctness of mapping we randomly selected 50 of the most commonly (from the first 20 %) and 50 of the most rarely (from the last 20 %) used terms from each clinic (in total 100 terms from each clinic). This sample of 200 terms was sent to two laboratory service physicians for independent expert review. The result of this expert review was used to calculate precision, recall, and F-measure [11]. We have calculated Cohen's kappa to rate the disagreement between experts [12]. Based on all 2563 terms, we calculated the coverage as a fraction of laboratory terms that we could map.

3 Results

The first task of the project was to map terms from two clinics to LOINC to enable semantic integration of heterogeneous laboratory data. 2563 terms were processed, and 2372 could be mapped to LOINC.

Table 1 presents the results of the mapping. The terms that were not mapped automatically were analysed and mapped by the experts. After the expert work have been finished the terms that were left unmapped were analysed for the reason why they could not be mapped. All the terms that could not be mapped were either service terms that could not be mapped to LOINC or were not in LOINC at the time of the analysis.

Table 1. Mapping results

Clinic	Source terms	Automatically mapped terms	Manually mapped terms	Unmapped terms
A	1358	1163 (86 %)	95 (7 %)	100 (7 %)
B	1205	1046 (87 %)	96 (8 %)	63 (5 %)
Total	2563	2372 (93 %)	191 (7 %)	163 (6 %)

As described in the methods section a random sample of 100 terms from each clinic (200 terms in total) was selected and independently reviewed by two laboratory physicians of the laboratory service. The results of evaluation (e.g. precision, recall and F-measure) for each clinic are presented in Table 2. Cohen's kappa was calculated to check the inter-rater agreement between the two laboratory physicians. The physicians showed disagreement in the case of two terms mapped in the clinic B. No disagreement was found in the sample from the clinic A.

Table 2. Mapping quality

Clinic	Terms	Mapped	Unmapped	Mistakes	Precision	Recall	F-measure	Cohen's kappa
A	100	96	4	1	0.99	0.95	0.96	1
B	100	97	3	1	0.99	0.96	0.97	0.96

The third goal of the study was to investigate the effort and conditions for maintaining LOINC as a coding system for integration with external HIS. To achieve a sustainable use we need to minimize the effort to map the currently used terms and the effort to map new terms in the future.

To check how many of the terms that were in use in the year 2014 we queried both clinics HISes to check how many of the terms used in the year 2014 could be mapped (automatically and semi-automatically). The query showed the coverage of 99 % (Table 3) for the most recently used terms.

Table 3 presents the results of the classification of unmapped terms. They could all be classified to three categories: comments (e.g. "hemolytic blood sample" or "clotted blood sample"), service (e.g. blood sampling performed by mobile laboratory service) and internal use codes (e.g. test is made by an outsource lab). This characterizes the quality of the initial data set and these terms are not to be mapped to LOINC.

Table 3. Mapping results for the terms in use in the year 2014

Clinic	Terms used in 2014	Terms mapped
A	685	683 (99 %)
B	754	750 (99 %)

Turnover Rate. As was mentioned above a sustainable use of LOINC implies that the effort to map newly introduced terms is minimized. We measured the number of new interface terms introduced each year since 2010. The results are presented in the Fig. 1. We can see that only about 4 % of terms were introduced since 2010 (about 1 % a year or 23 average terms a year).

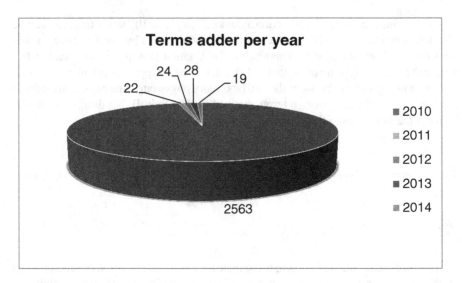

Fig. 1. Terms turnover rate

4   Discussion

We have been able to map the majority of more than 2500 Russian laboratory interface terms from two clinics to LOINC with a semi-automated approach using RELMA V. 6.6. The evaluation of mappings quality showed that only 3 out of the reviewed 400 terms were not correct. The application of LOINC as a canonical model for laboratory data exchange has shown its advantage in providing semantic interoperability. Furthermore, LOINC mapping and application of LOINC data in HIS can help structuring the displayed laboratory results in HIS.

The HISes of the Clinics A and B did not provide all the relevant data to perform mapping in every case. Even though many items could be mapped on the basis of the existing structured metadata and additional specifications in most cases analysis method were required to resolve some cases. The missing information, mostly the analysis methods, was available in standard operating procedures provided by the clinical laboratories or Helix laboratory system.

A high efficiency of mapping was achieved by implementing a semi-automated mapping approach with RELMA V.6.6, followed by manual mapping of items after no terms or multiple terms have been found automatically. Our project was limited by the Russian LOINC translation. From our experience we can assume that the process of mapping of English terms would have higher efficiency and it would need less manual work to be done.

The manual mapping was performed by an experienced laboratory doctor (with more than 10 years of experience). We managed to achieve the average mapping rate 15 terms per hour. The effort can be compared only to the Erlangen University Hospital project as other mapping projects did not report the effort. The efficiency of our project 15 terms per hour is higher than the efficiency of the German project [13]. This can be explained by the difference in the qualification of the experts. The Erlangen University Hospital project reported that the mapping was performed by a third year medical student.

Mapping validation was performed by an independent review of a sample of 400 interface terms to two laboratory doctors to check the feasibility of the approach. Different validation approached can be applied depending on the planned use of the LOINC codes. A partial validation that was used for our study was sufficient to check the feasibility of the approach and providing information for decision maker to establish LOINC as a routine coding system. If mapped terms are intended for use in routine clinical care, full validation of all mappings should be mandatory. We will run a full validation as soon as the decision will be made to employ LOINC for a routine use.

We were able to automatically map 86 % (Clinic A) and 87 % (Clinic B) of laboratory terms using RELMA V.6.6. as other terms were mapped manually to reach 94 % mapping rate. In our case all the actual laboratory terms were mapped to LOINC. The terms that could not be mapped characterize more a dataset than a mapping method (see Table 3 for unmapped terms classification). Lin et al. [14] reported a coverage of 44 %, 78 % and 79 % at three different sites. Khan et al. [15] reported a coverage of 67 % with their fully automated mapping tool. Their manual review showed that, after automated mapping, there were many unmapped terms remaining for which a precise LOINC existed, but the tool did not find it. Zunner et al. [13] reported 82 % and 75 % of terms in a semi-automated mapping using RELMA V.5.

So our semi-automated mapping using RELMA V.6.6 was even more efficient than the manual mapping of Lin et al. [14], and a semi-automated method using RELMA V. 5 by Zunner et al. [13]. The results of our project were much more efficient than the fully automated mapping of Khan et al. [15], where up to 27 % of terms could not be mapped.

As for mapping precision, Lin et al. [14] reported a precision of 0.95, with 40 mistakes in a sample of 884 terms. Khan et al. [15] did report on their mapping precision and error rate. These two projects did not report on their mapping errors. Zunner et al. [13] reported 0.98 precision with mapping errors no more than in one LOINC axes. In our mapping we have achieved 0.99 precision. The validation showed that the mapping errors never concerned more than one LOINC axis (e.g. specimen error "blood venous" instead of "blood cord venous").

This demonstrates the quality of mapping performed with RELMA is comparable to the quality of manual mapping. Of 163 unmapped terms only 47 concerned actual laboratory findings, with the others being mostly service codes and comments. This can be related to the quality of a dataset. Unfortunately we did not find any data set preparation procedures in the other studies. We have carefully checked the typos and the correctness of abbreviation before the mapping. So we recommend maintaining the consistency and quality of a dataset before mapping. Once the initial mapping has been completed, it appears that only a limited number of new laboratory tests have to be added per year to keep the mapping up to date. With approximately two new terms per laboratory and month, the time required to carry out these additional mappings should be less than an hour per month.

5   Conclusion

Our project has shown that a semi-automated approach based on RELMA V.6.6 is efficient for full mapping of Russian (non-English) routine clinical laboratory interface terms to LOINC. This was the first LOINC mapping project in Russia that allowed establishing LOINC as a coding method for two large clinics showing that the required effort is reasonable and the price of mapping and maintenance is relatively low.

References

1. Zhou, Q., He, J., Liu, J.: A study on the LIS and HIS integration. Sheng Wu Yi Xue Gong Cheng Xue Za Zhi **25**(6), 1294–1298 (2008)
2. Dixon, B.E., McGowan, J.J., Grannis, S.J.: Electronic laboratory data quality and the value of a health information exchange to support public health reporting processes. AMIA Annu. Symp. Proc. **2011**, 322–330 (2011)
3. Were, M.C., Meeks-Johnson, J., Overhage, J.M.: Enhanced laboratory reports: using health information exchange data to provide contextual information to laboratory results for practices without electronic records. AMIA Annu. Symp. Proc. 1174 (2008)
4. Kopanitsa, G.: Mapping Russian laboratory terms to LOINC. Stud. Health Technol. Inform. **210**, 379–383 (2015)
5. Hood, F.J.: Coding according to local medical review policy. South. Med. J. **94**(11), 1104–1106 (2001)
6. Wilson, P.S., Scichilone, R.A.: LOINC as a data standard: how LOINC can be used in electronic environments. J. AHIMA **82**(7), 44–47 (2011)
7. Vreeman, D.J., McDonald, C.J., Huff, S.M.: LOINC® - a universal catalog of individual clinical observations and uniform representation of enumerated collections. Int. J. Funct. Inform. Personal. Med. **3**(4), 273–291 (2010)
8. Co Jr., M.C., et al.: Using the LOINC semantic structure to integrate community-based survey items into a concept-based enterprise data dictionary to support comparative effectiveness research. Nurs. Inform. **2012**, 88 (2012)
9. Forrey, A.W., et al.: Logical observation identifier names and codes (LOINC) database: a public use set of codes and names for electronic reporting of clinical laboratory test results. Clin. Chem. **42**(1), 81–90 (1996)
10. Vreeman, D.J., et al.: Enabling international adoption of LOINC through translation. J. Biomed. Inform. **45**(4), 667–673 (2012)
11. Kawada, T.: Sample size in receiver-operating characteristic (ROC) curve analysis. Circ. J. **76**(3), 768 (2012). author reply 769
12. Berry, K.J., Johnston, J.E., Mielke Jr., P.W.: Weighted kappa for multiple raters. Percept. Mot. Skills **107**(3), 837–848 (2008)
13. Zunner, C., et al.: Mapping local laboratory interface terms to LOINC at a German university hospital using RELMA V. 5: a semi-automated approach. J. Am. Med. Inform. Assoc. **20**(2), 293–297 (2013)
14. Lin, M.C., et al.: A characterization of local LOINC mapping for laboratory tests in three large institutions. Methods Inf. Med. **50**(2), 105–114 (2011)
15. Khan, A.N., et al.: The map to LOINC project. AMIA Annu. Symp. Proc. 890 (2003)

Automation of Colorblindness Detection in Computer-Based Screening Test

Maciej Laskowski[✉]

Institute of Computer Science,
Lublin University of Technology, Lublin, Poland
m.laskowski@pollub.pl

Abstract. Despite popular belief, color vision disorders do have an impact on the life of the persons affected, on both professional and private, everyday level. It is important to be aware of the possessed disorder, as in severe cases colorblindness may even endanger one's life, as e.g. protanopes may perceive red traffic lights as extinguished.

Computer games and simulations, although broadly present in medical education for at least fifteen years, have not been yet used as an accepted diagnostic tool. This article discusses the possibility of using serious game for diagnosing color vision disorders with a author-developed disorder-dependent palette of colors, which are difficult to tell apart by colorblind. An experiment, involving simple web browser based game was conducted. The analysis of its results are discussed, especially the problem of false positives and negatives, which is always present in automatic diagnostic systems.

Keywords: Colorblindness · Color vision disorders · Serious games · Diagnostic systems · Gamification

1 Introduction

In the most broad definition, colorblindness is the inability (or reduced ability) to distinguish between certain colors or shades under normal lighting condition [6]. It may differ from total color blindness (monochromacy), through dichromacy (where one out of three types of retinal cones are missing or strongly underdeveloped), up to reduced visible color spectrum – anomalous trichromacy, where the aforementioned types of retinal cones are underdeveloped or not working properly [13].

Despite its name, colorblindness does not affect vision itself, just one's color perception. Color vision disorders may be caused by several different factors – the main cause being a faulty gene carried on the X chromosome (that's the reason why colorblindness affects mostly males, since they have only one X chromosome [11]), but it may also be caused (permanently or temporarily) by trauma to the optical nerve or brain as well as by some chemicals, including drugs [11].

About 10 % of the whole human population is affected with some kind of color vision disorder, with deuteranomaly being the most common (see Table 1), although it has to be noticed that this value is not distributed evenly among the human population – as colorblindness affects more men than women (except for monochromacy, tritanopia

© Springer International Publishing Switzerland 2015
G. Dregvaite and R. Damasevicius (Eds.): ICIST 2015, CCIS 538, pp. 45–56, 2015.
DOI: 10.1007/978-3-319-24770-0_5

and tritanomaly, the last two caused by mutation carried on gender-independent chromosome 7). Moreover, it affects Caucasians more often than any other human race [9]. The estimated geographical distribution of colorblind population is presented in Fig. 1.

Table 1. The distribution of color vision disorders in human population (source: [6, 9])

Color vision disorder	Type	% Males affected	% Females affected
Monochromacy	Rod monochromacy	0,001	
	Cone monochromacy	0,00001	
Dichromacy	Protanopia	1,1	0,02
	Deuteranopia	1,2	0,01
	Tritanopia	0,003	0,002
Anomalous trichromacy	Protanomaly	1,3	0,02
	Deuteranomaly	6	0,4
	Tritanomaly	0,01	

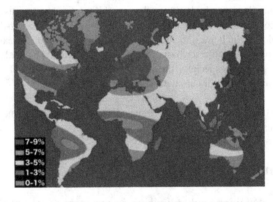

Fig. 1. Geographical distribution of colorblind population (source: [9])

Despite popular belief, color vision disorders do have an impact on the people affected. This does not only apply to the professional aspects of life, but mainly applies to everyday life, e.g. people with protanopia may perceive red traffic lights as extinguished or cannot distinguish raw meat from fried one. However, while discussing the impact of color vision disorders on professional aspects of life, it should be noticed, that this applies not only to drivers or pilots, but also to physicians [12], chemists or firemen [11].

Examples of simulated vision of a colorblind person is presented in Figs. 2 a–d and 3 a–d. As it can be seen, it is very important for the person affected with color vision disorder to be aware of this fact, as it may affect their personal safety.

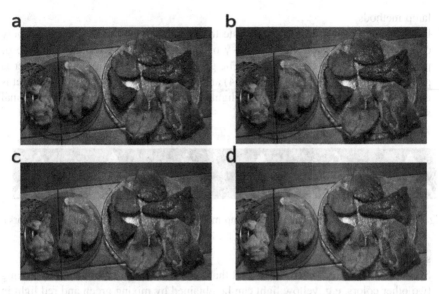

Fig. 2. Raw and fried pieces of different meats, as seen by a) person with normal color vision, b) with protanopia, c) with deuteranopia, d) with tritanopia (own work, simulation using vischeck.com)

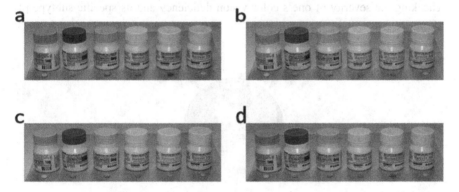

Fig. 3. Medicine bottles as seen by a) person with normal color vision, b) with protanopia, c) with deuteranopia, d) with tritanopia (own work based on [8], simulation using vischeck.com)

2 Overview of Currently Used Colorblindness Detection Methods

Colorblindness detection methods can be divided into four main groups (according to: [4, 14]):

- arrangement methods
  These methods requires the examinee either to select a number of samples with color matching (or close to) to the one given by the examiner or to arrange the samples in a certain order (e.g. from the lightest to the darkest).

- lamp methods

  Lamp methods are used to demonstrate the examinee's ability to distinguish only certain signal colors (e.g. used in navy or aviation), not to determine the type of potential color vision disorder [14]. The general method is pretty simple – user is presented with a set of lights (see Fig. 4) and his task is to determine which subset is currently turned on. The colors of the lights matches the colors used in navigational systems.

Fig. 4. An example of light sets used in lamp method – Wilczek's lamp (source: own work)

- spectral methods

  Spectral methods are based on the fact that certain color can be obtained by mixing two other colors, e.g. yellow light can be obtained by mixing green and red light in a certain ratio (see Fig. 5). Spectral methods are considered to be one of the most accurate diagnostic methods, as they allow – by analyzing the mixing ratio – checking the severity of one's color vision deficiency and its specific subtype [3].

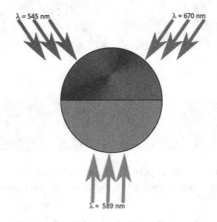

Fig. 5. Obtaining yellow light by mixing green and red lights in certain ratio (source: own work) (Color figure online)

- pseudoisochromatic plates

  Pseudoisochromatic plates usually contain a circle of points appearing randomized in color and size. Within the pattern there are dots forming a number or shape clearly visible to people with normal color vision and invisible or difficult to see to people with color vision disorders [14]. There are various sets of plates, dedicated to different groups of users, with sets developed by Shinobu Ishihara in 1917 being the most popular.

All of those methods differ on equipment needed, accuracy, examination cost and circumstances of use. The pseudoisochromatic plates are the most commonly used, due to relatively low cost and high accuracy (about 90–95 %), although are often criticized for being ambiguous and relatively inaccessible for certain groups of users, e.g. children or people with limited capabilities, despite having special plates for illiterates [2, 7].

Moreover, due to equipment wear each diagnostic method has a period of top accuracy, ranging from 18 months in case of pseudoisochromatic plates up to 5 years in case of lamp methods. This means that after this time, the diagnostic equipment should be replaced in order to provide best results.

The problem of ensuring diagnostic accuracy is especially important in case of the countries where being diagnosed as colorblind may result in preventing one's career in certain occupations as driver or pilot, as well as having non-professional driving license [5]. It is also worth noticing, that in some cases people tend to pretend to have color vision disorder, as this will allow them to be transferred into different position – e.g. in Indian railways the colorblind are not allowed to work as motormen, but are employed as a conductors, what usually means extra income [5].

All of those factors contribute to a need of new, reliable (possibly automatized) and relatively cheap diagnostic method for detecting color vision disorders.

3 Setting the Experiment

Planning the experiment, the authors wanted to answer the following question: is it possible to diagnose the potential color vision disorder while analyzing the actions and decisions made by player during the game? If so, which actions should and which shouldn't be taken into account?

3.1 Previous Attempts

The idea of using games for detecting color vision disorders was at first postulated by one of the authors in paper [1]. The primary method was focused on detecting colorblindness in candidates for drivers and was limited to player choosing the right traffic light positioned randomly on the screen (see Fig. 6).

Fig. 6. An example set of 20 randomly positioned traffic lights (source: own work)

Despite rather simple experimental presumption (using only three predefined colors), the experiment itself turn out to be quite successful, as it allowed to detect four potential dichromates in population of 80 tested persons. However, it has to be noticed that there was no attempt to corroborate the experiment results using further medical examination, as the diagnosis was only confirmed while interviewing the participants.

The described experiment should be treated only as a proof-of-concept and required further, more planned development, especially considering technical background, which was realized during the experiment described in this paper.

3.2 Technical Background

Color representation is one of the most puzzling problems in computer graphics. Depending on the graphical and display hardware, the colors presented to users may differ noticeably. Usually those differences are corrected by Color Management System implemented into OS, although some applications have their own CMS-s.

Authors decided to create a web-browser based application with HTML5 and JavaScript for detecting color vision disorders due to two main reasons:

- Color Management System implemented in some browsers (e.g. Mozilla Firefox). CMS is the controlled conversion between the color representations of various devices, like monitors, TV screens and corresponding media. Its primary goal is to obtain a good match across various devices, e.g. the colors of a photograph should appear the same on a computer monitor, a camera display, and in a printed form;
- availability of the application to the widest test group possible – anyone interested should be able to test his color vision without using special equipment (as only computer is required) or previous training (due to simple rules of a game and automation of the diagnostic process).

The application's core was written in PHP and all collected data is stored in MySQL database.

3.3 Color Schemes

Defining color scheme for each color vision disorder was another important issue. A set of colors hard to tell apart by people with certain type of colorblindness, but relatively easy to distinguish by people with normal color vision or another type of color vision disorder had to be compiled basing on data from literature and own research. This required working with actual colorblind persons, as color vision disorders cannot be fully simulated.

Author assumed that seven different color sets have to be created: one neutral (where colors can be told apart by anyone, regardless of the correctness of their color vision), three for each type of dichromacy and three for each type of anomalous trichromacy.

Moreover, developed sets should be complementary in corresponding types of color vision disorders: e.g. people with protanomaly should be able to distinguish colors, which are perceived wrongly by people with protanopia.

In order to develop discussed color sets, author used so-called "confusion axes" – intersecting lines (for each type of dichromacy) going through CIE 1931 color space.

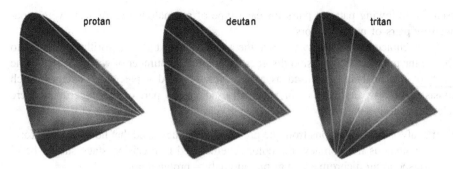

Fig. 7. Schematic representation of the CIE color triangle with the confusion lines for protan, deutan, and tritan defects (source: [10]) (Color figure online)

Colors placed on those lines are hard (or in case of severe color vision disorders – impossible) to distinguish by people with certain type of dichromacy [11] (Fig. 7).

3.4 Experiment Setup

The experiment was based on a simple game, which required its players to choose one of two colors displayed on the screen at the same time in order to match the model color. This test was to be simple in order to make it easy and understandable to the widest group possible (in opposition e.g. to Ishihara plates which are targeted at people over 6 years of age and at appropriate cognitive and language development level [7]). The participants were presented with 125 color pairs in total, having 5 s to make each choice (in comparison to 3 s in case of Ishihara plates).

The program interface is presented in Fig. 8.

The experiment was conducted in a controlled environment, using the same hardware configuration for each participant. The LCD computer screen used in the experiment was calibrated according to the producer's guidance and the latest driver available was used.

The experiment itself was divided into four stages. The first introductory stage (6 pairs) used only neutral color scheme. The second stage, consisting of 84 pairs in total,

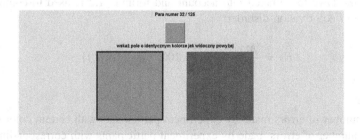

Fig. 8. Application interface: user has chosen the first color from a presented pair (source: own work)

used the following pattern: pairs for each type of anomalous trichromacy were separated by pairs of neutral colors.

User choices were analyzed after the second stage by an algorithm in order to choose the potential color vision disorder, basing on the number of wrong choices. The result of this analysis was used as a basis for the third – precision – stage, which consisted of 30 pairs. The color schemes used in this part of the experiment were selected as following:

- if analysis of user actions from the previous stage suggested that he has certain form of anomalous trichromacy, the color scheme used in precision stage should be of corresponding dichromacy (e.g. protanomaly – protanopia);
- if analysis of user actions from the previous stage was inconclusive (e.g. it was impossible to tell which type of anomalous trichromacy is present), two types of dichromacy were chosen, basing of the highest error ratio;
- if analysis of user actions from the previous stage showed that participant had correct color vision, the order of color schemes from the previous stage is repeated.

After completing the third stage, the results were analyzed again in order to diagnose the potential color vision disorder.

The fourth, final stage consisted of five pairs of colors, in the following order: protanomaly, deuteranomaly, tritanomaly, the diagnosed disorder and neutral. In case no disorder was detected, neutral color scheme was used.

After the final stage the diagnostic algorithm was run for the third and final time to confirm the diagnosis from third stage. Each diagnosis had its probability computed, according to the formula 1.1

$$E_v = \frac{M_v}{T_v} * 100, \quad v \in \{p, d, t\} \tag{1.1}$$

where:

M_v – number of errors made by experiment participants with certain color scheme
T_v – total number of color pairs in certain scheme displayed
p, d, t – dichromacy or anomalous trichromacy color scheme (p – protanous, d- deuteranous, t - tritanous)

In case of dichromacy, the errors made with corresponding anomalous trichromacy color scheme have to be taken into account and formula 1.2 is used to compute the probability of color vision disorder:

$$E_v = \frac{(M_v + M_{v2})}{(T_v + T_{v2})} * 100, \quad v \in \{p, d, t\} \tag{1.2}$$

where:

M_v – number of errors made by experiment participants with certain color scheme
M_{v2} – number of errors made by experiment participants with corresponding color scheme
T_v – total number of color pairs in certain scheme displayed

T_{v2} – total number of color pairs in corresponding scheme displayed

All of the diagnosed cases of color vision disorders were then tested offline using Ishihara pseudoisochromatic plates (as a widely used method in medical examination rooms) in order to corroborate the diagnosis done by the system.

Despite simplistic interface and rules, the presented game itself is quite extensible – as it allows quick implementation of elements for raising the attractiveness of the play or rewarding the playes, such as points or badges. However, it should be noticed that some gamification elements may not be usable due to the application purpose as screening test, e.g. leaderboards – due to the fact that the user will play the game only once, thus may not be willing to compete against other players. In this context also badges implementation is discussable.

4   Experiment Results and Analysis

Total number of 143 persons participated in the experiment, 37 females and 106 males, ranging from 17 to 57 years of age. Upon completing the test, before displaying the results, system required the participants to complete a short survey, asking about being previously diagnosed with colorblindness and about their opinion on the system itself. This feature will be removed from the final version of the system, as it is not vital for the diagnostic process and may be perceived as an unnecessary element in the screening test.

37 participants were diagnosed with color vision disorders – over 25 % percent of the tested population, which exceeded the usual percentage (see Table 1) over twice. Analysis of those results showed that 23 persons were characterized with very low probability of different color vision disorders, which means that one or two mistakes were made during the game. Moreover, the validation of the results survey results and using Ishihara plates showed no sign of color vision disorders in those persons – this corroborated the hypothesis that those low-probability diagnoses were caused by random mistake, not by wrong perception of colors.

Experiment results (for the potential colorblind users) are shown in Table 2.

Table 2. Experimental results for the potential colorblind users (source: own work)

Id	Sex	Potential CVD	% of errors (total)	Confirmed by expert
1	M	Protanopia	45	Yes
2	M	Protanopia	19	Yes
3	M	Protanopia	19	Yes
4	M	Protanopia	6	No
5	M	Protanopia	6	No
6	F	Protanopia	8	No
7	M	Protanomaly	63	Yes
8	M	Protanomaly	41	Yes

(*Continued*)

Table 2. (*Continued*)

Id	Sex	Potential CVD	% of errors (total)	Confirmed by expert
9	M	Protanomaly	31	Yes
10	M	Protanomaly	6	No
11	M	Protanomaly	6	No
12	M	Protanomaly	6	No
13	M	Protanomaly	6	No
14	M	Deuteranopia	50	Yes
15	M	Deuteranopia	42	Yes
16	M	Deuteranopia	6	No
17	M	Deuteranomaly	63	Yes
18	M	Deuteranomaly	31	Yes
19	M	Deuteranomaly	6	No
20	M	Deuteranomaly	6	No
21	M	Tritanopia	19	Yes
22	F	Tritanopia	6	No
23	M	Tritanopia	6	No
24	F	Tritanomaly	56	Yes
25	M	Tritanomaly	25	Yes
26	F	Tritanomaly	6	No
27	F	Tritanomaly	6	No
28	M	Tritanomaly	6	No
29	F	Tritanomaly	6	No
30	M	Tritanomaly	6	No
31	F	Tritanomaly	6	No
32	M	Tritanomaly	6	No
33	M	Tritanomaly	6	No
34	F	Tritanomaly	6	No
35	M	Tritanomaly	6	No
36	M	Tritanomaly	6	No
37	M	Tritanomaly	6	No

The analysis of the raw experimental data showed that an error threshold should be implemented into system before computing the final diagnosis. Implementing the threshold on earlier stages of diagnostic algorithm may be erroneous, as it may affect detection of mild anomalous trichromacy.

After analyzing the experiment results the error threshold was computed as an average error rate for all the unconfirmed cases (6 %). The experiment results with values above the error threshold are shown in Table 3.

Table 3. Experimental results for the potential colorblind users after implementing error threshold (source: own work).

Id	Sex	Potential CVD	% of errors (total)	Confirmed by expert
1	M	Protanopia	45	Yes
2	M	Protanopia	19	Yes
3	M	Protanopia	19	Yes
6	**F**	**Protanopia**	**8**	**No**
7	M	Protanomaly	63	Yes
8	M	Protanomaly	41	Yes
9	M	Protanomaly	31	Yes
14	M	Deuteranopia	50	Yes
15	M	Deuteranopia	42	Yes
17	M	Deuteranomaly	63	Yes
18	M	Deuteranomaly	31	Yes
21	M	Tritanopia	19	Yes
24	F	Tritanomaly	56	Yes
25	M	Tritanomaly	25	Yes

As it can be seen, implementing the error threshold removed almost all of the unconfirmed cases, except for one (with ID = 6). Moreover, it has to be noticed that no confirmed colorblind cases were removed from the list.

According to the survey, users graded the quality of working with the system with average of 4.13 (in a Likert scale of 1–5, where 1 – the worst, 5 – the best).

5 Conclusions

The analysis of the experiment results proved the system to be a useful tool for detecting color vision disorders, although it requires additional work on determining and corroborating the acceptance (error) threshold and lie scale (especially in case of tests on larger population). Nevertheless the proposed system proved to be a useful tool for screening tests, as even without implementing the acceptance threshold and lie scale, the number of patients requiring examination by medical personnel decreased significantly – by almost 75 %. This proves that automation of diagnostic process does improve its overall time consumption.

Although the method itself proved to be successful, mainly due to the automation of the diagnostic process, the problem of using a game as a diagnostic tool (or – in broader context – implementing game elements into diagnostic process) should be researched further. The described system can serve as a basis for more complicated applications with more game elements implemented. However, it should be noticed that the more complicated the game, the more elements have to be taken into account during the diagnosis (e.g. the influence of personal features like agility or reflex on the results obtained).

According to the survey, users confirmed that the game-based diagnostic method is an interesting alternative to traditional medical examination, as participants focused more on completing the game than on the examination itself, feeling like a subject to, not as an object of the test.

The described system can serve as an interesting and relatively cheap alternative to currently used colorblindness tests. It should be noticed, that although the proposed method requires a computer, which may be seen as expensive factor, the overall examination cost per capita is very low (almost equal to the cost of power consumed). Moreover, the computer can be used – if necessary – also for different purposes than colorblindness detection in contrast to any kind of currently used color vision disorders detection equipment, which are solely designed for this purpose.

References

1. Bober, D., et al.: Interactive method of detecting color vision disorders in candidates for drivers. In: Polish Association for Knowledge Management, Series: Studies and Proceedings no. 42, 2011, Bydgoszcz 2011, pp. 5–15 (2010)
2. Birch, J.: Diagnosis of Defective Colour Vision. Elsevier, Amsterdam (2003)
3. Fluck, D.: RGB anomaloscope color blindness test (2008). http://www.colblindor.com/2008/03/11/rgb_anomaloscope_color_blindness_test
4. Fluck, D.: Color blindness tests (2010). http://www.colblindor.com/2010/03/23/color_blindness_tests
5. French, A.L., et al.: The evolution of colour vision testing. Aust. Orthoptic J. **40**(2), 7–15 (2008)
6. Kaiser, P.K., Boynton, R.M.: Human Color Vision. Optical Society of America, Washington, D.C. (1996)
7. Laskowski, M.: A comparative cost and accuracy analysis of selected colorblindness detection methods. Actual Probl. Econ. **3**(141), 327–333 (2013)
8. L.A. Times: Color-coded pills often don't work for the colorblind, LA Times. http://latimesblogs.latimes.com/booster_shots/2009/08/colorcoded-pills-often-dont-work-for-the-colorblind.html. Accessed 28 August 2009
9. McIntyre, D.: Colour Blindness: Causes and Effects. Dalton Publishing, Chester (2002)
10. Optical Diagnostics. http://www.opticaldiagnostics.com/info/color_vision_defects.html
11. Shevell, S.K.: The Science of Color, 2nd edn. Optical Society of America, Oxford (2003)
12. Spalding, J.A.B.: Confessions of a colour blind physician. Clin. Exp. Optom. **87**(4–5), 344–349 (2004)
13. Szymczyk, T., Laskowski, M.: Method of supporting the CAPTCHA-based registration process for the visually impaired people. Pol. J. Environ. Stud. **18**(3B), 363–367 (2008)
14. Yates, J.T., Heikens, M.F.: Colour vision testing methodologies: update and review. In: Menu, J.P., Ivan, D. (eds.) RTO technical report 16. NATO, Neuilly sur Seine (2001)

GMM-Based Molecular Serum Profiling Framework

Małgorzata Plechawska-Wójcik$^{(\boxtimes)}$

Lublin University of Technology, Nadbystrzycka 38D,
20-618 Lublin, Poland
m.plechawska@pollub.pl

Abstract. The paper presents GMM-based molecular serum profiling framework dedicated to complete analyzing of Maldi-ToF mass spectrometry data. The presented Matlab-based framework is a comprehensive, self-adapting solution dedicated to different kind of spectra datasets. The process of mass spectrometry data analysis consists of several procedures, like data preparation, data pre-processing including baseline correction, detection of outliers and noise removal. The mean spectrum is calculated, modeled with GMM and decomposed using the Expectation-Maximization algorithm. In this process localization of the mean spectrum peaks is done with the dedicated adaptive procedure. Results of the mean spectrum decomposition in the subsequent step are applied into each single spectrum in the dataset in the form of Gaussian mask. The result is a data set ready for further statistical analysis.

Keywords: Biomedical signal processing · Gaussian mixture models · Spectrometry data analyzing · Biomedical data statistics

1 Introduction

Proteomic data profiling is a multitasking challenge which involve work with large data sets of high dimensionality. Analysis of such data needs for specially dedicated computer support systems enabling data cleaning, preprocessing, appropriate analysis, statistical interpretation and classification. Proteomic approaches give possibilities for interpretation of biological phenomenon, especially for medical diagnosis. One of areas which make use of proteomic analysis is oncology. The proteomic analysis gives promise for positive results of research over the process of tumor development in human organism and its response to the therapy. What is more, proteomics gives hope for improving diagnosis and developing of new and more efficient treatment methods.

Today development of computer-supported diagnosis and treatment enables to perform efficient statistical inference [7, 20]. Proteomic methods must be able to deal with large amount of data which are obtained in, usually extended, process of data gathering and preliminary analyzing. The raw data, however, must be subjected to complex and computationally demanding analysis. Such advanced techniques are needed to be applied especially in high-bandwidth mass spectrometry analysis, in studies of protein mixtures and evaluation of proteins expression. One of common

© Springer International Publishing Switzerland 2015
G. Dregvaite and R. Damasevicius (Eds.): ICIST 2015, CCIS 538, pp. 57–70, 2015.
DOI: 10.1007/978-3-319-24770-0_6

problems is efficient and adjusted to the different spectra identification of protein complexes. Development of proteomic techniques and tools gives opportunities for more efficient and accurate proteins detection and analysis of their influence on particular medical phenomena, primarily in terms of medical diagnosis and new methods of treatments. Also statistical analysis, especially classification plays an important role in the process of the analysis of those large data sets. There are ongoing search for efficient methods of dimensional reduction and classification fulfilling requirements for high sensitivity and specificity.

Complexity of proteomic data analysis lies in number of factors to be considered [28] (not always unique amino acid sequences, possible several different coding genes, existence of polymorphism genes resulting in different proteins variants, posttranslational modifications, etc.). Proteomics methods are able to examine complex interactions between proteins and their modifications in terms of simultaneous analysis of high-dimensional data. A typical proteomic approach is identification of proteins and their dependencies in biological tissues [5, 6]. Proteins identification is usually carried out by comparing the measured properties of the protein to those known and documented, available in biological (proteomic) databases, what enables low or non-invasive study of protein profiles in blood, plasma or urine.

The aim of this paper is to present a framework for complex analysis of proteomic mass spectra enabling efficient and automatic data processing. Presented framework is composed of the set of methods dedicated to preliminary data processing, dealing with outliers and noised data, peaks detection and static analysis. The paper presents also results of applying framework's methods to spectra obtained from serum of gastric cancer patients.

The novelty of the presented framework lies in the fact that it provides features and adjustments enabling comprehensive process of analysis automatically adjusted to the data. It provides complete preprocessing covering noise reduction and extended, three-step outlier detection including technical repetitions alignment. The framework applies the specified order of the analysis which was tested and analyzed for several different datasets. Those procedures are applied fully automatically, all parameters are adjusted based on the analyzed dataset. However, they may be corrected also manually. Applied peak detection method is based on the GMM model method presented in our previous studies [23–25]. However, the peak detection procedure is improved. It was turned to be adaptive – it automatically adjust parameters (for instance number of peaks) to data and it gives fully repetitive results. The framework, due to its flexibility, might be applied to various datasets such as: human datasets (head cancer, stomach cancer, prostate cancer data) and animals datasets (mice).

The rest of the paper is structured as follows. Section 2 provides a brief introduction to 2. Maldi-ToF mass spectra and analysis. Section 3 contains the description of the method applied in the case study. The main method dedicated to peaks identification is based on the Gaussian Mixture Model (GMM). Section 4 presents the complex mass spectra analysis procedure applied. It contains data preparation, data pre-processing, peaks identification, and statistical analysis. Result of the gastric cancer analysis is presented in Sect. 5. Conclusions are presented in Sect. 6.

2 Maldi-ToF Mass Spectra Analysis

The molecular profiling of the serum proteome, especially its low-molecular-weight component, is a potential method cancer diagnostics. The process presented in the paper is dedicated to MALDI-ToF-based profiling applied to identify serum proteome component associated with cancer data.

Maldi-ToF is one of the most popular mass spectrometry type willingly applied in the proteomic research. Mass spectrometry is an analytical technique dedicated for accurate measurement of mass to charge ratio (M/Z) of the proteins. This method is used to identify chemical compounds and to determine their structure and elemental composition. Maldi-ToF is used primarily to determine the composition of complex mixtures. It is widely applied in proteomics, to proteins identification. Typical mass spectrometer works in three phases. They are: ionization of molecules, selection of charged particles and their detection.

Maldi-ToF mass spectrometry is based on using of matrix absorbing the laser beam. This process causes ions sputtered and spared in the electric field. Ions hit a detector which determines intensities for particular M/Z value. The detector works based on the mass of ions on the basic of their velocities and time of flight through the spectrometer [21]. Mass spectrometer returns results in the form of the mass spectrum. The mass spectrum presents the dependence of mass-to-charge ratio (M/Z) and intensity. Intensity determines the number of ions that hit the detector in a small, fixed time interval. This interval is determined is the time resolution of the instrument.

Before the proper analysis, mass spectrometry data need to be pre-processed and prepared. Preprocessing steps have major impact on the further process of analysis and for quality of obtained results. Pre-processing steps and their parameters may vary depending on the specific type of data and applied data exploration method. However, proteomic analysis studies of mass spectrometry data usually apply: noise correction, baseline correction, normalization, spectra alignment. The type and sequence of steps is the result of years of research and studies [21]. Usually also missing data need to be handled. Noise removal and baseline correction are usually necessary due to noise of spectrometry matrix or contamination and instability of data samples. The level of noise in the spectrum is a spectrum quality determinant. Both, noise and baseline correction can be performed with methods based on multiple shifted window with defined width, discrete-wavelet transformation (especially undecimated discrete-wavelet transformation, UDWT [12, 18], the least-squares digital polynomial filter (Savitzky and Golay filters) or nonparametric smoothing (locally-weighted linear regression with specified window size and type of kernel) [17]. There are also methods considering peaks shape and localization, based on the rule the higher the weight, the wider and lower peaks. The important issue is also resolution of the device. Resolution is determined the percentage of the weight. While the weight increases, the device resolution worsens. That is why spectra of low molecular mass have better resolution and their peaks are more separable. The shape of the peaks, however, varies along with the spectrum. The higher the M/Z is, the lower and wider peaks may become. The most popular method of normalization consists in scaling all spectra to total ion current

(TIC) value or to constant noise. Sometimes also trimming, binning and the mean spectrum calculation is performed.

The primary source of information about proteins, their sequences and the genes encoding them constitutes biological databases. Data contained in such databases come from research experiments and their interpretation, publications and other databases. Research centers which undertake the construction and maintenance of biological databases often cooperate and exchange data. The problem of biological databases is the huge growth of information and the associated need of standardization and structuring of stored information. Biological data, in particular protein data, are difficult to manage because of the continuous flow of information and lack of uniform standards and methods of naming classification. Continuous exchange of data contained in different databases enable frequent updates. On the other hand, there is a need of continuous control of data quality and consistency. There are conducted works on automation of this process and developed of new comparison and integration methods. The best-known biological databases are:

- UniProt [26, 34] containing detailed information about proteins, such as entry name, status of reviewing process, organism, gene names and identifiers, features or GO annotations;
- NBCI [10], where searching is based on the gene identifier and it returns precise information about a particular gene, its role, status, lineage and related data;
- KEGG (Kyoto Encyclopedia of Genes and Genomes) [16] database giving details about genes pathways, structures, sequences, references to other databases;
- EPO-KB (Empirical Proteomic Ontology Knowledge Base) [2] database, where names of proteins and peptides might be found based on M/Z values given with a specified percentage tolerance;
- and many others, like EXPASY or HPRD.

One of the most essential tasks in the mass spectrometry data analysis is peaks identification. There are different models used to perform this task. The most popular one is based on local maxima and minima chosen from the mass spectrum [27, 33]. The real peaks can be chosen only among local maxima which are higher than a the signal to noise ratio (S/N) [8, 19]. It enables detection of peaks with the highest values of intensity [31]. Other methods distinguish between noise and the real peaks considering the shape of peaks [13, 14].

A model proposed by Coombes et al. [5], Morris et al. [21] defines distribution of the mass spectrum signal into baseline, normalization ratio and noise. This model uses sum of independent, sometimes overlapped peaks, each of which corresponds to a single protein. Peak shapes can be estimated empirically on the based on physical simulation of the ToF analyzer process. The noise is defined as white noise [5]. Baggerly et al. [1] considering the inclusion of the additional noise model time-dependent factor. The method assumes using of the mean spectrum, undecimated discrete wavelet transformation (UDWT) denoising and local minima and maxima analysis. There is also a group of methods modeling spectra with a set of member functions. Decomposition may be based on the wavelet transformations [11] or composition of Levy processes [4].

3   Applied Methods

Mixture model is a popular way of modeling large data sets. They are usually applied to model natural phenomena and biological processes. They can be also applied in image processing and clustering. Mixture models are often complex, they consist of many individual probability distributions. Mixture models allow to interpret the whole population as a composition of adequate number of sub-populations. This technique enables to decompose modeled data and perform detailed analysis to obtain better estimation. In practice, the most commonly used mixture models are based on Gaussian distributions. Such mixtures are known as Gaussian Mixture Models (GMM).

Appling GMM presents the data in parameterized way. Usually model's parameters are unknown and the main task of the analysis of mixture models is to determine their parameters. The number of unknown GMM parameters is 3k-1, where k is the number of Gaussian mixture's components. For each mixture component one need to estimate both its Gaussian parameters (mean and standard deviation) as well as its weight. The parameters estimation task may occur to be complex. The more components are included in the mixture, the harder and more time consuming is the estimation task.

The task of mixture models parameters solving can be treated as a missing data problem. This problem might be formulated as a task of determining the membership of a group of data points to one of the mixture distributions. This membership is unknown and needs to be estimated. Parameters of the model should therefore be selected in such a way as to find the best data representation by their membership to the individual components of the mixture.

The method chosen for mixture model parameters estimation needs to handle the missing values. Typical estimation methods are based on the maximum likelihood. However, complex models with large number of parameters to be estimated cannot be efficiently solved by maximum likelihood-liked methods. An additional difficulty is the existence of many local likelihood extremes of applied modeling function. Therefore, likelihood maximization of the Gaussian mixture model fit can be performed with Expectation-Maximization algorithm (EM) [9]. The EM method assumes the existence of hidden variables. Those hidden variables represent variables defining affiliation of the each observation to one of the GMM components.

EM algorithm is an iterative method, consisting of a repeated measures (E and M). E and M steps are executed in a loop until the defined accuracy is reached. In each subsequent step new parameters values are calculated. If the number of components is known, the initiation step of the algorithm consists in determination of the initial conditions.

The use of GMM for spectra modeling is based on the assumption that one peak is represented by a single Gaussian distribution. Each Gaussian defines and models one component of the spectrum. To calculate the model parameters one need to use a modified version of the algorithm Expectation-Maximization. This version is adjusted to the nature of spectrometry data.

Application of the EM algorithm requires adjustment of input data, because the standard version of EM requires a one-dimensional input vector. For the purposes of spectrometric data a weighted version of the algorithm was implemented. It considers the intensity of the spectrum characterizing the repetition number of the corresponding M/Z values.

4 Applied Analysis Procedure

The whole process of proteomic data profiling is based on four tasks: data preparation, data pre-processing, peaks identification and statistical analysis. All parameters are adjusted automatically. The set of parameters relate to:

- binning window
- dataset trimming and correction of noised high peak detected at the beginning of spectra
- interpolation type
- noise correction parameters including smooth method, window size and step size
- outliers detection based on GMM including signal-to-noise ratio, area under the curve and Dixon test.

4.1 Data Preparation

Before the analysis the aim of the process must be defined and raw dataset needs to be initially evaluated. Each dataset might be composed of dozens or even hundreds of data files. Single data file contain raw MALDI-TOF data obtained for single sample (for one patient). Single data file contain M/Z values and corresponding identities.

Cancer data might came from few groups of people: patients in different stage of disease (for example: locally advanced cancer and metastatic gastric cancer) and healthy donors. Depending on number of analyzed groups the whole process might vary especially in the context of the statistical analysis, which is performed using different methods for two analyzed groups and different for more than two of them. Data sets might also contain data repeatedly generated for single patient. This practice helps to avoid exclusion of patients' results caused by of noisy or improperly generated data. Before the analysis a researcher must know the characteristics of technical repeated data.

The analysis process must be verified at each level. Before the analysis it is good practice to generate and check the mean spectrum of the dataset. It enables to verify the dataset: the range of data, peaks shape and height. However, to generate the mean spectrum one needs to obtain X axis standardized for all data. It is also needed to performed further calculations. In proposed procedure it is done by checking all M/Z sets for all files and finding the most common one. It is possible, because if data were generated in one mass spectrometry process, they usually have similar sets of M/Z values. This chosen M/Z set acts as the X axis of the mean spectrum. In further step it needs to be trimmed, because several first and last points of the axis might occur impossible to adjust to other data files. The last step is to use linear interpolation to adapt other spectra to the chosen axis. This X axis determined in the described process is used in further calculations as M/Z value set of all spectra in the dataset.

4.2 Data Pre-processing

Pre-processing of proteomic data is a multistage process. It is composed of several stages whose order is fixed. The order is a standard which has been developed over the last few years of research in this field. In addition to the order of pre-processing steps, also their parameters adjustment is significant process. After each step the mean spectrum is calculated for the validation purpose.

Pre-processing steps applied in the procedure are:

1. Baseline correction – a procedure of identification and subtraction of a base level of intensity present in a spectrum.
2. Outliers detection – a procedure of removing outliers data and files.
3. Noise removal – a standard procedure of data smoothing.

Baseline correction flattens the base profile of a spectrum. This process often determines success of further analysis. This kind of algorithms uses such methods and techniques as: simple frame with fixed size and quintiles. The baseline is estimated within multiple shifted windows of set width. The varying baseline is regressed to the window points using a spline approximation.

Outliers detection is consisting of several steps. The first one is based on detection of noised signals, performed on the entire dataset. It is based on Signal-to-Noise (SNR) ratio calculated as median divided by MAD (median absolute deviation). SNR ratio is calculated for all spectra. A SNR threshold value describing noised spectra is calculated using Bayesian Information Criterion (BIC) on SNR ratio modeled by Gaussian Mixture Model. Spectra with SNR higher that the obtained threshold are removed. The second step of outliers detection is based on AUC (Area Under Curve) value. AUC value is calculated for all spectra of the dataset. Spectra are regarded as outliers if the AUC value exceeds a threshold. The threshold is calculated based on quartiles (Q1, Q3) and IQR value.

Results of those two independently conducted outliers detection steps are joined and summarized. Remained files are grouped according patients. This operation is done in order to revise technical repeats of individual patients. Alignment procedure is applied to those technically repeated spectra as well as Dixon test is performed to check possible outliers within single patient groups. After this process only one average spectrum is obtained for each patient.

Noise removal is a procedure performed on each spectrum remained in the dataset. Denoising is performed based on Savitzky and Golay filters smoother with span of 300 and Gaussian kernel.

4.3 Peaks Identification

The protein mass spectra decomposition methodology is based on Gaussian Mixture Models. This way of mass spectra processing is possible and gives good results, which has been confirmed by the results of the analysis of real data (presented later in this paper).

This mass spectral analysis method is based on peaks modeling with Gaussian distributions. Such modeling involves the appropriate choice of distributions' parameters. It enable to represent peak shapes and to model the spectra in the easy way.

Using of Gaussian distributions to model peaks allows to consider measurement errors which also can be modeled using Gaussian distributions. In most of the known methods these errors must be corrected by the difficult process of alignment of the peaks in different spectra collections. Gaussian distributions modeling does not need the aligning process, because when probability distributions are used, measurement ambiguities are allowed for a single spectrum.

The procedure is applied only to the mean spectrum calculated after performing pre-processing steps. GMM decomposition is performed with EM algorithm. This procedure is computationally demanding, so applying it only to the mean spectrum increases calculations performance. As a result of this process it is obtained a set of m/z values indicating on peaks localization.

The decomposition process is performed fully automatically. The adaptive procedure adjust to the dataset and apply fits such parameters such as number of peaks.

GMM decomposition result is regarded to each patient's spectrum by applying of Gaussian mask calculated a product of his spectrum and Gaussians obtained from the decomposition of the mean spectrum. For every patient it is obtained as many features as there are Gaussians in the mean spectrum. This process reduces dimensionality of data and prepares them to further analysis.

4.4 Statistical Analysis

Depending on the needs statistical analysis might be reduced to performing statistical tests or can be extended into statistical inference.

Typical statistical tests performed for groups of the dataset are:

1. Tests for normality of distribution: Kolmogorov-Smirnov, Lillietest and Shapiro-Wilk tests
2. T-test checking if data come from independent random samples from normal distributions with equal means and equal but unknown variances
3. Wilcoxon rank sum test returning the result of the test
4. Mann-Whitney-Wilcoxon - non parametric test for two unpaired groups, used to evaluate the difference between unpaired samples.
5. F test checking of independent samples come from normal distributions with the same variance, against the alternative that they come from normal distributions with different variances.
6. Welch test – checking if the homoscedasticity was met
7. Variance analysis: ANOVA performed for combinations of analyzed groups (in case of more than two groups)
8. Kruskal-Wallis checking if at least one sample median is significantly different from the others.

The analysis of data groups may be based on different kind of method such as cauterization (unsupervised learning method), classification and regression. Proteomic, data are often analyzed with support vector machines (SVM [3, 30]). Highly multi dimensional data need also dimension reduction techniques like PCA (Principal Component Analysis) [29], PLS (Partial Least Squares) [32], ICA (Independent Component Analysis [15] or MDS (multidimensional scaling). They enable to choose statistically the most significant features.

5 Results

The analyzed dataset was composed of 1124 data files, each of which contains single mass spectrum. Data files contain mass spectra of serum samples collected from 268 patients divided into three groups, depending on the development of disease stages:

1. 89 healthy donors;
2. 77 patients with locally advanced gastric cancer;
3. 102 patients with metastatic gastric cancer.

Data were obtained from blood samples collected by the Institute of Oncology in Gliwice, Poland according the procedure described in [22].

For each patient four technical repetitions were generated. For each patient material for research has been collected twice and each of taken sample was analyzed twice by a spectrometer.

After preliminary data processing involving the x axis standardization, data inter-polation and initial data trimming the demonstrative mean spectrum was generated (Fig. 1a). Afterwards the baseline correction was applied sequentially for all spectra. Figure 1b presents example baseline correction applied to a single spectrum.

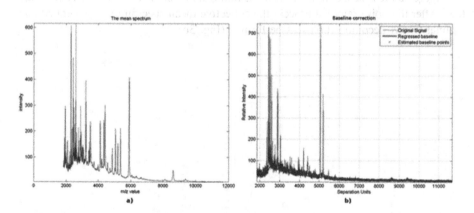

Fig. 1. Pre-processing steps: (a) the initial mean spectrum; (b) the baseline correction

Next step of the analysis process was dedicated to outliers detection. This process was composed of two parts. The first part of this process was based on GMM decomposition of SNR calculated for all spectra (Fig. 2a). The proper number of

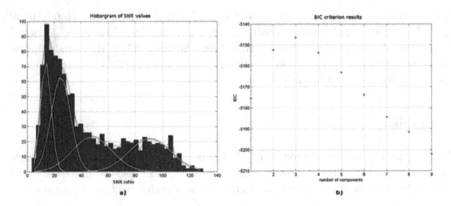

Fig. 2. Pre-processing steps: (a) the initial mean spectrum; (b) the baseline correction

components in this model was estimated with the BIC criterion to be 4 (Fig. 2b). Files with SNR of the last GMM component was removed (281 files).

The second part was outlier detection based on AUC (Area Under Curve), performed on the entire dataset with criterion based on quartiles (Q1, Q3) and IQR. 51 files was removed in this process.

After integration of outlier detection process results data of one patient was completely removed. After this operation detection of outlier of technical repeats for single patient was done. Technical repeats of individual patients were checked, alignment procedure and outlier correction with 90 % Dixon test were applied. As a result single mean spectrum for each patient was obtained.

Figure 3a presents example of the noise removal procedure using Savitzky & Golay filer. After the noise removal process the collective mean spectrum was generated and its final GMM decomposition was performed (Fig. 3b).

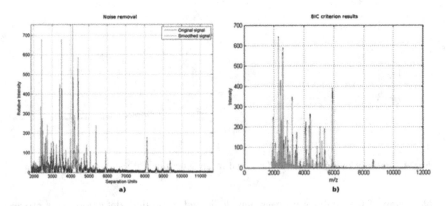

Fig. 3. Further analysis process: (a) noise reduction; (b) GMM decomposition

Table 1 present chosen fragment of statistical results. Obtained results proved that there are statistical difference between healthy controls and cancer patients. Presented results regard the Mann-Whitney U (MWU) and ANOVA (ANN) tests.

Table 1. Gastric data analysis results. A - the comparison between healthy donors and patients with locally advanced gastric cancer; B - the comparison between healthy donors and patients with metastatic gastric cancer; C - the comparison between patients with locally advanced gastric cancer and patients with metastatic gastric cancer.

m/z	MWU p-val A	MWU p-val B	MWU p-val C	ANN p-val A	ANN p-val B	ANN p-val C
1847,21	0,99483	0,03153	0,01792	0,05579	0,06727	2,47E-05
1861,37	1,14E-09	4,26E-27	2,81E-18	2,32E-09	3,17E-16	1,14E-10
1878,02	5,81E-23	7,89E-32	8,12E-22	1,92E-25	1,44E-16	3,67E-09
1900,94	7,64E-08	0,014947	9,89E-22	0,000256	0,071731	0,000111
1906,65	8,28E-10	0,938301	2,75E-10	5,79E-06	0,221696	2,58E-05
1921,64	1,19E-19	0,000368	5,07E-24	1,93E-11	0,000156	3,10E-11
1927,78	1,64E-17	0,002719	7,67E-20	2,66E-07	0,000236	4,96E-08
1933,97	2,85E-16	1,90E-12	3,44E-23	2,65E-13	2,17E-07	4,06E-08
1942,52	9,29E-19	0,032799	5,12E-20	4,62E-06	0,024467	0,000639
1947,88	3,49E-17	0,005348	1,50E-14	0,000273	0,006809	0,000507
1962,74	6,32E-15	3,32E-05	2,69E-26	3,47E-09	0,053390	5,43E-24
1979,19	1,92E-15	5,84E-09	2,86E-26	2,18E-11	7,47E-06	9,93E-29
2001,12	3,08E-12	4,50E-12	5,03E-23	1,28E-08	3,53E-10	2,43E-18
2013,22	2,22E-21	0,015165	1,05E-20	6,87E-10	0,013290	1,89E-09
2017,78	3,57E-23	0,000435	8,79E-16	1,88E-12	0,037242	1,02E-06
2030,98	9,70E-24	5,06E-05	1,68E-24	5,33E-22	0,042761	0,002545
2056,70	1,40E-05	9,12E-22	8,23E-26	0,000407	1,17E-20	7,54E-26
2077,72	9,78E-26	2,18E-09	7,17E-21	2,28E-10	2,67E-06	6,51E-10
2078,32	1,16E-24	1,99E-05	8,73E-23	7,01E-10	0,000171	4,20E-14
2096,76	0,000511	6,60E-16	2,72E-23	0,000839	9,36E-12	8,06E-24
2110,81	0,007774	5,35E-25	4,60E-21	0,079458	1,19E-25	1,13E-20
2143,72	6,66E-06	3,73E-12	2,57E-23	0,005216	3,05E-05	3,61E-10
2155,63	1,05E-07	7,80E-29	8,11E-19	1,90E-07	2,42E-34	4,58E-19
2167,87	0,003245	3,04E-24	3,36E-15	0,001468	7,00E-19	7,33E-12

6   Conclusions

The paper presents the framework dedicated to proteomic data profiling. The procedure is composed of several steps involving initial data preparation, preprocessing, peaks detection and statistical analysis.

The presented framework provides features enabling comprehensive process of analysis automatically adjusting procedure parameters to the dataset. Automatically set parameters relate to all preprocessing steps: binning, interpolation and noise correction. The extended process of outlier detection including three steps based on signal-to-noise ratio, area under the curve and Dixon test.

The framework also adapts the improved peak detection method based on the GMM model method. The improved procedure automatically adapts to the dataset choosing the correct number of peaks. The GMM-based method provides flexibility analysis of different types of datasets with different peak shapes and locations including overlapped peaks.

In comparison to other available methods (for example Prepms or Matalb-based Mspeaks, the presented tool is more generalized. It supports complete analysis including automatically adjusted number of peaks. Many methods applied in other applications need specifying the peaks number. What is more, majority of tools are based on local maxima what is useful only in case of datasets with separable peaks.

The method was applied to geriatric cancer data set. However, the presented framework can be applied to different dataset with varying shapes of spectra including narrow peaks as well as overlapped peaks characterized by a large variance. Presented procedure is completed, comprehensive process enabling peaks detection and statistical analysis of data including hard task of reducing the dimensionality of data.

References

1. Baggerly, K.A., Morris, J., Wang, J., Gold, D., Xiao, L.C., Coombes, K.R.: A comprehensive approach to the analysis of matrix-assisted laser desorption/ionization time of flight proteomics spectra from serum samples. Proteomics 1667–1672 (2003)
2. Barnhill, S., Vapnik, V., Guyon, I., Weston, J.: Gene selection for cancer classification using support vector machines. Mach. Learn. **46**, 389–422 (2002)
3. Boster, B., Guyon, I., Vapnik, V.: A training algorithm for optimal margin classifiers. In: Fifth Annual Workshop on Computational Learning Theory, pp. 114–152 (1992)
4. Clyde, M.A., House, L.L., Wolpert, R.L. Nonparametric models for proteomic peak identification and quantification. ISDS Discussion Paper, 2006–2007 (2006)
5. Coombes, K., Baggerly, K., Morris, J.: Pre-processing mass spectrometry data. In: Dubitzky, W., et al. (eds.) Fundamentals of Data Mining in Genomics and Proteomics, pp. 79–99. Kluwer, New York (2007)
6. Coombes, K.R., Koomen, J.M., Baggerly, K.A., et al.: Understanding the characteristics of mass spectrometry data through the use of simulation. Cancer Inform. **1**, 41–52 (2005)
7. Comon, P.: Independent component analysis – new concept? Sig. Proc. **36**, 287–314 (1994)
8. Fung, E.T., Enderwick, C.: Proteinchip clinical proteomics: computational challenges and solutions. Biotechniques **32**(Suppl 1), 34–41 (2002)
9. Dempster, A.P., Laird, N.M., Rubin, D.B.: Maximum likelihood from incomplete data via the EM algorithm. J. R. Stat. Soc. **39**(1), 1–38 (1977)
10. Dijkstra, M., Roelofsen, H., Vonk, R., Jansen, R.: Peak quantification in surface-enhanced laser desorption/ionization by using mixture models. Proteomics **6**, 5106–5116 (2006)
11. Du, P., Kibbe, W., Lin, S.: Improved peak detection in mass spectrum by incorporating continuos wavelet transform-based pattern matching. Genome Anal. **22**, 2059–2065 (2006)

12. Gentzel, M., Kocher, T., Ponnusamy, S., Wilm, M.: Preprocessing of tandem mass spectrometric data to support automatic protein identyfication. Proteomics **3**, 1597–1610 (2003)
13. Gyaourova, A., Kamath, C., Fodor, I.K.: Undecimated wavelet transforms for image de-noising. Technical Report UCRL-ID-150931, Lawrence Livermore National Laboratory, Livermore, CA (2002)
14. Hubert, M., Van der Veeken, S.: Outlier detection for skewed data. J. Chemometrics **22**, 235–246 (2008)
15. Jutten, C., Herault, J.: Blind separation of sources, part I: an adaptive algorithm based on neuromimetic architecture. Sig. Process. **24**, 1–10 (1991)
16. Kempka, M., Sjodahl, J., Bjork, A., Roeraade, J.: Improved method for peak picking in matrix-assisted laser desorption/ionization time-of-flight mass spectrometry. Rapid Commun. Mass Spectrom. **18**, 1208–1212 (2004)
17. Koziel, G.: Fourier transform based methods in sound steganography. Actual Probl. Econ. **6**(120), 321–328 (2011)
18. Lang, M., Guo, H., Odegard, J.E., Burrus, C.S., Well Jr, R.O.: Noise reduction using an undecimated discrete wavelet transform. IEEE Sig. Process. Lett. **3**, 10–12 (1996)
19. Mantini, D., Petrucci, F., Del Boccio, P., et al.: Independent component analysis for the extraction of reliable protein signal profiles from Maldi-ToF mass spectra. Bioinformatics **24**, 63–70 (2008)
20. Miłosz, M.: Performance testing of new enterprise applications using legacy load data: a HIS case study. In: ICEIS 2013 - 15th International Conference on Enterprise Information Systems, pp. 269–274 (2013)
21. Morris, J., Coombes, K., Kooman, J., Baggerly, K., Kobayashi, R.: Feature extraction and quantification for mass spectrometry data in biomedical applications using the mean spectrum. Bioinformatics **21**(9), 1764–1775 (2005)
22. Pietrowska, M., Marczak, L., Polanska, J., Behrendt, K., Nowicka, E., Walaszczyk, A., Widlak, P.: Mass spectrometry-based serum proteome pattern analysis in molecular diagnostics of early stage breast cancer. J. Transl. Med. **7**(60.10), 1186 (2009)
23. Polanska, J., Plechawska, M., Pietrowska, M., Marczak, L.: Gaussian mixture decomposition in the analysis of MALDI-TOF spectra. Expert Syst. **29**(3), 216–231 (2012)
24. Plechawska, M., Polanska, J.: Simulation of the usage of Gaussian mixture models for the purpose of modelling virtual mass spectrometry data. In: MIE, pp. 804–808 (2009)
25. Plechawska, M., Polańska, J., Polański, A., Pietrowska, M., Tarnawski, R., Widlak, P., Stobiecki, M., Marczak, Ł.: Analyze of Maldi-TOF proteomic spectra with usage of mixture of gaussian distributions. In: Cyran, K.A., Kozielski, S., Peters, J.F., Stańczyk, U., Wakulicz-Deja, A. (eds.) Man-Machine Interactions. AISC, vol. 59, pp. 113–120. Springer, Heidelberg (2009)
26. Randolph, T., et al.: Quantifying peptide signal in MALDI-TOF mass spectrometry data. Mol. Cell. Proteomics MCP **4**(12), 1990–1999 (2005)
27. Tibshirani, R., Hastiey, T., Narasimhanz, B., Soltys, S., Shi, G., Koong, A., Le, Q.T.: Sample classification from protein mass spectrometry, by 'peak probability contrasts'. Bioinformatics **20**, 3034–3044 (2004)
28. Tversky, A., Hutchinson, J.W.: Nearest neighbor analysis of psychological spaces. Psychol. Rev. **93**(1), 3–22 (1993)
29. Vapnik, V.N.: The Nature of Statistical Learning Theory. Springer, New York (1995)
30. Vapnik, V.N.: Statistical Learning Theory. Wiley, New York (1998)

31. Windham, M.P., Cutler, A.: Information ratios for validating cluster analyses. J. Am. Stat. Assoc. **87**, 1188–1192 (1993)
32. Wold, H.: Estimation of principal components and related models by iterative least squares. Multivar. Anal. 391–420 (1966)
33. Yasui, Y., Pepe, M., Thompson, M.L., Adam, B.L., Wright, G.L., Qu, Y., Potter, J.D., Winget, M., Thornquist, M., Feng, Z.: A data-analytic strategy for protein biomarker discovery: profiling of high-dimensional proteomic data for cancer detection. Biostatistics **4** (3), 449–463 (2003)
34. Zhang S.Q., et al.: Peak detection with chemical noise removal using Short-Time FFT for a kind of MALDI Data. In: Proceedings of OSB 2007, Lecture Notes in Operations Research, vol. 7, pp. 222–231 (2007)

Energy Efficient Method for Motor Imagery Data Compression

Darius Birvinskas[1]([✉]) and Vacius Jusas[2]

[1] Department of Computer Science, Kaunas University of Technology,
Studentu St., 50-210 Kaunas, Lithuania
darius.birvinskas@ktu.lt
[2] Department of Software Engineering, Kaunas University of Technology,
Studentu St., 50-404 Kaunas, Lithuania

Abstract. Electroencephalogram (EEG) is a popular method for measuring the electrical activity of the brain, and diagnose a variety of neurological conditions such as epileptic seizure. Furthermore, most Brain - Computer Interface systems provide modes of communication based on EEG, usually signals are recorded with several electrodes and transmitted through a communication channel for further processing. In order to decrease communication bandwidth and transmission time in portable or low cost devices, data compression is required. In this paper we consider the use of fast Discrete Cosine Transform (DCT) algorithms for lossy EEG data compression. Using this approach, the signal is partitioned into a set of 8 samples and each set is DCT-transformed. The least-significant transform coefficients are removed before transmission and are filled with zeros before an inverse transform. We conclude that this method can be used in low power wireless systems, where low computational complexity and high speed are required.

Keywords: Fast DCT · Data compression · Electroencephalography · EEG

1 Introduction

Electroencephalogram (EEG) is a popular method for measuring the electrical activity of the brain, and diagnose a variety of neurological conditions such as epileptic seizure or sleep disorder. In recent years have seen an increased interest in the use of ambulatory EEG monitoring using portable recording devices. An advantage of this is that the patient can remain at home in their normal environment during periods of observation [2]. Services that provide support for people to remain in their homes are called Ambient Assisted Living (AAL). Typically, these services provide additional information though location-awareness, presence-awareness, and context-awareness capabilities, arising from the prolific use of telecommunications devices [14].

Another use of EEG signals is the Brain - Computer Interface (BCI), which aim is to create communication channel between the human brain and an external device. Most BCI systems provide modes of communication based on electro - encephalogram (EEG) [20]. The EEG signal has become the main data source of BCI study due to its

G. Dregvaite and R. Damasevicius (Eds.): ICIST 2015, CCIS 538, pp. 71–80, 2015.
DOI: 10.1007/978-3-319-24770-0_7

low cost and non-invasive nature. It is possible to record different electrical potential from the nervous system of a human, depending on mental task. Motor imagination is an often used mental task for BCI purposes. Its popularity is based on a fact that imagination of movements is a very intuitive task [21]. An example of motor imagery task could be imagining left hand movement when want to go left and right hand movement when want to go right.

Due to the large data size of the EEG resulting from large number of electrodes, long recording time and usually high sample rate, data compression is required for an efficient transmission and archiving of data. Efficient compression of the EEG signal is a difficult task due to inherent randomness in the signal, and hence high compression rates cannot be achieved with lossless compression methods [5, 19]. Furthermore, portable EEG recording devices like Emotiv EPOC, use wireless technology to transmit to a host device and their working time is limited by a battery capacity. In this case lossy compression techniques may be acceptable as long as the reconstructed signal preserves enough information about the user's mental state [12]. For these applications, simple, low complexity, embedded data compression methods are required, even if it might effect accuracy.

In this paper we consider the use of fast Discrete Cosine Transform (DCT) algorithms for a lossy EEG data compression in order to decrease communication bandwidth and transmission time. This method could be useful in portable or low cost devices where data compression is required and small data loss is acceptable. For the experiment we will use fast DCT models implemented in Matlab environment, however these models are proven to be equivalent of VHDL implemented and FPGA-proven models [13].

2   Related Works

Compression techniques practically aim at obtaining maximum data volume reduction while preserving the significant information for reconstruction. Data compression can be lossless, when the signal waveform fidelity is totally preserved, or lossy, in cases where a certain amount of distortion in the decompressed data is allowed.

High compression rates cannot be achieved with lossless compression methods due to randomness of EEG signal. In some cases conventional compression algorithms, like TAR or ZIP can be used however, as shown in [22] specialized algorithms can achieve higher compression ratio.

Unlike lossless compression, lossy algorithms does not allow perfect reconstruction of the signal, but can achieve higher compression ratio and use less computation resources. Related works on lossy EEG compression includes the use of Wavelet Packet Transform [1]. This Cardenas-Barrera et al. proposed method is designed to be low-power and can be used in portable devices. Another approach with Wavelet dictionaries is presented in [6]. The compression is based on a superposition of dictionary elements, by minimizing the norm of the error.

Higgins et al. suggest the use of JPEG2000-based algorithm for lossy EEG compression [7]. The JPEG2000 algorithm is designed for image compression however, applications are not limited to image files only. Core components of algorithm include: Discrete

Wavelet Transform (DWT), quantisation and an Arithmetic Coder. The DWT replaces the Discrete Cosine Transform (DCT) of the original JPEG format. Using different compression parameters compression ratio of 11:1 was achieved by [7].

Furthermore, recent works based on wavelet-SPIHT [4] and finite rate of innovation technique [15] has been published. These approaches have shown some improvement in the compression performance at the expense of computation resources.

Several compression methods have been reported recently however, to the best of our knowledge none of these approaches uses Discrete Cosine Transform and fast DCT implementation for EEG data compressions. Furthermore, only a few of them consider energy efficiency as an important property of the method.

3   Material and Method

In this section we will provide description of discrete cosine transform, data recording procedure, proposed method for compression and evaluation parameters.

3.1   Discrete Cosine Transform

The discrete cosine transform is a transformation method for converting a time series signal into basic frequency components. Low frequency components are concentrated in first coefficients, while high frequency – in the last ones.

The DCT input $f(x)$ is a set of N data values (EEG samples, audio samples, or other data) and the output $Y(u)$ is a set of N Discrete Cosine Transform coefficients. The one-dimensional DCT for a list of N real numbers is expressed by Eq. (1):

$$Y(u) = \sqrt{\frac{2}{N}} \cdot \alpha(u) \cdot \sum_{x=0}^{N-1} f(x) \cdot cos\left(\frac{\pi \cdot (2x+1) \cdot u}{2N}\right),$$ (1)

where

$$\alpha(u) = \begin{cases} \frac{1}{\sqrt{2}}, & u = 0, \\ 1, & u > 0. \end{cases}$$

From Eq. (1), we can see, that if $u = 0$ then $Y(0) = \sqrt{\frac{1}{N}} \sum_{x=0}^{N-1} f(x)$. This, the first, coefficient contains mean value of original signal thereby, it is called the DC coefficient and rest are referred to as AC coefficients [17].

Inverse DCT takes transform coefficients $Y(u)$ as input and converts them back into time series $f(x)$. For a list of N DCT coefficients inverse transform is expressed by the following Eq. (2):

$$f(x) = \sqrt{\frac{2}{N}} \cdot \alpha(u) \cdot \sum_{u=0}^{n-1} Y(u) \cdot cos\left(\frac{\pi \cdot (2x+1 \cdot u)}{2N}\right).$$ (2)

In Eq. (2) notations are the same as in (1).

DCT exhibits good energy compaction for correlated signals. If the input data consists of correlated quantities, most of the N transform coefficients produced by the DCT are zeros or small numbers, and only a few coefficients are large. These small numbers can be quantized coarsely, usually down to zero. Since EEG has low frequency oscillations, most of the relevant information is compressed into the first coefficients, while the last ones usually contain noise.

During the transform small values of N such as 3, 4, or 6 result in many small sets of data items and small sets of coefficients where the energy of the original signal is concentrated in a few coefficients, but there are not enough small coefficients to quantize. Large values of N result in a few large sets of data. The problem in this case is that individual data items of a large set are normally not correlated and therefore result in a set of transform coefficients where all the coefficients are large. Popular data compression algorithms, that employ the DCT, use the value of N = 8 [17].

The direct implementation of DCT and IDCT formulas are highly computational intensive. The measure of algorithm effectiveness is the number of mathematical operations needed to perform it. The number of multiplications is extremely important, since it is a relatively complex and power consuming operation, to be performed in hardware. The number of computations can be reduced from N^4 to $Nlog_2 N$ using fast DCT algorithms. Many fast one-dimensional algorithms was proposed over the years for N data points where $N = 2^m$, $m \geq 2$. These algorithms are based on the sparse factorizations of the DCT matrix and many of them are recursive. Popular algorithms are Chens [3], Loeffler et al. [11], and BinDCT [10]. The theoretical lower bound on the number of multiplications required for 1-D 8-point DCT has proven to be 11. In this sense, the method proposed by Loeffler et al., with 11 multiplications and 29 additions [11]. However, in case of BinDCT, a multiplier-less computation is possible using a scheme of lifting steps, which in turn use only logic shift and addition [10].

3.2   Experimental Set-up for Data Acquisition

Experiment conducted here is a single subject experiment for the motor imagery paradigm, we have employed OpenViBE to implement stimulus representation and record EEG data. It is a free and open-source software platform which enables researchers to design, test, and use Brain - Computer Interfaces (BCI) [16]. The platform consists in a set of software modules that can be integrated easily to design various BCI experiments such as steady-state visual evoked potentials, P300 speller or motor imagery. For this experiment we will use Emotiv EPOC recording device. It is a low cost, portable, off-the-shelf EEG recording device. The electrodes are mounted on a semi-flexible plastic structure which does not allow large moves to change the electrodes' positions described using international 10–20 system. The whole recording system combines the headset and a software development kit (SDK) to obtain data to computer. Becouse of its low cost, this recording device is popular in recent BCI studies [9]. Due to limitation of the headset the sampling frequency is 128 Hz and 14 fixed EEG channels can be recorded. Channel names are based on the international 10–20 electrode location system: AF3, F7, F3, FC5, T7, P7, O1, O2, P8, T8, FC6, F4, F8, and AF4.

Using OpenViBE a cued motor imagery stimulus with online feedback was implemented. This experimental set up is often called Graz Motor Imagery BCI since it was proposed by University of Technology Graz group [18]. A duration of every trial was 9 s. Timing scheme of the experiment is shown in Fig. 1. The first 2 s was quite, and then an acoustic stimulus indicates the beginning of the trial. At the beginning a fixation cross was presented at the center of the screen it is shown for 1 s. At second 3, an arrow, pointing either to the left or right representing one of two different motor imagery tasks (left hand or right hand respectively), appeared on the screen for 6 s. The order of left and right cues was random additionally, the period between trials varied randomly between 1 and 3 s. Depending on the received stimulations, subject must imagine left or right hand movement. Afterwards, a pause of random length is present and new trial begins.

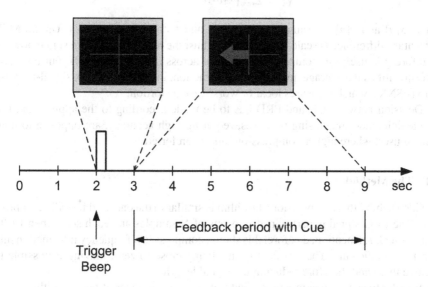

Fig. 1. Timing scheme of the experiment

3.3 Evaluation Parameters

Lossless data compression are usually evaluated using Compression Ratio (CR) [17], which is defined as (3):

$$CR = \frac{L_{comp}}{L_{orig}} \qquad (3)$$

where L_{orig} and L_{comp} is the length of original and compressed signals. Length can be measured in bits, bytes, or integers, as long as both parameters have the same dimension. In systems with wireless data transmission it is preferable to use bytes since many popular serial communication protocols use byte as the smallest unit.

However for lossy data compression ratio is not the only parameter that need to be take into account. While investigating this kind of algorithms reconstruction quality must be measured. Quantities, such as mean square error (MSE) and peak signal-to-noise ratio (PSNR), are used to measure the distortion caused by lossy compression. It is well known that higher data compression can be achieved by reducing the quality of reconstructed data. In this paper, we validate the quality of reconstructed signal as a percent of root-mean-square difference (PRD).

Let X and $\tilde{X}$ be the original and the reconstructed signals respectively, and N is its length. The PRD is defined as (4):

$$PRD = \sqrt{\frac{\sum_{n=1}^{n} (x[n] - \tilde{x}[n])^2}{\sum_{n=1}^{n} (x[n])^2}} \cdot 100\,\% \qquad (4)$$

where $x[n]$ and $\tilde{x}[n]$ are samples of original and reconstructed signals. Unlike MSE percentage difference is scale-independent (adjust the result for absolute signal power), therefore it is useful to compare performance across different data sets. Furthermore, PRD quantifies the average quality of reconstruction, in contrast to peak signal-to-noise ratio (PSNR), which measures local or worst-case distortion.

Decision between CR and PRD has to be made according to the application. For telemedicine and diagnosing purposes, requiring high accuracy, are opposite to non-clinical uses, where higher compression ratio is preferred.

3.4   The Method

The idea behind this compression algorithm is similar to the one used in audio compression. The EEG signal is partitioned into sets of N samples and each set is then DCT-transformed. As mentioned before, this should compress low frequency information into first few coefficients. The last coefficients being close to zero, making it possible to remove them and therefore reducing the signal length.

In order to speed up computation and save energy a number of fast algorithms were proposed. In our experiments the following DCT/IDCT computation algorithms are used:

– Matlab native function.
– Chen's [3] mathematical model using fixed point numbers.
– Loeffler's [11] mathematical model using fixed point numbers.
– BinDCT [10] mathematical model using fixed point numbers.

Matlab native functions use floating point numbers and direct implementation of Eqs. (1) and (2), so it is expected to be slow, but more accurate. Fast DCT algorithms are implemented in Matlab using fixed point numbers. As a result, fixed point mathematical models are less accurate, but less computationally demanding, and are possible to implement in hardware using VHDL description language. Loeffler's mathematical model used in this experiment has already been FPGA-proven and shown to be accurate [13].

There are two important parameters that must be chosen in order to compress a signal. The first one is the signal partition size N. Since fast DCT computation algorithms use a length of 2^m, where m is a positive integer, an obvious choice for partition size is $N = 8$. As mentioned, this size is used in the most of compression algorithms [17].

Another parameter considered is the number of DCT coefficients to truncate (we denote by R). We can achieve higher compression ratio by removing more coefficients however, this would reduce the quality of the reconstructed signal. The trade-off between compression ratio and quality of reconstructed signal is the subject of our experiment. We chose an R value of 2, 3, 4, 5 and 6. Since compression ratio depends on this value, formula (5) can be rewritten as:

$$CR = \frac{N - R}{N} \qquad (5)$$

Since parameters N and R are DCT coefficients, reduction of bandwidth and/or storage space depends on bit length of fixed-point coefficients. Our implemented fast DCT models use 16 bit numbers so by removing two coefficients a considerable amount of raw data can be saved.

Our experiments follow these steps:

1. Each trial is partitioned into sets of 8 samples. Convert numbers to fixed-point where necessary.
2. DCT transform is applied to every set of samples.
3. Number R of last DCT coefficients is removed and a new shorter data vector is constructed.
4. Removed coefficients are filled up with zeros.
5. Inverse DCT transform is applied to every set of coefficients.
6. PRD of each trial is computed.
7. Average PRD is computed.

These steps can be divided in 3 groups: signal compression (steps 1–3), signal reconstruction (steps 4 and 5) and quality assessment (steps 6 and 7). Four experiments were carried out using a pair of all previously mentioned DCT/IDCT algorithms (Matlab native function, Chen's, Loeffler's and BinDCT).

4   Results and Discussion

The experiment was carried out using Matlab and a PC running Debian Linux with an Intel Pentium Dual-Core E5700 (3.00 GHz) processor and 6 GB RAM. Data from all 14 recorded EEG channels were used to form a data set of 200 trials 896 samples each.

In Table 1, relation between compression ratio (CR) and quality of reconstructed signal is shown. This quality is measured using PRD as shown in formula (4). The table also present time taken to compress and decompress whole data set. This time was measured using Matlab internal stopwatch timer.

We can see in Table 1 and Fig. 2, there is a very small difference in terms of reconstruction quality while using different DCT models. As expected, reconstruction quality is decreasing as compression ratio is increasing. This support our initial claim, that higher compression ratio can be achieved, while sacrificing some original data. Besides,

Table 1. Results of self recoded data reconstruction

CR	Float-point DCT		Loeffler DCT		Chen DCT		Bin DCT	
	PRD, %	Time, s	PRD, %	Time, s	PRD, %	Time, s	PRD, %	Time, s
1.33	1.68	3.00	2.04	1.13	1.85	1.04	1.84	1.04
1.6	3.14	3.00	3.31	1.13	3.24	1.04	3.23	1.04
2	5.05	3.00	5.15	1.13	5.11	1.04	5.11	1.04
2.66	7.49	3.02	7.54	1.15	7.54	1.05	7.54	1.04
4	10.45	3.02	10.47	1.16	10.47	1.06	10.47	1.07

PRD is varying from 1.68 % to 10.47 %, it is in-line with other author's works. Therefore, DCT based algorithms show similar results across various datasets, and can be used low cost recording devices, like Emotiv EPOC.

Another parameter shown in Table 1 is time taken to compress and decompress whole dataset. First of all, we can see that time does not depend on compression ratio. This is true for all DCT models and are following: Float-point ~3 s, Loeffler ~1.13 s,

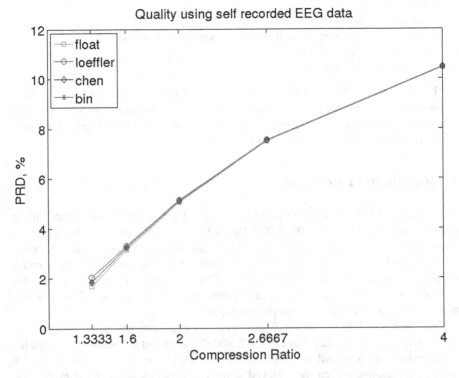

Fig. 2. Quality of reconstructed signal (self recorded motor-imaginary data)

Chen ~1.04 s, BinDCT ~1.04 s. This draw the conclusion that the use of hardware DCT models computation time is reduced three times. This lead to the conclusion that any dataset can be compressed faster using fast DCT models and computation time depend on used hardware rather than data recording method.

5 Conclusions

In this paper, we have conducted an experiment designed to investigate the possibility to use fast Discrete Cosine Transform for EEG data compression. Beside that we compare the performance of fast DCT models implemented in VHDL hardware description language and direct implementation of formulas (1) and (2). The first noticeable result is very small decrease in reconstruction quality when using fast algorithms instead of direct implementation. Usually the decrease is no more than 1 %. However, computation time is 2–3 times faster when using fast algorithms. This shows that hardware models are accurate and can be used in a real world application.

In addition to that reconstruction quality, expressed in percent of root-mean-square difference (PRD), is about 10.5 % at compression ratio 4:1. These quality results are in line with other authors, using more complex compression algorithms (Higgins et al. [7] used JPEG2000 and Dauwels et al. [5] used matrix and tensor decomposition). Furthermore, study made by [1] suggest that 99.5 % of EEG signal information is maintained when PRD is below 7 %. Other authors state that even higher PRD is tolerable for some application, like automated epileptic seizure detection [8]. Therefore we can conclude that purposed method for EEG data compression is efficient as well as fast.

As a result conclusion that fast fixed-point DCT algorithms implemented in VHDL can be used for EEG data compression. Since tested models can easily be transformed into a low power electronic chip, possible applications are primarily in low power wireless systems, for example portable EEG recording devices.

References

1. Cardenas-Barrera, J.L., Lorenzo-Ginori, J.V., Rodriguez-Valdivia, E.: A wavelet-packets based algorithm for EEG signal compression. Med. Inform. Internet Med. **1**, 15–27 (2004)
2. Casson, A., Yates, D., Smith, S., Duncan, J., Rodriguez-Villegas, E.: Wearable electroencephalography. Eng. Med. Biol. Mag. IEEE **29**(3), 44–56 (2010)
3. Chen, W.H., Smith, C.H., Fralick, S.: A fast computational algorithm for the discrete cosine transform. IEEE Trans. Commun. **25**, 1004–1009 (1977)
4. Daou, H., Labeau, F.: Pre-processing of multi-channel EEG for improved compression performance using SPIHT. In: Engineering in Medicine and Biology Society (EMBC), 2012 Annual International Conference of the IEEE. pp. 2232–2235, August 2012
5. Dauwels, J., Srinivasan, K., Reddy, M., Cichocki, A.: Near-lossless multichannel EEG compression based on matrix and tensor decompositions. IEEE J. Biomed. Health Inform. **17**(3), 708–714 (2013)
6. Fira, M., Goras, L.: Biomedical signal compression based on basis pursuit. In: Proceedings of the 2009 International Conference on Hybrid Information Technology, ICHIT 2009, pp. 541–545. ACM, New York, NY, USA (2009)

7. Higgins, G., Faul, S., McEvoy, R., McGinley, B., Glavin, M., Marnane, W., Jones, E.: EEG compression using JPEG2000: how much loss is too much? In: 32nd Annual International Conference of the IEEE EMBS, pp. 614–617 (2010)

8. Higgins, G., McGinley, B., Faul, S., McEvoy, R., Glavin, M., Marnane, W., Jones, E.: The effects of lossy compression on diagnostically relevant seizure information in EEG signals. IEEE J. Biomed. Health Inform. 17(1), 121–127 (2013)

9. Holewa, K., Nawrocka, A.: Emotiv EPOC neuroheadset in brain - computer interface. In: Control Conference (ICCC), 2014 15th International Carpathian, pp. 149–152 (2014)

10. Liang, J., Tran, T.D.: Fast multiplierless approximations of the DCT with the lifting scheme. IEEE Trans. Sig. Process. 49, 3032–3044 (2001)

11. Loeffler, C., Lightenberg, A., Moschytz, G.S.: Practical fast 1-D DCT algorithms with 11 multiplications. In: Proceedings of the International Conference on Acoustics, Speech and Signal Processing (ICASSP 1989), pp. 988–991 (1989)

12. Madan, T., Agarwal, R., Swamy, M.: Compression of long-term EEG using power spectral density. In: 26th Annual International Conference of the IEEE Engineering in Medicine and Biology Society, IEMBS 2004, vol. 1, pp. 180–183, September 2004

13. Martisius, I., Birvinskas, D., Jusas, V., Tamosevicius, Z.: A 2-D DCT hardware codec based on Loeffler algorithm. Electron. Electr. Eng. 7, 47–50 (2011)

14. Mulvenna, M., Carswell, W., McCullagh, P., Augusto, J., Zheng, H., Jeffers, P., Wang, H., Martin, S.: Visualization of data for ambient assisted living services. Commun. Mag. IEEE 49(1), 110–117 (2011)

15. Poh, K.K., Marziliano, P.: Compressive sampling of EEG signals with finite rate of innovation. EURASIP J. Adv. Sig. Process. 2010(1), 183105 (2010). doi:10.1155/2010/183105

16. Renard, Y., Lotte, F., Gibert, G., Congedo, M., Maby, E., Delannoy, V., Bertrand, O., Lécuyer, A.: OpenViBE: an open-source software platform to design, test, and use brain-computer interfaces in real and virtual environments. Presence: Teleoperators Virtual Environ. 19(1), 35–53 (2010)

17. Salomon, D.: Data Compression. The Complete Reference, 3rd edn. Springer, New York (2004)

18. Schloegl, A., Lugger, K., Pfurtscheller, G.: Using adaptive autoregressive parameters for a brain-computer-interface experiment. In: Engineering in Medicine and Biology Society, Proceedings of the 19th Annual International Conference of the IEEE, vol. 4, pp. 1533–1535, October 1997

19. Sriraam, N.: Quality-on-demand compression of EEG signals for telemedicine applications using neural network predictors. Int. J. Telemedicine Appl. 2011, 13 (2011)

20. Wolpaw, J.R., Birbaumer, N., McFarland, D.J., Pfurtscheller, G., Vaughan, T.M.: Brain - computer interfaces for communication and control. Clin. Neurophysiol. 113(6), 767–791 (2002)

21. Yi, W., Qiu, S., Qi, H., Zhang, L., Wan, B., Ming, D.: EEG feature comparison and classification of simple and compound limb motor imagery. J. Neuro Eng. Rehabil. 10(1), 106 (2013)

22. Ylostalo, J.: Data compression methods for EEG. Technol. Health Care 7(4), 285–300 (1999)

Comparison of Feature Extraction Methods for EEG BCI Classification

Tomas Uktveris[✉] and Vacius Jusas

Software Engineering Department, Kaunas University of Technology,
Studentu St. 50, Kaunas, Lithuania
{tomas.uktveris,vacius.jusas}@ktu.lt

Abstract. This work analyzes several feature extraction methods used in today's EEG BCI (electro-encephalogram brain computer interface) classification systems. Comparison of multiple EEG energy algorithms is presented for solving a 4-class motor imagery BCI classification problem. Furthermore, multiple feature vector generation techniques are employed into analysis. The effectiveness of CSP (common spatial pattern) filtering method in preprocessing step is shown. Channel difference feature extraction method is presented. It is discussed that key aim in today's EEG signal analysis should be dedicated to finding more accurate techniques for determining better quality features. Initial tests prove that static feature extraction methods are not optimal and adaptive algorithms are required to overcome subject specific EEG signal variations. Further work and new dynamic feature extraction methods are required to solve the problem.

Keywords: Common spatial patterns · Brain-computer interface · Laplace filtering · Feature extraction · Channel difference

1 Introduction

BCI systems try to narrow the gap between human and computer interaction. Direct control of computer applications using only human mind and mental abilities can help solve many rehabilitation, multimedia and gaming challenges. One of the key parts for a BCI system is accurate and fast algorithms, that are capable of analyzing electro-encephalogram (EEG) signal potentials recorded along the human scalp. Such signals contain noise and other unwanted artifacts, which prevent from correctly determining-classifying imagined motoric actions (imagery). Though, many algorithms were developed to overcome such issues, still the problem requires extensive work.

To be able to classify motoric actions with great accuracy, correct and significant features must be extracted from the EEG signal for classifier training. In the process of motor imagery, various regions of the brain are induced differently – signal energy decreases or increases. This is called Event-Related (De-) Synchronization – ERD or ERS. Since ERD/ERS describes transient changes in the brain signal oscillatory activity, a correct pattern of such information allows classification of motor imagery tasks. However, pattern extraction is error-prone due to the nature and highly non-deterministic brain activity even for the same test subject. This work further

© Springer International Publishing Switzerland 2015
G. Dregvaite and R. Damasevicius (Eds.): ICIST 2015, CCIS 538, pp. 81–92, 2015.
DOI: 10.1007/978-3-319-24770-0_8

discusses the use of various signal processing algorithms for EEG feature extraction. In Sect. 2 various feature extraction techniques for EEG signal analysis are presented along with a new Channel difference feature extraction method. Section 3 gives an overview of the classification methods applied in practice, while Sect. 4 provides more detail about the experiment procedure and data selected to assess the algorithms. Finally, Sect. 5 presents results and findings, concluding remarks are given in the last Sect. 6.

2 Techniques for Feature Extraction

Over the years many multi-class BCI solutions were proposed that use different feature extraction methods. A feature extraction algorithm is one of the most critical parts in EEG classification task or any BCI system processing pipeline. Since BCI system accuracy directly depends on the quality of extracted feature vectors, care must be taken to ensure quality. The pipeline can be viewed as an EEG signal processing filters chain as shown in Fig. 1.

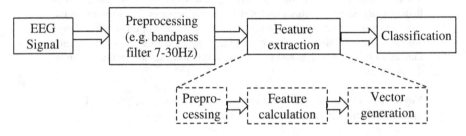

Fig. 1. EEG signal processing filter pipeline

After initial required signal preprocessing (that must be done for all signal channels) feature extraction stage comes into play. For each extraction algorithm, such stage can be decomposed into three distinct processing blocks that influence total performance of the algorithm:

1. *Preprocessing* [optional] – additional signal filtering (e.g. into different frequency bands).
2. *Feature calculation* – process EEG channel data (e.g. channel energy calculation).
3. *Vector generation* – compute elements of the final vector (e.g. mean of channel energy)

By controlling and changing the implementation in blocks many algorithm variations can be acquired for evaluation. This schema is handful in order to analyze subtle algorithm discrepancies also. Five EEG signal feature extraction methods were implemented and analyzed using this method in this work – Band Power features (BP), Time Domain Parameters (TDP), Teager-Kaiser Energy Operator, Signal power and Channel difference. Additional EEG preprocessing step was done using Common Spatial Patterns (CSP) filtering. Each of the algorithms will be briefly detailed further.

2.1   Signal Power Features

One of the simplest methods for signal energy calculation. The power of a signal is the sum of squares of its time-domain samples divided by the signal length (1). The power is computed for every EEG channel and the result is used further as a feature vector.

$$P = \frac{1}{N} \sum_{k=1}^{N} x^2[k] \tag{1}$$

where x – the discrete single EEG channel signal values, N – number of EEG signal samples taken.

2.2   Band Power Features

Algorithm calculates multiple band power by band-pass filtering [1] the signal. To apply the algorithm, the signal frequency range must be divided into multiple regions. First, initial EEG signal is filtered using a band-pass filter designed for each frequency band, e.g. 4-th order Butterworth finite impulse response (FIR) filter. The resulting signal is squared (2) to obtain its power.

$$p[t] = x^2[t] \tag{2}$$

here x –the filtered single band EEG signal values, p – resulting bandpower values.

A w-sized smoothing window operation is performed (3) to smooth-out (average) the signal. Finally a logarithm of the processed signal is taken. Computed result is used for feature vector generation. Such method is already implemented in MATLAB signal processing library.

$$\bar{p}[n] = ln\left(\frac{1}{w} \sum_{k=0}^{w} p[n-k]\right) \tag{3}$$

here $\bar{p}$ – resulting smoothed bandpower values, w – the smoothing window size.

Three different frequency bands were used in the work: 8–14 Hz, 19–24 Hz and 24–30 Hz which correspond to *Mu*, *Alfa* and *Beta* brain waves. A similar approach was used in a closed loop system for navigating in a virtual environment via ERD-BCI [2]. Complex band power features were selected from three major frequency bands of cortical oscillations: μ (8–12 Hz), sensorimotor rhythm (12–15 Hz) and β (15–30 Hz).

2.3   Time Domain Parameters

Similar to the BP algorithm, time domain parameters computes time-varying power of the first k derivatives of the signal. Obtained derivative values (4) are smoothed using exponential moving average and a logarithm is taken as given by (5). The resulting signal is used in feature vector generation.

$$p_i(t) = \frac{d^i x(t)}{dt^i}, \quad i = 0, 1, \ldots, k \tag{4}$$

$$\bar{p}_i[n] = \ln(u \cdot p_i[n] - (1 - u) \cdot p_i[n - 1]) \tag{5}$$

here x – initial EEG signal, p – signal derivative values, u – moving average parameter, $u \in [0; 1]$, $\bar{p}$ – smoothed signal derivatives.

2.4   Teager-Kaiser Energy Operator (TKEO)

A non-linear algorithm for a more accurate signal energy calculation was presented by Teager and further analyzed by Kaiser [3]. Advantage of TKEO is the ability to discover high-frequency low-amplitude components and take into account frequency component and signal amplitude of the signal [4]. The algorithm for a continuous signal can be written as shown in the (6) equation, while an approximation (7) exists for discrete signals.

$$\Psi[x(t)] = \left(\frac{\partial x}{\partial t}\right)^2 - x(t) \cdot \frac{\partial^2 x}{\partial t^2} \tag{6}$$

$$\Psi[x[n]] = x^2[n] - x[n - 1]x[n + 1] \tag{7}$$

here x – the EEG signal, $\Psi[x[n]]$ – energy values computed for discrete signal.

The algorithm was applied for each of EEG channels then final feature vectors were generated.

2.5   Channel Difference Method

Channel difference algorithm is a new method presented in this paper for extracting EEG signal features. The method is an extension to the Band power feature algorithm with an extra signal filtering step. The algorithm works by computing filtered features only for EEG channels that have at least four neighboring electrodes around each of them. In this work four EEG channels, that match this criteria, i.e. electrodes C3, Cz, C4 and Pz (in international system 10–20), were selected for this as shown in Fig. 2. The locations were chosen to be symmetric and to cover both hemispheres in order to be able to capture all energy changes induced by motor-imagery for different sides of the body [5]. It was already shown that Laplace signal filtering is effective at enhancing EEG spatial resolution [6] and discerning EEG signals from the background [7] noise. Each of the selected channels was filtered by using a Laplace filter (8) in a single channel radius neighborhood with weight kernel as given in (9).

$$S = \sum_{i=1}^{3} \sum_{j=1}^{3} K_{ij} E_{ij} \tag{8}$$

$$K = \begin{bmatrix} -0.5 & -1 & -0.5 \\ -1 & 6 & -1 \\ -0.5 & -1 & -0.5 \end{bmatrix} \tag{9}$$

where E_{ij} – the neighboring EEG channel signal, K_{ij} – the corresponding weight in the kernel matrix. For example, by taking Cz as the selected channel, the K_{11} element would denote a weight of -0.5 for the 3rd EEG channel and K_{22} would denote weight 6 for the Cz channel and so on. For non-existing channels zero weight was used. Larger kernel sizes were not analyzed as they would require more EEG channels.

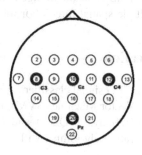

Fig. 2. EEG channels from the 10–20 system used in calculation

After filtering, the band power of frequency ranges: 8–14 Hz, 14–19 Hz, 19–24 Hz, 24–30 Hz was computed for each of the four signals. The 16 resulting energy bands were used for feature vector generation.

2.6 CSP Preprocessing

Common spatial patterns (CSP) is a preprocessing technique (filter) for separating a multivariate signal into subcomponents that have maximum differences in variance [8]. Separation allows for easier signal classification. In general, the filter can be described (10) as a spatial coefficient matrix **W**:

$$S = W^T E \tag{10}$$

where S – the filtered signal matrix, E – original EEG signal vector. Columns of **W** denote spatial filters, while inverse of, i.e. W^{-1}, are spatial patterns of EEG signal. Criterion of CSP for a two C_1, C_2 class problem is given by:

$$maximize \; tr\left(W^T \sum\nolimits_1 W\right) \tag{11}$$

$$subject \; to \; W^T\left(\sum\nolimits_1 + \sum\nolimits_2\right)W = I \tag{12}$$

here

$$\sum_1 = exp_{E_n \in C_1}\left(\frac{E_n E_n^T}{tr\left(E_n E_n^T\right)}\right) \quad (13)$$

$$\sum_2 = exp_{E_n \in C_2}\left(\frac{E_n E_n^T}{tr\left(E_n E_n^T\right)}\right) \quad (14)$$

The solution can be acquired by solving generalized eigenvalue problem of by decomposing the problem into multiple standard eigenvalue sub-problems. Multiclass solutions are combined of multiple spatial filters. For more information see [9].

3   Methods for Classification

From an extensive list of known EEG signal classifiers most commonly used ones were selected for analysis – Support Vector Machine (SVM), Linear Discriminant Analysis (LDA), Quadratic Discriminant Analysis (QDA) and k-Nearest Neighbors (kNN). A brief overview of the classification algorithms will be given further.

3.1   Linear and Quadratic Discriminant Analysis

A classifier that employs the Bayes' theorem for classification. Discriminant analysis estimates the parameters of a Gaussian distribution for each class and the trained classifier finds the class with the smallest misclassification cost. The posterior probability that a point x belongs to class C is the product of the prior probability and the multivariate normal density. The density function of the multivariate normal with mean μ_c and covariance Σ_c at a point x is given by:

$$P(x|C) = \frac{1}{(2\pi|\Sigma_c|)^{1/2}} exp\left(-\frac{1}{2}(x - \mu_c)^T \Sigma_c^{-1}(x - \mu_c)\right), \quad (15)$$

where $|\Sigma_c|$ is the determinant of Σ_c and Σ_c^{-1} is the inverse matrix.

Let $P(C)$ represent the prior probability of class C. Then the posterior probability that an observation x is of class C is given by:

$$P(C|x) = \frac{P(x|C)P(C)}{P(x)}, \quad (16)$$

where $P(x)$ is a constant equal to the sum over C of $P(x|C)P(C)$.

The Linear discriminant (or Fisher discriminant) analysis model is named for its inventor, Fisher [10]. Linear method (LDA) has the same covariance matrix for each class and only the means vary. For quadratic discriminant analysis (QDA), both means and covariances of each class vary.

3.2   Support Vector Machine (SVM)

The Support Vector Machines were introduced by Boser et al. [11] in 1992. SVM is a two-class algorithm that classifies data by finding the best hyperplane (17) separating all one class points (Fig. 3) from all of the other class (with the largest margin).

$$w^T x + b = 0 \tag{17}$$

The problem is of dual quadratic programming nature and can be reduced to Lagrangian optimization problem. A scheme of One vs All or One vs One is used if more than two classes are needed.

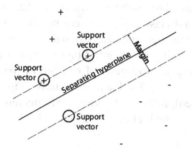

Fig. 3. Finding separating SVM hyperplane between features

3.3   k-Nearest Neighbors

kNN is one of the simplest algorithms for classification. A feature vector is classified by a majority vote of its neighbors. The object class is assigned to the most common one found among *k* nearest neighbors (e.g. to class "square" as given in Fig. 4).

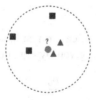

Fig. 4. Classifying object with a kNN classifier *(k = 5)*

4   Data Selection and Experiment

4.1   Evaluation Procedure

Feature extraction methods mentioned in Sect. 2 were implemented and compared in the experiment. All experiments were completed using MATLAB numerical computation environment, BioSig library for biomedical signal processing and libSVM for multiclass SVM classification tasks. The ideas of using different EEG signal energy processing methods and CSP filtering (with initial code implementation) were acquired from an earlier work of Piotr Szachewicz [12]. Classifiers were trained and validated using tenfold cross-validation. Default parameters were used for LDA and QDA classifiers as provided by MATLAB package. Grid search method was used for SVM RBF (radial basis function) gamma and cost parameter optimization [13], used values were: $C = 10$, $\gamma = 0.25$.

4.2   BCI IV 2a Dataset

A BCI signal database [14] from the BCI IV competition held in 2008 was selected for classifier training and testing. The analyzed experiment data was used from the freely available "2a" dataset for a 4-class motor imagery problem. The data consisted of 22 channels of 250 Hz sample rate recorded EEG signal for 9 test subjects and 288 motor imagery trials per subject. Using a cue-paced (synchronous) mode of operation, test subjects were asked to imagine movement of one out of four different motions (left hand, right hand, feet, tongue) for 3 s. Each of the trials (Fig. 5) in the dataset started with an audible signal (beep), followed by visual information (cue) to perform one of the mental tasks and a short break after the mental task.

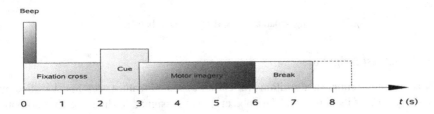

Fig. 5. Single trial timing scheme

4.3   Accuracy Calculation

The accuracy of the BCI data classification results was computed by calculating the Cohen's kappa [15] coefficient κ as given by equation:

$$\kappa = \frac{p_0 - p_e}{1 - p_e} \tag{18}$$

here p_0 – the classification accuracy, p_e – hypothetical accuracy of a random classifier for the data ($p_e = 0.25$ for four classes).

5   Results

All experiment results are given in Tables 1 and 2. As can be seen from the tables, by using simple EEG features the mean kappa for the LDA method almost everywhere scores highest accuracy (and average). This could be an indication of good linearization

Table 1. Average classification results (kappa values) using CSP filtering

Classifier	Ch.diff	Teager	TDP	Mean power	BP	C-Avrg
kNN	N/A	0,3890	0,4327	0,4249	0,3393	0,3965
LDA	N/A	**0,4437**	**0,4950**	**0,4638**	**0,4154**	**0,4545**
QDA	N/A	0,3868	0,4344	0,4259	0,3515	0,3997
SVM	N/A	0,3645	0,3835	0,4605	0,4075	0,4040
F-avrg	N/A	0,3960	0,4364	**0,4438**	0,3784	

Table 2. Average classification results (kappa values) without CSP filtering

Classifier	Ch.diff	Teager	TDP	Mean power	BP	C-Avrg
kNN	0,3678	0,1538	0,2045	0,1867	0,1225	0,2071
LDA	0,4346	**0,4147**	**0,4134**	**0,4400**	**0,2487**	**0,3903**
QDA	0,3179	0,2864	0,2790	0,3185	0,1480	0,2700
SVM	**0,4372**	0,1553	0,1791	0,2950	0,1877	0,2509
F-avrg	**0,3894**	0,2525	0,2690	0,3101	0,1767	

or good linear separation of the EEG features. Still, a combination of CSP filtering and SVM classification beats the LDA for single feature type, but the difference is negligible. A maximum average kappa of 0.495 was reached in tests (i.e. accuracy of 62 %), which is still far from 90 % accuracy achieved in other [16] work that uses more advanced techniques. Since Channel difference method does not support CSP filtering, so N/A values are presented.

Average feature performance (F-avrg) indicates that Mean power and TDP features are the best feature methods when using CSP filtering. However, Channel difference method achieves best result when CSP filtering is not being done. Band power algorithm was the worst performer in tests. A graphical view of the same data is given further in Fig. 6 where CSP filtering normalization influence can be seen better.

It should be noted, that Channel difference method performance follows along Band Power performance when CSP is used due to obvious reason – the method needs to extract different signal frequency bands by using the BP algorithm. This can be seen in Fig. 7 further. Since Channel difference method cannot use CSP filtering, one result bar is not shown.

Quite important is the view showing method accuracy per subject as in Fig. 8. Some subjects are resistant to existing EEG methods, so subject-specific (adaptive) techniques are required in order to achieve higher classification accuracy. The positive normalizing effect can be seen for the CSP case - giving greater average accuracy.

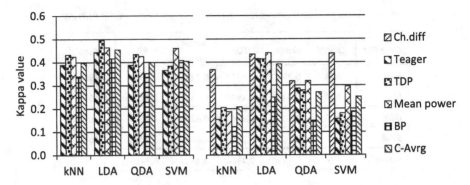

Fig. 6. Average feature results for classifiers (left – with CSP, right – no CSP)

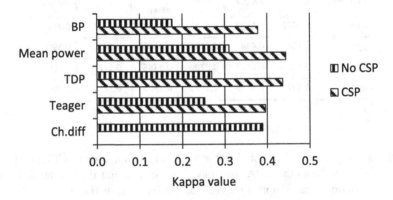

Fig. 7. Average accuracy per feature type

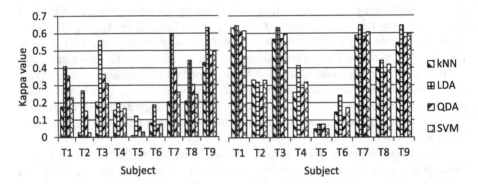

Fig. 8. Average accuracy per subject (left – no CSP, right – with CSP)

6 Conclusion

This work analyzed multiple signal energy feature extraction methods and their usage for 4-class motor imagery BCI classification problem. Tested algorithms showed that simple EEG signal energy feature extraction methods such as Mean power or TDP are one of the best when doing EEG signal classification with CSP filtering. A positive influence on accuracy and test results were visible when the CSP filter was applied.

Presented results also confirmed that the Linear Discriminant analysis (LDA) algorithm can be successfully used for EEG signal classification. Best classification performance was demonstrated by LDA among tested classifiers. Such results also provide insight, that EEG features can be linearly separable.

Proposed Channel difference algorithm for signal feature extraction was able to achieve best average classification result among other tested feature extraction algorithms. Ability to reach classification results close to CSP by using simpler filtering is one of the advantages of the method. However, many optimization possibilities exist for future work including development of better feature extraction algorithms and adaptation to subject specific EEG information.

All experiment source code, test data and detailed results can be acquired from repository: https://github.com/tomazas/icist2015.

References

1. Brodu, N., et al.: Comparative study of band-power extraction techniques for motor imagery classification. In: IEEE Symposium on Computational Intelligence, Cognitive Algorithms, Mind, and Brain (CCMB), pp. 1–6 (2011)
2. Pfurtscheller, G., et al.: Graz-Brain-Computer Interface: State of Research, pp. 65–84. MIT Press, Cambridge (2007)
3. Kaiser, JF.: On a simple algorithm to calculate the energy of a signal. In: IEEE International Conference on Acoustic Speech Signal Process, Albuquerque, NM (1990)
4. Martišius, I., et al.: Using higher order nonlinear operators for SVM classification of EEG data. Elektronika ir Elektrotechnika 119(3), 99–102 (2012)
5. Dolezal, J., Cerny, V., Stastny, J.: Online motor-imagery based BCI. In: International Conference on Applied Electronics (AE), pp. 65–68, 5–7 (2012)
6. Tandonnet, C., Burle, B., Hasbroucq, T., Vidal, F.: Spatial enhancement of EEG traces by surface Laplacian estimation: comparison between local and global methods. Clin. Neurophysiol. 116, 18–24 (2005)
7. Qin, L., He, B.: A wavelet-based time-frequency analysis approach for classification of motor imagery for brain-computer interface applications. J. Neural Eng. 2, 65–72 (2005)
8. Müller-Gerking, J., et al.: Designing optimal spatial filters for single-trial EEG classification in a movement task. Clin. Neurophysiol. 110(5), 787–798 (1999)
9. Thang, L.Q., Temiyasathit, C.: Increase performance of four-class classification for motor-imagery based brain-computer interface. In: 2014 International Conference on Computer, Information and Telecommunication Systems (CITS), pp. 1–5, 7–9 (2014)
10. Fisher, R.A.: The use of multiple measurements in taxonomic problems. Ann. Eugenics 7, 179–188 (1936)

11. Ben-Hur, A., Weston, J.: A user's guide to support vector machines. In: Carugo, O., Eisenhaber, F. (eds.) Data Mining Techniques for the Life Sciences. Methods in Molecular Biology, vol. 609, pp. 223–239. Humana Press, New York (2010)
12. Szachewicz, P.: Classification of Motor Imagery for Brain-Computer Interfaces. Master's thesis, Poznan University of Technology, Poznan (2013)
13. Hsu, C.-W., et al.: A Practical Guide to Support Vector Classification. National Taiwan University, Taiwan (2010)
14. Brunner, C., et al.: BCI Competition 2008 – Graz data set A (2008). https://www.bbci.de/competition/iv/desc_2a.pdf
15. Schlogl, A., et al.: Evaluation criteria in BCI research. In: Dornhege, G., del Millan, J.R., Hinterberger, T., McFarland, D.J., Muller, K.-R. (eds.) Toward Brain-Computer Interfacing, pp. 327–342. MIT Press, Cambridge (2007)
16. Ang, K.K., et al.: Filter bank common spatial pattern (FBCSP) in brain-computer interface. In: Neural Networks, IJCNN 2008. IEEE World Congress on Computational Intelligence, pp. 2390–2397, 1–8 June 2008

Best Practices for e-Learning in On-Campus and Distance Education – A Case Study of Karlstad University

Prima Gustiené and Monika Magnusson[✉]

Karlstad Business School, Karlstad University, Karlstad, Sweden
{Prima.Gustiene,Monika.Magnusson}@kau.se

Abstract. For the last decades e-learning has enabled new modes of learning and teaching in higher education. However, there seem to be relatively few case studies comparing and analysing how e-learning could be applied in different teaching modes. The main purpose of this paper is therefore to study how e-learning may be used in on-campus and distance educations respectively, and hybrids of these, and what the advantages and disadvantages of different teaching modes are. A case study of the Information Systems department at Karlstad University indicates that e-learning may be successfully applied in both on-campus and distance education and it may also be used to create flexible or blended learning. However, some caution is necessary to avoid creating information overload among on-campus students or to reduce the highly appreciated flexibility in time and space for distance students.

Keywords: e-Learning · Distance education · On-campus education · Flexible learning · Blended learning · Higher education

1 Introduction

Market changes, global competition, and distributed environments as well as sophisticated technologies force educators to provide their services with better quality and more flexibility [6], which makes it necessary to rethink and redesign old teaching methods and introduce new technological solutions. E-learning, or "the use of telecommunication technology to deliver information for education and training" [15] provides new teaching and learning methods. The flexibility in time and space enabled by e-learning fits our modern society (ibid.). However, for educational institutions to overcome the old traditional 'one size-fits-all' approach that mainly focuses on face-to face teaching is not an easy task. There are still a great many institutions that mostly use face-to-face teaching methods, or supplement these with Learning Management Systems (LMS) such as Moodle, using them only as repositories for course material. According to Jona [8] many traditional or classroom-based teaching methods suffer from problems such as passive learning, artificial divide between practice and instruction, irrelevant subject matter and inappropriate assessment that hinder effective learning. Education is not just a transmission of learning material and instructions. The process of how human learning takes place is of the utmost importance (ibid.). Blended learning is a combination of face-to-face and online teaching methods [7] and is rapidly gaining interest in practice

© Springer International Publishing Switzerland 2015
G. Dregvaite and R. Damasevicius (Eds.): ICIST 2015, CCIS 538, pp. 93–103, 2015.
DOI: 10.1007/978-3-319-24770-0_9

and in research (ibid.). With so many ways to approach teaching and numerous supporting technologies, it may be difficult to choose the best options. Course content, location and facilities can all influence the choice of teaching methods [3]. Sometimes the solution can be found not just in one approach but in a combination of approaches.

The purpose of this paper is to describe how e-learning technologies may be used in both on-campus and distance education and to analyse its advantages and disadvantages.

2 Different Types of Teaching Methods

It is increasingly clear that it is no longer possible to develop human capital such as knowledge with just a single approach. Digital technology changes the conditions of higher education in several ways. In this chapter we discuss different teaching methods in the conventional classroom, or on-campus education, and distance education, also called online learning, and the combination of these.

2.1 On Campus Education

Face-to-face (F2F) or classroom-based learning is the tradition in on-campus education. Most of us were taught by this method at school and at the university. According to Smith et al. [13] the classroom-based teaching and learning process is often based on "the information that passes from the notes of the teacher to the notes of the students without passing through the mind of either one". The problem here is that the teaching process should engage students in a learning process. Education is not just the transmission of information; rather this process has some important characteristics that need to be considered [8]; human learning process should be *goal-driven*, driven by *expectation failure* (i.e. by allowance to make mistakes), and *case-based*. According to Jona [8] the following problems with classroom-based learning hinder the effectiveness of education:

- *Passive learning*: classroom-based approach places learners in a passive role where they are expected just to sit and absorb knowledge.
- *Artificial divide between practice and instruction*: learners are presented with a great deal of information in form of concepts, theories, principles that the learners are supposed to remember and apply. The problem is that learners do not retain abstract concepts that they can relate to specific cases.
- *Irrelevant subject matter is inappropriate to assess:* very often the content of lecture-based courses are driven by what can be easily tested and measured.

The advent of sophisticated computer and networking technologies has afforded educational institutions to translate courses onto online courses, delivered on the Internet. But often online courses suffer from the same problems as classroom-based courses. Jona [8] presents three key principles that should be taken into consideration in creating effective learning environments: *learning by doing*, *learning by mistakes*, and *learning from stories*. These principles of effective learning could be applied both in classroom and online courses.

2.2 Distance Education

Technological and social changes require people to constantly develop and upgrade their knowledge. Distance education, as a method of teaching, is a necessity in order to reach wider groups in society. Thoms and Eryilmaz [17] define distance education as "any form of learning where individuals are not physically present in a traditional setting, such as a classroom". According to Lindh [11], distance education is a rational way to make time for advanced education when time is a scarce resource. Distance education allows the students to learn at their own pace and in their own space [17], thus enabling students in rural areas and/or with a family or a work situation that is difficult to combine with on campus education to study. Thompson et al. [18] claim that teaching methods such as online programs often attract non-traditional students that have "multiple competing demands on their time, including families and other job responsibilities".

A life situation with competing demands along with no or few physical interactions with teachers/instructors emphasizes the need for students to develop effective self-management or self-regulation skills. It is well known that student dropout rates are considerably higher in distance education than in conventional learning environment [10]. Lee et al. [10] found self-regulation skills to be one discriminator between students that dropped out of their distance educations and those that did not. Simpson [12] argues that advances in technology might not improve this situation. Rather, institutions need to find ways to strengthen the students' motivation in the light of the problems connected to part-time studies and a sense of isolation.

Setting learning goals and monitoring progress in reaching them are the cornerstones of self-regulation [8]. Furthermore, according to Lindh [11], making a time plan for studies is critical for distance learning. There are mainly three things that need to be scheduled: *reading the course literature, time to reflect and work with assignments, communication and discussion with other students.* The schedule is the aspect to evaluate if short time goals have been achieved. Distance education is thus much about students taking responsibility for their studies. This does not mean that the students should be left alone in the learning process. Different technology-based systems provide possibilities to communicate with teachers and other students. However, the first steps in developing effective on-line courses involve matching the content of the course with course structure, technical possibilities and the skills to be taught [8].

2.3 Blended and Flexible Learning

The competition between universities increases as does students' expectations to meet a digitally literate learning environment [2]. Nowadays the line between distance education and campus education is blurred as the same technologies are used in both. Hybrid forms of education models based on e-learning exist in a number of modes, ranging from technology-enhanced on campus (classroom based) education to distance education that offers supplementary or optional F2F contact [4]. When technology is used to reduce F2F contact time, it is sometimes called blended learning (ibid.) and when students "can choose whether or not to attend face-to-face sessions, 'with no attendant learning deficit'" the concept of flexible learning is sometimes used [16]. Thorne [19] describes blended learning as a workable solution that allows learners and teachers to integrate online learning with a broad range of more traditional learning techniques. "Blended learning represents an opportunity to integrate the innovative and technological advances offered by online learning with the interaction and participation offered in the best of traditional learning" (ibid.)

Taylor and Newton [16] claim that blended learning is not an ultimate solution. Instead they suggest a 'Converged Delivery' where "every student should have a range of pedagogically sound study options to best suit their learning preferences and their work and life demand" [16]. They argue that the real challenge is to provide students with equitable access to learning independent of the blend of delivery mode.

3   Research Method

The department of Information Systems at Karlstad University (KAU IS) was selected as an appropriate case to study due to its long experience of using e-learning in both on campus and distance education. An inductive study searching for themes in usage, advantages and disadvantages, was performed through a content analysis of different documents; strategic plans and decisions, policy documents, student course evaluations and statistics of applications and dropouts. The student course evaluations selected came from three introductory courses (for the years of 2013–2014), offered both as on-campus and as distance education. Also, the course evaluations in two mixed courses (combination of on campus and distance education students) were analysed for the same years. Statements related to e-learning were categorised into themes through an iterative coding process.

4   The Use of e-Learning at KAU IS - from Campus Courses to Flexible and Blended Learning Courses

Karlstad University is a fairly young but progressive university in providing different types of teaching methods. The university, for example, includes blended learning in their strategic plan: "In order to offer education with high availability, the University will especially focus on flexible education, so-called blended learning" [9]. There is thus a good support of e-learning at the strategic level of the university. However, at the IS department there are no formal guidelines on how to implement these strategies. There are three study programs at KAU IS. These are the two on-campus programs: *IT design* (ITD), *Web and Multimedia* (WOM) and one distance learning program *IT, project management and ERP system* (IPA). All three programs lead to a Bachelor's degree (180 credits) in Information Systems. The two latter also offer the option of choosing a higher education qualification (120 credits) after two years of study. IPA has two modes: full-time studies or part-time studies. The first semester contains the same courses in all three programs. After that a specialisation takes place even if there are some joint courses later on. This means that a number of courses are offered in both an on-campus and an online version. Examination formats are normally constructed to fit both modes.

4.1   e-Learning in on Campus Education at KAU IS

For approximately 7–8 years, all courses at the department, including face-to-face-based ones, have been using a LMS platform called itslearning www.itslearning.com. This LMS is paid for at university level and is the only LMS supported by the organization. A strategic decision was made in 2011 to close down a competing web page and phase out another LMS due to itslearing's perceived relative advantages in functionality, spread and prospects. Itslearning is web based and free of charge for all students. A virtual classroom is constructed for each course event. New instances of a course may be created through copying and pasting the content of earlier courses and adding new content. Only earlier discussions and submissions need to be removed. New folders may be added and files uploaded in the tree-based structure. Among the features are tests/ quizzes, links, notes, discussion, conferences and different games. The use of itslearning in all courses was initially not the result of a formal decision, but rather a grass-root initiative that has developed into a de facto-standard at the department. Teachers who had seen the advantages of using the platform in distance education courses decided that the possibility to gather all information in the same place could be advantageous also for on campus students. All information about a course is uploaded to the platform: schedule, literature, slides from lectures, booking lists for tutoring, assignments/tasks etc. The students may also submit exams and laboratory tasks via this platform. This way both student and teacher can monitor the process, present and view results. Furthermore, all courses have a platform discussion forum where students can ask questions to teachers and peers or merely socialize. Since itslearning was introduced, material that traditionally was reserved for distance students has been applied also in on-campus courses. This material is literature study instructions, filmed lectures, quizzes etc. In particular, students appreciate filmed lectures and literature study instructions, according to student course evaluations. The amount of course material is among the less appreciated aspects because it may become overwhelming and difficult to navigate in.

4.2   E-Learning in Distance Education at KAU IS

KAU IS has long experience of distance courses as well as flexible ways of teaching. The first distance learning courses started more than twenty years ago and a pure distance education program was launched in 2007. As Information Communication Technology (ICT) plays an important part in online education, the design of courses always takes into account three main concepts of ICT. Figure 1 presents the diagram of ICT as a foundation of distance courses.

Information, communication and technology are three important components in the structure of distance courses. Information concerns the content of the course: video lectures, instructions/study guides, course literature, slides and lecture notes, tasks, complementary material such as links, quizzes etc. Providing a clear and intuitive structure of the content at the LMS platform is essential in our experience. Failure to do this results in critical comments in student course evaluations. The structure can preferably be similar between different courses as this facilitates students' navigation. Furthermore, long-term planning in presenting the content is very much appreciated, according to student course

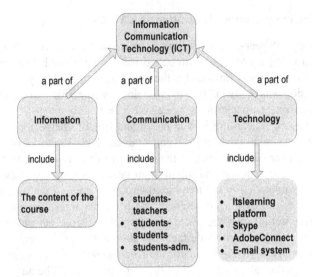

Fig. 1. ICT is the foundation of distance courses.

evaluations. Moreover, communication is an especially important concept in distance education. Communication in distance learning takes place between different sets of actors: *student-teacher, student-student, student-administrator*. It is very important that communication channels work properly. A common experience among the teachers and course administrators, which is also mentioned in student evaluations, is that it is extremely important to answer the students' questions quickly. Moreover, a recurrent theme in the course evaluations is that it is vital to distance education students to have maximum flexibility in time and space, which means that physical meetings and even synchronous virtual meetings should be avoided. Also technical support is essential to on-line communication and distance education in general. Workshops, tutorials, and seminars take place via Skype or Adobe Connect and generally work well. An important factor has been the recent Swedish increase of access to broadband.

4.3 Blended and Flexible Learning at KAU IS

Recently, the blended learning teaching methods were introduced in KAU courses. An important strategy issue at KAU is thus how the entire teaching staff can work systematically to achieve a high pedagogically qualified expertise in integrating digital technology in the learning environment. This is a core issue to achieve effectiveness and to switch between different modes of education delivery [5]. Besides from using LMSs in on-campus courses, the KAU IS department also uses flexible learning or hybrids in campus courses and online courses. Flexible learning is essentially about providing learners with freedom of choice regarding when, where, and how to study, that is, pace, place and delivery mode.

In practice this is handled in two ways. First, there are fewer courses that are open to both on-campus and distance learning students. All lectures and other on-campus activities are optional and if possible recorded on video and uploaded to the itslearning platform shortly after the physical event. Tutoring is accessible either on campus or via Skype or Adobe Connect. All material is uploaded to the itslearning platform where discussions between all students are encouraged. There is also a 'light-version' of flexible learning where distance learning students are invited to campus lectures and workshops. It means that the students who want to study at a distance but live near Karlstad University can have workshops, seminars and tutorials at the university. Furthermore, both campus and distance learning students have occasionally 'switched' mode. It means that students from the on-campus programs have studied single courses online and vice versa. The 'mixed' or flexible courses are both appreciated and criticised in student evaluations. Students appreciate the increased options although some on-campus students want more face-to-face lectures. Some occasional use of web 2.0 technologies, such as dedicated Facebook pages, has been used but mainly for networking reasons (e.g. a network for female IT students). Requests for social media and other web 2.0 technologies have so far been low both from students and teachers. However, a blended learning design is being developed for one of the introductory on campus courses. The aim is to use 'flipped classroom' together with filmed lectures and literature study guidelines. This approach will be tested and evaluated during the autumn of 2015.

4.4 Student Statistics in Different Learning Approaches

A comparison of student statistics from the three study programs shows that a large increase has taken place in the number of first choice applications to the distance learning program during the last five years while the application rate to the two on-campus programs is rather stable [14], see Fig. 2.

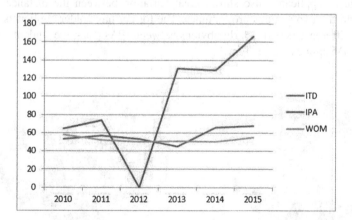

Fig. 2. First choice applications to KAU IS degree programs 2010–2015 [Source: Swedish Council for Higher Education 2015].

During 2012, the program start of IPA was cancelled due to a need for budget cut downs at the faculty. The figures for 2015 are based on the total number of first choice applications and may be higher than the finally approved applications, which are shown for 2010–2014. The number of study places for 2015 are 35 for ITD (previously 45),

35 for WOM (previously 40) and 30 for IPA. What is also apparent is that the dropout rate is higher among IPA students. Among the 80 students that were accepted in 2014 (a planned increase was made to correct for dropouts) approximately 55 students were still studying at the beginning of the second semester while ITD and WOM had approximately 5–10 student dropouts in the same period. The dropout rates were significantly higher in IPA also for students starting in 2011 and 2013. However, the share of female applicants is significantly higher in the distance learning program (IPA), 43 % for the year 2014 compared with the applicants to WOM (23 %) and ITD (12 %), see Fig. 3 [14]. The previous years have a similar distribution.

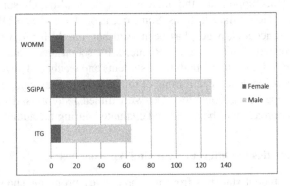

Fig. 3. Applicants to KAU IS degree programs by gender. [Source: Swedish Council for Higher Education 2015].

The age of applicants also shows great variation between the distance learning program and the two campus programmes. The former have older applicants than the latter. The difference is particularly obvious between IPAs part-time student applicants and the WOM applicants, see Fig. 4.

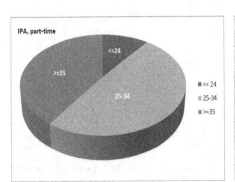 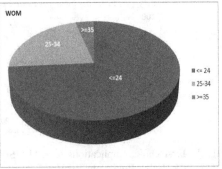

Fig. 4. Age distribution among first choice applicants in 2014. IPA to the left and WOM to the right. [Source: Swedish Council for Higher Education 2015].

5 Advantages, Disadvantages and Best Practices

The use of e-learning technology such as LMSs in the conventional on-campus courses and programmes may facilitate for students to structure their studies and plan their time. Furthermore, if they are prevented to attend a lecture they can still access the content. In addition, the possibility to submit assignments, project reports and other examination tasks and to monitor the progress may be added value to the students. A potential disadvantage to students is that the addition of an e-learning platform and distance learning features, such as literature study instructions and filmed lectures in on-campus courses, may increase the workload and cause stress. Although it is not mandatory to use the material, the students may feel obligated to do so. Also the instructors, who need to make sure that learning material, schedules, lecture notes and assignments are presented in a pedagogically and timely manner, may experience an increased workload. They also need to monitor discussion forums and respond swiftly to questions.

The advantage of the pure distance education is that it enables students of all ages with complex family or job situations to study regardless of time and space [17, 18]. The fact that the KAU IS department's distance learning students are older and that the programme attracts more female students indicate that distance learning options are important to reach non-traditional student groups or students that may not be able to attend campus courses. A major disadvantage of distance education is that the social processes often are hampered by the lack of face-to-face-communication [1]. Accordingly, distance education puts great demands on the students' self-regulation skills and students that are not strong in this area may drop out [10]. The dropout rate is considerably higher in the department's distance education programme than in the two on-campus programmes, especially during the first semester. The reason may be that many distance education students have a complex work and family situation and/or do not feel comfortable with the study situation that requires a high level of self-regulation [10] and may be quite lonely [12].

6 Conclusion

Based on the results of the case study done at KAU IS, it appears that one of the advantages of the pure distance education is that it enables students of all ages with complex family or job situations to study regardless of time and space. Another advantage is that the distance education programme at KAU IS department attracts older students as well as female students to a greater extent. The results thus indicate that distance education is important in reaching non-traditional student groups or students that may not be able to attend on-campus instruction. A major disadvantage with distance education is the high dropout rate. The students provide several reasons for that. The most common reasons are that some students have complex work and family situations, and/or they do not feel comfortable with the study situation that requires a high level of self-regulation. A disadvantage with adding e-learning platform and distance education features to on-campus education, such as written literature study instructions and recorded lectures, is that it may increase the workload and cause stress. However, the students also appreciate the increased flexibility and access to material outside of the classroom. Overall, the tendency towards integrating the two on-campus programmes with the distance education programmes in joint flexible courses seems mainly beneficial to both parties. Resources can be saved and students are offered greater flexibility and value added services. A recommendation is that institutions use the same LMS in all courses, on campus and distance, so that it becomes a natural way of working for both teachers and students. A further recommendation is, to offer different possibilities for students to mix on campus and distance education but to avoid mandatory face-to-face meetings or too many synchronous virtual meetings for distance students. Regarding the e-learning platform it is important to have long-term planning and to create clear and intuitive structures for the content. Finally, it is commendable if students' questions in digital media are answered as soon as possible.

References

1. Akkoyunlu, B., Soylu, M.Y.: A Study of student's perceptions in a blended learning environment based on different leaning styles. Educ. Technol. Soc. **11**(1), 183–193 (2008)
2. Duncan-Hawell, J.: Digital mismatch: expectations and realities of digital competency amongst pre-service education students. Aust. J. Educ. Technol. **28**(5), 827–840 (2012)
3. Ferriman, J.: Blended Learning is Better Learning? http://www.learndash.com/types-of-learning-infographic (2005)
4. Graham, C.R., Woodfield, W., Harrison, J., Buckley, J.: A framework for institutional adoption and implementation of blended learning in higher education. Internet High Educ. **18**, 4–14 (2013)
5. Gråsjö, F.: Policy Document: Strategy for Developing Blended Learning at Karlstad University. Karlstad University, Vice-Chancellor's Office (2014)
6. Gustiené, P., Carlsson, S.: How models and methods for analysis and design of information systems can be improved to better support communication and learning. In: Pankowska, M. (ed.) Infonomics for Distributed Business and Decision-Making Environment: Creating Information System Ecology, pp. 44–63. IGI Global, New York (2010)
7. Halvorsen, L.R., Graham, C.R., Spring, K.J., Drysdale, J.S., Henrie, C.R.: A thematic analysis of the most highly cited scholarships in the first decade of blended learning research. Internet High. Educ. **20**, 20–34 (2014)
8. Jona, K.: Rethinking the design of online courses. In: Proceedings ASCILITE 2000 Conference (2000)
9. Karlstad University. Strategisk plan för Karlstads universitet. http://www.intra.kau.se/dokument/upload/C10B9497076071FFBAvkFF9CC9F8/C2014_608Strategisk%20plan%202015_2107_2.pdf
10. Lee, Y., Choi, J., Kim, T.: Discriminating factors between completers of a dropouts from online learning courses. Br. J. Educ. Technol. **44**(2), 328–337 (2013)
11. Lindh, M.: Study Guide for Distance Learning. Karlstad University, Department for Political and Historical Studies (2009)
12. Simpson, O.: Student retention in distance education: are we failing our students? Open Learn. **28**(2), 105–119 (2013)
13. Smith, K.A., Sheppard, S.D., Johnson, D.W., Johnson, R.T.: Pedagogies of engagement: classroom-based practices. J. Eng. Educ. **94**(1), 1–15 (2005)
14. Swedish Council for Higher Education. Application statistics. http://statistik.uhr.se/

15. Sun, P.C., Tsai, R.J., Finger, G., Chen, Y.Y., Yeh, D.: What drives a successful e-Learning? An empirical investigation of the critical factors influencing learner satisfaction. Comput. Educ. **50**(4), 1183–1202 (2008)
16. Taylor, J.A., Newton, D.: Beyond blended learning: a case study of institutional change at an Australian regional university. Internet High. Educ. **18**, 54–60 (2013)
17. Thoms, B., Eryilmaz, E.: How media choice affects learners interaction in distance learning classes. Comput. Educ. **75**, 112–126 (2014)
18. Thompson, N.L., Miller, N.C., Franz, D.P.: Comparing online and face-to-face learning experiences for non-traditional students. Q. Rev. Distance Educ. **14**(4), 233 (2013)
19. Thorne, K.: Blended Learning: How to Integrate Online and Traditional Learning. Kogan Page, London (2003)

Information System of Students' Knowledge Test Control

Olga Aleksenko, Iryna Baranova, Svitlana Vashchenko[✉], and Andrii Sobol

Sumy State University, Sumy, Ukraine
sveta@opm.sumdu.edu.ua
{aleksenko.olga,baranova.iryna}@gmail.com

Abstract. The paper focuses on the improvement of the test control technology of mastering the educational material by the students.

The main aim of this work is to elaborate the information system for training and methodological support of learning by teacher.

This text presents the functional requirements list for the system as a result of review of existing testing systems. The design of the information system was built on the conceptual and UML use-cases models. In the work were analyzed four methods of pseudo-random numbers generating to provide a high level of tasks variability. According to this analysis the linear congruent method of randomization was chosen.

The information system of tests formation has been worked out as educational software.

Keywords: Testing · Model of test control technology · Test information system · Pseudo-random number generator · Linear congruent method

1 Introduction

The unified European education area requires the improvement of the educational technologies. A university student has to learn large amounts of information and to demonstrate competence in solving professional problems. To achieve a sufficient level of education quality the results control tools are needed. The use of written tests is best approach to ensure impartiality of the students attestation [1–3]. Also the learning results test control provides input information to improve the educational materials and forms profound knowledge of the students.

It is necessary to analyze the knowledge test technology (Fig. 1) to create an information technology (IT) for the tests formation. The important attribute of the testing system is the possibility of a computer knowledge control (e-tests), the ability to print test items and their saving in the archive. The test system also should provide a high level of tasks variability and reorder answers while displaying an item in different variants. The test system should generate test keys and be capable of paper tests automated inspection to simplify and accelerate the results checking. Also the working out of the balanced variants according to their complexity is an important task when creating test items.

© Springer International Publishing Switzerland 2015
G. Dregvaite and R. Damasevicius (Eds.): ICIST 2015, CCIS 538, pp. 104–114, 2015.
DOI: 10.1007/978-3-319-24770-0_10

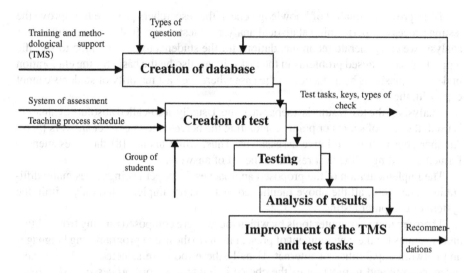

Fig. 1. The model of test control information technology

The making test database with a large number of questions with high variability and simultaneously the provision of the maximum level of educational material coverage is relevant up to today. Manual test tasks formation is not appropriate and does not provide the necessary quality of the control [1, 3].

The solving of this issue is working out information system of the testing tasks automated formation. In this case it is possible to use special mathematical methods for making the test question variety.

In research it will be used the following methods. The methods of system analysis will be used for the IS functional requirements formulation and making IS conceptual model. The methods and theories to support software production will be used for IS design and realization. The level of tasks variability will be increased by the methods of pseudo-random numbers generating.

2 Related Work

Computer-based testing systems allow you to create a variety of question types: from simple selection of correct answers to the tasks of compliance, ordering or filling gaps [4]. One way of widening test technologies is by types of tasks – using multi option testing tasks [5]. For this test question type the formation of a set of possible input values and the set of questions of the relevant results are provided. Due to this, each test task redo changes its content every time the test is passed. This approach will enhance the objectivity of the evaluation of the students. By analyzing answers to the following multi-option questions we can make a reliable conclusion on a student's mastering of a particular topic and exclude the possibility of guessing that is one of the negative aspects of testing. To avoid the possibility of guessing the probabilistic components can be taken into account when analyzing and evaluating the answers [6].

To improve the quality of knowledge check the researchers propose to improve the testing process by performing statistical analysis of test results [6–9]. As a result of this analysis we can generate recommendations for the students to pay attention to specific topics that have caused problems in the tasks. It can also be the basis for the elaboration of definite questions by a teacher, in the case where the vast majority of students cannot cope with the task.

Analysis of the test results is a separate issue. Usually, a so-called absolute evaluation is used: the sum of scores or points calculating the percentage of correct answers [5, 6]. Another approach is a relative assessment. Thus, while testing [8] the assessment is formed according to the best results to the set of answers.

The implementation of the proposed approaches for paper testing raises many difficulties. Therefore, all the above mentioned methods are implemented only within the system of computer testing.

There are many computer tools by which the tests are composed ranging from editors and programs for the development of presentations to the use of programming languages and network capabilities of internet. Usually these tools are selected by the teachers independently and in most cases the choice is limited to word processors. Moreover, this approach causes the problem of accumulation and processing of the base of questions.

The last problem can be solved by using special software. Almost each system is result of schools' development and is not in the free access. To solve the problem of finding a testing system that will automate the process of testing both automated and writing, five test systems have been analyzed [10–15]. Table 1 provides a list of nominated functional requirements and demonstrates the compliance of the analyzed systems according to these requirements.

Table 1. Functional capabilities of the similar software

Functional requirements	Software					
	AdTester	FastTEST	VeralTest	Exam	OpenTEST	INDIGO
Computer testing	+	+	+	+	+	+
Variability of the test	+/-	+	+/-	+/-	+/-	+/-
Formation of the paper tests	-	+	+	-	+	+
Automation module of the paper test check	-	-	-	-	-	-
Formation of "keys" for manual tests check	-	-	-	-	-	-
Archive of the existing questions	-	-	-	-	-	-
Mixing answer items in different variants	-	+	+	-	-	+

As shown in Table 1, none of the reviewed software implements all the requirements. None of the software can form the "keys", automate the check of "paper" tests, save previously created options in the archive. Also a significant drawback of existing testing software is that they select questions using the standard mechanism of the random number generation (RNG) that do not provide a sufficient level of variability.

3   Research Goals

To solve the pointed above problem the decision is made to work out an information system of the options formation for testing, providing a sufficient level of variability that will ensure the implementation of information technology of test control of students' knowledge.

The system puts forward the following functional requirements:

- the creation and editing of database with a list of questions to the disciplines with the distribution of questions according to the topics. The questions has to be distributed by the level of difficulty;
- formation and storage of options for the tests according to the themes indicated by the user, and you can choose whether to take into account the complexity of the questions in options formation;
- to provide the tests variety;
- export of the options in documents MS Word;
- formation of "keys" according to the created options, output to working window filed or saving in MS Excel;
- to enable automation inspection of "paper" tests.

To build information system we must first create its model and determine the method of creation of tasks variants using RNG.

4   Model of Test Control Systems

4.1   Conceptual Model of Information System

Testing Information System (IS) is a combination of:

$$IS = <DB, RNG, UI, ID>$$ (1)

Where DB ia a database, RNG is a generating module of random numbers, UI is an user interface, ID is an input data.

In turn, the database is a set of questions (SQ) formed from a plurality of created options (CO):

$$DB = <SQ, CO>$$ (2)

The set of questions consists of a range of disciplines (*Rd*), topics (*Rt*) in the subjects and questions (*Rq*) in the subject.

The input data to the system are the discipline, list of necessary topics, quantity of options for the formation and the number of questions in the variant.

In Fig. 2 the principle of the system work is presented. The user (teacher) collects database of questions that are divided into the disciplines and topics within the discipline, and sets the input data to form necessary test task. According to the information received from a plurality of questions the sample of all numbers is created that match the criteria. RNG module creates a sequence of random numbers obtained from the sample. Then from the set of questions the user (teacher) selects such questions that correspond to the data of generated sequence and a test task variant is created in accordance with the input data.

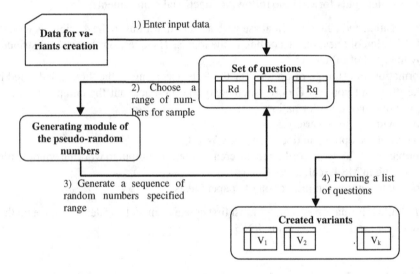

Fig. 2. The general principle of the information system

4.2   Model of IS

Project IS is built using UML as a set of diagrams which from different perspectives form the idea of testing the system with a gradual increase of the level of details.

In the system two categories of actors are defined: administrator and teacher-user. Figure 3 shows a fragment of diagram of the variants of use describing precedents important for the actor "teacher" who initiates efforts to create multivariate tests.

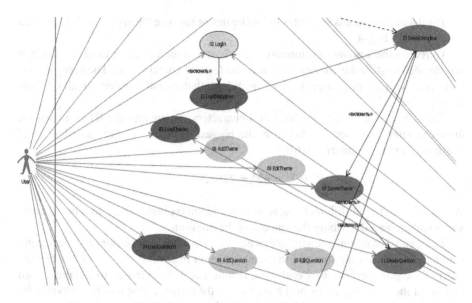

Fig. 3. Fragment of diagram of variant use

4.3 Database

One of the key elements of the information system is a database that will be stored on the server. The database stores data about users (teachers), subjects, topics, questions, tests and options.

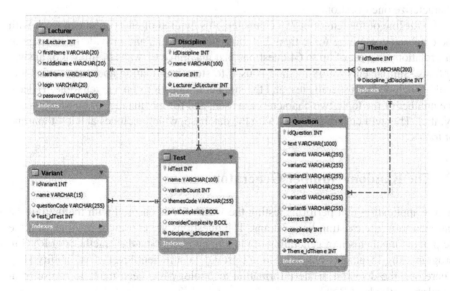

Fig. 4. Scheme of database

The database contains six tables linked by ties of the type "many to one". Chart data is presented in Fig. 4.

To reduce the amount of information that is stored on the server in the database, it was decided to store the created options in the form of encoded line. The encryption is performed with the help of capital and small Latin letters and numbers (in all 62 characters).

The line includes a set of groups of 4 characters. To encrypt the ID of a question three characters are used. In this case, the biggest question number (possible ID of questions from a database) is [16]:

$$N_q = k^l = 62^3 = 238328 \qquad (3)$$

Where k is number of different characters used in encryption, l is the number of characters (categories) describing the number of the question.

The method of mixing is encrypted as the fourth symbol in the group. This parameter is required so that using one and the same question in several variants of the test the order of the proposed answers each time is different. It is supposed to use predefined options of the rearrangements of the answers in the question that will be encrypted by the numbers. For example, 1 – in the order that is in the database, 2 – possible answers go in reverse order, etc.

The total amount of questions, the information of which may contain one line (that is one variant from the database is calculated according to the formula (4) [17]

$$N_v = \frac{L}{p} = \frac{256}{4} = 64 \qquad (4)$$

Where L is the maximum length of the line, p is number of characters (categories) that characterize one question.

So for line of the length in 256 characters this method of encryption can work with the database containing more than 238 thousand questions and provide the storage of information for a set of up to 64 questions that may have 62 ways of mixing of answer options. Similar encryption method is used to store information about the topics that will be included in a specific test and the number of questions on a given topic. To save the number of the topic two characters are used, and for the quantity of questions – one symbol. This will ensure the work with the database, which includes about 4 thousand of topics.

5   The Random Number Generator

In any application that performs testing the variability is ensured with the help of the samples from the existing list of items. The questions are chosen at random with the help of the mechanism of generating of random numbers. Standard methods of RNG in programming languages typically do not provide a sufficient level of variability [18]. Therefore, the decision in the information technology has been made to refuse from standard methods of RNG.

The search of a necessary method has been performed among the three main methods [19]: linear congruent method (LCM), Blum-Blum-Shub algorithm (BBSH), Fibonacci method of delays (MFD). For this test software in Visual C# language has been created. Additionally the built in the programming language method RNG (Random) has been considered.

The model of the system of testing has been worked out for choosing of the method of generation. The base of questions consisted of 30 questions that have IDs from 1 to 30. Using each of these methods the blocks of 15 options have been created. The number of questions in a variant ranged from 10 to 30 with step 5. In each series 8 experiments have been conducted.

The effectiveness of the method was evaluated by comparison to a standard case. The case is considered to be standard when each question in the block occurs the same number of times.

After the experiment the analysis of the received samples has been conducted. For every experimental method according to the formula (5) the score is calculated [16]:

$$K = \sum k_i \tag{5}$$

Where K is resulting score, k_i is the score of the experiment, which was calculated according to the formula:

$$k_i = \sum (n_j - n_e) \tag{6}$$

Where n_j is frequency of the j-th question in the created block, n_e – standard frequency of question repetition.

To choose the method of RNG the evaluation results were accumulated in the tables, the sample of which is shown in Table 2.

Table 2. Test results for samples from 20 and 30 questions

Exper \ Q-ty	Random	LCM	BBSH	MFD	Random	LCM	BBSH	MFD
		20				30		
1	1024	766	1720	988	1484	1176	2700	1600
2	1104	746	1280	1076	1554	1162	2160	1560
3	1048	778	1520	1026	1596	1134	2790	1530
4	1000	762	1960	1032	1502	1182	2250	1554
5	1070	740	4000	1050	1636	1144	2670	1468
6	1012	762	1940	998	1568	1130	5700	1590
7	1050	784	1360	1072	1502	1126	2400	1508
8	1038	780	3200	1034	1546	1138	2760	1528
	8366	6118	16980	8276	12418	9192	23430	12338

The analysis of the received data showed that in all the experiments linear congruent method showed the best results. That is the allocation of the sequence generated by the algorithm LCM is more uniform compared to other sequences in each series of experiments.

Based on this, for the creation of the test options linear congruent method has been selected. In this method, each following data Xn + 1 is calculated according to the formula (7):

$$X_{n+1} = (aX_n + c) \; mod \, m \tag{7}$$

Where m is module ($m \geq 0$), the maximum range of numbers; a is multiplier ($0 \leq a < m$), c – increase ($0 \leq c < m$).

To ensure the highest level of variability of the generated sequences, all data are from special tables.

6   Testing System Realization

In accordance with the created information system model the software modules "Organizer of tests" have been designed. The system has the classic two-level client-server architecture.

The user works with the client part (Fig. 5), which communicates with the server.

The database is placed on the server required for the system work, and images that are in questions.

The created software modules provide the implementation of all functional requirements put forward.

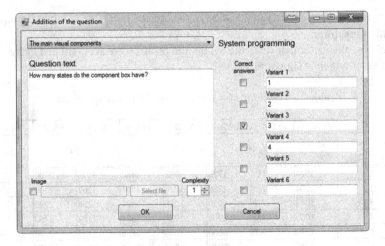

Fig. 5. User's interface

7   Conclusions and Future Work

The paper solved the relevant problem of improving the current students' knowledge testing technologies by using the developed information system. The IS has been made on the basis of the created model and it has been designed as software.

The review of existing testing systems was conducted. The functional requirements list for IS was formulated as the result of it. To elaborate the IS was built the conceptual model, which presents the principle of the system work. The made UML use-cases model describes the requirements to the IS. To provide a high level of tests tasks variability were analyzed four methods of pseudo-random numbers generating. The linear congruent method of randomization was chosen.

The use of developed information system can significantly save teachers' time during the test variants formation: the process of formation of 30 variants with 20 questions takes a few seconds. The use of the linear congruent method provides a higher level of variability compared to most similar software products. For the analysis of the effectiveness of the developed information system two samples assignments have been compared, obtained with the help of the standard RNG and linear congruent methods. The study found that the linear congruent method showed a 35 % better result.

The next stage of the IS development is the addition of the automated testing module with the archiving of results which will provide the teacher with the analysis tools of the test results to monitoring of the students' knowledge level.

References

1. Chmel, V.: Testing – as a method of pedagogical control. http://www.rusnauka.com/11_EISN_2008/Philologia/30455.doc.html. Accessed 10 March 2015
2. Hämäläinen, W., Vinni, M.: Comparison of machine learning methods for intelligent tutoring systems. In: Ikeda, M., Ashley, K.D., Chan, T.-W. (eds.) ITS 2006. LNCS, vol. 4053, pp. 525–534. Springer, Heidelberg (2006)
3. Hwang, G.-J., Hsiao, C.-L., Tseng, J.C.R.: A computer-assisted approach to diagnosing student learning problems in science courses. J. Inf. Sci. Eng. 19(2), 229–248 (2003)
4. Volkov, N., Alexeyev, A.: Test control of knowledge, Sumy (2004)
5. Lukina, T.: Technology of the development of questionnaires for monitoring research of educational problems. http://lib.iitta.gov.ua/4157/1/Технологія_розробки_анкет_для_моніторингових_досліджень_освітніх_проблем-метод_посібник.pdf. Accessed 30 March 2015
6. Avanesov, V.: Introduction to statistical and mathematical methods of educational measurement. Pedagogical Meas. 4, 91–116 (2005)
7. Romero, C., Ventura, S.: Educational data mining: A survey from 1995 to 2005. Expert Syst. Appl. 33(1), 135–146 (2007). doi:10.1016/j.eswa.2006.04.005
8. Mysnyk, L.: Methods and models of management of test technologies of universities in the implementation of the Bologna process. Thesis, Cherkasy (2010)
9. Damaševičius, R. Analysis of academic results for informatics course improvement using association rule mining. In: Information Systems Development: Towards a Service Provision Society, pp. 357–363, Paphos, Cyprus (2009)
10. ADTester homepage. http://www.adtester.org. Accessed 30 March 2015
11. FastTEST Professional Testing System homepage. https://assess.com/xcart/product.php?productid=17. Accessed 30 March 2015
12. Veralsoft homepage. http://veralsoft.com. Accessed 30 March 2015
13. Exam homepage. http://pisoft.ru/exam. Accessed 30 March 2015
14. OpenTEST homepage. http://opentest.com.ua. Accessed 30 March 2015
15. INDIGO homepage. http://indigotech.ru. Accessed 30 March 2015

16. Basalova, H.: Basics of cryptography, Tula (2009)
17. Korobeinikov, A: Mathematical basics of cryptology, St. Petersburg (2004)
18. Knut, D.: The Art of Computer Programming: Seminumerical Algorithms, vol. 2. Addison-Wesley, Boston (1997)
19. Ivanov, M.: The theory, application and evaluation of the quality of pseudo-random sequences generators, Moscow (2003)

CVLA: Integrating Multiple Analytics Techniques in a Custom Moodle Report

Bogdan Drăgulescu(✉), Marian Bucos, and Radu Vasiu

Politehnica University Timişoara, Timişoara, România
{bogdan.dragulescu,marian.bucos,radu.vasiu}@upt.ro

Abstract. Increased usage of information technologies in educational tasks resulted in a high volume of data that can be exploited to offer practical insight in the learning process. In this paper, we proposed a system architecture of integrating learning analytics techniques into an educational platform. To test the approach, three analysis scenarios were implemented into a custom report for our educational platform built on Moodle. The implementation steps with chosen solutions are discussed. The significance of this research lies in the potential of this approach to build analytics systems that can use multiple data sets and analytics techniques.

Keywords: Learning analytics · Sna · Machine learning · Moodle

1 Introduction

The increased usage of information technologies in the educational process has led to collect high volumes of data. This data can be used to provide educators with feedback about their online educational course and empower them to take informed decisions to improve the educational process. Recognizing the potential that educational data analysis has to improve the learning process, the new research area of learning analytics (LA) has emerged. Adam Cooper described in a report regarding the evolution of data analysis in educational platforms, the research field from which Learning Analytics borrows methods [1]. Some of this research fields and their usage in LA are business intelligence to process and present the data, machine learning for identifying patterns in the data, social network analysis to measure students' involvement. However, contemporary LCMSs do not provide tools to run learning analytics, they rely on simple statistics to provide feedback [2]. This is also the case with Moodle, the LCMS used in our University educational platform. In this paper, we present our approach of integrating three methods of data analysis into a custom Moodle report and discuss how this approach can be applied to other systems.

The remainder of this paper is organized as follows. In Sect. 2, shows some relevant concepts and findings from the field of learning analytics. Section 3 highlights the main steps needed to integrate data analysis into an educational platform. In Sect. 4, we discuss the proposed schematic system architecture used in the process of running data analysis

© Springer International Publishing Switzerland 2015
G. Dregvaite and R. Damasevicius (Eds.): ICIST 2015, CCIS 538, pp. 115–126, 2015.
DOI: 10.1007/978-3-319-24770-0_11

scenarios. The following section describes the integration of data analysis: social network analysis (SNA) in Sect. 5.1, predicting assignment submission in Sect. 5.2, and data visualization in Sect. 5.3. In Sect. 6, there is a discussion of this work, and finally Sect. 7 summarizes the main conclusions.

2 Background

In an article from 2012 [3], George Siemens described his vision on Learning Analytics research domain development. He stresses the interdisciplinary of LA and the need to extend connections to related fields that define analytics. Such fields include machine learning, educational data mining, learning sciences, and statistics. In addition to connecting various research fields, the author argues the need to address the following challenges: development of new tools and techniques, addressing ethic issues regarding user anonymity, exploring the interaction with education systems and stakeholders.

One technique that can be applied in Learning Analytics is Social Network Analysis. It may help in identifying patterns of relationship between people, and by analyzing them to discover the flow of information in a social network [4]. Educational researchers use data collected through educational applications to test the impact of social interactions in the learning process. Dawson has employed SNA to explore the relationship between the student sense of community and their position in the classroom social network. Closeness and degree centrality metrics were found as positive predictors of an individual sense of community. Another study proved by analyzing 10 years of data from a master's degree program, that students social capital is positively associated with their academic performance [5]. Ferguson and Shum present the advantages of social network analysis in education and found that knowledge acquisition is influenced by social interactions. To use the above findings in the pedagogical process by the actors involved (tutors, students, and administrators), custom tools need to be built. Some examples of such tools are: UCINET, it enables users to analyze network routines and general statistics [6]; GEPHI, an open source tool that uses a 3D render engine to display large networks in real-time [7]; SNAPP, a tool that infers networks from forum structures, designed as a client-side bookmarklet [8]. The first two tools require that the data handling to be done by the practitioner. The latter has limited access to the data collected by the educational system, only the data rendered in the browser.

The second group of techniques that are making an impact in the LA field contains those that are adapted from machine learning and data mining domains. Peña-Ayala in a review article that studied 240 works published between 2010 and 2013, categorizes the approaches of educational data mining in [9]:

- Student modeling – represent the user and adapt teaching experiences to meet the learning requirements of the individual.
- Student behavior modeling – predict particular pattern behaviors to adapt the system to users' tendencies.
- Student performance modeling – estimates the learner accomplishment of a given task or his ability to reach a specific learning goal.
- Assessment – the purpose is to differentiate student proficiency at a finer grained level through static and dynamic testing.

- Student support and feedback – support given by the computerized educational system and tracking of students' feedback.
- Curriculum, domain knowledge, sequencing and teachers support – represents the services devoted to facilitate the ordinary work performed by academics.

Tools have been developed that can perform specific labors in the context of educational data mining. A Java desktop Moodle mining tool is proposed in a paper from 2011 [10], that can be used by an instructor to run basic data mining process. Rodrigo et al. proposed an educational data mining workbench that can perform data labeling and feature distillation, usable in automated detectors of student behavior. A tool that supports tutors analysis of learning results and performance records of their students is proposed by Devine et al. [11]. Another approach is to employ a general data mining tool like Weka or RapidMiner, powerful tools but cumbersome for an educator to use.

Finally, another technique that has been employed in learning analytics is information visualization in dashboard applications for learners and teachers. Such dashboards provide graphical representations of the current and historical state of a student or a course. The majority of these applications gives the teacher a better overview of course activity, provide a means to reflect on their teaching practice, and find students at risk [12].

The first two techniques are applied in learning analytics outside of the confinement of an educational platform and require some knowledge to operate (data acquisition, pre-processing, using the appropriate tool, interpretation of the results). The common educator may have some difficulties in using the aforementioned techniques. In this paper, we propose a method of integrating such techniques in the educational platform interface, providing the teacher with easy access to analytics results.

3   Approach

In general, a learning analytics task is an iterative cycle and consists of three major steps [13]: data collection and pre-processing, analytics and action, and post-processing.

The first step of data collection is critical to the successful application of various learning analytics techniques. Educational data is collected and stored by the educational environments and systems, in our particular case the University educational platform based on Moodle. From the collected data, many irrelevant attributes need to be removed or pre-processed. In addition, in this stage the data needs to be transformed in a correct format for input in a particular LA method. In educational data mining the following pre-processing task need to be addressed [14]: data cleaning, user identification, session identification, path completion, data transformation and enrichment, data integration, and data reduction. If multiple educational data sources are available, a coherent data structure may be used to simplify information extraction.

Using the pre-processed data in the analysis and action step, different LA techniques can be applied to discover patterns that can help improve the learning process. This step requires custom tools or libraries that implement the required techniques. For scenarios where a user needs to be informed to take an action, the results produced in the analysis need to be presented to the targeted users of that particular scenario. Some examples are monitoring students' activities and generate reports, predict learner knowledge and future performance, personalization, and recommendation.

The final step, post-processing, is fundamental for the continuous improvement of the analytical task. A better performance may be obtained by adding a new data source, optimizing the attributes used, identifying new indicators or choosing a new analytics technique [13].

In this paper, an approach of integrating learning analytics methods in an educational platform is proposed. We aimed to define a system that can handle multiple data sets and not to consume the computing resources from the LMS platform. To achieve these desiderates and considering the general steps of a learning analytics process, we propose a modular approach to design the LA system. To overcome the multiple data sets constraint for some scenarios, the data was converted from SQL to RDF format by employing an educational ontology. Using the proposed system architecture, a Moodle module was developed that integrates three LA techniques: social network analysis, data mining, and data visualization.

4   System Architecture

When designing the system architecture that was employed in the process of integrating learning analytics in our university educational platform, we first needed to define the requirements.

The first concerned was regarding the processing power needed to run the analytical processes. We presume that the system needs to have access to live data and the data from archived versions of the educational platform from previous academic years. With this in mind, the tasks of extracting relevant data from the database may slow the queries from the educational platform. To counteract this problem, the educational platform database is hosted in a master-slave architecture. The database master server is used in the platform execution, and the slave server is used to back up the database and to facilitate running statistical queries. Other computational intensive tasks are the pre-processing and analysis of the selected features. To ensure that these tasks do not slow the educational platform, they need to be run on a different machine.

In some scenarios, the system has to access multiple data sources to complete the analytics task. Our educational platform is based on Moodle and it is upgraded to the latest version of the software before each start of a new academic year. Because changes are made in each subsequent upgrade to the database structure, the platform instances databases can be treated as individual data sources. In previous research, we explored the possibility of building a coherent data set by imploring an educational ontology [15].

Finally, an important concern is to ensure that access to the collected data and results produce from the analysis is only available to the correct parties. Additionally, ethic issues regarding user anonymity must be addressed.

With regard to the above concerns and the LA process steps, we defined a system architecture for learning analytics integration, structured in three layers: data storage, processing, and platform integration layer. The rest of this section contains the description for each layer, the blocks they contain, and the role the blocks have in the system. A representation of the system architecture is presented in Fig. 1.

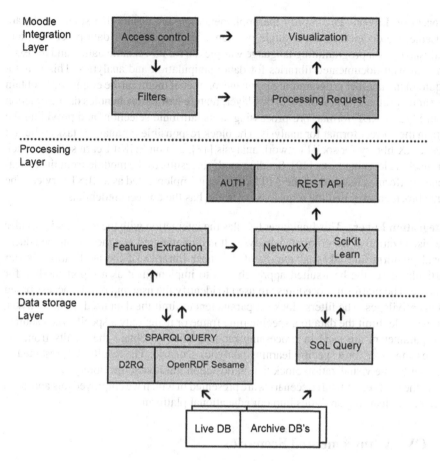

Fig. 1. Schematic architecture of LA Moodle integration

Data storage Layer. This layer is responsible for storing and providing access to the collected educational data. As described above the live and archive databases are accessible through the slave server. MySQL database management server is used and is responsible for SQL query execution. To facilitate access in a unified manner across data from all databases, the ontology proposed in Drăgulescu Ph.D. thesis [16] was used to convert the data. The relevant data from archived databases can be converted into RDF format and loaded in a triple store. For this task employed the use of the OpenRDF SESAME framework. On the other hand, for the live database the data in RDF format needs to be up to date. To accomplish this, the D2RQ platform is used. This software defines a way to access relational data in RDF format by using a declarative language to map the ontological concepts to SQL tables and attributes [17]. Thus, the data can be accessed through two RDF endpoints that can execute SPARQL queries and the default MySQL server for the relational data.

Processing Layer. To simplify the implementation and ensure that some blocks are reusable, we decided to use a single programming language for data processing and analysis. Python programming language was picked for its versatile nature and the existence of well-documented libraries for data manipulation and analytics. This is not a requirement, another programming language, or a set of them, can be employed to obtain the same results. The first block in this layer, feature extraction, handles data extraction from SQL or RDF format, pre-processing tasks, attribute selection, and providing the data in the correct format for analysis. The block responsible for analysis tasks relies on NetworkX library for social network analysis [18], and on SciKit Learn software pack for machine learning tasks [19]. Sending analysis results to the module from the educational platform is handled by the API block that is implemented as a REST service. The same block ensures that the request is valid and has the correct credentials.

Integration Layer. This final layer handles the interaction with the users and provides the visualization of the computed analysis. It is implemented as a module in the educational platform and takes advantage of the inner libraries of the application. In our particular case, the best-suited approach was to implement it as a report module for Moodle. The platform procedures are used to identify the user and restrict access based on his privileges. The filters block set parameters to limit the data used in the analysis, for example, limit the data to a specific time frame or using only a specific data source. The parameters are used in processing request block to obtain the results from the processing layer for a specific learning analytics scenario. The results are presented to the user by the visualization block that builds upon the JavaScript library D3.

In the next section, three scenarios are presented in which we employed this approach to integrate learning analytics into our educational platform.

5   CVLA Implemented Scenarios

Following the system architecture described above, we implemented three LA scenarios that constitute at the moment the CVLA Moodle report module. We choose to integrate all the scenarios in one module, organized using tabs (one tab for each scenario). These are the social network analysis tab, the prediction of assignment tab, and the central panel or dashboard tab. In the next subsections, a brief description of each implementation is presented, addressing the topics: aimed functionality, building the relevant data set, feature extraction, running the analysis, visualization, and security.

5.1   Social Network Analysis

From the application of SNA for educational purposes two metrics were selected, degree centrality and betweenness centrality. People with higher degree centrality are more likely to have access to more social resources, which can enable them to improve their performance [20]. High betweenness centrality is associated with brokerage positions, individuals in these positions have the potential to produce more innovative results [21]. The aimed functionality of this part of the module is to provide to the educator a visual analysis of the social interactions using the above two metrics.

A teacher can run SNA on the social interactions from one of his courses. On the other hand, an administrator should have the possibility to run SNA on multiple courses and multiple academic years. To facilitate access to a coherent data structure for all databases, in this scenario we used the data converted in RDF format. The applications that accomplish this task, OpenRDF Sesame and D2RQ, are hosted on a separate machine.

From evaluating the usage of communication tools in the educational platform, we discovered that the most used are forum, blog and IM. To obtain data for SNA three SPARQL queries patterns were designed, one for each communication tool. In order to filter the data for a specific case, the academic year context, time constraints, or course URI can be inserted in the SPARQL query patterns.

Social network analysis on the extracted data is run by using the NetworkX library. The results are made available in JSON format as a REST web service. The data selection, analysis, and web service are implemented in Python and hosted on a separate machine.

In the Moodle report, the results are provided to the user as shown in Fig. 2. Degree centrality is represented in the social graph through the size of the nodes; the individual represented by the bigger node has more social ties and, therefore, a higher degree centrality. The color of the nodes is correlated with betweenness centrality, blue for high value and red for low value. To produce this graph we make use of the JavaScript library D3. By selecting a node, the values of the metrics for that particular individual are displayed to the user. In the settings section, the user has the possibility to filter the data by selecting the data sources used in the analysis and the time interval in which the interactions took place.

The analysis is limited to the social interactions in the course from which the report is accessed. To view the report the user has to have at least the role of non-editing teacher in that particular course. This constraint is implemented using Moodle core functions.

5.2 Predicting Assignment Submission

In this learning analytics task, we aimed to provide to the educator predictions on whether or not the learners will submit an assignment on time. This is applicable only to the assignment activities that have a deadline set. With this information, an educator can take the necessary decisions to maximize the students' success rate: send reminders or extend the deadline if overtime predictions are made.

Building the data set to train the prediction model from the archived versions of the educational platform is done only the first time and then stored on the processing machine. In this case, we do not need to use a unified structure and query the data from the default MySQL database. From the live database, the data extraction is done at the end of each semester and added to the training set. An entry in the training set consists of the appropriate label representing the submission status of an assignment for a particular user involved in that activity and the corresponding values for attributes selected in the features extraction process. The selected attributes quantify the interaction of the user with that particular course (course hits, activities hits, course resources hits, and assignments hits). In order to ensure compatibility with entries from different courses, the attributes were normalized. From the last five academic years, we build a training set of 36.000 entries.

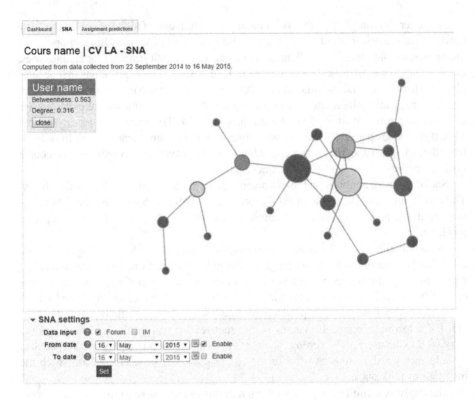

Fig. 2. SNA integration into CVLA Moodle block

We chose to predict if the user submits the assignment before the deadline, with a time delay or not at all. This is a multi-class classification problem in machine learning. To build the prediction model we used SciKit Learn software package. We evaluated the performance of six algorithms from this software that can solve multiclass classification problems: Naive Bayes, Linear Discriminant Analysis, Decision Trees, Random Forests, Nearest Neighbors and Logistic Regression. The best performing algorithm for this particular problem was Random Forests with a cross-validation accuracy of 0.86, kappa of 0.73, a precision of 0.85, and recall of 0.86. Using the Random Forests, we trained the prediction model and ensured model persistence by saving it to disk (because loading the model is substantially faster that to retrain it). The resulted predictions for a requested list of users are sent to the report module through the same web service used for SNA. On the educational platform side, the predicted labels are displayed for the user accompanied with the model confidence in that prediction. Access to the prediction is restricted to users with the role of non-editing teacher and above.

5.3 Central Panel

To display alerts and custom visualizations to participants in the course, we developed a central panel or dashboard. The aim of this task is to provide tools for learners and

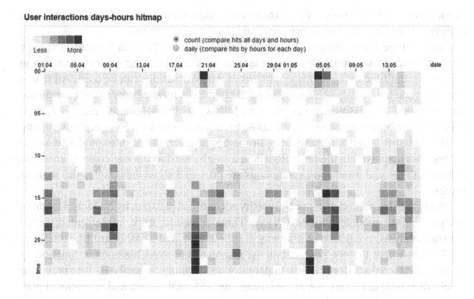

Fig. 3. User interaction hit map section from central panel

educators for self-evaluation, failure alerts, and pattern discovery. For data processing, we used the same analysis server to extract, clean, and deliver the resulted data to the educational platform. The tab integrated in the report module is structured in three blocks. First is the alerts section that notifies the teacher if students are inactive, the number of outliers in the social network analysis, and status of the assignment submissions predictions. The second block contains a visualization of interactions with different components of the course by each user. This can be used by the teacher to evaluate the quality of course resources (if a particular resource is not accessed it may not be visible to the students), and visualize students involvement.

Third, consists of a visualization of the user interactions with the platform summarized on time intervals (Fig. 3). One scenario in which a teacher can use this graph is to identify the best hours to offer support online. The implementation of the visualizations was done by using the same JavaScript library D3.

6   Discussions

As Siemens argues in an article from 2012 [3], learning analytics has the potential to dramatically impact the educational process by providing new insights into what works and does not work in teaching and learning. To capitalize this potential, the challenges involve the development of new tools, techniques, and people. The author also stipulates that ideally, an integrated analytics system would use multiple data sets and analytics techniques in a single interface for presenting data to practitioners.

In this paper, we address the challenge of integrating prior developed techniques into an educational platform. First, we designed a system architecture that can ensure the application scalability and easy extension of its functionalities. The system is structured in three layers: data storage, processing, and platform integration.

Data storage layer contains, in addition to the default educational platform storage method, a block that republish the relevant data in RDF. This approach ensures that in the case of multiple data sets same patterns of data extractions can be used. All that is needed to add a new data set is a mapping file that links its attributes to the educational ontology used. Processing layer contains the following blocks: feature extractions, analysis, and distribution of the result. We chose to use for this task the Python programming language, but it is not a requirement. In the upper layer, the results produced in the analysis are displayed to the practitioners in a single interface. Some controls are made available to the end users and explanations are provided about the insights the analysis brings.

We tested this approach in our University educational platform by building a learning analytics report module entitled CVLA. Three scenarios were implemented: social network analysis, prediction of assignment submission, and a dashboard-like interface.

To ensure that the need computational resources are available and the functioning of the educational platform is not impaired when running an analysis, we spread the blocks over four machines. Two preexisting ones (MySQL server and educational platform server) and two dedicated ones (RDF storage server and processing server). Another consideration that is worth mentioning is we used a master-slave topology for MySQL in order to ensure that the analysis system will not slow the performance of the educational platform.

Our educational platform is built on Moodle, so the developed module is specific to this system. Nonetheless, the proposed approach is valid in any educational platform. Even more, the majority of the code can be reused for other educational systems. What needs to be redeveloped are components of the integration layer, the mapping files to produce RDF data, and the query patterns used in data extraction.

Several researchers are trying to solve the same challenges with: a Java desktop tool addressed to non-data-mining experts [10], an e-learning web miner with plans to offer the analysis as a service [22], an exploratory Learning Analytics Toolkit that enables teachers to monitor and analyze their teaching activities [23], or CourseV is a tool that uses visualization approaches to support instructors in Web-based distance education [24]. Our approach contributes to this effort by providing a means of using multiple data sets and a modular system architecture that can facilitate future developments.

We intend further to develop the system by adding more analysis scenarios and methods like student dropout alerts, recommender systems, and more visualization techniques. In addition, the impact of this module in the educational process needs to be evaluated.

7   Conclusions

This paper presents a method of integrating learning analytics techniques into an educational platform. Components of this system are organized into layers: data storage, processing, and platform integration. The conversion of the relevant data into RDF is proposed to facilitate the use of multiple data sources in the analysis. Three scenarios were implemented into a custom report module to test the proposed system architecture. The significance of this research lies in the potential of this approach to build an integrated analytics system that can use multiple data sets and analytics techniques in a single interface for presenting data to learners and educators.

Acknowledgements. This work was partially supported by the strategic grant POSDRU/159/1.5/ S/137070 (2014) of the Ministry of National Education, Romania, co-financed by the European Social Fund – Investing in People, within the Sectoral Operational Programme Human Resources Development 2007-2013.

References

1. Cooper, A.: A brief history of analytics. Anal. Ser. **1**, 3–21 (2012)
2. Ali, L., Hatala, M., Gašević, D., Jovanović, J.: A qualitative evaluation of evolution of a learning analytics tool. Comput. Educ. **58**, 470–489 (2012)
3. Siemens, G.: Learning analytics: envisioning a research discipline and a domain of practice. In: Proceedings of the 2nd International Conference on Learning Analytics and Knowledge, pp. 4–8. ACM, Vancouver, Canada (2012)
4. de Laat, M., Lally, V., Lipponen, L., Simons, R.-J.: Investigating patterns of interaction in networked learning and computer-supported collaborative learning: a role for social network analysis. Int. J. Comput. Support. Collaborative Learn. **2**, 87–103 (2007)
5. Gašević, D., Zouaq, A., Janzen, R.: "Choose your classmates, your GPA is at stake!": the association of cross-class social ties and academic performance. Am. Behav. Sci. **57**, 1460–1479 (2013)
6. Borgatti, S., Everett, M., Freeman, L.: Ucinet for Windows: Software for Social Network Analysis. Analytic Technologies, Nicholasville (2002)
7. Bastian, M., Heymann, S., Jacomy, M.: Gephi: an open source software for exploring and manipulating networks. In: ICWSM, San Jose, California, pp. 361–362 (2009)
8. Dawson, S., Bakharia, A., Heathcote, E.: SNAPP: realising the affordances of real-time SNA within networked learning environments. In: Proceedings of the 7th International Conference on Networked Learning, Aalborg, Denmark, pp. 125–133 (2010)
9. Peña-Ayala, A.: Educational data mining: a survey and a data mining-based analysis of recent works. Expert Syst. Appl. **41**, 1432–1462 (2014)
10. Pedraza-Perez, R., Romero, C., Ventura, S.: A java desktop tool for mining Moodle data. In: Proceedings of the 3rd Conference on Educational Data Mining, pp. 319–320. ERIC, Pittsburgh, PA, USA (2011)
11. Devine, T., Hossain, M., Harvey, E., Baur, A.: Improving pedagogy by analyzing relevance and dependency of course learning outcomes. In: Proceedings of the KDD 2011 Workshop: Knowledge Discovery in Educational Data, San Diego, CA, pp. 83–90 (2011)
12. Verbert, K., Duval, E., Klerkx, J., Govaerts, S., Santos, J.L.: Learning analytics dashboard applications. Am. Behav. Sci. **57**, 1500–1509 (2013)
13. Chatti, M.A., Dyckhoff, A.L., Schroeder, U., Thüs, H.: A reference model for learning analytics. Int. J. Technol. Enhanced Learn. **4**, 318–331 (2012)
14. Romero, C., Ventura, S.: Educational data mining: a survey from 1995 to 2005. Expert Syst. Appl. **33**, 135–146 (2007)

15. Bucos, M., Dragulescu, B., Veltan, M.: Designing a semantic web ontology for e-learning in higher education. In: 2010 9th International Symposium on Electronics and Telecommunications (ISETC), pp. 415–418. IEEE, Timisoara, Romania (2010)
16. Dragulescu, B.: Semantic web technologies in educational context. Ph.D. thesis, Ed. Politehnica (2012)
17. Bizer, C., Seaborne, A.: D2RQ-treating non-RDF databases as virtual RDF graphs. In: Proceedings of the 3rd International Semantic Web Conference (ISWC 2004), Hiroshima, Japan, pp. 26–27 (2004)
18. Schult, D.A., Swart, P.J.: Exploring network structure, dynamics, and function using NetworkX. In: Proceedings of the 7th Python in Science Conferences (SciPy 2008), Pasadena, CA, pp. 11–16 (2008)
19. Pedregosa, F., Varoquaux, G., Gramfort, A., Michel, V., Thirion, B., Grisel, O., Blondel, M., Prettenhofer, P., Weiss, R., Dubourg, V.: others: Scikit-learn: machine learning in Python. J. Mach. Learn. Res. **12**, 2825–2830 (2011)
20. Sparrowe, R.T., Liden, R.C., Wayne, S.J., Kraimer, M.L.: Social networks and the performance of individuals and groups. Acad. Manage. J. **44**, 316–325 (2001)
21. Burt, R.S.: Structural holes and good ideas1. Am. J. Sociol. **110**, 349–399 (2004)
22. García-Saiz, D., Zorrilla, M.E.: E-learning web miner: a data mining application to help instructors involved in virtual courses. In: Proceedings of the 4th International Conference on Educational Data Mining, Eindhoven, The Netherlands, pp. 323–324 (2011)
23. Dyckhoff, A.L., Zielke, D., Bültmann, M., Chatti, M.A., Schroeder, U.: Design and implementation of a learning analytics toolkit for teachers. J. Educ. Technol. Soc. **15**, 58–76 (2012)
24. Mazza, R.: Evaluating information visualization applications with focus groups: the CourseVis experience. In: Proceedings of the 2006 AVI Workshop on BEyond Time and Errors: Novel Evaluation Methods for Information Visualization, pp. 1–6. ACM, Venezia, Italy (2006)

The Value of Video Lectures in the Classroom - UPT Study Case

Mihai Onița[✉], Camelia Ciuclea, and Radu Vasiu

Politehnica University of Timisoara, Timisoara, Romania
{mihai.onita,camelia.ciuclea,radu.vasiu}@cm.upt.ro

Abstract. As teachers, we have the responsibility to assist students in understanding the basic concepts and details (when necessary) upon a subject. We must offer them the right materials to achieve the information and the possibility to hear, try, see and think. In our study, conducted in Politehnica University of Timisoara (UPT) environment, we chose a target group consisting of approximately 200 students, divided into two subgroups. We had classroom meetings with all. We offered the first group printed material for home study and to the second group - video lectures. We evaluated students and analyzed the results. We conducted face-to-face post exam discussion and a survey to extract the advantages and disadvantages of video and printed from student's angle/perspective. This paper provide related work in the field, video lectures design, ours study findings and conclusions.

Keywords: Video lectures · Classroom · Interactivity · Blended learning · Printed educational resources

1 Introduction

1.1 Background Information

Constant and continuous transformation in Information and Communications Technology (ICT) area open new ways and opportunities to enhance teaching and educational methods. On one hand, teacher's abilities leave enough room to update to present and to deliver information in an attractive way. On the other hand, this might help students by offering them the information in channels and manners easier to understand, work with, and retrieve [1]. Comparing face-to-face learning (traditional classroom) with online teaching was and it is further the subject of many research studies. Wieling and Hoffman [2] stated that there is no "significant difference between the average performances of learners in the case of face-to-face learning as compared to learners exposed to distance learning methods". More, the comparison targets the effectiveness of printed material as exponent for the classroom (home study material) and the use of video, for the e-Learning purpose [3]. What happens in the case of matching up the face-to-face meeting with video recordings [2] and computer generated materials? Video is a rich and strong element in eLearning. It has also emerged as a dominant factor for educational goals in many MOOC (Massive Open Online Course) platforms [4, 5]. Is it possible to

© Springer International Publishing Switzerland 2015
G. Dregvaite and R. Damasevicius (Eds.): ICIST 2015, CCIS 538, pp. 127–137, 2015.
DOI: 10.1007/978-3-319-24770-0_12

become an important player for the after classroom study, and take the place of printed materials or complete them? This was our starting point of research.

Merkt et al. [3] stated that besides having an important role in students' media experience in their free time, videos are one of the most frequently accessed media in classroom setting and could very well serve as a promising measure to diversify the students learning experience. Videos give students the opportunity to gaining sight into events that they usually cannot experience in real life. Clark and Mayer [6] sustain that video seems to be more effective for beginners in the problem-solving process and more "fruitful" for learners at a more advanced stage of learning to solve problems. From educational psychology`s perspective, the role of video as an effective learning medium did not skip the opportunity to be undisputed, especially if we take as comparison element the print. So far, the studies in which the knowledge acquisition was lower for video than for text, typically presented video in a broadcast mode in which it was not possible for the viewers to control the video's flow of information [7, 8].

The status changed, as recent digital forms of video offer the viewers the opportunity to interact with the presentation: this being the way to generate interactive video materials as a major feature of well-designed multimedia courseware. In fact, researchers have proven that an interactive learning environment - "a multi-modal instruction is more efficient than using any single mode" [9]. To say it otherwise, this finding shows that "interactive media has an impact on learning, through the instructional possibilities that they enable" [1]. Moreover, Carnegie Mellon University's just-in-time lecture project suggests that video-based education and interactive training systems support "the same level of teaching and learning effectiveness as face-to-face instruction" [10].

1.2 Literature Approaches - Related Work

The applications and possible revenue/benefits of the use of video in teaching and learning were discussed since a few decades ago. Now, under the influence of the broad use of digital technology, video can definitely be considered a powerful medium that, first, can provide narrative visualization, and second, can engage multiple senses of learners simultaneously. Educational applications incorporating CD-DVD, digital video and online video can be found in various disciplines and mediums [11]. We extract from literature and other research work some examples based on video lectures.

Bayhan et al. [12] explored the use of computers at home to develop mathematical ideas. Chiu et al. [13] researched the viewing behavior of students in a Chinese grammar course with online post-class lecture videos made available. Evans et al. tried to find the effects of [14] "adding interactivity to computer-based learning packages of business and management" on a small sample of undergraduate students (22 males, and 11 females). In Gonzales et al. [11] paper is mentioned a European program that have the goal to improve engineer's ability to design and construct renewable energy systems in buildings and communities. Holzinger et al. [15] addressed the effects of using simulation to teach complex physiological models to 96 students of the college of medicine. Lage et al. [16] introduced in 2000 the concept of "the inverted classroom" (watch videos before live meeting), and applied it to a course in Microeconomics. In Marsh et al. [17] paper it is described the University of Sussex In-School Teacher Education Project (INSTEP) and it is about the using interactive video technologies to enhance initial teacher education programs for science trainee teachers. Phelps and Evans [18] findings consisted in using a supplemental instruction program in order to improve student performance in developmental mathematics. Ross and Bell [19] compared the perform- ance of students in a quality management course. Stith [20] study speaks about the benefice of animation in teaching cell biology and all fields of biology. At long last, online universities and especially MOOC platforms have the video as the most important element of teaching [5] "in many global languages" [4]. A list of popular MOOCs is offered by Onita et al. [21] and it also includes the "leaders" mention in Mihaescu et al. [22]: Coursera, edX, Udacity, MiriadaX, Canvas Network, FutureLearn, CourseSites, iversity, Open2Study and NovoEd.

2   Research Questions

Our main question was: face-to-face meetings between students and tutors and printed materials for further home study should be complemented or replaced by video lectures? Is it the way to pass from a passive learning to active learning? These lectures should follow the logic of the face-to-face meeting or rely on examples close to the concept but different from it? What are the desired elements in a video lecture? What kind of lecture is preferred? Do they bring value in terms of results after the evaluation of the students? We choose a teaching material (a combination of text, charts and pictures) for Television Systems discipline, taught in the 3rd year of the Faculty of Electronics and Telecommu- nications in Politehnica University of Timisoara (UPT). In the classroom, we have a theo- retical discussion and offer some examples from the production field. We teach and run (face-to-face) this material with two different generations: 2013–2014, 2014–2015, approximately 100 students/generation. For the first one, we offer for home study the print material and for the second one the instructor developed video lectures. We eval- uate the students and analyze the results.

We have built a survey (Q1–Q10), based on multiple-choice answers; that aims to strengthen the value of an (interactive) video that served as support for the traditional classroom. We have addressed to the students the following instructions and copyright agreement before completing the survey: "By completing this form you agree to the use of anonymous responses in the future papers or publications". Our survey was distrib- uted after the exam (evaluation) to all 200 students, via the UPT Virtual Campus (https:// cv.upt.ro). They used their login credentials. We used Google Forms to create the survey, and it consists of subjects: print vs. video and video (interactive) technical environment.

Q1: Do you consider as necessary that the printed materials specific to the preparation for the face-to-face meeting to be duplicated by video lectures on the same topic? Yes; No.
Q2: Do you consider the accumulation of knowledge by watching printed material as beneficial because: Visualization of video lectures is boring; The effort for viewing video lectures is much higher than the pursuit of printed material; Printed material provides detailed information that cannot be included in a video lecture.
Q3: If the study material for home will be a video lecture, in the face to face meeting, the tutor should: Follow the logical structure of the video lecture; Build on examples close as concept but different from the video lecture.

Q4: In a video lecture do you consider as necessary the presence of: The tutor (recorded); Interactive elements; Animations; Self-assessment questions; Further reading suggestions.

Q5: I prefer receiving information as: Charts, graphs and text; Images and voice.

Q6: In a book with many pictures and graphs, I prefer: To concentrate on text; To closely monitor graphs and images.

Q7: I remember the most: What I try; What makes me think; What I hear; What I see.

Q8: What type of video material is more attractive to you: Voice over presentation; Animated instructional video; Talking head video; Interactive video; Tutorial.

Q9: What is the ideal length of an educational video material? Under 10 min; Between 10 and 15 min; 15 to 20 min; Over 20 min.

Q10: What kind of interactivity do you prefer/expect in a video: custom video player; overlay video subtitle; interactive transcript; graphics overlay; hotspots; timeline with hot points; a visual key frame map; downloadable transcript; self-assessment quiz; FAQ.

A part of the questions raised are of our own, and a part was extracted from ASSIST forms: Approaches and Study Skills Inventory for Students [23] and Index of Learning Styles Questionnaire [24].

3 Video Lectures Design

Based on the software and equipment available at the research center where we work, it was possible to develop the types of lectures listed and described in the next paragraphs. We will use further the acronym VL for Video Lecture. We choose a storage and distribution medium fit to the number of users. We used UPT Virtual Campus in combination with Vimeo and YouTube solutions.

VL1 - Talking head video consists of close-up shots of the instructor. He speaks directly to the recording equipment (Logitech Webcam C250) and is filmed at his office with no audience, during which he talks about the subject matter. The audio part lets the voice do the teaching [25]. Preparation of our talking head video includes the setting up of a web camera and a script for the lecture, used in all lectures, except tutorial. The recording process with Logitech Recording Software was flexible, with a few breaks from recording. The unnecessary information was cut out, and new fragments of speech were recorded again. The editing part and the export in a specific format was made using Adobe Premiere. The value of the teacher enthusiasm, humor, intonation, face language and articulation can certainly be improved.

VL2 - Voice over Presentation includes a presentation of slides, supplemented by a voice over that gives details/explains the slides. Technically speaking the slides are created in PowerPoint and voice over was created with a microphone and Audacity Software. The combination of visual information (text, graphics, diagram and images) with audio narration makes learning operative. It allows using verbal skills to explain the subject reflected in the objects inserted in each slide. The result was edited in Adobe Presenter and was exported in the specific video format for student view.

VL3 - Tutorial proposes a video screen capture with the teacher's voice over, where the instructor demonstrates a concept (time-lapse in the current case). We used Adobe Captivate for the screen capture and editing tutorial itself and for time-lapse demonstration. Time-lapse photography is a cinema photography technique whereby the frequency at which film frames are captured (the frame rate) is much lower than the one that will be used to play the sequence back [26]. The chosen topic will help student familiarize with the video recording, capture, and editing techniques. This lecture is partially tested with students, is yet under construction.

VL4 - Animated instructional video implies advanced technical skills. During the animated instructional video lectures whether they include or not the voice, the instructor does not appear. In order to achieve the animation, we chose Sparkol Video Scribe software with a one-year license (VideoScribe EDU on a yearly subscription, https://my.sparkol.com). The interface have the functionalities (Fig. 1): Save button (1); Insert image (2); Create animated title (3), Insert graphics (4); Background sound (5); Recording sound (6); Working space texture and color (7); Animation basic settings (8); Preview (9); Rendering (10); Working space (11); Timeline (12); Panel Tools (13); Help (14).

Fig. 1. Sparkol video scribe interface

We created a Power Point presentation, each slide representing one frame that we then animated with specific Video Scribe tools. As worktable, we had chosen a gray crumpled paper texture and used as elements mostly imported materials from the online bookshop, the processed audio component being imported from a personal computer, after Audacity processing. As animation, we chose something that represents "a student", a hand with a pen, but also some special animations to enhance the movement.

VL5 - Interactive Lecture is the most complex material developed with content elements such as: text, images, charts, recorded voice, video, external links towards text type bibliographic sources, colored areas to attract attention on certain information, downloadable transcript at the end of the lecture, self-assessment test. We have started with the PowerPoint type material, Audacity for voice recording, Captivate and Zaption for interactive elements. In Captivate there were made audio synchronization with slides (tutor speech), insertions of dynamic and interactive elements, insertion of contents and saving as SWF, HTML 5, and video. The interactive part can be completed with manual or (semi)automatic annotation as the results of specific video annotations system [27, 28].

4   Study Findings

4.1   Factors Related to Evaluations Results

To see the impact of using video materials on education, we choose, as shown in Methodology, to evaluate, 200 students, two different generations. The first one, 2013/2014 we called it from now "the print generation". We had a face-to-face meeting, we prepared for this group the printed material for home study and evaluated them. In the next year, with the second generation, called it from now "video generation" we discussed live at the classroom, we prepared different types of video lecture on the same topic (VL1, VL2, VL3, VL4 and VL5) and also evaluated them. The evaluation was based on an exam with short answers, same grade of difficulty.

The global result is revealed in Fig. 2. We have the columns with the average notes from our evaluation and the columns with multiannual grade (after the first and the second year of study) at all disciplines. The video "generation", even the multiannual is under the "print generation", obtain in our evaluation a +0.63.

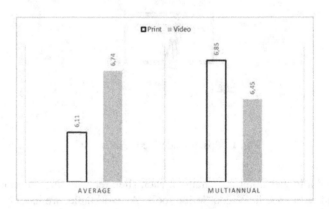

Fig. 2.   Evaluation average notes and multiannual grade

Deeper, in Fig. 3 we offer a statistic regarding the grades ranges in a notation system from 1 to 10. There are two major aspects that we want to mention: under 5 - print 22 % and video 7 %; between 6 and 7 we have printed 13 % and video 22 %. The video material, for sure, leading to fewer students failing the exams and more students with medium grades.

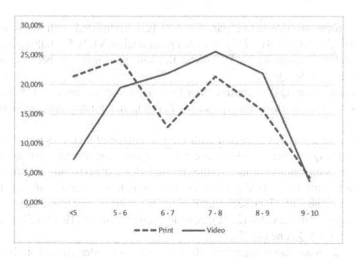

Fig. 3. Distribution grades after evaluation

4.2 Factors Related to Print

There are advantages and disadvantages for learning new information via print as compared to other ways such as videos. Students prefer receiving information as charts, graphs, and text (53 % - Q5) or a combination of images and voice (63 % - Q5). More exactly from the print point of view, in a book the students concentrate on the text information (30 % - Q6) and they closely monitor graphs and images (65 % - Q6), diagrams and other simulation charts. "Specifically, the benefits of print materials are that they allow learners to control their rate of learning and the order in which they choose to pay attention to information" [29]. Print was found to be better suited for detailed information that cannot be included in a video lecture (76 % - Q2), some believe that the effort for viewing video lectures is much higher than the pursuit of printed material (18 % - Q2) or visualization of them may be boring (2 % - Q2). "Not only do skilled readers adapt their reading pace to the complexity of the text and their cognitive needs, but they also actively reread important or difficult passages, skip unimportant or uninteresting passages, quickly browse through comprehensive texts, and stop reading for a moment to engage in self-explanations" [30]. Students used their prior knowledge accumulated in the laboratory and course experience, in what they try (48 % - Q7), what they hear (32 % - Q7), what they see (68 % - Q7), to understand the texts and actively used backtracking and rereading of difficult passages they did not understand [3] and to make them think for generating solutions.

4.3 Factors Related to Video Style, Interactivity and Length

The hypothesis of using video lectures has been validated with the higher percent of "yes" answer (90 %) of Q1 survey question. After collecting the data from the survey and having some post-evaluation discussion with students, the following characteristics regarding video itself can be exposed:

- Students focus on interactive part 66 % (VL5), completed with 24 % animated instructional video (VL4), 17 % voice over presentation(VL2), 5 % talking head video (VL1) and 6 % tutorial (VL3), maybe the low percentage is because of under construction mode (Q8).
- Student expect for (Q4): recording tutor (31 %), interactive elements (75 %), animations (45 %), self-assessment questions (71 %), and further reading suggestions (34 %).
- The interactive part is completed with the percentage of elements prefer/expect in such a video (Q10):custom video player with playback controls and buttons like mute, full screen, annotations on/off, subtitles on/off (81 %); overlay video subtitle (22 %); interactive transcript (30 %); graphics and animations overlay (46 %); hotspots (35 %); timeline with video segmentation (27 %); a visual key frame map with static image/frame from the video (22 %); downloadable transcript (19 %); self-assessment quiz (49 %); FAQ zone (46 %);
- Shorter videos are more engaging: 10 % of them are under 10 min' influence, the higher percent 46 % lead to 10–15 min gap. The landscape includes as well 43 % of 15–20 min (but segmentation - subchapters are included) and 6 % more than 20 min of video content (Q9); Student testimonial underlined: "the videos are good when they are neither too long or too short, when it captures our attention"
- If the study material for home will be a video lecture, in the face to face meeting (Q3), the tutor should follow the logical structure of the video lecture (45 %) or build on examples close as concept but different from the video lecture (55 %);

    On the other hand:

- We try to provide more intimate and personal feel to the videos, but we must coach ourselves for a better use of humor and enthusiasm where possible;
- We must familiarize the students with the videos` feature before browsing the content;
- For increasing learning engagement we should use more division of the timeline, segment the course content in smaller pieces, enable random access to this parts;
- We must invest more time in the pre-production planning phase. If we have difficulty with using computers and software, support is needed from the user's university technical-support staff.
- We must identify exactly the type of video lectures depending on the topic and on the message we want to transmit.

5   Discussions and Conclusions

As teachers we have the responsibility to assist students in understanding the basic concepts and when it is necessary to deepen information upon a subject, the principles, and particular facts and to give them the possibility to hear, try, see (Q4), make them think and achieve the information. Putting in a balance print material with video educational elements is a challenging task (Q1, Q2), a process that is not always straightforward and easy to be done. From our perspective, as educators, the videos may extend the courses and laboratories` viability to students in ways that print does not support. Other researchers claim: "Online video lectures and attending lectures in person are approximately equal" and propose the "blended learning approach" [2]. Using recorded or generated video lectures in combination with face-to-face meeting (classroom) and for detailed information the print material, interchanged all of these, can improve the student performance, and lead to a better student efficiency and University attractiveness. Foertsch et al. [31] envisioned the idea that "if all of a professor's lectures, syllabi, and assignments were digitized and put online, professors could spend less time lecturing and more time assisting students."

In our study, conducted in Politehnica University of Timisoara environment, videos complement classroom meeting and are valuable digital materials in helping students for their evaluation. The video lectures were prepared by the tutor (Mihai Onita) for one of his disciplines and had the same content as the classroom lectures, with some additional information for those who want to deepen. The videos reduce student dropout rates compared to print (4.1 Factors related to evaluations results), significantly increase the number of grades between 6 and 7, only few grades between 7 and 9, and maintain or decrease the grades between 5 and 6, 9 and 10. Overall, grade distribution curve is better than the distributions for the print, no-videos sample (Fig. 3). Five video designs were tested: talking head video, voice over the presentation, tutorial (still under construction), animated instructional video and interactive material. The student could choose any of them, depending on the desired experience: a linear video approach or a more complex one with interactivity alternative. In the second case, we offered a combination of recorded voice and materials, animations, self-assessments questions, table of contents, highlights area, external links (Q4).

We can conclude as, Brecht [32], that "student attentiveness and engagement in studying is sensitive to the videos" "learning environment" (Q8). Also we can share the enthusiasm of one of our student: "it is great to transform a classical presentation into an interactive experience, a challenging presentation mode, certainly a lovely choice for digital student like us. The (interactive) video is the most powerful materials used for studying in 16 years of education". In the opposite part, for an educator may be hesitant to allocate his time to developing video lectures and integrating into a course, especially when one has no technical skills, nor the necessary equipment or he is not rewarded (in any way) by the university to invest in such material preparation. Volunteering and the satisfaction to have better students in the class? With these closing remarks, it is obvious that there are many questions waiting for answers, and a lot of work to do in the present and the future of video and print learning.

Acknowledgments. This work was partially supported by the strategic grant POSDRU/159/1.5/ S/137070 (2014) of the Ministry of National Education, Romania, co-financed by the European Social Fund – Investing in People, within the Sectoral Operational Programme Human Resources Development 2007-2013.

References

1. Nusir, S., Alsmadi, I., Al-Kabi, M., Sharadgah, F.: Studying the impact of using multimedia interactive programs at children ability to learn basic math skills. Acta Didactica Napocesnia **5**(2), 17–31 (2012)
2. Wieling, M.B., Hofman, W.H.A.: The impact of online video lecture recordings and automated feedback on student performance. Comput. Educ. **54**, 992–998 (2010)
3. Merkt, M., Weigand, S., Hiere, A., Scwan, S.: Learning with videos vs. learning with print. The role of interactive features. Learn. Inst. **21**, 687–704 (2011)
4. Diwanji, P., Simon, B.P., Märki, M., Korkut, S., Dornberger, R.: Success factors of online learning videos. In: International Conference on Interactive Mobile Communication Technologies and Learning (IMCL), pp. 125–132 (2014)
5. Vasiu, R., Andone, D.: OERs and MOOCs-the romanian experience. In: 2014 International Conference on Web and Open Access to Learning (ICWOAL), pp. 1–5. IEEE (2014)
6. Clark, R.C., Mayer, R.E.: 10 brilliant design rules for e-learning. http://donaldclarkplanb.blogspot.ro/2013/01/mayer-clark-10-brilliant-design-rules.html
7. Gunter, B., Furnham, A., Leese, J.: Memory for information from a party political broadcast as a function of the channel of communication. Soc. Behav. **1**(2), 135–142 (1986)
8. van der Molen, J.W., van der Voort, T.: Children's and adults' recall of television and print news in children's and adult news formats. Commun. Res. **27**(2), 132–160 (2000)
9. Norhayati, A.M., Siew, P.H.: Malaysian perspective: designing interactive multimedia learning environment for moral values education. Educ. Technol. Soc. **7**(4), 143–152 (2004)
10. Zhang, D., Zhou, L., Briggs, R.O., Nunamaker, J.F.: Instructional video in e-learning: assessing the impact of interactive video on learning effectiveness. Inf. Manage. **43**, 15–27 (2006)
11. González, M.J., Montero, E., Beltrán de Heredia, A., Martínez, D.: Integrating digital video resources in teaching eLearning engineering courses. In: Education Engineering (EDUCON), pp. 789–793. IEEE (2012)
12. Bayhan, P., Olgun, P., Yelland, N.J.: A study of pre-school teachers' thoughts about computer assisted instruction. Contemp. Issues Early Child. **3**(2), 298–303 (2002)
13. Chiu, C.F., Lee, G.C., Yang, J.H.: A comparative study of post-class lecture viewing. In: Proceedings of the 5th IASTED International Conference on Web-Based Education, pp. 126–130 (2006)
14. Evans, C., Gibbons, N.J.: The interactivity effect in multimedia learning. Comput. Educ. **49**(4), 1147–1160 (2007)
15. Holzinger, A., Kickmeier-Rust, M., Wassertheurer, S., Hessinger, M.: Learning performance with interactive. Simulations in medical education: lessons learned from results of learning complex physiological models with the HAEMOdynamics SIMulator. Comput. Educ. **52**(2), 292–301 (2009)
16. Lage, M.J., Platt, G.J., Treglia, M.: Inverting the classroom: a gateway to creating an inclusive learning environment. J. Econ. Educ. **31**(1), 30–43 (2000)
17. Marsh, B., Mitchell, N., Adamczyk, P.: Interactive video technology: enhancing professional learning in initial teacher education. Comput. Educ. **54**, 742–748 (2010)
18. Phelps, J.M., Evans, R.: Supplemental instruction in developmental mathematics. Commun. Coll. Enterp. **12**(1), 21–37 (2006)
19. Ross, T.K., Bell, P.D.: No significant difference only on the surface. Int. J. Inst. Technol. Distance Learn. **4**(7), 3–13 (2007)
20. Stith, B.: Use of animation in teaching cell biology. Cell Biol. Educ. **3**, 181–188 (2004)

21. Oniţa, M., Mihaescu, V., Vasiu, R.: Technical analysis of MOOCs. TEM J. **4**(1), 60–72 (2015). ISSN: 2217-8309 (print), eISSN: 2217-8333 (online), Index Copernicus ICID: 1144333

22. Mihaescu, V., Vasiu, R., Andone, D.: Developing a MOOC-the romanian experience. In: The 13th European Conference on e-Learning ECEL, pp. 339–346, Aalborg, Denmark (2014)

23. ASSSIST: Approaches and study skills inventory for students survey. http://www.dcu.ie/surveys/assist.html

24. Soloman, B., Felder, R.M.: Index of learning styles questionnaire. https://www.engr.ncsu.edu/learningstyles/ilsweb.html

25. Udemy: Video lecture format: quality standards. https://support.udemy.com/customer/portal/articles/1505390-udemy-online-course-lecture-types?b_id=3150

26. Liu, W., Li, H.: Time-lapse photography applied to educational videos. In: Consumer Electronics, Communications and Networks (CECNet), pp. 3669–3672 (2012)

27. Petan, S., Mocofan, M., Vasiu, R.: Enhancing learning in massive open online courses through interactive video. In: Proceedings of the 10th International Scientific Conference "eLearning and Software for Education", Bucharest (2014)

28. Gabor, A.M, Vasiu, R., Loghin, G.: Video data use in interactive e-learning courses. A modern method of learning organizing process. In: 6th International Conference of Education, Research and Innovation ICERI 2013, pp. 2184–2190, Seville, Spain, 18–20 November 2013. ISBN 978-84-616-3847-5, ISSN 2340-1095, WOS:000347240602035

29. Wilson, E.A.H., Makoul, G., Bojarski, E.A., Bailey, S.C., Waite, K.R., Rapp, D.N., Baker, D.W., Wolf, M.S.: Comparative analysis of print and multimedia health materials: a review of the literature. Patient Educ. Couns. **89**, 7–14 (2012)

30. McNamara, D.S., Levinstein, I.B., Boonthum, C.: iSTART: interactive strategy training for active reading and thinking. Behav. Res. Meth. Instrum. Comput. **36**(2), 222–233 (2004)

31. Foertsch, J., Moses, G., Strickwerda, J., Litzkov, M.: Reversing the lecture/homework paradigm using eTEACH web-based streaming video software. J. Eng. Educ. **91**(3), 267–274 (2002)

32. Brecht, H.D.: Learning from online video lectures. J. Inf. Technol. Educ. Innovations Pract. **11**(2012), 227–250 (2012)

An Ontology Oriented Approach for E-Learning Objects Design and Improvement

Armantas Ostreika[1(✉)], Radu Vasiu[2], Daina Gudoniene[1], Rytis Maskeliunas[1], and Danguole Rutkauskiene[1]

[1] Kaunas University of Technology, Studentu str. 50, 51392 Kaunas, Lithuania
{armantas.ostreika,daina.gudoniene,rytis.maskeliunas,
danguole.rutkauskiene}@ktu.lt
[2] Politehnica University Timisoara, Piata Victoriei No. 2,
300006 Timisoara, Romania
radu.vasiu@cm.upt.ro

Abstract. A Semantic Web is one of the most emerging research areas nowadays. Ontology is a formal specification of the particular domain that describes a set of objects and properties that the objects might have. The development of learning objects for integrated learning environments based on Semantic Web services (SWS) are still at a very early stage. The SWS technology allows teachers to design and personalize learning objects (LO) presented for the necessary content. The aim of this paper is to outline the state-of-the-art research along those lines and to suggest a realistic way towards the educational Semantic Web. With regard to the aim we first propose a LO design (or redesign) model on service-based interoperability framework, in order to open up, share and reuse educational systems' content and knowledge components. The research will focus on LO design and redesign by proposing ontology-driven possibilities that reflect the modularization in the educational information systems. Some brief examples of implementation on the Virtual Campus platform of the Politehnica University Timisoara are also given.

Keywords: Learning objects · Semantic technologies · Ontology · Applications

1 Introduction

Successful e-learning strategies and scenarios may require dozens of software products chosen from hundreds of candidates sprawling across several categories. The learning content needs to be supported semantically as well as other open educational resources and practices dedicated to enrich learning objects with extra study process material semantically related to other LO of Semantic Web. In order to support a content and richer set of educational functions and increase their effectiveness, learning systems need to interoperate, collaborate and exchange content or reuse functionality. Independent on the purpose or functionality, all tools and systems are used to be integrated into a virtual learning environment (VLE). The aim there is that the virtual learning

G. Dregvaite and R. Damasevicius (Eds.): ICIST 2015, CCIS 538, pp. 138–150, 2015.
DOI: 10.1007/978-3-319-24770-0_13

environment can reflect the discipline by providing a well-designed visually stimulating environment that genuinely supports the real world learning environment. Semantically education suits well - it provides more flexibility and intelligence. However, developments in the Semantic Web, while contributing to the solution to these problems also raise new issues that must be considered if we are to progress [3]. Semantic Web ontologies have always been a challenging problem in multimedia environment. Various architectures of multimedia databases have been developed in past but still there is a need to refine them to get the desired results of users' interest, to extract semantics from images in a way the user perceives them.

Aroyo et al. [10] states, that the research on e-learning and web-based educational systems (WBES) traditionally combines research interests and efforts from various fields. The traditional Intelligent Tutoring Systems (ITS), are moving towards Web-based and hypermedia systems, we witness a growing interest in applying adaptation and personalization of the information offered to the users (e.g. learners, instructors and educational content authors) [10]. In order to achieve improved adaptation and flexibility for single and group users, education community tend to employ Semantic Web technologies.

Dhuria and Chawla [25] analysed Semantic Web as a content-aware intelligent web where Semantic Web technologies will influence the next generation of e-learning systems and applications. The importance of structuration and meta descriptions of learning objects and it's material is growing and ontology is a key constituent in the structural design of the Semantic Web. Ontology is a formal specification of a particular domain that describes set of objects, properties that objects can have and various ways how these objects are related to each other.

Today we can generate a set of requirements for the architecture to support and allow integration of Learning objects' design model for distributed e-Learning environments based on Semantic Web services (SWS). That enables the implementation of a successive learning process by developing semantic technologies based LOs that combine variety of multimedia elements and other learning material as well as structural basement for advanced learning methods. This paper presents e-learning objects design model ontological relations with future Semantic Web.

2 Research Methodology

The authors of this paper are analysing functionality of a modern LO to find out the ontology for the problem identified and to demonstrate the outline of our model which is explained in detail below. The model for learning objects design and ontologies for the model implementation into practice should be handy for any LO practical design in any curriculum area or scenario.

It is also important to recognize that while we refer to the "session", the need for this not necessarily occur in a single classroom session – it may be extended over time and space to encompass remote work, individual and group work outside the classroom or asynchronous work.

For the research it was selected descriptive research method what is typically depicted in research texts as being on the lowest rung of the quantitative research design hierarchy. In this hierarchy, "true" experiments aimed at prediction and control are the gold standard and any other design is non-experimental and weak [24]. The view of description in quantitative research has negatively influenced researchers engaging in qualitative research, many of whom have felt obliged to defend their efforts as it is something more than mere description. That is why they have sought epistemological credibility by designating their work as phenomenology, grounded theory, ethnography or narrative study. One of the descriptive research methods is correlational method where correlational research comprises of collecting data to determine whether and to what extent a relationship exists between two or more quantifiable variables. Correlational research uses numerical data to explore relationships between two or more variables.

The research was designed with overtones from other methods that can describe what these overtones were, instead of inappropriately naming or implementing these other methods.

3   Related Works

Dhuria and Chawla [25] stated that ontology provides a link between the learning material and its conceptualization results in individualized learning paths [13] and it is primary and most important part of Semantic Web because it focuses on relationship rather than information. Semantics in educational knowledge domain is very emerging. Benefits of using Semantic Web as a technology for e-learning: Replacing query-based search with query answering, organising knowledge in conceptual spaces according to its meaning, enabling automated tools to check for inconsistencies and extracting new knowledge [14]. Researchers [11, 19, 26] also emphasizes that ontological technologies for education based on two different perspectives technological and application.

Ontology for Semantic Web was analysed by Dhuria and Chawla [25]. Ontology provides a link between the learning material and its conceptualization results in individualized learning paths [30]. It allows develop a dynamic learning environment with improved access to specific learning Ontologies (Fig. 1).

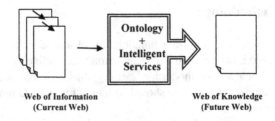

Web of Information
(Current Web)

Web of Knowledge
(Future Web)

Fig. 1. Realization of current web to future web.

Technological perspective defines role of ontology and in what manner the technology is implemented in a project. It describes knowledge representation technology, information retrieval technology and Semantic Web technology. Application perspective defines type of knowledge and ontology as a cognitive tool in education domain. It describes knowledge construction, knowledge communication and knowledge assessment for learning purposes.

The researchers generally defines ontologies as a representation of a shared conceptualization of a particular domain, and is a major component of the Semantic Web. It is anticipated that ontologies and Semantic Web technologies will influence the next generation of e-learning systems and applications [11, 12, 26]. The relation between new opportunities for e-learning created by the advent of ontologies and the Semantic Web is essential in order to explore new topics and engage into further development.

Researchers are discussing how ontology provides a common vocabulary, and an explication of what has been often left implicit. According to the authors [23, 25, 26] who states that systematization of knowledge and the standardization constitutes the backbone of knowledge within a knowledge-based system. They also pointed out that a meta model functionality specifies the concepts and relations among them, which are used as the main building blocks [16–18]. Ontology engineering has contributed several interesting aspects to modelling. Usually research on ontologies focuses on upper-level i.e. the equivalent of the meta-level in modeling. Some authors [25, 26, 29] pay attention that ontologies could be considered as metadata schemas providing a controlled vocabulary of concepts. The several researchers have tried to justify a scientific way for developing ontologies. The authors [6] also propose design criteria and a set of principles that have been proved useful in the development of ontologies: Clarity and Objectivity, Completeness, maximum monotonic extensibility, Minimal ontological commitments, Ontological Distinction Principle, Diversification of hierarchies, modularity, minimization of the semantic distance and standardization of names.

There are various classification systems presented in the literature for ontologies. The authors [4, 20, 27] present several types of ontologies, and one of them is based on the subject of the conceptualization. This classification distinguishes between four types of ontologies: domain ontologies, task ontologies, domain-task ontologies, and application ontologies (Fig. 2).

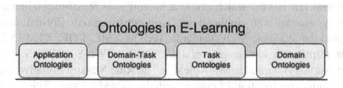

Fig. 2. Ontology classification

Furthermore, it is important to mention common standards in E-Learning. The authors [30–32] state that given advancements in web technology, global agencies, organizations, and publishers began proposing and promoting the use of standards for representing E-Learning content associated with E-Learning systems or educational content. Educational metadata standards have emerged to define a standard specification of a learning resource or component. A Learning Object (LO) is an example of a resource used to facilitate accessibility, interoperability, and reusability of learning materials. Using such standards enables education content publishing with rich, education-specific metadata. This enhances the possibility that major search engines, making it more accessible to learners, recognize the content. Common standards in the domain of E-Learning include the following: IEEE LOM (Learning Object Metadata), Dublin Core, SCORM, IMS Question and Test Interoperability (IMS QTI), and IMS Content Packaging. LOM includes a hierarchy of elements represented in Fig. 3 in the form of the nine categories, each of them containing sub-elements that can be simple or may contain sub-elements to their other sub-elements, the semantic of each element being determined by the context.

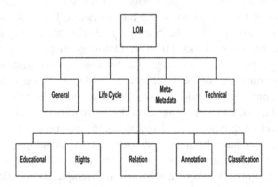

Fig. 3. LOM elements hierarchy [32]

Aroyo et al. [10], Dicheva et al. [23], Bajec [12] introduce new possibilities and challenges for E-learning educational systems. Researchers tackle several problems concerning Semantic Web. The authors Scott et al. [28], Garrido et al. [9] and Raju et al. [15] discussed about the technologies for developing next generation learning objects repositories for personalized learning. Within the context of Semantic Web, there are several hot issues, which allow achieving this reusability, shareability and interoperability among web applications. Conceptualizations (formal taxonomies), ontologies, and the available Web standards, such as XML, RDF, XTM (XTM: XML Topic Maps http://www.topicmaps.org/xtm/), OWL, OWL-S (OWL-S: OWL-based Web service ontology), and RuleML RuleML: The Rule Markup Initiative http://www.ruleml.org/), allow specification of components in a standard way. The notion of web services offers a way to make such components mobile and accessible within the wide sea of web information and applications.

Researchers Dimitrova [1] and Magnisalis et al. [7] in the works state, that E-learning is an area which can benefit from Semantic Web technologies. Current approaches to e-Learning implement the teacher-student model: students are presented with material (in a limited personalized way) and then tested to assess their learning. However, e-learning frameworks should take advantages of semantic services, interoperability, ontologies and semantic annotation. The Semantic Web could offer more flexibility in e-learning systems through use of new emergent Semantic Web technologies such as collaborative/discussion and annotations tools.

The ontologies, the Semantic Web, and the social Semantic Web offer a new perspective on intelligent educational systems by providing intelligent access to the management of web information, and semantically richer modelling of applications and their users [2, 3, 5, 6]. In addition, the learning technology community is quickly adopting many of the web technologies (XML, OWL), streaming video, etc.). Simultaneously, the educational technology standardization is moving forward at a rapid pace, with the IMS and the ADL having become the specification consortia that are tracked by vendors, implementers and academia. Both bring important contributions with respect to the management of educational resources. There is a growing concern, though towards the need of extending the existent educational standards, such as the IEEE/IMS LOM standard (http://ltsc.ieee.org/wg12/), in the context of the Semantic Web this allow to improve semantic annotation of learning resources [21, 22].

4 Design and Implementation

4.1 Ontological Generalization and Specialization of Concepts

Here we present the ontology, which analyzes relevant entities and organizes them into concepts and relations being represented respectively by unary and binary predicates, where the backbone of an ontology consists of a generalization and specialization of concepts taxonomy. A conceptualization is an abstract, simplified view of the world that we wish to represent for some purpose with the ontology language (Fig. 4).

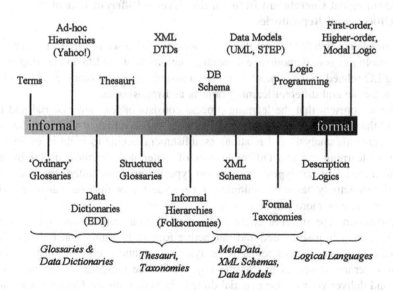

Fig. 4. Different approaches to the ontology language [32].

The researchers are working on the model for learning objects design where learning objects model has ontology for material, learning material, test activity, metadata, copyrights information, relation to similar material.

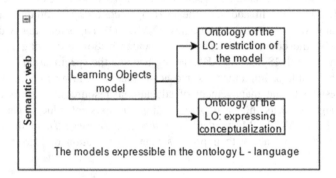

Fig. 5. Model expressible in ontology language.

According to the problem of the research, there is very important sharing of conceptualization but not possible to share whole conceptualizations, which are private to the mind of the individual. —What can be shared between several learning objects approximate conceptualizations based on a limited set of examples and showing the actual circumstances where a certain conceptual relation holds by expressing in ontology language (Fig. 5).

4.2   Ontological Correlation Between the Several Different Learning Objects and Repositories

The principle schema for LO ontologies in Semantic Web see in Fig. 6. The main idea of the ontologies is to demonstrate semantic relations between LO and reusing already existing LO related to the content and how to assure successful ontological correlation between the several different learning objects and repositories.

Here we present that the learning process consists of learning material and tests, tests and the semantic relations between learning objects enriched with metadata what enables semantic analysis and relations establishment engine to build-in external references to learning objects. Different types of material to be most useful by using learning material of the types: presentation type material and interactive video type material; test activity based on multiple choice – question with several answer variants from which one or more can be correct.

Presentation type material could be used when you want to package a piece of learning content in a structured and interactive format. Learning material is enriched with metadata what enables semantic analysis and relations establishment engine to build-in external references to learning objects. Course presentations enables you to author and deliver your course material directly in your browser. Course presentations

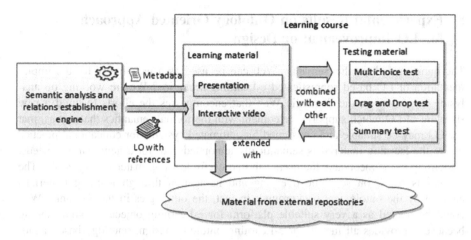

Fig. 6. Principle scheme for LO ontologies in Semantic Web.

contain slides where you can add various multimedia- and interactive elements to engage the learner. Presentation type material could be used when you want to package a piece of learning content in a structured and interactive format. Learners swipe through slides to experience the learning material, while solving various quizzes or watching videos along the way.

4.3   Improvement LO Based on Semantic Web Technologies

To make relation to similar material, semantic analysis should be made. In order to make relations the following components are necessary: learning object metadata; repositories of learning objects with search capability; functionality to set relations to learning object. We can call this part as "Semantic analysis and relations establishment engine".

For learning object to be lightweight and portable as possible decided to have semantic engine on authoring tool and after learning object is finished relations to similar material would be defined and included into the object.

In general relations establishment engine will work in such a way: engine will have flexible functionality to add new repositories and search engines, call to repository or search engine will be formed using construction algorithms responsible to form queries using strings, variables and placeholders.

In order to create flexible engine, the ability to add variables and define variable-value relations with search query formation rules will be created. From beginning relations establishment engine will be prepared to work with such a repositories and search engines. Semantic analysis and relations establishment engine will be seamlessly integrated to learning object construction functionality and will work autonomous. No user intervention is required – learning object creator has to define objects metadata and relations establishment engine will form queries to know repositories and search engines.

5 Experimental Results on Ontology Oriented Approach for LO Improvement or Design

The question is how the Semantic Web can be used as a technology for the implementation of LO based sophisticated e-Learning scenarios? We are working on analysing ontologies in the Semantic Web that encompasses the efforts to build a new structure of LO which supports the content with the formal semantics that means, that the LO may be suitable and consumed by automated systems for educational practice where the learning material is semantically annotated and, for a new learning needs. According to the meta data, the users can find useful learning material very easily. The process is based on semantic querying and navigation through learning materials, enabled by the ontological background. In fact, the ontologies in the Semantic Web could be treated as a very suitable platform for e-Learning objects implementation, because it provides all means for e-Learning ontology design, ontology-based annotation of e-learning materials, their composition in e-learning courses and proactive delivery of the learning materials through e-Learning information systems. The learning object needs to be described in metadata and restored in the repositories for open education resources.

The ontology enables the use of knowledge provided in various forms by semantic annotation of all the content. Distributed nature of the Semantic Web enables continuous improvement of learning materials - learning objects. The implementation of Semantic Web is as decentralised as possible. Personalized content is determined by the individual user's aims, therefore is able to satisfy the needs of the every user. The ontology is the link between the user aims and characteristics of the learning material. In such way, using personalised agent searches for learning material, user will be able to customise according to his/her exclusive needs.

The learning objects and tests contain metadata, i.e. the information to classify, identify learning objects. Metadata is a part of learning object and will be visible to object users. Also, learning object metadata is used to generate relations to similar learning objects hosted in outside repositories (Table 1).

Figure 7 presents an example of implementation for the sub-ontology "Full course", made on the Virtual Campus platform running at the Politehnica University of Timisoara, platform based on Moodle. The course materials have been considered as course resources and instances of the class *edu: CourseResource*. Those might be documents or packets of educational objects, on the condition to keep the link between them and the information describing them. This is why the properties *edu:resourceLocation* (the url location of the educational document), *edu: hasResource* (ensuring the link between a course section and a document). In order to give supplementary description of the documents (pdf, doc, html) the Dublin Core vocabulary can be used. For packets of educational objects (SCORM, IEEE LOM, IMS) the structured information according to each standard can be extracted and it can be converted into the RDF format.

A similar implementation has been done for the sub-ontology "Activities". According to the delivery process determined by students, it became clear that learning

Table 1. Metadata.

The types of metadata are identified						
Subject Area	Material Type	Assignments	Strategies	Primary User	Level	Media format
Arts Business English Language Arts Humanities Mathematics and Statistics Science and Technology Social Sciences Educational Use Curriculum/Instru ction Assessment Professional Development Other Informal Education	Activities and Labs Assessments Audio Lectures Case Study Data Full Course Games Homework	Images and Illustrations Instructional Material Interactive Lecture Notes Lesson Plans Primary Source Readings Reference Resource Review Simulations Specimen Student Guide Syllabi Teaching and Learning	Textbooks Unit of Study Video Lectures Other	Student Teacher Parent Other	Primary Secon dary Post- second ary	Audio Braille/BNF Downloadable docs eBook Graphics/Photos Interactive Mobile Text/HTML Video Other

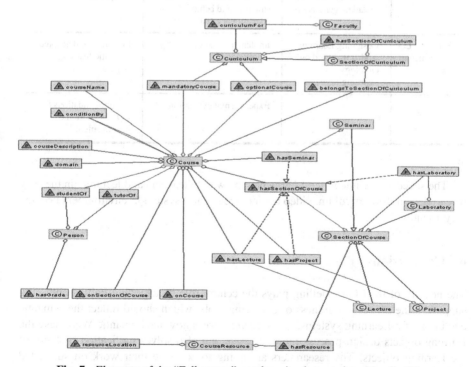

Fig. 7. Elements of the "Full course" ontology implemented on Moodle [8]

objects are distributed on the web, but they are linked to commonly agreed ontologies. This enables construction of a user-specific course.

Software agents on the Semantic Web may use commonly agreed service language, which enables coordination between agents and proactive delivery of learning materials in the context of actual problems. However, the aim to make the relations between learning objects and Semantic Web services is becoming realistic. Architectural model for learning objects design and delivery, as the Semantic Web (semantic intranet) offers the potential to have an integration platform for all business processes in an organisation, including learning activities.

The specific requirements for IS insertion of different LOs were intended, such like e-books, audio material, video material, self-assessment, etc., necessary information for study process that will be stored in VLE IS data storage. The idea was to standardize the learning objects that could be later transferred, stored in another format (Table 2).

Table 2. Components for standardization.

Framework	Components	Methods	Results
Semantic LO design	Conceptual domains for: knowledge space, students and Semantic Metadata, Metadata generation	Ontologies development according to ontology creation methodologies Description of the overall structure and behavior of the educational environments	Ontologies and relationships among educational system's components
Semantic LO experimentat ion	Designing Learning workflow based on Ontology, Learning timetable.	Implementation of ontologies	Improved and adapted semantic learning objects
	-	Experimental evaluation	Recommendations for LO design model improvement

The successfully integrated LO opened the way to teachers and lecturers in the easy way to design the curriculum, video conference support system IS environment become very friendly to use.

6   Conclusions

The novelty of the LO modelling plays the central role in achieving unified authoring support in the process-awareness of authoring tools, which should reflect the semantic evolution of e-Learning systems. The research shows how the Semantic Web make the learning objects design process more effective and also solves unification problem of the learning objects. The researchers are going to continue their work on suggested templates for users by designing LO content based on Semantic Web services and technologies.

We have determined that the ontology oriented approach for e-learning improvement is very important and can offer a perfect technology for individualized learning based on interactive learning objects not only for teachers but for the learners as well, they can be uniquely identified, the content can be specifically personalized, and learner progress can be monitored, supported and assessed.

We also identified that the ontologies, the Semantic Web and the Social Semantic Web offer a new perspective on intelligent educational systems by providing the intelligent access and the management of Web information, and semantically richer modelling of applications and their users. This is the next step for our research.

References

1. Dimitrova, V.: Semantic social scaffolding for capturing and sharing dissertation experience. IEEE Trans. Learn. Technol. **4**(1), 74–87 (2011)
2. Rutkauskienė, D., Mark, R., Kubiliūnas, R., Gudonienė, D.: Functional architecture of a service-oriented integrated learning environment. In: Proceedings of ECEL 2013 - 12th European Conference on e-Learning, pp. 431–439. Sophia Antipolis (2013)
3. Sakarkar, G., Deshpande, S.P., Thakare, V.M.: Intelligent online e-learning systems: a comparative study. Int. J. Comput. Appl. **56**(4), 21–25 (2012)
4. Alsultanny, Y.A.: e-learning system overview based on semantic web. Electron. J. e-Learn. **4**(2), 111–118 (2010). www.ejel.org
5. Ermalai, I., Dragulescu, B., Ternauciuc, A., Vasiu, R.: Building a module for inserting microformats into Moodle. Adv. Electr. Comput. Eng. **13**(3), 23–26 (2013). Timisoara, Romania
6. Ermalai, I., Mocofan, M., Onita, M., Vasiu, R.: Adding semantics to online learning environments. In: Proceedings of 5th International Symposium on Applied Computational Intelligence and Informatics – SACI 2009, pp. 569–573. Timisoara (2009)
7. Magnisalis, I., Demetriadis, S., Karakostas, A.: Adaptive and intelligent systems for collaborative learning support: a review of the field. IEEE Trans. Learn. Technol. **4**(1), 5–20 (2011)
8. Dragulescu, B.: Semantic web technologies used in education. PhD thesis, Politehnica University of Timisoara (2012)
9. Garrido, T., Onaindia, E.: Assembling learning objects for personalized learning: an AI planning perspective. IEEE Intell. Syst. **28**, 64–73 (2013)
10. Aroyo, L., Dicheva, D.: The new challenges for e-learning the educational semantic web. Educ. Technol. Soc. **7**(4), 59–69 (2013)
11. Ramadhanie, M.A., Aminah, S., Hidayanto, A.N., Krisnadhi, A.: Design and implementation of learning object ontology for e-learning personalization. In: International Conference on Advanced Computer Science and Information System, pp. 428–433 (2009)
12. Bajec, M.: A framework and tool-support for reengineering software development methods. Informatica **19**(3), 321–344 (2008)
13. Abdul Hamid, O., Abdul Qadir, M., Iftikhar, N., Ur Rehman, M., Uddin Ahmed, M., Ihsan, I.: Generic multimedia database architecture based upon semantic libraries. Informatica **18**(4), 483–510 (2007)

14. Gøtze, P., Engelund, C., Mortensen, R.L., Paszkowski, S.: Cross-national interoperability and enterprise architecture. Informatica **20**(3), 369–396 (2009)
15. Raju, P., Ahmed, V.: Enabling technologies for developing next-generation learning object repository for construction. Autom. Constr. **22**, 247–257 (2012)
16. Damasevicius, R., Stuikys, V.: High-level models for transformation-oriented design of hardware and embedded systems. Adv. Electr. Comput. Eng. **8**(2), 86–94 (2008)
17. Santiago, R., Raabe, A.L.: An architecture for learning objects sharing among learning institutions - LOP2P. IEEE Trans. Learn. Technol. **3**(2), 91–95 (2010)
18. Robu, D., Sandu, F., Petreus, D., Nedelcu, A., Balica, A.: Social networking of instrumentation – a case study in telematics. Adv. Electr. Comput. Eng. **14**(2), 153–160 (2014)
19. Kruk, S.R., Gzella, A., Dobrzański, J., McDaniel, B., Woroniecki, T.: E-learning on the social semantic information sources. In: Duval, E., Klamma, R., Wolpers, M. (eds.) EC-TEL 2007. LNCS, vol. 4753, pp. 172–186. Springer, Heidelberg (2007)
20. Repp, S., Linckels, S., Meinel, L.: Towards to an automatic semantic annotation for multimedia learning objects. ACM 1-59593-361-1/07/0003, pp. 19–26 (2006)
21. Dagiene, V., Jevsikova, T., Kubilinskiene, S.: An integration of methodological resources into learning object metadata repository. Informatica **24**(1), 13–34 (2013)
22. Rodriguez, V., Ayala, G.: Adaptability and adaptability of learning objects interface. Int. J. Comput. Appl. (0975–8887) **37**(1), 6–12 (2012)
23. Dicheva, D., Mizoguchi, R., Greer, J. (eds.): Semantic Web technologies for E-Learning, p. 252. IOS Press, Amsterdam (2009)
24. De Vaus, D.A.: Surveys in Social Research, p. 379. Psychology Press, New York (2002)
25. Dhuria, S., Chawla, S.: Ontologies for personalized e-learning in the semantic web. Int. J. Adv. Eng. Nano Technol. (IJAENT) **1**(4), 13–18 (2014). ISSN: 2347-6389
26. Dicheva, S., Sosnovsky, S., Gavrilova, T., Brusilovsky, P.: Ontological web portal for educational ontologies. In: Proceedings of "Applications of Semantic Web Technologies for E-Learning Workshop (SW-EL 2005)" in conjunction with 12th International Conference on Artificial Intelligence in Education (AI-ED 2005). Amsterdam (2004)
27. Gasevic, D., et al.: An approach to folksonomy-based ontology maintenance for learning environments. IEEE Trans. Learn. Technol. **4**(4), 301–314 (2011)
28. Scott, K., Benlamri, R.: Context-aware services for smart learning spaces. IEEE Trans. Learn. Technol. **3**(3), 214–227 (2010)
29. Baader, F., McGuinness, D.L., Nardi, D., Patel-Schneider, P.F.: The Description Logic Handbook: Theory, Implementation, and Applications. Cambridge University Press, New York (2003). ISBN 0-521-78176-0
30. Snow, E., Moghrabi, C., Fournier-Viger, P.: Assessing procedural knowledge in free-text answers through a hybrid semantic web approach. In: Proceedings of 25th IEEE International Conference on Tools with Artificial Intelligence, pp. 698–706 (2013)
31. Hatala, M., et al.: Ontology extraction tools: an empirical study with educators. IEEE Trans. Learn. Technol. **5**(3), 275–289 (2012)
32. Guizzardi, G.: Ontological Foundations for Structural Conceptual Models, p. 441. Centre for Telematics and Information Technology, Enschede (2005)

The LO Sequencing Problem and Its Solution Using Meta-Programming-Based Approach

Vytautas Štuikys, Renata Burbaitė$^{(\boxtimes)}$, and Kristina Bespalova

Kaunas University of Technology, Studentų 50, 51368 Kaunas, Lithuania
{vytautas.stuikys,renata.burbaite,
kristina.bespalova}@ktu.edu

Abstract. This paper presents a meta-programming-based approach to solve learning objects (LOs) sequencing task. The task is dealt with by introducing a framework, formal analysis of the problem. The approach includes: (i) task formalization, (ii) description of the method and algorithm, (iii) implementation and case study for computer science education. The approach enables the automatic generation and flexible adaptation on demand and has been approved in the real teaching setting. Some characteristics and future work are indicated.

Keywords: Learning object · Generative learning object · Learning objects sequencing · Metadata · Meta-programming

1 Introduction

At the core of e-learning is pedagogical competence, learning content and technology. Here we focus mainly on learning content. To name the learning content, one can meet a plethora of related terms in the e-learning literature (e.g., instructional material, course material, teaching recourse, etc.); however, the most general term by which we express the learning content is *learning object* (LO) or learning objects (LOs). This term is used in association with global reuse of the content, which, for example, is anticipated and exploited by standardization initiatives [23]. The key objective is to improve the metadata specifications that will ensure wide acceptance of the content (e.g., ADL, 2001; ARIADNE, 2002). According to Gibbons et al. [9], LO strategies will fulfill the long promised benefits of e-learning by offering improved ways to make instruction *adaptive* to individual learners, *generative* (able to compose individually appropriate instruction on the fly), and, above all, *scalable* (able to extend to large audiences without a proportional increase in cost).

At this point, LOs are to be delivered to learners in some well-defined (meaning pedagogy-driven) sequence. The ordered set of LOs is called sequence, so the process or task is called LO sequencing. The problem has many interrelated aspects such as: (1) structure of LO; (2) metadata standards; (3) selection of LO from knowledge (digital) libraries; (4) topic/lesson construction (LO aggregation) with regard to adaptation to learner's context, learning style used, etc.; (5) the whole course construction.

The aim of our research is to analyze LOs sequencing problem and introduce meta-programming-based approach to its solution. The approach brings the new way in creating content sequences, i.e. automatic generation and flexible adaptation on demand.

G. Dregvaite and R. Damasevicius (Eds.): ICIST 2015, CCIS 538, pp. 151–164, 2015.
DOI: 10.1007/978-3-319-24770-0_14

The structure of the paper is as follows. Section 2 analyzes related work. Section 3 presents LOs sequencing specification and formalization using feature diagrams. Section 4 introduces the proposed approach. Section 5 presents case study with examples explaining how sequences of LOs can be constructed. Section 6 gives conclusions and perspectives for future work.

2   Related Work

As the LO sequencing task has a wide context, we categorize the related work into the following groups: **I.** LO's properties and models; **II.** LO description using metadata; **III.** Suggested LOs sequencing models.

I. In e-learning systems LO is defined as an independent and separate unit of the learning content that is used and reused in different contexts. The main principle in constructing of the learning material is the flexible using of *small information chunks* that are called also reusable LOs [18, 21]. This principle is closely related to principles in software engineering. The concept *'aggregated learning object'* is widely used in e-learning with respect to granularity levels [18, 21].

Littlejohn et al. [15] and Nikolopoulos et al. [21] define the requirements for LOs: (1) *accessibility* requires defining LOs by using metadata to ensure effective search in repositories and databases; (2) *reusability* ensures using of LOs in different educational contexts; (3) *interoperability* states that LOs should be independent of the representation tools and knowledge management systems; (4) LOs should to increase the learner's motivation and to ensure active learning; (5) LOs should comply with the quality's requirements.

The general attributes of reusable LOs: (1) the modular structure, independence from applications and environments; (2) non sequential connection of modules [18]; (3) LO cover one or more learning goals [21]; (4) LOs are accessible to a wide audience [18]. Littlejohn et al. [15] adapted Wiley LOs taxonomy for e-learning resources and defined relationships among parameters of the learning process. The most important influence in LOs using have the relation between subject concepts and learning goals. Sakarkar et al. [24] distinguishes learning object models based on using: (1) semantic metadata; (2) item response theory; (3) reusability of previous content object; (4) web services; (5) multimedia tools; (6) collaborative learning approach; (7) learner's profile based recommendation; (8) self-directed; (9) implemented the concept of relationship.

II. The search in repositories and effective reusability of LOs are tightly related to using metadata to describe LOs. NISO (*National Information Standards Organization*) defines metadata as structured information that describes, explains and facilitates the search, using and management of learning resources [2]. The significance of metadata is closely related to the rapid development of e-learning, LOs repositories and libraries. The comparative analysis of metadata models performed by Roy et al. [23] shows that the most popular standards are IEEE LOM, Dublin Core and CanCore.

In IEEE LOM model elements have a hierarchical structure and semantics is based on elements context. This model is widely used in LOs repositories as an international standard and is related to other accepted specifications such as IMS Global Learning Consortium, ADL (SCORM). The LOM standards have been adapted in JORUM, JISC repositories, etc. The main disadvantage of IEEE LOM is that the conceptual scheme of the data: (1) is not related to abstract model which connects different schemes of metadata; (2) is not coordinated with essential standards (RDF) of the semantic interoperability. The same requirements in various systems are described differently. The listed reasons restrict the possibilities for sharing and adapting of LOs [20]. The CanCore standard is similar to IEEE LOM and it is popular in Canada [23]. DCMI (*Dublin Core (DC) Metadata Initiative*) standards describe a big set of LOs with various goals of use. DCMI consists of abstract model, metadata concepts, Singapore framework and Resource Description Framework. This standard has not pedagogical attributes and can be used in general applications only. Roy et al. [23] note that IEEE LOM is used in 7 repositories, Dublin Core and SCROM standards are used in one repository, respectively.

III. LOs sequencing problem became the important research issue in e-learning in recent years. The researchers suggest various models to implement LOs sequences. Brusilovsky and Vassileva [4] adapt traditional course sequencing techniques for large-scale web-based education. Researchers use dynamic planning of the course content and sequencing technique to verify the consistency of courses. The main disadvantage of the proposed approach is the initial knowledge representation issues. To produce adaptive course, the designer needs a large LOs database with well-indexed learning content. Farrell et al. [8] implement dynamic assembly of LOs that is adapted to the learner's needs. The authors present a system that automatically generates individualized learning path using LOs from the repository. The developed system is highly dependent on the search engine. Users can select a relevant set of LOs manually from the search results. Wiley and Waters [27] propose the unified framework what enables to shift responsibility for plugging the content into an instructional structure from the designer to the learner. The presented framework constructs taxonomies and groups sequencing rules and then connects them into entirety. This approach supports discourse-based, technology-mediated learning.

Karampiperis and Sampson [13] analyze adaptive learning resources sequencing in educational hypermedia systems. The authors propose a sequencing method that enables to generate all possible sequences of LOs, and then a suitable sequence is selected for a learner. Marcos et al. [16] suggest competency-driven content generation model. In this model competencies serve for defining constraints among LOs and a sequence of LOs is represented by relations among LOs and competencies. The sequencing problem is characterized as a Constraint Satisfaction Problem (CSP) and artificial intelligence techniques are used to solve it. The paper [7] specifies and generates LO sequences using feature diagrams and meta-programming techniques. Learning sequences are composed of LO instances generated from a generative LO. The proposed approach enables to extend capabilities of a learner to follow individualized learning paths.

Idris et al. [12] suggest an adaptive course sequencing approach based on using neural networks to identify similar LOs to select the most suitable of them for a learner. Boyle [3] introduces layered learning design framework. The layers cover: course design, session planning, activity design and designing LOs. A reference model of "layered learning design" helps to solve sequencing problem in "top-down" way: from high-level goals to concrete learning activities. Harden et al. [11] offer an approach to add commentaries to describe LOs to be used in an appropriate sequence. The commentary is treated as a local context in linking the LOs, and facilitating the student's learning. Limongelli et al. [14] propose a framework in which an automatic sequencing of LOs is performed according to the learner's initial and run-time knowledge, and learning style. The teacher can focus on specifying and producing learning resources. Navarro et al. [19] introduce a semi-automatic formation of a sequence starting from search of relevant LOs in different repositories, and their positioning process including micro-context attributes. Grubišić et al. [10] present an approach that is based on the automatization of courseware adaptivity in every stage of learning and teaching process by applying stereotypes, Bayesian networks and the Bloom's knowledge taxonomy. The developed system needs a more friendly interface to facilitate LOs sequencing. Queirós et al. [22] implement sequencing of educational resources that depends on the score obtained by the learner on solving exercises. Changuel et al. [5] provide a construction of LOs sequences based on previous knowledge of learners. The sequence of LOs selected to the learner should be such that each new LOs relies on concepts that have been already defined in previous LOs.

All listed approaches, models and frameworks emphasize adaptability and personalization issues in solving the sequences formation task. In the next section we present sequencing specification and formalization.

3   LOs Sequencing Specification and Formalization

First, to deal with the task, we introduce a framework (Fig. 1). It was adapted from [17]. The changes made are that we have also included generative LOs (GLOs) along with LO instances. The GLO model was adapted from our previous paper [25]. The framework was constructed also taking into account Churchill's LO taxonomy [6] and content models [26]. Therefore, we have a *hierarchical* model of the whole course or of a particular topic.

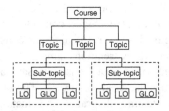

Fig. 1. A framework for analyzing LOs sequencing problem

Some underlying pedagogical principles are at the core of the task: (1) at the very beginning, student should know the goal of a topic (task) to be provided by the teacher; (2) he/she should also be aware about the scenario to be used in the process, including teaching model; (3) the teaching content should be delivered in pieces (chunks) (meaning a low granularity level) and the pieces should be delivered in the order "first the simpler ones and the subsequent pieces more complex". The principles can be seen as pre-specified constraints of dealing with the sequencing problem. The problem is constrained by the time because each activity is a time-consuming process. We need also to accept some preliminary assumptions. They are as follows: (1) the pedagogical principles used in the process are *expressed explicitly* (e.g., by textual statement, picture, etc.), meaning that they are a *chunk (piece) of knowledge* to be transferred for learners too; (2) with regard to assumption 1, this chunk of knowledge may have a *few variants* also expressed explicitly; (3) formally, any piece of knowledge (to be delivered or learnt), either the pedagogy-related or content-related one, can be expressed uniformly (e.g., through some metadata); (4) if some variant of pedagogy-related knowledge has been selected, it will be influential on selecting content-based chunks (we admit that variability space for content is much larger).

As a result of the stated assumptions, now it is possible to refine the framework using the feature diagram notation [1] (Fig. 2).

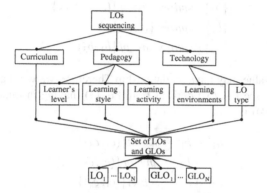

Fig. 2. Generalized feature diagram (GFD) for LOs sequencing specification

Further formalize the task in the following way. Let we have three knowledge chunks A, B, C and their variants $\{a_1, a_2\}$, $\{b_1, b_2, b_3\}$ and $\{c_1, c_2,..., c_n\}$ meaning A - the pedagogy-related chunk of knowledge, B – the chunk of theory (principles) of the topic to be learned, and C – practice–related content to be learned correspondingly. With regard to the introduced constraints, the most likely sequence of delivering knowledge chunks is as defined by Eq. (1):

$$A \to B \to C \qquad (1)$$

Equation (1) can be easily rewritten as (2):

$$\left\{ \begin{array}{c} a_1 \\ a_2 \end{array} \right\} \to \left\{ \begin{array}{c} b_1 \\ b_2 \\ b_3 \end{array} \right\} \to \left\{ \begin{array}{c} c_1 \\ ... \\ c_i \\ ... \\ c_n \end{array} \right\} \qquad (2)$$

If there are no more constraints, we can construct the following sets of sequences (3):

$$a_1 \rightarrow b_1 \rightarrow any\_of\{c_i\}; \ a_1 \rightarrow b_2 \rightarrow any\_of\{c_i\}; \ a_1 \rightarrow b_3 \rightarrow any\_of\{c_i\};$$
$$a_2 \rightarrow b_1 \rightarrow any\_of\{c_i\}; \ a_2 \rightarrow b_2 \rightarrow any\_of\{c_i\}; \ a_2 \rightarrow b_3 \rightarrow any\_of\{c_i\}, \tag{3}$$

Thus, theoretically, we will have $6n$ sequences in total, or in general– $|A| \times |B| \times |C|$. In practice, however, the number of sequences is much less, because there are other constraints such teacher preference or students' abilities that might be influential in selecting variants from A, B and C. Furthermore, the time constraints have to be taken into account. We assume that those additional constraints (except time constraints) can be expressed explicitly using some mechanism for representing the constraint relationships through the constraint operators *requires* and *excludes*, as follows:

$$\{a_1\} \ requires \ any\_of\{b_1, b_2\}$$
$$\{a_1\} \ excludes \ \{b_3\}$$
$$\{b_2\} \ requires \ any\_of\{(c_2, c_3), c_5\} \tag{4}$$
$$\{b_1\} \ requires \ \{(c_1, c_4)\}$$
$$\{a_2\} \ requires \ any\_of\{b_1, b_3\}$$

Note that one value may have a relationship Therefore, we will have the following eligible sequences (see Eq. (5)) derived from Eq. (3) (having in mind that $n = 5$ and $B = \{b_1, b_2\}$ and (4)) is valid:

$$a_1 \rightarrow b_1 \rightarrow subset\{(c_1, c_4)\}$$
$$a_1 \rightarrow b_2 \rightarrow any\_of\{(c_2, c_3), c_5\} \tag{5}$$
$$a_2 \rightarrow b_1 \rightarrow subset\{(c_1, c_4)\}$$

Rule 1. If some elements of the subset of values are independent, then the sequencing of the subset elements is arbitrary. For example, the last sequence in (5) can be rewritten as $a_2 \rightarrow b_1 \rightarrow c_1 \rightarrow c_4$ or $a_2 \rightarrow b_1 \rightarrow c_4 \rightarrow c_1$, if c_1 and c_4 are independent.

Rule 2. If some elements of the subset of values are dependent, then the sequencing of the subset elements follows this dependency. For example, the last sequence in (5) can be rewritten as $a_2 \rightarrow b_1 \rightarrow c_1 \rightarrow c_4$, if c_1 must appear strongly before c_4.

Equation (5) defines 7 eligible sequences. Now we will show how these sequences can be automatically generated using meta-programming-based (MPB) GLO as it is described in the next section.

4   Meta-Programming-Based Approach to Generate LOs Sequences

Sequencing Task Formulation. Let we have the following items:

(i) A predefined sequence $A \rightarrow B \rightarrow C \dots$ of knowledge chunks A, B, C, ... to be delivered for learning.

(ii) Variants of the knowledge chunks adequately: $A = \{a_1, a_2, ..., a_{n1}\}$, $B = \{b_1, b_2, ..., b_{n2}\}$ and $C = \{c_1, c_2, ..., c_{n3}\}$.

(iii) A set of constraints in using variants of the knowledge chunks, which are expressed by a set of constraint operators *require* and *exclude* as it is illustrated for Eq. (5) and pre-determined *constraint rules*.

Then the sequencing task is formulated as follows. We need *to specify an eligible sequence* of knowledge variants for learning in a given context, which are derived from the predefined sequence (i) by substitution each knowledge chunk with its possible variant taken from (ii) under given constraints (iii).

As the knowledge chunks *A*, *B*, *C*, ... are treated as formal items, we need to present a semantic interpretation of the task from the teacher's perspective. This interpretation depends on the level at which the problem is to be analyzed. There could be the following levels:

(1) The whole course level (it is defined as a set topics anticipated by the teaching program).

(2) The topic level (it is defined as a set of sub-topics within the given teaching program).

(3) The sub-topic level (it is defined as a set of LOs with the lowest level of granularity). For example, if we consider *Level 1*, then the knowledge chunks can be interpreted adequately: *A* – pedagogical aspects of learning the course, including objectives, pre-requisites, activities and teaching model; *B* - full list of topics (names of topics); *C* – full list of sub-topics; *D* – content of a given sub-topic, etc. The sequence $A \rightarrow B \rightarrow C...$ then can be interpreted as *a teacher's plan* for teaching the course. If we consider *Level 2*, then the knowledge chunks can be interpreted as follows: *A* – may be the same as previous but adapted to this level depending on a teaching topic and the learner's context; *B* - full list of sub-topics (names of sub-topics); *C* – content of the first sub-topic, *D* – content of the second sub-topic, etc. The sequence $A \rightarrow B \rightarrow C...$ then can be interpreted as *a teacher's plan* for teaching the topic. The identified sequence $a_i \rightarrow b_j \rightarrow c_k \rightarrow ...$ can be interpreted as a learning content to be delivered to learners depending on context/content parameters i, j, k.

(4) A-, B- list of sub-topics of a selected topic from A; - D – set of LOs to describe a sub-topic.

As it follows from the task definition and semantic interpretation, there are some assumptions or restrictions to form sequences. For instance, we use a predefined sequence of knowledge chunks which can be interpreted as a lesson structure or a topic structure containing within smaller parts (i.e., we exploit a granularity aspect of the content) identified here as variants. Next, we assume that we can select *only one variable* for each knowledge chunk at a time when the substitution operation is performed. The restriction appears because of variants within a given knowledge chunk are closely related (they are actually of the same kind and thus are excluded each other; it is especially true for the higher-level chunks).

Method to Solve the Task. The tasks can be solved manually as it is done in most cases in real teaching settings; though there are many efforts to deal with the task using some advanced methodologies and tools (see related work). We use the meta-programming-based approach to solve the task. We argue that the sequencing task can be pre-programmed using this approach. As this approach is general enough and can be applied in different domains, we first indicate some key attributes of the approach.

In the large, meta-programming can be conceived of as a technique for expressing learning variability at a higher abstraction level explicitly. To express a particular variant (e.g., a concrete LO), we use some language (e.g., either programming language such as C++, C#, Java, or even informal such as text, pictures, etc.; this language is called a *lower-level* or domain language. The learning variability, when represented, can be viewed as a set of LO variants. Due to this reason, learning variability is to be represented at a higher (meta) abstraction level using another language, called *meta-language*. Such a specification is the MPB GLO.

Now we consider *some strategies* of using MPB GLOs for the e-learning domain. Here, we identify the strategy as a foreseen objective to design and apply a particular GLO.

Strategy 1. The objective is to design a *stand-alone GLO* for the local use of the teacher as a pre-programmed meta-content to generate a particular LO instance on demand depending on the context, when the course topic (e.g., to teach CS) is to be delivered to learners within some teaching and learning setting.

Strategy 2. The objective is to design a local teacher's library of a pre-programmed meta-content (i.e. GLOs) to generate a particular LO instance (for various purposes, such as self-testing, self-learning, etc.) or a *set of interrelated instances* on demand, when the course topics (e.g., to teach CS) are to be delivered to learners. The background of the approach (based on the use of *Strategy 2*) is the representation of variants and substitution operations at a higher (meta) abstraction level and the process of extraction of the needed sequence at a lower level. More generally, we need to use a meta-program of the following structure:

$$GLO = Meta - interface \times Meta - body \qquad (6)$$

The meta-interface is defined as a set meta-parameters (identified here as a set of variants of knowledge chunks) and their values and a set of given constraints. The meta-body is defined as a set of meta-operations, which use meta-parameters as arguments to specify the eligible substitutions. Both structural units are specified using some meta-language. Such a specification hides the low-level representation, i.e. the concrete knowledge chunks obtained after substitution operation. The representation becomes visible after the execution of the specification. Formally, on this basis, we can create a meta-program template as it is described below.

A Meta-Programming-Based GLO Template to Implement the Task. First, we introduce some notation and describe an algorithm of the meta-program template.

Let we have the knowledge fragments that are dependent upon the given variants for each chunk as follows:

$$\{f_a(a_1),f_a(a_2),\ldots\}; \{f_b(b_1),f_b(b_2),f_b(b_3,\ldots)\}; \{f_c(c_1),f_c(c_2),f_c(c_3),f_c(c_4),f_c(c_5),\ldots\}\ldots, \tag{7}$$

where $f_x(x_i)$ is the full representation of fragment content indentified by its metadata (meta-parameter x_i).

The *algorithm* contains the following steps.

Step 1. Identify all needed information as it is described in the task formulation by (*i*) and (*ii*). For example, the length m of the sequence (*i*), the numbers $n_1, n_2, \ldots, n_m$ for (*ii*).

Step 2. Select the first chunk A in sequence (*i*) (see task formulation), introduce meta-parameter p_a, and identify its initial value from the set of its variants $\{a_1, a_2 \ldots\}$ and assign this value to the parameter. Note that the identification of the initial value) from the set of possible values is based on teaching goals and learning context. It is assumed that we always select the only one value for the chunk A.

Step 3. Form constraints (*iii*) using constraint operators and *Rules 1* and *2*.

Step 4. Analyze constraints of the type "constraints between A and B" and identify eligible selection for the set B.

Step 5. Select the next chunk B in sequence (*i*), introduce meta-parameter P_b, and choose its eligible values from the set of its variants $\{b_1, b_2, b_3 \ldots\}$ and assign those values to the meta-parameter. Note that the meta-parameter is a set. Analyze the selected parameter values and form constraints for the set B. To do that, we need to analyze for each parameter value the remaining chunks in (*i*) and their values because there might be dependencies between the parameter values and the values of remaining chunks.

Step 6. Select the next pair of sequential chunks from (*i*), analyze the pair and its constraints as it is described in *Step 5* until the last chunk is analyzed.

(Note that at this step the forming of meta-interface is completed and further, we start the meta-body formation procedure at *Step 7*).

Step 7. Form the sequence of meta-body fragments in the following way:

$$Meta-body = \forall_{i\in[1,m]}\{f_a^1(ML(P_a)) \Rightarrow f_b^2(ML(P_b)) \Rightarrow \ldots \Rightarrow f_k^m(ML(P_k))\} \tag{8}$$

Where "$\Rightarrow$"- the concatenation operation between two subsequent items; $f_x^i(ML(P_x))$-the knowledge fragment i ($i > 1$) representing its content x, which is expressed through meta-language (*ML*) constructs dependent upon the subset P_x of meta-parameter values.

5   Case Study: LOs Sequencing in CS Education

In Fig. 3, we present a feature-based sequencing model of LOs used in Computer Science (CS) education derived from Fig. 2. We analyze the MPB GLO that was used to teach the CS course (Topic "The While loop") at the Gymnasium level. The

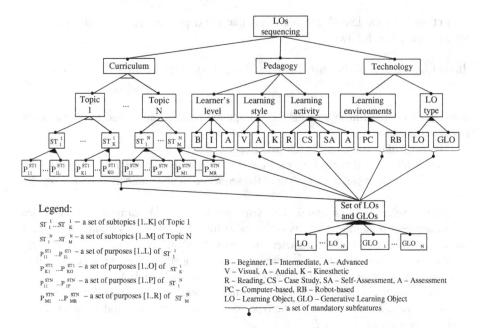

Fig. 3. Feature-based sequencing model of learning objects in CS education

pedagogical aim is to teach students of the *while-loop* construct in programming and to provide graphical visualization of the concepts in the form of ornaments in order to increase student engagement in the topic. The details of the pure technological implementation are left out of this paper. The MPB GLO is a meta-program implemented in PHP that has the two-level interface. Figure 4 exhibits the highest level interface (parameter's names on the left, their values on the right), where context information (course topic, student's level, learning objective and learning style) is at the focus.

The second level interface (Fig. 5) contains the task visualization-related parameters (radius and angle of the shape as wells as the shape type, shape colour and background colour) and their values (where radius in pixels, and angle in degrees are given). Here, we have 7 parameters whose default values are given within boxes. A user can change the default values by first selecting the new ones on demand, and then, by submitting them to the specification. The entire parameter space includes 11 parameters (4 at the first level, and 7 at the second level). Using all possible combinations of the parameter values (see Fig. 5), the user can derive a large number (25920) of LOs from the given specification. Moreover, the learner with good backgrounds in IT can become a co-designer (apprentice of a designer/teacher) of a LO by doing simple activities such as selecting the pre-specified values from the menu or introducing new parameters. Of course, the introduction of new parameters requires re-designing of the body. In this case, MPB GLO per se becomes a learning content for CS students.

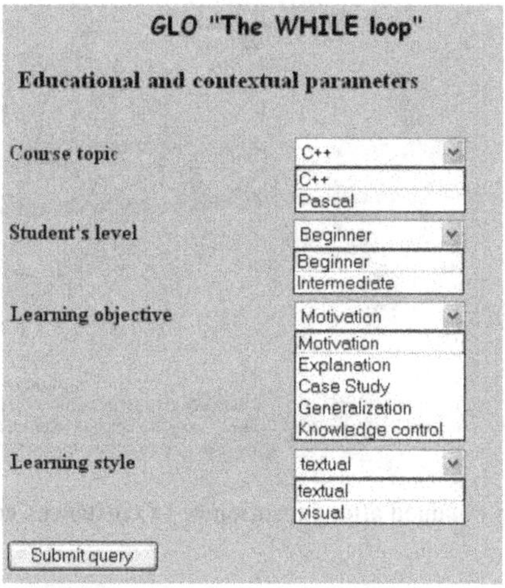

Fig. 4. The first level of hierarchical interface

Note that a user selects/inputs the parameter values from the interface only, while the tool extracts (i.e., generates) a specific LO from the specification automatically. This activity is generic because: it is independent upon the topic and student's profile, and it can be repeated by making the other selections. However, the result of this activity is the learning topic related. For example, in our case, the generated LO is a program. First, it should be understood by CS students and then executed to obtain the task solving results. Some examples are given in Fig. 6.

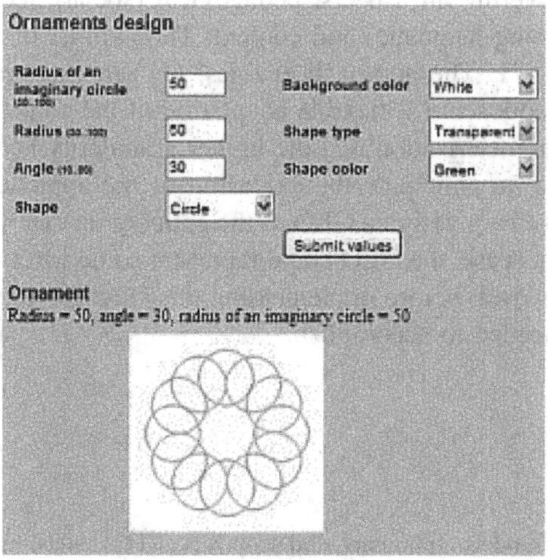

Fig. 5. The second level of hierarchical interface

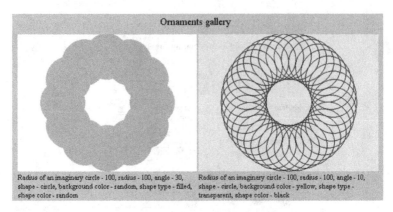

Fig. 6. Task solving results obtained after execution of LO instances generated from MPB GLO

The MPB GLO enables to enhance e-learning by automatic generation of the context-dependable content (LO) and the possibility to make a choice from the large range of variants. These include not only the generated programs as LOs but also a variety of visual representation forms of the LOs (results of program execution, the use of different colours, etc.).

6   Discussion and Conclusion

Currently the approach has been implemented at the topic level, covering three topics. In the presented case study (one topic), we have obtained the following characteristics: the number of possible sequences – 25920; the average sequence length contains – 8 knowledge chunks covering all aspects: pedagogical (social), technological (such as selection of programming language) and content. The number of learners involved in the experiment was – 71. The approach enables: (1) semi-automatic generation and re-generation of the sequence; (2) flexible adaptation of the content to learners' needs by the user-driven parameterization; (3) the higher granularity level of the content.

As a future work, we anticipate the extension of the approach by implementing *Strategy 3*. Its objective is to design a GLO as the entity of an external digital library for wide-scale reuse. In this case, the GLO could represent some part of the course, or even the whole course. However, before implementing this strategy, a great deal of research efforts has been yet needed to accomplish.

References

1. Batory, D.: Feature models, grammars, and propositional formulas. In: Obbink, H., Pohl, K. (eds.) SPLC 2005. LNCS, vol. 3714, pp. 7–20. Springer, Heidelberg (2005)
2. Barker, P., Campbell, L.M.: Metadata for learning materials: an overview of existing standards and current developments. Technol. Instr. Cogn. Learn. **7**, 225–243 (2010)

3. Boyle, T.: Layered learning design: towards an integration of learning design and learning object perspectives. Comput. Educ. **54**(3), 661–668 (2010)
4. Brusilovsky, P., Vassileva, J.: Course sequencing techniques for large-scale web-based education. In. J. Continuing Eng. Educ. Life Long Learn. **13**(1), 75–94 (2003)
5. Changuel, S., Labroche, N., Bouchon-Meunier, B.: Resources sequencing using automatic prerequisite-outcome annotation. ACM Trans. Intell. Syst. Technol. (TIST) **6**(1), 6 (2015)
6. Churchill, D.: Towards a useful classification of learning objects. Educ. Tech Res. **55**, 479–497 (2007)
7. Damasevicius, R., Stuikys, V.: Specification and generation of learning object sequences for e-learning using sequence feature diagrams and metaprogramming techniques. In: Ninth IEEE International Conference on Advanced Learning Technologies, ICALT 2009, pp. 572–576. IEEE (2009)
8. Farrell, R., Liburd, S.D., Thomas, J.C.: Dynamic assembly of learning objects. In: WWW 2004, pp. 162–169, New York, USA (2004)
9. Gibbons, A.S., Nelson, J., Richards, R.: The nature and origin of instructional objects. In: The Instructional Use of Learning Objects. Association for Educational Communications and Technology, Bloomington (2000)
10. Grubišić, A., Stankov, S., Žitko, B.: Adaptive courseware model for intelligent e-learning systems. In: 2nd International Conference on Computing, E-Learning and Emerging Technologies (ICCEET 2014) (2014)
11. Harden, R.M., Gessner, I.H., Gunn, M., Issenberg, S.B., Pringle, S.D., Stewart, A.: Creating an e-learning module from learning objects using a commentary or 'personal learning assistant'. Med. Teach. **33**(4), 286–290 (2011)
12. Idris, N., Yusof, N., Saad, P.: Adaptive course sequencing for personalization of learning path using neural network. Int. J. Adv. Soft Comput. Appl. **1**(1), 49–61 (2009)
13. Karampiperis, P., Sampson, D.: Adaptive learning resources sequencing in educational hypermedia systems. Educ. Technol. Soc. **8**(4), 128–147 (2005)
14. Limongelli, C., Sciarrone, F., Temperini, M., Vaste, G.: The lecomps5 framework for personalized web-based learning: a teacher's satisfaction perspective. Comput. Hum. Behav. **27**(4), 1310–1320 (2011)
15. Littlejohn, A., Falconer, I., Mcgill, L.: Characterising effective eLearning resources. Comput. Educ. **50**(3), 757–771 (2008)
16. Marcos, L., Martínez, J.J., Gutierrez, J.A.: Swarm intelligence in e-learning: a learning object sequencing agent based on competencies. In: Proceedings of the 10th Annual Conference on Genetic and Evolutionary Computation, pp. 17–24 (2008)
17. Morales, R., Aguera, A.S.: Dynamic sequencing of learning objects. In: Proceedings of ICALT, pp. 502–506 (2002)
18. Nath, J.: E-learning methodologies and its trends in modern information technology. J. Glob. Res. Comput. Sci. **3**(4), 48–52 (2012)
19. Navarro, S.M.B., Graf, S., Fabregat, R., Méndez, N.D.D.: Searching for and positioning of contextualized learning objects. Int. Rev. Res. Open Distrib. Learn. **13**(5), 76–101 (2012)
20. Nilsson, M., Johnston, P., Naeve, A., Powell, A.: The future of learning object metadata interoperability. In: Learning Objects: Standards, Metadata, Repositories, and LCMS, pp. 255–313. Information Science Press, California (2007)
21. Nikolopoulos, G., Solomou, G., Pierrakeas, C., Kameas, A.: Modeling the characteristics of a learning object for use within e-learning applications. In: Proceedings of the Fifth Balkan Conference in Informatics, pp. 112–117. ACM (2012)
22. Queirós, R., Leal, P.J., Campos, J.: Sequencing educational resources with Seqins. Comput. Sci. Inf. Syst. **11**(4), 1479–1497 (2014)

23. Roy, D., Sarkar, S., Ghose, S.: A Comparative study of learning object metadata, learning material repositories, metadata annotation and an automatic metadata annotation tool. Adv. Semant. Comput. **2**, 103–126 (2010)
24. Sakarkar, G., Deshpande, S.P., Thakare, V.M.: Intelligent online e-learning systems: a comparative study. Int. J. Comput. Appl. **56**(4), 21–25 (2012)
25. Stuikys, V., Brauklyte, I., Damasevicius, R.: How to integrate generative learning objects into teaching and learning processes (2009)
26. Verbert, K., Duval, E.: Towards a global architecture for learning objects: a comparative analysis of learning object content models. In: World Conference on Educational Multimedia, Hypermedia and Telecommunications, vol. 2004, no. 1, pp. 202–208 (2004)
27. Wiley, D., Waters, S.: Scoping and sequencing educational resources and speech acts: a unified design framework for learning objects and educational discourse. Interdisc. J. E-Learning Learn. Objects **1**(1), 143–150 (2005)

Business Intelligence for Information and Software Systems

A Strategy Map of Tacit Knowledge
for Manufacturing Companies.
An Empirical Study

Justyna Patalas-Maliszewska[1(✉)] and Irene Krebs[2]

[1] University of Zielona Góra, ul. Licealna 9, 65-417 Zielona Góra, Poland
J.Patalas@iizp.uz.zgora.pl
[2] Brandenburg University of Technology Cottbus-Senftenberg,
101344, 03013 Cottbus, Germany
krebs@iit.tu-cottbus.de

Abstract. The implementation of business strategies in an enterprise requires the engagement of all employees, but especially of knowledge workers. In this way, many organizations are focusing on knowledge sharing within the company. Knowledge sharing among knowledge workers could be a critical enabler of an effective implementation of business strategies. This study analyzes the links between the knowledge sharing of knowledge workers and the success of the implementation of business strategies in Polish manufacturing enterprises. It focuses on defined groups of knowledge workers in a manufacturing company and is based on a survey and on data obtained from 119 Polish manufacturing enterprises. This is followed by a discussion of the results of the empirical studies and of the supporting literature.

Keywords: Tacit knowledge · Business strategy · Manufacturing company

1 Introduction

Knowledge workers can create, distribute, or apply knowledge within their work in an organization. To achieve a strategic objective, knowledge workers should be encouraged to share useful knowledge across the organization. Knowledge sharing reflects the dynamic aspect of a strategic level of a company [16]. According to Hong et al. [10] it is a distinguished practice (what knowledge workers do) and possession (what knowledge workers know) of knowledge. We tried to clarify and analyze knowledge-sharing practices by conducting a study with 119 Polish manufacturing enterprises.

Bolman and Deal [3] explained that an effective implementation of business strategies should integrate a company's structure and also human resources. Organizational challenges are very often related to knowledge sharing within a company [7]. Tacit knowledge sharing among knowledge workers can create more added value for the organisation than explicit knowledge [4]. Argote et al. [2] stated that to enhance tacit knowledge sharing within a company, it should create a flexible social structure. To achieve a more contextually-rooted discussion, this paper defines groups of

© Springer International Publishing Switzerland 2015
G. Dregvaite and R. Damasevicius (Eds.): ICIST 2015, CCIS 538, pp. 167–174, 2015.
DOI: 10.1007/978-3-319-24770-0_15

knowledge workers in a manufacturing company, looks at how they could influence the achievement of strategic objectives and explores the impact of tacit knowledge sharing among knowledge workers on the defined objectives of a business strategy.

The proposed strategy map of tacit knowledge for manufacturing companies supports the selection of a group of knowledge workers who may have an impact on the success of the implementation of business strategies. The proposed map was based on data gathered from 119 Polish manufacturing companies. This study tries to ascertain the effects of knowledge sharing by knowledge workers on a strategy realization process in a manufacturing company.

The remainder of this paper is organized as follows: Sect. 2 presents the theoretical background of the study. Section 3 describes the research model, explains the research methodology and examines the research results. Section 4 provides a conclusion.

2 Theoretical Background

In the literature, three types of tacit knowledge are defined: somatic tacit knowledge (physical engagement with the working matter), contingent tacit knowledge (collection of projects), and collective tacit knowledge (social relationships between workers) [5, 6, 15]. A knowledge worker can be motivated to share their knowledge by appropriate organizational support [1, 14].

Tacit knowledge can be shared within an organization by using different methods; supported or not supported by information and communication technology tools. The structure of tacit knowledge sharing in a manufacturing company includes the externalization of knowledge by the knowledge transmitter and the internalization of knowledge by the receiver [11]. Tacit knowledge sharing of knowledge workers refers to the degree of communication and sharing of tacit knowledge, such as experiences, ideas, and expertise among employees within an organization [12, 13, 18].

This study posits that tacit knowledge is shared by knowledge workers to other knowledge workers in each department of the manufacturing company by the use of methods not supported by ICT, i.e. daily face-to-face meetings and coffee breaks [17].

To support tacit knowledge sharing among knowledge workers within a company, a strategy map of tacit knowledge was formulated in this study. The strategy map links strategic business objectives with knowledge-sharing practices [8]. This study takes the position that a strategy was realized if a set of defined and desired strategic business objectives were achieved. The following strategic business objectives in a manufacturing company are defined:

- Strategic Objective 1: Building a culture of inter-cooperation (SO1).
- Strategic Objective 2: Increasing the potential for innovation (SO2).
- Strategic Objective 3: Increasing the sales volume (SO3).
- Strategic Objective 4: Improving the efficiency of business processes (SO4).

The conceptual model shown in Fig. 1 depicts the relationships among knowledge workers in a manufacturing company that it is examined (see Fig. 1).

In order to facilitate the description of the defined relationships, the strategy map of tacit knowledge for manufacturing companies should be organized in a standardized way, shown as follows:

Table 1. The strategy map of tacit knowledge for manufacturing companies

Tacit knowledge sharing among knowledge workers by the use of the methods of daily face-to-face meetings and coffee breaks (TKS)	The achievement of strategic objective 1 (SO1)	The achievement of strategic objective 2 (SO2)	The achievement of strategic objective m, $m \in N$ (SOm)
KWP	R(KWP,SO1)	R(KWP,SO2)	R(KWP,SOm)
KWS	R(KWS,SO1)	R(KWS,SO2)	R(KWS,SOm)
KWD	R(KWD,SO1)	R(KWD,SO2)	R(KWD,SOm)
KW_n, $n \in N$	R(KW$_n$,SO1)	R (KW$_n$,SO2)	R(KW$_n$,SOm)

where:
- KWP - the set of Knowledge Workers in the Production Department in a manufacturing company.
- KWS - the set of Knowledge Workers in the Sales Department in a manufacturing company.
- KWD - the set of Knowledge Workers in the Research and Development Department in a manufacturing company.
- KW - the n-set of Knowledge Workers in a manufacturing company.
- R – relationship (correlation) between tacit knowledge sharing among knowledge workers and the achievement the strategic business objectives.

3   Research Methodology and Research Results

Before the survey was carried out, the main departments: production, sales and research and development in a manufacturing company in which knowledge workers collaborate with each other according to the assumption proposed in Fig. 1, were defined by five managers and the survey items were modified based on their feedback. The data for this study were collected from 119 Polish manufacturing companies (see Table 1) in which there is a significant use of the methods of daily face-to-face meetings and coffee breaks which can be exploited in order to share tacit knowledge among knowledge workers.

The research model posits, from the aforementioned argument, that when tacit knowledge is shared by knowledge workers in a manufacturing enterprise, they are able to contribute to the achievement of the strategic business objectives of that enterprise. Before the survey was carried out, it was assumed that those companies which took part in the research would have a business strategy and be able to realize it.

The list of factors for the achievement of strategic business objectives were based on feedback surveys and its sources are listed here.

The achievement of strategic business objectives: the degree is the output that results from strategy realization which is formalized and documented within an manufacturing enterprise.

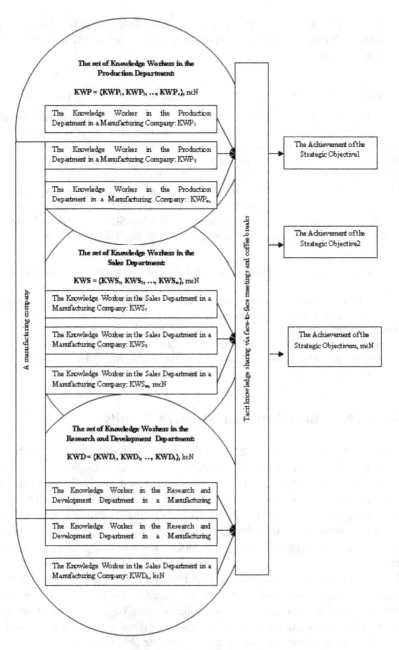

Fig. 1. A conceptual model

Sharing tacit knowledge among knowledge workers: The degree to which the use of the methods of daily face-to-face meetings and coffee breaks in an enterprise facilitates knowledge sharing among the organization's employees.

The surveys used for testing the research model were developed by defining scales to fit the knowledge codification context. A five-point scale was used for survey items. The data for this study were collected from 119 Polish manufacturing companies between January to September, 2014 (see Table 2).

Table 2. Profile of companies and respondents

	Items	Frequency (N = 119)
Manufacturing companies	Industry	88 (74 %)
	Construction	16 (13 %)
	Others	15 (13 %)
Department of the company in which the respondent works	Management	95 (80 %)
	Sales and Marketing	24 (20 %)

The strategy map of tacit knowledge for manufacturing companies (see Table 1) was formulated using a correlation approach in order to estimate the relationships between tacit knowledge sharing among knowledge workers and the achievement of strategic business objectives. A moderated correlation approach using Statistica ver.10.0 was used to test the hypotheses. The data were carefully examined with respect to linearity, equality of variance and normality. No significant deviations were detected. Table 3 presents descriptive correlations for the main variables.

In accordance with the data received from 119 Polish manufacturing companies, finding the correlation value of the outcome of a realized business strategy, as expressed by tacit knowledge sharing among knowledge workers, enables for the formulation of the strategy map of tacit knowledge for manufacturing companies (see Table 4).

The proposed strategy map of tacit knowledge for manufacturing companies shows that the critical enabler of the effective implementation of business strategies is tacit knowledge sharing among knowledge workers in the Research and Development Department, especially for the achievement of the strategic objective: Increasing the potential for innovation.

Knowledge plays a special role in the innovation creation process. According to Garvin [9], a knowledge-oriented company means that the cooperation of knowledge workers enables the achievement of a competitive edge for the organization. Therefore, it can be stated, that tacit knowledge sharing among knowledge workers in a production department in a manufacturing company could be one of the main determinants in the growth of the innovation level of that company.

Like all studies, this one has certain limitations that further research should aim to overcome. Firstly, because the intention is to analyze tacit knowledge sharing among knowledge workers, but separately in each department of the manufacturing company, this study focuses on sets of knowledge workers who use the methods of daily face-to-face meetings and coffee breaks to share their tacit knowledge. Furthermore, all the variables are measured at the same moment in time. So, it would be useful to

Table 3. The strategy map of tacit knowledge for manufacturing companies: research results

TKS	SO1	SO2	SO3	SO4
KWP	0.2141 (r2=0.0458/t=2.370 4/p=0.0194)	0.3249 (r2=0.1055/t=3.7157/p =0.0003)	0.2183 (r2=0.0476/t=2.4191/ p=0.0171)	0.23600 (r2=0.0557/t=2.6270 p=0.0097)
KWS	0.1179	0.2417 (r2=0.058/t=2.6946/p= 0.0081)	0.1369	0.0606
KWD	0.2422 (r2=0.0587/t=2.700 4/p=0.0080)	**0.4754** (r2=0.02260/t=5.8451/ p=0.0000)	0.0993	0.2476 (r2=0.0613/t=2.7642 p=0.0066)

Table 4. The recommended strategy map of tacit knowledge for manufacturing companies

Tacit Knowledge Sharing among Knowledge Workers/Strategic Objectives for a Manufacturing Company	SO1	SO2	SO3	SO4
Knowledge Workers in the Production Department				
Knowledge Workers in the Sales Department				
Knowledge Workers in the Research and Development Department				

where,

• Green – Tacit Knowledge Sharing among Knowledge Workers in the indicated department in a manufacturing company influences the achievement of strategic objectives.
• Yellow – Tacit Knowledge sharing among Knowledge Workers in the indicated department in a manufacturing company relatively influences the achievement of strategic objectives.
• Red - Tacit Knowledge sharing among Knowledge Workers in the indicated department in a manufacturing company does not influence the achievement of strategic objectives

provide such research in the whole company to analyse the relationship between tacit knowledge sharing among knowledge workers in a whole company and over a longer time period. These limitations suggest proposals for future research directions, such as exploring additional methods that could improve the effect of tacit knowledge sharing among knowledge workers.

4   Conclusions

The results of this study demonstrate the measurable existence of a positive relationship between tacit knowledge sharing among knowledge workers in the Research and Development Department via daily face-to-face meetings and coffee breaks for the achievement of the strategic objective: Increasing the potential for innovation.

Transparent tacit knowledge sharing among knowledge workers in the research and development department supported only by face-to-face meetings and coffee breaks is needed to enhance innovation at the company level. This study suggests that it may be a good idea to support tacit knowledge sharing because it could increase the outcome of realized business strategies in manufacturing companies.

References

1. Allen, D.G., Shore, L.M., Griffeth, R.W.: The role of perceived organizational support and supportive human resource practices in the turnover process. J. Manag. **29**(1), 99–118 (2003)
2. Argote, L., McEvily, B., Reagans, R.: Managing knowledge in organizations: an integrative framework and review of emerging themes. Manag. Sci. **49**(4), 571–582 (2003)
3. Bolman, L.G., Deal, T.: Reframing Organisations: Artistry Choice and Leadership. Prentice-Hall, Englewood Cliffs (2003)
4. Wei, C.C., Choy, S.C., Chew, G.G.: Inter-organizational knowledge transfer needs among small and medium enterprises. Libr. Rev. **60**, 37–52 (2011)
5. Collins, H.: Bicycling on the moon: collective tacit knowledge and somatic-limit tacit knowledge. Org. Stud. **28**(2), 257–262 (2007)
6. Collins, H.: Tacit and Explicit Knowledge. The University of Chicago Press, Chicago (2010)
7. Ding, X.-H., Liu, H., Song, Y.: Are internal knowledge transfer strategies double-edged swords? J. Knowl. Manag. **17**(1), 69–86 (2013)
8. Eppler, M.J.: Making knowledge visible through knowledge maps: concepts, elements, cases. In: Holsapple, C.W. (ed.) Handbook on Knowledge Management, pp. 187–205. Springer, New York (2003)
9. Garvin, D.A.: Building the learning organization. Knowledge Management. Helion, Gliwice (2006)
10. Hong, J.F.L., Snell, R.S., Easterby-Smith, M.: Knowledge flow and boundary crossing at the periphery of an MNC. Int. Bus. Rev. **18**, 539–554 (2009)
11. Liu, M., Liu, N.: Sources of knowledge acquisition and patterns of knowledge sharing behaviors-an empirical study of Taiwanese high-tech firms. Int. J. Inf. Manag. **28**(5), 423–432 (2008)
12. Muljadi, H., Takeda, H., Shakya, A., Kawamoto, S., Kobayashi, S., Fujiyama, A., Ando, K.: Semantic Wiki as a Lightweight Knowledge Management System. In: Mizoguchi, R., Shi, Z.-Z., Giunchiglia, F. (eds.) ASWC 2006. LNCS, vol. 4185, pp. 65–71. Springer, Heidelberg (2006)
13. Patalas-Maliszewska, J., Krebs, I.: The impact of the use of web 2.0 technologies on the performance of polish manufacturing companies. In: Abramowicz, W., Kokkinaki, A. (eds.) BIS 2009. LNBIP, vol. 183. Springer, Heidelberg (2009)

14. Patalas-Maliszewska, J.: Knowledge Worker Management: Value Assessment, Methods, and Application Tools. Springer, Heidelberg (2013)
15. Ribeiro, R.: The language barrier as an aid to communication. Soc. Stud. Sci. **37**(4), 561–584 (2007)
16. Teece, D.J., Pisano, G., Shuen, A.: Dynamic capabilities and strategic management. Strateg. Manag. J. **18**(7), 509–533 (1997)
17. Young, R.: Knowledge Management Tools and Techniques Manual. Asian Productivity Organization, UK (2010)
18. Zhang, C., Hu, Z., Gu, F.F.: Intra- and interfirm coordination of export manufacturers: A cluster analysis of indigenous Chinese exporters. J. Int. Mark. **16**(3), 108–135 (2008)

Rule-Based Table Analysis and Interpretation

Alexey Shigarov[✉]

Matrosov Institute for System Dynamics and Control Theory SB RAS,
Lermontov Str. 134, 664033 Irkutsk, Russia
shigarov@icc.ru

Abstract. Today, a huge amount of tables are presented in web pages, word documents, and spreadsheets. Many of them are unstructured tabular data. They are intended to be understood by humans but not to be interpreted by machines. At the same time, we often need to have that information in a structured form, e.g. relational databases. We propose a rule-based approach to table analysis and interpretation and demonstrate how it can be applied to transform tabular data from unstructured (spreadsheets) to structured (relational databases) form. The paper discusses representing tabular data as facts in the working memory of a rule engine, a formal language for defining rules of table analysis and interpretation, and its implementation.

Keywords: Table analysis and interpretation · Table understanding · Information extraction from tables · Unstructured tabular data integration

1 Introduction

Today, a huge amount of tables are presented in web pages, word documents, and spreadsheets. Many of them are unstructured tabular data. It refers to any tabular information, which is not organized as a table of a relational database. These tables are intended to be interpreted by humans but not designed for high-level machine processing like SQL queries.

In practice, the transformation of tabular data from unstructured to structured form is required in many cases. For example, tables presented in unstructured form are often the only available source of statistical or financial information. To use that information in business intelligence we need to transform data from these tables to structured form like relational databases.

The conversion of unstructured tabular data to structured form can be considered as table understanding [1,2], which consists in recovering relationships among entries (data values), labels (attributes), and categories (dimensions) presented in a table. Our work is devoted to the issues of recovering semantic relationships of a table. In terms of Hurst [1], we deal with the following steps of table understanding: functional analysis separating cells into entries and labels, structural analysis recovering relationships between cells, and interpretation recovering relationships between entries, labels, and categories.

© Springer International Publishing Switzerland 2015
G. Dregvaite and R. Damasevicius (Eds.): ICIST 2015, CCIS 538, pp. 175–186, 2015.
DOI: 10.1007/978-3-319-24770-0_16

There are several challenges in the table understanding. A table can be produced or generated by a huge amount of ways. Table features originate from typographical standards, corporative practice, ad hoc software, data formats, and human inventiveness. To reduce the complexity of table understanding the existing methods use various assumptions (heuristics) about tables. Usually those assumptions are entirely embedded in their algorithms. This constrains a range of tables, which can successfully be understood by them.

We propose a rule-based approach for transforming unstructured tabular data to relational databases [3]. The main idea we exploit is that tables produced by the same vendor often have similar structures, styles, and content. It allows defining a set of production rules for describing how these tables can be analyzed and interpreted. We propose to develop separate sets of table interpretation rules (knowledge bases) for different sets of similar tables. In that case, the process of the table analysis and interpretation is performed as rule firing. It provides processing of a wide range of tables having various complex structures and features.

Based on the approach we develop a table model for presenting tabular data as facts in the working memory of a rule engine and a formal language for defining rules of table analysis and interpretation, called CRL (Cells Rule Language). These rules map what we know, i.e. spatial (topological), style (typographical), and textual (natural language) information of a table, into what we do not know, i.e. its semantic relationships (label-entry, label-label, and label-category pairs). Our language is implemented as domain specific language for the rule engine "Drools Expert" [4]. It allows translating CRL rules to DRL (Drools Rule Language) [4] and firing them in this rule engine. The concepts of CRL language are examined with our prototype of the system for conversion of unstructured tabular data from spreadsheets to structured (canonical) form.

The remainder of this paper is organized as follows. In Sect. 2 we discuss the studies devoted to the issues of table analysis and interpretation. Section 3 describes our data structures for representing tabular data as facts in the working memory of the rule engine. The CRL language is considered in Sect. 4. In Sect. 5 we demonstrate several typical and complex table structures, and how they can be analyzed and interpreted by CRL rules.

2   Related Work

Existing methods for table analysis and interpretation can be divided into two groups: domain-specific [5–7] and domain-independent [9–14].

The domain-specific methods are based on using ontologies or knowledge bases describing a particular domain. These methods allow binding natural language content of a table with concepts of the particular domain. For instance, the method from the TANGO project [5] is based on a library of frames containing knowledge about lexical content of tables. Each frame describes a data type using regular expressions, dictionaries, and open resources like the lexical database WordNet. Embley et al. [6] use ontologies developed specially for information extraction. In addition to objects, relationships and constraints the extraction ontology includes a set of data frames, which are associated with sets of objects. Those data frames allow binding table content with objects of the ontology using regular expressions. Wang et al. [7] consider the problem of understanding a web table as associating the table with semantic concepts presented in the "Probase" [8] knowledge base.

The methods listed above [5–7] principally use the analysis of natural language content from tables. It is not always sufficient in practice. Information extraction from tables often requires the analysis of spatial and style information for high accuracy.

The domain-independent methods [9–14] are based on the analysis and interpretation of spatial, style and text information from tables instead of using external knowledge on a specific domain. For instance, Gatterbauer et al. [9] propose to use only the analysis of spatial and style information in CSS2 format. Their method is based on assumptions about style information designed for several common types of web-tables. Also Pivk et al. [10,11] suggest the methodology and TARTAR system for automatic transforming HTML tables into logical structured form (semantic frames). The TARTAR system uses heuristics on structure and text content of a table, which are designed for three typical table types. Kim et al. [12] use the analysis of spatial, style, and natural language information from web tables based on embedded rules and regular expressions for five table types. The recent papers [13,14] discuss the method for transforming data from web tables to a relational database. The method provides grouping attributes into categories, using only the analysis of table structure. It is based on several embedded in algorithms assumptions on regular structure of pivot tables.

The mentioned above domain-independent methods [9–14] are based on using a limited set of assumptions on table structures, styles, and content which originate from a few common types of tables. These assumptions are embedded in the proposed algorithms. They limit classes of tables, which can be analyzed and interpreted by those methods with high accuracy.

3   Tabular Data Facts

To design data structures representing table facts, we are inspired by the Wang's table model [15]. We use partially terminology of [15] to describe a table: entries (data values), labels (attributes), and categories (dimensions). These concepts and their relationships are shown in Fig. 1.

Cell is a main structure for representing input tabular data facts extracted from a cell of a table. Each cell characteristic is accessible through the corresponding field. The cell structure includes the following main fields (hereafter, they are marked by monospaced font):

– Positions: `cl` — left column, `rt` — top row, `cr` — right column, and `rb` — bottom row. Note that a cell located on several consecutive rows and columns

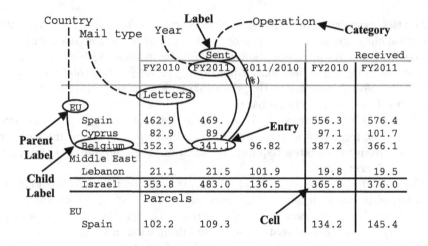

Fig. 1. Table concepts and their relationships

covers a few grid tiles, which always compose a rectangle. Moreover, two cells cannot overlap each other.

- Style settings `style` are encapsulated in the style structure. The main of them are: `font` contains all typical font characteristics; `horzAlignment` and `vertAlignment` indicate types of horizontal and vertical alignments respectively; `rotation` defines text rotation; `bgColor` and `fgColor` represent background and foreground colors; `leftBorder`, `topBorder`, `rightBorder`, and `bottomBorder` specify types (thin, medium, dashed, etc.) and colors of four corresponding cell borders.
- Content: a cell can contains text, image, or RTF. However, the current cell structure supports only textual content through the field `text`.
- There are several additional characteristics: `cellType` — data type (numeric, date, string, etc.), `indent` — number of space characters in the beginning of the textual content, `width` in units of 1/256th of a character width and `height` in twips (1/20th of a point), `mark` — word marking the cell, `table` — reference to the corresponding table structure, `entries` — ordered set of entries and `labels` — ordered set of labels generated from the cell. Note that, a cell can contain one or more entries and/or one or more label in the same time.

Entry structure serves to present data values from a table. Entry consists of the following fields: `value` — textual value, `cell` — reference to the related cell, `labels` — set of labels associated with the entry. Moreover, an entry can be associated with only one label in each category.

Label structure represents labels, which are values describing entries. A label is defined by the fields: `value` — textual value, `cell` — reference to the related cell if it exists. Also, each label is associated with only one category: `category` — reference to it. Labels of a category can be organized as one or more trees. Therefore, a label can have a parent and a set of children. They can be accessible through the fields: `parent` and `children`.

Category structure intends to represent categories (dimensions). One or more labels are combined into a category. This structure includes the following fields: `name` — textual value, `labels` — set of related labels.

4   CRL Rules

A CRL rule defines how we analyze and interpret a table. The left hand side of the rule defines conditions using known facts about a table. Its right hand side contains consequences (actions) to recover its unknown semantic relationships. The specification of the CRL language is defined as a set of DSL definitions, which map CRL sentences to DRL constructs. It is available at the following address: http:// cells.icc.ru/pub/crl. The key CRL constructs are presented in the paper.

4.1   Conditions

The condition elements allow querying cells, entries, labels, and categories asserted as facts into the working memory:

```
cell $cell : constraints
entry $entry : constraints
label $label : constraints
category $category : constraints
```

A condition element consists of three parts. In its order of occurrence, the first is a keyword which denotes one of the following fact types: `cell`, `entry`, `label`, or `category`. The second is a variable name that starts with a dollar sign ('$'). The third optional part defines constraints restricting the requested facts. They follow the colon character (':'). A constraint is an expression that returns "true" or "false". These constraints conform to the DRL syntax. Therefore, in essence, they are Java expressions with some enhancements. Also, they can be separated by the comma character (',') that is logical conjunction for them. A condition element without constraints allows querying all facts of specified type.

4.2   Consequences

Cell Marking is an optional action which allows binding a cell `$cell` with a mark `@mark`, that is a word with the first character '@':

```
set mark @mark -> $cell
```

Using marks allows developing more understandable rules when it is possible to divide cells into several meaningful groups and apply different subsets of rules for them. In these cases, a constraint on a mark can substitute several constraints on other cell characteristics.

The typical practice is to set a mark to all cells, which play the same function or are located in the same table region. For example, if a table has the following parts: "head", "stub", and "body", we can mark each cell with one of the marks: `@head`, `@stub`, or `@body`, depending on their location in the table. Subsequently, we can use these marks in other rules, instead of using constraints on cell location in table regions.

Label and Entry Creating consequences generate entries and labels in a cell `$cell` respectively, using the string expressions `entry_value` and `label_value` usually extracted from its textual content:

```
new entry entry_value -> $cell
new label label_value -> $cell
```

Each created entry or label is asserted into the working memory as a new fact. Moreover, the following short form can be used to set entry and label values respectively, using a cell text without string processing:

```
new label $cell
new entry $cell
```

Label Categorizing is to associate a label `$label` with a category `$category`:

```
set category $category -> $label
```

Furthermore, a string expression `category_name` presenting the name of a category can be used as the argument:

```
set category category_name -> $label
```

In the latter case, we try to find the category with this name in the current table instance. If it exists, then the label is associated with it. Otherwise, we try to create locally in the table the new category with this name and then associate the label with it.

Label-Label Associating allows connecting two labels `$label1` and `$label2`:

```
set parent label $label1 -> $label2
```

In the consequence above, the argument `label1` is considered as the parent and the addressee `$label2` respectively is its child. This action mainly intends to support hierarchical categories. Two or more labels can be connected, organizing a tree. An attempt of creating a cycle in label-label relationships causes that the table processing cannot perform the further rule firing. Additionally, we suppose that all labels connected in the tree must be associated with the same category. The contrary case brings the table processing to a halt.

Label Grouping places two labels `$label1` and `$label2` in one group:

```
group $label1 -> $label2
```

A group is a set of labels, that can be considered as an anonymous category. In some tables, we can define that several labels are related to the same category, without knowing what the category is. For example, we may know that labels, which are located in the same row, are related to the same category. Placing two or more labels in the group means that they are related to the same category.

In time of the rule firing, one or more labels from a group can be associated with a category. When it happens, we assume that all the rest labels from the group also must be associated with the category. After the rule firing, we try to associate these labels with the category. The case, when two labels are grouped together but associated with different categories, is not allowed and leads to the crash of the table processing. After the rule firing, if in a group all labels are not categorized, then the category with automatically generated name is created and these labels are associated with it.

Entry-Label Associating is used to relate an entry `$entry` with a label `$label`:

```
add label $label -> $entry
```

As is mentioned above, any entry can be associated with only one label from each category. The interruption of this is considered as the failure that does not allow the further table processing. Moreover, it means that the label must belong to a category. If the added label is uncategorized then it is not associated with the entry at that moment. At first, it becomes a candidate which may be associated automatically with the entry only after it is categorized.

There are two additional forms for the consequence. The first serves to associate an entry `$entry` with a label having the value specified by the first argument `label_value` from a category with the name defined by the second argument `category_name` (both of them are string expressions):

```
add label label_value from category_name -> $entry
```

First, to process this consequence, we examine if the current table instance has the category with this name. If it does not exist, we try to create this category. After that, we look for the label with the specified value in the founded or created category. When there is no label, we create it, using this value. At last, the entry is associated with the founded or created label. Note that, this form allows to generate labels independently of cells.

The second form is similar to the first, but the second argument `$category` is a variable that refers to a category:

```
add label label_value from $category -> $entry
```

In this case, we try to find or to create the label specified with the value `label_value` in the category `$category`, and then to relate the entry `$entry` to it.

Auxiliary Consequences. There are several auxiliary consequences, including the following: cell splitting and merging; editing textual content of a cell; editing a value of an entry or label; and updating facts such as cells, entries, and labels in the working memory.

5   Applying CRL

We demonstrate several typical and complex table structures, and how they can be analyzed and interpreted by CRL rules. More examples of CRL rules can be found at the address http://cells.icc.ru/pub/crl/samples.

5.1   Marking, Creating, Grouping, and Categorizing

In tables like the ones shown in Fig. 2, *a*, cells can be separated into three region: column headings, row headings, and data values. Actually, two labels, where one is produced from a column heading and other is generated from a row heading, belong to different categories. We can use the empty cell in the top-left corner to allocate cells among these regions. For example, the rule below can be used to mark column headings (any cell $cell located on the right of $corner, but in the same rows) and to create corresponding labels:

```
when
      cell $corner : cl == 1, rt == 1, blank
      cell $cell : cl > $corner.cr, rb <= $corner.rb
then
      set mark @ColumnHeading -> $cell
      new label $cell
```

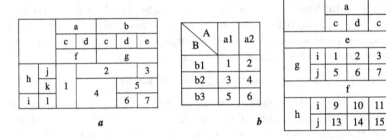

Fig. 2. Pivot tables: the table contains the data values indicated as numbers ('1',...,'7'), column ('a',...,'g') and row ('h',...,'l') headings (*a*) presented by Latin characters for convenience; the cell in the top-left corner contains two headings 'A' and 'B', describing the headings in the boxhead ('a1','a2') and stub ('b1','b2','b3') respectively (*b*); and the cut-in headings 'e' and 'f' appear between data cells (*c*)

Furthermore, we suppose that two labels, which are generated from either two column headings located in one row or two row headings situated in one column, are connected with the same category. So, the labels in Fig. 2, *a* belong to the five categories as follows: {'a', 'b'}, {'c', 'd', 'e'}, {'f', 'g'}, {'h', 'i'}, and {'j', 'k', 'l'}. Using this assumption, labels can be grouped and associated with corresponding anonymous categories. For example, the following rule allows grouping the labels related to column headings:

```
when
      label $l1 : cell.mark =="@ColumnHeading", $c : cell
      label $l2 : cell.(mark == "@ColumnHeading", rt == $c.rt)
then
      group $l1 -> $l2
```

For tables like Fig. 2, *b*, we assume that the top-left corner contains headings (like 'A' and 'B'), which define two category names: the first ('A') for labels created from boxhead cells, and the second ('B') for labels originated from the stub cells. We can use them for categorizing labels. For example, the rule, where we set a category to column headings, can be written as follows:

```
when
    cell $corner : cl == 1, rt == 1, $t : text
    label $label : cell.rb <= $corner.rb
then
    set category token($t, 0) -> $label
```

Here, the function `token` returns the first ('0') token of a text '$t' of the top-left corner cell `$corner`.

In tables like Fig. 2, *c*, supposing that a cut-in heading cell spans all columns, we can write the following rule for marking these cells:

```
when
    cell $cell : cl == 1, cr == table.numOfCols
then
    set mark @CutInHeading -> $cell
```

In this rule, the nested field `table.numOfCols` is a number of columns of the table.

5.2 Processing Multi-valued Cells and Footnotes

In a bilingual table as Fig. 3, *a*, a cell can contain two labels or two entries in both languages. For example, the rule for generating labels from cells located in the leftmost column or the topmost row, where the first phrase is written in Greek language and the second is Chinese phrase, may have the form:

```
when
    cell $cell : cl == 1 || rt == 1, !blank, $t : text
then
    new label extract($t, "\\p{IsGreek}+") -> $cell
    new label extract($t, "\\p{IsHan}+") -> $cell
```

Here, the function `extract` returns all occurrences of a text $t which are matched to the regular expression "\p{IsGreek}+" Greek and "\p{IsHan}+" for Chinese language respectively.

In this example, we suppose that the first entry in a cell can be related exclusively to the first label in other cell, as well as the second entry only to the second label. The rule implementing this assumption is shown below:

```
when
    cell $c1 : containsLabel()
    cell $c2 : containsEntry(), cl == $c1.cl || rt == $c1.rt
```

```
then
    add label $c1.label[0] -> $c2.entry[0]
    add label $c1.label[1] -> $c2.entry[1]
```

For tables similar to the one shown in Fig. 3, b, where any cell under the topmost row contains a text as "key=value", the following rule creates a label from the "key" part and an entry from the "value" part:

```
when
    cell $cell : rt > 1, $t : text
then
    new label left($t,'=') -> $cell
    new entry right($t,'=') -> $cell
```

In the first consequence above, the function **left** returns a substring of a text $t before the '=' character. In the second, the function **right** returns a substring after this character.

Recovering relationships between a label ("key") and an entry ("value") can be realized as follows:

```
when
    cell $cell : rt > 1
then
    add label $cell.label -> $cell.entry
```

Footnotes can be interpreted differently, depending on the requirements of target representation. In our example (Fig. 3c), the footnotes ('u' and 'v'), which are related to the entries ('2' and '5') through the references ('*', '**') respectively, are considered as labels. The following rule shows how to create a label from a footnote and relate it to a corresponding entry.

```
when
    cell $footer : rb == table.numOfRows, $footnotes : text
    entry $entry : cell.text matches ".+\\*+",
        $reference : extract(cell.text, "\\*+")
then
    add label between($footnotes, $reference, '\n')
        from "Footnote" -> $entry
```

In the first condition above, we query a text $footnotes of the cell $footer located on the bottommost row. The second condition: we try to find all cells having a text ending by one or more asterisk ('*') character. The text $reference corresponds the footnote reference extracted from the text by the regular expression "*+". In the consequence, the function **between** returns a substring of the text $footnotes between the reference $reference and the newline character. We create a label in the category named "Footnote", using the substring as its value, and associate the entry $entry with it.

	α 阿爾法	β 公測
γ 伽馬	1 —	2 二
δ 三角洲	3 三	4 四

a

C1	C2
a = 1	b = 2
c = 3	d = 4
e = 7	f = 8
g = 10	h = 11

b

	a	b	c
d	1	2*	3
e	4	5**	6
f	7	8	9
* u ** v			

c

Fig. 3. Tables with multi-valued cells: the bilingual table, where each non-empty cell has either two labels or two entries (*a*); a text like "key=value" in a cell can be interpreted as a label ("key" part) and a related entry ("value" part) (*b*); footnotes 'u' and 'v' in the footer

6   Conclusions

Our rule-based approach to table analysis and interpretation is implemented in the CRL language. CRL rules can be translated to the DRL format and executed by the "Drools Expert" rule engine.

As in existing methods, we also use assumptions about structures, styles and content of tables. But, in contrast to them, we divide assumptions into two parts: general and special. General assumptions are embedded in our data structures described in Sect. 3. Special assumptions are written with the CRL language. They are combined into sets (knowledge bases), which are designed for different classes of tables. That approach allows reaching high or even absolute accuracy for particular classes of tables.

Furthermore, the CRL rules provide possibilities of dealing with not typical table features, including the following: headings and data cells can be located anywhere (e.g. footers, cut-in heads), non-numerical data values; multi-valued cells (several entries and/or labels can be placed in a cell); hierarchy of labels built by indents in text; footnotes.

The CRL language can be used in developing software for unstructured tabular data integration, populating databases from spreadsheets, and extracting information from tables.

Acknowledgments. The research work was financially supported by the Russian Foundation for Basic Research (Grant No. 15-37-20042) and the Council for grants of the President of the Russian Federation (Grant No. SP-3387.2013.5).

References

1. Hurst, M.: Layout and language: challenges for table understanding on the web. In: 1st International Workshop on Web Document Analysis, pp. 27–30, Seattle (2001)
2. Embley, D.W., Hurst, M., Lopresti, D., Nagy, G.: Table-processing paradigms: a research survey. IJDAR **8**(2), 66–86 (2006)
3. Shigarov, A.O.: Table understanding using a rule engine. Expert Syst. Appl. **42**(2), 929–937 (2015)

4. Drools Expert. http://www.drools.org
5. Tijerino, Y.A., Embley, D.W., Lonsdale, D.W., Ding, Y., Nagy, G.: Towards ontology generation from tables. World Wide Web Internet Web Inf. Syst. **8**(3), 261–285 (2005)
6. Embley, D.W., Tao, C., Liddle, S.W.: Automating the extraction of data from HTML tables with unknown structure. Data Knowl. Eng. **54**(1), 3–28 (2005)
7. Wang, J., Wang, H., Wang, Z., Zhu, K.Q.: Understanding tables on the web. In: Atzeni, P., Cheung, D., Ram, S. (eds.) ER 2012 Main Conference 2012. LNCS, vol. 7532, pp. 141–155. Springer, Heidelberg (2012)
8. Probase. http://research.microsoft.com/en-us/projects/probase
9. Gatterbauer, W., Bohunsky, P., Herzog, M., Krpl, B., Pollak, B.: Towards domain-independent information extraction from web tables. In: 16th International Conference on World Wide Web, pp. 71–80. ACM, Banff (2007)
10. Pivk, A., Cimianob, P., Sure, Y.: From tables to frames. Web Seman. Sci. Serv. Agents World Wide Web. **3**(2–3), 132–146 (2005)
11. Pivk, A., Cimiano, P., Sure, Y., Gams, M., Rajkovic, V., Studer, R.: Transforming arbitrary tables into logical form with TARTAR. Data Knowl. Eng. **60**(3), 567–595 (2007)
12. Kim, Y.-S., Lee, K.-H.: Extracting logical structures from HTML tables. Comput. Stan. Interfaces **30**(5), 296–308 (2008)
13. Embley, D.W., Nagy, G., Seth, S.: Transforming web tables to a relational database. In: 22nd International Conference on Pattern Recognition, pp. 2781–2786. IEEE Computer Society, Washington (2014)
14. Nagy, G., Embley, D.W., Seth, S.: End-to-end conversion of HTML tables for populating a relational database. In: 11th IAPR International Workshop on Document Analysis Systems, pp. 222–226. IEEE Computer Society, Troy (2014)
15. Wang, X.: Tabular Abstraction, Editing, and Formatting. PhD Thesis. University of Waterloo, Waterloo (1996)

The Forecasting of the Daily Heat Demand of the Public Sector Buildings with District Heating

Yuliia Parfenenko, Vira Shendryk[✉], Svitlana Vashchenko,
and Natalya Fedotova

Sumy State University, Sumy, Ukraine
{yuliya_p,ve-shen,sveta}@opm.sumdu.edu.ua

Abstract. This study is devoted to the increasing of the heat energy demand forecasting accuracy for district heating of the public sector buildings.

The authors have analyzed forecasting techniques used for the heat energy demand forecasting for buildings with district heating. The system model for description the forecasting process as a part of the information support of the heat energy management process in the public sector institution is proposed.

The mathematical model of the heat energy demand forecasting of a public sector building have been developed. It is based on the usage of the artificial neural networks technology. It takes into account both meteorological and social components of impact on the heat energy demand. The computational experiments that prove its accuracy have been carried out. The proposed models have been implemented in the forecasting subsystem of the information and analysis system «HeatCAM».

Keywords: Forecasting · Heat energy demand · Neural network · Information system · Energy management

1 Introduction

One of the important conditions for the sustainable development of the city is the efficient functioning of the housing and communal services in general and district heating in particular. The district heating system of any city is a complex technological and socio-economic system that produces heat energy, which is used to support comfort indoor air temperature in heated rooms. The consumers of the heat energy from the district heating systems in cities are usually houses, public sector buildings (institutions of education, science, culture and health) and some industrial enterprises.

Today, due to the shortage of primary energy resources and constantly increasing of their value, the solving of the energy conservation problem is urgent. One way to reduce the heat energy consumption for district heating is the implementation of energy management measures. In relation to the public sector buildings the timely regulation of the heat energy demand for heating buildings eliminates the excess of the heat consumption due to the fluctuations in temperature of the environment and the work schedule of public sector buildings. The decisions on regulation of the heat energy demand need to be taken on the basis of the current heat energy demand and the forecasting data.

© Springer International Publishing Switzerland 2015
G. Dregvaite and R. Damasevicius (Eds.): ICIST 2015, CCIS 538, pp. 187–198, 2015.
DOI: 10.1007/978-3-319-24770-0_17

The improving of the efficiency of the heat energy management, the reduction of the heat energy consumption by the public sector buildings requires the development and usage of the models for forecasting of the heat energy consumption a high forecasting accuracy. The heat energy demand of the public sector buildings depends on the weather conditions and the institution schedule. Reducing the heat energy demand at the weekends allows reducing total heat consumption every heating season while maintaining comfortable indoor air temperature. Therefore, the combination of these factors of influence on heat energy demand both the input parameters of the neural network allows to build a forecasting model that is able to consider these features. Thus the development and implementation of the neural network forecasting model that takes into account the peculiarity of heat energy demand for public sector buildings is one of the of energy saving measures, so the solving of this task is urgent.

This paper is organized as follows. Section 2 describes related works of methods on heat demand forecasting. Section 3 presents the functional model for forecasting. The model of the neural network for the daily heat energy demand forecasting is presented in Sect. 4. Section 5 presents the architecture of the forecasting subsystem. The conclusions are presented in Sect. 6.

2   Related Work

The improvement of the heating efficiency of the public sector buildings might be achieved by the implementation of the energy management system under the standard ISO 50001: 2011 [1]. This standard regulates the management of the heat energy demand. The organizational structure of the ISO 50001: 2011 is shown in Fig. 1.

This standard specifies requirements for the energy management system and provides an opportunity to carry out the energy saving policy for the public sector buildings which lies in transition from technical energy efficiency measures (replacement of the windows, wall insulation, etc.) whose implementation requires significant investment, to the management measures of the energy efficiency achievement.

To monitor the functioning parameters of district heating in public sector buildings the information-analysis system «HeatCAM» [2] has been developed. The standard ISO 4472: 2005 specifies the requirements for the information support of the energy management [3], including the use of the modern analytical methods for decision making in energy conservation and forecasting the amounts of the heat energy demand. Thus it is necessary to develop the forecasting subsystem using advanced intelligent technologies to implement it into the information and analysis system «HeatCAM».

In the study of energy systems the forecasting techniques based on the formal models and algorithms for data processing and analysis are widely used.

Initially the forecasting techniques in district heating were focused on the forecasting of the volume of heat energy from the heating source to the consumers [4, 5]. However, the solving of the problem of the heat energy demand regulation in the individual heating plant as one of the energy management measures requires the forecasting of the heat energy consumption on the consumers side.

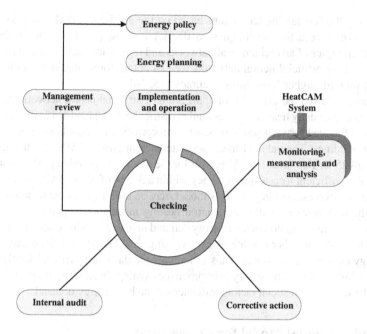

Fig. 1. Energy management according to ISO 50001

The implementation of regional monitoring systems of the energy resources consumption, the equipment of public sector buildings with the heat meters provides the access to large data amounts of the short-term consumption of the heat energy. This allows using this data for development of short-term forecasting models of heat consumption which are consumer-oriented [5]. This approach takes into account different needs in heat energy demand for each public sector building separately. The development of the short-term forecasting models provides necessary data to support the decision-making process for the regulation of heat energy demand of the public sector buildings on the consumer side, which allows reducing the consumption of the heat energy.

In recent years a large amount of techniques for solving the problems of the short-term forecasting in heating system [6] has appeared. For forecasting the heat energy demand methods of the time series analysis are used that allow, based on a model that describes the behavior of the time series, determination its future data [7]. The regression methods are used to establish relationships between the amount of the heat energy demand, temperature, flow rate and such parameters as the type of the building, the heated area and the time of day, the day of the week (working day or weekend), and period of the heating season [8, 9]. Also the Box-Jenkins methodology (autoregressive models ARIMA), used for correlation analysis of the stationary time series with marked seasonal fluctuations, is widely spread. ARIMA models are based on the construction of linear function according to the parameters of time series of the previous data. Such methods are unable to take into account the influence of the independent variables and have a limited ability to model non-linear and non-stationary characteristics [6, 10, 11].

Currently the forecasting techniques based on the artificial neural networks are the most common forecasting techniques in district heating [12–14]. The studies that compare techniques of artificial neural networks and regression techniques indicate that with usage of the artificial neural networks we can obtain forecasted data of the energy consumption with higher forecasting accuracy [15, 16].

We have reviewed the examples of application of artificial neural networks for short-term forecasting of daily heat energy demand in district heating [12–14, 17, 18]. In [17] the authors used the feed forward neural network for forecasting the heat load for multifamily apartment buildings. The value of mean absolute percent error (MAPE) for this model is from 5 % till 25 %. The value of MAPE error for the model, proposed in [18], is from 10 % till 20 %. The sufficient forecasting accuracy within a 3–5 % of error MAPE is achieved in forecasted model presented in [14]. This model may be used in a system to automatically regulate the temperature, feeding the central heating installation depending on external temperature. But in regulation of heat energy demand in «HeatCAM» system are taken into account changes in weather conditions and working schedule that allows decreasing the heat energy demand in weekends. Thus to forecast the daily heat demand for the public sector buildings given it is necessary to improve the existing forecasting models taking into account the weather and social factors influence on the heat energy demand.

3   The Functional Model for Forecasting

Let us conduct a function decomposition of the forecasting process using the standards IDEF [19]. We present the system model for solving the problem of the heat consumption forecasting of the public sector buildings with artificial neural networks based on the notations IDEF0 and IDEF3. The context diagram A0 of the forecasting process in IDEF0 notation is shown in Fig. 2.

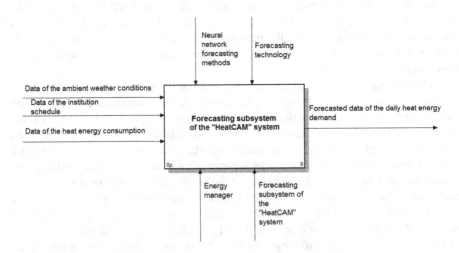

Fig. 2. The context diagram A0 of the forecasting process

The diagram A0 is the general description of the forecasting process undertaken by the forecasting subsystem of the information and analytical system «HeatCAM» and the interaction with the environment. The decomposition of the forecasting process into separate function boxes has been conducted: «Data collection and preparation», «building of the model for forecasting», «Definition of the forecasted data». The child diagram A1 of the forecasting process in IDEF0 notation is shown in Fig. 3.

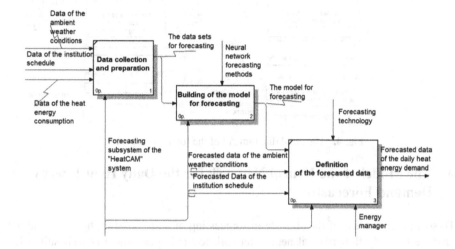

Fig. 3. The child diagram A1 of the forecasting process

The process «Data collection and preparation» is implemented by the monitoring subsystem IAS «HeatCAM» [20]. Empirical data about the climatic conditions of the environment and the monitoring data of the heating supply system parameters are stored in the database. The process «Building of the model for forecasting» is a structural and parametric synthesis of neural network based on the historical monitoring data. A mathematical model of the forecasting of the daily heat energy consumption by the public sector buildings is described below in Sect. 4. The child diagram A2 of the process "Building of the model for forecasting" is shown in Fig. 4.

The process "Definition of the forecasted data" implements the call of the neural network with the parameters established during the process of training.

The process "Definition of the forecasting data" is called to perform by the energy manager if it is necessary to calculate the forecasted data of the consumed heat by the building for the implementation of the measures of the mode supplies adjustment. To enable the access to the forecasting data online the forecasting subsystem should be built based on the considered forecasting process that must be introduced to the information system «HeatCAM».

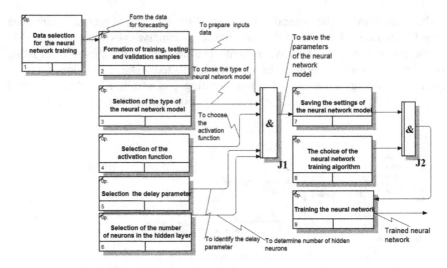

Fig. 4. The child diagram A2 of the forecasting process

4 The Model of the Neural Network for the Daily Heat Energy Demand Forecasting

To solve the problem of the short-term forecasting of daily building heat demand we propose to apply the artificial neural network technologies, which is well suited for modeling nonlinear dependences [21].

The proposed model of artificial neural network represents the model of dependence between the data about meteorological conditions, data of the institution schedule and the daily building heat demand.

The input data for the forecasting are the heat energy consumption data collected from the meters installed in the buildings of the university, data of the ambient weather conditions and data of the institution schedule.

The data sets that are used for building the neural network model can be divided into two subsets. The first subset is formed from the data of the daily building heat demand in accordance with the date of its monitoring and the type of the day of the week (the working day or the day off) for the previous heating seasons. The second subset includes data of meteorological conditions (the ambient temperature, wind speed, the atmospheric pressure, and the air humidity) by date of their monitoring for the previous heating seasons.

The data sets that are used in process of the neural network forecasting are formed from monitoring data of daily building heat consumption of the public sector buildings during these previous heating seasons.

The data that are involved in the neural network forecasting are formed on the basis of monitoring data of heat consumption of the public sector buildings during the previous heating season.

In this work we chose the nonlinear autoregressive network with exogenous inputs model (NARX). The literature review has shown that the NARX architecture could provide the bigger forecasting accuracy in comparison with the other architectures which are used for forecasting [15, 21].

The NARX is a nonlinear discrete-time system and its mathematical expression is:

$$\hat{y}(t) = F(y(t-1), y(t-2), \ldots, y(t-n), x(t-1), x(t-2), \ldots, x(t-n)), \tag{1}$$

where $\hat{y}(t)$ is an output signal of the model, $y(t-1), \ldots, y(t-n))$ are data of the output signal during the previous periods of time, $x(t-1), \ldots, x(t-n)$ are the current and the previous data of the inputs of the neural network, t is discrete moment of time, n is the data of time delay of the forecast.

The Eq. (1) shows that the NARX network combines both input variables, and data from the previous forecasts.

The general algorithm of the building of the neural network forecasting model of the daily heat energy demand of the public sector buildings is shown in Fig. 5.

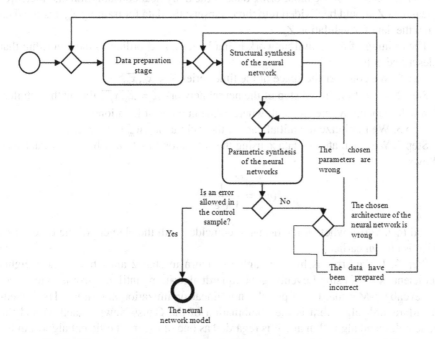

Fig. 5. The general algorithm for the building of the neural network model

In accordance with this algorithm, the process of the neural network model's construction can be divided into three stages. These stages are performed until the forecasting error will not be reduced to the minimum value. The forecasting error must not exceed 5 %. In this case it indicates to the high forecasting accuracy.

The data preparation stage is required for the selection of monitoring data relevant to the normative heat supply modes and its validation.

At the stage of the structural synthesis of the neural networks we chose the multilayer feed-forward network with one input layer, one hidden layer and one output layer.

The components of the input variables vector $x(t)$ are:

x_1 – the ambient temperature, C;
x_2 – the wind speed, m/s;
x_3 – the atmospheric pressure, mm. Hg. c.;
x_4 – the air humidity, %;
x_5 – the type of the day of the week (working day or weekend).

The output variable of the NARX model $\hat{y}(t)$ is the daily heat energy demand, Gcal.

At the stage of the parametric synthesis the parameters of the neural network model are tuned as a result of training. The procedure of training is the reflection of the monitoring data on the weights of the neural network that may be written as $Z \rightarrow \hat{w}$ to obtain the optimal, according to the established criteria, forecasting heat demand data as the output signal of neural network $\hat{y}(t)$. For realization of the neural network training process the data set of the monitoring data of the daily heat consumption and meteorological data Z should be divided into three subsets: the data for training Z_{tr}, testing data Z_t and the data for validation Z_v.

The training of the neural network is implemented according to the algorithm that is described below.

Step 1. We consider the space of the time series $X = \overline{x_0, x_n}$.

Step 2. We set the initial step of the neural network $\bar{X} = \overline{x_0, x_{j-1}}$ that with each iteration will reduced by one element, where j- the number of iterations.

Step 3. We minimize the initial data of the weights $\overline{w_1, w_m}$ in neurons.

Step 4. We calculate the data x_i using the activation function, which is evaluated as follows:

$$f(\psi) = \frac{1}{1 + e^{\psi x}}$$

and then verify whether the decision coincides with the element of the time series which is known earlier.

Step 5. If the error is high enough we return to step 2 and change the weights coefficients $\overline{w_1, w_m}$ using Levenberg-Marquardt algorithm, until the error is minimized.

Levenberg-Marquardt is a popular non-linear optimization algorithm. The Levenberg-Marquardt algorithm is the combination of the Gauss-Newton method and the gradient descend algorithm and it is regarded as one of the most efficient algorithm for the neural network training.

The essence of the Levenberg-Marquardt algorithm is a sequential approximation of the given initial data of the parameters to the desired local optimum [22]. It is necessary to set the following data of the parameters that would find a local minimum of the error function using the least squares method which is defined as follows:

$$E = \sum_{i=1}^{n} (y_i - f(w, x_i))^2 \rightarrow \min$$

The Levenberg-Marquardt algorithm begins with the setting of the initial data of the weights of the neural network w, and with each step of the iteration we change the set data to the data δw that are calculated by the following formula:

$$(w + \delta w) \approx f(w, x) + J\delta w$$

where J is Jacobian of the function $f(w, x_i)$ at a point w.

As a result of transformations, we obtain that δw may be found from the system of linear equations:

$$\delta w = (J^T \cdot J)^{-1} \cdot J^T \cdot (y - f(w))$$

With using the Marquardt regularization parameter in order to find the inverse matrix, we rewrite the equation as follows:

$$\delta w = (J^T \cdot J + \lambda diag(J^T \cdot J))^{-1} \cdot J^T \cdot (y - f(w))$$

The training of the neural network has been carried out according to this algorithm on the set of the monitoring data of three last heating seasons reflecting changes in daily heat demand depending on the institution schedule and on the weather conditions. The historical data for the neural network training are formed by means of the subsystem of the monitoring of the information and analysis system «HeatCAM» [2]. These data are formed a data set Z for the neural network training which have been divided into three subsets: Z_{tr}- 70 %, Z_t- 20 %, Z_v- 10 %.

To assess the validity of the proposed forecasting model of the daily heat demand of the public sector buildings it have been realized in the Matlab Neural Network Toolbox. By means of the computational experiments we chose the number of the hidden neurons L that equal 10, the number of delays that determines the number of the previous data to be used in forecasting d equals 7. To assess the forecasting accuracy of the developed model the experiments for forecasting of the daily heat energy demand for one of the buildings of the university were conducted. We calculated the forecasting errors:

– The mean absolute percent error MAPE, which is calculated according to the formula:

$$MAPE = \frac{1}{N} \sum_{t=1}^{N} \left| \frac{y(t) - \hat{y}(t)}{y(t)} \right| \cdot 100\% \qquad (2)$$

– The mean absolute percent error MAE, which is calculated according to the formula:

$$MAE = \frac{1}{N} \sum_{t=1}^{N} |y(t) - \hat{y}(t)| \qquad (3)$$

While carrying out the numerical experiments to prove the reliability of the proposed model according to the Eqs. 2 and 3 the errors MAE and MAPE have been calculated for the evaluation of the forecasting accuracy of the heat energy demand in the heating season 2014–2015.

The daily heat energy demand of the building for which we have calculated the forecasting errors is from 20 to 50 Gcal per day depending on the institution schedule and on the weather conditions.

The MAE error, calculated according to the Eq. 2 does not exceed 1.06 Gcal per day. It is between 2 and 5 % of the daily heat energy demand of this building. The average data of the mean absolute percent error MAPE, calculated according to the Eq. 3 is less 5 %. Thus the high forecasting accuracy of the proposed model is proved.

5   The Architecture of the Forecasting Subsystem

The architecture of the forecasting subsystem of the «HeatCAM» system is shown in Fig. 6. The request for the data calculation of the forecasted heat energy demand is carried

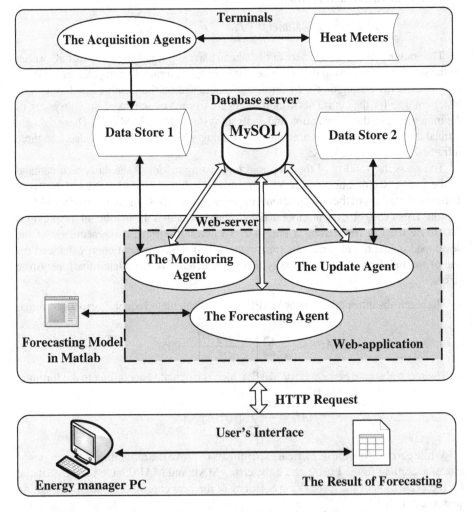

Fig. 6. The architecture of the forecasting subsystem

out by the energy manager. The forecasting subsystem interacts with the monitoring subsystem that provides data collection from the sensors and the heat energy meter, their validation and their placement into the database.

Data collection is carried out by the Acquisition agents in the set intervals. Initially, the collected data are placed in the «Data store1» where the verification and their placement in the database of the «HeatCAM» system are performed. This process is performed by the Monitoring Agent. The data used for the neural network training are located in the «Data store2». They are updated periodically by the Update agent. On the basis of these data the testing, training and validation sets for the neural network forecasting are defined. The Forecasting agent is started up at the energy manager request. It provides the calculation of the heat energy demand forecast. It interacts with the Matlab module, which realizes the forecast of the heat energy demand using the trained neural network. The result of the heat consumption forecast is displayed on the web- page of the «HeatCAM» system.

6   Conclusion

This paper is devoted to solving the problem of the improvement of short-term heat energy demand forecasting for the public sector buildings. We explored the forecasting techniques which may be used for forecasting the daily heat energy demand. The neural network models are more suited for forecasting but existing models either do not take into account the peculiarities in heat energy demand for public sector buildings due to working schedule either do not provide the high forecasting accuracy.

The functional model of forecasting process and the model of daily heat energy demand forecasting have been developed. The daily heat energy demand forecasting model based on the NARX neural network architecture. The proposed model, unlike existing, combines both social and meteorological components as inputs of the neural network. The experimental results proved its high forecasting accuracy. They were compared with the results [14, 17, 18]. The comparison showed the advantage of the developed model over the forecasting models, which have been studied in literature review, for forecasting the daily heat energy demand in public sector buildings.

Based on the developed models the forecasting subsystem has been implemented into the information and analysis system «HeatCAM». As future work we plan to design the decision support system for regulation of the daily heat energy demand on the basis of the monitoring and forecasted data.

References

1. ISO 50001:2011: Energy management systems – Requirements with guidance for use. https://www.iso.org/obp/ui/#iso:std:iso:50001:ed-1:v1:en
2. Shendryk, V., Nenja, V., Parfenenko YU., Okopnyi, R.: The Author's Certificate of Ukraine on Computer Program "Information-analytical system for monitoring and forecasting of heat consumption", No 51299 (2013)
3. State Standard DSTU 4472: 2005 Energy. Energy Management Systems. General Requirements. http://esco.od.ua/wp-content/uploads/2013/03/%D0%94%D0%A1%D0%A2%D0%A3-4472-2005.doc. In Ukrainian

4. Voropai, N.I.: System Research in the Energy Sector, p. 685. Nauka, Novosibirsk (2010). In Russian
5. Grzenda, M.: Consumer-oriented heat consumption prediction. Control Cybern. **41**(1), 213–240 (2012). Systems Research Institute, Polish Academy of Sciences
6. Buhari, M., Adamu, S.: Short-term load forecasting using artificial neural network. In: Proceedings of the International MultiConference of Engineers and Computer Scientist (2012)
7. Chramcov, B., Baláte, Ja, Princ, M.: Heat demand forecasting for concrete district heating system. Int. J. Math. Models Methods Appl. Sci. **4**(4), 231–239 (2010)
8. Komass, T., Sniders, A., Laizans, A.: Statistical analysis of municipal heat supply. In: Proceedings of 11th International Scientific Conference, vol. 11, pp. 1–8 (2012)
9. Nielsen, H.A.: Predicting the heat consumption in district heating systems using meteorological forecasts. Technical University of Denmark, IMM, Lyngby, p. 147 (2000)
10. Bacher, P., Madsen, H.: Short-term heat load forecasting for single family houses. Energy Build. **65**, 101–112 (2013)
11. Grosswindhager, S., Voigt, A., Kozek, M.: Online short-term forecast of system heat load in district heating networks. In: Proceedings of the 31st International Symposium on Forecasting, pp. 1–8 (2011)
12. Dostál, P. Chramcov, B., Baláte, J.: Prediction of the heat supply daily diagram via artificial neural network. In: Proceedings of the East West Fuzzy Colloquium, pp. 178–183 (2002)
13. Moon, J.W., Jung, S.K., Kim, J.-J.: Application of ANN (artificial-neural-network) in residential thermal control. In: Proceedings of the Eleventh International IBPSA Conference, pp. 64–74 (2009)
14. Wojdyga, K.: Predicting heat demand for a district heating systems. Int. J. Energy Power Eng. **3**(5), 237–244 (2014)
15. Mitrea, C.A., Lee, C.K.M., Wu, Z.: A comparison between neural networks and traditional forecasting methods: a case study. Int. J. Eng. Bus. Manag. **1**(2), 67–72 (2009)
16. Datta, D., Tassou, S.A., Marriott, D.: Application of neural networks for the prediction of the energy consumption in a supermarket. In: Proceedings of Clima 2000 Conference, pp. 1–11 (1997). http://www.aivc.org/resource/application-neural-networks-prediction-energy-consumption-supermarket
17. Idowu, S., Saguna, S., Ahlund, C., Schelen, O.: Forecasting heat load for smart district heating systems: a machine learning approach. In: Proceedings of the IEEE International Conference on Smart Grid Communications, pp. 554–559 (2014)
18. Park, T.C., Kim, U.S., Kim, L.-H., Jo, B.W., Yeo, Y.K.: Heat consumption forecasting using partial least squares, artificial neural network and support vector regression techniques in district heating systems. Korean J. Chem. Eng. **27**(4), 1063–1081 (2010)
19. Menzel, C., Mayer, R.J.: The IDEF family of languages. Handbook on Architectures of Information Systems, pp. 215–249. Springer, Berlin (2006)
20. Parfenenko, Y., Shendryk, V., Nenja, V., Vashchenko, S.: Information system for monitoring and forecast of building heat consumption. In: Dregvaite, G., Damasevicius, R. (eds.) ICIST 2014. CCIS, vol. 465, pp. 1–11. Springer, Heidelberg (2014)
21. Haykin, S.: Neural Networks – A Comprehensive Foundation. Prentice Hal, New Jersey (2005)
22. Yu, H., Wilamowski, B.M.: Levenberg–Marquardt training. In: Irwin, J.D. (ed.) The Industrial Electronic Handbook: Intelligent Systems, Chapter 12. Taylor & Francis Group, CRC Press, Boca Raton (2011)

Implementation of the AHP Method in ERP-Based Decision Support Systems for a New Product Development

Sławomir Kłos[✉]

Department of Computer Science and Production Management,
University of Zielona Góra, Zielona Góra, Poland
s.klos@iizp.uz.zgora.pl

Abstract. Effective management of R&D projects determines the competitiveness of manufacturing enterprises. The proper choice of product prototypes that might be manufactured and sold forms part of the critical, strategic decisions of each company. These decisions have a direct impact on the financial results of the enterprise, development possibilities and its competitive position. Depending on the size and characteristics of companies, an enterprise can make a variety of decisions annually, from a few to several dozen, regarding the introduction of new products into production. Therefore, the development of a decision support system for the selection of the best prototypes is very important especially for manufacturing enterprises that bring many new products onto the market. The decision support system should be based on an analysis of technical and business factors of new products and enable the improvement of effectiveness and reduce decision time. To automate the process of decision-making the data required for the decision support system should be acquired from the ERP (enterprise resource system). The proposed decision support system is based on the AHP method. An illustrative example is given.

Keywords: Analytical hierarchy process (AHP) · Product research and development · Enterprise resource planning system (ERP) · Product lifecycle management (PLM)

1 Introduction

The development of manufacturing enterprises is determined by the introduction of new products on the market. Product development departments are constantly creating new products. From many alternative prototype products, the best solution should be selected. The best choice enables the selection of the prototype of a new product that could guarantee market success; funding further research and development in the future. Therefore, the decision process of new product selection should be integrated with product lifecycle management (PLM). PLM is an essential tool for coping with the challenges of more demanding global competition and ever-shortening product and component lifecycles [6]. PLM support entails the modeling, capturing, manipulating, exchanging, and use of information in all product lifecycle decision-making processes, across all application domains [5]. Effective product lifecycle management includes the following stages:

© Springer International Publishing Switzerland 2015
G. Dregvaite and R. Damasevicius (Eds.): ICIST 2015, CCIS 538, pp. 199–207, 2015.
DOI: 10.1007/978-3-319-24770-0_18

1. Product concept,
2. Product design,
3. Prototype of product,
4. Technology and quality control,
5. Organization the manufacturing and cooperation processes,
6. Production and maintenance,
7. Product recycling.

   The decision about the selection of a new product should be taken by the product design or prototype of the product stages. The later the stage of the decision-making, the greater costs of the research and development process. However, in the case of simple products, the decision could be taken in the stage of technology and quality control design. In the stage of new product concept, many alternatives can be taken into account. In the subsequent stages, the number of alternatives is decreased to several variants. In the stages of prototype or technology design, only two or three alternatives are analyzed. Of course, the decision process depends on the branch and size of the enterprise and especially on its financial potential. During the decision-making process, all aspects of the product life cycle should be taken into account, such as: available technology, quality level, production capacity, manufacturing costs, impact on the environment, etc. New product development should be based on the knowledge and experiences of manufacturing companies registered as data in the ERP and PLM databases [2, 3]. To evaluate different variants of products, access to the data of similar products from the ERP system is required. In the next chapter a description of the AHP method is presented.

2 The Analytic Hierarchy Process

The AHP was elaborated by Thomas Saaty in 1980 [4]. The method can be success-fully used for investment or development decision support in manufacturing companies [1]. It is an effective method for dealing with complex decision making, and may aid the decision maker to set priorities in order to support the best decision. By reducing complex decisions to a series of pairwise comparisons, and then synthesizing the results, the AHP enables us to capture subjective and objective aspects of a decision. In addition, the AHP encompasses a useful technique for checking the consistency of the decision maker's evaluations, thus reducing any bias in the decision making process [4]. The AHP considers a set of evaluation criteria, and a set of alternative options among which the best decision is to be made. The AHP can be implemented in the three following steps [4]:

1. Computing a vector of criteria weights.
2. Computing a matrix of option scores.
3. Ranking the options.

   In order to compute the weights for the different criteria, in the first step, the AHP starts by creating a pairwise comparison matrix A. The matrix A is a $m \times m$ real matrix, where m is the number of evaluation criteria considered. Each entry a_{jk} of the matrix

$\mathbf{A}$ represents the importance of the jth criterion relative to the k-th criterion. If $a_{jk} > 1$, then the jth criterion is more important than the k-th criterion, while if $a_{jk} < 1$, then the jth criterion is less important than the k-th criterion. If two criteria have the same importance, then the entry a_{jk} is equal to 1 [4]. The entries a_{jk} and a_{kj} satisfy the following constraint:

$$a_{jk} \cdot a_{kj} = 1 \tag{1}$$

wherein $a_{jj} = 1$ for all j. The relative importance between two criteria is measured according to a numerical scale from 1 to 9, where [4]:

1. 1 - j and k are equally important,
2. 3 - j is slightly more important than k,
3. 5 - j is more important than k,
4. 7 - j is strongly more important than k,
5. 9 - j is absolutely more important than k.
6. 2, 4, 6, 8 - are intermediate values.

On the basis of matrix $\mathbf{A}$, we can be create a normalized pairwise comparison matrix $\mathbf{A}_{norm}$ by making the sum of the entries on each column equal to 1, i.e. each entry $\bar{a}_{jk}$ of the matrix $\mathbf{A}_{norm}$ is computed as:

$$\bar{a}_{jk} = \frac{a_{jk}}{\sum_{i=1}^{m} a_{ik}} \tag{2}$$

Next, the criteria weight vector w (that is an m-dimensional column vector) is built by averaging the entries on each row of $\mathbf{A}_{norm}$, i.e. the elements of the vector are computed as follows [4]:

$$w_j = \frac{\sum_{i=1}^{m} \bar{a}_{ik}}{m} \tag{3}$$

In the next step, a matrix $\mathbf{S}$ of option scores should be created ($n \times m$ real matrix). Each entry s_{ij} of $\mathbf{S}$ represents the score of the ith option with respect to the jth criterion. In order to derive such scores, a pairwise comparison matrix $\mathbf{B}^{(j)}$ is first built for each of the m criteria, $j = 1, \ldots, m$. The matrix is a $n \times n$ real matrix, where n is the number of options evaluated. Matrix $\mathbf{B}^{(j)}$ is a $n \times n$ real matrix, where n is the number of options evaluated. Each entry of the matrix represents the evaluation of the ith option compared to the hth option with respect to the jth criterion. If $b_{ih}^{(j)} > 1$ then the ith option is better than the hth option, while if $b_{ih}^{(j)} < 1$, then the ith option is worse than the hth option. The entries $b_{ih}^{(j)}$ and $b_{hi}^{(j)}$ satisfy the following constraint:

$$b_{ih}^{(j)} \cdot b_{hi}^{(j)} = 1 \tag{4}$$

wherein $b_{ii} = 1$ for all i. The AHP applies to each matrix $\mathbf{B}^{(j)}$ the same two-step procedure described for $\mathbf{A}$, i.e. it divides each entry by the sum of the entries in the same column, and then it averages the entries on each row, thus obtaining the score vectors **s**, $j = 1, \ldots, m$. The vector contains the scores of the evaluated options with respect to the jth criterion. The score matrix **S** is obtained as $\mathbf{S} = [\mathbf{s}^{(1)}, \mathbf{s}^{(2)}, \ldots, \mathbf{s}^{(m)}]$ i.e. the jth column of **S** corresponds to $\mathbf{s}^{(j)}$. The weight vector **w** and the score matrix **S** have been computed, the AHP method obtains a vector **v** of global scores by multiplying **S** and **w**, i.e.

$$v = S \cdot w \tag{5}$$

The ith entry v_i of **v** represents the global score assigned by the AHP to the ith option [4]. The AHP includes an effective technique for checking the consistency of the evaluations made by the decision maker when building each of the pairwise comparison matrices involved in the process, namely matrix **A** and matrices **B**$^{(j)}$. The Consistency Index (*CI*) is obtained by first computing the scalar x as the average of the elements of the vector whose jth element is the ratio of the jth element of vector $\mathbf{A} \cdot \mathbf{w}$ to the corresponding element of vector w. The CI index is computed as follows:

$$CI = \frac{x - m}{m - 1} \tag{6}$$

A perfectly consistent decision maker should always obtain CI = 0 but small values of inconsistency may be tolerated. In particular the inconsistencies are tolerable, if

$$\frac{CI}{RI} < 0,1 \tag{7}$$

and a reliable result may be expected from the AHP. In (7) the RI is *the random index* i.e. the consistency index when the entries of **A** are completely random. The values of RI for m ≤ 10 (small problems) are shown in Table 1.

In the next chapter the example of hierarchical structure of a new product selection for a manufacturing enterprise is described.

Table 1. Values of the random index (RI) for small problems.

m	2	3	4	5	6	7	8	9	10
RI	0	0.58	0.90	1.12	1.24	1.32	1.41	1.45	1.51

3   The Hierarchical Structure of the New Product Selection Problem

The decision about the selection of a new product for production is determined by both technical and economic factors. The impact of the factors on the final decision about the implementation of the new product into the manufacturing process depends on the branch, product specification and market requirements. In Fig. 2, the hierarchical structure of the selection of a new product is presented. The technical factors include: reliability, producibility, quality, functionality, safety and appearance. The business factors include: cost/price, investment related to the launch of new production, lifetime and the influence of the new product on the environment.

The selection of the new product is based on a procedure implemented in a medium-sized enterprise that produces equipment for the heat treatment of metals. The company introduces tens of new products into the market annually and both the selection process and an identification of priorities for different prototypes are very important. The most important factors in the new product selection are the business factors (four times more important than technical factors). Tables 2, 3 and 4 show pairwise comparison matrices relative to a new product selection, it includes technical factors and business factors.

Table 2. AHP attribute details – new product selection

	Technical factors	Business factors
Technical factors	1	0.25
Business factors	4.00	1

Table 3. AHP attribute details – technical factors

	RE	PR	FU	QA	SF	AP
RE	1.00	0.50	0.25	0.50	2.00	4.00
PR	2.00	1.00	0.50	2.00	3.00	4.00
FU	4.00	2.00	1.00	3.00	4.00	5.00
QA	2.00	0.50	0.33	1.00	0.33	2.00
SF	0.50	0.33	0.25	3.00	1.00	2.00
AP	0.25	0.25	0.20	0.50	0.50	1.00
Sum	9.75	4.58	2.53	10.00	10.83	18.00

Table 4. AHP attribute details – business factors

	CP	IN	EV	LT
CP	1.00	2.00	4.00	5.00
IN	0.50	1.00	3.00	5.00
EV	0.25	0.33	1.00	2.00
LT	0.20	0.20	0.50	1.00
Sum	1.95	3.53	8.50	13.00

Among the technical factors, of primary importance for the company are functionality and producibility and the least important are safety and appearance.

Among the business factors, the most important are costs and planned investments.

On the basis of the data presented in Tables 2, 3 and 4, criteria weight vectors can be calculated (Table 5).

For the matrices presented in Tables 3 and 4, the consistency indexes are calculated and presented in Table 6. The consistency condition is fulfilled in the case of both factors.

Table 5. Criteria weight vectors

New product selection	TF	BF				
Weights	0.200	0.800				
Technical factors	RE	PR	FU	QA	SF	AP
Weights	0.128	0.220	0.365	0.115	0.121	0.052
Business factors	CP	IN	EV	LT		
Weights	0.484	0.319	0.124	0.074		

Table 6. Analysis of inconsistency

	Technical factors	Business factors
Consistency index CI	0.11	0.02
Random index RI	1.24	0.90
CI/RI	0.09 < 0.1	0.02 < 0.1

The presented structures of the technical and business factors with calculated weights are a basis for the evaluation of different projects. In the next chapter, this paper presents a model of data acquisition from the PLM system based on the ERP database in order to evaluate different products.

4 A Model of the Comparison of a New Product Based on the PLM System and ERP Data

Many advanced ERP systems offer support of PLM functionality. PLM systems enable the support of the development processes of a product by an analysis of the following ERP data:

1. customer requirements,
2. sales offers and orders,
3. different product configurations,
4. variants of bills of materials,
5. CAD drawings and products visualizations,
6. technological variants,
7. the availability and cost of materials,
8. the availability and cost of manufacturing resources and tools,
9. service orders and product utilization,
10. customer complaints.

On the basis of an analysis of the data, different concept/prototypes of product can be compared with each other. In Fig. 2, a model of the product comparison is presented. The procedure supports the creation of pairwise comparisons matrices. To compare different products, product features related to technical and business factors should be defined. The concepts of new products should be prepared using ERP data repositories [7]. The concept of the product should be created by the configuration and selection of

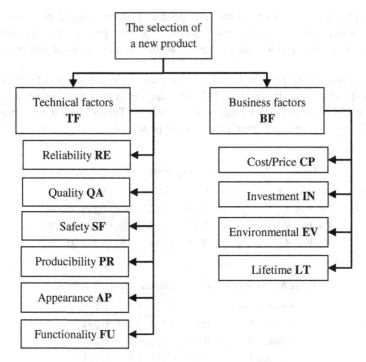

Fig. 1. AHP hierarchy of a new product system selection in a production enterprise

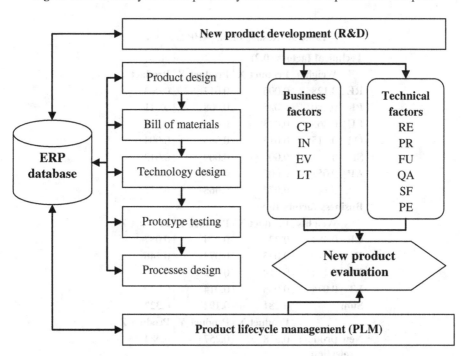

Fig. 2. A model of the evaluation of a new product.

different options. The concept of the new product is considered to be ready when a product designer checks all possible options – a new product configuration. The configuration of the product can be based on the hierarchical structure proposed in Fig. 1.

On the basis of the proposed model, AHP pairwise comparisons of different prototypes of products can be created. It is very important that the comparisons of the different products are able to be made automatically. In Tables 7 and 8, examples of the results of the comparison of three products are presented.

Table 7. AHP pairwise comparisons –technical factors

Technical factors	RE	PR	FU	QA	SF	AP
Product X	0.230	0.566	0.313	0.640	0.128	0.570
Product Y	0.648	0.192	0.333	0.206	0.360	0.259
Product Z	0.122	0.242	0.354	0.154	0.512	0.171

Table 8. AHP pairwise comparisons –business factors

Business factors	CP	IN	EV	LT
Product X	0.586	0.143	0.123	0.094
Product Y	0.190	0.286	0.320	0.234
Product Z	0.224	0.571	0.557	0.671

Table 9. Results of the AHP analysis

Technical factors (0.2)				
	Weights	Product X	Product Y	Product Z
RE	0.128	0.006	0.017	0.003
PR	0.220	0.025	0.008	0.011
FU	0.365	0.023	0.024	0.026
QA	0.115	0.015	0.005	0.004
SF	0.121	0.003	0.009	0.012
AP	0.052	0.006	0.003	0.002
	Sum	**0.077**	**0.065**	**0.057**
Business factors (0.8)				
	Weights	Product X	Product Y	Product Z
CP	0.484	0.227	0.074	0.087
IN	0.319	0.036	0.073	0.146
EV	0.124	0.012	0.032	0.055
LT	0.074	0.006	0.014	0.040
Sum		**0.281**	**0.192**	**0.327**
		Product X	Product Y	Product Z
New product selection		0.358	0.257	**0.384**

The numbers show how individual products fulfill defined technical and business factors.

For example; Product Y best meets the reliability criteria and Product X has the best cost/price relation. But for a proper evaluation of new products, the importance of the business and technical factors should be taken into account. Table 9 presents the final results of the evaluation of the three products.

An analysis of the data presented in the table shows us that Product X best fulfills the technical criteria of the evaluation, and Product Z best fulfill the business criteria. Because the business factors are more important, Product Z should be selected for production. Notably, the final results show that there is no significant difference between Product X and Product Y. The final decision should be made on the basis of a detailed data analysis.

5 Conclusions

The decision problem related to new product development is critical for every manufacturing company and is classified as a strategic decision. PLM and ERP systems contain a great data repository which enables the improvement of the decision-making process. In this paper, a model of new product evaluation and best product selection on the basis of AHP methodology and ERP/PLM data is proposed. For the decision support system, business and technical factors are proposed for the selection of the best products/prototypes from a set of alternatives. Of course, the same system can be used for the determination of priorities for different product development projects in production companies. The proposed list of technical and business factors in the paper and the hierarchical structure are able to be expanded. The proposed solution can be implemented, without the need for large expenditure, as an option of the ERP or PLM systems dedicated for research and development departments. Further research will focus on decision support systems for configurable products.

References

1. Kłos, S., Trebuna, P.: Using the AHP method to select an ERP system for an SME manufacturing company. Manage. Prod. Eng. Rev. **5**(3), 14–22 (2014)
2. Patalas-Maliszewska, J.: Managing Knowledge Workers: Value Assessment. Methods and Application Tools. Springer, Heidelberg (2013)
3. Patalas-Maliszewska J., Kłos S., Model evaluation of the effectiveness of business processes in terms of managing knowledge workers. Pomiary Automatyka Robotyka **2**, 143–146 (2013)
4. Saaty, T.L.: The Analytic Hierarchy Process. McGraw-Hill, New York (1980)
5. Silventoinen, A., Papinniemi, J., Lampela, H.: A roadmap for product lifecycle management implementation in SMEs. In: XX ISPIM Conference (2009)
6. Sudarsan, R., Fenves, S.J., Sriram, R.D., Wang, F.: A product information modeling framework for product lifecycle management. Comput. Aided Des. **37**(13), 1399–1411 (2005)
7. Wei, C.C., Wang, M.J.J.: A comprehensive framework for selecting an ERP system. Int. J. Project Manage. **22**, 161–169 (2004)

HYRE-ME – Hybrid Architecture
for Recommendation and Matchmaking
in Employment

Bruno Coelho[1(✉)], Fernando Costa[2], and Gil M. Gonçalves[1]

[1] INOVA+, Matosinho, Portugal
{bruno.coelho,gil.goncalves}@inovamais.pt
[2] Instituto Superior de Engenharia Do Porto, Porto, Portugal
fernando.maia.costa@gmail.com

Abstract. Nowadays people search job opportunities or candidates mainly online, where several websites for this end already do exist (LinkedIn, Freelancer and oDesk, amongst others). This task is especially difficult because of the large number of items to look for and the need for manual compatibility verification. What we propose in this paper is a recruitment recommendation system that considers the user model (content-based filtering) and social interactions (collaborative filtering, e.g. likes and follows) to improve the quality of its suggestions. The devised solution is also able to generate adequate teams for a given job opportunity, based not only on the needed skills but also on the social compatibility between their members.

Keywords: Recommender systems · Decision support systems · Match-making algorithms · Jobs · Employment · Work · Teams · User modeling · Content-based filtering · Collaborative filtering

1 Introduction

Social professional networks have had an exponential growth in the last few years, mainly due to the banalization of internet access. LinkedIn, created in 2003, is now the most relevant professional network platform; it has reached 300 million users in 2014 [13], being that 210 million were registered in the last 5 years. As LinkedIn allows the input of job opportunities, if someone is looking for the most suitable job, the universe of search is pretty vast. 3 million jobs vast, to be more precise [11]. These numbers were used as an example for the current job search scenario, but many other similar tools exist online, each having thousands and even millions of users interacting every day.

Of course that one can focus this job search to only one specific activity area, or search on an existing recommended jobs list. However, there is still a need for an extensive and manual analysis of each one of the job specifications (e.g. analyze required experience, technical skills, soft skills, educations, etc.) to know which jobs really are the most adequate to the candidate, or if we are what the opportunity really needs (opposite recommendation).

G. Dregvaite and R. Damasevicius (Eds.): ICIST 2015, CCIS 538, pp. 208–224, 2015.
DOI: 10.1007/978-3-319-24770-0_19

These job search platforms lack in features that could attenuate or even eliminate all this trouble: a precise Recommendation System (RS) that takes in consideration all the parameters that a human resources (HR) specialist would normally take when searching for the best opportunity or candidate. Also, they lack on a very relevant matter – team recommendation. This would represent a very efficient and useful way of searching all the best candidates and verifying which of them would probably make a good team together. Also, this could help an HR specialist finding a perfect fit for an existent team.

In this job search context, the main objective is the recommendation between entities of the domain: users and opportunities. On almost any type of situation where recommendations need to be calculated, one issue automatically arises – possible large volume of items to compare (similarity calculation) and consequently low speed in the recommendations calculation. In this scenario, speed is especially relevant because of the complexity that the entities can reveal. E.g. a user can have multiple professional experiences, soft skills and technical skills associated, so the similarity calculation can be as complex as the complexity of its profile and its interactions with the system. The same logic applies to the opportunities that can be characterized by the same dimensions. The search world dimension problem has special incidence in the team recommendation context, because of the large number of combinations that can be done with a small number of users (e.g. for 15 users, combined in 10 element groups, $15C10 = 3003$).

Another problem has to do with the known cold-start issue [9], that consists on having little to none information about the entities that are part of the recommendation calculation – in this case users and opportunities.

2   Related Work

In this chapter we present you some examples of previous research made within the scope of the same job recommendation problem. These endeavors have helped HYRE-ME immensely by providing excellent problem-resolution thinking, problem analysis and an overall experience when trying to tackle the same difficulties. It is believed that HYRE-ME has made good use of those examples and has improved upon some of the features made available by them.

2.1   A Recommender System for Job Seeking and Recruiting Website [5]

This research has some similarities to our solution, being that this is a hybrid RS that uses both content-based and interaction-based data to make recommendations. Based on that information, it creates a graph that relates all the entities involved and then, using that graph, calculates similarities. The main differences between this system and our solution are: (1) this system does not have the ability to make team recommendations; (2) profile similarity calculations are made using Latent Semantic Analysis (LSA) tools and (3) the system cannot inference new information. This tool analyzes text files that contain the content of profiles (instead of directly comparing each entity's profile characteristics), leading to less precise results.

2.2   The Zen of Multidisciplinary Team Recommendation [2]

This project consists on a framework that is based on a model characterized by three sets: individuals I, expertise areas EA and social dimensions SD. The elements of such sets are captured using three graphs: competence graph, social graph and history graph. This is an interesting approach, because it divides the content into three different data structures, so the content in each one of the graphs is more specialized. However, because the information is partitioned into various graphs, one cannot infer new knowledge that uses information from more than one graph (or at least the database cannot). Although, because the information in the platform has a simplified structure, the recommendation of teams can be executed relatively fast. This solution continues to have the same combination explosion problem already explained, because all the team combinations must be individually calculated and evaluated, as well as their members' compatibility. Also, there are several sources of information which are used for the team recommendation calculations; the quantity of information available is vast, leading to more complexity in the recommendation calculations.

2.3   Reciprocal Recommendation Algorithm for the Field of Recruitment [15]

This project makes two-way recommendations (between jobs and users), which is also exactly what HYRE-ME performs. To make recommendations, they perform the following steps: (1) use explicit information extracted from user résumés and jobs' attribute information and convert them to vector space models (VSM), in order to calculate the similarity of explicit preference (it is not very clear if the job entity is also described through a résumé); (2) they use all the other résumés that exist in the platform to locate implicit preference, according to the proportion of each of the attributes being compared. These steps are followed by similarity calculations, using those explicit and implicit information.

This solution has as main advantages the simplicity and efficiency of the similarity calculation, while giving to the user total freedom to input whatever he *likes* without using rigid forms for profile definition. Although, the use of VSM for the similarity calculations has some issues: (1) user résumés with similar context but different term vocabulary won't be associated; (2) the order in which the terms appear in the document is lost in the vector space representation; (3) keywords must precisely match the résumés' items and (4) words' substrings might result in a "false positive match" (e.g. 'program' and 'programs').

3   Concept and Architecture

HYRE-ME is part of a broader web platform that has the purpose of bringing together entities which can execute tasks and entities which have the need to have those tasks executed. The overall architecture of our solution is represented in Fig. 1.

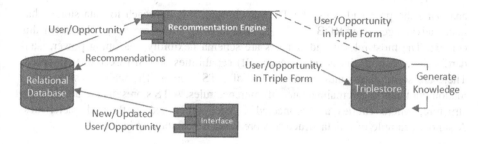

Fig. 1. Components diagram

In the next subsections these components are explained in some detail, before diving into the most important aspect of HYRE-ME: recommendations made in the scope of the Recommendation Engine.

3.1 RDB (Relational Database)

The RDB component consists on a SQL Server relational database that contains all the data from the operational system. Only some information (present in this component) related with the characteristics and interactions between the various entities is needed for recommendations. Some attention was paid as to not overload this component for the sake of recommendations, since the most important criteria for the availability of the database is the end-user interface (see next section). At this moment, the database still lacks some features that could, at a later stage, further improve the performance of recommendations (such as clustering and indexing), so this has to be considered too.

3.2 Interface

The interface refers to the web portal/application that is publicly available for users to interact with and that ultimately uses the features made available by the RS. As users interact with it, the information in the RDB is updated, triggering the recommendation calculations on the Recommendation Engine component. This app has many of the typical features found today on similar-themed platforms, such as social network, badges, messaging, LinkedIn integration and more. One of the most interesting and powerful scenarios is the capability of any LinkedIn user to import some parts of its profile (the compatible ones) into the devised platform, therefore eliminating the so-called cold start problem explained earlier.

3.3 Triple Store

A study was conducted about the best option for the persistence of information of the platform's entities, which would at the same time enable for a fast recommendation generation without having an impact in the web app. Two possibilities were found: a RDB (another one or the same one presented earlier) or a Triple Store (TS). After analyzing the pros and cons, the TS was chosen. This approach to data storage has many advantages over RDB databases, and most of those are very relevant in this context. The most relevant advantages are schema flexibility, reasoning power, standardization, cost, Business Intelligence (BI) capabilities and SELECT queries speed. There are some disadvantages on the use of a TS though. The main ones are information duplication and maintenance of inference rules. A TS stores data in a graph-like structure, where entities are connected to each other and to their characteristics. A simple example of a data structure stored in a TS is showed in Fig. 2.

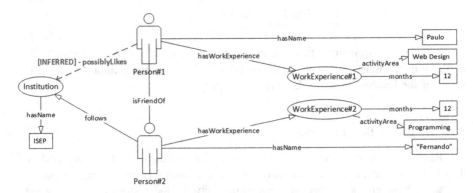

Fig. 2. Graph inference example

The TS contains all the data related with the entities that are relevant for the recommendations calculation. This data contains not only the data related with the characteristics of the entities but also the relations between them (e.g. user's friends, user's likes, followed entities, etc.). This information can then be used by the TS itself to infer new information. As an example, a TS can infer that a person possibly likes a certain institution if (1) a person X is friend of a person Y and (2) a person Y follows some institution Z. This can also be visualized in the Fig. 2.

3.4 Recommendation Engine

This component is the most important of all and is responsible for the recommendations' calculations and the conversions between the RDB and the triple format (for the TS). These actions are triggered for some entity that is either added or updated in the database, therefore only operating when necessary. The recommendations are calculated for every possible combination of entities in the platform (user-user, user-opportunity, opportunity-opportunity, user-group and opportunity-team), so that end users have all of this useful data when navigating through the web app in a general purpose. These calculations are then originally made for all the elements present, with no restrictions made to the universe of search. Conversions between the database and TS are made for every dimension related with the entities that are later used for recommendation. So users/opportunities are completely "converted" to the TS, including not only their fields but also their interactions with the system; this means that after the conversion is made, the RDB is no longer necessary and thus the system is completely free to attend web requests from users. After that, similarities between entities are calculated offline, so that there is no noticeable delay in the user interface. As soon as an entity is modified, all their similarities related to every other entity in are recalculated.

4 Recommender System Algorithms

The core component of the devised work is a set of heterogeneous data blocks that make up for the most important part of the recommendation calculation. It was started by defining which information pieces to attach to each one of the entities involved in the recommendation context and by streamlining that data into common blocks that would be used in a modular way in all recommendation scenarios. We have defined the following large information dimensions: (1) Education; (2) Languages; (3) Soft Skills; (4) Technical Skills; (5) Work Experience and (6) Physical Location. These dimensions are the basis of the similarity calculation between entities, and thus the basis for the more advanced forms of recommendation referred later. The fact that these dimensions are shared between entities eases and fastens the similarity calculation, while increasing precision. The dimensions of an entity "Opportunity" refer to the needed specifications for the related job opportunity; as for the entity "User", they refer to personal characterists of human candidates (users). With the aforementioned structure in place, we will now present how we calculate the most basic kind of recommendation.

4.1 Singular Entity Recommendations

We make singular entity recommendations (SER) by calculating the similarity between one instance of any of the basic entities involved in the job search scenario: user and opportunity; therefore we have the following types of recommendations: **user-opportunity**, **user-user** and **opportunity-opportunity**. User-group recommendations can also be obtained by going through the user-user recommendations of the respective group members (using the average). These calculations take into consideration all the dimensions associated with each one of the entities being compared. Using those similarities, we then calculate a final one that sets a weight to each one of them and then aggregates them all, as shown in Fig. 3. We now explain in detail each one of the dimensions' similarity calculations.

Educations. Educations refer to the academic background related with the entities; at the current time only more formal types of formations are supported. When calculating their similarity, the compared attributes are: institution, activity area (compared based on the semantic distance between them, using Eq. (1) [1]), grade (numeric distance) and degree (numeric distance).

$$sim_{semantic} = \frac{1}{hierarchy_{distance} * b} \tag{1}$$

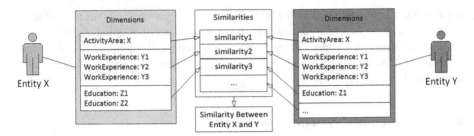

Fig. 3. Entities' similarity calculation

The semantic distance between two entities of the same type is performed in the following dimensions: activity areas (used in their own similarity and within experience and education) and technical skills. The variable $hierarchy_{distance}$ is the number of levels in the hierarchy that separate both concepts, while b can act as the value 1 or 2 depending on whether the comparing entity is a superclass or a subclass of the comparison target respectively (i.e. we gave more importance to specialization rather to generalization).

$$sim_{edu} = (sim_{institution} * 0.2) + (sim_{actarea} * 0.5) + (sim_{grade} * 0.15) + (sim_{degree} * 0.15) \tag{2}$$

In a single education element comparison, the activity area is what most relates two different items (50 % of the weight), while the remaining similarities are auxiliary and imply less relationships between those.

Languages. Languages refer to language skills that entities possess. Compared attributes are the language id and proficiency level (numeric distance).

$$sim_{lang} = \frac{1}{proficiency_{difference}} \tag{3}$$

The above formula relates to a single language, so it is replicated and averaged for all matching language skills being compared.

Soft Skills. Soft skills (SSs) are personal traits and human characteristics that play an important part in the job search problem. Because SSs can be completely defined only by its id (i.e. the existence of that skill), the comparison is directly made. $\#shared_{SS}$ is the number of shared SSs between comparing entities, while $\#total_{SS}$ is the total number of SSs available in the system; this means that similarity is given for matching SSs and the inexistence of SSs (even in both entities) is not classified as similarity.

$$simSS = (\#shared_{SS})/(\#total_{SS}) \tag{4}$$

Technical Skills. Technical skills (TSs) are one of the most important and used information pieces in recruitment and, in the scope of HYRE-ME, are compared based on the next attributes: technical skill id (semantic distance, i.e. Eq. (1)) and proficiency.

$$sim_{tech} = \left(sim_{skill} * 0.7\right) + \left(sim_{proficiency} * 0.3\right) \tag{5}$$

In this comparison, the sheer existence of the technical skill (or a relating one) has most of the used weight (70 %), while the proficiency if left at 30 %.

Work Experience. Work experiences possessed by people or required by opportunities are compared based on the next attributes: activity area and duration.

$$sim_{we} = \left(sim_{actarea} * 0.7\right) + \left(sim_{months} * 0.3\right) \tag{6}$$

Regarding work experiences, the activity area that they relate to (or a relating one) also uses most of the weight (70 %), while the number of months in which it was carried on is less important (30 %).

Physical Location. The physical location is compared based on the real distance between the locations of the compared entities. This distance is more relevant when calculating a user-user similarity because of the *propinquity*, studied by the social sciences, that relates interpersonal attraction with the physical or psychological proximity between people [7].

$$sim_{location} = \left(sim_{city} * 0.9\right) + \left(sim_{country} * 0.1\right) \tag{7}$$

Since the city is not mandatory and it could not be available, some weight has to be put in the country alone (10 %). However, most of the importance in this formula is given to the specific city/region (90 %), depending on the granularity applied to a particular country.

Activity Area. The activity area to where the entity belongs to can have a relevant importance in the similarity between entities. Therefore it is compared based on its semantic distance to other areas, using Eq. (1).

Likeability Ratio. Unlike the other dimensions, which are explicit profile components of each one of the entities, the likeability is an indirect value that measures the relationship between a user and an institution related with a certain opportunity. Equation (8) shows a part of that likeability, which deals with the number of *likes* made to posts from institution members; however, that equation may still add some additional conditions, such as (1) if the user follows that institution or (2) if he is a member of that same institution (hence the following formula has only 30 % of its weight).

$$likeabilityratio = \frac{log(\#postsLiked + 1)}{(log(100 + \#postsLiked))} * 0.3 \tag{8}$$

Final Similarity Calculation. The final similarity calculation weights each one of the explained dimensions with an almost- equal distribution; we have also made these weights configurable through a configuration file, so that they can be further tweaked/refined. We have defined the weights with the following values shown in Fig. 4.

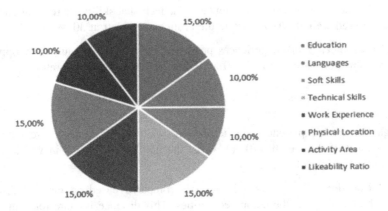

Fig. 4. SER weights

By using all of the previously explained formulae, the final similarity value is then given by (9). Given that the overall formula has 8 components and to stretch their importance without extreme ups and downs, it was decided to put more weight into the most classical elements of job spec profiles (education, work experience, technical skills) and less into lesser complex/important components such as activity area and the devised likeability.

$$
\begin{aligned}
entity_{similarity} = {} & (sim_{edu} * 0.15) + (sim_{lang} * 0.1) + (sim_{ss} * 0.1) \\
& + (sim_{tech} * 0.15) + (sim_{we} * 0.15) + (sim_{location} * 0.15) \\
& + (sim_{actarea} * 0.1) + (sim_{like} * 0.1)
\end{aligned}
\tag{9}
$$

4.2   Team Recommendations

Teams are groups of people; however, not all groups are teams, because a team is so much more than just a set of people together and that fact alone triggers all sorts of changes and interactions between people that otherwise wouldn't happen. With that in mind, we have studied which are the concepts and human traits that may have an influence in achieving the perfect group of users that can make up a good team for a certain opportunity (i.e. only those related with the job domain). Based on a number of different studies, our research has come up with the following four upper-level components that, when combined, are able to distinguish one good team from a simple/plain group of people: (1) number of team members, (2) team cohesion, (3) required competences and (4) physical location of team members. In the next sections we thoroughly detail the research and nature of these components in the scope of team recommendations, as well as how we use them in HYRE-ME.

Number of Team Members. How many people does the team have is one of the major variables to consider, not only because of resources to be allocated for the project but also because it has an impact on the rest of the variables. We have analyzed some previous studies on the subject that have helped us reach a more grounded concrete idea for the team member number.

References [8, 14] have researched, through a simple rope-pulling test, the relationship between the number of team members and the individual member's average performance. The results were surprising, demonstrating that, as new members were added to the team, the average effort by each member actually decreased. This is related with a known phenomenon called "social loafing" (SL) that happens when people exert less effort to achieve a goal when they work in a group rather than alone [10]. Reference [12], that had also studied the SL phenomenon, said that the ideal number of team members is somewhere between 5 and 12, being the number 6 the most relevant in his studies. In [4] it is considered that the maximum number of team members should be 4 or 5. Teams with less than 4 are too small to be effective and teams over 5 are non-efficient. A study made by [6] (that includes as metrics concepts such as size, time, effort and detected defects) showed that in short term projects, bigger teams (with an average of 8.5 workers) reduced only 24 % of the execution time relative to smaller teams (with an average of 2.1 workers), i.e. a direct relationship between the number of people in a team and the productivity (increase) was not found.

Based on the aforementioned literature, we chose to define the number of team members to a maximum of ten. This is the top number of people suggested that a team working together must have, having in consideration productivity maximization and team inefficiency minimization. We also suggest 6 as the number of optimum team size for projects which necessarily will be multi-people, but we enable people to refine that number as they please in the web interface.

Team Cohesion. Groups, as all living creatures, evolve over time. Initially a group is just an agglomerate of people who happened to work together, but the uncertainty eventually gives place to cohesion as the members bond with each other through strong social connections. Cohesion depends essentially on how well people relate with one another, as pairs and as groups; it is what keeps a team together after the presence of relationships between all the members. It prevents team fragmentation, keeping its members in a constant state of bonding, as well as avoids (or at least more easily and rapidly) problems and animosities.

Reference [14] defends that there exist a clear distinction between the individual and the group when one talks about team cohesion. For one, there is the attraction of the individual to the group – how much he/she wants to be a part of it. Then there is the group aspect, represented by a set of perceptions/features that consist, e.g. in the degree of proximity, similarity and union inside the group. Widmeyer also defends that there is a clear distinction between social cohesion and task cohesion. While social cohesion refers to the motivation to develop and maintain social relations with a group, task cohesion refers to the motivation of reaching company or project goals. We can conclude that the ideal scenario would be when both cohesions exist, since they are both positive; indeed, the existence of only one is a bad omen for low cohesion in the long run. In the proposed solution, we chose not to calculate task cohesion, since the detection of this kind of psychological trait is difficult based on the existing data from the operational system. The best way to identify it is analyzing/monitoring the physical behavior of a person when working on a certain task; also, in the context of team recommendation, this variable does not have that much relevance, since people can have a very high cohesion on a certain task and very low on another one.

Social Cohesion. A way of detecting team cohesion is analyzing the social cohesion, since a team is a form of social interaction. We reach this by using a formula that appears in [9]. This $social_{score}$ combines all the following variables:

- Shared projects: the number of projects that each person has in common with other team members (this has a very direct relationship with his/her interpersonal or emotional connection)
- Friendship relations: friendship/contact relationships between team members (just like in Facebook or LinkedIn) are one of the most obvious pieces of information for probable likeability between people
- Shared interests: if team members share the same interests or tastes (if they *follow* the same entities in the social network, such as people, groups and institutions), frequented the same institutions, etc.

Next we describe the approach that was used in each one of the defined variables, in order to make them ready to be included on the $social_{score}$ equation.

Shared Projects. Consider $C = \{c_1, \ldots, c_m\}$ as being the group of connections between elements of a certain group of people. Each element of C connects two people and has an associated weight p relative to the number of shared projects between them. Consider also *max* as being the heaviest weight of the C set and n representing the number of elements contained in that same set. Let U be the set of users that are related in the C set's connections. Based on these statements, we obtained (10, which is a value representing how familiar a team is regarding past projects that their members have been a part of.

$$familiarity_{score(U)} = 1 - \frac{\sum_{i=1}^{|n-1|} |p_i - \max|}{|n-1| * \max}, \forall \max \geq 1; \forall n > 2 \qquad (10)$$

Friendship relations. Consider the set of friendship connections between users from the team being analyzed $R = \{r_1, \ldots, r_m\}$. We represent the number of elements of the R set using the *na* (number of friendships) variable. Consider also the number of all the possible combinations of relations between those users represented by n. With this, we have defined a $friendship_{score}$ that represents, in a certain way, the overall friendship assumption between all the elements from a particular team (11).

$$friendship_{score(G)} = \frac{na}{n}, \forall n \in [0, +\infty], \forall na \in [0, +\infty], na \leq n \qquad (11)$$

Shared Interests. One important step in the team cohesion calculation is the analysis of their members' shared interests/tastes (when in the scope of job-related matters). We have made this calculation using the following connections:

- *Likes* to the same *posts*
- *Follows to* the same entity
- Frequency of the same scholar institution (or same course)

For the sake of brevity, the underlying assumptions about these variables were left out. Equation (12) is the one that handles all these variables. *Likes*, as a more specific indicator, were provided with more weight (40 %).

$$shared_{interests} = likes_{score} * 0.4 + follows_{score} * 0.3 + academic_{similarity} * 0.3 \qquad (12)$$

We have then defined in Eq. (13) how to calculate the final score related with the social cohesion. Consider a certain set $P = \{p_1, \ldots, p_n\}$ that contains a group of people. We have also set weights for the three components mentioned before, such as that shared projects and friendship relations are both 25 % important; these 2 pieces are most probably less existent and frequent in a normal snapshot of the user population than shared interests (which happen more and were thus given more weight).

$$social_{cohesion(P)} = familiarity_{score} * 0.25 + friendship_{score} * 0.25 + tastes_{score} * 0.5$$
$$\qquad (13)$$

Required Competences. For a team to be able to complete a certain task, their members' competences need to cover the ones required by that same task [3] – "If a set of people do not provide complete coverage, then they cannot form a legitimate team by themselves". This means that at least one of their members must fulfill each one of the required competences. In order to calculate a numeric value representative of a team's competence ($competence_{score}$), we use Eq. (14) presented by [3].

$$competence_{score(T)} = \sum_{j=1}^{|C_m|} \Omega_{i=1}^{|P_m|} e(p_i, c_j) \qquad (14)$$

We now explain how the $competence_{score}$ formula works. Consider a group of people $P = \{p_1, \ldots, p_m\}$, a group of key competences $C = \{c_1, \ldots, c_n\}$, and a function $e : P \times C \rightarrow Value$ that allows to calculate the value of a person P related with a C competence. Now consider also the Ω possible values, so that $\Omega \in \{max, min, avg\}$, that helps quantifying the value of the skills of a person according to indicated preferences. The *max* value gives more importance to the existence of experts in a certain skill, while the *avg* gives more relevance to the existence of a balanced team on each of the required skills. The *min* usage gives more importance to minimizing "weakest links".

With the objective of reducing the number of combinations to be calculated (i.e. avoiding using the whole universe of search), we've considered only the top 15 candidates for a given opportunity. These candidates are obtained through the already calculated similarities (SERs) stored in the RDB. This way, we limit the number of combinations to be analyzed to a maximum of $15C7 = 6435$. There is the clear understanding that this kind of limitation may leave out some excellent teams; a great team may not necessarily be composed of the very best of the best, nor can HYRE-ME (or any platform for that matter) predict particular types of problems that may happen between teams (such as psychological disorders). Furthermore, the more the user base increases, the more a specific value limitation is risky and ungrounded, so it is being tried to come up with some techniques to be able to relax this constraint in the medium/long run. Some examples may be the use of artificial intelligence (AI) techniques related with the analysis of long-term data (such as neutral networks and case-based reasoning), the clustering of data regarding any of the information pieces that describe entities, the explicit filtering of data through the web interface, amongst others.

Physical Location of Team Members. In the context of virtual teams[1], the physical proximity of their members can still have a big influence on its success; one of the main reasons is the fact that people's *propinquity* ends up influencing their similarity. This means that not only people's personality plays a role on this likeability, but also their culture/history, easing the interpersonal relations between them. To calculate the similarity between team members related with their geographical location, we have created Eq. (15). In this formula, we sum up the averages of the distances between each pair of team members and we divide this result by the squared number of people, therefore getting a global distance average. The final $location_{similarity}$ is achieved by checking, in a logarithmic scale, how the $avg_{distance}$ stacks up against the overall distance curve.

$$avg_{distance} = \frac{\frac{\sum_{i=1}^{n} d_1}{\#people-1} + \cdots + \frac{\sum_{i=1}^{nm} d_m}{\#people-1}}{(\#people - 1)^2} \quad (15)$$

$$location_{similarity} = -\frac{\log(avg_{distance} + 1)}{\log(100 + avg_{distance})} + 1 \quad (16)$$

Team Score Formula. After the description of all variables that come into play when we evaluate the recommendation of a team of people, we then present the final formula that aggregates them all (Eq. 17). We have distributed the weights this way: team cohesion (35 %), needed competences (50 %, i.e. still the most direct and important comparison made) and physical location (15 %).

$$team_{score} = social_{cohesion} * 0.3 + competence_{score} * 0.5 + location_{similarity} * 0.15 \quad (17)$$

---

[1] Virtual Teams - teams that do not work in the same physical space.

5 Testing and Validation

In order to evaluate HYRE-ME, we have made tests regarding recommendations' calculations. Because the system isn't still properly mature and there's not a lot of real data available, we had to build a dummy data set for this purpose.

5.1 Recommendation Speed

The first test is about the speed of recommendation's generation, i.e. the time it takes for the HYRE-ME algorithm to be run against a particular user or opportunity. Figures 5 and 6 show the calculation speeds for SERs (explained in Sect. 4.1) and team recommendations (explained in Sect. 4.2) respectively. This test was conducted on a machine with the following specifications: CPU Intel Core i7-3630QM, RAM 6 GB 1600 MHz and HDD 500 GB 5400 RPM.

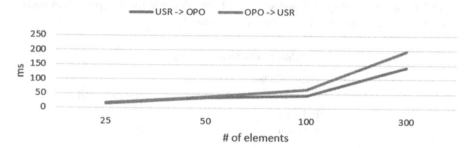

Fig. 5. Entity recommendation speed

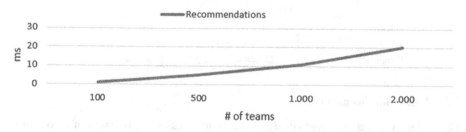

Fig. 6. Team recommendation speed

These obtained recommendation times are acceptable, as they are calculated offline (please check Sect. 3) and are not needed in real-time by the application user. However, as the number of entities in the database increases, this time delay can be a problem. As one can infer by analyzing Fig. 5, if there are 1.000.000 elements in the database, then the average time that would be required to do this calculation is approximately 500 s (∼8 min), which clearly is too high. We also have to take into consideration that we are making an extensive complex analysis to all possible combinations in the RDB. This is mainly due to the need for accuracy and precision of the recommendations' generation. Knowing these bottlenecks, we can make some improvements, such as: (1) increasing hardware processing power, (2) enabling multi-threading and (3) perform data clustering algorithms to split data using thoughtful criteria.

5.2   Precision

As the main goal in a RS is the interest of the recommendations themselves for the user who receives them, we have made a classic precision test to evaluate this matter. In this test, we started by defining 25 very different user and opportunity profiles (different activity areas and experience, etc.). We then calculated SERs between all of those entities and manually evaluated the obtained results, which are demonstrated in Table 1. Using this data we have calculated some metrics that help us evaluating, in a more precise manner, the quality of the obtained recommendations. These measures can be analyzed in the Table 2.

Analyzing the calculated metrics, we can conclude that the SERs obtained through the RS have a very high quality and so a very high relevance for the application users, although more tests are still needed (see next section).

Table 1. Confusion matrix.

Objective class	Predicted class		
		Suggested	Not suggested
	Relevant	21	4
	Irrelevant	0	0

Table 2. Evaluation metrics.

Metric	Result [0–1]
Recall	$21/(21 + 4) = 0,84$
Precision	$21/(21 + 0) = 1$
F-measure	$2 \times \frac{Precision \times Recall}{Precision + Recall} = 2 \times \frac{1 \times 0.84}{1 + 0.84} = 0,45$

5.3   Validation Scenario

The aforementioned tests were made primarily to assess the robustness of algorithms and the overall concept of the platform, which at the moment has been deployed only with the nature of a Minimum Viable Product (MVP) designation and approach. However, HYRE-ME also needs to be validated using other means, such as with real scenarios and more intensive needs. To this end, the following pilots are already being executed: (1) a real use-case of a company in need of freelance consultants in the IT sector (35 user profiles are already present) and (2) the dissemination of the platform into several consultancy companies/technology and business hubs in order to promote the use of the system in today's extremely dynamic, versatile and demanding job market scenarios.

6 Conclusions and Future Work

HYRE-ME is a system that is able to make suggestions, in an accurate and precise manner, between users and opportunities. It can also generate team suggestions for a particular opportunity, based on its complex description requirements. These recommendations are made based on: (1) explicit information from user and opportunity profiles (not only directly compared but based on their semantic distances); (2) social network interactions – e.g. shared *likes*, shared *follows* and items visualization and (3) implicit information, through inference of new knowledge using the TS discovery capabilities. Our tests so far have found out that, being a RS closely related to the content-based nature, it correctly recommends items with a fairly high precision and, since we have moved our most resource-intensive processes into an offline component, recommendations can be used in a real-time application with great success.

However, there is still a lot to be made in order to improve, above all, the recommendation mechanism. For instance, it will be tried to improve the recommendation's calculation **speed** both by increasing the server's hardware capabilities as well as using the server's multi-threading feature. Also, we want to use clustering techniques to reduce the universe of search – e.g. when trying to find the top candidates (or teams) to an opportunity, only calculate similarities to the 1000 closer users. It is also expected to improve the **accuracy** and **recall** of the recommendations by inferring more knowledge about user and opportunity entities. This new knowledge can be easily inferred through the addition of more knowledge rules into the TS. This evidently increases the calculation load of the TS; however, it does not make much difference in response times. In addition, work team search configurations will also be implemented (cohesiveness, competence, creativity, etc.) and make them available to the final user without losing much speed in the similarity calculations. These features will allow the platform users to search, in a more precise way, for the exactly kind of team profile they want. However, since the platform is still in MVP stage, some issues are yet to be dealt with, such as scalability, user acceptance, analysis on the validation scenario, analysis as to how the solution is actually use, etc. On the other hand, research into this area of study will not halt, so we expect to continue making progress into HYRE-ME.

Acknowledgements. This work has been supported by the project WorkInTeam, funded under the Portuguese National Strategic Reference Programme (QREN 2007-2013) under the contract number 2013/38566.

References

1. Blanchard, E., Harzallah, M., Briand, H., Kuntz, P.: A typology of ontology-based semantic measures. In: EMOI-INTEROP 2005 (2005)
2. Datta, A., Braghin, S., Yong, J.T.: The zen of multidisciplinary team recommendation. J. Assoc. Inf. Sci. Technol. (2013)
3. Datta, A., Yong, J.T., Ventresque, A.: T-RecS: team recommendation system through expertise. In: WWW 2011 (2011)
4. de Rond, M.: Why less is more in teams. Harvard Business Review (2012)

5. Lu, Y., Helou, S.E., Gillet, D.: A recommender system for job seeking and recruiting website. In: WWW 2013 (2013)
6. Putnam, D.: Haste makes waste when you over-staff to achieve schedule compression (2015)
7. Rauch, K.L., Scholar, M., University, P.S.: Human mate selection: an exploration of assortative (2003)
8. Ringelmann, M.: Recherches sur les moteurs animés: Travail de l'homme. In Annales de l'Institut National Agronomique (1913)
9. Sahebi, S., Cohen, W.: Community-based recommendations: a solution to the cold start problem. In: RecSys 2011 (2011)
10. Simms, A., Nichols, T.: Social loafing: a review of the literature. J. Manage. Policy Pract. (2014)
11. Smith, C.: By the numbers: 12 interesting LinkedIn job statistics (2015)
12. University, W.: Is your team too big? Too small? What's the right number? (2006)
13. Wagner, K.: LinkedIn hits 300 million users amid mobile push (2014)
14. Widmeyer, W.N., Brawley, L., Carron, A.: The measurement of cohesion in sport teams: the group environment questionnaire (1985)
15. Yu, H., Liu, C., Zhang, F.: Reciprocal recommendation algorithm for the field of recruitment. J. Inf. Comput. Sci. 8(16), 4061–4068 (2011)

Perceived Benefits, Risks and Trust on Online Shopping Festival

Yuan Xu[1](✉), Tristan W. Chong[1], Tomas Krilavičius[2],
and Ka Lok Man[1]

[1] Xi'an Jiaotong-Liverpool University (XJTLU), Suzhou, China
Yuan.xul1@student.xjtlu.edu.cn
[2] Baltic Institute of Advanced Technologies and Vytautas Magnus University,
Kaunas, Lithuania

Abstract. This paper investigated to what extent perceived benefits, risks and trust has influenced Chinese customers' attitude and purchasing intention towards online shopping festival on Alibaba.com. It seeks to investigate critical factors drive the huge business success of the company in 'Double 11 online shopping festival' from consumer point of view.

Keywords: Perceived benefits · Risks · B2C · Online shopping festival · Alibaba.com · Chinese online consumer · Purchase intention

1 Introduction

Alibaba.com is the largest operator of online and mobile marketplaces in wholesale and retail trade in China. The company reached revenues of CNY 52,504 million during the financial year ended March 2014, an increase of 52.1 % over FY2013 (Market Line 2015). This increase might be driven by the continued growth of the retail business of Alibaba.com in China. The company also runs a various range of marketplaces, which attract sellers and buyers with diverse interests. Meanwhile, Taobao.com marketplace is the largest online shopping website in China, meanwhile, Tmall.com is stated as China's most powerful third-party platform for retailors and brands, in terms of gross merchandise value (GMV). In addition, in FY2014, the marketplace of Alibaba.com had GMV of $296 billion with 14.5 billion annual orders (MarketLine 2015).

China's Singles Day is originally created in the 1990s by college young adults who believe the date 11/11 looked as four solitary stick figures. As other holidays, this strange day became noteworthy and strong, somehow, became an excuse for the Chinese to go online shopping (International business times 2013). Consequently, Alibaba.com launched the OSF in 2009 with 27 participating brands to light up an inanimate shopping period between National Day and Chinese lunar New Year in January or February; while in 2013, over 30,000 players including western companies were involved in the 'Double 11 OSF'. More than 20,000 merchants on Tmall.com and Taobao.com are promising 50 % discounts on 'Double 11 OSF' (Lynch 2014).

In 2014, the country's largest e-commerce giant Alibaba.com smashes an online sales record of $9.3 billion on 'Double 11 Single Day' in 24 h (Lynch 2014).

© Springer International Publishing Switzerland 2015
G. Dregvaite and R. Damasevicius (Eds.): ICIST 2015, CCIS 538, pp. 225–235, 2015.
DOI: 10.1007/978-3-319-24770-0_20

Shopaholic singles have stimulated the E-business giant Alibaba.com set this new record for highest online sales revenue generated in one day. In the meantime, one of Alibaba's online platforms Tmall.com set its own record for the most mobile phones sold in 24 h, with selling a miraculous 1,894,867 handsets (Lynch 2014). In this respect, Alibaba.com 'Double 11 OSF' has become one of the biggest OSFs in the world.

There is no literature directly investigated the potential customer attitudes and intentions on Chinese OSF except the research did by Swilley and Goldsmith (2013) who investigated the customers intentions on Black Friday and Cyber Monday. Alibaba.com 'Double 11 OSF' provides 50 % off discount to lure online customers has been popular in China for around 6 years, however, research in this field is extremely limited. There are some previous studies investigated the factors influencing consumers' intentions to participate in online shopping (Hsu et al. 2013); even in the online group buying (Liu et al. 2012). Consumers can purchase online in various ways, thus some people viewed online shopping as an online marketplace, while some others perceived it to be something else such as online auctions, online retailing, online group buying and even OSF, leading analysis of incorrect measurements. Thus, in order to obtain an accurate representation of results, it is necessary to focus on a certain type of online shopping.

This research is the pilot to explore from the consumer and online user perspective how perceived benefits, risks and trust influence Chinese consumers' attitude and intention on Alibaba.com 'Double 11 OSF'. The purpose of this paper is to explore the critical factors influencing behavioral decisions in OSF by analyzing the perceived Chinese customers' benefits, risks and trust. In this regard, this study will help to fill the research gaps through both quantitative and qualitative methods, which means both semi-structured interview and questionnaire survey are conducted to explore the hypotheses proposed in the theoretical model. The data were analyzed by factor analysis and regression analysis through SPSS. Thus, through the statistical results, all the 4 hypotheses were supported. To be specific, the customer attitude positively leads to purchase intention on 'Double 11 OSF', meanwhile, intentions are influenced by perceived benefits, risks and trust. Interestingly, the product and price both showed risks and benefits that influence customer intention. Thus, the results provided concentrated evidence and analysis about OSF and online consumer preference in China. Further, the finding of this paper enables the OSF initiator (i.e. Alibaba.com), even online retailers to gain a better comprehension of the online customer preference and barriers for OSF. The online business managers should not only consider the product and price benefits during the transaction, but also the perceived risks on the opposite.

2 Research Methodology

Quantitative research and qualitative research are not mutually exclusive but interrelated and complementary reinforcing. Combining the two approaches enables researchers discover potential problems and study the same theme from different angles (Smith 1975). Therefore, if we want a comprehensive understanding of antecedents influencing OSF, both quantitative and qualitative research should be conducted.

The main method used is quantitative research enables researchers to evaluate their hypotheses by analyzing and measuring the casual associations between variables (Denzin and Lincoln 2005). To be specific, the emphasis of this research method is on cause-and-effects of behavior. The mathematical procedure is the standard for testing the numeric empirical observation, the information generated from numbers can be demonstrated and qualified, and overall outcomes are presented in statistical terminologies (Denzin and Lincoln 2005). Considering the objectives of this research and characteristics of quantitative research, this study conducted a quantitative survey questionnaire approach to collect data for testing the conceptual model and to find empirical support for research hypotheses.

In the meantime, qualitative research method is also employed to support the quantitative research. Denzin and Lincoln (2005) asserted that qualitative method investigates how and why of the decision making, not just where, when and what, meanwhile, it is an explosive research and a procedure of investigating new things widely used in different fields such as for social science and in marketing research (Smith 1975). Furthermore, the qualitative research interview was used aims to describe the meanings of critical themes in the subject and the main task in interviewing is to seek and understand the potential information of what the interviewees said (Kvale 1996). Thus, this method is used to seek customer in-depth understanding and perception, and to get the story behind participants' experiences in OSF.

3 Data Analysis and Findings

3.1 Descriptive Statistics

A total 203 valid questionnaires were received. The demographic characteristics of the respondents are presented as follows: The sample contains considerably more female respondents (n = 115) than male respondents (n = 88). Female customers compromise 57 % of the age, while male customers compromise 43 % of the age. Regarding the age, 87 % of the sample are aged from 18–27, this sample is just the main target sample of this study. Mean-while, thinking of the popularity among various age group participating the OSF in China, this study also concluded a small number of sample aged from 28–37, which compromise 10 % of the sample and even 6 respondents aged from 38 to 47. As for experience on OSF, 95 % of the respondents have the shopping experience on OSF. This sample characteristic could better represent the customers' attitude and intention for OSF. The details are shown in Table 1.

3.2 Preliminary Analysis

Data analysis found a good fit for the proposed model and gained support statistically for all the hypotheses. In this study, principal components factor analysis with varimax rotation was adopted to every variable in order to ex-am the fundamental components of the model. Factor analysis is applied to find a method to decrease a group of original variables into a smaller spectrum of underlying variables with imperative information as a data reduction technique (Gorsuch 1983). Factor analysis is essential lies in the

Table 1. Descriptive data

	Frequency	Percent
Gender		
Male	88	43.3 %
Female	115	56.7 %
Total	203	100 %
Age		
under 18	2	1 %
18–27	176	86.7 %
28–37	19	9.4 %
38–47	6	3.0 %
Total	203	100 %
Experience on online shopping festival		
Yes	193	95.1 %
No	10	4.9 %
Total	203	100 %

following aspects, identifying the analysis's groups, achieve data reduction and vari-able selection and adopting the results generated from factor analysis to other multi-variate approaches. Therefore, Table 2 shows the collected final results of the factor analysis including 8 items separately explained the internal reli-ability and validity of the gathered data.

Reliability Test. The Cronbach's alpha coefficient is used to calculate internal reli-ability of each variable and construct. According to Hair et al. (1998) higher reliability leads to higher stability. Based on the various value categories of Cronbach's alpha, George and Mallery (2003) provided an accepted empirical rule to explain the internal consistency. The internal consistency is excellent when the value is between 0.9 and 1.0, is good when the value is between 0.8 and 0.9, when between 0.7 and 0.8, it is acceptable. The extent to which the item correlates with the total score shows the construct validity of the items (Hair et al. 1998). In this research, as presented in the Table 2, the Cronbach's alpha value of perceived benefit got 0.657; perceived risks got 0.813; while the trust during the purchase process got 0.770; finally, the purchase intention got 0.804. Regarding on the previous statement of Hair et al. (1998), all the variables in this study were considered to be reliable, thus, the clustering structure of the factors for each potential variable is in accordance with that proposed theoretical framework.

Validity Test. After ensuring the reliability of the collected data, validity test is also concerned in this study as showed in Table 2. To evaluate the adequacy of the correlation construct, Kaiser-Meyer-Olkin (KMO) measure of sampling adequacy and Bartlett's test of sphericity were measured, meanwhile, eigenvalues and factor loadings were investi-gated in order to ensure the concept is well defined by the measures (Hair et al. 1998).

Table 2. Factor analysis results

Variable	Mean	Std.	KMO	Bartlett's test	Eigen-value	Factor loading	Variance explained	Cronbach alpha
Perceived benefits	3.2808	0.75410						
Price benefit	3.34	1.062	0.699	122.606	1.991	0.859	49.779 %	0.657
Product benefit	3.41	1.023				0.694		
Recreation benefit	3.1823	0.95766				0.457		
Perceived risks	3.5616	0.75791						
Product risk	3.62	1.029	0.750	433.891	3.113	0.959	51.889 %	0.813
Price risk	4.06	0.965				0.824		
Delivery risk	3.7020	0.96913				0.491		
Privacy risk	3.22	1.110				0.320		
Financial risk	3.06	1.093				0.293		
Trust	3.2771	0.86738						
Trust on initiator's web site	3.26	1.124	0.758	207.764	2.377	0.697	59.414	0.770
Trust on social networking system	3.37	1.172				0.496		
Trust on friends	3.2365	0.96254				0.430		
Purchase intention	3.5345	0.88653						
Purchase attitude	3.38	1.020	0.500	122.221	1.676	1.676	83.779	0.804
Willingness to return	3.68	0.917				0.324		

Based on Kaiser and Rice (1974), the KMO value set in the 0.90 s was 'extraordinary', in the 0.80 s was perceived as 'meritorious', in the 0.70 s is showed as 'middling', while below 0.50 is viewed as 'unacceptable'. As for KMO value in this study, perceived trust listed in this survey is the most significant one with the highest score 0.758, meanwhile perceived benefit and perceived risk got 0.699 and 0.750 score separately. In addition, the variable 'purchase intention' is not as significant as other variables in this analysis with a low score 0.500. Considering the above analysis, the construct validity of this research is satisfactory. In the meantime, the critical test for significance of all relations in a correlation matrix known as Bartlett's test of sphericity also indicated significant results for validity in this study. The Bartlett's test of sphericity measure of sampling adequacy of the four selected variables are all higher than 120, among which perceived risks got the highest score of 433.891(p = 0.000), other results also seems significant (X perceived benefits = 122.606, p = 0.000, X trust = 207.764, p = 0.000, X purchase intention = 122.221, p = 0.000). This result supporting the fitness of the factor analysis for the fata from the survey based on the criteria discussed previously.

Moreover, the eigenvalues are all qualified (>1.0) with no cross-construct loadings, and most of the factor loadings for items are over 0.5, however, with the statements from researchers, the factor loadings in 0.50 or higher than 0.50 are viewed as practically statistical and significant, while the items with eigenvalue lower than 1.0 or components with rotated factor loading less than 0.50 should be dropped if necessary (Hair et al. 1998). In this sense, from the results showed in factor loading and eigenvalue measure, financial risk and privacy risk with extremely low factor loading results (0.320 and 0.293) should consider to be removed from the perceived risks in this research. Considering the comparatively satisfied eigenvalue of the perceived risks, the privacy and financial risks perceived as security risks in the OSF was dropped from potential risk. Nevertheless, the security risks would be discussed in the discussion section. Apart from that, the scale still indicates suitable validity according to statements from previously researchers.

3.3 Correlation

After confirming the reliability and validity of the quantitative data, correlation analysis was conducted to measure the conformity accuracy of the 4 hypothetic relationships proposed in the previous sections: relations between perceived benefits and purchase intention; correlations lie in perceived risks and purchase intention; relations between trust (on friends, social networking sites, website initiator) and purchase intention, between customer attitude and purchase intention.

It is defined by Hair et al. (1998) that Correlation analysis is the evaluation of relationship between two mathematical variables or measured data, and conducted as one of the most pervasive reported and applied statistical approaches for analyzing research data involving, usually referred to as bivariate correlation. Researchers often use 'r' coefficient (referred as Pearson's product-moment r) to test whether the relationship between any two variables exists and to evaluate how strong or how significant of that relationship (Taylor 1990). Correlations have two significant attributes including direction and strength. Positive correlations emerge while the variables move in one direction, which indicates a direct relationship between the metric two variables. When the correlation efficient at zero indicates that no association exists between the two measured variables, while negative demonstrates inverse relationship among which an increase in the first variable leads to a decrease of the other corresponded variable (Taylor 1990).

The correlation results were showed in Table 3 consisted of Pearson's product-moment correlation efficient and p value which indicated the significant level of the results. All the r values ranged from 0.229 and 0.676 were positive under the p-values of each outcome were smaller than 0.001. According to the theoretical principles discussed before, such results support the appropriateness of the hypothesized relationships in the proposed model. To be specific, the association between purchase attitude and purchase intention was extremely significant (r = 0.676, p = 0.000). As hypothesized in before, the perceived benefits are positively associated with the purchase attitude as well as purchase intention with 0.649 and 0.490 (p = 0.000) r coefficient values separately. The perceived risks are also positively related to the purchase attitude and intention (r = 0.330 and 0.229). Meanwhile, the significant positive association between trust and purchase attitude and intention were confirmed (r = 0.552 and 0.406).

Table 3. Correlation results

		Perceived benefits	Perceived risks	Trust	Purchase attitude
H1: Perceived benefits	R Coefficient		0.372	0.581	0.649
	Sig. (2-tailed)		0.000	0.000	0.000
H2: Perceived risks	R Coefficient	0.372		0.453	0.330
	Sig. (2-tailed)	0.000		0.000	0.000
H3: Trust	R Coefficient	0.581	0.453		0.552
	Sig. (2-tailed)	0.000	0.000		0.000
H4: Purchase intention	R Coefficient	0.490	0.229	0.406	0.676
	Sig. (2-tailed)		0.000	0.000	0.000

** Correlation is significant at the 0.01 level (2-tailed)

3.4 Regression Analysis

After ensuring the associations in the hypothesized relationships in the model by correlation analysis, the cause-and-effect relationship was measured via the process which is known as regression analysis. To start with, simple linear regression is a widely used method to check out the hypotheses via testing the usefulness of one independent variable as a predictor of the corresponding dependent variable (Kirchner 1996). This method aims to identify one variable's value from another variable's value to interpreting the linear dependence of one variable on the other. At the same time, this analysis approach can make corrections for the linear relationship between two factors (Kirchner 1996).

According to Steel and Torrie (1960), the coefficient of determination, R-square, illustrated to what extent the data points statistically fit the proposed model and aims to test the hypotheses and forecasting the potential outcomes. In this study, the four main relationships proposed in the conceptual model are measured separately through the R-square, in order to explain how significant the regression illustrated the variance. In addition, Brace et al. (2012) illustrated that except for R-square, adjusted R-square is recognized as the modification of R-square that adjust the number of participants and variables in this model.

With the theoretical knowledge, R-value, R-square and adjusted R square of four proposed relationships are showed in the Table 4 after running the SPSS. According to the interpretation of R-square referred above, it is evident that the coefficient of item was 0.388, which indicate nearly 38.8 % of the variance in attitude towards OSF was interpreted by variance in perceived benefits. In a similar way, 27.4 % of variance in attitude towards OSF was explained by variance in trust, and 45.6 % of variance in purchase intention was accounted for by the variance in consumer attitude towards OSF. Nevertheless surprisingly, only 9.3 % of variance in attitude towards OSF was interpreted by perceived risks.

Table 4. Coefficients of determination

Model	R	R square	Adjusted R square
H1	0.623	0.388	0.385
H2	0.306	0.093	0.089
H3	0.523	0.274	0.270
H4	0.676	0.456	0.454

In the same time, the standardized coefficients and t-value were also conducted to measure the coefficients. Brace et al. (2012) have asserted that standardized coefficient, which also known as Beta coefficients with the purpose to investigate the strength of the influence of the independent variable on the dependent variable, which also suggest that how many standard deviations that a dependent variable changes, resulting in per standard deviation rise in the independent variable. Upon these implications, the Beta coefficients of the hypotheses reached positive values ranged from 0.306 to 0.676 as shown in Table 5.

The significant degree and the cause-and-effect relationship were explored in this research, by combining the beta coefficient and t-value that associated with how strength the relationships are. As the hypotheses indicated, the perceived benefits have a positive effect on the consumer purchase intention on OSF. (B = 0.623, t = 11.282) Furthermore, the trust on website, social networking platforms and even friends have a positive influence on online shopping intention in 'Double 11' (B = 0.523, T = 8.707). Interestingly, the path from perceived risks to purchasing intention was not as significant as perceived benefits and trust do. (B = 0.306, t = 4.552). However, on the whole, the total four propositions were confirmed (Fig. 1).

Table 5. Simple Linear Regression

Model		Coefficients			
Dependent	Independent	Beta	t	Sig.	Hypotheses
Purchase intention	Perceived benefits	0.623	11.282	0.000	H1: Yes
Purchase intention	Perceived risks	0.306	4.552	0.000	H2: Yes
Purchase intention	Trust	0.523	8.707	0.000	H3: Yes
Purchase intention	Overall attitude	0.676	12.991	0.000	H4: Yes

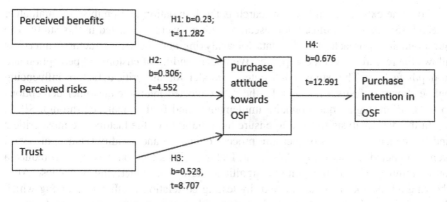

Fig. 1. Conceptual model with hypotheses

4 Discussion

This study is the first to explore the theoretically customer perceived benefits, risks and trust on holiday shopping, particular on the most profitable Chinese online shopping day 'Double 11 OSF'. Data analysis found an appropriate fit for the model proposed in the literature section and obtained support statistically for the 4 hypotheses. The results indicate that the perceived benefits of participating in the 'Double 11 OSF' including relatively low price, variety of commodities and enjoyment of hunting the products in one day. A significant number of people perceive the risk from bloated price during the 'Double 11 OSF'.

This study makes a quantity of theoretical contributions, which will be demonstrated as three demonstrations: Customer perceived benefits and purchase intention on OSF; customer perceived risks and purchase intention on OSF; customer perceived trust and purchase intention on OSF; as well as customer attitude towards OSF and shopping intention on OSF.

Based on the TPB, this research shows a strong connection between customer attitude and purchase intention with the r square value at 0.456, which can be interpreted as nearly 45.6 % of the variance in purchase intention was resulted from the purchase attitude. This result is consistent with Ajzen (1991)'s model. The regression analyzing result (b = 0.676, t = 12.991) also indicated customer attitude has positive effect on purchase intention in OSF.

5 Conclusions

At a first glance, online shopping processes advantages (i.e. convenience, time-saving, easy to search etc.) compared with offline shopping as a new purchase channel, especially in China. Nowadays, the 'Double 11' has become the country's annual OSF and everyone considers it as the best day to do online shopping thanks to thousands of giant discounted products promoted online. As a result, huge benefits were gained by both online venders and consumers. This study focused on OSF and verifies significant perceived benefits, perceived risks and trust on OSF.

To some extent, quantitative research is the foundation and premise of qualitative research (Smith 1975), thus, both research methods were conducted in this study. The questionnaire approach provides data for analyzing and the semi-structured interview allows the researcher get a comprehensive understanding of customers' perception and in-depth feeling. This study contributed a model for the critical factors influencing online shopping festival meanwhile, the data collected intensive customer perceptions to the OSF through a questionnaire implemented and further analyzed through SPSS.

In the data analysis section, to ensure the reliability of the factors, the most critical and fundamental features of measure process reliability and validity (Hair et al. 1998) were conducted in this study. After that, factor analysis method was used to reduce a large number of variables into a significant array of underlying variables. After showing all the four associations exit by testing correlation coefficients, among which the relationships between shopping intention and perceived risks is most significant. In sequence, cause-and-effect relationships are measured. Finally, by using the single linear regression analysis, the hypotheses proposed in the model were confirmed statistically.

As shown in the results section, the most significant factor influence customer attitude and intention to participate in OSF are perceived price benefits and product benefits. The price risk and product risks are perceived to be the most serious hinders negatively influence customer attitude. Meanwhile, trust is configured as the one of the significant antecedents encouraging customer repeat purchase intentions. Thus, the OSF host Alibaba.com should try to increase the website quality, service quality and information system quality in order to maintain the well-built reputation and allure repeat purchase on OSF.

In a nutshell, the results of this study will bring a long-term influence to both practitioners and literature in understanding the roles of perceived benefits, perceived risks and trust in customer attitude and purchasing intention in OSF. The analyzing will serve as foundations of future research in the online shopping promotion area, in particular, OSF.

References

Ajzen, I.: The theory of planned behavior. Organ. Behav. Hum. Decis. Process. **55**, 179–211 (1991)

Brace, N., Snelgar, R., Kemp, R.: SPSS for Psychologists, 5th edn. Psychology Press, New York (2012)

Denzin, N.K., Lincoln, Y.S.: The Sage Handbook of Quantitative Research, 3rd edn. Sage, Thousand Oaks (2005)

George, D., Mallery, P.: SPSS for Windows Steps by Step, 4th edn. Allyn and Bacon, Boston (2003)

Gorsuch, R.L.: Factor Analysis. Lawrence Erlbaum Associates, Hillsdale (1983)

Hair, J.F., et al.: Multivariate data analysis, 7th edn. Prentice Hall, Upper Saddle River (1998)

Hsu, M.H., Chuang, L.W., Hsu, C.S.: Understanding online shopping intention: the roles of four types of trust and their antecedents. Internet Res. **24**(3), 332–352 (2013)

International Business Times: China in buying frenzy on singles day, Alibaba cashes in with online purchases (2013). http://eds.b.ebscohost.com/eds/detail/detail?sid=59701ac2-fb53-434c-9813-79a3b647fc75%40sessionmgr114&vid=2&hid=105&bdata=JnNpdGU9ZWRzLWxpdmU%3d#db=bwh&AN=521525.20131112. Accessed 9 November 2014

Kaiser, H., Rice, J.: Little Jiffy, Mark IV. Educ. Psychol. Measur. **34**(1), 111–117 (1974)

Kvale, S.: Interviews an Introduction to Qualitative Research Interviewing. Sage Publications, Thousand Oaks (1996)

Kirchner, J.: Data Analysis Toolkit #10: Simple linear regression [Online] (1996)

Liu, T.M., Brock, J.L., Shi, G.C.: 'Perceived benefits, perceived risks, and trust: influences on consumers' group buying behavior. Asia Pac. J. Mark. Logistics **25**(2), 225–248 (2012)

MarketLine: Company Profile Alibaba Group Holding Limited Swot analysis 2015 (2015)

Steel, R., Torrie, J.: Principles and Procedures of Statistics with Special Reference to the Biological Sciences, vol. 187, p. 287. McGraw Hill, New York (1960)

Swilley, E., Goldsmith, R.E.: Black Friday and cyber Monday: understanding consumer intentions on two major shopping days. J. Retail. Consum. Serv. **20**, 43–50 (2013)

Smith, T.W.: Strategies of Social Research: The Methodological Imagination. Prentice Hall, Englewood Cliffs (1975)

Taylor, R.: Interpretation of the correlation coefficient: a basic review. J. Diagn. Med. Sonography **6**(1), 35–39 (1990)

Agent-Based Modelling and Simulations as an Integral Functionality of the Business Intelligence Framework

Vladimír Bureš[(✉)], Petr Blecha, and Petr Tučník

University of Hradec Kralove, Hradec Kralove, Czech Republic
{vladimir.bures,petr.blecha,petr.tucnik}@uhk.cz

Abstract. The Business Intelligence concept has been subject of interest in the realm of computer science and business administration for several years. While various analytical tools have been developed and focus on historical data has represented the main stream of research, inclusion of simulations-based forecasts and predictions have been somehow neglected. Therefore, this paper introduces the business intelligence framework in association with agent-based simulations. Moreover, it supports it with the demonstration, in which particular functionality of the Broker agent is used. Finally, the paper also depicts possibilities of further research that can elaborate and further progress the use of agent-based simulations in business intelligence.

Keywords: Agent · Broker · Business intelligence · Virtual economy · Economic model

1 Introduction

Modelling socio-economic systems and consequent simulations represent quite intensive stream of study in the realm of computer science. But quite surprisingly, usage of simulations in Business Intelligence (BI) domain is still under-researched. BI refers to an organisation's capability to gather and analyse data about business operations and transactions in order to evaluate its performance [11]. Several practical tools have already been developed ranging from data integration [13] to BI mark-up language development [10]. Furthermore, diverse features such as adaptability [12], or various technologies such as mobile technologies or visualisation tools for dashboards have been integrated under this umbrella concept. BI systems have both historical and real-time data available. However, as it is apparent from the definition above, the attention is mostly focused on the past and current situation on the market or in the company. Therefore, the aim of this paper is to explore possibilities of agent-based (AB) modelling and simulation in the business environment and based on specific example depict potential application of selected tools into the BI concept. The rest of the paper is structured as follows. Firstly, the brief introduction of research focused on AB modelling and simulation in the business settings is provided. In addition, the virtual economy, which serves as a platform for relevant experiments, is introduced in this section. Secondly, specific functionality named Broker and its basic features are put into context of BI.

© Springer International Publishing Switzerland 2015
G. Dregvaite and R. Damasevicius (Eds.): ICIST 2015, CCIS 538, pp. 236–245, 2015.
DOI: 10.1007/978-3-319-24770-0_21

Thirdly, limitations and research pathways are outlined. Lastly, the paper is concluded with final remarks.

2 AB Modelling and Simulation in the Business Environment

In general, AB modelling is a quite favourite approach, which has already been applied in various fields of study. There are three main tenets associated with this approach [1]:

- there is a multitude of objects that interact with each other and with the environment;
- objects are autonomous (hence, they are called agents), no central or "top down" control over their behaviour is admitted; and
- the outcome of their interaction is numerically computed.

Socio-economical systems have represented a subject of AB modelling for several years, where several features might be successfully used in the BI framework. For example, in the second half of 1990s Vidal and Durfee [17] applied an economic AB system to determine when agent should behave strategically (i.e. learn and use models of other agents), and when it should act as a simple price-taker. They found out mechanisms how savvy buyers can avoid being deceived by sellers, how price volatility can be used to quantitatively predict the benefits of deeper models, or how particular types of agent populations affect system behaviour. In the same year, Janssen and de Vries [8] published their study, in which they describe a simple dynamic model consisted of three main parts: economy; energy; and climate. They prove that the adaptive behaviour can be included in global change modelling. Since this pioneering era, the application area in the business and economy field has been extended. For example, Rao et al. [14] explore general possibilities of AB systems in the e-business realm, Guessoum et al. [7] propose a new adaptive AB model that concludes the organisational forms into the economic models, or Wilkinson and Young [18] employ AB simulation models for recognising and modelling under-lying mechanisms and processes in the marketing domain. In their study, Dama-ceanu and Capraru [5] conduct 11 computer experiments and study the evolution of various banking market indicators. Dosi et al. [6] develop an evolutionary model of output and investment dynamics yielding endogenous business cycles. The model describes an economy composed of particular organisations and consumers. Whereas firms belong to two industries, consumers sell their labour and consume their income. Simulation results show that the model is able to deliver self-sustaining patterns of growth characterised by the presence of endogenous business cycles. Other studies can be used in the BI domain as well, e.g. procurement system described by Lee et al. [9], or management of supply costs [2].

The created model presented in this paper is based on and continuously elaborates models depicted in the previous paragraph. For instance, buyer-seller relation-ships are reflected, or supply chains are established. However, the next sections are focused primarily on one particular functionality, which is used as an example how AB modelling might be used in BI. Nevertheless, the overall system comprises four types of agents: (a) consumer agent, (b) factory agent, (c) mining agent and (d) transportation agent. In general an agent is described as a vector of eight observed parameters

$$AGENT = (pos, w, k, s, con, e, pro, mob, a) \tag{1}$$

where

- *pos* represents the agent's position in the 2-D Cartesian coordinates during the simulation;
- *w* means wealth with the assumption $w_{agent} > = 0$, i.e. no debts are allowed;
- *s* represents storage capacity, which is any type of container in which material can be saved;
- *con* gives an agent's consumption, in case of consumer agents it represents combination of production manufactured by factory agents, in case of mining and transportation agents it represents consumption of capital required for production, and in case of factory agent it expresses combination of products on inputs and labour;
- *e* stands for efficiency (i.e. technological level in case of factor, mining and transportation agents, and qualification of consumer agents);
- *pro* represents a production function, which represents combination of inputs used by factory and mining agents;
- *mob* gives mobility, i.e. working efficacy of a transport agent; and
- *a* stands for agent's affiliation to a colony (defined below), whereas agent → COL that express that each agent belongs to just one colony in the model.

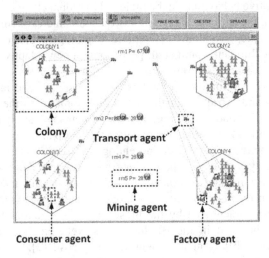

Fig. 1. Visual presentation of the AB model utilisable for BI simulations [adopted from [4]]

Then, particular agents are formally described by the selection of vectors included in the Eq. (1):

- consumer agent: $C = (pos, a, w, s, con, e_C)$,
- factory agent: $F = (pos, a, w, s, con, e_F, pro)$,
- mining agent: $M = (pos, w, s, con, e_M, pro)$,
- transportation agent: $T = (pos, a, s, con, e_T, mob)$.

Moreover, a colony is added as the fifth type of agent (meta-agent) and has the parameters described in the Eq. (2).

$$COL_{metaagent} = (pos, s, w, cw, CP) \qquad (2)$$

where

- cw reports the creditworthiness of a colony; and
- CP indicates the colony population, i.e. size of the colony in terms of number of agents.

The visualisation of the system might be seen in the following Fig. 1. Further details associated with the AB model used in this paper can be found in [4].

3 Demonstration Settings: Using Broker Agent as a Part of BI Functionality

BI can be considered as an umbrella concept, in which several tools, methods or approaches are applied (see Fig. 2). The basic level is represented by transactional system (e.g. Enterprise Resource Planning – ERP, or Customer Relationship Management – CRM), in which raw data are generated. Then, data are transmitted with the help of the data integration level (Extract/Transform/Load – ETL, or Enterprise Applications Integration – EAI) to the upper BI level. At this level, data are stored in various types of databases, where data warehouses represent the main component. Consequently, the analytical level uses data for analytical procedures, either predefined (reporting), or ad-hoc (On-Line Analytical Processing – OLAP). Also, new patterns or knowledge can be discovered here (data mining). Up to now, merely historical data are used and analytical tools are used for evaluation of the past. The last BI level comprises end users tools that can ease human-computer interaction, support decision making, or process outcomes from the analytical component. At this level, simulations based on appropriate AB models might be successfully applied and used in practice.

Facility agents like Broker are used in the AB models for coordination of markets with products and services. The broker is consequently used by agents that belong to the corresponding colony (M-agents and F-agents in the simulation model, or employees, teams, or departments in BI application). Therefore, each agent has an access to one broker only. Broker manages and organises markets with products or services, which are used by specific agents. In this specific case, M-agents and F-agents do not represent end agents, while C-agents are end ones. This structure is inspired by study published by Singh et al. [15].

Usage of the broker agent for coordination activities significantly decreases computations. Single agents (in the form of both buyer and seller) do not need to keep their own

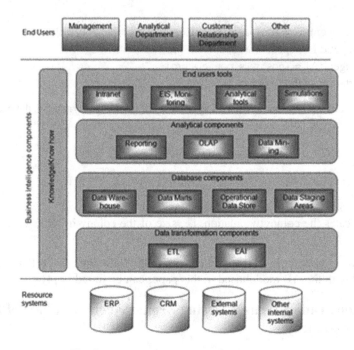

Fig. 2. Business Intelligence structure [3, 16]

databases with information about other agents included. The only information they need to know is location (address) of the broker, which might be initialised, when there is any market-related requirement (product distribution, product procurement). Broker's behaviour is depicted as the flowchart in Fig. 3.

Broker keeps several databases that it uses during work:

1. **SaveRequests** – Database of new products, which should be placed on the market.
2. **NewOrders** – Database of new product orders, which has not been processed yet, neither were they manipulated in any way.
3. **UnexecutableOrders** – Saved orders, which could not have been met during the last execution (e.g. due to lack of products on the market).
4. **CompletedOrders** – Successfully completed orders.
5. **WholesaleMarket** – Products that are traded on wholesale market.
6. **RetailMarket** – Products that are traded on retail market.

New classes Product and SaveRequest were created in order to develop an order structure. While product is defined as name (String) and amount (double), SaveRequest is defined as client (Agent), product (Product), and price (double).

When the system is initialised only one Broker agent is created in each colony. This agent has to go through initialisation (see state Init in Fig. 3). Here, the link to Broker's city is saved (for more effective access) and new Microsoft Excel file is created. This file saves statistics acquired at the end of each simulation round. After the certain period of time (determined in brokerInitialized) Broker gets into the state updateMarket. At this point of

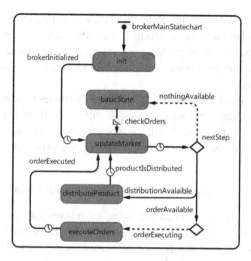

Fig. 3. Statechart diagram of Broker in Anylogic.

time, particular products that are stored by agents are distributed (StoreAgent is created with partially full store). After successful distribution of products on the market, Broker gets itself to the state basicState for the first time. At this moment, thanks to transition checkOrders (e.g. eight time per day) regularly it checks its request databases (SaveRequests, or NewOrders), which are obtained from other agents.

Broker checks size of SaveRequest and NewOrders databases in the decision-maker nextStep after the next achievement of the state updateMarket. The database SaveRequests is scanned in order to prompt distribution of new products that might be part of particular orders. Then, if there are new requests for distributions, Broker gets to the state distributeProduct, in which the function launching products on the market is executed (see Fig. 3). In addition to this, Broker is able to decide, which parameter should be used, i.e. if there it is handling with wholesale products, or retail products. Function distributeProduct (as seen in Fig. 6) scan the whole SaveRequest list. Based on the parameter it decides whether it deals with wholesale or retail products and compare items on the market with the actual one. When the identical item is found (i.e. item with the same provider, name and price), it increases its amount by the requested value. If the opposite case takes place, it creates a new record in the database. After processing of all requests the number of successful distributions is increased and the list is erased. In this way, duplicity records cannot be distributed.

Broker checks the NewOrders database after meeting all requirements for SaveRequests. If there are any requests for product transactions Broker moves to the state executeOrders. In this state availability of each request is checked. If the request cannot be met (i.e. it is not on the market, or not in the sufficient amount), it is shifted to the database UnexecutableOrders, where it is saved to the next day when its availability can be re-checked (this re-checking takes place once in a day by returning of items from UnexecutableOrders to NewOrders).

Once the request can be satisfied, the mechanism for optimisation of the order is run. This mechanism is adjusted to the client's requirement to find the best total sum, which it has to pay. There are various items on the market, which are identical but priced differently. Therefore, Broker uses the function PriceSorter, which orders individual items based on the price. Acquired list of items is consequently processed from the cheapest items to the most expensive ones. Additionally, required and available amount is compared for each item.

If required item amount exceeds the offer, Broker calculates the price and charge to the customer. Apparently, the purchased amount is subtracted from the available amount. This algorithm is repeatedly applied until the whole required amount is purchased. At the end the order is shifted to the database CompletedOrders. Eventually, the database Orders will equal:

$$Orders = UnexecutableOrders \cup CompletedOrders \qquad (3)$$

Therefore, Broker always erases actual list during the transmission back to the state updateMarket. The final outcome from the Broker agent might be seen in Fig. 4. The list comprises items sold on both the Wholesale market, and the Retail market (particular items' parameters are represented by item name : amount : price : providing agent). Apparently, this functionality might be successfully used in the BI systems. In this way, simulations associated with trading and market activities in general could improve decision making. End users from the business or analytical departments can use developed models for supporting their decisions.

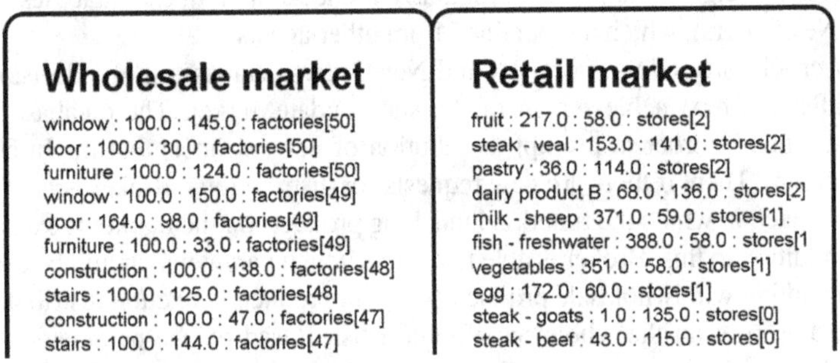

Wholesale market

window : 100.0 : 145.0 : factories[50]
door : 100.0 : 30.0 : factories[50]
furniture : 100.0 : 124.0 : factories[50]
window : 100.0 : 150.0 : factories[49]
door : 164.0 : 98.0 : factories[49]
furniture : 100.0 : 33.0 : factories[49]
construction : 100.0 : 138.0 : factories[48]
stairs : 100.0 : 125.0 : factories[48]
construction : 100.0 : 47.0 : factories[47]
stairs : 100.0 : 144.0 : factories[47]

Retail market

fruit : 217.0 : 58.0 : stores[2]
steak - veal : 153.0 : 141.0 : stores[2]
pastry : 36.0 : 114.0 : stores[2]
dairy product B : 68.0 : 136.0 : stores[2]
milk - sheep : 371.0 : 59.0 : stores[1]
fish - freshwater : 388.0 : 58.0 : stores[1]
vegetables : 351.0 : 58.0 : stores[1]
egg : 172.0 : 60.0 : stores[1]
steak - goats : 1.0 : 135.0 : stores[0]
steak - beef : 43.0 : 115.0 : stores[0]

Fig. 4. Example of the outcome form the Broker agent.

Apparently, historical data from relevant transactional systems located at the lower level of the BI framework might be combined with the simulation outcomes. For instance, it could be experimented with the size of orders in order to find out if it is more profitable to realise big orders on a one-time basis, or buy in parts. The former will include higher prices with savings on transportations, the latter will be associated with lower prices and relatively higher transportation costs. This would increase system effectivity and meaningfulness of its application in practice.

4   Further Research

As already indicated at the end of the previous section, there are research pathways, which are open and should be explored. Firstly, optimisation of the whole agent functionality can be reconsidered. For instance, the initial version had its functionality embedded in the transition between states updateMarket and distributeProducts (see Fig. 5). Later, this functionality has been substituted by the "for-cycle", which is embedded in the state distributeProduct depicted in Fig. 6. In this way, the execution speed increased significantly and thus practical usability as well. Secondly, other item's parameters can be added in order to make simulations more realistic. For instance, sales and discounts represent an alternative that can be inserted in the decision-making process. Furthermore, determination of minimal price or maximal price during trading can be considered. In addition to this, the decision-maker symbol situated at right bottom part of the Fig. 3 might be used for negotiation mechanism, which should ensure the best trading conditions for both buyers and sellers. Therefore, this element has only one outcome at the moment. Lastly, in relation to sales and discounts, functionality enabling price discrimination can be developed. This would enable decision-makers to better evaluate potential impacts of their decisions.

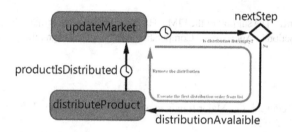

Fig. 5. Product distribution in the former version of the Broker agent.

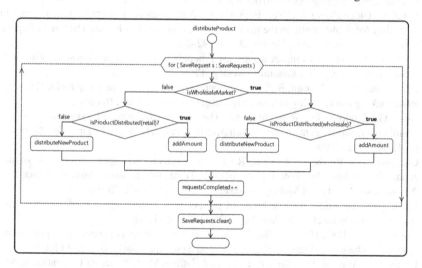

Fig. 6. Broker – action chart diagram of distribution in Anylogic

5   Conclusions

Business intelligence systems have experienced quite significant boom recently. Both researchers and practitioners have already developed various tools helping to process data from transactional systems in organisations. However, in comparison to other analytical tools simulation-oriented research does not blossom. Therefore, this paper depicts how agent-based modelling and consequent simulations might be helpful in the business intelligence domain. Based on the model of virtual economy the paper outlines possibilities of its inclusion into the decision-making processes made by managers. Broker agent serves as an example. This trading agent can help to explore trading strategies or setting of orders' volume or prices. In the current form, the Broker can help decision-makers, however, its elaboration and optimisation might be done in future. In this way, it would become a useful tool applicable in practice.

Acknowledgement.   The support of the FIM UHK Specific Research Project "SCM and Control of Markets and Production in Agent-based Computational Economics" is gratefully acknowledged.

References

1. Bargigli, L., Tedeschi, G.: Major trends in agent-based economics. J. Econ. Interac. Coord. **8**(2), 211–217 (2013)
2. Bunata, E.: Using business intelligence to manage supply costs. Healthc. Finan. Manag. J. Healthc. Finan. Manag. Assoc. **67**(8), 44–47 (2013)
3. Bureš, V., Otčenášková, T., Čech, P., Antoš, K.: A proposal for a computer-based framework of support for public health in the management of biological incidents: The Czech Republic experience. Perspect. Public Health **132**(6), 292–298 (2012)
4. Bureš, V., Tučník, P.: Complex agent-based models: application of a constructivism in the economic research. E M Ekonomie a Manag. **17**(3), 152–168 (2014)
5. Damaceanu, R.-C., Capraru, B.-S.: Implementation of a multi-agent computational model of retail banking market using netlogo. Metalurgia Int. **17**(5), 230–236 (2012)
6. Dosi, G., Fagiolo, G., Roventini, A.: The microfoundations of business cycles: an evolutionary, multi-agent model. Schumpeterian Perspect. Innov. Competition Growth **18** (3–4), 413–432 (2009)
7. Guessoum, Z., Rejeb, L., Durand, R.: Using adaptive multi-agent systems to simulate economic models. In: Proceedings of the Third International Joint Conference on Autonomous Agents and Multiagent Systems, vol. 1, pp. 68–75 (2004)
8. Janssen, M., de Vries, B.: The battle of perspectives: a multi-agent model with adaptive responses to climate change. Ecol. Econ. **26**(1), 43–65 (1998)
9. Lee, C.K., Lau, H.C., Ho, G.T., Ho, W.: Design and development of agent-based procurement system to enhance business intelligence. Expert Syst. Appl. **36**(1), 877–884 (2009)
10. Leonard, A., Masson, M., Mitchell, T., Moss, J., Ufford, M.: SQL Server Integration Services Design Patterns. Apress, New York (2014)
11. Lipika, D., Ishan, V.: Text-driven reasoning and multi-structured data analytics for business intelligence. In: Integration of Data Mining in Business Intelligence Systems, pp. 143–173 (2015)

12. Michalewicz, Z., Schmidt, M., Michalewicz, M., Chiriac, C.: Adaptive business intelligence: three case studies. Evolutionary Computation in Dynamic and Uncertain Environments, pp. 179–196. Springer, Berlin (2007)
13. Petermann, A., Junghanns, M., Müller, R., Rahm, E.: Graph-based data integration and business intelligence with BIIIG. In: Proceedings of the VLDB Endowment, 7(13) (2014)
14. Rao, M., Jain, M.B., Shukla, P.: The use of multi agent paradigm to build an agent based architecture for e-commerce application. Res. J. Eng. Technol. 2(1), 5–9 (2011)
15. Singh, A., Mishra, P.K., Jain, R., Khurana, M.K.: Design of global supply chain network with operational risks. Int. J. Adv. Manuf. Technol. 60(1–4), 273–290 (2012)
16. Tučník, P., Bureš, V.: Inclusion of complexity: modelling enterprise business environment by means of agent-based simulation. Int. Rev. Model. Simul. 6(5), 1709–1717 (2013)
17. Vidal, J.M., Durfee, E.H.: Learning nested agent models in an information economy. J. Exp. Theor. Artif. Intell. 10(3), 291–308 (1998)
18. Wilkinson, I.F., Young, L.C.: The past and the future of business marketing theory. Ind. Mark. Manag. 42(3), 394–404 (2013)

Risks and Benefits of Cloud Business Intelligence

Petra Maresova[✉]

Faculty Informatics and Management, University of Hradec Kralove, Rokitanskeho 62, Hradec Kralove, Czech Republic
petra.maresova@uhk.cz

Abstract. Current market is dynamic. Customer needs change, too. Global competition is also developing and market subjects must be able to interpret information correctly and make decisions instantly. Business Intelligence (BI) tools are based on the ultimate exploitation of data ownership and their transformation into information and knowledge. The increasing amount of data makes it necessary to develop linking business intelligence and cloud computing. This phenomenon brings about new opportunities as well as risks. This contribution is to analyse suitability of linking BI and cloud computing with respect to risks and benefits of cloud technologies. It should result in a group of criteria enabling to provide relevant information about suitability of this technology for organizations. An analysis of accessible studies on decision-making models and cloud computing and an analysis of companies' attitudes to cloud computing and information technologies both served as starting points of the proposal.

Keywords: Cloud computing · Business intelligence · Decision-making · Risks · Benefits

1 Introduction

Business Intelligence (BI) is a set of processes, applications and technologies, whose aim is to efficiently support processes in companies. BI application covers analytical and planning functions of most areas of company management, namely sale, purchase, marketing, financial management, control, property, human resource management, production, or IS/ICT [1]. According to "The Data Warehousing Institute", Business Intelligence unites data, technologies, analytics and human knowledge in order to optimize business decisions in order to achieve company success. BI programs usually combine company data stores and BI platforms of a set of tools in order to transform data into useful business information [2].

BI environments require a large capital layout to implement and support large volumes of data as well as massive processing power, which inflict tremendous pressure on corporate resources. In recent years, cloud computing has made BI tools more accessible as compared to traditional BI. It is expected that customers will slowly but surely migrate from inhouse BI to BI in the cloud [3, 4]. According to Mell and Grance [5] cloud computing is a convenient distribution model for realizing network access to shared computing sources (e.g. networks, servers, data stores, applications and services). The access to these sources

© Springer International Publishing Switzerland 2015
G. Dregvaite and R. Damasevicius (Eds.): ICIST 2015, CCIS 538, pp. 246–256, 2015.
DOI: 10.1007/978-3-319-24770-0_22

may be granted as well as revoked to its users quickly and with the minimal use of means for managing the operation or an intervention of the provider. The whole concept is based on permanent accessibility of shared means. The company Forrester [6] widens the definition by the standardization of IT tools on the service supplier side and by self-service principles on the user side. Cloud computing is a set of standardized IT capacities (services, software solutions or infrastructure) accessible via the Internet on the self-service basis (Staten [6]). Marks and Lozano [7] understand standardization, particularly on the hardware level, as a necessary prerequisite to the initial development of cloud computing. Cloud deployment strategies are often categorized either as Infrastructure-as-a-Service (IaaS), Platform-as-a-Service (PaaS), or Software-as-a-Service (SaaS). Paas service model offers complex hardware as well as software platforms. It is therefore sometimes called cloudware. The PaaS service usually facilitates creating user interfaces and includes tools and services for developing applications and makes it possible to design, develop, test, implement and host [8]. Software as a Service is an application licensed as a service rented to a user. The SaaS model has a great potential among small and medium enterprises that need flexible IT supporting their growth. Large enterprises use the SaaS model in most cases as a solution to their supporting processes. Infrastructure as a Service is a model that enables the provider to provide data storage, computing performance for data processing, network infrastructure and other basic computing sources that enable the user to implement and run any software – whether operation systems or applications [9]. Figure 1 depicts linking BI and cloud computing.

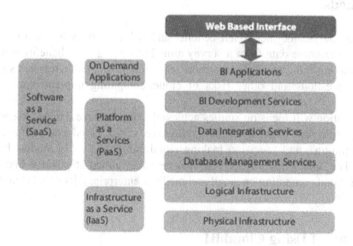

Fig. 1. Linking BI and cloud computing, source: [10]

BI has become an important asset with the advent of knowledge economy and the need to store and process enormous amounts of data, which is evidenced by the following figures. Worldwide business intelligence (BI) software revenue will reach $13.8 billion in 2013, a 7 percent increase from 2012, according to Gartner, Inc. The market is forecast to reach $17.1 billion by 2016. Cloud-based Business Intelligence (BI) is projected to grow from $.75B in 2013 to $2.94B in 2018, attaining a CAGR of 31 % (Fig. 2).

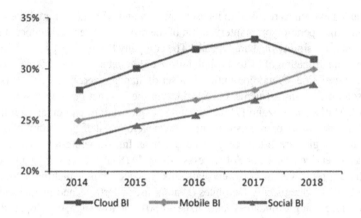

Fig. 2. Global business intelligent market, by technologies, 2013–2018, source: [10]

Business Intelligence in connection with cloud computing may create new opportunities. It also provokes asking questions concerning data safety. This contribution therefore aims to analyse the suitability of linking BI and cloud computing with respect to risks and benefits of cloud technologies.

2 Methods

In order to analyse the mentioned benefits and risks, retrospective analysis will be employed to examine data from a survey aimed at finding what benefits and barriers cloud computing bring about. Furthermore, research of accessible resources related to legislative questions and other risks of cloud computing implementation will be employed.

The attention will focus on studies achieved from database named Science Direct under the keywords "cloud business intelligence", "risk cloud computing", "benefit cloud computing", and "decision making cloud computing". 112 studies have been analysed. The author also uses a previous research, aimed at positive and negative impacts of cloud computing on small and medium enterprises. Its results can be found in [11].

3 Benefits of Using Cloud BI

Advantages of using BI in cloud are clear when a quick response to instant changes of market conditions or an analysis of immediate business opportunity is required [12]. Its benefit is undeniable in the field of marketing and business when it is necessary to analyse data within hours, or days after finishing a marketing campaign. In case of traditional IT solutions such a speed is unthinkable as traditional BI cannot usually enable expeditious processing of external data by the company's own employees from various departments. On the other hand, it is necessary to closely cooperate with the internal IT department, which is responsible for the data store. Moreover, such changes are very expensive.

This technology can potentially improve the company's position on the market. Among the frequently mentioned benefits belong lower costs of IT departments, an ability to flexibly change requirements for provided services and data access from anywhere. There are however many more advantages [13]. The main idea of cloud computing is the fact that the user pays just for what they consume. Generally speaking, it results in potential **lowering the costs** of the following items:

- personnel – it is possible to either lower the number of IT specialists or more efficiently use their time,
- hardware, real estate, energy, cooling and maintenance,
- software and software licences – from the financial point of view, in the long-term the SaaS model operation is not necessarily much cheaper, there is however the fact of even distribution of costs in time without unexpected costs and with savings of indirect costs.

The provider offers an **instant access** to a wide range of services. The flexibility enables to flexibly react to changing business requirements.

The implementation of IT capacities usually requires a big initial investment, particularly into hardware. Providers often offer accounting models on the basis of the amount of used system means. They charge according to the time the company spends in the cloud system, or according to its consumption of sources (connection, transmitted data, use of storage space). In the cash flow model all these items are subsequently clearly depicted, which enables the company to have a detailed and clear list of their expenditures. It may lead the company to reassess its demand for IT services and optimize it.

Cloud computing provides new opportunities for sharing and cooperation. For example, a general overhaul of e-mailing system, using virtual space and web conferences. Such forms of cooperation accelerate and improve communication among individual companies or within a company as well as labour productivity.

Providers will manage competences and services which are not key to most companies' activities and their managements. Consequently, they may refocus their attention from constant repairs of software and other computing problems to new strategic objectives and technologies, which are important for achieving their business objectives. Data stored in cloud remain accessible all the time, no matter what happens to the user's physical device (e.g. theft). Moreover, enciphering used by big companies providing cloud services may ensure better safety than the company's own safety arrangements.

The above mentioned benefits are described in the following studies: [14–21].

4 Risks of Using Cloud BI

Cloud computing, as any other technology, has its disadvantages and related risks. The three risks of cloud computing that are most frequently mentioned in international studies are as follows: risk of mistakes and higher costs during the implementation of the system, problems with possible inaccessibility of the service and data safety at the provider. In practice, in relation to cloud computing other questions (e.g. that of trust in this new technology, legislative risks, geopolitical risks, dependence on the provider, or interoperability among providers) are being asked and discussed.

Data safety has lately been a hotly debated topic not only in cloud computing but in the whole field of information technologies. A lot of studies focusing on cloud computing technologies show that companies consider data safety to be extremely important. According to a survey done by IDC, a business analytics company, among 244 IT department managers, problems related to data safety featured as number one problem in almost 75 % of responses [22]. Another survey, done by CIO Research among 173 IT specialists in managerial positions arrived at a similar conclusion – data safety is most significant for 45 % of respondents [23].

Geopolitical risks must be considered in relation to political decisions or changes in the country in question which have negative influence on interests of other countries, companies and individuals. From the service provider's and its customer's points of view there are risks resulting from the geographical position of servers and other computing tools that serve to providing a service and storing users' data. Such risks may include physical destruction, switching off or a violent takeover of a part or the whole of the provider's computing infrastructure, which may bring about a threat to data safety.

There is a form of defence against risks linked to the above mentioned events. It is a reliable and consistently applied replication and data backup in a location other than the source server. To limit the loss of data accessibility related to geopolitical risks, the customer should know the geographical location of servers (at least within the country in question) and the provider's infrastructure. The customer should ask if both data and cloud services are replicated into other servers in geographically distant locations to ensure sufficient redundancy. A request for replication and data backup in other locations should be a matter of course. Even if that is the case, it is advisable to know at least in what countries the replicated data are located.

Data accessibility is also related to legislative risks that arise from the legislation of the country where the user of the service has its headquarters. There may also be laws facilitating data access to the third parties (police, state institutions), for instance the Electronic Communications Privacy Act in the USA [24], or laws that limit storing the data of enumerated institutions in computing systems located in certain countries, e.g. Data Protection Act in Great Britain [25].

Legislative risks linked to data safety rests on the problems of ownership and protection of data stored in cloud services. The European Parliament and The European Council passed the Data Protection Directive 95/46/EC in 1995. Its purpose was to ensure and unify personal data protection regulations concerning European citizens from all EU countries [26]. This directive orders that EU citizens' personal data transferred outside the EU can get only to countries providing an adequate level of protection. The list however does not contain countries where there are data centres for cloud services often located, including the USA, China, India, the Philippines and others [27]. Moreover, in the USA all companies are obliged to make all data available to the Government, which means that cloud computing providers have to make their customers' data available to the US Government, no matter what country these customers come from. It may be a problem for non-American users. Similarly, there is a problem with personal data protection duty. It is recommended to classify data that a company works with according to the levels of protection (public, internal, personal data). It is necessary to get acquainted with the legislation of the country where the cloud provider is headquartered and the country, into which the data may potentially be transferred. Based on the gathered information, the user has to assess the legislative risks and decide what data they will store in their own computing environment and what data they will transfer to the computing infrastructure of the provider.

5   Decision Making Criteria for Cloud Computing

Due to the above mentioned facts, the company considering the implementation of BI on cloud computing has to be able to decide correctly on how to use this technology and what data to store in this way. There are certain decision-making models and criterion-related questions.

The Open Group [28] in cooperation with NIST provides a decision-tree, a scheme of questions which gradually lead to the recommendation whether or not to use cloud computing. The questions are as follows:

- Is your company structure horizontal or vertical?
- Are the processes differentiated?
- Do there exist any barriers to cloud computing?
- Are the key entrepreneurial activities in harmony with this technology?
- Is IT in company isolated from company processes?

Other questions aim at technology and they treat the following problems: distribution model (mainly PaaS), current state and functionality of HW, technical requirements for the system and performance. The organization has to decide which processes are key and therefore should be managed by the company itself. Then, risks should be specified. Potential benefits of the technology are as follows: lowering the figure of the TCO indicator, improved cash flow, transition from investment costs to OPEX, improving the function of the domain or an increase of its expert knowledge.

According to Ross [28], the existing decision-making model contains the following questions which the company should be able to answer before implementing BI on cloud computing.

- Does the company work with sensitive or critical data?
- Does the current company infrastructure correspond to this situation?
- Is the solved – is it possible to locate data with the third party?
- Is it possible to implement cloud computing with respect to inner directives?
- Is this solution effective as for its costs?
- Are the SLA parameters set?

Another set of questions is linked to the implementation of the technology and to the possibilities and requirements of the system restore.

The decision-making model according to Vivanco et al. [29], which is based on the situation of small and medium enterprises in Spain, focuses on the benefits and suitability of cloud computing in the field of SaaS for organizations. The preliminary parameters are:

- the characteristics of the company (number of employees, industry),
- the company's priorities in strategic decision-making.

The organization should specify its priorities in certain areas by matching importance to the offered criteria. On this basis, solutions are recommended within the frame of SaaS.

The McKinsey company's [30] decision-tree for determining the distribution model is based on questions about technological aspects of choosing a platform in relation to the financial possibilities of the company and its return on investment (ROI) requirement. Then, two principal areas are specified, namely *safety* (accessibility, authorization, recovery from mistakes) and *management* in relation to individual models (risk management, determining responsibilities and competences). The decision-tree is based on the SaaS model and its acceptability.

- Is SaaS a suitable option for the organization?
- Are there any acceptable providers?
- Is the ROI for SaaS acceptable?
- Is the ROI for PaaS acceptable?

Based on the answers, the user is recommended either SaaS, or PaaS, or IaaS distribution model.

According to Marešová and Klímová [31] three areas should be specified: the company characteristics, strategic objectives, technical requirements.

In relation to the first area, if the company has more subsidiaries in various locations, its employees work in the field or from home, and if recently there has not been any substantial investment in its IT system, it is advisable to recommend cloud computing. Then it is important how the inner directives for data treatment are set, whether companies work with their clients' sensitive data and it is necessary to take into account various countries' legislative directives that regulate personal data protection. Strategic management of companies aims at the good description of the company's IT equipment flexibility in relation to the strategic objectives and their changes. Companies should be aware of whether their IT is resilient in case of a breakdown, whether it is feasible to increase data storage capacity, whether their IT sufficiently supports business continuity. When there are any weaknesses, then the corresponding company processes and data has to be specified and possible solutions proposed with respect to the distribution model. Last but not least, technical parameters of component capacity and performance should be defined.

6   Discussion

To sum up, three basic questions – those related to technical, operational and economic criteria – appear in decision-making models [32].

Technical criteria represent a wide spectrum of parameters and features of information technologies and infrastructure. It is usually possible to exactly quantify or specify these criteria. *Operational criteria* are important operational effectiveness indicators of the current/final solution. Problems of an effective proposal and smooth operation of information technologies in organizations are addressed by various methods and approaches (ITIL, TOGAF, FCAPS, or IT Governance). All these approaches share an emphasis on linking technological and economic views of implementing information technologies in company processes. Among the most significant qualitative factors belong the user affability and a system of user support, platform flexibility, speed and difficulty of development of new applications and requirements. For this reason, Service Level Agreements (SLAs), where the requirements are stated, are used. *Economic-financial criteria* are primary indicators of economic effectiveness of the final solution in relation to the current one. Among the most significant quantifiable criteria belong investments into infrastructure and software solutions. Economic criteria fundamentally influence the selected model of cloud computing services.

At the same time, it is impossible to make a decision without applying this kind of information on the actual processes, including their characteristics, in the company (Fig. 3).

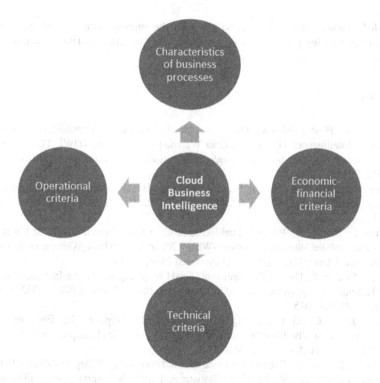

Fig. 3. Criteria for the use of cloud business intelligence, source: author

7   Conclusion

Business Intelligence, which was established in the 1980s, is used as a supporting tool in many a decision-making process. It is predicted that it will be increasingly used particularly together with other technologies like mobile applications, social networks or cloud computing. This is due to the fact that modern technologies increase efficiency in business processes and in learning to the new generally [33–38]. This contribution aims to analyses whether it is suitable to link BI and cloud computing with respect to risks and benefits of cloud technologies. A lot of analysts consider this connection to be promising or they specify benefits and risks [39] or conditions suitable for cloud deployment [40]. In this paper several criteria and criterial questions in relation to the risks and benefits of cloud computing has been proposed. This criteria can help to managers to make correct decision whether and how to transfer data to the cloud and which form should be chosen. Nonetheless, there are still several unresolved legislative problems related to data safety and many are scared of handing their data over to the third party. It is therefore essential to analyse company processes, specify possible benefits and technical requirements in order to make the right final decision about the range of using cloud-based Business Intelligence.

Acknowledgement. The paper was written with the support of the specific project grant "Determinants affecting job satisfaction" granted by the University of Hradec Králové, Czech Republic.

References

1. Novotný, O., Pour, J., Slánský, D.: Business Intelligence. Czech Republic, Grada (2005)
2. Business Intelligence: TDWI -The Data Warehousing Institute. TDWI. TDWI: The Data Warehousing Institute. http://tdwi.org/portals/business-intelligence.aspx (2012). Accessed 28 Mar 2015
3. Tamer, C.H., Kiley, M., Asharfi, N., et al.: Risks and Benefits of Business Intelligence in the Cloud. http://www.nedsi.org/proc/2013/proc/p121023001.pdf (2013). Accessed 28 Mar 2015
4. Menon, L., Rehani, B.: Business Intelligence on the Cloud: Overview and Use Cases. http://www.tcs.com/SiteCollectionDocuments/White%20Papers/HighTech_Whitepaper_Business_Intelligence_Cloud_0412-1.pdf (2012). Accessed 28 Mar 2015
5. Mell, P., Grance, T.: The NIST Definition of Cloud Computing. In National Institute of Standards and Technology. http://www.sciencedirect.com/science/article/pii/S0167923610002393 (2009). Accessed 28 Mar 2015
6. Staten, J.: Is Cloud Computing Ready For The Enterprise? In: Forrester. https://www.forrester.com/Is+Cloud+Computing+Ready+For+The+Enterprise/fulltext/-/E-RES44229 (2008). Accessed 28 Mar 2015
7. Marks, E., Lozano, B.: Executive's guide to cloud computing. Wiley, Hoboken (2010)
8. Horalek, J., Sobeslav, V., Pavlik, J.: Statistic and analysis of service availability in cloud computing. In: IDEAS 2014, pp. 310–313. BytePress, Porto (2014)
9. Mell, P., Grance, T.: The NIST Definition of Cloud Computing (Draft): Recommendations of the National Institute of Standards and Technology. http://csrc.nist.gov/publications/nistpubs/800-145/SP800-145.pdf (2011). Accessed 28 Mar 2015
10. Gartner. Gartner Says Worldwide Business Intelligence Software Revenue to Grow 7 Percent in 2013. http://www.gartner.com/newsroom/id/2340216 (2013). Accessed 28 Mar 2015
11. Marešová, P., Hálek, V.: Deployment of cloud computing in small and medium sized enterprises in The Czech Republic. E+M Ekonomie Manage. **17**(4), 159–174 (2014)

12. Tamer, Ch., Kiley, M., Ashrafi, N., et al.: Risks and benefits of business intelligence in the cloud. http://sitic.org/wp-content/uploads/Risks-and-Benefits-of-Business-Intelligence-in-the-Cloud.pdf (2011). Accessed 17 Jun 2015

13. Marešová, P.: Potential of ICT for Business in the Czech Republic. Professional Publishing, Hungary (2013)

14. Armburst, M. et al.: Above the Clouds: a Berkeley View of Cloud Computing. http://www.eecs.berkeley.edu/Pubs/TechRpts/2009/EECS-2009-28.html (2009). Accessed 28 Mar 2015

15. Goncalves, V., Ballon, P.: Adding value to the network: mobile operators' experiments with software-as-a-service and platform-as-a-service models. Telematics and Inform. **28**(1), 12–21 (2011)

16. Marston, S., Zi, L., Bandyopadhyay, S., Zhang, J., Ghalsasi, A.: Cloud computing – the business perspective. Decis. Support Syst. **1**(51), 176–189 (2011)

17. Marešová, P.: Knowledge management in the Czech companies. E+M Ekonomie Manage. **13**(1), 131–143 (2010)

18. Marks, E.A., Lozano, B.: Executive's Guide to Cloud Computing. Wiley, New Jersey (2010)

19. Hogan, M.: How databases can meet the demands of cloud computing. http://www.scaledb.com/pdfs/CloudComputingDaaS.pdf (2008). Accessed 28 Mar 2015

20. Rosenthal, A., Mork, P., Li, M.H., Stanford, J., Koester, D., Reynolds, P.: Cloud computing: s new business paradigm for biomedical information sharing. J. Biomed. Inform. **12**, 342–353 (2010)

21. Velte, T., Velte, A., Elsenpeter, R.: Cloud Computing: a Practical Approach. McGraw-Hill Companies, New York (2010)

22. Gens, F.: IT Cloud Services User Survey, pt. 2: Top Benefits & Challenges. IDC. IDC eXchange. http://blogs.idc.com/ie/?p=210 (2008). Accessed 28 Mar 2015

23. Mather, T., Kumaraswamy, S., Latif, S.: Cloud Security and Privacy: an Enterprise Perspective on Risks and Compliance, pp. 240–245. O'Reilly, Sebastopol (2009)

24. Lanois, P.: Privacy in the age of the cloud. Journal of Internet Law. Business Source Complete, pp. 8 (2011)

25. Choo, R.: Cloud computing: challenges and future directions. Trends & Issues in Crime & Criminal Justice. http://search.ebscohost.com (2010). Accessed 28 Mar 2015

26. Hradilová, J.: Ochrana osobních údajů v Evropské unii. Ikaros. http://www.ikaros.cz/node/4552 (2008). Accessed 28 Mar 2015

27. The OpenGroup, Making standards work: Cloud Buyers' Decision Tree. The Open Group Guide. https://downloads.cloudsecurityalliance.org/initiatives/guidance/Open-Group-Cloud-Computing-Book.pdf (2010). Accessed 28 Mar 2015

28. Ross, L.: The University of Queensland. Cloud deployment model decision tree. https://www.its.uq.edu.au/filething/get/12331/Cloud%20deployment%20model%20decision%20tree.pdf. Accessed 28 Mar 2015

29. Vivanco, Z.J., Belver, R.R., Cillerelo, E., Osa, A.F.J., Garechana, G.: INSISOC. Decision tool based on cloud computing technology. In: Book of Proceedings of the 7th International Conference on Industrial Engineering and Industrial Management - XVII Congreso de Ingeniería de Organización, pp. 137–146

30. Kundra, V.: Getting ahead in the cloud. Federal cloud computing strategy, Washington, DC (2011)

31. Marešová, P., Klímová, B.: Investment evaluation of cloud computing in the European business sector. Appl. Econ. **47**(36), 3907–3920 (2015)

32. Marešová, P., Kuča, K.: Assessing the effectiveness of cloud computing in European countries. In: Proceedings of the 4th International Conference on Computer Engineering and Networks, pp 769–775. Springer International Publishing, Switzerland (2015)

33. Bartuskova, A., Krejcar, O., Selamat, A., et al.: Framework for managing of learning resources for specific knowledge areas. In: 13th International Conference on Intelligent Software Methodologies, Tools, and Techniques (SoMeT), Frontiers in Artificial Intelligence and Applications, vol. 265, pp. 565–576 (2014)

34. Bartuskova, A., Krejcar, O.: Evaluation framework for user preference research implemented as web application. In: Bădică, C., Nguyen, N.T., Brezovan, M. (eds.) ICCCI 2013. LNCS, vol. 8083, pp. 537–548. Springer, Heidelberg (2013)

35. Mohelská, H., Sokolová, M.: Effectiveness of using e-learning for business disciplines: the case of introductory management course. E&M Ekonomie Manage. 17(1), 82–92 (2014)

36. Mohelská, H., Sokolová, M.: The competence and roles of territorial administration: the results of primary research. In: 9th International Conference on Hradec Economic Days 2011 - Economic Development and Management of Regions Location (2011)

37. Brunet-Thornton, R., Bures, V.: Cross-cultural management: establishing a Czech benchmark. E&M Ekonomie Manage. 15(3), 46–62 (2012)

38. Bures, V., Jasikova, V., Otcenaskova, T., et al.: A comprehensive view on evaluation of cluster initiatives. In: 8th European Conference on Management Leadership and Governance (ECMLG), pp. 74–79. Neapolis Univ Pafos, Paphos (2012)

39. Kasen, M., Hassanein, E.E.: Cloud Business intelligence survey. Int. J. Comput. Appl. 90(1), 23–29 (2014)

40. Mircea, M., Micu, B., Stoica, M.: Combining Business Intelligence With Cloud Computing To Delivery Agility In Actual Economy. http://www.ecocyb.ase.ro/12011%20pdf/Marian %20Stoica.pdf (2011). Accessed 17 Jun 2015

Enterprise Resource Planning Systems as a Support Tool of Increasing of Performance of the Company

Helena Jacova[✉] and Josef Horak[✉]

Faculty of Economics, Technical University of Liberec, Liberec, Czech Republic
{helena.jacova,josef.horakl}@tul.cz

Abstract. Nowadays, enterprises increasingly rely on modern Enterprise Performance Management (EPM) systems. These systems are used to improve the performance, quality and transparency of a company's financial management, as well as to reduce the company's costs and expand its customer base. These systems are part of Business Intelligence and they include metrics and methodologies aimed at improving the company's performance. One way to improve a company's performance is to implement Enterprise Resource Planning Systems into the corporate environment. The present article includes an assessment of a questionnaire survey that was carried out among enterprises in the Czech Republic, namely in the geographical areas of central and north-east Bohemia. It contains responses concerning the implementation of ERP systems, opinions on the use and operation of such systems and the information they provide, and – above all – it deals with problems that are encountered by ERP system users in corporate practice.

Keywords: Enterprise resource planning systems · Performance of the company · Implementation of ERP systems · Problems connected with the usage of ERP systems · Survey

1 Introduction

Nowadays, being able to successfully operate in a competitive environment is crucial to any enterprise. This requires having material information available at the right time and in the right place, i.e. something that can be facilitated through introducing an appropriate information system in the company. Information systems are based on monitoring and recording individual events that have occurred as part of the operation of an organisation. A system that is conceived in this way mainly relies on internal information sources. Obviously, an organisation needs a much broader range of information for business management. An organisation must therefore also monitor the external environment and respond flexibly to any on-going changes in it.

Each company is looking for ways to significantly and radically improve the effectiveness of business processes to a point where the costs can be reduced to a minimum level while maintaining the required quality of the goods or services produced. One possible way to reduce costs is to implement an Enterprise Resource Planning System into the company's environment.

© Springer International Publishing Switzerland 2015
G. Dregvaite and R. Damasevicius (Eds.): ICIST 2015, CCIS 538, pp. 257–267, 2015.
DOI: 10.1007/978-3-319-24770-0_23

To enable effective financial management of the company, business information systems are continuously improved. These information systems provide the management of the company with required information which are necessary for right decision making and successful management of the company. For this purpose, new or modified Enterprise Resource Planning (ERP) systems are used. These systems enable a faster reaction to the current situation of the company as well as changes in its environment.

A correctly set information system allows for quickly and efficiently identifying a company's weaknesses that underlie the company's inefficiencies or might cause problems in the future, and also to recognise the strengths that need to be promoted and that the company can build upon in the future. For an entity to be successful, it cannot rely solely on the given information system, trusting that its implementation will improve the effectiveness of the company's production activities. Unless each key management process works well in a given entity, no information system can guarantee its success [1]. The actual integration of an information system is very expensive, which is precisely why it is necessary to consider whether it is necessary to implement the system at all and, if so, how to select the optimal system that will serve as an effective tool in competition.

However, it is important to keep in mind that no information system is able to generate high-quality and reliable information unless processes and algorithms have been set correctly by administrators, company owners or key users. In the subsequent phase, the proper operation of the system is dependent on relevant data entered by end users. And ultimately, the company's decisions depend on the management's experience and knowledge in the relevant area of business, but they also rely greatly on the results and the data that are provided by the information system.

2 Methodology

The methodology of the paper is based on the literature overview; the methodology of the research is based on the survey. For the purpose of this article an electronic survey was implemented back in February and March 2014 in companies situated in the Czech Republic. The vast majority of analysed companies were located in the Central and North-East part of Bohemia. The survey consisted of 3 main parts: first part contained basic information about a business entity, second part was focused on evidence of environmental costs in these companies and the last part analysed usage of ERP Systems and problems of financial management. The main goal of the survey was to monitor present situation in practical use of performance measurement systems, mainly with focus on innovated approaches of strategic management, monitor present situation in practical usage of performance measurement systems, mainly with focus on innovated approaches of strategic management.

The survey was prepared in the electronic form and it contained 38 questions. To obtain relevant information about the analysed companies, both closed and open questions were used. The task of the respondents was to answer open questions with no options available. These answers were selected by companies at their sole discretion. Closed questions included some options to be used by respondents. Within the scope of the survey, 137 companies were contacted and we obtained 117 completed question-naires back. 110 of them were usable. There was a certain risk that respondents may understand the questions wrongly, which could affect the results of the survey. The data collected by questionnaires were subject to a thorough analysis. These data were processed with the help of an Excel spreadsheet application [2].

3 Enterprise Resource Planning Systems

Enterprise Resource Planning Systems (ERP systems) are enterprise information systems that are developed by commercial entities and offered as products intended for individual enterprises. This is enterprise resource planning, where the main idea is to unify enter-prise sub-functions across the enterprise. These applications are sometimes referred to as enterprise-wide applications, because they express the effort to integrate individual programmes meeting the information needs of individual departments or employees within the company into a single application that shares a common data base [3].

Enterprise Resource Planning systems are the information base and support tools that a company's management uses for making decisions. The aim of these tools is to support a decrease in the consumption of raw materials, energy and other limited resources, which in turn increases the company's performance of. This is mainly due to lower costs and increased corporate profitability.

Early ERP systems can be traced back to the early 1990s, when these systems were gradually implemented and interconnected with the databases in use and, above all, with financial and managerial accounting systems. Given the high financial cost of these systems, they were initially implemented and used within multinational corpo-rations. At present, the concept of ERP systems is used to refer to much more com-prehensive information systems that include transactional applications covering most of a company's processes and functions. The vast majority of commercial, financial, material and other transactions are conducted through these transaction applications. ERP is an information system that brings together and automates a large number of corporate processes. These mainly include production, logistics, distribution, sales, accounting, corporate asset management and controlling processes. Modern ERP systems include portals, managed corporate processes, mobile applications, analytical tools and tools for external communication and integration [4, 5].

These systems are based on the partial customisability of standard software applications according to a company's various requirements. Generally speaking, there are predefined templates that are specific to a given area of business, i.e. a company that decides for a given information system receives the template. This is a very effective tool that streamlines enterprise activities at all levels of management, i.e. from the operational to the strategic level.

3.1 Requirements for an ERP System

An Enterprise Resource Planning System must meet the needs of the company's management. Generally speaking, it should meet at least the following requirements. These include security, information gathering, the possibility of system extensions and modifications based on end user requirements, connection to other companies' information systems (e.g. suppliers, customers), utilisation of existing and planned hardware and software [6].

The security of ERP systems lies in ensuring the security and reliability of operation for all enterprise processes, including e.g. logistics, shipping, financial accounting, materials management, long-term asset record keeping etc. Security should be ensured based on the significance and sensitivity of the data in terms of their potential theft or misuse or, if applicable, physical data loss. The required system must provide the capability to recover in the event of interruption or failure [7, 8].

Information gathering is a necessary requirement for an information system, since up-to-date information about all enterprise processes – i.e. at the desired time, detail and structure – is crucial to the company's management. An important requirement is that information needs to be gathered efficiently. The possibility of extensions and modifications to the system lies in adapting the system to both internal and external requirements. As a result, the system needs to be modifiable and extensible as easy as possible, without major difficulties or financial cost. Connecting the information system to other companies allows the seamless exchange of required information between business partners and, in turn, its efficient use. These systems are used to settle mutual receivables and payables and to provide information necessary for the company's production activities. The aim is to integrate electronic data exchange.

The utilisation of current and planned hardware and software is, yet again, an essential requirement for an information system. The aim is to minimise the cost for new hardware, providing that the hardware should be renewed in accordance with the company's plans. As a result, there should be no extreme expenditure on investment solely due to implementing the information system into the corporate environment [9]. Therefore, it should be possible to use the new information system on existing hardware, without any conflicts with existing software being caused by the information system. The aim is to streamline and speed up economic processes, increase data security, centralise data and reduce potential errors, quickly generate reports for corporate management, achieve long-term savings in operating and investment costs, support for bookkeeping in accordance with IFRS (International Financial Reporting Standards).

3.2 Risks Associated with the Implementation of ERP Systems

Musaji states that the risks associated with the project for implementing an ERP system must be identified, analysed, defined and eliminated systematically, depending on the assigned priority that is determined according to the urgency of the risk and the degree of the threat and extent of potential damage. The objective of the activities is to ensure that risks are understood and evaluated properly and that measures to prevent them are taken in a timely manner [10].

A risk can be viewed as a factor that may negatively affect the achievement of the objectives that are associated with the implementation of ERP systems into the company. The risks jeopardising implementation itself may result from a wide range of activities, for example from incorrect definition/interpretation of corporate strategy, underestimation of system testing, failure to meet hardware installation deadlines, insufficient scope of training for future users of the system concerned, incorrect system documentation, lack of resources to fund the ERP systems' implementation into the corporate environment.

These risks need to be identified, analysed, defined and eliminated systematically in advance, depending on the assigned priority that is determined by the urgency of the risk and the degree of the threat and extent of potential damage. Risk identification and management is an integral part of the entire implementation process, at all its levels.

3.3 SAP Enterprise Resource Planning System

One of the most widespread ERP systems that are used by multinational corporations operating in the Czech Republic is the "SAP R/3" software product. Therefore, the above system has been chosen as the underlying product for the analysis presented in this article. This will be a software solution in the B2B, B2A, B2E, B2G and B2C segments [11, 12].

The SAP ERP system has an integrated environment in which information is only stored in a single database for efficiency reasons. The different modules work with that database, and employees using the relevant modules only have access to information that is essential to the performance of their jobs. The above facts result in cost optimisation in the processing of individual transactions, and the data available to users are always up-to-date, with no duplication. Given the wide use of this system, it is important to point out another equally important feature that improves the efficiency and reduces the cost of the various business processes, namely that the present system also offers control over individual links between suppliers and the given company and, of course, the same links can be found between the company and its customers [13].

SAP consists of the following modules, which work with each other and obtain data from a single database. The **Human Resources (HR)** module is mainly used by a company's HR department and it mainly deals with human resource planning and management in the company (personnel development, personnel cost plan, training, payroll costs, travel costs, recruiting etc.). The **Financial Accounting (FI)** module consists primarily of the general ledger, business partners (suppliers, customers), financial planning, consolidation, electronic banking. The **Fixed Asset Management (AM)** module is used both for financial accounting purposes and for the purposes of managing all fixed tangible and intangible assets. It also includes investment controlling. The **Quality Management (QM)** module is mainly used in the area of logistics, where it is used for monitoring, analysing, controlling and managing quality, from the beginning to the end of the logistics chain [14].

The **Production Planning (PP)** module contains comprehensive planning and management of all production within the company (BOMs, production capacity optimisation etc.). The **Sales & Distribution (SD)** module is very important for the purposes of financial and managerial accounting, because this is where products are billed to customers. In addition, it deals with the pricing, sale and the actual shipping and distribution of the products offered. The **Materials Management (MM)** module is another very important component of the SAP R/3 system – it is used for logistics purposes (the purchase, storage, pricing and use of inventory). The **Project System (PS)** module deals with project management from the long-term perspective. The **Workflow (WF)** module deals with the circulation of all documents within the company. It is mainly used for organising all business processes.

The **Controlling (CO)** module serves the needs of corporate controlling. It draws data from underlying documents that are provided by financial and managerial accounting. It is used to thoroughly analyse the results of operations and the performance and profitability of the company, it deals with cost optimisation and it analyses and evaluates differences. At the same, outputs are produced for corporate managers. The **Plant Maintenance (PM)** module deals with the maintenance of and repairs to technical systems and industry-specific solutions [13].

However, it is very important as a comprehensive part of the SAP corporate information system. SAP is able to flexibly and quickly plan, create and implement new business processes and strategies. In addition, it contains an entire range of configured integration and business scenarios that provide an opportunity for process innovations as part of the launch of new implementations. All applications are compatible with each other. Thanks to the above facts, a custom-tailored information system can be created – within a relatively short period of time – for any entity wishing to implement an ERP system into its corporate environment.

4   Results of the Survey

The survey took place in companies based in the Czech Republic that are located in the geographical area of central and north-east Bohemia. The structure of the companies analysed was as follows: micro enterprises accounted for 32.73 %, small enterprises for 10.91 %, medium-sized enterprises 18.18 % and large enterprises 38.18 %. The above information is shown in Fig. 1.

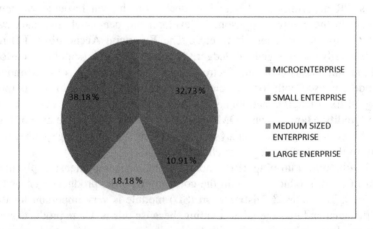

Fig. 1. The structure of analysed companies (Source: own work)

The most common legal forms were Ltd. and Plc., each accounting for 38.18 %, cooperatives represented 2 % and other legal forms of entrepreneurs accounted for 22 %. These mainly included individual entrepreneurs. The data are presented in Fig. 2.

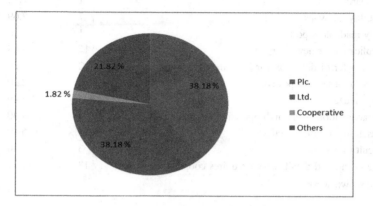

Fig. 2. The structure of analysed companies according to their legal form of business (Source: own work)

Of the companies surveyed, 38.18 % stated that they were using the SAP ERP system for their activities. For this reason, for the purposes of this article, the following data only relate to the SAP information system. Table 1 presents the Advantages of the ERP System SAP. The companies could choose more answers from the list.

Table 1. Advantages of SAP

Category	Number	Share [%]
It is a complex and interconnected system	27	28.13
Ease of operation and control	2	2.09
Filtering capability	6	6.25
No extensive inspection required on part of user	9	9.38
Can be interconnected with MS Excel	5	5.20
Fast data acquisition	6	6.25
Cancellation capability	2	2.08
Reliability	20	20.83
Flexibility	7	7.29
Clarity	12	12.50

(Source: own work)

Table 2 presents the disadvantages that are connected with the usage of ERP System SAP. The companies chose more possibilities from the list.

The analysed companies evaluated the quality of output information from SAP and the results are presented in Table 3.

Table 2. Disadvantages of the SAP ERP System

Category	Number	Share [%]
No complaints	31	34.07
Poor clarity	1	1.10
Instability, slowness	7	7.69
Poorly readable reports	1	1.10
Complicated for new users	17	18.68
Poor transfer of data, e.g. for large data volumes	2	2.20
Filter cannot be transported	2	2.20
Easily freezes	5	5.49
High acquisition costs, high operation and maintenance costs	4	4.40
Restrictions on user privileges	5	5.49
Difficult to set up	3	3.30
Large extent and detail, which requires cooperation with IT	13	14.28

(Source: own work)

Table 3. Quality of output information

Category	Number	Share [%]
High quality	19	24.36
We are satisfied	23	29.49
Can be adapted to the needs	12	15.38
Satisfactory	17	21.78
Condensed and small font	7	8.97

(Source: own work)

Table 4. The system can be recommended to other enterprises

Category	Number	Share [%]
Yes	36	94.74
No	2	5.26

(Source: own work)

Table 4 presents the opinion of the financial managers if the ERP System SAP is recommendable.

The above advantages and limitations of ERP systems are examined in more detail in the discussion section of this article.

5   Discussion

Within the questionnaire survey, companies that were using the SAP ERP system responded to additional questions relating to their use of the ERP system. The goal was to determine how long SAP has been used in the company, whether the company has experience with another information system, what advantages and disadvantages it sees in its use, how the functionality and clarity of the system is evaluated, to what degree the company is satisfied with the quality of the output information, whether there are specific ideas for changes to the system in order to improve it, and whether the company would recommend the system to other enterprises. The companies viewed the complexity and interconnectedness of the SAP system as its biggest advantage – the system brings together many different areas within its modules, which are interconnected with each other. However, complexity comes with one disadvantage, namely that the system is very extensive and complicated for new users, and whenever new transactions are used, it is necessary to cooperate with the IT department and employees specialising in each module.

According to the respondents, another advantage is the system's clarity. Also, the companies see another advantage in the fact that no extensive inspection is required on the part of the user (e.g. unless all necessary information has been filled in, the system will not allow the accounting transaction to be entered into the books etc.). According to the companies, an equally important advantage lies in the fact that the SAP system can be interconnected with MS Excel. An employee can prepare the underlying data in MS Excel and then convert them to the SAP system. However, a certain disadvantage is that if we wanted to convert the sorted (filtered) data from SAP to MS Excel, MS Excel would not be able to accept such modified data. The user needs to download all data from SAP and then sort (filter) the data in MS Excel according to their needs. Another advantage of the system is its extensibility using additional programmes that can be interconnected e.g. with banking institutions (e.g. SEPA payments that may be used between different EU countries). According to users, other advantages of the system include its reliability, clarity, fast processing of data and reports etc.

Besides advantages, the system also has its disadvantages. One major disadvantage that was indicated by the respondents is that the system is very complicated for new users, which is why new employees should receive training in order to understand all the functionalities the SAP system provides for their work. Another disadvantage is seen in the extent and detail of the system, which requires cooperation with the IT department. Reduced system functionality and system instability mainly occur in cases where the system is overloaded and, in turn, data processing slows down. Also, another deficiency can be experienced when processing large volumes of data for a certain time period, e.g. one year, where the system is not able to download the data required. Another problem occurs when the company's accounting year spans two calendar years, i.e. it uses a financial year (e.g. from 1 April 20X0–31 March 20X1) [9]. In this case, too, users encounter problems when downloading the necessary data for the financial year. Some users also see the poor appearance and clarity of default reports as a disadvantage, as the resulting document is condensed, confusing and in small type. However, this is because the SAP system is saving space when printing.

A certain disadvantage may also be that there are different privilege levels, which may result in a situation where each user configures their own version of displaying documents, but a user with higher privileges may change all display versions, thus deleting the versions of all other users. Each user must then reconfigure their document display version, which is an unnecessary loss of time. Most of the companies surveyed would recommend the SAP system to other companies. They only point out the high acquisition and maintenance costs.

6 Conclusion

Increasing companies' performance is an issue that has been debated constantly for many years. One very important factor that adds to the pressure towards companies' performance is the effect of the globalisation of business activities and rapidly developing competition at both the local, international and global level. Therefore, companies are looking for tools and informatics applications to help them succeed in such a demanding market environment. It is the use of information and communication technologies that helps businesses in their management, increases their competitiveness and enhances their activities to a superior qualitative level.

Enterprise Resource Planning systems allow businesses to accurately and efficiently monitor the costs of the company. These costs can be managed by the company. Cost Management enables more efficient use of inputs and leads to a reduction of corporate costs, which leads to better financial performance.

The actual selection and introduction of the correct information system is an important moment in the life of any company, as it affects its operations for several years to come, which is why it needs to receive adequate attention from the companies. A new information system is a large-scale investment whose success or failure always has a significant effect on the future of the entire company. By properly selecting and adequately implementing an IS, the company gains not only a competitive advantage in the market, but also new opportunities for cooperation with business partners. When implemented properly, the information system can also play a positive role in motivating and improving the satisfaction of employees and in stimulating their interest in the company's development, as well as in improving the effectiveness and quality of production processes. An important part of successful implementation lies in ensuring significant participation of human resources on the part of the company being implemented, respecting the size of the organisation, taking into account corporate culture and other important factors. In the event the information system is selected incorrectly or its implementation is wrong or incomplete, such a system not only results in considerable additional costs for the company, but it also causes the following risks: insufficient preparation, inadequate timing and a delay in launching the implementation of the new IS, wrong setting of the IS, supplies to customers are jeopardised, dissatisfaction of users of the new IS and, last but not least, lack of information for management and corporate management decision-making, which could ultimately lead to a collapse and problems threatening the company's existence. In most cases, the life of corporate ERP systems does not end with their implementation. Companies constantly change their structure and processes, expand or respond to changes in legislation. Such cases (situations) make it necessary for these systems (software) to be gradually yet constantly adapted to the existing conditions.

Acknowledgement. This paper was created in accordance with the research project entitled "The analysis of current approach of companies to evaluation of productivity and financial situation using company information systems" undertaken by The Technical University of Liberec, The Faculty of Economics.

References

1. Malíková, O., Černíková, M.: Environmental impact identified from company accounts in the Czech Republic. In: WIT Transactions on Ecology and the Environment. WIT Press, Ashurst Lodge (2013)
2. Horák, J., Jáčová, H.: Application of strategic management in enterprises located in the czech republic as a tool of resources management support. In: WIT Transactions on Ecology and the Environment. WIT Press, Ashurst Lodge (2013)
3. Gelinas, U., Dull, R., et al.: Accounting Information Systems. South-Western Cengage Learning, Mason (2011)
4. Stair, R., Reynolds, G.: Principles of Information Systems. Course Technology Cengage Learning, Boston (2014)
5. Olson, D.L., Kesharwani, S.: Enterprise Information Systems Contemporary Trends and Issues. World Scientific Publishing, Singapore (2010)
6. Hall, J.A.: Accounting Information Systems. South-Western Cengage Learnging, Mason (2013)
7. Boddy, D., Boonstra, A., Kennedy, G.: Managing Information Systems Strategy and Organisation. Prentice Hall, Harlow (2009)
8. Mei-Yeh, F., Lin, F.: Measuring the performance of ERP system – from the balanced score card perspectives. J. Am. Acad. Bus. **10**(1), 256–263 (2006)
9. Randáková, M., Bokšová, J., Strouhal, J., et al.: Current issues of reorganization process in the Czech Republic. J. Econ. Bus. Manage. **1**(2), 68–73 (2014)
10. Musaji, Y.F.: Integrated Auditing of ERP Systems. Wiley, New York (2002)
11. Weske, M.: Business Process Management. Springer, Heidelberg (2012)
12. Sabau, G., et al.: Information systems in university learning. Informatica Economia **14**(4), 171–182 (2010)
13. Maynard, J.: Financial Accounting, reporting and analysis. Oxford University Press, Oxford (2013)
14. Maasen, A., Schoenen, M.: Lern – und Arbeitsbuch SAP/R3. Springer Fachmedien, Wiesbaden (2002)

The Emergence of Public Intelligence: Penetration of Business Intelligence into the Public Administration Realm

Tereza Otčenášková[1](✉), Vladimír Bureš[1], Pavel Čech[1], and Fridrich Racz[2]

[1] University of Hradec Kralove, Hradec Kralove, Czech Republic
{tereza.otcenaskova,vladimir.bures,pavel.cech}@uhk.cz
[2] Vysoká škola manažmentu, Bratislava, Slovakia
fridrich.racz@gmail.com

Abstract. The current organisations face the challenge to gain and sustain the competitive advantage. The Business Intelligence tools support the organisational processes and enhance their efficiency. Nevertheless, these still have not penetrated to satisfactorily extent to the public administration realm. Therefore, this paper introduces the framework focused on the Business Intelligence implementation in the public administration. Firstly, the basic concepts linked with Big Data and Business Intelligence are described. Afterwards, the specific characteristics of public administration are considered. Finally, the practical model of Business Intelligence in context of the discussed issues is provided.

Keywords: Business intelligence · Czech Republic · Public administration · Technology penetration

1 Introduction

Decision-making approaches matter and occur in public administration at all levels (from federal to local). These are significantly different compared to business firms and large companies. Additional legislative regulations, objectives that do not aim at financial performance targets, the election of top management staff, the assessment process, the factors that are influencing particular decisions, or decision-making methods can serve as examples of influential factors contributing to this difference [1]. Decision-making in public administration represents a complex process which needs to be supported by any available tool [2]. Modern Information and Communication Technologies (ICTs) provide managers with a set of methods, techniques, tools, principles and procedures, which have already been successfully applied in various kinds of business oriented issues ranging from business process management [3] to knowledge management implementation [4]. New concepts such as New Public Management [5, 6], Good Governance [7, 8], or Public Private Partnership [9, 10] are more or less successfully introduced in public administration bodies around the Globe. Nevertheless, public administration lacks the experience with projects related to the advanced and sophisticated tools such as mobile-oriented architecture [11], or Smart Environments [12].

© Springer International Publishing Switzerland 2015
G. Dregvaite and R. Damasevicius (Eds.): ICIST 2015, CCIS 538, pp. 268–277, 2015.
DOI: 10.1007/978-3-319-24770-0_24

Moreover, growing requirements on public administration effectiveness, efficiency, and strategic planning force to implement the methods and tools that are mostly common in the business environment. Obviously, a specific approach with potential to support the existing public administration issues still lacks of attention nowadays. Bulk of available data obtainable from several resources enables the concept of Business Intelligence (BI) to be deployed [13]. Several exceptions might be identified. For instance, Wickramasuriya et al. suggest that Geospatial Business Intelligence (Geo-BI) can be adapted to meet the requirements of an integrated solution for local and regional governance of infrastructure services [14]. Geo-BI is an improvement of the traditional BI approach. It is possible thanks to the integration of Geographic Information Systems (GIS) with BI [15]. This example represents the starting point for other initiatives, which would use the bottom-up approach. In this vein, existing BI tools might be extended by public administration systems, data sources, and applied technologies in order to meet specific end users' needs. However, general framework that could be used as a basis for top-down methodological development is still missing. This statement is based on the assumption that the necessity to work appropriately with data resources is not exclusively tied to business environment. General principles and methods can be applied also in environments, which main objective is not to gain profit or increase the market share. The latter imply the need and usefulness of BI penetration into the public administration. Therefore, these principles are introduced and outlined within the paper.

The paper is organised as follows. Next section discusses the Big Data phenomenon and its implications for public sector in particular. Afterwards, a case study is analysed in detail. It suggests a potential framework for BI tools and implementation approach to be used in the discussed context. The value added in the form of BI framework from the public administration perspective is concluded in the last section.

2   Big Data as an Enabler

BI tools are closely tied to data availability and amount. Fortunately, it might be stated that Big Data represents one of the current and future research frontiers. Not surprisingly, public administration is also included in this phenomenon. Each nation has relatively large population. Within this and no matter for example age, gender or work position, all people need and require certain level of public services. Children and teenagers should be provided with the education whereas the elderly need higher level of health care. Moreover, the needs usually overlap particular areas of public services. Each society and also each individual within it generates a lot of data in most of the mentioned public sector areas. This implies the huge the number of public administration data. US Library of Congress can serve as an illustration when it collected three terabytes of data by 2011 [16].

Not only business organisations, but also governmental institutions chase the opportunity to face the adverse conditions in pursuit to improve their productivity and fight against global recession. Public administration definitely belongs to areas which could be more effective and support consequently the decrease of budget deficits and reduction of national debt levels. According to McKinsey's report [17], Big Data functionalities, such as reserving informative patterns and knowledge, provide the public sector a chance to improve productivity and higher levels of efficiency and effectiveness. European's public sector has the aim to reduce expenditure of administrative activities by 15–20 %, increasing 223 billion to 446 billion values, or even more. The latter should accelerate productivity growth by 0.5 % point over the next decade [16]. The public sector organisations are large consumers of information technologies [18]. Governments in the Czech Republic at all levels - national, regional, and local levels - should strategically use IT for a variety of purposes ranging from the maintenance of operational infrastructures to delivery of responsive public services and interaction with citizens. BI is the next approach waiting for its utilisation.

3   The Case Study

Apparently, BI within public administration realm requires attention. Therefore, the research question was linked with the applicability of BI concepts use in these settings. The study is established in the context of the Czech Republic. The following section discusses the implications of the aforementioned issues.

3.1   Problems in Public Administration in the Czech Republic

Currently, the Czech Republic consists of 14 regions and more than 6 200 municipalities. The Czech public administration typically focuses on various activities. These comprise for example the support and advancement of people's preferences and interests, provision of public estates, creation of conditions for social and economic development of a region, execution of civil services, and coordination of relations municipality - region; municipality - state; and region - state. Considering the national background, there are particular specifics linked with the discussed issues.

Firstly, current situation is strongly influenced by existing model of public services which is employed in the country. The so called "mixed model", based on parallel execution of both local administration and civil services, is applied.

Secondly, another specific of the Czech public administration is the procedure of decision-making processes. These are realised by "managers" who are elected. They make decision related not only to strategic issues of municipalities or regions, but also to operational activities without relevant vocational qualification. It is not required in the Czech Republic to acquire at least minimum of managerial competencies when one wants to perform a function. Elected "managers" are allowed to make decisions only based on democratic consensus. Such situation is almost unknown in the business realm except from the decision-making processes based on the shareholding.

Thirdly, the aforementioned is related to the so-called "double-level" management in public administration. The elected "managers" represent the first level, whereas the professionals create the second one. These professionals are usually head of particular departments, deputies, or directors of public organisations. This level of management is limited in its responsibility by boundaries set by the first level of elected managers. Therefore, the main role of professionals is the preparation of materials and sources for strategic decision-making of elected managers, who have the final decision-making power. This situation is not unique to the Czech Republic. For instance, Määtä and Ojala describe similar principles in Finland [19] (see Fig. 1).

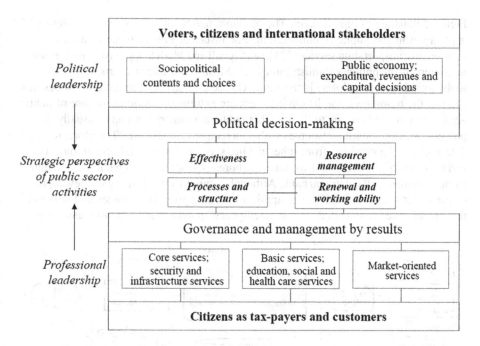

Fig. 1. "Double-level" management in public administration (Source: [19]).

Finally, there is wide latitude in decision making in the business environment, whereas public administration is firmly tied to the existing legislation. Moreover, decisions are mostly based not only on objective and unbiased information. These also have to represent a certain type of agreement among ruling parties with different political goals, aspirations and priorities.

All these attributes of situation in the Czech public administration significantly influence strategic decision making. In pursuit to improve the latter, any available tools should be used. Measurement, management and evaluation of performance cannot only improve quality of information available for strategic decisions, but it can also provide benefits in the following areas:

- Transparency, which is the basic stimulus for innovations.
- Rewarding performance and prevention of bureaucracy.
- Orientation on the external environment.

3.2 Business Intelligence in Public Environment: Public Intelligence

BI might be described as a complex of ICT approaches and applications, which almost exclusively support only the analytical and planning activities in an enterprise and which are based on the principle of multidimensionality that represents the ability to investigate reality from several perspectives [20]. The field of BI is well developed and particular technologies are applied, scrutinised and further elaborated. There are various approached to the BI decomposition from the technological and process perspective.

Figure 2 illustrate of one of them. The literature review offers several examples of BI application in the public administration. For instance, Poister presents a case study focused on transportation services [21], or Brignall and Modell apply BI to performance measurement in public administration [22]. Mostly, the internal structure (methods, tools, techniques, principles) is the same. On the contrary, the external resources that connect the framework and its environment are extremely important in case of public administration. This is due to the fact that public administration bodies usually do not possess sufficient internal resources with data required for analysis. Therefore, relevant data needs to be obtained from other public, state or commercial institutions. These include external resources such as statistical bureaus, insurance companies, local administration bodies, or the national bank. Although commonly used during the development of particular Business Intelligence applications, their overall attributes and structures that are suitable for so called "public intelligence" purposes are generally unknown.

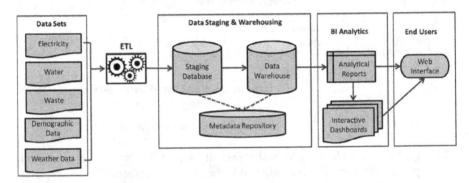

Fig. 2. Technical architecture of business intelligence components (Source: [14]).

Nevertheless, attention linked with external resources of "public intelligence" is not its only specific feature. Another issue that has to be taken into consideration is the strategic perspective. The difference between business organisations and public administration bodies is obvious. Both types of organisations have similar structure including managers, employees, objectives, processes, or financial resources. However, they differ in the purpose, customers, or limitations they face. In case of public administration, profit or revenues are not the primary reasons why particular institutions are established, or there are strong legislative boundaries and limitations. These should be considered during the everyday decision-making processes. As stated by Becker et al. [23], such specifics of the public sector include, among others:

- Complexity of political decision processes. Recent research focused on the relationship between politics and administration [24] has proven the specific conditions of decision-making processes in public organisations which necessitate an effective domain-specific adaptation of BI concepts.
- Complexity of BI addressees. The addressee of BI is not only the management (e.g. majors or public managers), but also major stakeholder groups. These comprise for example citizens, suppliers, partners or parliaments acting in the public sector decision-making process.

- New approach of public management. Old attitude has been replaced by a new one through various reform approaches in the area of the public sector over the last two decade. Managerial thinking, as reflected in the term new public management, seems to be today's paradigm. However, managerial issues have been largely addressed before. As a result, today's BI solutions have to deal with legacies, for instance, distributed strategic competencies and fragmented planning capacities.

Figure 3 is based on Kaplan and Norton's work [25] and depicts basic strategic processes conducted in the public administration and their mutual relationship. Apparently, there are six major processes connected with development, realisation and modification of two basic documents - Strategy and Operational plan.

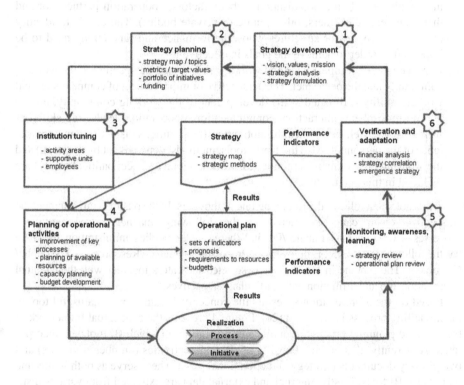

Fig. 3. Strategic planning in public administration (Source: [2]).

3.3 Potential of BI Introduction in the Czech Public Administration

BI represents an appropriate and helpful tool no matter type or sector of business. Therefore, its utilisation in the Czech public administration is outlined. The main aim is to improve the situation in the Czech public administration. Nevertheless, BI application should be adapted considering the aforementioned specifics. BI comprises several perspectives, methods or tools. In pursuit to deploy BI successfully, the following attributes should be taken into account (adapted from [19]).

1. Effectiveness - the perspective of the citizen and the political decision-maker. The extent to which a public organisation achieves its goals based on its social responsibility is manifested in the results or external achievements of the organisation.
2. Resources and the economy - the purpose of resource management is to convince political decision-makers and tax-payers, citizens and stakeholders that the organisation is using the economic inputs and other resources of society entrusted to it (personnel, capital, premises and property, economic resources, etc.) in an economic, productive and cost-effective way in order to ensure even better effectiveness.
3. Processes and structures - the perspective refers to processes and structures owned and controlled by the organisation itself or its cooperation partners. The processes may begin outside the organisation (subcontractors, cooperation partners) or end there (citizens, customers, other public or private bodies). The aim is to identify processes, activities or structures whose performance and functioning need to be improved in order to achieve the goals in effectiveness.
4. Improvement of competencies and working ability - the perspective of the working community and the personnel. The perspective of improvement of competencies and working ability is directed at the development of the working community, unit or teams (atmosphere, interaction, communication, cooperation, leadership skills) as well as at the well-being, health, motivation (rewarding, satisfaction) and competence of the personnel. Also the work (tools, methods, demands set by the work) and the working environment (ergonomics, work hygiene and occupational safety) are included in this perspective.

The whole idea follows the following line of thoughts. In the business environment the perspective chain can be ordered in the following manner: Employees → Processes → Customers → Finance/Profit. Whereas in the public administration, the chain has the following sequence: Employees → Processes → Finance/Resources → The public/ Customers. The scheme in Fig. 3 depicts selected indicators together with their mutual interrelationship and affiliation with particular perspectives.

Based on the aforementioned results the conceptual framework as a useful tool in the modelling process is proposed [26]. Figure 4 presents the conceptual framework of the strategic planning process in public administration, in which BI tools are incorporated. Apparently, this process consists of six main activities (numbered in stars) and two primary documents (strategy and operational plan). These serve as both inputs and outputs for BI tools. Firstly, internal and external data are extracted from various institutions. Statistical offices, ministries, geographic information and other external systems can serve as an example. Afterwards, these are proceeded, analysed and transformed through BI tools. These might be structured to several levels, in which, for instance, data transformation, database, analytical and end-users tools are applied. The final step represents the adapted use of the outputs by different stakeholders exemplified by general public, ministries and municipalities, or organisations and institutions within public and private sector.

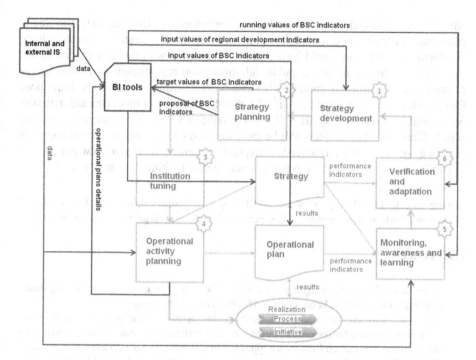

Fig. 4. Conceptual framework of strategic planning process in public administration connected with Balanced Scorecard (BSC) and BI (Source: author's research).

3.4   Limitations and Further Research

Apparently, the BI principles might be applied in various public sector areas, in which big data volumes can be generated (e.g. transportation [21] or education [27]). Although this idea is generalizable to a certain extent, it is foreseeable that the introduced framework would work in countries where the European framework of public administration is used. Nevertheless, other countries should amend it considering the existing conditions and possibilities. Among other factors, technological or legislative preparedness should be reflected. Therefore, further research should be focused on different contexts. Moreover, other managerial methods and their interpretation within the public administration realm should be introduced. The utilizable methods might be exemplified by tools for data mining, decision support, workflow monitoring, predictions or performance management.

4   Conclusions

As outlined above, the BI tools are crucial for all types of organisations, no matter the sector and field they operate in. In the business environment, the BI issues are vividly discussed and incorporated within organisational processes. This leads to particular efficiency increase and competitive advantage enhancement. Unfortunately, the area of public administration is still omitted significantly in a lot of countries even though the employment of BI tools would be useful. The implications of this fact depend on the extent of maturity of particular public administration organisation as well as of the preparedness of particular country where such organisation operates. The introduced framework should help organisations with the identification of processes and activities which will be supported by BI tools to a maximum extent. Consequently, not only stakeholders, but other subjects will be more satisfied with the organisational approach as well as services. The introduced conceptual framework represents new perspective of public decision and strategic processes management within the public sector.

Acknowledgement. The support of the FIM UHK Specific Research Project "SCM and Control of Markets and Production in Agent-based Computational Economics" is gratefully acknowledged.

References

1. Viorel, B.B., Radu, I.: Intelligence cycle integration within decisional system among public administration. Procedia Econ. Finance **15**(2014), 864–870 (2014)
2. Bureš, V.: Balanced scorecard and business intelligence in the public administration: framework proposal for the Czech settings. In: The 19th International Business Information Management Association Conference, pp. 142–147, Barcelona, Spain, 12–13 Nov 2012a
3. Slavíček, V.: Enhancing business process management with knowledge. E+M Econ Manage. **14**(1), 123–134 (2011)
4. Bureš, V.: Knowledge management and its implementation. In: 2nd International Conference on Web Information Systems and Technologies (WEBIST 2006), pp. 115–118. INSTICC Press, Setubal, Portugal (2006)
5. Young, R., Young, M., Jordan, E., O'Connor, P.: Is strategy being implemented through projects? Contrary evidence from a leader in New Public Management. Int. J. Project Manage. **30**(8), 887–900 (2012)
6. Schubert, T.: Empirical observations on New Public Management to increase efficiency in public research - Boon or bane? Res. Policy **38**(8), 1225–1234 (2009)
7. Lockwood, M.: Good governance for terrestrial protected areas: a framework, principles and performance outcomes. J. Environ. Manage. **91**(3), 754–766 (2010)
8. Griffin, L.: The limits to good governance and the state of exception: a case study of North Sea fisheries. Geoforum **41**(2), 282–292 (2010)
9. Grimsey, D., Lewis, M.K.: Are public private partnerships value for money?: evaluating alternative approaches and comparing academic and practitioner views. Acc. Forum **29**(4), 345–378 (2005)
10. Shaoul, J.: 'Sharing' political authority with finance capital: the case of Britain's Public Private Partnerships. Policy Soc. **30**(3), 209–220 (2011)
11. Kozel, T., Mohelská, H.: Models of firms with mobile oriented architecture. E+M Econ. Manage. **13**(4), 135–142 (2010)
12. Mikulecký, P.: Learning in smart environments - from here to there. In: 10th European Conference on e-Learning, pp. 479–484, Brighton, United Kingdom (2011)
13. Bureš, V.: External data resources for public administration intelligence services. In: The 19th International Business Information Management Association Conference, pp. 115–120, Barcelona, Spain, 12–13 Nov 2012b

14. Wickramasuriya, R., Ma, J., Berryman, M., Perez, P.: Using geospatial business intelligence to support regional infrastructure governance. Knowl.-Based Syst. **53**, 80–89 (2013)
15. Angelaccio, M., Basili, A., Buttarazzi, B., Liguori, W.: Using geo-business intelligence to improve quality of life. In: IEEE 1st AESS European Conference on Satellite Telecommunications, Rome, pp. 1–6, 02–05 Oct 2012
16. Chen, C.I.P., Zhang, C.-Y.: Data-intensive applications, challenges, techniques and technologies: a survey on big data. Inf. Sci. **275**, 314–347 (2014)
17. Manyika, J., Chui, M., Brown, B., Bughin, J., Dobbs, R., Roxburgh, C., Byers, A.H.: Big data: The Next Frontier for Innovation, Competition, and Productivity. McKinsey Global Institute (2012)
18. Pang, M.-S.: IT governance and business value in the public sector organizations - the role of elected representatives in IT governance and its impact on IT value in U.S. state governments. Decis. Support Syst. **59**, 274–285 (2014)
19. Määtä, S., Ojala, T.: A Challenge for Balanced Success in the Public Sector: Towards more proactive Strategic Management. Ministry of Finance, Helsinki (1999)
20. Novotný, O., Pour, J., Slánský, D: Business Intelligence: Jak využít bohatství ve vašich datech (in Czech, translated title in English: Business Intelligence: How to use the richness of your data), 1st ed. Grada Publishing, Prague, Czech Republic (2005)
21. Poister, T.H.: Strategic planning and management in state departments of transportation. Int. J. Public Adm. **28**, 1035–1056 (2005)
22. Brignall, S., Modell, S.: An institutional perspective on performance measurement and management in the "new public sector". Manage. Acc. Res. **11**, 281–306 (2000)
23. Becker, J., Niehaves, B., Müller-Wienbergen, F., Matzner, M.: Open source public sector business intelligence systems. In: Wojtkowski, W., Wojtkowski, G., Lang, M., Conboy, K., Barry, C. (eds.) Information Systems Development, pp. 379–391. Springer, New York (2009)
24. Nalbandian, J.: Politics and administration in local government. Int. J. Public Adm. **29**, 1049–1063 (2006)
25. Kaplan, R.S., Norton, D.P.: Strategy Maps: Converting Intangible Assets into Tangible Outcomes. Harvard Business School, Boston (2004)
26. Otčenášková, T., Bureš, V., Čech, P.: Conceptual modelling for management of public health in case of emergency situations. In: Proceedings of the International Conference on Knowledge Engineering and Ontology Development (KEOD) 2011, pp. 344–348, Portugal (2011)
27. Grulich, P.: Computer technology in teaching Archiving. Archiving J. (Archivní časopis) **64**, 210–215 (2014)

Software Engineering

The Theoretical Connections Between Agile Software Development and Innovative Climate

Tomi Juhola[✉], Sami Hyrynsalmi, Tuomas Mäkilä,
and Ville Leppänen

Department of Information Technology, University of Turku, Turku, Finland
{tkjuho, sthyry, tusuma, ville.leppanen}@utu.fi

Abstract. Agile software development methods are claimed to fully expose the innovation capabilities of a software development team. In the current business world, where the new innovations are seen as keys for survival and growth of the firm, these development methods have been welcomed and widely adapted. There, however, is a lack of understanding how these methods drive innovation. Therefore, in this study we analyse agile principles and practices against established innovation climate dimensions. The mapping used in analysis is done by the authors and provides a starting point for further scientific discussion. The results show that there is a clear link between practices and several classical innovation climate dimensions. However, a few dimensions are only covered by the agile principles. The study concludes by proposing new avenues for further work in agile software development research.

Keywords: Agile software development · Agile practice · Agile principle · Innovation · Innovation factor · Innovation climate

1 Introduction

Agile software development has become the dominant software development method in the industry. Lack of empirical evidence related to the effectiveness of these methods seems to have little impact on the adoption. Early on the agile software development was referred as a way to drive innovation [1]. However, as [2] showed in their review, there is almost no theoretical or empirical evidence of this. As the agile methods have risen as the *de facto* development methods in the industry, it is crucial to understand do the methods drive innovation–and if they do, what are the certain practices and principles that are the most important ones for the innovation capabilities of a team. Careless adaption of these kinds of practices would not unveil the full potential of the agile software development methods.

The aim of this paper is to map current known agile principles and practices to proven innovation factors. In this study, we use conceptual analysis [3] to study agile software development methods' ability to drive innovation. We will identify what innovation drivers are emphasized by agile software development and what innovation factors are not well addressed implicitly in agile software development body of knowledge. Thus we will increase theoretical knowledge of the connections between agile software development methods and innovations.

G. Dregvaite and R. Damasevicius (Eds.): ICIST 2015, CCIS 538, pp. 281–292, 2015.
DOI: 10.1007/978-3-319-24770-0_25

Our aim is to answer to the following research questions:

- RQ1: Are there agile principles or practices that can have a *positive* effect on innovation climate factors?
- RQ2: Are there agile principles or practices that can have a *negative* effect on innovation climate factors?
- RQ3: Are there some innovation climate factors that *are not affected* by any agile principles or practices?

By answering these questions, we are able to show what practices and principles are crucial for innovation climate of a development team. While these results serve as a starting point for further academic work, the results also might help the industry experts in evaluating what practices and principles they should adapt. Furthermore, the results show what innovation climate factors are not affected by the agile principles and practices, and thus point the practitioners in which area there might be a possibility to improve.

The rest of the paper is structured as follows. We will start with reviewing the relevant existing literature on agile software development and innovation. Then we describe the methods used to conduct the research, followed by the results. The paper is wrapped in discussion and key findings are highlighted finally in conclusion.

2   Literature Review

In this section we will describe the key terms: agile software development and innovation. We will proceed by identifying the principles and practices what agile software development consists of. Finally, we will take a look into known innovation factors.

2.1   Agile Software Development

The term 'agile software development methods' refers to modern lightweight software development processes that emerged during 1990s and 2000s. Agile software development proposes an alternative view of software development than the old methods: the traditional methods are seen as formal and inflexible tools that are not able to answer nowadays business needs for rapid changes [4]. Thus, these new methods treat unpredictability and changing requirements as an opportunity [5].

The common nominator for agile software development methods is the Agile Manifesto [6]. The manifesto lists four values and twelve principles (principles are shown in Table 2) that should "uncover better ways of developing software". Agile software development methods are supposed to support and follow these values and principles.

While there exist a plethora of different agile software development methods [4, 5], the different methods share similar constructions and advices. Furthermore, agile software development methods are often meant to be tailored for the need of an adopting company and project. Thus, comparing the development methods would not draw correct picture as the actual effect of a certain method depends on the practices utilized. Therefore, in this study we do not analyse through different agile development methods but rather we focus on agile practices. The practices [7] are concrete ways of working (e.g. pair programming) or advices (e.g. timeboxing, cross-functional team) that should support agile software development's values and principles. In this study, we utilize Appelo's list of agile practices [8]. This is, to the authors' best knowledge, the largest existing collection of agile practices.

2.2 Innovations and Innovation Climate Factors

An innovation is a commercialized idea that leads to e.g. better product, process, business model or service. Innovations were identified as the key driver in economic change by Schumpeter [9] already a hundred years ago. As the importance of innovations has grown also the innovation management has become critical. In order to manage innovation, also large number of different measurement frameworks has been created and innovation factors have been identified [10–12].

Each framework takes a specific viewpoint where the measurement is done from. Due to this the variance in factors is large, and the target for the measurement can be anything from overall economy and company's market to team climate and individual creativity. Due to the large variance, and the emphasis on team in agile development, we choose to concentrate on the innovation climate on team level in this research.

The criticality of correct kind of innovation climate has been identified as a difference between an innovative organization and non-innovative organization [11, 13, 14]. Especially [13–15] consider organizational structure and innovation climate important for creativity and innovation. Ekvall [13] has identified 10 factors of innovation shown in Table 1. We will use these high level factors as a baseline in this paper as they are well validated, often referenced, stable, and used as a baseline for many industry used innovation measurement frameworks, e.g. Situational Outlook Questionnaire SOQ and Innovation Climate Questionnaire ICQ.

Table 1. Ekvall's 10 innovation climate factors (adapted from [14])

Challenge	"The degree to which people are involved in daily Involvement operations, long-term goals, and visions. High Challenge/Involvement implies better levels of engagement, commitment, and motivation."
Freedom	"The degree of independence shown by the people in the organization. High levels of Freedom imply more perceived autonomy and ability for individual discretion."
Idea support	"The way new ideas are treated. In a high Idea Support situation people receive ideas and suggestions in an attentive and professional manner. People listen generously to each other."
Trust/openness	"The emotional safety in relationships. In high Trust/Openness situations people feel more comfortable sharing ideas and being frank and honest with each other."

(Continued)

Table 1. (*Continued*)

Dynamism/liveliness	The eventfulness of life in an organization
Playfulness/humour	"The spontaneity and ease displayed within the workplace. Good-natured joking and laughter and a relaxed atmosphere (lower stress) are indicators of higher levels of Playfulness and Humor"
Debates	"The occurrence and open disagreement between viewpoints, ideas, experiences, and knowledge. In the Debating situation many different voices and points of view are exchanged and encouraged."
Conflicts	"The presence of personal and emotional tensions (a negative dimension — in contrast to the debate dimension). When Conflict is high people engage in interpersonal warfare, slander and gossip, and even plot against each other"
Risk taking	"The tolerance of uncertainty and ambiguity. In a high Risk-Taking climate people can make decisions even when they do not have certainty and all the information desired. People can and do "go out on a limb" to put new ideas forward."
Idea time	"The amount of time people can, and do, use for elaborating new ideas. When Idea-Time is high people can explore and develop new ideas that may not have been included in the original task."

3   Methods

The purpose of this study is to identify theoretical supporting or hindering connections between agile software development and innovation factors. We will only look one-directional relationships (agile practice improves/harms innovation factor). Through this investigation we will identify gaps, clusters and patterns in these relationships.

We use conceptual analysis approach in this study. In this method, the concepts are broken down into their building parts to gain insight into the study object [3]. The key concepts in this study are agile principles and practices, and innovation climate dimensions.

The current agile principles and practices were mapped to known innovation factors. The practices mapped are based on Appelo's Big List of Agile Practices [8] and the principles are the 12 principles of Agile Manifesto [6]. Both are first of all high level enough to make the mapping feasible, but at the same time close enough to actual software development work, so that they can be treated as practical guidance to developers.

The innovation factors are the ones identified by Ekvall [13]. We decided to use these factors as they have been studied and used widely after their publication in the 1990s (more than 800 citations by April 2015 according to Google Scholar).

After the key concepts are broken down into the constituent parts, we study how these can be mapped against each other. This mapping is done based on the following questions:

1. Which agile practices can improve an innovation factor?
2. Which agile principles can directly improve an innovation factor?
3. Which agile principles can indirectly improve an innovation factor?

The directly improving principles and practices are such that the logic was clearly identified by two researchers. The indirect effect of principles and practices was identified by a researcher and agreed by another researcher. The researchers discussed on a few disagreement cases until a common understanding was found. The resulting mapping was analysed together by the researchers. Especially gaps, strong points, differences between principles and practices, as well as, possible patterns were listed and discussed.

4 Results

The mapping with principles that directly or indirectly improve one or multiple innovation factors is shown in Table 2. The notable areas are highlighted with grey in order to identify both innovation factors with most supporting principles and with zero supporting principles. The indirectly mapped agile principles are shown in **bold**.

We can see that *Trust/Openness*, *Freedom* and *Debates* gather most principles, with *Conflicts* and *Challenge* trailing behind. *Risk taking* and *Playfulness/humour* did not get any principles mapped. Principles 3 and 10 are not mapped to any innovation factor. On the other hand, principles 4 (3 factors), 11 (3 factors), 2 (2 factors), 5(2 factors), 6 (2 factors) and 12 (2 factors) are mapped to multiple innovation factors.

When looking at the principles that can be seen as indirectly affecting the innovation factors, we notice that it only adds 3 principles to the mapping, each of these affecting Trust/Openness (Principles 1, 2 and 3). This leaves only principle 10 without direct or indirect effect on innovation factors.

The Table 3 shows the big list of agile practices mapped to Ekvall's [13] innovation factors. The mapping of practices was similar to the mapping of agile principles. As an example, *Pair programming* is an agile practice where software is programmed simultaneously by two persons in a single computer. This practice supports Debates, Dynamism/Liveliness and Conflicts dimensions (two programmers discuss while they are coding, and the pairs are regularly changed), Idea Support (the practice encourages programmers to listen new ideas) and Trust/Openness (the practices promote openness of ideas and solutions). However, we do not see any link between the practice and Challenge, Playfulness/Humour or Risk Taking. The practice seems to harm Freedom of a single developer as his degree of independence will decrease.

Each of the innovation factors has at least four practices mapped to it. The factor with most practices is *Trust/Openness* with 28 practices, followed by *Debates* (16 practices) and *Dynamism/Liveliness* (16 practices). The factors with least practices are *Playfulness/Humour* (4 practices), *Freedom* (5 practices) and *Idea time* (4 practices).

The practices that are mapped to most innovation factors are *Pair-Programming/Pairing*, *Collective Code Ownership*, *Retrospective/Reflection Workshop* and *Colocated Team/Sitting Together/Common Workspace*. There are also 6 practices that were not mapped to any innovation factor: *Use Cases, Design by Contract, Refactoring, Software Metrics/Code Metrics & Analysis, Issue Tracking/Bug Tracking* and *Velocity*.

Table 2. Direct and Indirect mappings from Agile Manifesto principles to Ekvall's factors of innovation.

Agile principle (Direct mapping / **Indirect mapping**)	Innovation factor
1. Customer satisfaction by rapid delivery of useful software	Challenge
9. Continuous attention to technical excellence and good design	
11. Self-organizing teams	Freedom
5. Projects are built around motivated individuals, who should be trusted	
12. Regular adaptation to changing circumstance	
4. Close, daily cooperation between business people and developers	Idea support
1. Customer satisfaction by rapid delivery of useful software	Trust/openness
2. Welcome changing requirements, even late in development	
3. Working software is delivered frequently (weeks rather than months)	
4. Close, daily cooperation between business people and developers	
5. Projects are built around motivated individuals, who should be trusted	
6. Face-to-face conversation is the best form of communication (co-location)	
7. Working software is the principal measure of progress	
2. Welcome changing requirements, even late in development	Dynamism/liveliness
	Playfulness / humour
6. Face-to-face conversation is the best form of communication (co-location)	Debates
11. Self-organizing teams	
2. Welcome changing requirements, even late in development	
4. Close, daily cooperation between business people and developers	
12. Regular adaptation to changing circumstance	Conflicts
11. Self-organizing teams	
	Risk taking
8. Sustainable development, able to maintain a constant pace	Idea time
10. Simplicity—the art of maximizing the amount of work not done—is essential	

Practices with negative effect have been marked with N and grey cells in Table 3. Only *Pair-Programming, Timeboxing, On-Site Customer, Frequent Delivery* and *Velocity* were identified as practices that can hinder innovation factors. Most of these might affect negatively to *Risk taking* and *Idea time* as they create schedule pressure. *On-site customer* can create a desire to avoid conflicts as the customer could see it and *Pair programming* can hinder the freedom of individual developers.

Principles 1 (*Customer satisfaction by rapid delivery of useful software*) and 3 (*Working software is delivered frequently (weeks rather than months)*) can also hinder *Risk taking* and *Idea time* mainly due to the schedule pressure.

Table 3. Mapping of big list of agile practices [5] to Ekvall's [4] innovation factors

Practice	Challenge	Freedom	Idea support	Trust/openness	Dynamism/liveliness	Playfulness/humour	Debates	Conflicts	Risk taking	Idea time
Product Vision / Vision Statement	X									
Product Backlog					X					
User Stories	X				X					
Use Cases										
Usage Scenarios			X		X					
Personas			X		X	X				
Planning Poker						X	X	X		
Requirement Prioritization							X	X	X	
Architectural Spikes / Spike Solutions	X							X	X	X
Domain Driven Design	X						X			
Emergent Design / Evolutionary Design	X						X	X		
CRC Cards					X	X				
Design by Contract										
System Metaphor		X	X							
Coding Style / Coding Guidelines / Coding Standard							X			
Test Driven Development	X			X						
Behavior Driven Development				X						
Pair-Programming / Pairing		N	X	X	X		X	X		X
Refactoring										
Collective Code Ownership		X		X	X		X	X		
Daily Builds / Automated Builds / Ten-Minute Builds				X						
Continuous Integration				X						
Code Reviews / Peer Reviews			X	X			X	X		
Software Metrics / Code Metrics & Analysis										
Source Control / Version Control				X					X	
Issue Tracking / Bug Tracking										
Configuration Management									X	
Frequent Delivery / Frequent Releases	X			X					N	N
Unit Testing				X					X	
Smoke Testing / Build Verification Test				X					X	

(*Continued*)

Table 3. (*Continued*)

Practice	Challenge	Freedom	Idea support	Trust/openness	Dynamism/liveliness	Playfulness/humour	Debates	Conflicts	Risk taking	Idea time
Integration Testing				X					X	
System Testing				X					X	
Exploratory Testing				X	X				X	
Test Automation				X					X	
Storytesting / Acceptance Criteria / Acceptance Testing				X					X	
Timeboxing / Fixed Sprints / Fixed Iteration Length	X	X					X	X	N	N
Release Planning	X									
Iteration Planning / Planning Game / Sprint Planning	X									
Sprint Backlog					X					
Task Board					X		X	X		
Definition of Done / Done Done				X						
Daily Stand-up Meeting / Daily Scrum				X						
Velocity									N	N
Sprint Review / Iteration Demo	X			X			X			
Value Stream Mapping							X	X		
Root Cause Analysis / 5 Whys							X	X		
Burn Down Charts / Burn Up Charts					X					
Big Visible Charts / Information Radiators	X			X						
Retrospective / Reflection Workshop		X		X	X				X	X
Small Team				X	X		X	X		
Cross-Functional Team				X	X		X	X		
Self-Organizing Team / Scrum Team		X								
Colocated Team / Sitting Together / Common Workspace				X	X	X	X	X		
On-Site Customer / Product Owner			X	X	X			N		
Scrum Master			X	X	X					
Sustainable Pace										X
Move People Around	X		X							
Scrum of Scrums	X			X					X	

5 Discussion

The research questions of this paper uncovers which agile principles and practices have positive or negative effect on innovation climate; and which of the innovation factors are not affected by any of the agile principles or practices.

5.1   Principles and Practices with Positive Effect on Innovation

Close, daily cooperation between business people and developers alongside of self-organizing teams affect most innovation factors and thus can be argued to have largest impact on innovativeness of the team. These key principles are supported by pair-programming, collective code ownership, retrospectives and collocated teams. All of these are very communication-oriented principles and practices with mostly emphasis on the team. The only technical practices (pair-programming and collective code ownership) are also very communication intensive.

When looking from a higher level, each of the key principles and practices that support innovation factors, are related to two agile values: Individuals and interactions over processes and tools, Customer collaboration over contract negotiation. These emphasize both the communication inside the team and towards the stakeholders.

Surprisingly, the agile principles support mainly trust and debates, with little impact on e.g. playfulness or risk taking. We can see that the clear emphasis on agile practices is currently in creating a safe environment where people trust each other and are open about their opinions. This will then have a positive boost on the innovation factors.

5.2   Negatively Affecting Agile Principles and Practices

The negatively affecting principles and practices were mainly ones that will create some schedule pressure. Thus as a practical implication, using some way to create slack time or agreed time for experimentation could be beneficial.

The current trend in innovation management is Open innovation [16]. Conboy and Morgan have examined the compatibility of agile principles and open innovation principles [17]. They resulted that there seems to be distinct problems with combining these, e.g. openness is compromised by competitive element and lack of transparency [17]. We did not observe similar hindrances when mapping agile principles towards more traditional innovation climate factors. This however requires further studies to conclude if Open innovation principles change the innovation mechanisms so much that it becomes incompatible with agile software development.

5.3   Innovation Factors not Related to Agile Principles and Practices

Risk taking and Playfulness are not supported by agile principles at all. However, many agile practices support risk taking. As such, these practices are recommended to use, as simply following principles does not seem to improve risk taking climate.

Playfulness is not currently supported by any practices and principles and should be addressed by other means. In practice, this might mean e.g. that the team's manager creates playfulness into different meetings, or humour is kept high through common relaxed coffee breaks.

In addition to playfulness, also idea time and freedom are not well supported by practices. Again these can partly be improved by following agile principles, but also management should emphasis and enable these factors in the work environment.

5.4   Other Notable Findings

Especially debates, trust and openness are well supported by agile principles. These factors can also be seen as very tightly coupled. It seems that the emphasis of open communication in agile software development at least in theory leads to open and trusted workplace where debates occur often.

We can also see the need for both principles and practices in factors like dynamism and risk taking. Both are only supported by certain practices, but not that much by principles.

Surprisingly, principle 10 (Simplicity—the art of maximizing the amount of work not done—is essential) was not mapped to any innovation climate factors. This might be due to more technical nature of the principle.

Following practices were not mapped to any innovation factor: Use Cases, Design by Contract, Refactoring, Software Metrics/Code Metrics & Analysis, Issue Tracking/Bug Tracking and Velocity. Again, most of these can be seen as either rather technical practice (Refactoring, Design by Contract) or a tool (Use cases, software metrics, issue tracking, velocity). Thus they do not necessarily create suitable climate for innovation, but rather are used to keep the technical standards high or to analyse situation.

The practices and innovativeness are highly contextual. Just moving to agile software development and taking the practices into use will have very different impacts in large corporations compared to small companies. What is highly innovative for a banking giant can be seen as old fashioned for modern web companies.

5.5   Limitations and Further Studies

Naturally, there are limitations that should be acknowledged. First, this study bases on conceptual analytical approach and on qualitative analysis, i.e. mapping, done by the authors. Although we have done our best to remove researcher bias in the study process, the evaluation is subjective and further work would be needed to verify the results. In future work, external innovation climate and agile software development methods experts should evaluate the presented mapping in, e.g., a focus group discussion, or in a wider survey, to verify the results. However, this study provides the first steps for these kinds of continuation studies.

Second limitation is the lack of empirical evidence. In this study, the analysis was based on the ideal implementation of each practice; however, in reality, ideal implementation is rarity and often practices are more or less adapted in the development environment. Also only agile practices were included in the mapping which leaves out many important traditional practices. This means that not all innovation potential of a single practice might be utilized. Further empirical studies are needed to address do (and how) agile practices support or hinder innovation climate.

Overall, this study opens new paths for future research. In addition to seeking further confirmation of our results by e.g. reviews from agile practitioners and experts, future work should drive to improve those innovation climate dimensions which were found lacking the most. For the industry practitioners, we showed that there are theoretical links between improved innovation climate and certain practices might improve innovation climate of a development team. Furthermore, practitioners should also note the innovation climate dimensions that are not covered by the agile principles or practices; i.e. supporting also these dimensions might improve the innovations capabilities of the team more.

6 Conclusion

In this study, we addressed agile software development methods to drive innovation climate of a company. The conceptual analysis reveals that there are theoretical links between several different innovation climate factors and agile practices and principles. The results show that agile methods aim to build a safe environment where workers can trust each other and share their new ideas and opinions freely. However, the methods do not directly take into account playfulness dimension that is also showed to improve innovation climate. Managers of software development teams should note this limitation. Finally, this paper requested empirical research to support the findings from the conceptual analysis and proposed new avenues for further work in the field of agile software development.

Acknowledgment. Tomi Juhola is grateful for Turku University Foundation and Ulla Tuominen Foundation for financially supporting his dissertation work on innovations in agile software development context.

References

1. Highsmith, J., Cockburn, A.: Agile software development: business of innovation. Computer **34**(9), 120–127 (2001)
2. Juhola, T., Hyrynsalmi, S., Leppänen, V., Mäkilä, T.: Agile software development and innovation: a systematic literature review. In: Proceedings of 6th ISPIM Innovation Symposium: Innovation in the Asian century, pp. 1–19. ISPIM (2013)
3. Beaney, M.: Analysis, Stanford Encyclopaedia of Philosophy. http://www.plato.stanford.edu/entries/analysis/ (2014). Accessed April 2015
4. Abrahamsson, P., Salo, O., Ronkainen, J., Warsta, J.: Agile software development methods: review and analysis. VTT Publications 478, VTT, Espoo, Finland (2002)
5. Cohen, D., Lindvall, M., Costa, P.: An introduction to agile methods. Adv. Comput. **62**, 1–66 (2004)
6. Agile manifesto. http://www.agilemanifesto.org (2001). Accessed April 2015
7. Guide to Agile Practices. http://guide.agilealliance.org/. Accessed April 2015
8. Appelo, J.: Big list of agile practices. http://noop.nl/2009/04/the-big-list-of-agile-practices.html (2009). Accessed April 2015
9. Schumpeter, J.A.: The Theory of Economic Development. Transaction Publishers, New Brunswick (1934)
10. Edison, H., Bin Ali, N., Torkar, R.: Towards innovation measurement in the software industry. J. Syst. Softw. **86**(5), 1390–1407 (2013)

11. Adams, R., Bessant, J., Phelps, R.: Innovation management measurement: a review. Int. J. Manage. Rev. **8**(1), 21–47 (2006)
12. Regnell, B., Höst, M., Nilsson, F., Bengtsson, H.: A measurement framework for team level assessment of innovation capability in early requirements engineering. In: Bomarius, F., Oivo, M., Jaring, P., Abrahamsson, P. (eds.) PROFES 2009. LNBIP, vol. 32, pp. 71–86. Springer, Heidelberg (2009)
13. Ekvall, G.: Organizational climate for creativity and innovation. Eur. J. Work Organ. Psychol. **5**(1), 105–123 (1996)
14. Anderson, N.R., West, M.A.: Measuring climate for work group innovation: development and validation of the team climate inventory. J. Organ. Behav. **19**(3), 235–258 (1998)
15. Isaksen, S.G., Akkermans, H.J.: Creative climate: a leadership lever for innovation. J. Creative Behav. **45**(3), 161–187 (2011)
16. Chesbrough, H.W.: Open Innovation: the New Imperative for Creating and Profiting from Technology. Harvard Business School Press, Boston (2003)
17. Conboy, K., Morgan, L.: Beyond the customer: opening the agile systems development process. Inf. Softw. Technol. **53**(5), 535–542 (2011)

Inheritance in Object-Oriented Knowledge Representation

Dmytro Terletskyi[✉]

Taras Shevchenko National University of Kyiv, Kyiv 03680, Ukraine
dmytro.terletskyi@gmail.com
http://cyb.univ.kiev.ua/en/departments.is.terletskyi.html

Abstract. This paper contains the consideration of inheritance mechanism in such knowledge representation models as object-oriented programming, frames and object-oriented dynamic networks. In addition, inheritance within representation of vague and imprecise knowledge are also discussed. New types of inheritance, general classification of all known inheritance types and approach, which allows avoiding in many cases problems with exceptions, redundancy and ambiguity within object-oriented dynamic networks and their fuzzy extension, are introduced in the paper. The proposed approach bases on conception of homogeneous and inhomogeneous or heterogeneous class of objects, which allow building of inheritance hierarchy more flexibly and efficiently.

Keywords: Single inheritance · Multiple inheritance · Strong inheritance · Weak inheritance · Full inheritance · Partial inheritance

1 Introduction

Nowadays the design and development of knowledge-based systems for solving problems in different domains are important tasks within area of artificial intelligence. Currently there are many different knowledge representation models (KRM), the most famous of which are logical models, production models, semantic networks, frames, scripts, conceptual graphs, ontologies, etc. All of these KRMs have their own specifics and allow representing of some types of knowledge. However, the certain programming paradigm should be chosen for implementation of any particular KRM. For today the most famous and commonly used programming paradigm is an object-oriented programming (OOP). It gives us an opportunity of efficient implementation of many existing KRMs, in particular those that are object-oriented, e.g. frames, scripts. We should take into account that the knowledge in forms of any KRM must be somehow represented in the database. Object-oriented approach to knowledge representation is very suitable for this purpose, because it provides such powerful tool, as inheritance mechanism. It allows building of inheritance hierarchies and avoiding of redundancy of knowledge representation in database, because it partially implements the conception of reusability. In its turn, inheritance hierarchy as a type of knowledge structure provides an efficient mechanisms of reasoning about knowledge. Furthermore, the modern versions of most OOP-languages support such

G. Dregvaite and R. Damasevicius (Eds.): ICIST 2015, CCIS 538, pp. 293–305, 2015.
DOI: 10.1007/978-3-319-24770-0_26

programming technique as object-relational mapping (ORM), which provides convenient interaction among object-oriented programs and databases.

However, despite all advantages of object-oriented approach to knowledge representation, it also has some drawbacks. Firstly, inheritance mechanism leads three main kinds of problems, such as *problem of exceptions*, *problem of redundancy* and *problem of ambiguity* [1,13]. They arise during constructing of inheritance hierarchies and reasoning within them. Secondly, a lot of human knowledge have vague and imprecise nature [2,6] and OOP does not support representation of such knowledge. Thirdly, OOP provides an opportunity to create and to operate only with homogeneous classes [10], that is why we need to create new class for every new type of objects, even when some of them are similar.

2   Inheritance in Object-Oriented Programming

Nowadays there are two main approaches in modern OOP, which are implemented within *class-based* and *prototype-based* programming languages [3]. The main idea of first approach is an identification of common properties of some quantity of objects and their description within such structure as class. Objects exist only in runtime as a result of instantiating of a class. Within the second approach, the objects are results of cloning operation, which is applied to *prototypes*, where prototypes define stereotypical objects. The new prototype can be obtained as a modification of copy of other prototype. Currently, class-based programming approach is more commonly used than prototype-based one and most of modern OOP-languages support exactly class-based style. That is why all future considerations concerning OOP will be done within class-based programming approach.

In paradigm of OOP, class defines a kind of a concept, and objects are instances of it. Each class consists of fields and methods, where fields define the structure of the class and methods define its behavior. In other words, fields define properties of the concept and methods are functions that give an opportunity to manipulate them. When the program creates an object as an instance of some class, this object has the same fields, as its class and each method of the class can be called for this object. In such a way, class implements the mechanism of encapsulation, because the object has the same structure and behavior, but it has its own values of the fields, which can differ from corresponding values of class's fields and can be changed during program execution.

2.1   Single Inheritance

Class-based approach provides an ability to define the class using the existing definition of another class. In this case, one class can inherit specifics of another one. Moreover, it can extend or specialize the inherited specifics by adding its own features. This process is called *single inheritance* [3]. Using this mechanism, we can build inheritance hierarchies, where concepts that are more general will have higher position in the hierarchy than those that are less general. Class which inherits another class is called a *subclass* of that class and the class, which was inherited by another class, is called a *superclass*. Single inheritance can be graphically represented as a tree.

According to [3] there are at least three different interpretations of inheritance. We will consider inheritance in the context of modeling of classification hierarchies in the chosen application domain. Such interpretation is more common in OOP and is used in object-oriented knowledge representation.

Proposed approach has some benefits. Usage of inheritance allows more efficient using of computer memory and memory in a database by avoiding duplication of similar information, during description of classes. Almost all modern OOP-languages support single inheritance. However, it also has some drawbacks. When one class inherits another one, it inherits all its properties. There are some cases when it causes some redundancy of description of subclasses, moreover sometimes it causes conflicts among concepts, described by subclass and superclass. All these problems will be considered and discussed in more detail later.

2.2 Multiple Inheritance

Under single inheritance, each subclass can have only one superclass, however class can have more than one superclass and there are cases when single inheritance is insufficient. For this purpose there is another form of inheritance, which is called a *multiple inheritance* [3]. It allows class to inherit specifics of many other classes. Multiple inheritance hierarchy can be graphically represented as an acyclic directed graph, or simply an direct inheritance graph.

Multiple inheritance has almost the same benefits, as a single one. Moreover, it gives an opportunity to create more complex classes and objects via inheritance. However, multiple inheritance also has some drawbacks. Usage of multiple inheritance sometimes causes two types of semantic conflicts within the subclasses. In the first case, the class can simultaneously inherit a few copies of the same method or different values of the equivalent properties from different superclasses. In the second case, the subclass can inherit semantically incompatible properties and methods. In addition, in contrast to single inheritance, not every OOP-language supports multiple inheritance. Languages, which support multiple inheritance, are C++, Common Lisp, Eiffel, Scala, Perl, Python, etc. However, for example such commonly used OOP-languages as C#, Java, Objective-C, Ruby, Php do not do it. Most of them use an alternative approaches to multiple inheritance such as interfaces, that allow partial modelling of multiple inheritance principles.

3   Object-Oriented Knowledge Representation

The main idea of object-oriented knowledge representation approach is representation of knowledge about a domain in terms of objects, classes and relations among them. OOP provides all opportunities for such representation, however in many books where models of knowledge representation are described, OOP is not mentioned. Nevertheless, we consider models, which are ideologically close to

OOP, such as frames and object-oriented dynamic networks (OODN). We briefly consider these KRMs and implementation of inheritance mechanism within them.

3.1 Frames

Frame is a data-structure for representation of knowledge about stereotypical situations [7]. Frame consists of set of slots, where each slot has its own filler. Name of a frame, relationships with other frames, attributes of frame, procedural attachments can be fillers for frame's slots. Every slot with its value represents particular property of object or class, which is represented by frame. Generally, there are two types of frames: individual or *instance-frames* for representation of single objects, and generic or *class-frames* for representation of classes [9].

Different frames can be merged into one system via relationships [7]. There are three main types of relations among frames: *generalization*, *aggregation* and *association*. Generalization represents relationship between subclass and super-class or object and class, when subclass is a kind of superclass or object is an instance of its class. This type of relationships can be denoted using *is-a*, *an-instance-of*, *a-kind-of*, etc. links. Aggregation represents relationship among several subclasses and their superclass, when subclass is a part of superclass. Usually aggregation can be denoted as *a-part-of*, *part-whole*, etc. Association describes some semantic relationship among different classes, which are unrelated otherwise. Examples of such kind relationships are *have*, *can*, *own*, etc.

Usually, frames can have some methods associated with them. They are called procedural attachments. Every procedure is a set of some instructions, which are associated with a frame and can be executed on request.

Similarly to OOP, frames use the inheritance mechanism for building frames-systems, which also have hierarchical structure [9]. The conception of inheritance within frames is the same as in OOP. There is difference only between representation of structure of classes and objects within these approaches. OOP is more flexible and powerful for representation of class structure, because in contrast to frames, it has some set of basic built-in primitive data types, which can be used for creating more complex data structures, while frames has only three built-in primitive types: numeric, string and logical. However, frames have such feature as compound attributes which take a value from some set of values, which elements can have different types.

In terms of frames, class can inherit specifics of another class through generalization relationship, i.e. *is-a* slot. However, single and multiple inheritance cause the same problems in frames as in OOP [9,13].

As we can see, problems of inheritance are common for all object-oriented KRMs, but they are related only to the specifics of inheritance mechanism.

3.2 Problem of Exceptions

The first known problem of inheritance is the problem of exceptions. There are some classical examples, which illustrate it. They are known as examples about flying penguins or ostriches and about three-legged or white elephant [1,13]. In general, the problem can be formulated as a situation, when superclass contains properties, which are not true for all its subclasses.

After formulation of this problem, a few approaches to its solving were proposed. For example, in frame-based systems, subclasses can override the values of inherited slots from their superclass [9]. However, this approach is not efficient, because overriding of values of slots leads to the situation when the subclass goes beyond its superclass. After it, this class cannot be viewed as the subclass of its superclass, because all subclasses must inherit all properties of their superclass.

The main idea of another known approach is the usage of *not-is-a* links for modelling of exceptions [1,13]. Such solution differs from others, because its main idea is not to avoid the exceptions in the hierarchy, but to describe them somehow. The conception of *not-is-a* link came from logical approach of knowledge representation and on the first glance such solution does not cause any suspicions. However it causes appearing of the contradictory classes, formation of inconsistent knowledge base and as result contradictory reasoning [1].

In OOP, solving of this problem relies on the programmer. In other words, the programmer should somehow constrain the generality of the superclass.

3.3   Problem of Redundancy

One more kind of problem related to inheritance is the problem of redundancy. It appears within the inheritance tree, when the class inherits specifics from more than one related superclass [1,13]. In this situation, there is a vertical chain of inheritance, where top level contains most general class and each of lower levels contains less general class, than its superclass. On the bottom level there is the most specific class of the hierarchy. The main features of this class is that it inherits all properties from its predecessors. Sometimes such inheritance is redundant, because the class can inherit unnecessary properties or methods and all objects of this class will have the same specifics.

There are some approaches, which avoid the inheritance of redundant properties. One of them is the choosing of the nearest value. However, it is not an efficient way, because the result of such choosing depends on appropriate algorithm. Various systems have different algorithms, which can return different results in the same situation [1,13].

3.4   Problem of Ambiguity

Another kind of problem related to inheritance is the problem of ambiguity. There are a few classical examples, which illustrate this problem. They are known as examples about Quaker or Nixon and about elephant, who is a circus performer, etc. [1,13]. This problem appears, when the class inherits specifics from more than one unrelated superclass of the same level, and these superclasses contain properties and methods with the same names. In this situation, subclass should somehow choose one of these variants.

Concerning properties, sometimes they can have only similar name, but not a type or value. Sometimes, they can have the same type and different values or they can have the same type and value. In all these cases there is an ambiguity, because it is unknown, which particular property should be chosen and different variants can have totally different semantic contexts. Methods, similarly to properties can have only the same names and very different semantic contexts. However, even if their semantics are similar or close to similar, they can be implemented in different ways.

There are a few approaches for solving this problem [1,13]. First of them uses the idea of choosing some particular version of property or method. In this case, there is a question how to choose them. There are appropriate algorithms, which are implemented in different systems, in particular in frame-based ones. However, they use different criteria for choosing the variant. Very often result depends on the behavior and time complexity of the algorithm. It means that different algorithms will give different results using the same inheritance structure. Second approach allows inheritance of all possible variations of properties and methods. In this situation results will be different in various systems [1]. However, both solutions are not efficient enough, because in the first case a system ignores some part of variants in different ways and in the second one, knowledge base becomes inconsistent.

3.5   Object-Oriented Dynamic Networks

Another kind of object-oriented knowledge representation model is object-oriented dynamic networks, which was proposed in [11]. In some aspects, this KRM is similar to OOP and frames, however, despite this, it has some specific peculiarities, which are not typical for other models. Let us consider structure of this model.

Definition 1. *Object-Oriented Dynamic Network is a 5-tuple*

$$OODN = (O, C, R, E, M),$$

where:
- *O – a set of objects;*
- *C – a set of classes of objects, which describe objects from set O;*
- *R – a set of relations, which are defined on set O and C;*
- *E – a set of exploiters, which are defined on set O and C;*
- *M – a set of modifiers, which are defined on set O and C.*

Analyzing this definition, we can conclude that usage of conceptions of objects, classes and relation among them is common for both OOP and frames. However, all these concepts have different implementations within mentioned KRMs. One of the main differences is the definition of the class. Within OOP, class is something like abstract description of some quantity of objects of the same nature [3]. According to this, such class is homogeneous, because all its instances have the same type. In this sense, definition of the class within frames is similar to appropriate one in OOP. However, there is another type of classes, which are inhomogeneous or heterogeneous [10]. Conception of a class, which is defined within OODN, takes into account both types of classes. Let us consider it in more details.

Definition 2. *Class of objects T is a tuple $T = (P(T), F(T))$, where $P(T)$ is specification (a vector of properties) of some quantity of objects, and $F(T)$ is their signature (a vector of methods).*

The next definition proposes some classification of classes.

Definition 3. *Homogeneous class of objects is a class of objects, which contains only similar objects.*

According to this, we can conclude that Definition 2 describes homogeneous classes.

Now let us consider the definition of inhomogeneous class.

Definition 4. *Inhomogeneous (heterogeneous) class of objects T is a tuple*

$$T = (Core(T), pr_1(A_1), \ldots, pr_n(A_n)),$$

where $Core(T) = (P(T), F(T))$ is the core of class of objects T, which includes only properties and methods similar to corresponding properties of specifications $P(A_1), \ldots, P(A_n)$ and corresponding methods of signatures $F(A_1), \ldots, F(A_n)$ respectively, and where $pr_i(A_i) = (P(A_i), F(A_i))$, $i = \overline{1, n}$ are projections of objects $A_1, \ldots, A_n$, which consist of properties and methods typical only for these objects.

This approach gives an opportunity to describe some quantity of objects, which have similar or even different nature within one class. While in OOP, we must define new class for each new type of objects, even if these types are close or similar.

Some of main features of OODN are a set of exploiters E and a set of modifiers M. Both of them contain methods which can be applied to the objects and classes of objects from set O and C respectively. The difference between these two types of methods is character of their action. Exploiters use objects and classes of objects, as the parameters for obtaining new knowledge, without any their changes, while, modifiers change the essence of objects and classes of objects and allow modelling of changes of basic knowledge over the time.

In general, OODN can be viewed as two conceptual parts. First of them is declarative, which includes sets O, C, R, and allows representation of knowledge about particular domain. Second part is procedural one, it includes sets E, M and provides the tools for obtaining new knowledge from basic ones.

4   Object-Oriented Representation of Fuzzy Knowledge

Currently there is variety of KRMs, which give an opportunity to represent the knowledge in different ways. Main of them were mentioned in the introduction part. However, a lot of human knowledge is vague and imprecise [2,6] and cannot be represented in efficient way, using existing KRMs. That is why most of them were extended to the case of fuzzy knowledge, through the use of fuzzy sets theory [14]. Currently there are fuzzy logic, fuzzy semantic networks, fuzzy rule-based models, fuzzy neural networks, fuzzy ontologies, fuzzy frames, fuzzy UML, etc. However, classical paradigm of OOP does not provide an opportunity for representing fuzzy objects and classes. That is why, a few attempts to do this were done within object-oriented approach to representation of fuzzy knowledge [2,6,8].

Similarly to object-oriented knowledge representation, main concepts of object-oriented representation of fuzzy knowledge are fuzzy objects, classes of fuzzy objects and relationships among them. The object and class are fuzzy, when they have at least one fuzzy property, i.e. property that is defined by a fuzzy set. The relations among fuzzy objects and classes of fuzzy objects, which are usually considered are similar to corresponded relations in frames and OOP, i.e. generalization, aggregation and association.

4.1   Fuzzy Frames

One of the most interesting extensions of classical KRMs to the case of fuzzy knowledge are fuzzy frames [4,5]. There are two main differences between frames and fuzzy frames. Firstly, within fuzzy frames slots can contain fuzzy sets as values. Secondly, the inheritance through *is-a* slot can be partial. Such extension of frames allows describing of objects and classes which have partial properties, i.e. properties which inherent with some measure. It means that such properties are not strictly true or false for the object or class. This kind of inheritance is called weak one.

Proposed kind of inheritance can solve problem with exceptions in some cases, when the subclass inherits all properties of its superclass, but some of them are inherited with measure less than 1. It means that these properties are less expressed within the subclass than in its ancestor. However, such approach does not solve problems with redundancy and ambiguity, because it allows only the flexible description of inheritance relationships among classes.

4.2   Fuzzy Object-Oriented Dynamic Networks

Similarly to OOP and frames, object-oriented-dynamic networks are not efficient for representation of fuzzy objects and classes. That is why concepts of object and class of objects, which are basic for OODN were extended to the case of fuzzy knowledge [12]. Taking into account these extensions, the definition of fuzzy object-oriented dynamic networks can be formulated in the following way.

Definition 5. *Fuzzy Object-Oriented Dynamic Network is a object-oriented dynamic network*

$$FOODN = (O, C, R, E, M),$$

for which at least one of the following conditions:

- $\exists A_k, \ldots, A_m \in O = \{A_1, \ldots, A_n\}$, *where* $1 \leq k \leq m \leq n$ *and* $A_k, \ldots, A_m$ *are fuzzy objects;*
- $\exists T_p, \ldots, T_q \in C = \{T_1, \ldots, T_w\}$, *where* $1 \leq p \leq q \leq w$ *and* $T_p, \ldots, T_q$ *are classes of fuzzy objects;*
- $\exists R_i, \ldots, R_j \in R = \{R_1, \ldots, R_v\}$, *where* $1 \leq i \leq j \leq v$ *and* $R_i, \ldots, R_j$ *are fuzzy relations among fuzzy objects and classes of fuzzy objects.*

is true.

The most important feature of this extension is that general structure of the object and class of objects, types of classes and relations are the same for OODN and FOODN. There only difference is the type of properties, because in FOODN some properties of objects or classes of objects can be fuzzy.

5 Types of Inheritance

As we can see from previous sections, there are two types of inheritance – single and multiple. Such inheritance types classification allows consideration of inheritance process in the context of different types of inheritance source. However, there is another classification, which divides inheritance on strong and weak. It allows consideration of inheritance from another point of view, namely how the inherited properties will be expressed within the subclass.

Nevertheless, there are other classifications. The common feature for single and multiple inheritance is that subclass inherits all properties and methods of inheritance source. We suppose that it is the source of majority of problems. In our opinion, if the class did not inherit all the properties of inheritance source, it would not cause the problems of redundancy and ambiguity. Moreover, such kind of inheritance allows building of inheritance hierarchy in more flexible way, without redundancy and ambiguity. According to this, we can conclude that inheritance can be also classified as full and partial. In the first case subclass inherits all the properties and methods from inheritance source, in the second case it inherits only selected properties and methods. All considered classifications of inheritance can be arranged within one classification, which is represented in the Table 1.

Now, let us consider the process of inheritance within OODN and FOODN. Suppose we have three classes of object A_1, A_2 and A_3, which are defined as follows

Table 1. Classification of inheritance types

		Inheritance					
	Single				Multiple		
Full		Partial		Full		Partial	
Strong	Weak	Strong	Weak	Strong	Weak	Strong	Weak

$$T(A_1) = (P(A_1), F(A_1)) = (p_1(A_1), p_2(A_1), f_1(A_1), f_2(A_1)),$$
$$T(A_2) = (P(A_2), F(A_2)) = (p_1(A_2), p_2(A_2), f_1(A_2)),$$
$$T(A_3) = (P(A_3), F(A_3)) = (p_1(A_3), f_1(A_3)).$$

Let us consider types of inheritance, which are shown in Table 1, within OODN and FOODN. According to Table 1, there are eight different types of inheritance, but all of them can be reduced to two main kinds – single and multiple. That is why, let us consider these two types as the most general ones.

5.1   Single Inheritance

Suppose we have the following sequence of inheritance

$$A_3 \xrightarrow{inherits} A_2 \xrightarrow{inherits} A_1.$$

The result of such inheritance is

$$A_3 \xrightarrow{inherits} A_2 \xrightarrow{inherits} A_1 = T = (Core(T), pr_1(T), pr_1(pr_1(T))),$$

where

$$Core(T) = (p_1(A_1), p_2(A_1), f_1(A_1), f_2(A_1)),$$
$$pr_1(T) = (p_1(A_2), p_2(A_2), f_1(A_2)),$$
$$pr_1(pr_1(T)) = (p_1(A_3), f_1(A_3)).$$

The structures of classes A_1, A_2 and A_3 in the heterogeneous class T can be expressed as follows:

$$A_1 = Core(T),$$
$$A_2 = Core(T) \cup pr_1(T),$$
$$A_3 = Core(T) \cup pr_1(T) \cup pr_1(pr_1(T)).$$

5.2   Multiple Inheritance

Suppose we have the following sequence of inheritance

$$A_3 \xrightarrow{inherits} A_1 \quad and \quad A_3 \xrightarrow{inherits} A_2.$$

The result of such inheritance process is

$$A_3 \xrightarrow{inherits} A_1 \quad and \quad A_3 \xrightarrow{inherits} A_2 = T =$$
$$= (pr_1(T), pr_2(T), pr_1(pr_1(T), pr_2(T))),$$

where

$$pr_1(T) = (p_1(A_1), p_2(A_1), f_1(A_1), f_2(A_1)),$$
$$pr_2(T) = (p_1(A_2), p_2(A_2), f_1(A_2)),$$
$$pr_1(pr_1(T), pr_2(T)) = (p_1(A_3), f_1(A_3)).$$

The structures of classes A_1, A_2 and A_3 in the heterogeneous class T can be expressed as follows:

$$A_1 = pr_1(T),$$
$$A_2 = pr_2(T),$$
$$A_3 = pr_1(pr_1(T), pr_2(T)).$$

5.3   Special Cases

Let us consider example of partial and weak inheritance, using previously described classes A_1, A_2 and A_3 for it. Suppose we have the situation, when the class A_2 partially inherits the class A_1, for example property $p_1(A_1)$ and method $f_1(A_1)$.

$$A_2 \xrightarrow{inherits\ (p_1, f_1)} A_1 = T = (Core(T), pr_1(T), pr_2(T)),$$

where

$$Core(T) = (p_1(A_1), f_1(A_1)),$$
$$pr_1(T) = (p_2(A_1), f_2(A_1)),$$
$$pr_2(T) = (p_1(A_2), p_2(A_2), f_1(A_2)).$$

The structures of classes A_1 and A_2 in the heterogeneous class T can be expressed as follows:

$$A_1 = Core(T) \cup pr_1(T),$$
$$A_2 = Core(T) \cup pr_2(T).$$

Suppose we have the situation, when the class A_2 weakly inherits the class A_1, for example property $p_1(A_1)$ with measure 0.5.

$$A_2 \xrightarrow{inherits\ (p_1/0.5)} A_1 = T = (Core(T), pr_1(T), pr_2(T)),$$

where

$$Core(T) = (p_2(A_1), f_1(A_1), f_2(A_1)),$$
$$pr_1(T) = (p_1(A_1)/1),$$
$$pr_2(T) = (p_1(A_1)/0.5, p_1(A_2), p_2(A_2), f_1(A_2)).$$

The structures of classes A_1 and A_2 in the heterogeneous class T can be expressed as follows:

$$A_1 = Core(T) \cup pr_1(T),$$
$$A_2 = Core(T) \cup pr_2(T).$$

6   Conclusions

This paper contains analysis of inheritance process and its specifics in the context of knowledge representation within OOP, frames and OODN. Such kinds of inheritance problems as problems of exceptions, redundancy, ambiguity and some approaches for their solving were considered in different perspectives. In addition, the various kinds of inheritance classifications were also considered.

New types of inheritance, which allow building of inheritance hierarchies in more flexible and efficient way, were proposed. Furthermore, general classification of all known inheritance types, which includes eight different types of inheritance, was introduced. The application of approach, which allows avoiding in many cases problems with exceptions, redundancy and ambiguity within OODN and FOODN was shown, using examples.

Proposed approach for organizing of inheritance hierarchies suggests new concepts, which can extend the OOP in many useful directions. However, despite all its benefits, it requires further research.

References

1. Al-Asady, R.: Inheritance Theory: An Artificial Intelligence Approach. Ablex Publishing Corporation, Norwood (1995)
2. Berzal, F., Marin, N., Pons, O., Vila, M.A.: Managing fuzziness on conventional object-oriented platforms. Int. J. Intell. Syst. **22**, 781–803 (2007)
3. Craig, I.D.: Object-Oriented Programming Languages: Interpretation. Springer, London (2007)
4. Graham, I., Jones, P.L.: A theory of fuzzy frames: part-1. Bull. Stud. Exch. Fuzziness Appl. **32**, 109–132 (1987)
5. Graham, I., Jones, P.L.: A theory of fuzzy frames: part-2. Bull. Stud. Exch. Fuzziness Appl. **32**, 120–135 (1987)
6. Leung, K.S., Wong, M.H.: Fuzzy concepts in an object oriented expert system shell. Int. J. Intell. Syst. **7**, 171–192 (1992)
7. Minsky, M.: A Framework for Representing Knowledge. Technical Report No. 306, AI Laboratory, Massachusetts Institute of Technology (1974)

8. Ndousse, T.D.: Intelligent systems modeling with reusable fuzzy objects. Int. J. Intell. Syst. **12**, 137–152 (1997)
9. Negnevitsky, M.: Artificial Intelligence: A Guide to Intelligent Systems, 2nd edn. Addison-Wesley, Harlow (2004)
10. Terletskyi, D.A., Provotar, O.I.: Mathematical foundations for designing and development of intelligent systems of information analysis. Sci. J. Probl. Program. **15**, 233–241 (2014)
11. Terletskyi, D.O., Provotar, O.I.: Object-oriented dynamic networks. In: Setlak, G., Markov, K. (eds.) Computational Models for Business and Engineering Domains, vol. 30, pp. 123–136. ITHEA IBS ISC (2014)
12. Terletskyi, D.A., Provotar, A.I.: Fuzzy object-oriented dynamic networks. I. Int. Sci. J. Cybern. Syst. Anal. **51**, 34–40 (2015)
13. Touretzky, D.S.: The Mathematics of Inheritance Systems. Morgan Kaufmann Publishers, Los Altos (1986)
14. Zadeh, L.A.: Fuzzy sets. Inf. Cont. **8**, 338–353 (1965)

QoS-Based Web Services Composition Optimization with an Extended Bat Inspired Algorithm

Serial Rayene Boussalia[1]([✉]), Allaoua Chaoui[1], and Aurélie Hurault[2]

[1] MISC Laboratory, Constantine 2 University, 25000 Constantine, Algeria
seriel.rayene@gmail.com, a_chaoui2001@yahoo.com
[2] IRIT Laboratory, University of Toulouse, 5505 Toulouse, France
Aurelie.Hurault@enseeiht.fr

Abstract. The QoS-Based Web services composition optimisation problem is an NP-Hard problem. So far, solving such a problem consists on finding its optimal solution, while optimizing an objective function using the QoS as an optimization criteria. In this paper, we propose an approach based on the use of a new Extended Bat Inspired Algorithm to deal with the QoS-Based Web Services composition optimization problem. The Bat Inspired Algorithm has the advantage of providing a very quick convergence at a very early stage by switching from exploration to exploitation. This makes it an efficient algorithm. The originality of the proposed approach is the designing and the built of the composition solutions by adjusting the main parameters of the algorithm. Then, to compare potential generated solutions, different QoS attributes are considered and aggregated at the complete composition level. A prototype has been realized and applied to a text translation case study. The results of experimentation are very encouraging and show that the approach is highly efficient in terms of optimality rate and running time.

Keywords: Quality of service(QoS) · Web service · Web services composition · Optimization methods · Bat Inspired Algorithm

1 Introduction

The composition of Web services is required when the user's needs are not met by one simple basic Web service, but by a complex one. However, the large number of Web services available on the internet with different implementations offering the same functionality led to many solutions of Web services compositions. So, for one user request, several potential compositions can be proposed [1]. For that, we need a Web services composition optimization to deal with this problem.

The Web services composition optimization is an NP Hard optimization problem [2] that can be modelled as a problem of multidimensional knapsack. Three factors determine the complexity of this problem: the number of tasks to be performed, the number of candidate services for each task and the number of parameters of quality of services to optimise [3].

© Springer International Publishing Switzerland 2015
G. Dregvaite and R. Damasevicius (Eds.): ICIST 2015, CCIS 538, pp. 306–319, 2015.
DOI: 10.1007/978-3-319-24770-0_27

The optimization of the Web services composition consists on finding the optimal combination of Web services satisfying a user request using optimization methods to optimize predefined QoS parameters [2]. In this context, the quality of service (QoS) attributes are the non-functional properties of Web services which emerge as the key differential factors for selecting and composing Web services [4].

The present study is designed to investigate the use of an extended Bat Inspired Algorithm (BA) to deal with the Web services composition problem. This efficient iterative approach performs a global optimization in the search space by building an optimal solution of the problem. During each iteration, the algorithm constructs new solutions trying to find the one that better satisfies the user's request. The solutions are constructed by adjusting some parameters of the BA algorithm while optimizing the QoS criteria.

In the literature, the problem of QoS-based Web services composition optimization has been intensively studied and different approaches have been proposed in the past few years. We can cite approaches using optimization methods to deal with the Web services composition problem: the Genetic Algorithm [5,6], Particle Swarm Optimization [7], the Ant Colony Algorithm [8], the Cuckoo Search algorithm [9].

Most of the approaches are statics [5–8], they are based on static workflows to realize the Web services compositions. But, in this paper a dynamic approach named BA-WSC is proposed. With this approach, the use of a new Extended Bat Inspired Algorithm (BA) is investigated to handle the Web services composition problem.

The particularity of BA-WSC approach is the use of the BA starting from an initial population generated according to the user's request with a new randomized heuristic. Likely many metaheuristic algorithms, Bat Inspired Algorithm has the advantage of simplicity and flexibility. The Bat Inspired Algorithm is easy to implement, and flexible enough to solve a wide range of problems as we have seen in the above review.

The remainder of this paper is organized as follows: Sect. 2 recalls the background required for developing the approach; Sect. 3 presents the context of QoS Web services composition optimization; Sect. 4 defines the formulation of the problem; Sect. 5 introduces the proposed approach based on dealing the composition problem with a new extended version of the Bat Inspired Algorithm; Sect. 6 discusses the experimentation and the obtained results. Finally, the paper is ended by some important conclusions and prospects, suggested in the use of optimization methods to find the best Web services composition.

2 Background

This section recalls the theoretical background required for developing the BA-WSC approach based on the use of an extended Bat Inspired Algorithm(BA) to optimize the QoS-based Web services composition.

2.1 Web Services Composition

The Web services composition refers to the process of combining the functionality of multiple Web services within the same business process, in order to meet the complex request that one Web service could not satisfy alone [10]. So, the process of Web services composition mainly focuses on finding the most appropriate Web services whose composition satisfies user requirements. Different works are interested of the Web services composition problem by proposing different approaches. Generally the proposed resolution methods are based on workflows, artificial intelligence planning or metaheuristics [11].

2.2 Web Services Composition Optimization

The optimization of Web services composition consists on selecting and interconnecting the appropriate Web services provided by different Web services providers, with the aim of optimizing a set of predefined parameters to guaranty the overall quality of this composition [12].

Selecting the appropriate Web services to be candidates in the best Web services composition is seen as a challenge [2]. Consequently some heuristics and biologically inspired optimization algorithms were proposed. The simplicity of these algorithms and their fast speed of convergence to the optimal or near-optimal solutions are their main advantage. Some algorithms were proposed to solve the Web services composition problem such as: the Genetic Algorithm [13], Particle Swarm Optimization [14], the Ant Colony Algorithm [15], the Cuckoo Search algorithm [16] and others.

2.3 Bat Inspired Algorithm

Bat Inspired Algorithm (Algorithm 1) is a new metaheuristic method proposed by Yang [17]. This algorithm is based on behaviour of the bats that can track their prey/foods using their capability of echolocation [18]. In order to model this algorithm, Yang [19] has idealized some rules, as follows:

1. All bats use echolocation to sense distance, and they also "know" the difference between food/prey and background barriers in some magical way.
2. A bat fly randomly with velocity v_i at position x_i with a fixed frequency f_{min}, varying wavelength λ and loudness A_0 to search for prey. They can automatically adjust the wavelength (or frequency) of their emitted pulses and adjust the rate of pulse emission $r \in [0, 1]$ depending on the proximity of their target.
3. Although the loudness can vary in many ways, Yang [19] assume that the loudness varies from a large (positive)A_0 to a minimum constant value A_{min}.

Firstly, the initial position x_i , velocity v_i and frequency f_i are initialized for each bat b_i of the population. For each time step t , being T the maximum number of iterations, the movement of the bats is given by updating their velocity and position using Equations 1, 2 and 3, as follow [17].

Algorithm 1. Bat Inspired Algorithm [19]

1: Objective function $f(x), x = (x_1, ..., x_n)$;
2: **Input :** Problem Data;
3: **Output :** Optimal solution x_*;

4: **begin**
5: Initialize the bat population x_i and v_i $(i = 1, 2, ..., n)$
6: Define pulse frequency f_i at x_i $(i = 1, ..., n)$
7: Initialize pulserates r_i and the loudness A_i $(i = 1, ..., n)$
8: **while** $t < $ T (Max number of iterations) **do**
9:    Generate new solutions by adjusting frequency;
10:    Updating velocities and locations/solutions (*Equation 1 to Eq. 3*);
11:    **if** $rand > r_i$ **then**
12:       Select a solution among the best solutions;
13:       Generate a local solution around the selected best solution;
14:    **end if**
15:    Generate a new solution by flying randomly (*Equation 4*);
16:    **if** $(rand < A_i$ and $f(x_i < f(x_*)))$ **then**
17:       Accept the new solutions;
18:       Increase r_i and reduce A_i (*Equation 5 and Eq. 6*);
19:    **end if**
20:    Rank the bats and find the current best x_*;
21: **end while**
22: Post process results and visualization ;

$$f_i = f_{min} + (f_{min} - f_{max}).\beta \tag{1}$$

$$v_i^j(t) = v_i^j(t - 1) + [v_*^j - v_i^j(t - 1)].f_i \tag{2}$$

$$v_i^j(t) = v_i^j(t - 1) + v_i^j(t) \tag{3}$$

where β denotes a randomly generated number within the interval $[0, 1]$. Recall that $v_i^j(t)$ denotes the value of decision variable for bat i at time step t. The result of f_i (Eq. 1) is used to control the pace and range of the movement of the bats. The variable v_*^j represents the current global best solution for decision variable j, which is achieved comparing all the solutions provided by the m bats [19].

In order to improve the variability of the possible solutions, Yang [17] has proposed to employ random walks in order to generate new solutions (Eq. 4).

$$x_{new} = x_{old} + \varepsilon \overline{A}(t) \tag{4}$$

In which $(\overline{A}(t))$ stands for the average loudness of all the bats at time t and $\varepsilon \in [-1, 1]$ attempts to the direction and strength of the random walk. For each iteration of the algorithm, the loudness A_i and the emission pulse rate r_i are updated, as follows:

$$A_i(t + 1) = \alpha A_i(t) \tag{5}$$

$$r_i(t + 1) = r_i(O)[1 - exp(-\gamma t)] \tag{6}$$

where α and γ are ad-hoc constants. At the first step of the algorithm, the emission rate $r_i(O)$ and the loudness $A_i(O)$ are often randomly chosen. Generally, $A_i \in [1,2]$ and $r_i \in [0,1]$ [19].

In the following, we recall the context and the basic ideas of our proposed approach.

3   QoS Based Optimization

The non-functional descriptions of a Web service called quality of service(QoS) correspond to the modalities for achieving its functionality. Generally their values are provided by the Service Provider while publishing the Web service [20]. The QoS model used in BA-WSC approach is composed of four criterion as parameters of quality of service: time, cost, availability and reputation. They represent a selection of relevant characteristics in the field of Web services. These criteria are presented below:

Time: Measures the execution time of the Web service between sending a request and receiving a response.

Cost: Is the amount that the service requester needs to pay to execute the Web service.

Availability: is the probability that the service is accessible.

Reputation: Measures the trustworthiness of the Web service. It depends on the user's experience using this service.

In this approach, the QoS characterize each Web service and lead to determine the candidate ones for each task of a complex user's request.

The computation of the overall QoS depends on the Web services composition. This composition is evaluated by computing the aggregated QoS function based on the values of its QoS parameters. Then, when the aggregated QoS functions of all possible Web services combinations are calculated, the best combination of Web services that does not violate the QoS constraints set by the user is selected [21].

4   Problem Formulation

For optimizing the composition problem, the QoS value of each candidate composition is based on the QoS values of its component services. Those values of QoS are aggregated into a single real value, in order to estimate the solution QoS. For such optimization, while we are aggregating the QoS attributes values, it's not feasible to minimize some criteria (time and cost) and maximize the others (reputation and availability). For this reason, we are interested about the complement of both reputation and availability which are respectively the bad-reputation and the unavailability in order to minimize all the QoS attributes.

Using a QoS aggregated function, a criteria can be privileged comparing to the others. For example, more importance can be given to time and less importance to the cost. Formally, the optimization problem is modelled as the minimization of the QoS as follows. For a composition $WSC = \{S_1, ..., S_m\}$ where m is the number of services in the composition, $S_i, i \in 1..m$ are the services in the composition, and w_k are the weight of each QoS attribute (Time, Cost, Badreputation, Unavailability), let define:

$$
\begin{aligned}
QoS(WSC) = {} & w_1 * Time(WSC) \\
& + w_2 * Cost(WSC) \\
& + w_3 * Badreputation(WSC) \\
& + w_4 * Unavailability(WSC)
\end{aligned} \tag{7}
$$

where:

$$Time(WSC) = \Sigma_{i=1}^{m} Time(S_i) \tag{8}$$

$$Cost(WSC) = \Sigma_{i=1}^{m} Cost(S_i) \tag{9}$$

$$Badreputation(WSC) = 1/m \Sigma_{i=1}^{m} Badreputation(S_i) \tag{10}$$

$$Unavailability(WSC) = \Pi_{i=1}^{m} Unavailability(S_i) \tag{11}$$

Subject to constraints:

$$Time(WSC) \leq Tmax \tag{12}$$

$$Cost(WSC) \leq Cmax \tag{13}$$

$$Badreputation(WCS) \leq BRmax \tag{14}$$

$$Unavailability(WCS) \leq Umax \tag{15}$$

In the above model the first objective function (Eq. 7) minimizes the aggregated QoS function of potential Web services compositions (WSC) that correspond to a user request. This function allows merging the attributes of QoS in one real value, by assigning a weight w_k to each attribute. The values of w_k are defined according to the user preferences.

Equations 8, 9, 10 and 11 present the QoS aggregated function for the attributes: time, cost, bad-reputation and unavailability respectively. These aggregated functions lead us to define the QoS constraints expressed in Eqs. 12, 13, 14 and 15. They represent the user's constraints that need to be satisfied.

5 Proposed Approach

In this section, an overview of the BA-WSC approach is presented. The basic concepts used for the resolution of the Web services composition optimization problem are explained.

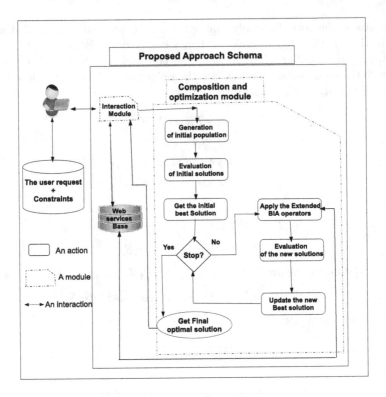

Fig. 1. The proposed approach schema

5.1 Schema of the Proposed Approach

The proposed approach (BA-WSC) is based on the use of a new version of the Bat Inspired Algorithm (BA) while optimizing the QoS descriptions of Web services. The objective is to build and determine the optimal Web services composition that satisfy a user request while respecting his constraints. This approach is realised by considering the QoS as an optimization criteria.

The schema of this approach (BA-WSC) is presented in Fig. 1, where the user is supposed to enter his request(input, output) and his QoS constraints. The best Web services composition is computed by the BA-WSC approach.

5.2 Representation of Solutions

In order to easily apply the BA operators to solve the Web services composition optimization problem, a binary representation is adopted. So, a Web services composition is represented as a binary vector satisfying the following criteria:

- For n Web services, the size of the binary vector (Fig. 2) that represents a composition is n, each element of the vector is a Web service.

$$\begin{bmatrix} 1\ 0\ 1\ 0\ 0\ 1\ 1\ 0\ 0\ 0 \end{bmatrix}$$

Fig. 2. A binary solution

- The presence of 1 in the position (i) of the solution's vector indicates that the Web service i is a candidate Web service in the current composition's solution.

5.3 The Extended Bat Inspired Algorithm for the Web Services Composition Optimization

To enable using the Bat Inspired Algorithm to deal with the Web services composition optimization problem, an extended version of the basic Algorithm [17] is proposed. Indeed, the BA uses a frequency-tuning technique for increasing the diversity of the solutions in the search space, it also try to balance exploration and exploitation during the search process by mimicking the variations of pulse emission rates and loudness of bats when searching for prey [17]. As a result, it proves to be very efficient with a typical quick start.

The main feature characteristics of the proposed algorithm consists on the adaptation of the BA to deal with the Web services composition optimization problem. A second feature is the use of a constructive heuristic that build and generate the initial population starting from the user request while satisfying his constraints. A measurement operation [9] has been added to transform the real solutions generated by the algorithm into binary vectors. Finally, a reparation heuristic verifies and corrects the results of the measurement operation.

The Proposed Stochastic Heuristic. The construction of the initial population is a crucial phase; it consists to build gradually feasible solutions that must fulfil the user's end-to-end QoS requirements and ensure its preferences. Within the aim of reducing the runtime complexity, a new efficient and scalable stochastic heuristic is used to generate the initial population of the Web services composition optimization problem.

For more details, the proposed random heuristic is described in Algorithm 2.

Outline of the BA-WSC Algorithm. The first step is the generation of the initial population using our proposed heuristic [9] to create gradually feasible solutions starting from the user request. The second step consists on initializing the parameters of the proposed algorithm (velocity, frequency, loudness and pulse rates). Next step is the evaluation of the solutions (compositions) with the objective function (Eq. (7)) and the selection of the best one using the selection operator which is similar to the elitism strategy used in genetic algorithms [13]. The developed algorithm called Extended Bat Inspired Algorithm progresses through a number of generations.

Algorithm 2. Heuristic for generating solutions [9]

1: **Input :** Existing Web services, $request_{input}$, $request_{output}$
2: **Output :** A Web services composition solution;

3: **begin**
4: Initiate Web services composition solution to zero;
5: Find randomly service S_i such as $request_{input} = Si_{input}$;
6: $S_{candidate} = S_i$;
7: Put the value 1 in the position i of the vector's solution;
8: **while** $request_{output}$ not found **do**
9:    Find randomly service S_i such as $Si_{input} = Scandidate_{output}$;
10:   $S_{candidate} = S_i$;
11:   Put the value 1 in the position i of the vector's solution;
12: **end while**
13: **end**

During each iteration, new solutions are generated by adjusting the parameters of the algorithm: frequencies, loudness and pulse emission rates. The new solution is accepted or not depends on the quality of the solutions controlled or characterized by loudness and pulse rate which are in turn related to the closeness or the fitness of the locations/solution to the global optimal solution. Then, the best composition solution is found and the global one is then updated if a better one is found. The whole process is repeated until reaching a stopping criterion.

For more details, the proposed algorithm can be described in Algorithm 3.

6   Prototype and Experimentation

The experiment of the BA-WSC approach is performed on the Pentium Dual-Core 3.0 GHz processor with 2.2 GB memory, using Java programming language with Net-Beans IDE 7.3. To evaluate and validate the contribution, the Java-based prototype has been tested on a text translation case study. Finally, to analyse it's performance, a comparison has been realized with the approach presented in [9]. This experiment study shows the feasibility and effectiveness of our approach.

6.1   Case Study and Experiments

The approach is illustrated by a text translation case study because it concretes clearly the process of the Web services composition.

The user enters his request (the input language, and the output language) and his QoS constraints. The role of the optimization approach is to meet his queries with the best Web services composition. The optimization approach is realized by composing the most appropriate Web services.

Algorithm 3. Proposed Bat Inspired Algorithm

1: Objective function $f(x), x = (x_1, ..., x_n)$;
2: **Input :** Problem Data;
3: **Output :** Optimal solution x_*;

4: **begin**
5: Initialize the velocity v_i for each position x_i $i = (1, ..., n)$
6: *Generate the bat population using the proposed generation heuristic;*
7: Define pulse frequency f_i at x_i $i = (1, ..., n)$
8: Initialize pulserates r_i and the loudness A_i for each position x_i $i = (1, ..., n)$
9: **while** Not stable **do**
10:    Generate new solutions by adjusting frequency;
11:    Updating velocities and locations/solutions (*Equation 1 to Eq. 3*) ;
12:    **if** $(rand > r_i)$ **then**
13:       Select a solution among the best solutions;
14:       Generate a local solution around the selected best solution;
15:    **end if**
16:    Generate a new solution by flying randomly (*Equation 4*);
17:    **if** $(rand < A_i$ and $f(x_i < f(x_*)))$ **then**
18:       Accept the new solutions;
19:       Increase r_i and reduce A_i (*Equation 5 and Eq. 6*);
20:    **end if**
21:    *Applying the measurement operation to have binary solution;*
22:    *Correcting obtained solutions using Reparation heuristic to have feasible compositions;*
23:    Rank the bats and find the current best x_*
24: **end while**
25: Post process results and visualization

In order to evaluate the BA-WSC approach, a data set of 1040 Web services text translators is used. Each Web service is defined by its input, output, and the QoS (Time, Cost, Unavailability and Bad-Reputation) parameters.

The values of each QoS attribute are generated by a uniform random process which respects the bounds specified in Table 1.

In the experiment, the Extended Bat Inspired Algorithm uses the following attributes chosen empirically:

Population size=100 bats.
Loudness value= 1.0.
Pulse Rate value = 0.5.
Minimum of Frequency =0.
Maximum of Frequency =2.

The stopping criterion is crucial, the Extended Bat Inspired Algorithm terminates when the set of solutions is stable and there is no improvement in the obtained results after a given number of iterations.

Table 1. The QoS bounds

QoS criterion	Bounds values
Time	[0 , 300] (sec)
Cost	[0 , 30](Dollar)
UnAvailability	[0.7 , 1.0]
BadReputation	[0 ,5]

6.2   Results and Discussion

Let's consider the following user's request (Table 2):

Table 2. The user request

Input Language	French
Output Language	Spanish
Tmax	500 sec
Cmax	100 dollars
Umax	0.5
BRmax	1

During the first phase, the system will respond to the user query by applying the proposed randomized heuristic to generate the 100 bats (solutions) of the population, and return the best initial Web services composition.

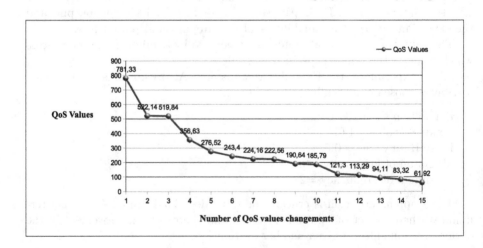

Fig. 3. The optimization evolution

Table 3. Request results

	The solution	QoS value
Best initial solution	(Spanish,portugese)	781.33246
	(Portugese,irish)	
	(Irish,breton)	
	(Breton,italian)	
	(Italian,galcian)	
	(Galcian,romanian)	
	(Romanian,french)	
	(French,english)	
Optimal Solution	(spanish,portugese)	61.919266
	(Portugese,french)	
	(French,english)	

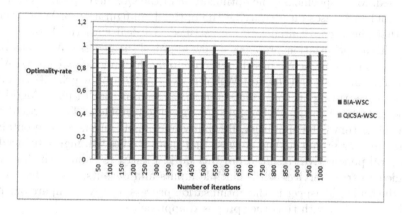

Fig. 4. The optimality rate

Once the best initial solution is defined, the system executes the optimization phase that consists on applying the adjustment of the algorithm parameters(velocity, frequency, loudness and pulse rate) using Eqs. 1, 2, 3, 4, 5 and 6 in order to generate new solutions and returns the final best Web services composition.

The results are presented in Table 3.

Figure 3 shows the evolution of the QoS function during the optimization phase (for the example's request). The quick convergence to the optimal solution illustrates the applicability and efficiency of the proposed approach (BA-WSC).

The optimality rate is defined as follows [9] (Eq. (16)):

$$Optimality_{rate} = 1 - \left(\frac{QoS_{optimal\ solution}}{QoS_{initial\ solution}}\right) \tag{16}$$

Figure 4 below indicates the optimality rate according to the iteration number, for the same example.

The BA-WSC approach can reach an optimality rate between 0.8 and 0.99 regardless of the number of iterations.

We note that the time of execution is relative to the number of iterations. Therefore, if the number of iterations increases, automatically the time of execution also increases and the complexity of the problem becomes greater.

Comparing to the optimality rate of the QICSA-WSC approach [9], we notice that the new proposed approach is more efficient. This observation confirms the effectiveness of our approach and its feasibility. We can see that BA-WSC is a very promising approach.

7   Conclusion and Perspectives

In this paper, the problem of the Web services composition optimization is addressed. More specifically the optimization of the QoS descriptions is studied. This problem focuses on identifying the optimal configuration of Web services such that the user requirements are satisfied. To deal with the Web services composition optimization problem, a new approach named BA-WSC has been proposed. This approach is based on the use of an Extended Bat Inspired Algorithm. The aim is to find the best Web services composition which satisfy a user request by capturing his constraints. For that, the basic Bat Inspired Algorithm has been adapted to the Web services composition problem. The particularity of this algorithm is its simplicity, flexibility and its effectiveness. The obtained results are very promising and suggest that more studies will highly be needed.

Several perspectives results from this work. Firstly, the approach should be extended to treat services with multiple inputs and outputs. Secondly, considering the semantic aspect in the optimisation process. Lastly, Compare our proposed approaches with the other proposed approaches.

References

1. Zeng, L., Benatallah, B., Ngu, A., Dumas, M., Kalagnanam, J., Chang, H.: QoS-aware middleware for web services composition. IEEE Trans. Softw. Eng. **30**(5), 311–327 (2004)
2. Wang, L., Shen, J., Yong, J.: A Survey on bio-inspired algorithms for web service composition. In: Proceedings of the International Conference on Computer Supported Cooperative Work in Design, pp. 569–574. IEEE (2012)
3. Alrifai, M., Risse, T.: Combining global optimization with local selection for efficient QoS-aware service composition. In: proceedings of the International World Wide Web Conference Committee, pp. 881–890. ACM (2009)
4. Parejo, J., Fernandez, P., Rueda, S., Cortes, A.: QoS-aware services composition using tabu search and hybrid genetic algorithms. Actas de los Talleres de las Jornadas de Ingeniera del Software y Bases de Datos 2(1) (2008)
5. Wang, J., Hou, Y.: Optimal web service selection based on multi- objective genetic algorithm. In: Proceedings of the International Symposium on Computational Intelligence and Design. Vol. 1, pp. 553–556. IEEE Computer Society (2008)

6. Tang, M., Ai, L.: A hybrid genetic algorithm for the optimal constrained web service selection. In: IEEE Congress on Evolutionary Computation, pp. 1–8 (2010)
7. Li, J., Yu, B., Chen, W.: Research on intelligence optimization of web service composition for QoS. In: Liu, C., Wang, L., Yang, A. (eds.) ICICA 2012, Part II. CCIS, vol. 308, pp. 227–235. Springer, Heidelberg (2012)
8. Radu, V.: Application. In: Radu, V. (ed.) Stochastic Modeling of Thermal Fatigue Crack Growth. Applied Condition Monitoring, vol. 1, pp. 63–70. Springer, ACM, Heidelberg (2015)
9. Boussalia, S.R., Chaoui, A.: Optimizing QoS-based web services composition by using quantum inspired cuckoo search algorithm. In: Awan, I., Younas, M., Franch, X., Quer, C. (eds.) MobiWIS 2014. LNCS, vol. 8640, pp. 41–55. Springer, Heidelberg (2014)
10. Gustavo, F., Casati, H., Kuno, H., Machiraju, V.: Web Services: Concepts, Architecture and Applications. Springer, Heidelberg (2004)
11. Rao, J., Su, X.: A survey of automated web service composition methods. In: Cardoso, J., Sheth, A.P. (eds.) SWSWPC 2004. LNCS, vol. 3387, pp. 43–54. Springer, Heidelberg (2005)
12. Lecue, F., Mehandjiev, N.: Seeking quality of web service composition in a semantic dimension. IEEE Trans. Knowl. Data Eng. 23(6), 942–959 (2011)
13. Holland, J.H.: Genetic algorithms and the optimal allocation of trials. SIAM J. Comput. 2(2), 88–105 (1973)
14. Kennedy, J., Eberhart, R.: Particle swarm optimization. In: International Conference on Neural Networks. IEEE (1995)
15. Dorigo, M., Maniezzo, V., Colorni, A.: Ant system: optimization by a colony of cooperating agents. IEEE Trans. Syst. Man Cybern. Part B Cybern. 26(1), 29–41 (1996)
16. Layeb, A.: A novel quantum inspired cuckoo search for knapsack problems. Int. J. Bio Inspired Comput. 3(5), 297–305 (2011)
17. Yang, X.-S.: A new metaheuristic bat-inspired algorithm. In: González, J.R., Pelta, D.A., Cruz, C., Terrazas, G., Krasnogor, N. (eds.) NICSO 2010. SCI, vol. 284, pp. 65–74. Springer, Heidelberg (2010)
18. Nakamura, R.Y.M., Pereira, L.A.M., Costa, K.A., Rodrigues, D., Papa, J.P., Yang, X.S.: BBA: a binary bat algorithm for feature selection. In: 2012 25th SIBGRAPI Conference on Graphics, Patterns and Images, Institute of Electrical and Electronics Engineers (IEEE) August 2012
19. Yang, X.S., He, X.: Bat algorithm: literature review and applications. Int. J. Bio Inspired Comput. 5(3), 141 (2013)
20. Bhuvaneswari, A., Karpagam, G.: QoS considerations for a semantic web service composition. Eur. J. Sci. Res. 65(3), 403–415 (2011)
21. Claro, D.B., Albers, P., Hao, J.: Selecting web services for optimal composition. In: Proceedings of the International workshop on semantic and dynamic Web processes, pp. 32–45 (2005)

Automated Distribution of Software to Multi-core Hardware in Model Based Embedded Systems Development

Lukas Krawczyk[✉], Carsten Wolff, and Daniel Fruhner

Dortmund University of Applied Sciences and Arts,
Emil-Figge-Str. 42, 44227 Dortmund, Germany
{lukas.krawczyk,carsten.wolff,daniel.fruhner}@fh-dortmund.de
http://www.amalthea-project.org

Abstract. Software-Mapping, i.e. the mapping of software elements to hardware components, is especially in the context of embedded multi-core systems a rather complex task. Usually, it is not sufficient to allocate tasks to hardware, since further types of allocations, e.g. communications to data paths or data to memories, exist. Accordingly, these allocations have a crucial impact on the performance. Since it is required to fulfill several constraints, e.g. deadlines or task ordering, it is furthermore necessary to select those allocations that result in a valid, but also efficient mapping. Such efficiency is usually not achieved by executing the application as quick as possible but e.g. as reliable or energy saving as possible. This can be achieved by using mathematical methods, e.g. Integer Linear Programming (ILP). ILP allows describing the mapping problem in terms of equations, which will be optimized towards a specific goal.

This work describes an exemplary integration of an existing mathematical method for embedded multi-core software to hardware mapping into the AMALTHEA Tool Platform, including its evaluation as well as adaptation, in order to provide an automated software mapping functionality.

Keywords: Model-based development · Multi-core · Automotive software · AMALTHEA

1 Introduction

The development of embedded multi-core systems is a complex process with several tasks. One of these tasks is finding a valid allocation of software to hardware, we call this step *software mapping*, that combines challenges from various domains. From an embedded point of view, the software has to be executed on very limited resources while meeting (hard) deadlines. Moreover, sporadic events

---

The work leading to these results has been founded by the Federal Ministry for Education and Research (BMBF) under Grant 01|S14029K within the ITEA3 EU-Project AMALTHEA4public.

© Springer International Publishing Switzerland 2015
G. Dregvaite and R. Damasevicius (Eds.): ICIST 2015, CCIS 538, pp. 320–329, 2015.
DOI: 10.1007/978-3-319-24770-0_28

(e.g. interrupts) also have to be considered. From a multi-core point of view, it is necessary to distribute the software to multiple processors or processor cores in due consideration of software dependencies, e.g. task ordering, or specific software requirements, like the availability of floating point units. Moreover, passing information between tasks, which are allocated to different cores, requires valid data paths and communication performance, which depends on the architecture and speed of the communication hardware. This communication can occur on various transfer speeds that depend on the underlying network. The communication network itself can be understood as shared resource, which may delay concurrent accesses, leading to additional bottlenecks if not considered appropriately. Heterogeneous architectures, which are common for embedded systems, increase the complexity of this step even further, since allocations to a non optimal core may change the run-time of the software drastically.

In order to cope with this complexity, it is necessary to utilize a proper tooling. Such tooling, with scope on *automotive embedded systems development*, is provided by the AMALTHEA Tool Platform [1], which guides through the respective development steps and provides design flow automation. This platform is the basis for our automated mapping integration and aims at developing tailored tool chains for automotive embedded multi-core systems development. It provides a variety of models for storing development artifacts, e.g. software, hardware, or constraint descriptions, as well as open source tools for a specific set of development steps, e.g. variability management, structural and behavioral modeling, partitioning, mapping, and code generation.

This paper presents one of the tools within this platform, which realizes an automated software mapping functionality for multi-core hardware by using mathematical methods. These methods allow describing the whole software mapping problem in terms of equations, which are merged into a larger mathematical model and optimized towards a specific goal. For this purpose, we specified a concept for the automated mapping approach and adapted an existing ILP strategie for energy minimization to the models of the AMALTHEA Tool Platform in order to enable an continuous tool-flow.

This paper is organized as follows. Section 2 presents related work, followed by a brief description of the concept for the automated mapping approach in Sect. 3. It lists the utilized information from the AMALTHEA Tool Platform as well as the different mapping strategies. The adaptation steps of the integrated ILP based energy minimization strategy are presented in Sect. 4. It shows how the required information can be synthesized in order to allow a seamless workflow and exemplary outlines how mapping strategies can be applied for embedded multi-core systems. Experimental results based on the approach are discussed in Sect. 5. Finally, a conclusion as well as an outlook on future work closes this paper in Sect. 6.

2   Related Work

The literature discussing the mapping-problem is rich [2] and utilizing a large variety of methods to solve the problem like e.g. Integer Linear Programing

(ILP), Genetic Algorithms, or Heuristics. A general decision, which method is best suited in finding a solution for the mapping problem, highly depends on the actual use case. Naturally, exact methods like ILP tend to require much more computation time compared to heuristic methods, although they are capable of providing optimal solutions. In contrast, heuristics and metaheuristics, like Genetic Algorithms, can determine good solutions very quick, but usually do not guarantee the determination of an optimal solution.

Since we aim at supporting the embedded multi-core system development process with an automated mapping functionality, higher computation times of the method are not considered an issue, which allows applying ILP based methods. Even if optimizing the mapping problem should become very time consuming, it can still be swapped over to a high performance computer. At the same time, the developed embedded system will highly benefit from optimal solutions, since e.g. a higher amount of resources can be saved or the cores fully utilized.

Regarding ILP based methods, a comparatively simple strategy to allocate tasks to processors while minimizing the total execution time is presented in [3]. This method is based on the machine scheduling problem [4] and supports multiple processors with equal processing speed (e.g. homogeneous processors). A downside of this strategy is the missing consideration of inter-task dependencies (e.g. waiting for the results of a task's predecessor(s)).

Another strategy is described in [5], presenting an approach for the parallelization of sequential applications containing loops by revealing loop-level and pipeline parallelism, as well as mapping the resulting parallel software to heterogeneous multi-core platforms. The allocations within this mapping are optimized towards the lowest execution time of an application, i.e. minimizing its overall run-time. Compared to our approach, the work from [5] utilizes so called hierarchical task graphs that are synthesized from C-Code, which is usually generated at a later design phase compared to our model based approach.

A strategy with a different goal is shown in [6]. It presents a framework, which aims at minimizing the energy consumption of variable voltage processors while executing real time dependent tasks. The strategy integrates a two-phased approach, which utilizes an heuristic for the allocation of tasks to cores and solves an ILP model for the selection of the optimal voltage levels.

3   Concept for an Automated Mapping

The concept of our automated mapping approach is shown in Fig. 1. It shows the three mandatory input models *(Software, Hardware, Constraints)*, which provide the required information about the software, hardware, and task ordering for the mapping generation process. An optional model containing allocation constraints *(Property Constraints)* can be used to reduce the solution space of the mapping.

The concepts aims at providing a diversity of mapping strategies for various optimization goals as well different problem sizes. Currently, these strategies are split into *Heuristic methods, Integer Linear Programming (ILP) based methods,*

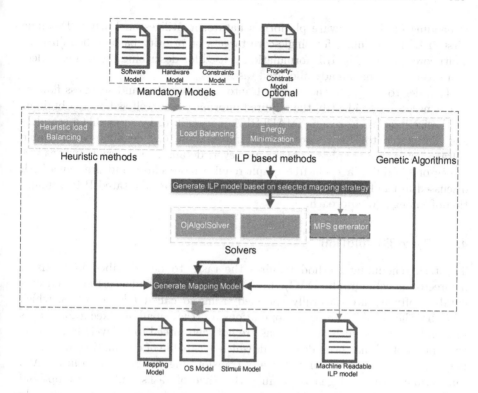

Fig. 1. Concept for an automated mapping approach using the AMALTHEA Tool Platform

and *Genetic Algorithm* based approaches. Unlike ILP based methods, Genetic Algorithm and Heuristic methods, such as the *Heuristic Data Flow Graph (DFG) load balancing*, will immediately create a mapping. ILP based methods on the contrary need to generate an ILP model of the mapping problem according to the selected mapping strategy, e.g. *ILP based load balancing* or *Energy aware mapping* in advance. Once the ILP model has been created, it can be solved by one of the mathematical *Solvers*, which in our case is provided by the open source project Oj!Algo [7]. An optional MPS[1] generator can be utilized for MPS file generation, which contains the whole mapping problem in terms of equations. This allows using external (e.g. commercial) solvers, which tend to be more efficient in solving larger models compared to open source Java implementations, without integrating them into the Tool Platform.

4   Automated and Seamless Software-Mapping Approach

The approach from Zhang [6], which is subject of our integration, consists of two methods for scheduling as well as an ILP formulation for the voltage selection.

---

[1] File format used to store linear programing or mixed integer programing problems.

Depending of the hardware platform's nature, it utilizes an Earliest Deadline First (EDF) scheduling for single-core targets or priority based scheduling for multi-core targets. The ILP formulation is used for describing the voltage selection problem of the already allocated tasks.

In order to integrate the approach into an automated and seamless flow, it is first necessary to identify the required information as well as how to obtain or synthesize it from the given AMALTHEA models in order to enable a seamless and automated tool flow. Most of the information, e.g. deadlines or available voltage levels, are simple to obtain. However, details like the switching capacitance or obtaining a cycle free graph require more effort and are henceforth discussed in the following subsections, followed by our adapted ILP formulation of Zhang's [6] approach.

4.1   Cycle Dissolution

The task scheduling method requires the tasks to be described in terms of a directed acyclic graph (DAG). In AMALTHEA, dependencies between executable software are naturally specified using so called *label accesses*, which describe the read- and write operations of the smallest executable units (*Runnables*). Since such descriptions are not guaranteed to be cycle free, a partitioning tool [8], has been developed, which is capable of eliminating any cycles between these *Runnables* and basically transforming the graph into in a DAG. Furthermore, the tool generates an early stage of tasks and suggest optimal agglomerations from *Runnables* to tasks. The resulting graph however is only cycle free between *Runnables*, but not tasks, as illustrated in Fig. 2(a).

In order to resolve this issue, we have decided to apply the software mapping approach on Runnable level instead of Task level. Otherwise the cycle elimination would remove additional edges of the graph (Fig. 2(b), dashed arrow), consequently decreasing the accuracy of the energy minimization approach and putting further overhead on the developer, who would have to replace the missing input values by e.g. values from previous iterations. An alternative strategy with less overhead could be achieved in allocating the *Runnables* in a manner which prevents bidirectional inter-task communication. This however comes at the cost of parallelism, as shown in Fig. 2(c). Ideally, Task 2 can be executed as soon as runnable R5 is finished. However, since the energy minimization algorithms operate at task level, the parameters for a tasks earliest start time are based on the finishing time of its predecessor task instead of the runnable, which in our example forces Task 2 to start after Task 1 has been finished.

4.2   Deriving the Application Deadline

The maximum amount of time the program may require (T_{Con}) is another essential parameter, which is required by the approach. Without this value, the application will have no timing constraints, allowing it to be executed at the lowest voltage level during each execution cycle.

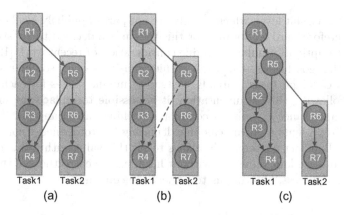

Fig. 2. (a) partitioned SW model, (b) SW model without inter-task cycles, (c) optimized allocation of Runnables to tasks

In order to allow an autonomous application of the approach, we derive the value for T_{Con} from existing data i.e. which is already present in the model. This is done by using the values of the software model's *activation* elements that specify the interval of a *Runnable*'s execution. In AMALTHEA, possible types for activation elements are

- `Periodic`, i.e. a Task is called e.g. each 20 ms.
- `SporadicActivation`, i.e. a Task is called randomly
- `CustomActivation`, i.e. a Task is executed at a customizable point

Since *SporadicActivation* and *CustomActivation* do not necessarily impose which data about the activation behavior has to be specified, it is possible that no concrete indicators when or how often a *Runnable* is executed are provided. This makes software utilizing this constructs impossible to schedule while guaranteeing meeting their deadlines [9]. At least some information, e.g. the minimal time between a *Runnable*'s recursions, has to be present.

Periodic activations on the contrary provide information about the recurrence, i.e. the time in between, of a *Runnable*'s execution. Since the first execution of a *Runnable* must be completed before it can be called a second time, it equals the T_{Con} value in periodically executed software models. In case of multiple specified *Periodic* activations, hyper perdiods[2] [10] are created and T_{Con} set accordingly to ensure satisfying the deadlines.

4.3   Switching Capacitance per Processor Cycle

The *switching capacitance* per cycle (C_u) for a specific task u is typically [11] used in energy consumption calculations. Usually, it contains an unique value for each of the executed tasks. However, it also depends on several device related

---

[2] Least common multiple of all periods among the tasks.

parameters at circuit level, which usually are not part of publicly available material and therefore hard to obtain. For this reason, we decided to substitute the energy consumption formulation in due consideration of recent work [12], which has shown that good results can also be achieved using a single common *switching capacitance* C for *all tasks* (threads) instead of unique values for each individual task. Following this argumentation, it is possible to replace the individual switching capacitance C_u with a common switching capacitance C. Thus, the constant C represents a linear scale in calculating the total energy consumption (see Eq. 2). This fact consequently allows to set this value within this method's context to any random value $\neq 0$ without harming the correctness of the energy minimization process, allowing us to neglect the constant.

4.4   Adapted ILP Formulation

The original [6] ILP formulation is listed in Eqs. (1)-(7) with D_x describing a node (task) x's start time. It should be noted that we had to rearrange and adapt some of the formulations in order to allow a simple integration of the model into the AMALTHEA Tool Platform.

$$minimize \sum_{u \in V} E_u \tag{1}$$

The objective of the formulation is shown in Eq. (1) and aims at minimizing the total power consumption of all tasks.

$$subject\ to\quad E_u = C_u(\sum_{i=1}^{m} N_{u,i}(V_i^2 - V_h^2) + N_u V_h^2)\ \forall u \in V \tag{2}$$

The power consumption E_u for each single Task u is described in Eq. (2). It is the sum of the respective voltages V_i times the number of cycles $N_{u,i}$ during a voltage level i, with N_u being the total number of cycles, V_h the highest available voltage level, and C_u a task's switching capacitance.

$$D_{Out} - D_{In} \leq T_{Con} \tag{3}$$

Equation (3) ensures, that the path from the first node of a graph D_{In} to it's last node D_{Out}, i.e. a single activation (call, execution) of the application, is executed within the time limit specified by T_{Con}.

$$D_v - D_u - \sum_{i=1}^{m} N_{u,i}(CT_i - CT_h) \geq T_u\ \forall e(u,v) \in E \tag{4}$$

Equation (4) is used to prevent the start of a successor v before its predecessor u is finished. The sum term represents the amount of time the task u is delayed by being executed at lower voltage cycles, with CT_i being the cycle time[3] at voltage

---

[3] Time required for a single cycle.

level i, whereas CT_h represents the cycle time for the highest voltage level. The
initial task execution time, i.e. the time task u requires if being executed only
at the highest voltage level, is represented by T_u.

$$\sum_{i=1}^{m} N_{u,i}(CT_i - CT_h) \geq 0, \; int, \; \forall u \in V \tag{5}$$

$$D_u \geq 0, \; N_{u,i} \geq 0, \; int, \; \forall u \in V \tag{6}$$

$$\sum_{i=1}^{m} N_{u,i} \leq N_u \; \forall u \in V \tag{7}$$

Finally, Eqs. (5)-(7) are used to constraint the values for the tasks duration
(Eq. (5)), constraint start times D_u as well as cycles for each voltage level $N_{u,i}$
to positive integer values (Eq. (6)), and prevent $N_{u,i}$ from exceeding a task u's
total number of cycles N_u (Eq. (7)).

5   Experimental Results

The goal of our conducted experiments lies in evaluating the mapping-approach
and its integration as well as its runtime and applicability to real-world problems.
For this, we set up two software mapping use cases, which are common for
the automotive domain. The first use case distributes a rather simple software
for controlling a heating, ventilation and air conditioning (HVAC) system to a
multi-core platform and consists of 11 *Runnables*. The second use case contains
43 *Runnables* and describes an engine control application, which is based on a
re-engineered ETAS DemoCar Project [13]. The common multi-core hardware
platform for both use cases is represented by a Freescale i.MX6 Board, which
contains two homogeneous cores operating at 792 MHz and specifies 2 voltage
levels (1.15 V for full speed, and 1.05 V for half speed) that can be applied for each
of the cores independently. Since the hardware platform exceeds the required
performance of our use cases, we reduced the time between the periods in order
to increase the hardware platforms utilization. Otherwise, the mapping would
have finished in a few milliseconds with simply slowing down *all* instructions. In
order to reduce the computation time, we specified a so called maximal gap of
10 % as break condition for the solver. This gap specifies the maximal difference
between the simple determinable LP-relaxation of the ILP model and a found
feasible solution, i.e. as soon as the value of a determined energy consumption is
not higher then 10 % compared to the LP-relaxation, the solver will accept the
solution and stop the optimization process. The average, minimal and maximal
run-time results of the mapping-tool for applying the approach to both use cases
are shown in Fig. 3.

As we can see, the ILP energy minimization approach finishes in less then
one second for both use cases, which makes it applicable for the development and
even for rapid prototyping, where changes to software may occur in very short

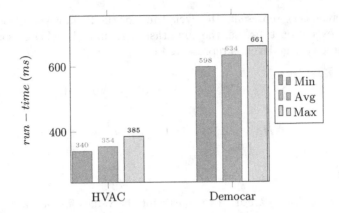

Fig. 3. Measured run-times of the mapping tool integration for applying the energy minimization on the *HVAC* and *Democar* use case (max gap of 10 %)

intervals. Usually, such situations highly benefit from the seamless tool flow as well as the automated mapping functionality.

Another interesting aspect is the growth in run-time for both use cases. While the solver's run-time only increases by a factor of approx. two, the number of distributed *Runnables* increased from 11 to 43, i.e. an approx. factor of 4. Based on the small increase in run-time, it can be expected, that the approach will grow similarly on even larger combinations, i.e. more cores and more allocatable targets (*Runnables*). Furthermore, the run-times remained stable during both test scenarios, which also indicates a support for larger problem sizes. These assumption however, are only based on estimations and naturally require an further analysis of the approaches and the solver's capabilities.

6   Conclusion and Future Outlook

In this work we presented how various mathematical mapping approaches can be implemented and integrated for an automated and continuous application within a tool chain. For this purpose, we exemplary analyzed one ILP based approach, which is capable of minimizing the total energy consumption of a developed software for a specific multi-core hardware platform as well as providing optimal solutions. This approach, among others, has been successfully integrated into the AMALTHEA Tool Platform and is capable of solving a mathematical model describing the mapping problem, which is automatically generated out of a set of AMALTHEA models. Our evaluation of this approach with regard to its seamless and automated execution on two real-world examples, which are represented by the Democar and HVAC projects, has shown that the integration supports even larger models and is capable of delivering quick solutions even for multi-core platforms with little to no additional interaction from the developer. Although the integrated approach could be successfully applied to the mapping problems, there is always room for improvement and future work.

One of the major opportunities for improvement lies in the mapping approaches themselves. As mentioned earlier, a large number of mapping strategies with various goals, degrees of freedom etc. exist, which exacerbate the process of finding a suitable integration candidate that supports a seamless tool flow. Ideally, a mapping strategy should accept most of the information from a development platform and allow generating software to hardware mappings with a larger amount of considered allocations, e.g. data to memories or communications to available communication paths. Henceforth, we intend to extend the platform with mapping approaches tailored towards the specific information, which is provided by the AMALTHEA Tool Platform. Moreover, more recent techniques, e.g. parallel hybrid generic algorithms, which will probably allow handling larger varieties of problems, such as many-core applications with multiple degrees of freedom, will be considered for these approaches.

References

1. AMALTHEA Tool Platform. http://www.amalthea-project.org/
2. Aleti, A., Buhnova, B., Grunske, L., Koziolek, A., Meedeniya, I.: Software architecture optimization methods: a systematic literature review. IEEE Trans. Softw. Eng. **39**, 658–683 (2013)
3. Drozdowski, M.: Scheduling for Parallel Processing. Computer Communications and Networks. Springer, London (2009)
4. Grigoriev, A., Sviridenko, M., Uetz, M.: Machine scheduling with resource dependent processing times. Math. Program. **110**, 209–228 (2007)
5. Cordes, D., Engel, M., Neugebauer, O., Marwedel, P.: Automatic extraction of pipeline parallelism for embedded heterogeneous multi-core platforms. In: 2013 International Conference on Compilers, Architecture and Synthesis for Embedded Systems (CASES), pp. 1–10 (2013)
6. Zhang, Y., Hu, X.S., Chen, D.Z.: Task scheduling and voltage selection for energy minimization. In: Proceedings of the 39th annual Design Automation Conference, pp. 183–188. ACM (2002)
7. oj! Algorithms Website. http://ojalgo.org/
8. AMALTHEA: D3.4 - Prototypical Implementation of Selected Concepts. https://itea3.org/project/amalthea.html
9. Sprunt, B., Sha, L., Lehoczky, J.: Aperiodic task scheduling for hard-real-time systems. Real-Time Syst. **1**, 27–60 (1989)
10. Yang, H., Ha, S.: ILP based data parallel multi-task mapping/scheduling technique for MPSoC. In: International SoC Design Conference (ISOCC), pp. 134–137 (2008)
11. Ishihara, T., Yasuura, H.: Voltage scheduling problem for dynamically variable voltage processors. In: International Symposium on Low Power Electronics and Design, pp. 197–202. IEEE (1998)
12. Li, P., Guo, S.: Energy minimization on thread-level speculation in multicore systems. In: 2010 Ninth International Symposium on Parallel and Distributed Computing (ISPDC), pp. 125–132 (2010)
13. Frey, P.: A timing model for real-time control-systems and its application on simulation and monitoring of AUTOSAR systems. http://vts.uni-ulm.de/doc.asp?id=7505

Risk Evaluation: The Paradigm and Tools

Aiste Balzekiene[1], Egle Gaule[1], Raimundas Jasinevicius[2],
Egidijus Kazanavicius[2], and Vytautas Petrauskas[2(✉)]

[1] Institute of Public Policy and Administration,
Kaunas University of Technology, Kaunas, Lithuania
{aiste.balzekiene,egle.gaule}@ktu.lt
[2] Center of Real Time Computer Systems,
Kaunas University of Technology, Kaunas, Lithuania
{raimundas.jasinevicius,egidijus.kazanavicius,
vytautas.petrauskas}@ktu.lt

Abstract. The paper is devoted to: (1) investigate risk as an inherently fundamental entity that exists in all aspects of our life; (2) show that up until now, the majority of available risk definitions are suitable only for particular application areas; (3) propose a relatively unified risk paradigm and a fuzzy logic based risk evaluation methodology and (4) to present a set of computerized risk evaluation tools. This paper confirms and strongly advocates the possibility to use the newly developed, unified/generalized and theoretically based risk control methodology and a set of networked ICT tools for risk evaluation, mitigation and monitoring. Our conclusions emphasize that such methodology, if delivered through a networked academic community would increase the competences of university graduates and enable professionals from governmental and public organizations to properly maintain problems associated with risk and risk control.

Keywords: Risk definition · Risk control · Risk evaluation · Computerized tool set · Risk governance training methodology

1 Introduction, Related Works and Motivation

Modern society is facing many local, national, and global challenges. Every challenge is associated with some kind risk. And because risk refers to likely damage (whether in health, environmental, economic, or other terms [1]), adequate solutions for dealing with those risks are required.

According to Slovic [2], modern societies face risk in three fundamental dimensions: "risk as feelings refers to our fast, instinctive, and intuitive reactions to danger. Risk as analysis brings logic, reason and scientific deliberation to bear on hazard management. When our ancient instincts and our modern scientific analyses clash, we become painfully aware of a third reality... risk as politics." These three dimensions of risk not only define the division between people's understanding of risk and expert assessment of risk, but also include a political dimension, related to the decision-making processes.

© Springer International Publishing Switzerland 2015
G. Dregvaite and R. Damasevicius (Eds.): ICIST 2015, CCIS 538, pp. 330–342, 2015.
DOI: 10.1007/978-3-319-24770-0_29

Many authors notice that there is no unified definition of risk. Aven et al. [1] tried to systemize various definitions taken both from natural sciences and social sciences, and provided three categories of a risk concept:

(a) risk as a concept based on events, consequences and uncertainties,
(b) risk as a modeled, quantitative concept, and
(c) risk measurements (risk descriptions).

Aven [3] also notes that in natural sciences, risk analysis is usually based on probabilistic approach, whereas in social sciences risk research is based on non-probabilistic understanding of risk (knowledge and perception). However, both paradigms include *uncertainty* as one of the main elements in risk analysis. Therefore, *uncertainty* should be regarded as the central dimension of risk in an interdisciplinary approach.

Risk includes both the potential for physical changes and the potential for social responses based on perceived dangers and hazards [4]. There are several options in terms of taking action (including doing nothing), each of which is associated with potential positive or negative consequences. Evaluation of risks helps to select an option that promises more benefit than harm compared to all other options [4]. However, the decision-making process is difficult as the challenges under consideration are characterized by limited and sometimes controversial knowledge with respect to their risk characteristics and consequences. Thus, an integrated approach from a multi-actor and a multi-objective perspective in terms of risk control is required. Sometimes, the term 'risk governance' is used for risk control. 'Risk governance' is based on transfer of the essence of governance and its core principles to the context of risk-related decision-making [1].

2 Risk Paradigm

2.1 Approach

Our contemporary world can be viewed as the evolving system of risky systems (SoS). More and more researchers realize that every single component of the SoS is a messy combination of many physical, technical and social subsystems (Fig. 1) [5].

Fig. 1. A system of a multitude of physical, technical and social subsystems

In this figure, "our world" – the reality under investigation – consists of several entities ω1, ω2, ω3, ω4, ω5; each entity can be characterized by its autonomy, heterogeneity, existence of individual objectives and goals, various activities, intelligence, risks under uncertain circumstances, adaptability and ability to evolve. A possible presence of human or social factors in these entities is the reason why such an entity can be considered as a certain socio-technical fabric.

The set of entities $\Omega = \{\omega1, \omega2, \omega3, \omega4, \omega5\}$ evolve and interact with the environment that has the same properties as the Ω itself. It means that in real life, the environment itself is a particular type of Ω; and only we (the observers, human beings, interest groups) divide, distinguish or separate them artificially with some degree of uncertainty and according to our scientific or pragmatic needs.

Consequently, "the reality" $\Omega = \{\omega1, \omega2, \omega3, \omega4, \omega5\}$ as a whole (and its entities ω) function according to a universal paradigm, the paradigm of causal risk and uncertainty. This paradigm determines any emerging behavior of "the reality" Ω that faces all possible risks.

Recent events (such as financial and economic crises), sudden outbreaks of the Ebola virus, military conflicts, acts of terrorism, and environmental disasters have revealed the necessity to use knowledge, innovation and education to boost safety and resilience, and to increase public awareness.

2.2   Definition

Risk research in general (and in social sciences especially) is performed in a very fragmented manner because there are many different and quite ambitious approaches used in different science fields. Despite the fact that risk research is very important, we still do not have any seriously based, unified risk definition and risk control methodology [6]. In science and in practical life, risk is still not considered as a certain fundamental entity. Social theories behind the contextual, psychological, structural and other factors are discussed in more detail in [7]. Risk perception is influenced by micro level factors, such as structural and psychological factors that vary across individuals within the society, and macro level factors, such as contextual factors (related to national, regional contexts) and risk sources (related to the nature and characteristics of risk sources).

Taking all this into consideration, we risk of proposing the following paradigmatic definition of risk. Let us consider that any risk depends on four overlapping entities: (1) **activities** (*EFF*), which include efforts/investments/etc. that are involved in the subject, work and situation under investigation; (2) possible **positive results** (*OP*) – such as achievements/profit/opportunities/joy … and so on; (3) possible **negative results** (*TH*) – such as losses/threats/disappointment … and so on; and (4) **uncertainty** (*HES*) – such as hesitancy/randomness/possibility/probability of a certain event … and so on [8, 9].

Considering this, the risk itself can be defined as a measureable level of uncertainty of the action results:

{RISK = LEVEL OF UNCERTAINTY OF ACTION RESULTS}. We advocate the following assumptions and a hypothesis: a measureable level of risk *R* can be calculated as a value of certain function $\mathbf{R}$ (.), depending on $\textbf{\textit{EFF}}$, $\textbf{\textit{OP}}$, $\textbf{\textit{TH}}$ and $\textbf{\textit{HES}}$ in the intuitive manner as is shown in (1):

$$R = \mathbf{R}(\textbf{\textit{EFF}} \uparrow; \textbf{\textit{OP}} \downarrow; \textbf{\textit{TH}} \uparrow; \textbf{\textit{HES}} \uparrow), \tag{1}$$

keeping in mind that $\uparrow$ and $\downarrow$ mean the increase and decrease of R correspondingly.

2.3   Control

The fact that it is possible to evaluate risk pushes us to develop a system of risk minimization, control and monitoring. Usually, risk control is based on the concept of general system control that advocates a closed loop feedback approach: environment – situation analysis (identification of threats) – risk level evaluation – risk treatment (prevention, detection, mitigation according to the goals of the user) – direct influence to the environment (according to the recommendations provided by tools and user's decisions) and risk monitoring (active evaluation of risk evolution over time), as it is shown in Fig. 2. Here, the environment under investigation is observed, and the results of those observations (received from the "SENSORS" part) represent actual evaluation of all possible $\textbf{\textit{TH}}$, $\textbf{\textit{OP}}$ and $\textbf{\textit{EFF}}$. It must be emphasized that the evaluation made is usually both quantitative (deterministic and/or stochastic) and qualitative (fuzzy and/or verbal), and the results must be normalized, summarized and transformed into certain non-dimensional data that is convenient for further processing in the RISK MEA-SUREMENT block for the evaluation of the real risk R_{real}. It must be noted that risk mitigation must play the most important role in the process of risk evaluation. So, the difference $\varDelta R$ between user's WISHES or CRITERIA R_0 (that concern the real risk value and its real numerical or verbal evaluation R_{real}) serves as data for online tuning of parameters in the environment under consideration:

$$\varDelta R = R_0 - R_{real} \tag{2}$$

Such an integrated approach proposed in this paper signifies a unified attitude towards risk as a fundamental entity inherent in every human activity and in nature in general.

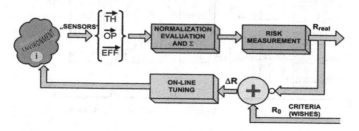

Fig. 2. Environmental risk control concept

3 Risk Evaluation

3.1 On Risk Analysis Tools

Nowadays, ICT experts have a large spectrum of computerized software tools suitable for various fragmented stages of risk control processes, such as: (1) analysis of risky situations, (2) risk evaluation, (3) risk mitigation models and implementation, (4) risk monitoring, and so on. And the main task for people working in a concrete problematic field is to select/adopt, put together and/or adapt adequate ICT tools. A generalized list of such ICT tools includes: (a) various commercialized products, (b) open source software products, and (c) "home-made" products. Namely, SWOT – analysis type tools for static and/or dynamic evaluation ("SWOT-expert", "WINSWOT", "SwotFcm", and many others), tools based on the concept of fuzzy cognitive maps ("FCMnew", "CubiCalc", "Fuzzy Logic Toolbox", "FUZZLE 3.0", and many others), tools based on fuzzy expert maps ("FCM App", "MEP_KRC_T", "fuzzyTECH 6.0", and so on) [10–12]. A lot of very efficient risk evaluation products are introduced in http://www.capterra.com/risk-management-software/ [13]. As it was emphasized above, these products were developed without taking into account the universality of risk as such and without consideration of taking an integrated approach to risk control problems. In this paper we propose the following: firstly, to fill this gap and secondly, to propose a new risk evaluation module based on the newly proposed paradigmatic risk evaluation methodology (1).

According to the risk control ideology depicted in Fig. 2, a certain set of ICT tools from the list mentioned above must be created at least for a forward information flow, as it is shown in Fig. 3.

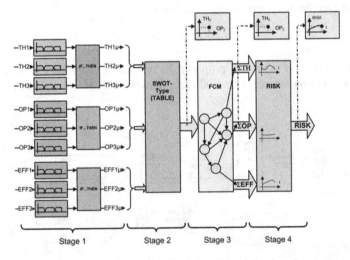

Fig. 3. A set of ICT tools for a forward information flow following the concept depicted in Fig. 2

Here, in the first stage, the integration and unification of tools is based on fuzzification of data concerning various *TH*, *OP* and *EFF*, and decision-making rules (created by an expert) followed by a corresponding deffuzification. So, the normalized and summarized information is gathered in a convenient non-dimensional form, ready to use for the SWOT-Type tables in the second stage. The third stage involves a fuzzy cognitive maps (FCM) tool serving as a dynamic extension of SWOT analysis, convenient for an interactive online risk mitigation and tuning of parameters. A risk evaluation module (RISK), that ensures continuous risk surveillance, completes the sequence of ICT tools in the fourth stage.

3.2 "Home-Made" Tools

A set of "home-made" tools used for risk evaluation and control was created under the frame of a research project "Generalized Methodology for Sociotechnical Risks Governance and Assumptions for the Establishment of RISK-LAB in KTU". The project was carried out by an interdisciplinary team of researchers from the Faculty of Social Sciences, Arts and Humanities and the Center of Real Time Computer Systems (CRTCS) of the Faculty of Informatics. The prototype tools and/or their models were developed at the CRTCS and then collected, adopted and adapted for risk control needs. The "SwotFcm" tool was used [11, 12] to tackle the problems connected to information processing in the 2nd and 3rd stages (Fig. 3). A block diagram of this tool is shown in Fig. 4.

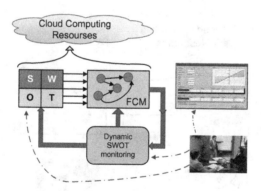

Fig. 4. The "SwotFcm" tool

Usually, the entities analyzed within the areas of multi-purpose and multi-disciplinary risk analysis are too complicated to be described strictly in quantitative terms. In such cases, it is impossible to avoid verbal expert estimates. For the evaluation of a risky behavior of the system, a mechanism similar to SWOT analysis is frequently employed. A detailed risk modeling, monitoring and prediction require a certain level of dynamics. To achieve optimal system parameters, *TH*, *OP* and *EFF* should be under the influence of dynamics. In order for the experts to affect them professionally, additional fuzzy situations and factors need to be analyzed. The most convenient tool for solving such a task today is to use the mechanism of fuzzy cognitive maps (FCM). The "SwotFcm" tool suggests combining the mechanisms of SWOT-Type analysis and FCM (fuzzy cognitive maps) and indicates that such hybridization provides experts with a new tool of system risk analysis. Experts select FCM elements of the monitoring structure, their dependency on the total values of *TH*, *OP* and *EFF* of the system for the nodes being modeled. Thus, the experts complete a gradual evaluation of risk dynamics by modelling and analyzing the simulation results.

Sometimes, we are able to introduce more sophisticated information concerning the risky situations under investigation into the nodes of FCM in stage 3 (Fig. 3). The fuzzy information available for the processing of risk consists of: (a) structurally described interactions between entities under consideration, (b) some nonlinearities that characterize the predicted behavior of entities, and (c) fuzzily prescribed evaluation of the influence of *TH*, *OP* and *EFF* on each other. Although sometimes researchers address much more complicated problems: when only the first (a) item is given, and the second and the third (b, c) items are usually supposed by experts, their guesses based on their experience. These elements are described by a set of fuzzy rules and the fuzzy logics of their composition [14]. Such a rule based extension of an ordinary FCM approach is defined as fuzzy expert maps (FEM). Here, every node of the FEM contains elements that are inherent in open-loop fuzzy control systems [15]: a fuzzification block, a block for fuzzy inference and a block of defuzzification. A schematic representation of this tool (called the "MEP_KRC_T") is given in the online risk analysis activity in Fig. 5.

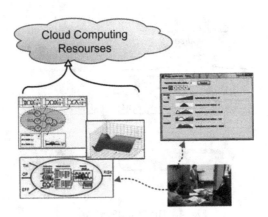

Fig. 5. A schematic representation of the "MEP_KRC_T" tool

A complete analysis of risky activities requires recognition and evaluation of *TH*, *OP* and *EFF* that describe the situation under consideration. Usually, all activities can be represented by several sets of different cases: one of them contains successful, another one – only tolerable, yet another one – just so-so or even bad samples. The case itself is very often described fuzzily even among the members of business community. This means that some parameters of a certain case are presented quantitatively (in numbers), whereas others – only qualitatively (using verbal expressions, such as, for example, "very good", "good", "acceptable", "bad" or "very bad"). The Center of Real Time Computer Systems (CRTCS) has developed a prototype of Pattern Recognition Based Scoring System (PR_BSS) that enables us to analyze even a fuzzy history of each case set, extract its decisively important typical features and use them later for scoring and evaluation of patterns of new cases (Fig. 6). The kernel of the PR_BSS software automatically performs the following: (1) carries out a certain preparation of cases (defuzzification, normalization, and so on), (2) gives a solution of a Linear Programming problem in order to determine the coefficients for a multiple scoring of the case pattern, and (3) recognizes the case pattern that permits to assign the case under consideration to one of the several predetermined sets (or classes).

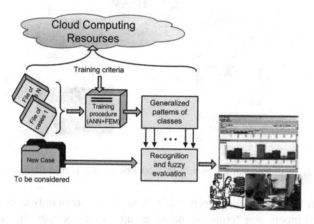

Fig. 6. A block diagram of the "PR_BSS" tool

The main features of the PR_BSS are as follows: (a) the PR_BSS does not require a huge amount of statistical data in any class set; (b) it can work even with a significantly limited history of business situations; (c) if the history is rich, the PR_BSS is able to generalize it and extract the most important data; (d) the PR_BSS is a self-training algorithm: while operating, it continuously improves the quality of recognition by analyzing the most recent historical data. All possible estimations and recommendations concerning the classification of risky situations are based soundly on the mathematics of linear programming instead of being based on a precarious rule of thumb. The PR_BSS can be easily integrated in different application fields, such as: financial market operations, various business evaluations, medical diagnosis, planning of military operations, earthquake predictions, signal and process recognition, and many others.

4   Risk Measurement Module

4.1   Generalized Structure

The prototype model of a tool used in the fourth stage of risk evaluation (module RISK in Fig. 3) based on the concept expressed by formula (1) was simulated using a commercial software package fuzzyTECH 6.06c. A block diagram of the structure of the RISK measurement tool is shown in Fig. 7. Here, normalized and summarized values of **TH**, **OP** and **EFF** are delivered to the corresponding inputs. They must be fuzzified automatically according to the fuzzy logic terms presented in advance by the expert team. The inference block, which contains a set of fuzzy rules, performs actions prescribed following the hypothesis that the risk $R = \mathbf{R}(EFF \uparrow; OP \downarrow; TH \uparrow; HES \uparrow)$. It must be emphasized that the hesitancy seen in this risk measurement formula is expressed by the shapes of membership functions used for fuzzification and defuzzification.

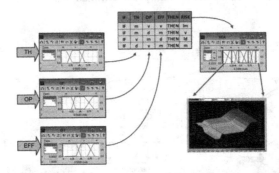

Fig. 7. A diagram of the prototype model of the RISK measurement tool

In this simplified diagram, as seen in Fig. 7, we have shown only three terms for the fuzzification of inputs, five terms for the defuzzification of outputs, and a fragment of fuzzy rules list. The software package fuzzyTECH 6.06c used for the simulation of the RISK measurement tool permits to evaluate the influence of both the changes in **TH**, **OP** and **EFF**, and the changes of hesitancy as well, all in online mode. All risk evaluation changes are conveniently displayed on a computer screen.

4.2 Experimental Case

A simplified example of the usage of a simulated **RISK-MEASUREMENT** module is presented in this section. Let us assume that we are measuring the risk of playing the lottery. In this case, experts (or one's family members) take into account the following aspects of this risky situation according to the paradigm presented in Sect. 2.

First of all: amount of money spent on tickets (TH1);
probability of possible lose (TH2);
amount of money to be won (OP1);
probability to win (OP2);
number of purchased tickets (EFF1);
number of different kiosks where the lottery tickets were purchased (EFF2).

The fuzzy membership functions μ (.) created for the terms of the *TH*, *OP* and *EFF* according to expert opinion are presented in Fig. 8, where S, M, and L stand for "small", "medium" and "large", respectively.

For the sake of simplicity of the case under consideration we use only three fuzzy terms for the defuzzification of normalized and summarized *THS*, *OPS* and *EFFS* (Fig. 9).

The module of normalization and summarization of the *TH*, *OP* and *EFF* is developed using the software package fuzzyTECH 6.06.c (Fig. 10). In the same figure, a block diagram of the calculation of risk *R* is shown as well.

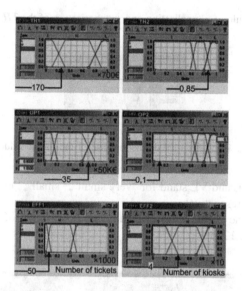

Fig. 8. Terms for fuzzification of the *TH*, *OP* and *EFF*

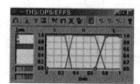

Fig. 9. Terms for defuzzification of the *THS*, *OPS* and *EFFS*

The process of normalization and summarization of the *TH* requires 3 × 3 = 9 rules; the same applies for the process of inference for *OP* and *EFF* as well. The lists of rules were generated, adapted according to the expert opinion and saved in the software package of fuzzyTECH 6.06.c. The result of normalized and summarized *TH*, *OP* and *EFF* is delivered in the last stage for risk *R* measurement. For the purpose of simplification, we used the following items in our example case: (a) the same input terms as shown in Fig. 9, (b) 3 × 3 × 3 = 27 rules for risk measurement inference process and (c) five terms for risk R defuzzification. These terms are presented in Fig. 11.

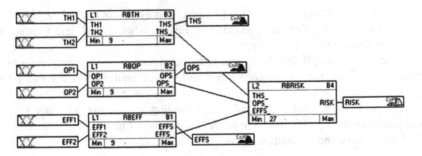

Fig. 10. A module of normalization and summarization of the *TH*, *OP* and *EFF*

Fig. 11. Terms for defuzzification of the risk *R* values

Here, VS, S, M, L and VL stand for "very small", "small", "medium", "large" and "very large" risk *R*, respectively.

An example of the presentation of results and possibilities of risk *R* analysis are demonstrated in Fig. 12.

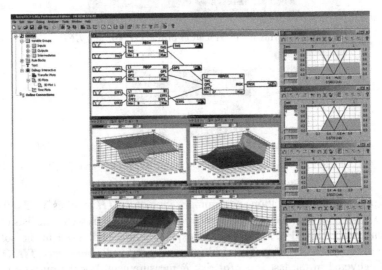

Fig. 12. Visualization of the processes of risk *R* analysis as seen on a computer screen

It is worth mentioning that the results shown in Figs. 8, 9, 10, 11 and 12 correspond to the case of purchasing 50 lottery tickets for 170 € that were bought in 4 different kiosks in hopes of winning at least 35,000 € when the probability to lose is 0.85 and the probability to win is 0.1.

A simulation of the described processes demonstrates the viability of our approach and the convenience and efficiency of the analysis of influences different changes have on risky situations.

5 Future Tendencies

Such a generality that the concept of risk presupposes requires a unified study of risk control fundamentals both at a university research and teaching level, and at a practical training and implementation level. Fundamental knowledge of the general risk control theory must be disseminated, adapted and adopted by practitioners in various fields and target groups of activities. So, a further development of the approach proposed in this presentation can be defined as follows:

(1) development of ICT based multi-modal educational network of academic communities for practice in risk and security governance (for example, in the Nordic – Baltic region);
(2) development of a methodology for active involvement and cooperation between universities and governmental, public, industrial and business institutions in partner countries for e-training activities in the field of risk and security governance;
(3) development of an open access curricula for risk and security governance course modules dedicated for different universities and relevant professional groups in different partner countries available through the common network data base that can be accessed by interested institutions and individuals (for example, in the Nordic – Baltic region);
(4) enhancement of competencies of governmental, public, industrial, business institutions, community leaders and individuals to prepare for possible risk analysis, computerized decision-making, risk treatment and monitoring.

6 Final Remarks

This presentation confirms and strongly advocates the possibility to use a newly developed, unified/generalized and theoretically based risk control methodology and a set of networked ICT tools for risk evaluation, mitigation and monitoring.

Such a methodology, if delivered through a networked academic community, would increase the competences of university graduates, and enable professionals from governmental and public organizations to properly maintain problems associated with risk and risk control.

Acknowledgments. This work is supported by KTU grant (2015) *"Generalized Methodology for Sociotechnical Risks Governance and Assumptions for the Establishment of RISK-LAB in KTU"* (RISK-LAB).

References

1. Aven, T., Renn, O., Rosa, E.A.: On the ontological status of the concept of risk. Saf. Sci. **49**(8), 1074–1079 (2011)
2. Slovic, P., Finucane, M.L., Peters, E., MacGregor, D.G.: Risk as analysis and risk as feelings: some thoughts about affect, reason, risk, and rationality. Risk Anal. **24**(2), 311–322 (2004)
3. Aven, T.: The risk concept—historical and recent development trends. Reliab. Eng. Syst. Saf. **99**, 33–44 (2012)
4. Renn, O.: Concepts of risk: an interdisciplinary review–part 2: integrative approaches. GAIA Ecol. Perspect. Sci. Soc. **17**(2), 196–204 (2008)
5. Jasinevicius, R., Petrauskas, V.: On fundamentals of global systems control science (GSCS). In: Sanayei, A., Zelinka, I., Rössler, O.E. (eds.) ISCS 2013: Interdisciplinary Symposium on Complex Systems, vol. 8, pp. 77–88. Springer, Heidelberg (2014)
6. White Paper: Risk Management - Concepts and Methods. Methods Commission/Espace Méthodes, 40 p. CLUB DE LA SECURITE DE L'INFORMATION FRANCAIS, Paris 2008–2009
7. Balžekienė, A.: Rizikos suvokimas: sociologinė konceptualizacija ir visuomenės nuomonės tyrimo prielaidos (Risk perception: sociological conceptualization and methodological approaches to public opinion research). FILOSOFIJA. SOCIOLOGIJA **20**(4), 217–226 (2009)
8. Atanassov, K.T.: On Intuitionistic Fuzzy Sets Theory. Springer, New York (2012)
9. Chen, L.-H., Tu, C.-C.: Dual bipolar measures of Atanassov's intuitionistic fuzzy sets. IEEE Trans. Fuzzy Syst. **22**(4), 966–982 (2014)
10. Jasinevičius, R., Petrauskas, V.: Sprendimų pagrindimo kompiuterizavimas (Computerization of Decision Making), 149 p. Technologija, Kaunas (2011). ISBN 978-609-02-0048-3
11. Jasinevicius, R., Petrauskas, V.: Dynamic SWOT analysis as a tool for environmentalists. Environ. Res. Eng. Manage. **1**(43), 14–20 (2008)
12. Jasinevicius, R., Petrauskas, V.: The new tools for systems analysis. Inf. Technol. Control **2**(27), 51–57 (2003)
13. http://www.capterra.com/risk-management-software. Accessed 20 April 2015
14. Jasinevicius, R., Petrauskas V.: Fuzzy expert maps: the new approach. In: Proceedings of 2008 IEEE International Conference on Fuzzy Systems (FUZZ 2008), pp. 1511–1517. IEEE (2008). ISBN 978-1-4244-1819-0/08
15. Passino, P.M., Jurkovich, S.: Fuzzy Control. Addison-Wesley, Boston (1998)

Weighted Classification Error Rate Estimator for the Euclidean Distance Classifier

Mindaugas Gvardinskas[✉]

Department of System Analysis, Vytautas Magnus University,
Vileikos St. 8, 44404 Kaunas, Lithuania
m.gvardinskas@if.vdu.lt

Abstract. Error counting estimators are among the best known and most widely used error estimation techniques. Perhaps the best known subcategory of error-counting estimators are k-fold cross-validation methods. Like most other error estimation techniques, cross-validation methods are biased. One way to correct this bias is to use a weighted average of cross-validation and resubstitution estimators. In this paper we propose a new weighted error-counting classification error rate estimator designed specially for the Euclidean distance classifier. Experiments with real world and synthetic data sets show that resubstitution, repeated 2-fold cross-validation, leave-one-out, basic bootstrap and D-method are outperformed by the proposed weighted error rate estimator (in terms of root-mean-square error).

Keywords: Error estimation · Classification · Resubstitution · Cross-validation · Bootstrap

1 Introduction

The probability of the classification error rate is the most commonly used measure of classifier performance. If the underlying class-conditional distribution is known, one can calculate the probability of the classification error rate exactly. However, in most real world pattern recognition problems this distribution is unknown and an estimator of the classification error rate must be used. One group of error estimation techniques is so called error-counting methods. According to this approach, error rate of a classification rule is estimated as the ratio between misclassified data vectors and total number of data vectors. Perhaps the best known subcategory of error-counting estimators are k-fold cross-validation methods. One popular form of cross-validation is leave-one-out, also known as N-fold cross-validation. This estimator is almost unbiased as an estimator of true probability of the classification error rate [2, 3, 8–11], however it has large variance [2, 3, 8]. Other forms of cross-validation typically have lower variance than leave-one-out, but they are more biased [2, 3, 8]. One way to correct this bias is to use a weighted average of optimistically biased cross-validation and pessimistically biased resubstitution estimators. A weighted error rate estimator is an estimator of the form [14, 16]:

© Springer International Publishing Switzerland 2015
G. Dregvaite and R. Damasevicius (Eds.): ICIST 2015, CCIS 538, pp. 343–355, 2015.
DOI: 10.1007/978-3-319-24770-0_30

$$\hat{\varepsilon}_N = \omega \hat{\varepsilon}_N^{(1)} + (1 - \omega) \hat{\varepsilon}_N^{(2)} \tag{1}$$

where $\hat{\varepsilon}_N^{(1)}$ and $\hat{\varepsilon}_N^{(2)}$ are error estimators, N is the data set size and $0 \le \omega \le 1$. Typically, the performance of weighted estimators is significantly superior to cross-validation and resubstitution [2, 14]. In addition, when weighted estimator is designed for specific classification rule, results can be even better [14]. However, there are only few specialized weighted estimators [11, 14].

In this paper we propose a new weighted error-counting classification error rate estimator. Similar to other weighted estimators, proposed method uses weights to balance biases of both component estimators, however contrary to the above mentioned estimators, new method uses weights that are calculated specially for the Euclidean distance classifier.

This paper is organized as follows. Section 2 presents Euclidean distance classifier and gives a brief review of the most common error estimation techniques. Section 3 introduces the new error estimation method. Section 4 reports the results of our simulation study. Section 5 contains concluding remarks.

2   Methods Investigated

2.1   Basic Definitions

Consider two category classification problem where class label $y \in \{0, 1\}$, feature vector $\mathbf{x} \in R^n$ and a classifier is a function f: $R^n \to \{0, 1\}$. An induction algorithm builds a classifier from a set of N independent observations $D_N = \{(\mathbf{x}_1, y_1), \dots, (\mathbf{x}_N, y_N)\}$ drawn from some distribution T. Formally, it is a mapping g: $\{R^n \times \{0, 1\}\}^N \times R^n \to \{0, 1\}$. The performance of a classifier is measured by conditional probability of misclassification (conditional PMC):

$$\varepsilon_N = P(g(D_N, \mathbf{x}) \ne y) \tag{2}$$

This error is conditioned on one particular training set D_N and induction algorithm g. In most real world pattern recognition problems conditional PMC is unknown, therefore an error estimator $\hat{\varepsilon}_N$ is used. Commonly used performance measures of an error estimator $\hat{\varepsilon}_N$ are the bias, deviation variance and root-mean-square error (RMS) [3, 14, 16]:

$$Bias[\hat{\varepsilon}_N] = E[\hat{\varepsilon}_N] - E[\varepsilon_N] \tag{3}$$

$$Var_{dev}[\hat{\varepsilon}_N] = Var(\hat{\varepsilon}_N - \varepsilon_N) = Var(\hat{\varepsilon}_N) + Var(\varepsilon_N) - 2Cov(\hat{\varepsilon}_N, \varepsilon_N) \tag{4}$$

$$RMS[\hat{\varepsilon}_N] = \sqrt{E[(\varepsilon_N - \hat{\varepsilon}_N)^2]}$$
$$= \sqrt{E[\varepsilon_N^2] + E[\hat{\varepsilon}_N^2] - 2E[\varepsilon_N \hat{\varepsilon}_N]} \tag{5}$$

The most important performance measure is RMS, because it combines bias and the deviation variance into a single metric.

2.2 Euclidean Distance Classifier

Euclidean distance classifier assigns a test vector x to the class of the closest arithmetic mean. In two category case, this classification rule can be written as a linear discriminant function [12]:

$$j(x) = \mathbf{V}^T \mathbf{x} + v_0, \tag{6}$$

where

$$\mathbf{V} = (\hat{\mathbf{M}}_1 - \hat{\mathbf{M}}_2),\ v_0 = -\frac{1}{2}(\hat{\mathbf{M}}_1 + \hat{\mathbf{M}}_2)^T \mathbf{V} \tag{7}$$

here $\hat{\mathbf{M}}_1$ and $\hat{\mathbf{M}}_2$ are estimates of class mean vectors. A new pattern x is classified according to the sign of the discriminant function j.

2.3 Resubstitution

The apparent error rate, or resubstitution estimator, was first suggested by Smith [15]. In the resubstitution method, the whole data set is used as the training set and then reused as the test set. The resubstitution estimated error is defined as:

$$\hat{\varepsilon}_N^{(R)} = \frac{1}{N} \sum_{i=1}^{N} |g(D_N, \mathbf{x}_i) - y_i| \tag{8}$$

This method is known to be optimistically biased ($E[\hat{\varepsilon}_N^{(R)}] < E[\varepsilon_N]$), especially for small data sets and complex classification rules [2]. Although the optimism of the resubstitution estimator declines as N increases [2, 3].

2.4 Cross-Validation

In k-fold cross-validation, the data set is randomly partitioned into k subsets of approximately equal size. Each subset is used as a test set and the remaining k-1 subsets are used as the training set. The cross-validation error estimate is defined as:

$$\hat{\varepsilon}_N^{(CV)} = \frac{1}{N} \sum_{i=1}^{k} \sum_{j=1 \wedge (\mathbf{x}_j, y_j) \in D_i}^{N} |g(D_N \backslash D_i, \mathbf{x}_j) - y_j| \tag{9}$$

where D_i is the i-th fold of the data set D_N, k is the number of folds and N is the size of D_N. The main drawback of cross-validation estimators is their variance [2, 3, 13]. Additionally, when the number of folds is small, the bias of cross-validation is large [8].

2.5 Bootstrap

Basic bootstrap estimator tries to correct the bias of resubstitution estimator. This bias can be expressed as $b = E[\varepsilon_N] - E[\hat{\varepsilon}_N^{(R)}]$. Since b is not known, it must be estimated from the given data set D_N. The estimation procedure is as follows. First, a bootstrap sample is formed by sampling N data points uniformly and with replacement from the original data set. Then, an induction algorithm is trained on the bootstrap sample and tested on the original data set D_N. These steps are repeated r times and the estimate of b is calculated as

$$\hat{b} = \frac{1}{r} \sum_{i=1}^{r} (\hat{\varepsilon}_N - \hat{\varepsilon}_N^{(R)^*}) \tag{10}$$

where $\hat{\varepsilon}_N^{(R)^*}$ is resubstitution error on the bootstrap data and $\hat{\varepsilon}_N$ is conditional error estimate obtained by testing the classifier on the original data set D_N. The bootstrap estimate of the conditional error rate is given by [4]

$$\hat{\varepsilon}_N^{(B)} = \hat{\varepsilon}_N^{(R)} + \hat{b} \tag{11}$$

where $\hat{\varepsilon}_N^{(R)}$ is resubstitution error on the original data set D_N. There are many variants of this basic bootstrap estimator. The one, which in various empirical studies has shown good performance is called the 0.632 bootstrap. Similar to basic bootstrap estimator, this method tries to correct the bias of zero bootstrap by doing a weighted average of resubstitution and zero bootstrap estimators [2]. The 0.632 bootstrap estimated error is defined as [5, 6]

$$\hat{\varepsilon}_N^{(0.632B)} = 0.632 \cdot \hat{\varepsilon}_N^{0B} + 0.368 \cdot \hat{\varepsilon}_N^{(R)} \tag{12}$$

where $\hat{\varepsilon}_N^{(0B)}$ is zero bootstrap estimate

$$\hat{\varepsilon}_N^{(0B)} = \frac{1}{r} \sum_{i=1}^{r} \sum_{j=1 \wedge (x_j, y_j) \in D_N \backslash D_{Bi}}^{N} |g(D_{Bi}, x_j) - y_j| \tag{13}$$

here r is the number of bootstrap samples and D_{Bi} is the i-th bootstrap sample. The 0.632 bootstrap estimator has low variance, but may fail when resubstitution is too low biased [2, 14].

2.6 D-Method

It is the first parametric classification error rate estimator, proposed in statistical pattern recognition literature. For the homoscedastic (equal covariance matrices) normal model for two classes with equal prior probabilities, the D estimator is given by [7]

$$\hat{\varepsilon}_N^{(D)} = \Phi \left\{ -\frac{\hat{\delta}}{2} \right\} \tag{14}$$

where Φ is a standard Gaussian cumulative distribution function, $\hat{\delta} = \sqrt{(\hat{\mathbf{M}}_1 - \hat{\mathbf{M}}_2)^T \hat{\boldsymbol{\Sigma}}^{-1} (\hat{\mathbf{M}}_1 - \hat{\mathbf{M}}_2)}$ is an estimate of Mahalanobis distance, $\hat{\boldsymbol{\Sigma}}$ is the estimate of common covariance matrix and $\hat{\boldsymbol{\Sigma}}^{-1}$ is its inverse. This method is known to have low variance but large bias [10]. The bias is especially severe when the data are non-Gaussian.

3 Proposed Method

3.1 Basic Expressions

Expected error of the Euclidean distance classifier can be expressed as [17]

$$E[\varepsilon_N] \approx P_1 \Phi \left\{ -\frac{\delta}{2} \frac{1 + \frac{n}{\delta^2} \left(\frac{1}{N_2} - \frac{1}{N_2} \right)}{\sqrt{1 + \frac{n}{\delta^2} \left(\frac{1}{N_2} + \frac{1}{N_1} \right)}} \right\} + \\ P_2 \Phi \left\{ -\frac{\delta}{2} \frac{1 + \frac{n}{\delta^2} \left(\frac{1}{N_1} - \frac{1}{N_2} \right)}{\sqrt{1 + \frac{n}{\delta^2} \left(\frac{1}{N_1} + \frac{1}{N_2} \right)}} \right\} \tag{15}$$

and expected resubstitution error can be expressed as

$$E[\varepsilon_N^R] \approx \Phi \left\{ -\frac{\delta}{2} \sqrt{1 + \frac{n}{\delta^2} \left(\frac{1}{N_1} + \frac{1}{N_2} \right)} \right\} \tag{16}$$

where N_1 is the number of instances from the first class, N_2 is the number of instances from the second class, the size of the data set D_N is $N = N_1 + N_2$, P_1 and P_2 are class prior probabilities, $\delta = \sqrt{(\mathbf{M}_1 - \mathbf{M}_2)^T \boldsymbol{\Sigma}^{-1} (\mathbf{M}_1 - \mathbf{M}_2)}$ is a Mahalanobis distance between two pattern classes, $\mathbf{M}_1$ and $\mathbf{M}_2$ are class mean vectors, $\boldsymbol{\Sigma}^{-1}$ is the inverse of the common covariance matrix.

3.2 Proposed Method

Unbiased weighted classification error rate estimator can be expressed as:

$$Bias[\hat{\varepsilon}_N] = \omega E[\hat{\varepsilon}_N^{(1)}] + (1 - \omega) E[\hat{\varepsilon}_N^{(2)}] - E[\varepsilon_N] = 0 \tag{17}$$

Now, assume that estimator $\hat{\varepsilon}_N^{(1)}$ is repeated k-fold cross-validation. In each run, repeated k-fold cross-validation uses $N^* = N - N/k$ vectors for classifier training, therefore we can write that $E[\hat{\varepsilon}_N^{(1)}] \approx E[\varepsilon_{N^*}]$. Also, suppose that estimator $\hat{\varepsilon}_N^{(2)}$ is repeated resubstitution and in each run it uses $N^* = N - N/k$ vectors to estimate resubstitution error. Now we can write that $E[\hat{\varepsilon}_N^{(2)}] \approx E[\varepsilon_{N^*}^R]$ and Eq. (17) can be rewritten as:

$$Bias[\hat{\varepsilon}_N] \approx \omega E[\varepsilon_{N^*}] + (1 - \omega)E[\varepsilon_{N^*}^R] - E[\varepsilon_N] \approx 0 \tag{18}$$

From (18) we have that

$$\omega \approx \frac{E[\varepsilon_N] - E[\varepsilon_{N^*}^R]}{E[\varepsilon_{N^*}] - E[\varepsilon_{N^*}^R]} \tag{19}$$

Now, suppose that the following preconditions are met:

(1) Classifier deals with two multivariate Gaussian pattern classes;
(2) the covariance matrix is the same for all classes;
(3) the covariance matrix is proportional to the identity matrix, i.e. $\Sigma = \sigma^2 I$;
(4) Mahalanobis distance is constant;
(5) the dimensionality n is fixed and very large;
(6) both values, $N, N^* \to \infty$.

Then from (15) and (16) we get that the weight is

$$\omega \approx \lim_{\frac{n}{N} \to 0} \frac{E[\varepsilon_N] - E[\varepsilon_{N^*}^R]}{E[\varepsilon_{N^*}] - E[\varepsilon_{N^*}^R]} \approx (1 - Q)\frac{N^*}{N} + Q, \tag{20}$$

where

$$Q = 8.5478 - 51.9959\,Z + 125.9721\,Z^2 - 136.5547\,Z^3 + 56.4591\,Z^4 \tag{21}$$

and

$$Z = \max(P_1, P_2) \tag{22}$$

The derivation of expression (20) is based on the Taylor series expansion of $E[\varepsilon_N], E[\varepsilon_{N^*}^R]$ and $E[\varepsilon_{N^*}]$. The proposed weighted classification error rate estimator (PWE) is defined as:

$$\hat{\varepsilon}_N^{(PWE)} = \frac{1}{r} \sum_{i=1}^{r} \left(\omega \cdot \hat{\varepsilon}_N^{(CV)} + (1 - \omega) \cdot \hat{\varepsilon}_N^{(R)} \right) \tag{23}$$

where r is the number of repetitions.

4   Simulation Study

4.1   Experimental Setup

Our experiments consists of two parts: synthetic experiments with Gaussian data and experiments with real world data sets. The error estimators studied are resubstitution, leave-one-out, basic bootstrap, 0.632 bootstrap, D-method, proposed weighted estimator and repeated 2-fold cross-validation. Proposed weighted estimator use repeated 2-fold cross-validation and repeated half sample resubstitution as component estimators. Note that these component estimators were chosen since they are highly biased [8]. In 0.632 bootstrap and basic bootstrap the number of runs (r) is set to 200. In proposed weighted estimator and repeated 2-fold cross-validation the number of runs is set to 100 and this makes the number of designed classifiers equal to 200.

4.2   Simulation Based on Synthetic Data

We use three data models to generate sample points. Data model 1 is two-class Gaussian data model with equally likely classes, common identity covariance matrix and class means located at $\mathbf{M}_1 = (m, m, \dots, m)^T$ and $\mathbf{M}_2 = (-m, -m, \dots, -m)^T$. Data models 2 and 3 are similar to model 1. The only difference is that different class prior probabilities are used. In model 2 we use $P_1 = 0.6$, $P_2 = 0.4$ and in model 3 we use $P_1 = 0.7$, $P_2 = 0.3$. For each data model we choose four values of m such that Bayes error is from 0.05 to 0.20. In each of these twelve cases 10000 independent samples of size $N = 40$, are generated (in all cases $n = 20$).

Experimental results for data models 1–3 are shown in Figs. 1, 2, 3, 4, 5, 6, 7, 8 and 9. Here we can see that resubstitution, D-method, repeated 2-fold cross-validation, basic bootstrap and 0.632 bootstrap are more biased than proposed estimator and leave-one-out. Also, we can see that proposed method works well in correcting the bias of repeated 2-fold cross-validation. The experiments also show that proposed method is less variable than repeated 2-fold cross-validation, basic bootstrap and leave-one-out but more variable than resubstitution, D-method and 0.632 bootstrap. The overall performance (RMS) of 0.632 bootstrap and proposed estimator is better than the overall performance of resubstitution, repeated 2-fold cross-validation, leave-one-out, basic bootstrap and D-method. Additionally, when $\varepsilon_{Bayes} > 0.10$ proposed method performs better than 0.632 bootstrap (in RMS sense).

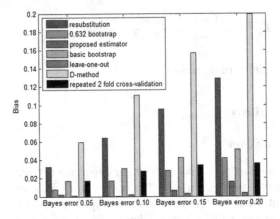

Fig. 1. Bias results (absolute values), data model 1.

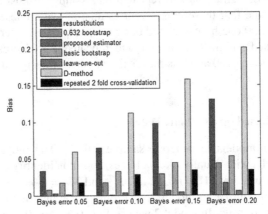

Fig. 2. Bias results (absolute values), data model 2.

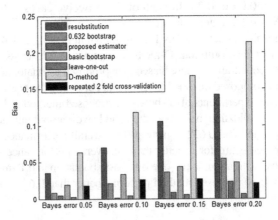

Fig. 3. Bias results (absolute values), data model 3.

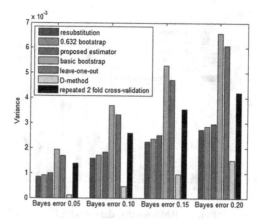

Fig. 4. Variance results, data model 1.

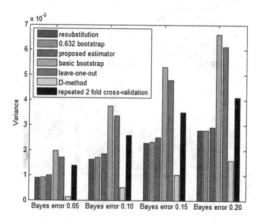

Fig. 5. Variance results, data model 2.

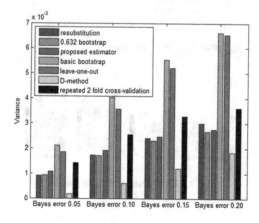

Fig. 6. Variance results, data model 3.

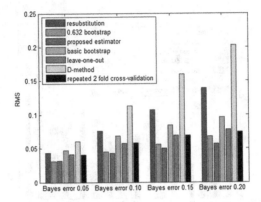

Fig. 7. RMS results, data model 1.

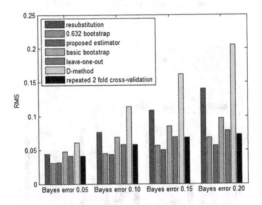

Fig. 8. RMS results, data model 2.

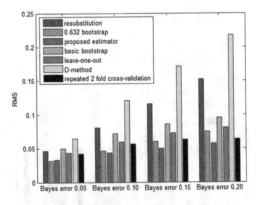

Fig. 9. RMS results, data model 3.

4.3 Simulation Based on Real Data

We conduct our experiments on 3 data sets from the UCI machine learning repository [1].

Magic Gamma Telescope data set. This data set is generated to simulate registration of high energy gamma particles in a ground-based atmospheric Cherenkov gamma telescope. The data set contains 19020 instances, of which 12332 are classified as signal and 6688 are classified as background. Each instance has 10 features. The size of the training/error estimation data set is 32.

Pima Indian Diabetes data set. This database is composed of 768 instances of which 268 are diabetes positive and 500 are diabetes negative. The size of the training/error estimation data set is 32.

Indian Liver Patient data. This data set contains 416 liver patient records and 167 non liver patient records. Each record is described by 10 features. The size of the training/error estimation data set is 20.

Euclidean distance classifier assumes spherical distribution of the data. However, none of the above data sets are distributed spherically. In order to make the data spherical, a whitening transformation is performed. After this transformation, the covariance matrix of each class is equal to the identity matrix (preconditions 2 and 3). However, none of the data sets shows Gaussian distribution (according to Mardia's and Henze-Zirkler tests). Each Monte Carlo simulation is designed in the following way: the data set is randomly split into two sets and one set is used for both, classifier training and error estimation, while the other (much larger set) is used to approximate conditional PMC. This procedure is repeated 10000 times.

Figures 10, 11 and 12 display experimental results based on real world data sets. Here we can see that D-method has the largest bias while resubstitution, repeated 2-fold cross-validation, basic bootstrap and 0.632 bootstrap are moderately biased. The least biased error estimation methods are proposed estimator and leave-one-out. However, leave-one-out has large variance. Experiments show that leave-one-out is more variable than repeated 2-fold cross-validation, proposed method, 0.632 bootstrap, D-method and resubstitution. Experiments also show that proposed method is less variable than

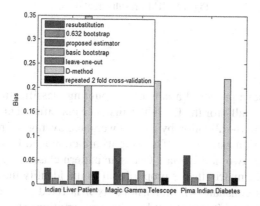

Fig. 10. Bias results (absolute values), real data.

repeated 2-fold cross-validation, basic bootstrap and leave-one-out but slightly more variable than 0.632 bootstrap. The overall performance (RMS) of the proposed method is similar to 0.632 bootstrap but better than resubstitution, repeated 2-fold cross-validation, leave-one-out, basic bootstrap and D-method.

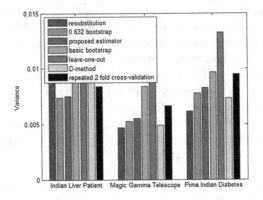

Fig. 11. Variance results, real data.

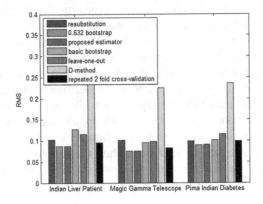

Fig. 12. RMS results, real data.

5   Conclusion

In this paper we have proposed a new error-counting classification error rate estimator designed specially for the Euclidean distance classifier. This method corrects the bias of k-fold cross-validation by using a weighted average of resubstitution and k-fold cross-validation estimators. The weights are computed by assuming that the classifier deals with two multivariate Gaussian pattern classes (1), all classes share the same covariance matrix that is proportional to the identity matrix (2, 3), Mahalanobis distance is constant (4), dimensionality n is fixed and very large (5) and sample size approaches infinity (6). When these assumptions are violated, proposed method may fail to correct the bias of cross-validation. This can be seen in some synthetic experiments where preconditions 5 and 6 are not met, and also in real world data sets, where preconditions 1, 5 and 6 are violated. However, in most cases, bias correction works well, even when some of the above preconditions are not met. The weights of the proposed method are not designed to minimize the RMS of the weighted estimator. However, experiments with real world and synthetic data sets show that resubstitution, repeated 2-fold cross-validation, leave-one-out, basic bootstrap and D-method are outperformed by the proposed weighted error rate estimator (in terms of RMS).

References

1. Bache, K., Lichman, M.: UCI machine learning repository. http://archive.ics.uci.edu/ml. School of Information and Computer Science, University of California, Irvine, CA (2015)
2. Braga-Neto, U., Dougherty, E.: Is cross-validation valid for small sample microarray classification? Bioinformatics **20**(3), 374–380 (2004)
3. Dougherty, E., Sima, C., Hua, J., Hanczar, B., Braga-Neto, U.: Performance of error estimators for classification. Curr. Bioinf. **5**(1), 53–67 (2010)
4. Efron, B.: Bootstrap methods: another look at the jackknife. Ann. Stat. **7**(1), 1–26 (1979)
5. Efron, B.: Estimating the error rate of a prediction rule: improvement on cross-validation. J. Am. Stat. Assoc. **78**(382), 316–331 (1983)
6. Efron, B., Tibshirani, R.: Improvements on cross-validation: the 632+ bootstrap method. J. Am. Stat. Assoc. **92**(438), 548–560 (1997)
7. Fisher, R.: The use of multiple measurements in taxonomic problems. Ann. Eugenics **7**, 179–188 (1936)
8. Kohavi, R.: A study of cross-validation and bootstrap for accuracy estimation and model selection. In: Proceedings of the Fourteenth International Joint Conference on Artificial Intelligence, pp. 1137–1143 (1995)
9. Krzanowski, W.J., Hand, D.J.: Assessing error rate estimators: the leaving-one-out reconsidered. Aust. J. Stat. **39**(1), 35–46 (1997)
10. Lachenbruch, P., Mickey, R.: Estimation of error rates in discriminant analysis. Technometrics **10**(1), 1–11 (1968)
11. McLachlan, G.J.: A note on the choice of a weighting function to give an efficient method for estimating the probability of misclassification. Pattern Recogn. **9**, 147–149 (1977)
12. Raudys, S.: Statistical and Neural Classifiers, An Integrated Approach to Design. Springer, London (2001)
13. Rodriguez, J.D., Perez, A., Lozano, J.A.: A general framework for the statistical analysis of the sources of variance for classification error estimators. Pattern Recogn. **46**, 855–864 (2013)
14. Sima, C., Dougherty, E.: Optimal convex error estimators for classification. Pattern Recogn. **39**(6), 1763–1780 (2006)
15. Smith, C.: Some examples of discrimination. Ann. Eugenics **18**, 272–282 (1947)
16. Toussaint, G., Sharpe, P.: An efficient method for estimating the probability of misclassification applied to a problem in medical diagnosis. Comput. Biol. Med. **4**, 269–278 (1975)
17. Zollanvari, A., Braga-Neto, U., Dougherty, E.: Analytic study of performance of error estimators for linear discriminant analysis. IEEE Trans. Signal Process. **59**(9), 4238–4255 (2011)

Application of Intelligent Algorithm to Solve the Fractional Heat Conduction Inverse Problem

Rafał Brociek and Damian Słota[✉]

Institute of Mathematics, Silesian University of Technology,
Kaszubska 23, 44-100 Gliwice, Poland
damian.slota@polsl.pl

Abstract. This paper describes an application of an intelligent algorithm to reconstruct the boundary condition of second kind in the heat conduction equation of fractional order. For this purpose, a functional defining error of approximate solution was minimized. To minimize this functional Ant Colony Optimization (ACO) algorithm was used. Calculations has been performed in parallel way (multi-threaded), so the computation time is significantly shortened. The paper presents examples to illustrate the accuracy and stability of the presented algorithm.

Keywords: Intelligent algorithm · Inverse problem · Identification · Time fractional heat conduction equation

1 Introduction

In recent years, many applications are based on the optimization algorithms artificial Intelligence [1–10]. Among the artificial intelligence algorithms we can distinguish optimization algorithms based on natural behavior of insects, for example Artificial Bee Colony algorithm [11–14], Ant Colony Optimization algorithm [15–17], firefly algorithm [3]. The advantage of artificial intelligence is that, besides the assumption of the existence of solution of the problem, does not have any restrictions, as well as providing better results from the solutions obtained by the classical methods.

Recently, the modeling of different types of phenomena in physics and technical sciences the fractional order derivatives was used [18–23]. For example, fractional derivatives are used in electrical engineering [24]. In paper [25] author described approximation method for a fractional order transfer function. Often mathematical models using fractional order derivatives better describe the process than conventional models derived from integer order derivatives [26]. One of the first papers, in which the method of fractional calculus was used in classical inverse heat conduction problem is [27]. The first works on the inverse problem for the heat conduction equation of fractional order was Murio works [28, 29]. In recent years, many of articles dealing with this problem, see for example [30–35].

This paper describes the application of parallel version of the Ant Colony Optimization algorithm to reconstruct heat flux at the boundary of the area, when the temperature distribution is described by the heat conduction equation of fractional order. For this purpose, a functional defining error of approximate solution was

© Springer International Publishing Switzerland 2015
G. Dregvaite and R. Damasevicius (Eds.): ICIST 2015, CCIS 538, pp. 356–365, 2015.
DOI: 10.1007/978-3-319-24770-0_31

minimized. The inspiration for the creation of the algorithm was to behavior the swarm of ants in search of the shortest path connecting the anthill with a source of food. Parallelization of the algorithm has significantly reduced computation time. The direct problem was solved by using the implicit finite difference method [36, 37]. The paper presents examples to illustrate the accuracy and stability of the presented algorithm.

2 Formulation of the Problem

We will consider the following heat conduction equation with a fractional derivative with respect to time

$$c\rho \frac{\partial u^\alpha(x,t)}{\partial t^\alpha} = \lambda \frac{\partial u^2(x,t)}{\partial x^2} \tag{1}$$

defined in region

$$D = \{(x,t) : x \in [0,L], t \in [0,t^*)\},$$

where c, ρ, λ denotes the specific heat, the density and thermal conductivity. To Eq. (1) the initial condition is posed

$$u(x,0) = f(x), \qquad x \in [0,L], \tag{2}$$

and boundary conditions of second and third kind

$$-\lambda \frac{\partial u}{\partial x}(0,t) = q(t) \qquad t \in (0,t^*), \tag{3}$$

$$-\lambda \frac{\partial u}{\partial x}(L,t) = h(t)(u(L,T) - u^\infty), \qquad t \in (0,t^*), \tag{4}$$

where h is the heat transfer coefficient and u^∞ is the ambient temperature.

Fractional derivative occurring in Eq. (1) will be Caputo derivative. For $\alpha \in (0, 1)$ Caputo derivative will be defined by formula

$$\frac{\partial^\alpha u(x,t)}{\partial t^\alpha} = \frac{1}{\Gamma(1-\alpha)} \int_0^t \frac{\partial u(x,s)}{\partial s}(t-s)^{-\alpha} ds, \tag{5}$$

where Γ is the Gamma function.

We assume that the function q, occurring in the boundary condition of the second kind, will be in the following form

$$q(t) = \begin{cases} a_1, t \in [0,t_1), \\ a_2, t \in [t_1,t_2), \\ a_3, t \in [t_2,t^*), \end{cases} \tag{6}$$

where a_1, a_2, $a_3 \in R$. Considered inverse problem consists on reconstruct a_1, a_2, a_3 (therefore the boundary condition) based on the selected values of the function u in the set points of the domain D. Known values of the function u (input data) in selected points (x_i, t_j) of the domain D will be denoted

$$u(x_i, t_j) = \hat{U}_{ij}, \quad i = 1, 2, \ldots, N_1, \quad j = 1, 2, \ldots, N_2, \tag{7}$$

where N_1 denotes number of sensor and N_2 denotes number of measurements at each sensor.

Solving the direct problem for fixed values of the coefficients a_1, a_2, a_3 we obtain values of approximation of function u in selected points $(x_i, t_j) \in D$. These values will be denoted by $U_{ij}(q)$. Using these values and input data $\hat{U}_{ij}$, we create functional defining error of approximate solution

$$J(h) = \sum_{i=1}^{N_1} \sum_{j=1}^{N_2} \left(U_{ij}(q) - \hat{U}_{ij} \right)^2. \tag{8}$$

Minimizing the functional (8), we reconstruct function q.

3 Method of Solving

Direct problem, defined by Eqs. (1)–(4), for fixed values of a_1, a_2 and a_3 was solved by using implicit finite difference method.

In order to reconstruct function q (boundary condition) we minimized functional (8) by using Ant Colony Optimization algorithm. It is a heuristic algorithm, so the calculation in each case need to be repeated certain number of times. In addition, calculations were performed in parallel (multi-threaded) way, which made it possible to significantly reduce the computation time.

The inspiration for the creation of ACO algorithm was the behavior of ant colonies, widely regarded as the efficient and intelligent community. The ants searching for the food sources communicate with each other by leaving the pheromone trace. Pheromone is a chemical substance produced and recognized by the most of ant species. This substance is leaved in the ground by the moving ant and smelled by the other ants which makes them to follow the marked trace. The more ants travel the trail, the stronger is the pheromone trace. The shorter the distance between the anthill and a source of food is, the pheromone trail is more intense. For long routes, and thus rarely frequented, the pheromone trail is faint and evaporates.

Such simple mechanism is imitated in the following way. For initializing the procedure we need to set up the number M of ants in one population, number I of iterations and the initial value α_1 of the narrowing parameter. The role of ants is played by the vectors x^k, $k = 1, \ldots, M$, for a start randomly dispersed in the considered region. And the goal of the procedure is to bring them closer to the source of food, that is to the sought minimum of function F. In each step one of the individuals is selected as the best one x^{best} - the one for which the minimized function F takes the lowest value, that

is the one which is the closest to the source of food. Next, to vector x^{best} there is added
M vectors dx randomly selected from the range $\left[-\alpha_j, \alpha_j\right]$. The vectors obtained in this
way represent the new locations of ants. Thus, in each iteration the vector representing
each ant is updated I^2 times. After each such cycle the ants dislocation range α is
tenfold decreased which simulates the process of the pheromone trail evaporation,
because thanks to this the ants are forced to gather more and more densely around the
best solution.

The presented approach is based on the algorithm presented in [17] and details of
the procedure, used in the current paper including the parallelization of ACO algorithm,
are listed below. Thanks to this procedure we intend to determine the values a_1, a_2, a_3
on the way of minimizing functional (8).

We assume the following symbols

$$F - \text{minimized function}, \mathbf{x} = (x_1, \ldots, x_n) \in D,$$

nT $-$ number of threads, $M = nT \cdot p$ $-$ number of ants in one population,
I $-$ number of iteration (in practice $I^2 \cdot I$), α_i $-$ narrowing parameters.
Below we present the steps of the algorithm.

Initialization of the algorithm

1. Setting parameters of the algorithm nT, M, I and α_j ($j = 1,2, \ldots, I$).
2. Generate starting population $\mathbf{x}^k = (x_1{}^k, x_2{}^k, \ldots, x_n{}^k)$, where $x^k \in D$, $k = 1, 2, \ldots,$
   M.
3. Dividing the population on nT groups (groups will be calculated in parallel way).
4. Determination of the value of minimized function for the each ant in population
   (parallel calculation).
5. Determination in the population best solution $\mathbf{x}^{best}$ (best ant).

Iterative process

6. Random selection of vector shifts $\mathbf{dx}^k = (dx_1{}^k, dx_2{}^k, \ldots, dx_n{}^k)$, where $-\alpha_j \leq dx_i{}^k \leq$
   α_j,
7. Generating a new location of ant colonies $\mathbf{x}^k = \mathbf{x}^{best} + \mathbf{dx}^k$, $k = 1, 2, \ldots, M$.
8. Dividing a population on nT groups (groups will be calculated in parallel way).
9. Determination of the value of minimized function for the each ant in population
   (parallel calculation).
10. Determining the best solution in ant colony. If this solution is better than $\mathbf{x}^{best}$, then
    we accept this solution as $\mathbf{x}^{best}$.
11. Steps 6 − 10 are repeated I^2 times.
12. Changing the values of narrowing parameters α_j: $\alpha_j = 0.1\alpha_j$.
13. Steps 6 − 12 are repeated I times.

4 Experimental Results

We consider Eq. (1) with following data

$$t^* = 500 \; [s], \qquad L = 1 \; [m], \qquad c = 2 \; [J/kg \cdot K], \qquad \rho = 2 \; [kg/m^3],$$
$$\lambda = 2 \; [W/m \cdot K], \qquad u^\infty = 0 \; [K], \qquad f(x) = 0 \; [K],$$
$$h(t) = 1400 \exp\left[\frac{t - 45}{455} \ln\left(\frac{7}{4}\right)\right] \; [W/m^2 \cdot K].$$

In ACO algorithm we set the following parameters

$$nT = 4, \; M = 12, \quad I = 3, \qquad \alpha_1 = 1.$$

Function q, will be in the following form

$$q(t) = \begin{cases} a_1, t \in [0, t_1),. \\ a_2, t \in [t_1, t_2),. \\ a_3, t \in [t_2, t^*).. \end{cases}$$

Exact values of a_1, a_2, a_3 are equal to 200, 800 and 1300, respectively.

Inverse problem will be consist on reconstruction a_1, a_2 and a_3 based on measurements data (input data) $\hat{U}_{ij}$. The grid used to generate these data was of the size 300×5000.

We assume only one measurement point xp = 0.1 (N_1 = 1), measured from this point will read every 0.5, 1, 2 s (N_2 = 1000, 500, 250). In order to investigate the effect of measurement errors on the results of reconstruction and stability of the algorithm, we perturbed the input data by the pseudorandom error of 1 and 2 % size.

In the process of minimizing functional, the direct problem need to be solve many times. Grid used to solve the direct problem has size 100×1000 and was different density than grid used to generate the input data.

To determine the minimum of the functional (8) ACO algorithm was used. This is a heuristic algorithm, therefore it is required to repeat calculations a certain number of times. In this paper, we assumed that the calculations for each case will be repeated ten times and population consists on twelve ants ($M = 12$).

Algorithm was adapted for parallel computations (multi-threaded), which significantly reduced the computation time. In the case of calculations without multi-threads, the time required for the execution of one algorithm was about 1826 s, while the use of four threads that time has reduced to about 477 s.

Tables 1, 2, 3 presents reconstruction of coefficient a_1, a_2, a_3 depending on the size of disturbance input data at the measurement point xp = 0.1.

As we can see from the tables the coefficients a_i (i = 1, 2, 3) are reconstructed very well. In each case, the relative error of restoring of these coefficients is not exceed 0.5 %.

One of the main indicators for evaluating the results of temperature reconstruction are errors in the measurement point xp = 0.1. Tables 4 and 5 shows errors of restoration

Table 1. Results of computation in case of measurements every 0.5 s in measurement point $\underline{xp} = 0.1$ ($\overline{a_i}$- reconstructed value of a_i, $\delta_{\overline{a_i}}$ - percentage relative error of a_i, σ - standard deviation ($i = 1,2,3$))

Noise	$\overline{a_i}$	$\delta_{\overline{a_i}}$ [%]	σ
0 %	199.67	0.17	0.57
	799.81	0.03	0.47
	1298.80	0.10	0.83
1 %	199.15	0.43	0.56
	799.63	0.05	0.60
	1299.34	0.06	0.77
2 %	200.29	0.15	0.46
	800.18	0.03	0.70
	1299.74	0.02	0.64

Table 2. Results of computation in case of measurements every 1 s in measurement point $\underline{xp} = 0.1$ ($\overline{a_i}$- reconstructed value of a_i, $\delta_{\overline{a_i}}$ - percentage relative error of a_i, σ - standard deviation ($i = 1,2,3$))

Noise	$\overline{a_i}$	$\delta_{\overline{a_i}}$ [%]	σ
0 %	199.75	0.13	0.20
	800.01	0.01	0.59
	1299.17	0.07	0.57
1 %	199.78	0.11	0.36
	799.26	0.10	0.41
	1300.05	0.01	0.80
2 %	200.06	0.03	0.45
	799.58	0.06	0.41
	1300.03	0.01	0.39

Table 3. Results of computation in case of measurements every 2 s in measurement point $\underline{xp} = 0.1$ ($\overline{a_i}$- reconstructed value of a_i, $\delta_{\overline{a_i}}$ - percentage relative error of a_i, σ - standard deviation ($i = 1,2,3$))

Noise	$\overline{a_i}$	$\delta_{\overline{a_i}}$ [%]	σ
0 %	199.29	0.36	0.38
	798.69	0.17	0.44
	1298.92	0.09	0.43
1 %	199.58	0.21	0.45
	799.58	0.06	0.41
	1299.09	0.01	0.49
2 %	199.64	0.18	0.30
	798.69	0.17	0.67
	1297.92	0.17	0.31

Table 4. Errors of temperature reconstruction in measurement point $x_p = 0.1$ for measurements every 0.5 and 1 s (Δ_{av} - average absolute error, Δ_{max} - maximal absolute error, δ_{av} - average relative error, δ_{max} - maximal relative error)

Noise	0 %	1 %	2 %	0 %	1 %	2 %
	0.5 s $x_p = 0.1$			1 s $x_p = 0.1$		
Δ_{av} [K]	0.1913	0.2696	0.1023	0.1130	0.1673	0.0830
Δ_{max} [K]	0.5206	0.3719	0.1269	0.3590	0.3254	0.1835
δ_{av} [%]	0.0940	0.2000	0.0711	0.0816	0.0123	0.0330
δ_{max} [%]	0.1651	0.4251	0.1451	0.1251	0.1101	0.0524

Table 5. Errors of temperature reconstruction in measurement point $x_p = 0.1$ for measurements every 2 s (Δ_{av} - average absolute error, Δ_{max} - maximal absolute error, δ_{av} - average relative error, δ_{max} - maximal relative error)

Noise	0 %	1 %	2 %
	2 s $x_p = 0.1$		
Δ_{av} [K]	0.4441	0.2233	0.4656
Δ_{max} [K]	0.5757	0.3974	0.9095
δ_{av} [%]	0.2253	0.1195	0.1696
δ_{max} [%]	0.3551	0.2101	0.1801

of temperature in measurement point for measurements every 0.5, 1, 2 s. Hence we can say that the temperature at the measurement point is reconstructed very well. The maximum relative error of reconstruction temperature in each case does not exceed 0.43 %, in turn, the average relative error is less than 0.23 %.

Figure 1 presents relative errors of reconstructing function q occurring in the boundary condition for the measurements every 0.5, 1, 2 s. In each case relative error of restoring function q is less than 0.65 %.

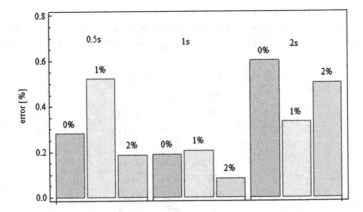

Fig. 1. Relative errors of reconstruction of function q for various perturbations of input data and for measurements every 0.5, 1, 2 s

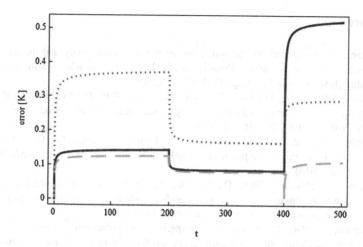

Fig. 2. Distribution of errors of temperature reconstruction in measurement point $x_p = 0.1$ for measurements every 0.5 s and for various perturbations of input data (0 % – solid line, 1 % – dashed line, 2 % – dotted line)

In Fig. 2 are shown distribution errors of reconstruction temperature in the measurement point $x_p = 0.1$ in case of measurements every 0.5 s.

We can see that error of temperature reconstruction slightly decreases between 0.5 and 1 s, but then it increases between 1 and 2 s. These differences are minimal. They are probably due to the probabilistic nature of the algorithm. In case of perturbed input data, additionally we have randomness disorders.

5   Conclusions

In this paper we considered the inverse problem for the heat conduction equation of fractional order. Boundary condition of the second kind was reconstructed. The direct problem was solved using implicit finite difference method, and to minimize the functional Ant Colony Optimization algorithm was used. By using the ACO algorithm, we have received a satisfactory approximate solution.

The function q defining the boundary condition of the second kind has been reconstructed very well. The errors of reconstruction did not exceed 0.65 % and do not exceed the input errors. Errors of reconstruction temperature in the measurement point are minimal and do not exceed 0.43 %.

It is worth mentioning that the used algorithm can be easily adapted to parallel computing which allows to significantly reduce the computation time. Executing algorithm for the 4 threads, the computation performed nearly 3.8 times faster than without multithreading approach.

364   R. Brociek and D. Słota

References

1. Ardakani, M., Khodadad, M.: Identification of thermal conductivity and the shape of an inclusion using the boundary elements method and the particle swarm optimization algorithm. Inverse Prob. Sci. Eng. **17**, 855–870 (2009)
2. Carvalho, A.R., Velho, H.F.D.C., Stephany, S., Souto, R.P., Sandri, J.C.B.S.: Fuzzy ant colony optimization for estimating chlorophyll concentration profile in offshore sea water. Inverse Prob. Sci. Eng. **16**, 705–715 (2008)
3. dos Santos, A., de Campos, V.H., Luz, E., Freitas, S., Grell, G., Gan, M.: Firefly optimization to determine the precipitation field on South America. Inverse Prob. Sci. Eng. **21**, 451–466 (2013)
4. Hetmaniok, E., Nowak, I., Słota, D., Zielonka, A.: Determination of optimal parameters for the immune algorithm used for solving inverse heat conduction problems with and without a phase change. Numer. Heat Transfer B **62**, 462–478 (2012)
5. Hetmaniok, E., Słota, D., Zielonka, A.: Experimental verification of immune recruitment mechanism and clonal selection algorithm applied for solving the inverse problems of pure metal solidification. Int. Comm. Heat Mass Transf. **47**, 7–14 (2013)
6. Hetmaniok, E., Słota, D., Zielonka, A.: Experimental verification of selected artificial intelligence algorithms used for solving the inverse Stefan problem. Numer. Heat Transfer B **66**, 343–359 (2014)
7. Hetmaniok, E., Słota, D., Zielonka, A.: Using the swarm intelligence algorithms in solution of the two-dimensional inverse Stefan problem. Comput. Math. Appl. **69**, 347–361 (2015)
8. Borowik, G., Woźniak, M., Fornaia, A., Giunta, R., Napoli, C., Pappalardo, G., Tramontana, E.: A software architecture assisting workflow executions on cloud resources. Int. J. Electron. Telecommun. **61**, 17–23 (2015)
9. Woźniak, M., Kempa, W.M., Gabryel, M., Nowicki, R.K.: A finite-buffer queue with single vacation policy – analytical study with evolutionary positioning. Int. J. Appl. Math. Comput. **24**, 887–900 (2014)
10. Woźniak, M., Połap, D.: On some aspects of genetic and evolutionary methods for optimization purposes. Int. J. Electron. Telecommun. **61**, 7–16 (2015)
11. Karaboga, D., Basturk, B.: A powerful and efficient algorithm for numerical function optimization: artificial bee colony (ABC) algorithm. J. Global Optim. **39**, 459–471 (2007)
12. Karaboga, D., Basturk, B.: On the performance of artificial bee colony (ABC) algorithm. Appl. Soft Comput. **8**, 687–697 (2008)
13. Karaboga, D., Akay, B.: A comparative study of artificial bee colony algorithm. Appl. Math. Comput. **214**, 108–132 (2009)
14. Özbakir, L., Baykasoglu, A., Tapkan, P.: Bees algorithm for generalized assignment problem. Appl. Math. Comput. **215**, 3782–3795 (2010)
15. Dorigo, M., Stützle, T.: Ant Colony Optimization. MIT Press, Cambridge (2004)
16. Dorigo, M., Blum, C.: Ant colony optimization theory: a survey. Theor. Comput. Sci. **344**, 243–278 (2005)
17. Toksari, M.D.: Ant colony optimization for finding the global minimum. Appl. Math. Comput. **176**, 308–316 (2006)
18. Carpinteri, A., Mainardi, F.: Fractal and Fractional Calculus in Continuum Mechanics. Springer, New York (1997)
19. Podlubny, I.: Fractional Differential Equations. Academic Press, San Diego (1999)
20. Das, S.: Functional Fractional Calculus for System Identification and Controls. Springer, Berlin (2008)

21. Caponetto, R., Dongola, G., Fortuna, I., Petras, I.: Fractional Order Systems. Modeling and Control Applications. World Scientific Series on Nonlinear Science, Series A, vol. 72. World Scientific Publishing, New Jersey (2010)
22. Klafter, J., Lim, S., Metzler, R.: Fractional Dynamics. Resent Advances. World Scientific, New Jersey (2012)
23. Mitkowski, W., Kacprzyk, J., Baranowski, J.: Advances in the Theory and Applications of Non-integer Order Systems. Springer Inter. Publ, Cham (2013)
24. Mitkowski, W., Skruch, P.: Fractional-order models of the supercapacitors in the form of RC ladder networks. Bull. Polish Acad. Sci. Tech. Sci. **61**(3), 581–587 (2013)
25. Oprzędkiewicz, K.: Approximation method for a fractional order transfer function with zero and pole. Arch. Control Sci. **24**(4), 409–425 (2014)
26. Obrączka, A., Kowalski, J.: Modelowanie rozkładu ciepła w materiałach ceramicznych przy użyciu równań różniczkowych niecałkowitego rzędu. In: Szczygieł, M. (ed.) Materiały XV Jubileuszowego Sympozjum „Podstawowe Problemy Energoelektroniki, Elektromechaniki i Mechatroniki", PPEEm 2012, vol. 32 of Archiwum Konferencji PTETiS, Komitet Organizacyjny Sympozjum PPEE i Seminarium BSE, pp. 133–132 (2012)
27. Battaglia, J.L., Cois, O., Puigsegur, L., Oustaloup, A.: Solving an inverse heat conduction problem using a non-integer identified model. Int. J. Heat Mass Transfer **44**, 2671–2680 (2001)
28. Murio, D.A.: Stable numerical solution of a fractional-diffusion inverse heat conduction problem. Comput. Math Appl. **53**, 1492–1501 (2007)
29. Murio, D.: Time fractional IHCP with Caputo fractional derivatives. Comput. Math Appl. **56**, 2371–2381 (2008)
30. Liu, J., Yamamoto, M.: A backward problem for the time-fractional diffusion equation. Appl. Anal. **89**, 1769–1788 (2010)
31. Zheng, G., Wei, T.: A new regularization method for the time fractional inverse advection-dispersion problem. SIAM J. Numer. Anal. **49**, 1972–1990 (2011)
32. Wang, J.-G., Zhou, Y.-B., Wei, T.: A posteriori regularization parameter choice rule for the quasi-boundary value method for the backward timefractional diffusion problem. Appl. Math. Lett. **26**, 741–747 (2013)
33. Yan, L., Yang, F.: Efficient Kansa-type MFS algorithm for time-fractional inverse diffusion problems. Comput. Math. Appl. (2014, in press)
34. Brociek, R., Słota, D., Wituła, R.: Reconstruction of the thermal conductivity coefficient in the time fractional diffusion equation. In: Latawiec, K.J., Łukaniszyn, M., Stanisławski, R. (eds.) Advances in Modeling and Control of Non-integer Order Systems. LNEE, vol. 320, pp. 239–247. Springer, Heidelberg (2015)
35. Obraczka, A., Mitkowski, W.: The comparison of parameter identification methods for fractional partial differential equation. Solid State Phenom. **210**, 265–270 (2014)
36. Murio, D.: Implicit finite difference approximation for time fractional diffusion equations. Comput. Math Appl. **56**, 1138–1145 (2008)
37. Brociek, R.: Implicit finite difference method for time fractional diffusion equations with mixed boundary conditions. Zesz. Nauk. PŚ., Mat. Stosow. **4**, 73–87 (2014)

Intelligent System for Detection of Breathing Disorders

Marcin Szczygieł[2($\boxtimes$)], Paweł Kielan[2], Edyta Hetmaniok[1], Damian Słota[1], Roman Wituła[1], and Adam Zielonka[1]

[1] Institute of Mathematics, Silesian University of Technology, Kaszubska 23,
44-100 Gliwice, Poland
{edyta.hetmaniok,damian.slota,roman.witula,
adam.zielonka}@polsl.pl
[2] Faculty of Electrical Engineering, Department of Mechatronics,
Silesian University of Technology, Akademicka 10A, 44-100 Gliwice, Poland
{marcin.szczygiel,paweł.kielan}@polsl.pl

Abstract. Breathing disorders during the sleep are different for the population of adults and for the population of children. Most frequently used method for detection of breathing disorders is the polysomnography. In this method many sensors must be used and, in fact, this method is uncomfortable for the patients. In this paper the Authors propose the intelligent system for detection of breathing disorders based on the sound analysis. Additionally, the applied mathematical methods used in this system are presented. Advantage of the proposed procedure is that it is less invasive for the patients and enables the continuous observation of breathing or its disorders.

1 Introduction

Sleep is a physiological state of the body, indispensable for every human being. We spend in this state about 30 % of all our life, and lack of a sleep can lead even to death [1]. Sleep can be divided into two basic phases [1]:

- nREM phase (*non-Rapid Eye Movement*) – phase of the slow movements of the eyeballs connected with the deep sleep, characterized by lesser brain activity and regular breath;
- REM phase (*Rapid Eye Movement*) – phase of the rapid movements of the eyeballs connected with shallow sleep, which translates into a greater brain activity and occurrences of irregular breath.

Simultaneously, the sleep is a strictly ordered state and the preservation of the deep sleep phase and the shallow sleep phase is necessary for the proper functioning of a body.

The sleep disorders can be caused by the occurrences of breath disorders, classified by the American Academy of Sleep Medicine (AASM) as the Sleep Disordered Breathing (SDB), the basic factors of which are the following [2]:

1. Central Sleep Apnoea (CSA) – in which during the sleep it comes frequently to the breath arrest because of the respiratory system insufficiency,

G. Dregvaite and R. Damasevicius (Eds.): ICIST 2015, CCIS 538, pp. 366–375, 2015.
DOI: 10.1007/978-3-319-24770-0_32

2. Obstructive Sleep Apnoea Syndrome (OSAS) – in which it comes frequently to the breath arrest (taking about 10 s–30 s) because of the airway obstruction (collapse or narrowing of the throat).

Breathing disorders during the sleep are different for the population of adults and for the population of children. The differences reveal in the clinical signs, treatment, diagnosis, therapy and its efficiency. The apnoea can cause the following diseases [3]: shallow breathing syndrome, upper airway resistance syndrome (UARS), primary snoring, respiratory effort-related arousal (RERA).

Breathing disorders, as the episodes occurring many times during the night, can lead, among others, to the appearance of the body general weakness, excessive daytime sleepiness, as well as to many diseases of the cardiovascular system [4].

Currently for OSAS (Obstructive Sleep Apnoea Syndrome – see above) there are distinguished three stages of the disease defined on the basis of index AHI (*Apnoea-Hypopnoea Index*) indicating the occurrence of apnoea or shallow breathing during one hour of sleep: soft stage for AHI $\geq$ 5 and < 15, moderate stage for AHI $\geq$ 15 and < 30 and, finally, the tough stage for AHI > 30.

Analysing the data concerning OSAS, with regard to various criteria referring to the age and diagnostics, it is estimated that about 5–15 % of human population suffer from OSAS, although the diseases connected with OSAS are of much greater range (for example, the snoring is a serious social problem and it affects about 40–60 % of adult people). As an example let us quote the results of research executed in Spain on the population of 1050 men and 1098 women [5]. In the group of 50–59 years old men it was stated the value AHI $\geq$ 15 at 19.4 % of tested persons, whereas AHI $\geq$ 30 at 11.4 %. In the group of 60–70 years old men the value AHI $\geq$ 15 was stated at 24.2 % of tested persons, whereas AHI $\geq$ 30 at 8.6 %. In the group of 50–59 years old women it was stated the value AHI $\geq$ 15 at 8.6 % of tested persons, whereas AHI $\geq$ 30 at 4.3 %, and in the group of 60–70 years old women AHI $\geq$ 15 was stated at 15.9 % and AHI $\geq$ 30 at 5.9 % of tested persons.

The most frequently used method for diagnosing OSAS is the polysomnographic study. Study of this kind is burdensome because of the necessary stay of the patient (an adult as well as a child) in hospital and, additionally, because of a big number of sensors needed for executing the tests. The standard parameters monitored in polysomnography are the following [6]:

- Electroencephalography (EEG)
- Electrooculography (EOG)
- Electromyography of muscles in the chin area (EMG)
- Air flow through the anterior nostrils
- Respiratory movements of the chest
- Respiratory movements of the abdominal wall
- Breath sounds (snoring) measurement (microphone)
- Cardiac function recording
- Recording of the arterial blood saturation (SaO$_2$)
- pCO$_2$ recording: transdermal (tc pCO$_2$) or in the exhaled air (ETCO$_2$)
- Sensor of the body position

- Sensor of the limbs movements
- Intraesophagus pH measurement (single-tract).

Method, less invasive and less burdensome for the patient – especially for the child, may be the method of breath monitoring on the basis of sound analysis.

2 Diagnostic Intelligent System

The acoustic signal is determined by many of parameters – frequency, amplitude etc., but in the context of apnoea detection analysis, the most important are the following:

- Pitch of a sound connected with the fundamental frequency,
- Timbre of a sound connected with the spectral structure of a sound,
- Variation of the sound volume in time, that is the sound envelope.

Monitoring and analysis of the presented parameters can indicate the anomaly in breathing, before the state of apnoea even occurs. Therefore it is essential that the elaborated device could give the possibility of precise analysis in relatively short time. The presented parameters determine the object-oriented quality, that is the physical quantity [8].

Analysis of these parameters is possible thanks to the algorithms for signal analysis in the time domain and in the frequency domain (spectral analysis). Time analysis of a signal enables to obtain the plot of amplitude in the function of time which, in turn, contributes in determining the variation of the volume of analysed sound. Frequency analysis of a signal enables to extract all the components of the signal frequency, thanks to which we can get the spectrum of the recorded sound signal.

In paper [7] there is presented a conceptual solution of a device for monitoring the breath of babies.

The next stage of developing the device, applying the sound analysis, is the monitoring-recording device for identifying the occurrences of apnoea, which is grounded on the four basic systems:

(a) Recorder/sound acquisition system, the components of which are: microphone, isolation system, system adjusting the voltage level. These elements are connected with the signal processor where the analog signal, recorded by microphone, is transformed into the digital signal.
(b) Analyser – in this part of the system the recorded signal is analysed in order to determine the "correctness" or "incorrectness" of a sleep. The algorithms of FFT and wavelet analysis, implemented on the signal processor, enable to identify the occurrence of breath by means of the comparison of the measurement data.
(c) Transmitter – the basic role of this part is to generate an alarm signal in case when the breath does not appear longer than the assumed time, for example 5 s.
(d) Receiver/archiving and presentation system – a device enabling to visualize and represent the measurement data in the form of plots, graphs, indices and so on.

Figure 1 presents the flowchart of the signal processing path with the basic elements of proposed system.

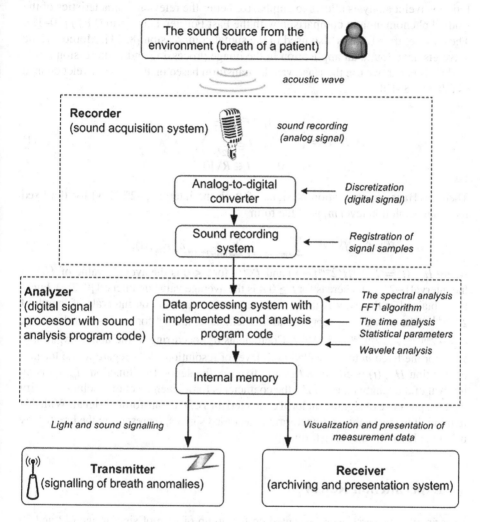

Fig. 1. Flowchart of the signal processing path

3 Mathematical Models

Signal transform is a transformation of the signal for obtaining a different representation of the same signal. The signal is transformed in order to enhance its essential features which in the primary signal representation may be invisible or hardly visible. In the last thirty years a wide popularity have been gained by the wavelet transform of a signal, since it gives the possibility of simultaneous analysis of the time and frequency properties of investigated signal. Thanks to this, the multi-resolution wavelet analysis allows to emphasize better the relevant characteristics of the studied phenomenon in comparison with the Fast Fourier Transform (FFT) [10–12]. The wavelet transform is also used in the signal compression [8, 11]. Moreover, the wavelets have found an application in the image processing and compression [10].

In this paper, we use the Haar wavelet transform based on the Haar wavelet defined as follows [8–10]:

$$
H(t) = \begin{cases} 1, & t \in \left[0, \frac{1}{2}\right), \\ -1, & t \in \left[\frac{1}{2}, 1\right), \\ 0, & t \in R \setminus [0, 1). \end{cases}
\tag{1}
$$

Then the Haar approximation of signal $f(t)$ on the interval $[-2^{m_0}, 2^{m_0})$ for the fixed maximal resolution level m_1 is of the form

$$
f^{m_1}(t) = f^{(-m_0)} + \sum_{m=-m_0+1}^{m_1} \sum_{n=-2^{m_1-m}}^{2^{m_1-m}} d_n^m H_{mn}(t),
\tag{2}
$$

where $H_{mn}(t) = 2^{-m/2} H(2^{-m}t - n)$ and $f^{(-m_0)}$ for $t < 0$ is the average value of $f(t)$ on the interval $[-2^{m_0}, 0)$ whereas for $t \geq 0$ it is the average value on interval $[0, 2^{m_0})$. Function obtained in this way is the piecewise constant function on intervals of length of $2^{-(m_1+1)}$. The new signal representation coefficients are d_n^m for $m = -m_0 + 1, \ldots, m_1$, $n = -2^{m_1-m}, \ldots, 2^{m_1-m}$ and $f^{(-m_0)}$. Coefficients d_n^m, occurring in the above expansion, form for the fixed m the so-called m-th level of resolution. With regard to the locality of function $H_{mn}(t)$ occurrence (for the fixed m the support of function $H_{mn}(t)$ is an interval of the length equal to 2^m) the coefficients for a given level of resolution clarify well the presence of significant local characteristics of the transformed signal. With this in mind, it is reasonable to transform the recorded signals, representing the breaths, by using the Haar wavelet transform.

4   Experimental Research

Experimental research were executed on the group of men of similar age (22 and 23 years old). The breaths were recorded by multidirectional microphone of bandwidth $f_r = 100 \div 16000$ Hz. To the recorded files the FFT (Fast Fourier Transform) analysis and the wavelet analysis were applied. Recorded spectra of the breaths were compared with the spectrum of a sound without any breath occurrence. Results obtained for 4 selected samples are presented in Figs. 2, 3, 4 and 5.

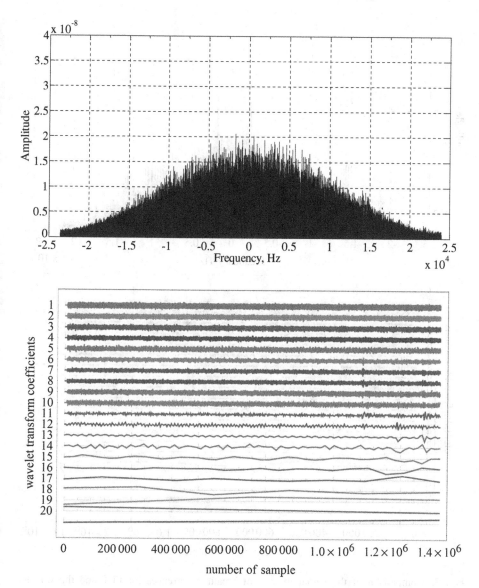

Fig. 2. Comparison of the signal in case of no breath occurrence for FFT and the wavelet decomposition

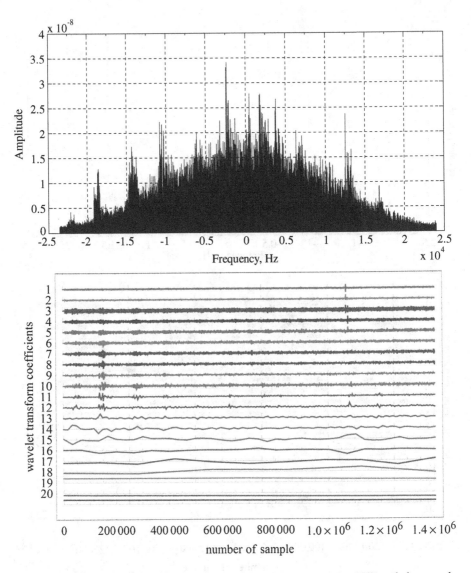

Fig. 3. Comparison of the signal in case of breath occurrences for FFT and the wavelet decomposition – sample I

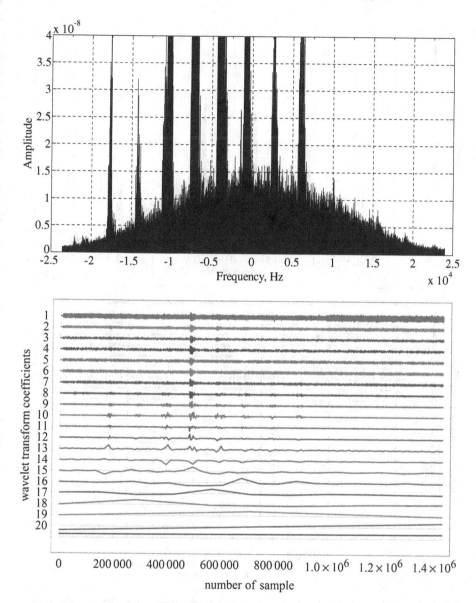

Fig. 4. Comparison of the signal in case of breath occurrences for FFT and the wavelet decomposition – sample II

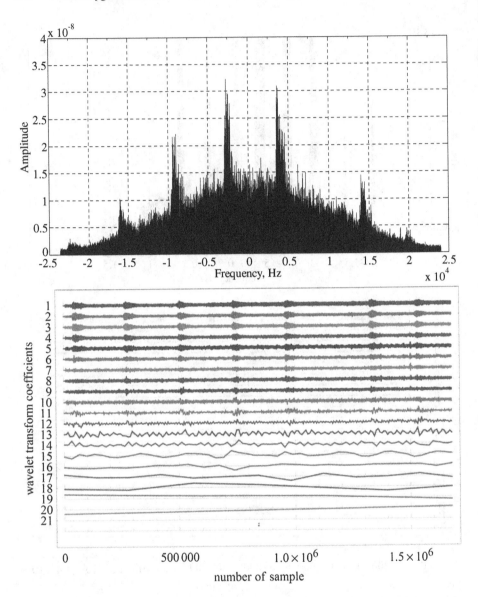

Fig. 5. Comparison of the signal in case of breath occurrences for FFT and the wavelet decomposition – sample III

5   Summary

The proposed recording-measuring system makes possible to monitor the breath continuously and completely with no contact with the patient body, as well as to record the breath for further analysis (determination of frequency of the apnoea occurrences in the given time interval). Analysing the results of executed tests one can select the signals characteristic for the given age group. On the basis of comparative analysis and statistic research this should lead to partitioning the breathing disorders with respect to the diseases which definitely can give the possibility to optimize the algorithms for devices of this class. Ultimately, the designed analyser system should give the opportunity to adopt the device individually to the patient needs, with additional possibility to use it at home.

References

1. Pływaczewski, R., Brzecka, A., Bielicki, P., Czajkowska-Malinowska, M., Cofta, S.Z., Jonczak, L., Radliński, J., Tażbirek, M., Wasilewska, J.: Guidelines of Polish respiratory society concerning diagnosis and treatment of breath disorders during the sleep in adults (Zalecenia Polskiego Towarzystwa Chorób Płuc dotyczące rozpoznawania i leczenia zaburzeń oddychania w czasie snu (ZOCS) u dorosłych). Pneumonologia i Alergologia Polska **81**(3), 221–258 (2013) (in Polish)
2. American Academy Of Sleep Medicine: International Classification of Sleep Disorders: Diagnostic and Coding Manual, 2nd edn. American Academy of Sleep Medicine, Westchester (2005)
3. Kukwa, W., Kukwa, A.: The nose and sleep – disordered breathing (Nos a zaburzenia oddychania podczas snu). Magazyn Otoryno-Laryngologiczny Z. **4**(48), T. XII, 107–111 (2013) (in Polish)
4. Kukwa, W.: Obstructive Sleep Apnea Syndrome and Sleep Apnoea -The Latest Definitions and Scale of Problem (Zespół snu z bezdechami i zaburzenia oddychania podczas snu – najnowsze definicje i skala problemu). Kwartalnik Zdrowie i Sen, Nr1, 2011 (in Polish)
5. Alper, C.M.: Decision making in pediatric OSAS and sleep studies in children (Zaburzenia oddychania podczas snu u dzieci – rozpoznawanie i leczenie). Magazyn Otoryno-Laryngologiczny, Z. **4**(48), T. XII, 121–128 (2013)
6. Lis, G.: Polysomnographic studies in infants and children (Badanie polisomnograficzne w diagnostyce zaburzeń oddychania u dzieci). Diagnostyka Kliniczna (2003) (in Polish)
7. Szczygieł, M., Kielan, P.: The concept of monitoring and recording the breath of infants based on sound analysis (Koncepcja monitorowania i rejestracji oddechu niemowląt na podstawie analizy dźwięku). Workshop PTZE "Bioelektromagnetyzm Teoria i Praktyka" Kraków – Warszawa, 12–14 Grudnia 2005 (in Polish)
8. Havelok, D., Sonoko, K., Vorlander, M.: Handbook of Signal Processing in Acoustics. Springer, New York (2008)
9. Koornwinder, T.H.: Wavelets: An Elementary Treatment of Theory and Applications. World Scientific, Singapore (1995)
10. Hoggar, S.G.: Mathematics of Digital Images. Cambridge University Press, Cambridge (2006)
11. Stranneby, D.: Digital Signal Processing: DSP and Applications. Newnes, Oxford (2001)
12. Nussbaumer, H.J.: Fast Fourier Transform and Convolution Algorithms. Springer, Heidelberg (1982)

Is the Colony of Ants Able to Recognize Graphic Objects?

Dawid Połap[1]([⊠]), Marcin Woźniak[1], Christian Napoli[2],
Emiliano Tramontana[2], and Robertas Damaševičius[3]

[1] Institute of Mathematics, Silesian University of Technology,
Kaszubska 23, 44-101 Gliwice, Poland
dawid.polap@gmail.com, marcin.wozniak@polsl.pl
[2] Department of Mathematics and Informatics,
University of Catania, Viale A. Doria 6, 95125 Catania, Italy
{napoli,tramontana}@dmi.unict.it
[3] Software Engineering Department,
Kaunas University of Technology, Studentu 50, Kaunas, Lithuania
robertas.damasevicius@ktu.lt

Abstract. This paper is to discuss a matter of ants swarm intelligence for 2D input images recognition systems. In the following sections we try to analyze possibility of using artificial ants colony algorithm to analyze input images. Experiments have been performed on a set of test images, to present and prove efficacy and precision of recognition.

Keywords: Image processing · Swarm algorithm · Object classifier

1 Introduction

Computer Science gives many dedicated methods or tailored solutions to solve classification of various objects. EC methods assist in complex problems solving: dynamic systems positioning [31], queueing systems modeling [6, 12, 23, 32, 34–36], benchmark tests [39] or heat transfer optimization [14, 15]. This knowledge is proper to be used by Decision Support System (DSS) [5, 9, 10, 13, 19–21, 24]. Image recognition is one of the processes, where dedicated computer systems may help to classify input objects. For this operation efficacy is of a paramount importance. In the following sections we try to analyze selected Evolutionary Computation (EC) method, in particular Artificial Ant Colony Algorithm (AACA) combined with a dedicated filtering to create object recognition system.

1.1 Related Works

EC methods are proven to efficiently assist in image preprocessing [8, 40], image compression [16], gray-scale image watermarking [22], key-point recognition [37], [38], intelligent video target racking [31], satellite image segmentation [4]. Therefore, in the following sections we discuss a novel approach to object extraction based on Artificial Ant Colony Algorithm (AACA). Ant-based optimization algorithms have

© Springer International Publishing Switzerland 2015
G. Dregvaite and R. Damasevicius (Eds.): ICIST 2015, CCIS 538, pp. 376–387, 2015.
DOI: 10.1007/978-3-319-24770-0_33

already been used for edge detection and shape recognition before. For example [27] have combined it with MRF (Markov Random Fields) for detection of edges. Reference [19] have used a cellular automata based method for segmentation of images. References [3, 11] have employed the algorithm based on the social behavior of ants for image segmentation. References [2, 29, 41] have proposed ant colony based image feature extraction algorithm for edge extraction. Reference [20] has employed ant-based swarm intelligence for detection of centers of objects in an image. Reference [28] have described the ACS-based algorithm to separate background and foreground components of an image.

2 Toward Novel Image Recognition

Image recognition is an important problem, with a wide range of applications in various DSS. Common graphic DSS are based on classic methods like SIFT or SURF [30, 38], which unfortunately demand complex mathematical operations to determine position of most important features. To simplify this process we can use EC. First experiments on EC application in image processing were presented in [35, 38, 40]. This article is devoted to improvements in recognition by benchmark on tailored filtering that together with AACA compose DSS.

2.1 Image Filtering

In the proposed solution, a sobel based filtering is obtained by an edge detection approach using derivative preprocessing. Input images are filtered using differential operator [1, 7, 40], which approximates two dimensional gradient of a luminance function by a convolution with an integer filter applied along the axial directions. For a continuous function $f : \mathbb{R}^2 \rightarrow \mathbb{R}$ and a given point $x_i = (x_{i,1}, x_{i,2})$, the gradient ∇ is computed using partial derivatives $\partial_1 f$ and $\partial_2 f$ calculated at each x_i pixel. An approximation is a convolution of kernels for a small area of neighbor pixels, where $\partial_1 f$ and $\partial_2 f$ use a separate kernel each

$$S1 = \begin{pmatrix} -1 & -2 & -1 \\ 0 & 0 & 0 \\ 1 & 2 & 1 \end{pmatrix}, \qquad S2 = \begin{pmatrix} -1 & 0 & -1 \\ 2 & 0 & 2 \\ -1 & 0 & 1 \end{pmatrix} \qquad (1)$$

combined into a gradient operator, one for a maximum response for the vertical edge and the other for a maximum response for the horizontal edge of the input object. To obtain the edges an associated luminance intensity matrix I is used to compute for every pixel $x_i = (x_{i,1}, x_{i,2}) \in I$ the following functions

$$g_1(x_i) = g_1(x_{i,1}, x_{i,2}) = \sum_{m=1}^{3} \sum_{n=1}^{3} S1_{mn} * I(x_{i,1} + m - 2, x_{i,2} + n - 2),$$
$$g_2(x_i) = g_2(x_{i,1}, x_{i,2}) = \sum_{m=1}^{3} \sum_{n=1}^{3} S2_{mn} * I(x_{i,1} + m - 2, x_{i,2} + n - 2), \qquad (2)$$
$$g(x_i) = g(x_{i,1}, x_{i,2}) = g_1^2(x_i) + g_2^2(x_i).$$

Once the values of the function in (2) are obtained for each pixel, the edges are defined as the pixels in the subset of points $\varepsilon \in T$ that

$$\forall x_i \in \varepsilon \Rightarrow \begin{cases} g(x_i) > 4g^2 \\ g_1(x_i) > g_2(x_i) \\ g(x_i) \geq g(x_{i,1}, x_{i2} - 1) \\ g(x_i) \geq g(x_{i,1}, x_{i,2} + 1) \end{cases} \text{OR} \begin{cases} g(x_i) > 4g^2 \\ g_1(x_i) < g_2(x_i) \\ g(x_i) \leq g(x_{i,1} - 1, x_{i,2}) \\ g(x_i) \leq g(x_{i,1} + 1, x_{i,2}) \end{cases}, \tag{3}$$

basing on the g_1, g_2 and g computed for each pixel $x_i \in I$ as in (2). When a sobel filter is applied to 2D input image T, a new indexed image is depicted as a plain representation of the points of $\varepsilon \in T$, as defined in (3). The indexed image coordinate system is a representation of T, whereby all the values are zeros, except for the coordinates of the point in ε which are ones. Finally the image is then processed to recognize the objects, where the bright patterns can become the shapes of object easy to recognize by AACA. Applied filtering is presented in Algorithm 1.

2.2 Artificial Ant Colony Algorithm

Artificial Ant Colony Algorithm (AACA) simulates behavior of ants when collecting food. Each ant moves in a random way. In case, when the ant finds food, it goes anthill leaving a trail of the pheromones. This pheromone help another ants to follow the trail. However, over the time the pheromones evaporate. Therefore i.e. short trails ensure that the potency of pheromones will be greater. This process is modeled to form an EC optimization algorithm.

Algorithm 1. Applied image filtering

Start,
Import image I to Im,
Calculate the number of pixels columns and rows in 2D input image Im,
Create the 3×3 filters $S1$ and $S2$ using (1),
while $n \leq rows$ **do**
  while $m \leq columns$ **do**
    $Grays[m][n] = $ ccvmean$(Im[m][n])$,
    Compute g, g_1 and g_2 on $Grays[m][n]$ using (2),
  end
end
Save g as a bitmap grayscale image GIm,
Stop.

Pheromones levels are updated in AACA according to

$$f^{t+1}(x_i, x_j) = (1 - \rho)f^t(x_i, x_j) + \Gamma^t_i, \tag{4}$$

where ρ is evaporation rate, t means number of iteration and n is the number of ants in population that must traveled to worker x_i over Γ_i^t distance. This distance, that each ant must travel, is modeled in equation

$$\Gamma_i^t = \sum_{i=1}^n \frac{1}{L_{ij}^t},$$

(5)

where L_{ij}^t means the length of traveled path by ant i to j. The length L_{ij}^t between any two ants i and j in the population of workers situated at points x_i and x_j in the image is defined using Cartesian metric

$$L_{ij}^t = \left\| x_i^t - x_j^t \right\| = \sqrt{\sum_{k=1}^2 (x_{i,k}^t - x_{j,k}^t)^2},$$

(6)

where notations in t iteration are: x_i^t, x_j^t – points in RxR space, $x_{i,k}^t$, $x_{k,j}^t$ – k-th components of the spatial coordinates x_i^t and x_j^t that describe image points in the space. The probability of choosing path from point x_i to x_j by worker ant determines

$$p^t(x_i, x_j) = \frac{\left[f^t(x_i, x_j)\right]^\alpha \left[\frac{1}{L_{ij}^t}\right]^\beta}{\sum_{\alpha \in N_i^k} \left(\left[f^t(x_i, x_j)\right]^\alpha \left[\frac{1}{L_{ia}^t}\right]\right)},$$

(7)

where α is the impact of left pheromones, L_{ij}^t is the distance between i and j, N_i^k is a set of locations, which ant k has not visited and which lead from i.

Having all these information population of worker ants can move over the image. This movement is based on the path choosing probability from point x_i to x_j by worker ant

$$x_i^{t+1} = x_i^t + sign(x_i^t(ind(t)) - x_j^t)),$$

(8)

here $ind(t)$ is an array of neighbor indices after sort. How does the movement is done? The worker ant which is situated at the certain image point has eight possible directions (locations) to move, see Fig. 1.

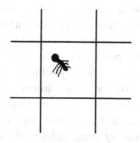

Fig. 1. Worker ant moves possibility in each iteration

In each t iteration the ant can move only one location (pixel) further toward the strongest pheromone source. The ant uses information about best location in each iteration, this information is calculated in (7), and moves toward this direction. This process is a simulation of the search that worker ants do while searching for food using pheromones left by other workers from the colony. Entire AACA is presented in Algorithm 2.

Algorithm 2. AACA to recognize 2D images

Start,
Define all coefficients: n size of workers population, α impact of left pheromones, ρ evaporation rate, number of *generations*,
Define fitness function for the algorithm using (9),
Create a random initial population P of *ants* in 2D image,
$t = 0$,
while $t \leq generation$ do
  Update pheromone values using (4),
  Calculate distances between worker ants (6),
  Calculate possible path to follow by worker i to location j $p^t(x_i, x_j)$ using (7),
  Evaluate population using (9),
  Determine the best position to follow,
  Move population of workers using (8),
  Next generation t++,
end
Values from last population with best fitness are the solution,
Stop.

2.3   Feature Extraction Method Based on Dedicated Filtering and AACA

Our research aim at finding a simple and efficient method for 2D image classification. First attempt to this task was presented in [37]. In this article we present novel approach combined of dedicated filtering and bio-inspired solution. Addition of filtering helps to increase efficiency for recognition of shapes. To preform classification on filtered images we use AACA defined in Sect. 2.2. Our attempt is based on nature. If we look closely at the colony of ants, we can see that there are roles that each ant has. Some of them carry of the queen, soldiers protect the anthill and others search for food. Worker ants have become the prototype of our method. In nature they search for food in the forest and bring it home. However they also provide an information about the source of food to other workers. This information is provided by the use of pheromones, which guide other workers to food. This process is modeled in (4). Each of the workers leave trace of pheromones that is recognized by others. After comparing pheromones intensity ants follow direction of the most strongest trace. This is modeled with probability (7). The source that the ants must find in the image are filtered images of various objects. After filtering, in the picture stay only most important features describing depicted objects. Among them colony of ants choose points of greater importance. These points are key for object extraction.

In the AACA worker ant is representing a single pixel of the image. A population of workers is simulated in order to move over the image to search for specific areas crucial for automatic recognition process. Using filtering we extract the borders of input objects, which are marked in white on a dark background what is perfect input for AACA recognition. Workers validate pixels using simplified fitness function that reflects the brightness of filtered points

$$\Phi(x_i) = \begin{cases} 0.1\ldots1, & saturation \\ 0, & other \end{cases}, \tag{9}$$

Where $\Phi(x_i)$ is the quality of the evaluated pixel reflected by a value in the scale from 0.0 to 1.0, where color saturation changes from black to white.

3   Experiments

In the research we have examine proposed solution. The recognition system was first filtering input images using method presented in Sect. 2.1. These images, after filtering were passed to next component. AACA method from Sect. 2.2 have been implemented on filtered images. Artificial ant colony was moved over the image to search for important features. The evolutionary method was performed with coefficients $\rho = 0.1$, $\beta = 0.3$. In the experiments we were trying to localize objects like cars, architecture construction (houses and their elements, bridges), nature elements and so on. Figures 2, 3, 4, 5 and 6 present classification. Leftmost top image presents the original input, going to the right we can see the image after first filtering and AACA recognition

Fig. 2. 2D input image recognition process over single objects (Color figure online)

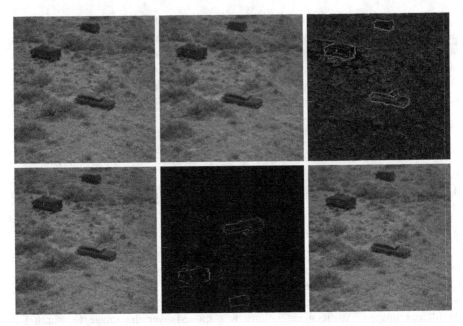

Fig. 3. 2D input image recognition process over landscape objects (Color figure online)

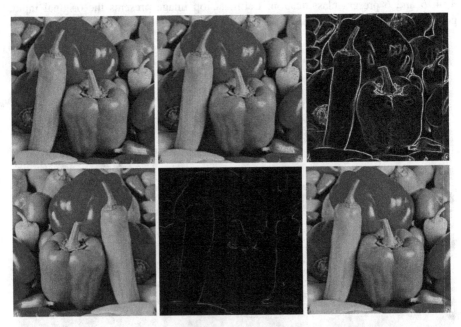

Fig. 4. 2D input image recognition process over still nature (Color figure online)

Fig. 5. 2D input image recognition process over architecture (Color figure online)

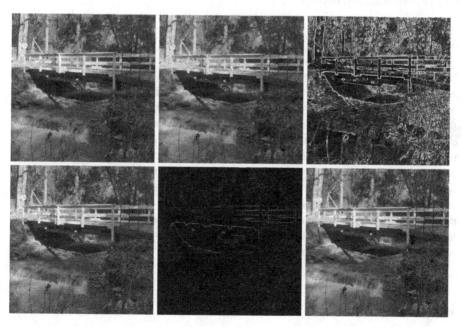

Fig. 6. 2D input image recognition process over nature object (Color figure online)

(in red). The second row shows the image after second filtering, AACA recognition (in red) and main classification result.

If we look at first AACA recognition without prefiltering, in each figure, we can see that the system is just covering objects in the picture with points. In this way we can only show location of the objects. However if we compare this with recognition after first and second filtering, we can see that AACA over filtered images is able not only to show place of the objects we are looking for but also show most important points of the shape. Sometimes AACA recognition over once filtered image has enough precision. However sometimes second filtering can help if we are classifying images where object have many details.

3.1 Conclusion

Novel approach to image recognition helps to simplify this process. The knowledge is useful for DSS. Because of flexibility of the proposed solution we can use the recognition in two ways. Location of classified points (recognition without filtering) can be used to help DSS in decision about size of the object, location or surroundings. If the filtering is applied, proposed classifier shows less points however these points are better for shape recognition. As now they are classified in most important points of input images DSS can use their location to calculate features important for shape recognition, etc. To classify objects using shape points we can use some rough and fuzzy methods [25, 26] or neural approach [10, 39].

4   Final Remarks

Novel feature extraction based on filtering and AACA is precise, easy to implement and fast. The solution can be used in two ways, with prefiltering or without it. Both recognitions are proper for various DSS. This makes it a very promising tool for Artificial Intelligence systems. The solution can work as a part of sophisticated image classifiers, where one needs to detect shape of objects or just simple detection systems where decision is taken only using the location of the recognized object. In both cases presented method gives proper results and recognition process is performed ad-hoc without complicated mathematical modeling. This makes it very important for DSS where we use simple computation devices without efficient processing units. The precision of AACA in recognition of objects is possible to increase, i.e. when we use larger population of ants or use some fast aggregation methods. This improvements will be considered in the future work.

References

1. Anusha, G., Prasad, T., Narayana, D.: Implementation of sobel edge detection on FPGA. Int. J. Comput. Trends Technol. **3**(3), 472–475 (2012)

2. Aydin, D.: An efficient ant-based edge detector. Trans. Comput. Collective Intell. **1**, 39–55 (2010)

3. Benatcha, K., Koudil, M., Benkhelat, N., Boukir, Y.: ISA an algorithm for image segmentation using ants. In: Proceedings of IEEE International Symposium on Industrial Electronics, pp. 2503–2507. IEEE (2008)

4. Bhandari, A.K., Singh, V.K., Kumar, A., Singh, G.K.: Cuckoo search algorithm and wind driven optimization based study of satellite image segmentation for multilevel thresholding using kapurs entropy. Expert Syst. Appl. **41**(7), 3538–3560 (2014)

5. Bonanno, F., Capizzi, G., Sciuto, G.L., Napoli, C., Pappalardo, G., Tramontana, E.: A cascade neural network architecture investigating surface plasmon polaritons propagation for thin metals in OpenMP. In: Rutkowski, L., Korytkowski, M., Scherer, R., Tadeusiewicz, R., Zadeh, L.A., Zurada, J.M. (eds.) ICAISC 2014, Part I. LNCS, vol. 8467, pp. 22–33. Springer, Heidelberg (2014)

6. Borowik, G., Woźniak, M., Fornaia, A., Giunta, R., Napoli, C., Pappalardo, G., Tramontana, E.: A software architecture assisting workflow executions on cloud resources. Int. J. Electron. Telecommun. **61**(1), 17–23 (2015). doi:10.1515/eletel-2015-0002

7. Canny, J.: A computational approach to edge detection. IEEE Trans. Pattern Anal. Mach. Intell. **6**, 679–698 (1986)

8. Napoli, C., Pappalardo, G., Tramontana, E., Marszałek, Z., Połap, D., Woźniak, M.: Simplified firefly algorithm for 2D image key-points search. In: Proceedings of the IEEE Symposium on Computational Intelligence for Human-like Intelligence – CIHLI 2014, Orlando, USA, pp. 118–125. IEEE, 9–12 December 2014, doi:10.1109/CIHLI.2014.7013395

9. Capizzi, G., Bonanno, F., Napoli, C.: A new approach for lead-acid batteries modeling by local cosine. In: Proceedings of International Symposium on Power Electronics Electrical Drives Automation and Motion (SPEEDAM), pp. 1074–1079, 14–16 June 2010. doi:10.1109/SPEEDAM.2010.5542285

10. Damaševičius, R.: Structural analysis of regulatory DNA sequences using grammar inference and support vector machine. Neurocomputing **73**(4–6), 633–638 (2010)

11. Etemad, S., White, T.: An ant-inspired algorithm for detection of image edge features. Electron. Lett. Comput. Vis. Image Anal. **11**(8), 4883–4893 (2011)

12. Gabryel, M., Nowicki, R.K., Woźniak, M., Kempa, W.M.: Genetic cost optimization of the *GI/M/1/N* finite-buffer queue with a single vacation policy. In: Rutkowski, L., Korytkowski, M., Scherer, R., Tadeusiewicz, R., Zadeh, L.A., Zurada, J.M. (eds.) ICAISC 2013, Part II. LNCS, vol. 7895, pp. 12–23. Springer, Heidelberg (2013)

13. Napoli, C., Pappalardo, G., Tramontana, E., Nowicki, R.K., Starczewski, J.T., Woźniak, M.: Toward work groups classification based on probabilistic neural network approach. In: Rutkowski, L., Korytkowski, M., Scherer, R., Tadeusiewicz, R., Zadeh, L.A., Zurada, J.M. (eds.). LNCS, vol. 9119, pp. 79–89. Springer, Heidelberg (2015)

14. Hetmaniok, E., Nowak, I., Słota, D., Zielonka, A.: Determination of optimal parameters for the immune algorithm used for solving inverse heat conduction problems with and without a phase change. Numer. Heat Transf. B **62**, 462–478 (2012)

15. Hetmaniok, E., Słota, D., Zielonka, A.: Experimental verification of immune recruitment mechanism and clonal selection algorithm applied for solving the inverse problems of pure metal solidification. Int. Commun. Heat Mass Transf. **47**, 7–14 (2013)

16. Horng, M.H.: Vector quantization using the firefly algorithm for image compression. Expert Syst. Appl. **39**(1), 1078–1091 (2012)

17. Horzyk, A.: Innovative types and abilities of neural networks based on associative mechanisms and a new associative model of neurons. In: Rutkowski, L., Korytkowski, M., Scherer, R., Tadeusiewicz, R., Zadeh, L.A., Zurada, J.M. (eds.). LNCS, vol. 9119, pp. 26–38. Springer, Heidelberg (2015)
18. Horzyk, A.: How does generalization and creativity come into being in neural associative systems and how does it form human-like knowledge? Neurocomputing **144**, 238–257 (2014). doi:10.1016/j.neucom.2014.04.046
19. Keshtkar, F., Gueaieb, W.: Segmentation of dental radiographs using a swarm intelligence approach. In: Proceedings of Canadian Conference on Electrical and Computer Engineering, pp. 328–331 (2006)
20. Lakehal, E.: A swarm intelligence based approach for image feature extraction. In: Proceedings of International Conference on Multimedia Computing and Systems, pp. 31–35 (2009)
21. Martisius, I., Birvinskas, D., Damasevicius, R., Jusas, V.: EEG dataset reduction and classification using wave atom transform. In: Mladenov, V., Koprinkova-Hristova, P., Palm, G., Villa, A.E.P., Appollini, B., Kasabov, N. (eds.) ICANN 2013. LNCS, vol. 8131, pp. 208–215. Springer, Heidelberg (2013)
22. Mishra, A., Agarwal, C., Sharma, A., Bedi, P.: Optimized gray-scale image water-marking using DWT SVD and firefly algorithm. Expert Syst. Appl. **41**(17), 7858–7867 (2014)
23. Napoli, C., Papplardo, G., Tramontana, E.: Improving files availability for bit-torrent using a diffusion model. In: IEEE 23rd International Workshop on Enabling Technologies: Infrastructure for Collaborative Enterprises - WETICE 2014, pp. 191–196, June 2014
24. Napoli, C., Pappalardo, G., Tramontana, E., Zappalà, G.: A cloud-distributed GPU architecture for pattern identification in segmented detectors big-data surveys. Comput. J. bxu147 (2014). doi:10.1093/comjnl/bxu147
25. Niewiadomski, A.: Imprecision measures for type-2 fuzzy sets: applications to linguistic summarization of databases. In: Rutkowski, L., Tadeusiewicz, R., Zadeh, L.A., Zurada, J.M. (eds.) ICAISC 2008. LNCS (LNAI), vol. 5097, pp. 285–294. Springer, Heidelberg (2008)
26. Nowak, B.A., Nowicki, R.K., Woźniak, M., Napoli, C.: Multi-class nearest neighbour classifier for incomplete data handling. In: Rutkowski, L., Korytkowski, M., Scherer, R., Tadeusiewicz, R., Zadeh, L.A., Zurada, J.M. (eds.). LNCS, vol. 9119, pp. 469–480. Springer, Heidelberg (2015)
27. Ouadfel, S., Batouche, M.: MRF-based image segmentation using ant colony system. Electron. Lett. Comput. Vis. Image Anal. **2**(2), 12–24 (2013)
28. Wang, Y., Wan, Q.: Detecting moving objects by ant colony system in a MAP-MRF framework. In: Proceedings of International Conference on E-product E-service and E-Entertainment, pp. 1–4 (2010)
29. Tian, J., Yu, W., Chen, L., Ma, L.: Image edge detection using variation-adaptive ant colony optimization. In: Nguyen, N.T. (ed.) Transactions on Computational Collective Intelligence V. LNCS, vol. 6910, pp. 27–40. Springer, Heidelberg (2011)
30. Uktveris, T.: Efficiency analysis of object position and orientation detection algorithms. In: Dregvaite, G., Damasevicius, R. (eds.) ICIST 2014. CCIS, vol. 465, pp. 302–311. Springer, Heidelberg (2014)
31. Walia, G.S., Kapoor, R.: Intelligent video target tracking using an evolutionary particle filter based upon improved cuckoo search. Expert Syst. Appl. **41**(14), 6315–6326 (2014)
32. Woźniak, M.: On applying cuckoo search algorithm to positioning GI/M/1.N finite-buffer queue with a single vacation policy. In: Proceedings of the 12th Mexican International Conference on Artificial Intelligence – MICAI 2013, Mexico City, Mexico, pp. 59–64. IEEE, 24–30 November 2013. doi:10.1109/MICAI.2013.12

33. Woźniak, M.: Fitness function for evolutionary computation applied in dynamic object simulation and positioning. In: Proceedings of the IEEE Symposium Series on Computational Intelligence – SSCI 2014: 2014 IEEE Symposium on Computational Intelligence in Vehicles and Transportation Systems – CIVTS 2014, Orlando, Florida, USA, pp. 108–114. IEEE, 9–12 December 2014. doi:10.1109/CIVTS.2014.7009485

34. Gabryel, M., Woźniak, M., Damaševičius, R.: An application of differential evolution to positioning queueing systems. In: Rutkowski, L., Korytkowski, M., Scherer, R., Tadeusiewicz, R., Zadeh, L.A., Zurada, J.M. (eds.). LNCS, vol. 9120, pp. 379–390. Springer, Heidelberg (2015)

35. Woźniak, M., Kempa, W.M., Gabryel, M., Nowicki, R.K.: A finite-buffer queue with single vacation policy - analytical study with evolutionary positioning. Int. J. Appl. Math. Comput. Sci. **24**(4), 887–900 (2014). doi:10.2478/amcs-2014-0065

36. Woźniak, M., Kempa, W.M., Gabryel, M., Nowicki, R.K., Shao, Z.: On applying evolutionary computation methods to optimization of vacation cycle costs in finite-buffer queue. In: Rutkowski, L., Korytkowski, M., Scherer, R., Tadeusiewicz, R., Zadeh, L.A., Zurada, J.M. (eds.) ICAISC 2014, Part I. LNCS, vol. 8467, pp. 480–491. Springer, Heidelberg (2014)

37. Woźniak, M., Marszałek, Z.: An idea to apply firefly algorithm in 2D image key-points search. In: Dregvaite, G., Damasevicius, R. (eds.) ICIST 2014. CCIS, vol. 465, pp. 312–323. Springer, Heidelberg (2014)

38. Woźniak, M., Połap, D.: Basic concept of cuckoo search algorithm for 2D images processing with some research results. In: Proceedings of the 11th International Conference on Signal Processing and Multimedia Applications – SIGMAP 2014, Vienna, Austria, pp. 64–173. SciTePress – INSTICC, 28–30 August 2014. doi:10.5220/0005015801570164

39. Woźniak, M., Połap, D.: On some aspects of genetic and evolutionary methods for optimization purposes. Int. J. Electron. Telecommun. **61**(1), 7–16 (2015). doi:10.1515/eletel-2015-0001

40. Woźniak, M., Połap, D., Gabryel, M., Nowicki, R.K., Napoli, C., Tramontana, E.: Can we process 2D images using artificial bee colony? In: Rutkowski, L., Korytkowski, M., Scherer, R., Tadeusiewicz, R., Zadeh, L.A., Zurada, J.M. (eds.). LNCS, vol. 9119, pp. 660–671. Springer, Heidelberg (2015)

41. Zhuang, X., Yang, G., Zhu, H.: A model of image feature extraction inspired by ant swarm system. In: Proceedings of International Conference on Natural Computation, pp. 553–557 (2008)

An Object-Oriented Neural Network Toolbox Based on Design Patterns

Christian Napoli[✉] and Emiliano Tramontana

Department of Mathematics and Informatics, University of Catania, Viale Andrea Doria 6,
95125 Catania, Italy
{napoli,tramontana}@dmi.unict.it

Abstract. Generally, the resolution of a problem by using soft-computing support requires several attempts for setting up a proper neural network. Such attempts consist of designing and training a neural network and can be a relevant effort for the developer. This paper proposes a toolbox that automates several steps for setting up a neural network, and provides high-level abstractions allowing a developer to choose classical network topologies and configure them as desired, as well as design a neural network from a scratch. A valuable aspect of our solution is given by the modularity of the whole design that builds on object-orientation and design patterns.

Keywords: Artificial intelligence · Soft-computing · Modularity · Software design · Software evolution

1 Introduction

The main characteristics of a neural network are the *topology* and the *working mechanism*. The topology characterises the neurons and their interconnections (synaptic links, feedbacks, delay lines, etc.), whereas the working mechanism consists of the algorithms used for training and, after that, to obtain coherent outputs. Such a working mechanism is chosen according to the topology of the trainee network. Different categories of topologies and training procedures have been proposed and are useful for categories of classification or prediction problems.

Generally, the best specific topology for solving a problem is unknown, therefore often the first training of a neural network is unsuccessful. In such a case, some policies of growth or pruning have to be applied, which involve the creation or elimination of one or more neurons. Moreover, each time a neuron is created or removed the network topology changes and a training phase is needed again (at least partially). Hence, while topology and training are functionally connected to each other, the set up for each should be made possible independently of the other. Hence, the developer should be able to choose abstractions and compose a novel behaviour by setting these up (Booch and Maksimchuk 2007).

As a solution to the above modularity requirement, this work presents an object-oriented toolbox that provides the user with a level of abstraction appropriate to design

G. Dregvaite and R. Damasevicius (Eds.): ICIST 2015, CCIS 538, pp. 388–399, 2015.
DOI: 10.1007/978-3-319-24770-0_34

neural networks for several classification and prediction problems. The proposed solution takes into account the important features of neural networks and supports their modular instantiation, hence providing reusable abstractions and modules where the training support can be reused and adapted to different topologies.

2 Neural Networks

A neural network is basically composed by a set of simple interconnected *functional units* called neurons. The topology resulting by the said connections allows us to have a specialised network performing some tasks such as: modelling physical phenomena (Bonanno et al. 2014c), performing predictions (Borowik et al. 2015), enhancing forecast correctness (Napoli et al. 2014a), filtering signals (Nowak et al. 2015; Gabryel et al. 2015) and images (Napoli et al. 2014b; Wozniak and Polap 2014; Wozniak et al. 2015a), etc. (Haykin 2004). A neural network processes data trying to emulate the human brain model, by partially reproducing the human connectome with the said functional units that we call neurons. Functionally, a neural network builds some knowledge out of training data and applies such a knowledge for further use on the same data domain. Hence, the field of neural networks gives us a different approach to problem solving with respect to standard algorithmic. This latter is based on a conventional set of instructions in well defined deterministic steps that are followed in order to reach the solution, while in general a neural network approach is not deterministic. In fact, it is not possible to program a neural network in order to perform a specific task without any need for training. Moreover, in the majority of cases, even the topology is unknown beforehand. Then, in order to use neural networks a user must be prepared to a try-and-check procedure that could require a certain amount of interactions.

Nevertheless, when a problem is successfully managed by a topology, such a topology could be used for a range of problems in the same domain. Moreover, a specifically trained neural network with such a topology could be reused to continue the computation on the same data domain. E.g. in order to predict the power generation of photovoltaic power plants the topology results similar among different plants, while each plant will use a specifically trained neural network that has learnt how to model the environmental conditions and variations on that specific site.

3 The Developed Toolbox

The presented toolbox is designed in order to be modular and robust to changes, and such properties have been achieved thanks to *design patterns*, i.e. software solutions that have been proven successful to solve recurrent problems in the field of object-oriented programming (OOP), described in terms of needed classes and their relationships (Gamma et al. 1994). In order to obtain a design for creating, training, using and managing neural networks, we have to take into account the big number of various topologies and training strategies available, the different sizes, and the different fields which the network can be applied to. The most important requirements are: (i) a neural network can have an arbitrary size and can use different kinds of neurons, (ii) neurons are usually organised into layers, and connected to each other in a custom way, (iii) connections between neurons have their own characterisation, e.g. a connection could link two neurons or link a delay to a neuron and vice versa, and finally, (iv) neurons could use different activation functions according to the layer they belong to.

Out of the said requirements, we have designed the following main class hierarchies, and connected them according to three design patterns.

- Class `NeuralNetwork` represents a neural network consisting of some layers.
- Class Layer represents a layer, i.e. a given number of neurons, and a matrix of weights for the synaptic links to each neuron.
- Class Topology is a class that is meant to create neural networks consisting of layers that are interconnected in some specific way.
- Class TransferFunc is the root of a class hierarchy where each class provides an activation function (e.g. Tansig, Logsig and Radbas) and implements the proper methods for training and computation.

The following design patterns are used.

- *Factory Method* is used to organise the creation and interconnection of neurons inside layers, hence the initialisation decisions that allow to establish a given topology.
- *Decorator* is used to customise the interconnections between neurons.
- *Bridge* is used to let neurons choose one among several activation functions.

The said classes and patterns (see Fig. 1) are detailed in the following sections.

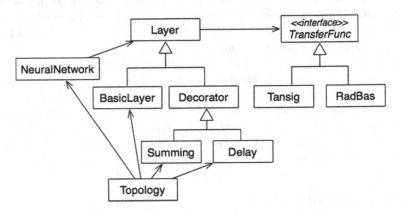

Fig. 1. The UML class diagram of the proposed toolkit

4   Details of Classes

4.1   Class Layer

The very core of the toolbox consists of class Layer and its subclasses. They are responsible to hold neurons and compute the output of such neurons. The main method is compute() and implements the algorithm that performs the computation on the neurons according to input data (stored into field inputs), and stores output data into field outputs, accessible by means of method getOutputs(). Typically, a layer calls getOutputs() on another layer, therefore an instance of Layer holds a reference to another instance of Layer as field source. Additional methods of Layer are: trainStep() performing a single iteration of computation during training, initWeights() and setWeights(w) giving values to weights. Method initWeights() is called when Layer is instantiated, in order to initialise the synaptic weights and store them into field weights, such weights would be modified and recomputed during each training epochs by method trainStep() and then stored by using method setWeights(), taking as input the new weights and updating the weights matrix. Class Layer plays the role of *Component* for design pattern Decorator, hence several responsibilities can be additionally executed, and available as implementations in proper *ConcreteDecorators* Summing and Delay (see Sect. 5.2 for details). Moreover, class Layer plays the additional role *Abstraction* for design pattern Bridge, in order to let the subclasses use different transfer functions (see Sect. 5.3 for details), and its subclasses have the additional role *RefinedAbstraction*. Therefore, Layer holds a reference to an instance of a class implementing a transfer function, i.e. interface *TransferFunc*, that will be used to compute the output of neurons. Having a separate class for computing the transfer function allows us to easily configure layers in order to use one among several available transfer functions.

4.2 Class TransferFunc

Since a neural network emulates the behaviour of its human counterpart, in the same manner an artificial neuron emulates the behaviour of a neural cell. The latter is a constantly stimulated cell that needs to reach some kind of threshold in order to activate itself. In an artificial neuron such a threshold is mathematically emulated by a so called *activation function* or *transfer function*. The two different names are used according to the point of view, i.e. whether we focus on the activity of one neuron only, or on the functionalities of the entire network of neurons. In the latter case, we call it a transfer function, since it will determine how the input data will change and interact while passing from a layer to the next. The neuron behaviour is then univocally identified by its activation function that gathers data from the linked neuron in the preceding layer and gives results to feed data into the neurons in the successive layer. A description both general and comprehensive of all activation functions is overwhelming since, a transfer function could be any function defined within a finite range and absolutely integrable, therefore any function in $L^1(\mathbb{R})$ (Gupta et al. 2004). Nevertheless, not all the functions in $L^1(\mathbb{R})$ are equally performant or reliable for a neural network. In general, in a feedforward neural network, a transfer function can be described as a function $f:\mathbb{R} \rightarrow \mathbb{R}$ so that the neuron returns an output in the form:

$$y_i = f\left(\sum_{j=1}^{N} wi_j x_j\right)$$

where index i identifies the computing neuron and index j the connected neurons from where the inputs x_j are coming. Each input is (in general) weighted before it is used to compute the output. It follows that when considering one input layer and two hidden layers, respectively of M and N neurons, then, the output will be in the form of

$$y_i = f_1 \left(\sum_{j=1}^{N} w_{ij} f_2 \left(\sum_{k=1}^{M} w_{jk} x_k \right) \right)$$

Then, it is possible to define the output of a neuron in the n-esime layer, recursively:

$$\begin{cases} y_{k_0}^{(0)} &= u_{k_0} \\ y_{k_1}^{(1)} &= f_1 \left(\sum_{k_0} w_{k_0}^{k_1} y_{k_0}^{(0)} \right) \\ y_{k_n}^{(n)} &= f_1 \left(\sum_{k_{n-1}} w_{k_{n-1}}^{k_n} y_{k_{n-1}}^{(n-1)} \right) \end{cases}$$

so that a neural network becomes a function

$$N[\mathbf{u}] = N\left[(u_{k_0})\right] = \left(y_{k_n}^{(n)}\right) = y.$$

For such a kind of topology a wide range of different transfer functions have been proven useful. Some excellent examples are the sigmoidal functions like

$$f(x) = \frac{A}{1 + e^{-k(x-u)}}$$

where A represents the maximum amplitude of the function, k is a fixed parameter and μ the value for the mean point of the sigmoid itself. Another kind of interesting activation function is represented by the radial basis function family. The most commonly used radial basis function is of gaussian type and is formalised as follows

$$\rho(x) = e^{-(\sigma x)^2}$$

on the other hand, a well enough approximation is used in the field of neural networks so that

$$f(x) = \sum_l w_l \rho\left(\|x - \mu_l\|\right) = \sum_l w_l e^{-(\sigma \|x - \mu_l\|)^2}$$

The latter function requires a different training procedure with respect to the previous one, it is indeed noticeable that also the set of parameters $\{\mu_l\}$, called centroids, must be adjusted during training.

It follows that different kinds of transfer functions require different training methods, also according to the number of fixed parameters. Moreover, certain transfer functions could be applied to different kinds of topologies which, sometime, not only differ on the number of neurons and links, but also, or solely, on the kind of computation which are performed on different layers (Haykin 2009). A typical example is given by the comparison between a feed forward network using radial basis functions and a radial basis network, i.e. while they use the same transfer function on the first hidden layer (as the name suggests), they use the second hidden layer in a completely different way (that is the reason why the neuron in the two hidden layers of a RBF network are traditionally called pattern units and summation units) (Musavi 1992).

While this description is far from comprehensive or complete, it should give an insight on how the different choices regarding the training and operation of a neural network strictly depends on the topology and the activation function itself. It is then paramount to structure the code in an appropriate manner in order to both encapsulate the transfer function and the related responsibilities, while being still able to change the behaviour of other modules according to the chosen topology and functions.

4.3   Class Topology

The first recognisable feature of a neural network is trivially the topology. In the past decades, an entire zoology of different topologies has been developed, some topology categories are standard (see Fig. 2), others are highly customised. Therefore, not all the neural networks are organised similarly, and, even when some networks present topological similarities the functionalities are sometimes very different, moreover different networks are trained and used in different manners.

The encapsulation of the algorithms specifying topology details for a neural network is achieved by means of class Topology. Such a class implements methods that instantiate and interconnect Layers in a specific way, and also neurons with each others, hence creating a topology. Each given classical neural network topology has its own method, such as e.g. getFeedForward(), named after the related topology. All the knowledge on the topology is encapsulated into such methods and all other classes unaware of the topology issues.

Class Topology implements a variant of design pattern Factory Method, therefore class Topology plays role *ConcreteCreator*, and class Layer plays role *Product*. Typically, several instances of Layer are needed at once to form a neural network, hence references to such instances are inserted into an instance of NeuralNetwork. Moreover, each instance of Layer is given a reference to another instance acting as the preceding layer, the *ConcreteCreator*'s factory methods *inject dependencies* into Layer classes. In the following we will give some examples of the factory methods implemented within class Topology (e.g. getFeedForward(), getRecurrent(), getHopfield(), etc.), which create topologies by interconnecting layers in different ways.

Feed Forward Neural Networks. The feed forward topology is depicted in Fig. 2(a) and presents the easiest concept. It is implemented by means of subsequent layers, each layer communicates the output of each constituting neuron to the neurons of the next layer (Bonanno et al. 2014b). Therefore, to obtain the said interactions among instances of layers, a factory method dubbed getFeedForward(int l, int[] nl) is provided to instantiate a number l of Layers (l is the first input parameter), each having the number of

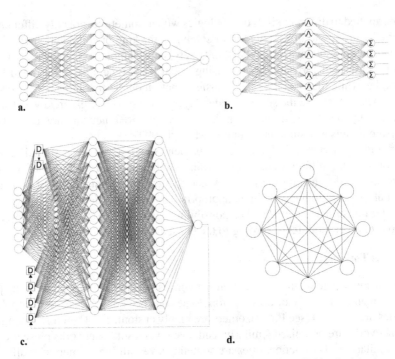

Fig. 2. Different neural network topologies: (a) feed forward, (b) radial basis, (c) recurrent, (d) Hopfield (1982). Note that networks (a), (b) and (c) are organised in layers, and belong to the same topology category, moreover, while (a), (b) and (c) share some topological commonalities their training and use is completely different.

neurons given as the i-sime position of array nl, and provide each Layer instance with a reference of the former Layer instance.

Radial Basis Neural Networks. Figure 2(b) shows a neural network using the radial basis configuration (Napoli et al. 2014c), in which each layer has its own purpose and functions in a different manner than another layer (Napoli et al. 2015). Therefore, a factory method getRadialBasis() provides the needed implementation for instantiating Layers and interconnecting them, similarly to getFeedForward(). Differently to the latter, getRadialBasis() sets the RBF transfer function for the instantiated layers, by providing the created instances of Layer with a reference to an instance of RadBas.

Recurrent Neural Network. Differently from the other categories, such a topology (Fig. 2(c)) presents feedbacks and delay lines (Williams and Zipser 1989; Bonanno et al. 2012). While a layer gets the outputs of a preceding layer in the same manner of a feed forward neural network, such a topology uses a different strategy to store delayed data and feed such data to the neurons linked to the related delay lines (Napoli et al. 2013b). For the related implementation, a layer is created by means of class Delay (appropriately storing data for a time step). Then such an instance of Delay is provided as reference to the other Layers.

The given examples are not comprehensive neither exhaustive of all the possible topology of a neural network. Such examples were intended to explain our design choices. Due to its high level of encapsulation and loose class coupling, our proposed toolbox can be easily expanded with other topologies and activation functions. Further application-dependent classes that implement custom topologies, functions and training methods can be also provided to our toolbox.

5   Details of Design Patterns

5.1   Factory Method

The main intent of design pattern Factory Method is to define an interface, *Creator*, and some classes, *ConcreteCreator*, to instantiate a class implementing a common interface *Product*. A *ConcreteCreator* encapsulates the algorithm selecting one among several implementations of *Product*, dubbed *ConcreteProduct*. As a result, client classes are unaware of the used *ConcreteProduct* class, and such classes can be freely changed with each other (Gamma et al. 1994).

We have used design pattern Factory Method, in our solution, to encapsulate the selection of the implementation of Layer that has to be instantiated, in such a way that client classes remain independent of the implementation. Moreover, each implemented *ConcreteCreator* will be responsible to provide instances of Layer with the reference to each other, and therefore *injects dependencies* into them.

A class playing as *Creator* and *ConcreteCreator* is Topology (see Fig. 1), which lets the client class obtain a NeuralNetwork. Additional topologies are implemented each as a factory method of Topology. This approach is far more flexible than connecting classes at design time to a specific implementation, e.g. giving a BasicLayer means to access type RadBas, which generates a tight coupling between such classes. Moreover, the number of dependencies for a class could expand, e.g. BasicLayer would have to handle both Tansig and RadBas. More generally, tight coupling generates undesired consequences and less reusable code.

5.2   Decorator

The main intent of design pattern Decorator is to have the possibility to add responsibilities to a class dynamically and with a more flexible mechanism than that provided by inheritance. The solution suggests the following roles for classes: *Component* defining the operations that all objects have, *ConcreteComponent* implementing the object to which functionalities are added, *Decorator* holding a reference to *Component*, *ConcreteDecorator* implementing an additional responsibility (Gamma et al. 1994). The abstraction provided by interface Layer let us keep a general representation of a layer, independent of its number of neurons and connections. The needed connections among neurons, possibly with delayed lines, are additional responsibilities that can be dynamically added to the basic behaviour of a layer. Accordingly, we have implemented the basic behaviour of a layer by class BasicLayer playing the role *ConcreteComponent* for the Decorator design pattern, then the additional responsibilities are implemented as classes Summing and Delay playing as *ConcreteDecorators*. Class Summing computes a weighted sum of the outputs, whereas class Delay stores the outputs for a time step. By means of the mechanisms provided by design pattern Decorator, the responsibilities of different classes can be accurately selected to extend the functionalities of instances of BasicLayer.

5.3   Bridge

The aim of design pattern Bridge is to decouple abstractions and implementations, in such a way that both can change independently. The solution provides role *Abstraction* defining the interface for client classes and holding a reference to *Implementor*, role *RefinedAbstraction* as a subclass of *Abstraction*, role *Implementor* defines the operations that the *Abstraction* uses, and its implementations are provided as role *ConcreteImplementor* (Gamma et al. 1994). While the other implemented patterns are concerned on the topology of the neural network in terms of layer sizing and connections (with special care for delays and feedbacks), the activation function for the neurons is selected by using the Bridge design pattern. The Bridge let us decouple the implementation of the different activation functions from the related abstractions. This behaviour is far more flexible with respect to the simple inheritance since this latter ultimately binds the implementation and the abstraction permanently in the code. The Bridge gives us means to separately modify, extend, manage and maintain the classes and methods related with the use of different activation function and, consequently, decoupling the topology of the network from its usage and the implemented functions. E.g., it is possible to have a simple multilayer topology with no feedbacks or delays: while this could be used for a feed forward neural network, the same topology could implement a radial basis neural network, although the use and training of those two network is completely different, as well as their purpose and management. It follows from the implementation of the Bridge pattern that the class Layer has to hold a reference to a *ConcreteImplementor*, therefore to an object of type TransferFunc, on the other hand it is possible in such a way to hide the implementation details to the client once again separating the concerns of the different classes (Tramontana 2013).

6   Related Works

Other object oriented solutions have been presented in projects and toolboxes for the implementation of neural networks. One of the most known is Neuroph (Ševarac 2012): a Java framework for creating, train and use neural networks with different topologies and training methods. This project, which begun in 2008, proposes an open source solution which is still evolving and expanding its potential. Such a software solution has increased its complexity during time, essentially because of the high degree of class coupling. While we agree on many of the identified abstractions, a better modularity could be achieved by using design patterns. Neuroph is mainly organised into three layers: one for the GUI and two for the neural network library and core. The library implements the supported neural networks, while the core consists of two packages containing the base classes, which provide structure and functionalities to the created networks, and the utilities for training and management. We note that in it several coding practices should have been avoided and some of them are actually *smells*, for refactoring techniques (Fowler et al. 1999; Pappalardo and Tramontana 2013). It should be stated that creating, managing and training a neural network is a complex task affected by several difficulties. The UML class diagram of Neuroph shows a cyclical dependency of classes Neuron, Layer, and NeuralNetwork. Other cyclical dependencies can be found e.g. for classes NeuralNetwork and LearningRule, and for classes Neuron and Connection. Such a practice should be avoided in a well engineered software system. Moreover, tight coupling could be avoided by recurring to some design patterns, e.g. for the dependencies among classes Layer and NeuralNetwork, as well as for class Connections. Of course, it is not straightforward to refactor such a mature software. The approach presented in this paper aims at having a highly maintainable system which can be further enhanced, thanks to its modularity (Napoli et al. 2013a). Consequently, by using design patterns, while encapsulating the different needed abstractions we also successfully manage to separate the different concerns. The resulting system has classes that depend on interfaces and not implementations. This in turn makes it possible to include new features (e.g. new kind of topologies, transfer functions, training methods, etc.). Finally, out approach aims to build a system that can be easily ported into a distributed and parallel infrastructure (Bonanno et al. 2014a; Napoli et al. 2014d), making good use of Java multithreading and distributed supports.

7 Conclusion

This paper has shown the design of a toolbox that allows instantiating a neural network and configuring it as desired. The provided components automate some important design decisions, such as the topology, while also allowing the developer to configure the network as desired, as well as create a neural network from a scratch. Our solution has put a high relevance on the modularity issues, hence the proposed components are loosely coupled and can be easily be refined, by adding more classes to the provided classes hierarchies. The devised design choices, based on design patterns Factory Method, Decorator and Bridge, will easily grip on new available classes, without additional connecting code. In our future work, the modularity in our design will support us in distributing objects implementing parts of a neural network on a parallel and distributed infrastructure.

Bibliography

Booch, G., Maksimchuk, R.A.: Object-Oriented Analysis and Design with Applications. Addison-Wesley, Reading (2007)

Bonanno, F., Capizzi, G., Napoli, C.,: Some remarks on the application of RNN and PRNN for the charge-discharge simulation of advanced Lithium-ions battery energy storage. In: International Symposium on Power Electronics, Electrical Drives, Automation and Motion (SPEEDAM), pp. 941–945 (20–22 June 2012). doi:10.1109/SPEEDAM.2012.6264500

Bonanno, F., Capizzi, G., Sciuto, G.L., Napoli, C., Pappalardo, G., Tramontana, E.: A novel cloud-distributed toolbox for optimal energy dispatch management from renewables in IGSs by using WRNN predictors and GPU parallel solutions. In: International Symposium on Power Electronics, Electrical Drives, Automation and Motion (SPEEDAM), pp. 1077–1084 (18–20 June 2014) (2014a). doi:10.1109/SPEEDAM.2014.6872127

Bonanno, F., Capizzi, G., Coco, S., Napoli, C., Laudani, A., Sciuto, G.L.: Optimal thicknesses determination in a multilayer structure to improve the SPP efficiency for photovoltaic devices by an hybrid FEM - Cascade Neural Network based approach. In: International Symposium on Power Electronics, Electrical Drives, Automation and Motion (SPEEDAM), pp. 355–362 (18–20 June 2014) (2014b). doi:10.1109/SPEEDAM.2014.6872103

Bonanno, F., Capizzi, G., Sciuto, G.L., Napoli, C., Pappalardo, G., Tramontana, E.: A cascade neural network architecture investigating surface plasmon polaritons propagation for thin metals in OpenMP. In: Rutkowski, L., Korytkowski, M., Scherer, R., Tadeusiewicz, R., Zadeh, L.A., Zurada, J.M. (eds.) ICAISC 2014, Part I. LNCS, vol. 8467, pp. 22–33. Springer, Heidelberg (2014c)

Borowik, G., Wozniak, M., Fornaia, A., Giunta, R., Napoli, C., Pappalardo, G., Tramontana, E.: A software architecture assisting workflow executions on cloud resources. Int. J. Electron. Telecommun. 61(1), 17–23 (2015). doi:10.1515/eletel-2015-0002

Fowler, M., Beck, K., Brant, J., Opdyke, W., Roberts, D.: Refactoring: Improving the Design of Existing Code. Addison-Wesley, Reading (1999)

Gabryel, M., Woźniak, M., Damaševičius, R.: An application of differential evolution to positioning queueing systems. In: Rutkowski, L., Korytkowski, M., Scherer, R., Tadeusiewicz, R., Zadeh, L.A., Zurada, J.M. (eds.) Artificial Intelligence and Soft Computing. LNCS, vol. 9120, pp. 379–390. Springer, Heidelberg (2015)

Gamma, E., Helm, R., Johnson, R., Vlissiders, J.: Design Patterns: Elements of Reusable Object-Oriented Software. Addison-Wesley, Reading (1994)

Gupta, M., Lian, J., Noriyas, H.: Static and Dynamic Neural Networks: from Fundamentals to Advanced Theory. Wiley, New York (2004)

Haykin, S.: Neural Networks: a Comprehensive Foundation. Pearson, London (2004)

Haykin, S.: Neural Networks and Learning Machines. Pearson, London (2009)

Hopfield, J.: Neural networks and physical systems with emergent collective computational abilities. Proc. Natl. Acad. Sci. 79(8), 2554–2558 (1982)

Musavi, M.T.: On the training of radial basis function classifiers. Neural Netw. 5(4), 595–603 (1992)

Napoli, C., Pappalardo, G., Tramontana, E.: Using modularity metrics to assist move method refactoring of large systems. In: IEEE International Conference on Complex, Intelligent, and Software Intensive Systems (CISIS), pp. 529–534 (July 2013) (2013a). doi:10.1109/CISIS.2013.96

Napoli, C., Pappalardo, G., Tramontana, E.: Improving files availability for bittorrent using a diffusion model. In: 23rd IEEE WETICE Conference (WETICE), pp. 191–196 (23–25 June 2014) (2014a). doi:10.1109/WETICE.2014.65

Napoli, C., Pappalardo, G., Tramontana, E., Marszalek, Z., Polap, D., Wozniak, M.: Simplified firefly algorithm for 2D image key-points search. In: IEEE Symposium on Computational Intelligence for Human-like Intelligence (CIHLI), pp. 1–8 (9–12 December 2014) (2014b). doi:10.1109/CIHLI.2014.7013395

Napoli, C., Pappalardo, G., Tramontana, E.:"An agent-driven semantic identifier using radial basis neural networks and reinforcement learning. In: XV Workshop Dagli Oggetti agli Agenti (WOA 2014), Catania, Italy (25–26 Sepember 2014) (2014c). doi:10.13140/2.1.1446.7843

Napoli, C., Pappalardo, G., Tramontana, E., Zappalà, G.: A cloud-distributed GPU architecture for pattern identification in segmented detectors big-data surveys. Comput. J. bxu147 (2014) (2014d). doi:10.1093/comjnl/bxu147

Napoli, C., Pappalardo, G., Tramontana, E., Nowicki, R.K., Starczewski, J.T., Woźniak, M.: Toward work groups classification based on probabilistic neural network approach. In: Rutkowski, L., Korytkowski, M., Scherer, R., Tadeusiewicz, R., Zadeh, L.A., Zurada, J.M. (eds.) Artificial Intelligence and Soft Computing. LNCS, vol. 9119, pp. 79–89. Springer, Heidelberg (2015)

Napoli, C., Pappalardo, G., Tramontana, E.: A hybrid neuro–wavelet predictor for QoS control and stability. In: Baldoni, M., Baroglio, C., Boella, G., Micalizio, R. (eds.) AI*IA 2013. LNCS, vol. 8249, pp. 527–538. Springer, Heidelberg (2013b)

Nowak, B.A., Nowicki, R.K., Woźniak, M., Napoli, C.: Multi-class nearest neighbour classifier for incomplete data handling. In: Rutkowski, L., Korytkowski, M., Scherer, R., Tadeusiewicz, R., Zadeh, L.A., Zurada, J.M. (eds.). LNCS, vol. 9119, pp. 469–480Springer, Heidelberg (2015)

Pappalardo, G, Tramontana, E.: Suggesting extract class refactoring opportunities by measuring strength of method interactions. In: IEEE Asia Pacific Software Engineering Conference (APSEC), pp. 105–110 (December 2013)

Ševarac, Z.: An open source software framework for neural network development. Neuroph. 11(43), 40–44 (2012)

Tramontana, E.: Automatically characterising components with concerns and reducing tangling. In: QUORS workshop at Compsac. IEEE, pp. 499–504 (2013)

Williams, R.J., Zipser, D.: A learning algorithm for continually running fully recurrent neural networks. Neural Comput. 1(2), 270–280 (1989)

Woźniak, M., Połap, D., Gabryel, M., Nowicki, R.K., Napoli, C., Tramontana, E.: Can we process 2D images using artificial bee colony? In: Rutkowski, L., Korytkowski, M., Scherer, R., Tadeusiewicz, R., Zadeh, L.A., Zurada, J.M. (eds.) Artificial Intelligence and Soft Computing. LNCS, vol. 9119, pp. 660–671. Springer, Heidelberg (2015a)

Wozniak, M., Polap, D.: Basic concept of cuckoo search algorithm for 2D images processing with some research results: an idea to apply cuckoo search algorithm in 2D images key-points search. In: International Conference on Signal Processing and Multimedia Applications SIGMAP 2014, pp. 157–164, Setubal (2014). doi:10.5220/0005015801570164

Rough Deep Belief Network - Application to Incomplete Handwritten Digits Pattern Classification

Wojciech K. Mleczko, Tomasz Kapuściński, and Robert K. Nowicki[✉]

Institute of Computational Intelligence, Czestochowa University of Technology,
Al. Armii Krajowej 36, 42-200 Czestochowa, Poland
{wojciech.mleczko,tomasz.kapuscinski,robert.nowicki}@iisi.pcz.pl
http://www.iisi.pcz.pl

Abstract. The rough deep belief networks (RDBN) are new modification of well known deep belief networks. Thanks to applied elements from Pawlak's rough set theory, RDBNs are suitable in processing of incomplete patterns. In this paper we present the results of adaptation of this class of networks for classification of handwritten digits. The samples of the pattern applied in the learning and working processes are randomly corrupted. This allows to study the robustness of classifier for various levels of incompleteness.

Keywords: Deep belief network · Rough set · Missing features

1 Introduction

The Restricted Boltzmann Machine [7,27] is one of sophisticated types of neural networks which can process probability distribution, and is applied to filtering, image recognition, and modelling [4]. Deep belief network [2,9] is a structure that contains RBMs. As other types of computational intelligence systems, DBNs can process real data, which often contain imperfections such as noise, inexactness, uncertainty and incompleteness. The easiest way to use such data is kind form of preprocessing. In the case of incompleteness there are two general ways, imputation and marginalization. They can take into consideration a class of incompleteness, for example MCAR (Missing Completely At Random), MAR (Missing At Random), MNAR (Missing Not At Random) [19]. An interesting way to process the data with a variable set of available values of input features is the rough set theory proposed by Pawlak [25,26]. It defines the approximations of the sets in form of the pair of sets, called the rough set, and consist of the lower and upper approximation. The quality of approximation depends on the usefulness of available knowledge. The theory has been extended by defining the rough fuzzy sets, fuzzy rough sets [5,6], covering rough sets [30,31] and other. It allows us to extend various types of a fuzzy systems [3,12–14,21,22], a nearest neighbor classifier [23], a decision tree [20] and other [2,24] to work with missing

G. Dregvaite and R. Damasevicius (Eds.): ICIST 2015, CCIS 538, pp. 400–411, 2015.
DOI: 10.1007/978-3-319-24770-0_35

data. The resulting systems have been called rough fuzzy systems, rough k-NN classifiers etc. In some solutions missing values are replaced by appropriate interval which can cover the whole domain of feature (MCAR) or its parts (MAR, MNAR). Answer of the systems is represented as an interval or, in the case of classification, information about assignment to one of three regions defined in rough set theory, i.e. positive, boundary and negative. It means that, using available input information, the classifier can decide that the object being classified definitely belongs to a class (positive region), definitely does not belong to a class (negative region) or that input information is insufficient to make a decision (boundary region). It also allows us to start the classification process with limited description of classified object and complement it until the answer is either positive or negative.

In the paper we introduce Rough Deep Belief Network (RDBN) which is created in similar way. It is a structure that contains rough restricted Boltzmann machines (RRBM) capable of processing information in the form of intervals as well as incomplete data. It should be noted that the vast majority of network-like architectures are suitable in various parallel implementations. It could be realized using many signal processors connected by dedicated serial bus [1] and multicore CPU architectures [28,29]. Nowadays, networks are even implemented in structures made of single molecules [17], for example distributed in mesoporous silica matrix [15,16]. RDBN like other rough hybrids uses answer "unknown" when input information is too incomplete to make a credible answer. In the same case, other classifiers give answer with low level of credibility — frequently incorrect.

The paper is organized as follows. The Sect. 2 brings the reader to architecture of DBN, followed by Sect. 3 describes RDBN. The following section describes the MNIST database of handwritten digits which was used in testing. Then, the obtained result is presented. Section 6 summarizes the work.

2   Deep Belief Network Architecture

Deep Belief Networks (DBN) are neural networks composed of multiple layers of latent stochastic variables which use Restricted Boltzmann Machines (RBMs) [27] as their basic building blocks. Deep Belief Networks were proposed by Hinton et al. along with an unsupervised greedy learning algorithm for constructing a network one layer at a time [9].

In summary, an RBM contains a set of stochastic hidden units h that are fully connected in an undirected model to a set of stochastic visible units v as shown in Fig. 1. The RBM - (l) defines the following joint distribution:

$$E^{(l)}(\mathbf{v}, \mathbf{h}) = \exp\left(-\sum_{i \in visible} b_{vi}^{(l)} v_i^{(l)} - \sum_{j \in hidden} b_{hj}^{(l)} h_j^{(l)} - \sum_{i,j} v_i^{(l)} h_j^{(l)} w_{ij}^{(l)}\right), \quad (1)$$

where v_i, h_j are binary states of visible unit i and hidden unit j, b_{vi}, b_{hj} are their biases and w_{ij} is the weight between them. The network assigns a probability to

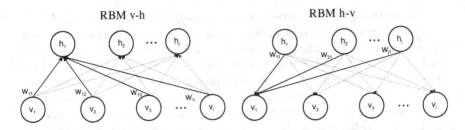

Fig. 1. Schematic representation of a Restricted Boltzmann Machine (RBM)

every possible pair of visible and hidden vectors via following energy function:

$$p^{(l)}(\mathbf{v}, \mathbf{h}) = \frac{1}{Z} e^{-E^{(l)}(\mathbf{v}, \mathbf{h})}, \tag{2}$$

where the *partition function* Z is given by summing over all possible pairs of visible and hidden vectors:

$$Z^{(l)} = \sum_{\mathbf{v}, \mathbf{h}} e^{-E^{(l)}(\mathbf{v}, \mathbf{h})}, \tag{3}$$

The probability which network assigns to a visible vector $\mathbf{v}$ is given by summing over all possible hidden vectors:

$$p^{(l)}(\mathbf{v}) = \frac{1}{Z^{(l)}} \sum_{\mathbf{h}} e^{-E^{(l)}(\mathbf{v}, \mathbf{h})}, \tag{4}$$

Given a random input configuration $\mathbf{v}$, the state of the hidden unit j is set to 1 with probability:

$$P^{(l)}\left(h_j^{(l)} = 1|\mathbf{v}^{(l)}\right) = \sigma\left(b_{hj}^{(l)} + \sum_i v_i^{(l)} w_{ij}^{(l)}\right), \tag{5}$$

where $\sigma(x)$ is the logistic sigmoid function $\frac{1}{1+\exp(-x)}$. Similarly, given a random hidden vector, the state of the visible unit i can be set to 1 with probability:

$$P^{(l)}\left(v_i^{(l)} = 1|\mathbf{h}^{(l)}\right) = \sigma\left(b_{vi}^{(l)} + \sum_i h_j^{(l)} w_{ij}\right). \tag{6}$$

The probability which network assigns to the training image can be raised by adjusting the weights and biases to lower the energy of that image and to raise the energy of other images, especially those that have low energies and therefore make a big contribution to the partition function. The derivative of the log probability of a training vector with respect to a weight is surprisingly simple.

$$\frac{\partial \log p^{(l)}(\mathbf{v})}{\partial w_{ij}^{(l)}} = \langle v_i^{(l)} h_j^{(l)} \rangle_0 - \langle v_i^{(l)} h_j^{(l)} \rangle_\infty, \tag{7}$$

where $\langle\cdot\rangle_0$ denotes the expectations for the data distribution (p_0) and $\langle\cdot\rangle_\infty$ denotes the expectations for the model distribution $(p_\infty^{(l)})$ [18]. It can be done by starting at any random state of the visible units and performing alternating Gibbs sampling for a very long time. One iteration of alternating Gibbs sampling consists of updating all hidden units in parallel using Eq. 5 followed by updating all visible units in parallel using Eq. 6 [7].

To solve this problem, Hinton proposed a much faster learning procedure - Contrastive Divergence algorithm [7,8]. This procedure can be applied in order to correct the weights and bias of the network:

$$\Delta w_{ij}^{(l)} = \eta \left(\langle v_i^{(l)} h_j^{(l)} \rangle_0 - \langle v_i^{(l)} h_j^{(l)} \rangle_\infty \right), \tag{8}$$

$$\Delta b_{vi}^{(l)} = \eta (v_{i0}^{(l)} - v_{i\infty}^{(l)}), \tag{9}$$

$$\Delta b_{hj}^{(l)} = \eta (h_{j0}^{(l)} - h_{j\infty}^{(l)}), \tag{10}$$

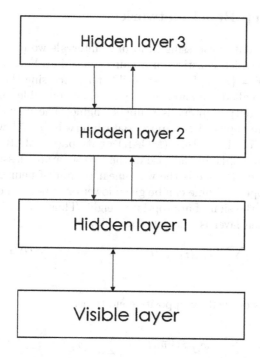

Fig. 2. DBN an example of architecture

Every next layer is stacked on top of the DBN as shown in Fig. 2. The training process is performed in an unsupervised manner allowing the system to learn complex functions by mapping the input to the output directly from data. All weights of DBNs must be pre-trained layer by layer as the RBM training.

After pre-training, the weights of DBNs are fine-tuned by the standard back-propagation algorithm and the steepest descent algorithm as the Multi-Layer Perceptron (MLP). For this purpose we create an additional layer using the output from last RBM layer which will represent a model of logistic regression in form of a probabilistic classifier. An additional layer forms a bilayer network which output units are defined as follows:

$$y_j^{(L)} = softmax_j(w_{ij}^{(L)} h_i^{(L)} + b_j^{(L)}), \tag{11}$$

where L is an additional layer, $y_j^{(L)}$ output from the network, $w_{ij}^{(L)}$ and $b_j^{(L)}$ weight and bias of extra layer, their initial value is set to 0, $h_i^{(L)}$ value is obtained from the last RBM layer with a scholar DBN. Softmax function is calculated as follows:

$$softmax_j(w_{ij}^{(L)} h_i^{(L)} + b_j^{(L)}) = \frac{e^{w_{ij}^{(L)} h_i^{(L)} + b_j^{(L)}}}{\sum_j e^{w_{ij}^{(L)} h_i^{(L)} + b_j^{(L)}}} \tag{12}$$

3   Rough Deep Belief Network

For the purpose of data processing in form of intervals we propose a version of RBM architecture which constsits of a pair of machines both using a common weight matrices $\mathbf{W} = \{w_{ij}\}$. Part responsible for processing the bottom ends of output intervals is called the lower engine, a part responsible for processing the upper ends of the output intervals – upper engine. The unavailable (missing) input values v_i are replaced by appropriate intervals $[\underline{v}_i, \overline{v}_i]$ which can cover the whole domain of the feature (MCAR) or its parts (MAR, MNAR). Thus the data is processes alike in the case of the two separate classic RBMs with a few exceptions. The first one is the way linear output of neurons is calculated. Both lower and upper machine can be given lower or upper end of intervals. The choice depends on the sign of appropriate weight. Thus, the lower linear output of neurons in hidden layer is calculated as follows:

$$\underline{s}_{hj}(t) = \sum_{\substack{i=0 \\ w_{ij}(t)>0}} w_{ij}(t) \cdot \underline{v}_i(t) + \sum_{\substack{i=0 \\ w_{ij}(t)<0}} w_{ij}(t) \cdot \overline{v}_i(t) + b_{hj}(t). \tag{13}$$

The upper value is derived by opposite conditions:

$$\overline{s}_{hj}(t) = \sum_{\substack{i=0 \\ w_{ij}(t)>0}}^{N} w_{ij}(t) \cdot \overline{v}_i(t) + \sum_{\substack{i=0 \\ w_{ij}(t)<0}}^{N} w_{ij}(t) \cdot \underline{v}_i(t) + b_{hj}(t) \tag{14}$$

Similar methodology is applied in the visible layer, i.e.

$$\underline{s}_{vi}(t) = \sum_{\substack{j=0 \\ w_{ij}(t)>0}}^{N} w_{ij}(t) \cdot \underline{h}_j(t) + \sum_{\substack{j=0 \\ w_{ij}(t)<0}}^{N} w_{ij}(t) \cdot \overline{h}_j(t) + b_{vi}(t), \tag{15}$$

and

$$\overline{s}_{vi}(t) = \sum_{\substack{i=0 \\ w_{ij}(t)>0}}^{N} w_{ij}(t) \cdot \overline{h}_j(t) + \sum_{\substack{i=0 \\ w_{ij}(t)<0}}^{N} w_{ij}(t) \cdot \underline{h}_j(t) + b_{vi}(t). \tag{16}$$

The output of j-th neuron in hidden layer of lower RBM is signed by $underline h_j(t)$, and $overline h_j(t)$ in the case of upper RBM. They are derived with the probability described by non-linear output of the neurons as follows:

$$P\left(\underline{h}_{0j}(t) = 1|\underline{y}_{hj}(t)\right) = \underline{y}_{hj}(t), \tag{17}$$

$$P\left(\overline{h}_{0j}(t) = 1|\overline{y}_{hj}(t)\right) = \overline{y}_{hj}(t), \tag{18}$$

but

$$\underline{h}_{0j}(t) \leq \overline{h}_{0j}(t). \tag{19}$$

The output of the neurons in visible layers is derived in the same way.

The common weights w_{ij}, biases in hidden layers $b_{hj}(t)$ and visible layers $b_{vi}(t)$ are corrected using correction values Δw_{ij}, $\Delta b_{hj}(t)$ and $\Delta b_{vi}(t)$ which come from both upper and lower RBMs.

The output of the classifier for the additional layer are defined as follows

$$\underline{y}_j^{(L)} = softmax_j(\underline{s}_i^{(L)}(t)), \tag{20}$$

and

$$\overline{y}_j^{(L)} = softmax_j(\overline{s}_i^{(L)}(t)), \tag{21}$$

where L is an additional layer, $\underline{y}_j^{(L)}$ and $\overline{y}_j^{(L)}$ are output from the network, $\underline{s}_i^{(L)}(t)$ and $\overline{s}_i^{(L)}(t)$ are values obtained from the last RBM with a scholar DBN. Softmax function is calculated using Eq. 12.

4   The MNIST Database of Handwritten Digits

In our work we used MNIST database which contains samples of handwritten digits. Samples are commonly used while testing machine learning, pattern recognition techniques, and their implementations. Database has been created from NIST's databases and is divided into 60,000 training samples and 10,000 testing samples. Each sample is a 28 by 28 gray-scale image representing a single handwritten digit. All samples have been scaled down to 20 by 20 bounding box while preserving their aspect ratio and positioned so the center of mass of the pixels is at the center of 28 by 28 image.

Data sets are stored in four files. Two files contain images for the data sets. Two remaining files contain labels for corresponding images. Images and labels are stored in custom, easy to read binary format. All images from given data set are kept as a sequence of bytes organized row-wise. Each byte defines a color for single pixel. Value 0 means white color (paper) and value 255 means black color (ink). Some samples are shown in Fig. 3.

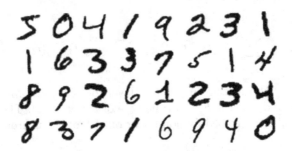

Fig. 3. Example samples taken from MNIST Database

Files containing labels have very similar format but instead of image data they only contain a single byte value for each image. Values are in range from 0 to 9 and describe what kind of digit corresponding image represents. Labels are specified in the same order as images data set.

5   Implementation and Experimental Results

For the purpose of our study, solution has been implemented in Matlab which allowed us to compare results with implementation presented by Karpathy [10,11]. In all our tests we used 6000 samples of hand-written digits from the data set described in Sect. 4.

5000 samples used for learning the system, and the remaining 1000 samples used for testing the system. In experiments, it has not applied any rotation of the sample. Missing data were obtained completely randomly by assigning pseudo-random data from the interval [0,1]. DBN and RDBN networks had 784-500-500-100-10 architecture. Last layers from tested networks used softmax activation function and all remaining layers used sigmoid function.

In RDBN, the result of digit recognition is based on comparison of results from upper and lower systems. Those systems are created at the beginning of algorithm. For complete data, results from those systems are identical and similar to results from DBN. Small differences originate from the stochastic nature of the algorithm. In case that we provide incomplete data to systems, results are calculated in accordance to model described in Eqs. 13–21. As a result, we obtain two systems that adequately recognize digits from testing data set.

Tested image is given classification when lower and upper systems provide the same answer. If the answers are different, RDBN informs us that it does not recognize the digit. This way system refrains from making possibly incorrect classification and reduces total number of mistakes. Resulting information is thereby more reliable and more accurate. Details describing how digit recognition is performed is shown on Algorithm 1.

System is able to correctly classify most images when little information is missing. When the amount of missing information exceeds 25 % system starts being unable to correctly classify majority of samples and the number

---

Algorithm 1. Recognition of digits

1: **procedure** DBNPREDICTROUGH
2:     $numSamples \leftarrow$ number of $sample$
3:     $i \leftarrow sample$
4:     $W \leftarrow$ the weight of the learned model
5:     $b \leftarrow$ the bias of the learned model
6:     $dataD \leftarrow$ sample down systemu
7:     $dataT \leftarrow$ sample top systemu
8:     **while** $(i < numSample)$ **do**
9:         $Response\_down\_system(i) =: softmax(dataD(i) * W + b)$;
10:       $Response\_top\_system(i) =: softmax(dataT(i) * W + b)$;
11:      **if** $(Response\_down\_system(i) == Response\_top\_system(i))$ **then**
12:          $Response\_system(i) =: Response\_down\_system(i)$
13:      **else**
14:          $Response\_system(i) = sample\_Unknown$
15:      **end if**
16:     **end while**
17:     **return** $Response\_system$
18: **end procedure**

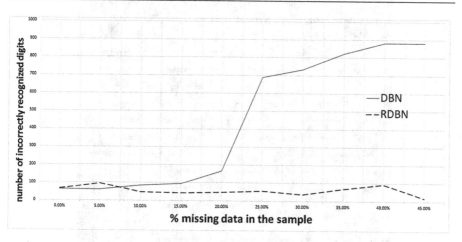

Fig. 4. Comparison of incorrectly recognized digits

of "unknown" answers increases. Unknown answers represent different type of classification and are therefore not counted in diagrams representing correct and incorrect answers. Thanks to extending the range of possible answers by response "unknown", total number of mistakes for RDBN system has been significantly reduced which is shown in Fig. 4. Results show that RDBN system provides noticeably fewer incorrect answers than DBN. Comparison of correct classification results between RDBN and DBN is shown in Fig. 5. RDBN gives a similar number of correctly classified digits as DBN which proves comparable level of efficiency.

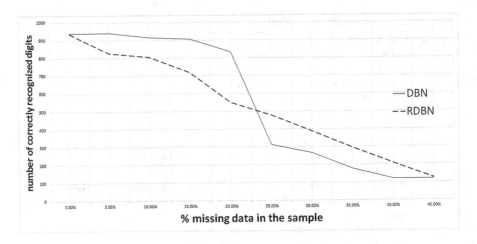

Fig. 5. Comparison of correctly recognized digits

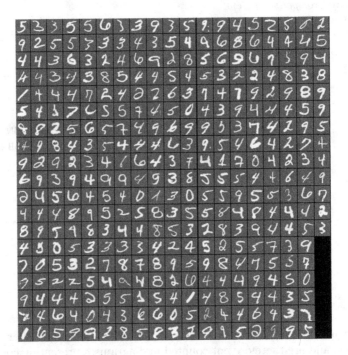

Fig. 6. Samples which were incorrectly classified by RDBN with 5 % of the missing data

Some of the samples used for testing are particularly difficult to classify due to irregularities of handwriting. Removing randomly information can turn a digit into different one or make it unrecognizable. Figure 6 shows tested samples with randomly removed 5 % of information which RDBN could not correctly

Fig. 7. Samples which were considered unknown by RDBN at 5 % of the missing data

recognize and gave incorrect answer. Figure 7 shows samples which system could not classify and instead gave answer "unknown".

6 Conclusions and Future Work

In the paper we examined rough deep belief network as a system for recognition of handwritten digits in samples with missing values. The investigation was processed for various level of missing input information to evaluate the robustness of the classifier. The obtained results confirm again that the rough set theory is a useful to extend traditional computational intelligence systems. The digits were recognized with quite high level of missing pixels. The indisputable advantage of RDBN and other system extended using rough set theory is the possibility to apply the incomplete information also in the developing (e.g. learning) phase. The future step in the investigation is to use RDBN with data containing other forms of imperfection, for example patterns with erroneous values and noise.

References

1. Bilski, J.: Momentum modification of the RLS algorithms. In: Rutkowski, L., Siekmann, J.H., Tadeusiewicz, R., Zadeh, L.A. (eds.) ICAISC 2004. LNCS (LNAI), vol. 3070, pp. 151–157. Springer, Heidelberg (2004)
2. Chu, J.L., Krzyzak, A.: The recognition of partially occluded objects with support vector machines and convolutional neural networks and deep belief networks. J. Artif. Intell. Soft Comput. Res. 4(1), 5–19 (2014)

3. Cpaka, K., Nowicki, R., Rutkowski, L.: Rough-neuro-fuzzy systems for classification. In: The First IEEE Symposium on Foundations of Computational Intelligence (FOCI 2007) (2007)
4. Dourlens, S., Ramdane-Cherif, A.: Modeling & understanding environment using semantic agents. J. Artif. Intell. Soft Comput. Res. 1(4), 301–314 (2011)
5. Dubois, D., Prade, H.: Rough fuzzy sets and fuzzy rough sets. Int. J. Gen. Syst. 17(2–3), 191–209 (1990)
6. Dubois, D., Prade, H.: Putting rough sets and fuzzy sets together. In: Słowiński, R. (ed.) Intelligent Decision Support: Handbook of Applications and Advances of the Rough Sets Theory, pp. 203–232. Kluwer, Dordrecht (1992)
7. Hinton, G.: Training products of experts by minimizing contrastive divergence. Neural Comput. 14(8), 1771–1800 (2002)
8. Hinton, G.: A practical guide to training restricted Boltzmann machines. Momentum 9(1), 926 (2010)
9. Hinton, G., Osindero, S., Teh, Y.W.: A fast learning algorithm for deep belief nets. Neural Comput. 18(7), 1527–1554 (2006)
10. Karpathy, A.: Code for training restricted Boltzmann machines (RBM) and deep belief networks in MATLAB. https://code.google.com/p/matrbm/
11. Karpathy, A.: CPSC 540 project: Restricted Boltzmann machines
12. Korytkowski, M., Nowicki, R., Rutkowski, L., Scherer, R.: AdaBoost ensemble of DCOG rough–neuro–fuzzy systems. In: Jędrzejowicz, P., Nguyen, N.T., Hoang, K. (eds.) ICCCI 2011, Part I. LNCS, vol. 6922, pp. 62–71. Springer, Heidelberg (2011)
13. Korytkowski, M., Nowicki, R., Scherer, R.: Neuro-fuzzy rough classifier ensemble. In: Alippi, C., Polycarpou, M., Panayiotou, C., Ellinas, G. (eds.) ICANN 2009, Part I. LNCS, vol. 5768, pp. 817–823. Springer, Heidelberg (2009)
14. Korytkowski, M., Nowicki, R., Scherer, R., Rutkowski, L.: Ensemble of rough-neuro-fuzzy systems for classification with missing features. Proc. World Congr. Comput. Intell. 2008, 1745–1750 (2008)
15. Laskowski, L., Laskowska, M.: Functionalization of sba-15 mesoporous silica by cu-phosphonate units: probing of synthesis route. J. Solid State Chem. 220, 221–226 (2014)
16. Laskowski, L., Laskowska, M., Balanda, M., Fitta, M., Kwiatkowska, J., Dzilinski, K., Karczmarska, A.: Mesoporous silica sba-15 functionalized by nickel-phosphonic units: raman and magnetic analysis. Microporous Mesoporous Mater. 200, 253–259 (2014)
17. Laskowski, L., Laskowska, M., Jelonkiewicz, J., Boullanger, A.: Spin-glass implementation of a hopfield neural structure. In: Rutkowski, L., Korytkowski, M., Scherer, R., Tadeusiewicz, R., Zadeh, L.A., Zurada, J.M. (eds.) ICAISC 2014, Part I. LNCS, vol. 8467, pp. 89–96. Springer, Heidelberg (2014)
18. Le Roux, N., Bengio, Y.: Representational power of restricted boltzmann machines and deep belief networks. Neural Comput. 20(6), 1631–1649 (2008)
19. Little, R., Rubin, D.: Statistical Analysis with Missing Data. Wiley, New York (1987)
20. Nowak, B.A., Nowicki, R.K., Mleczko, W.K.: A new method of improving classification accuracy of decision tree in case of incomplete samples. In: Rutkowski, L., Korytkowski, M., Scherer, R., Tadeusiewicz, R., Zadeh, L.A., Zurada, J.M. (eds.) ICAISC 2013, Part I. LNCS, vol. 7894, pp. 448–458. Springer, Heidelberg (2013)
21. Nowicki, R.: Rough-neuro-fuzzy structures for classification with missing data. IEEE Trans. Syst. Man Cybern.-Part B: Cybern 39(6), 1334–1347 (2009)

22. Nowicki, R.: On combining neuro-fuzzy architectures with the rough set theory to solve classification problems with incomplete data. IEEE Trans. Knowl. Data Eng. **20**(9), 1239–1253 (2008)
23. Nowicki, R.K., Nowak, B.A., Woźniak, M.: Rough k nearest neighbours for classification in the case of missing input data. In: Proceedings of the 9th International Conference on Knowledge, Information and Creativity Support Systems, Limassol, Cyprus, pp. 196–207, November 2014
24. Pawlak, M.: Kernel classification rules from missing data. IEEE Trans. Inf. Theory **39**, 979–988 (1993)
25. Pawlak, Z.: Rough sets. Int. J. Comput. Inform. Sci. **11**(5), 341–356 (1982)
26. Pawlak, Z.: Rough Sets: Theoretical Aspects of Reasoning About Data. Kluwer, Dordrecht (1991)
27. Smolensky, P.: Information processing in dynamical systems: foundations of harmony theory. In: Rumelhart, D.E., McLelland, J.L. (eds.) Parallel Distributed Processing: Explorations in the Microstructure of Cognition: Vol. 1 Fundations, pp. 194–281. MIT Press, Cambridge (1986)
28. Staff, C.I., Reinders, J.: Parallel Programming and Optimization with Intel® Xeon PhiTM Coprocessors: Handbook on the Development and Optimization of Parallel Aplications for Intel® Xeon Coprocessors and Intel® Xeon PhiTM Coprocessors. Colfax International, Sunnyvale (2013)
29. Szustak, L., Rojek, K., Gepner, P.: Using Intel Xeon Phi coprocessor to accelerate computations in MPDATA algorithm. In: Wyrzykowski, R., Dongarra, J., Karczewski, K., Waśniewski, J. (eds.) PPAM 2013, Part I. LNCS, vol. 8384, pp. 582–592. Springer, Heidelberg (2014)
30. Zhu, W., Wang, F.Y.: Reduction and axiomization of covering generalized rough sets. Inform. Sci. **152**, 217–230 (2003)
31. Zhu, W., Wang, F.Y.: On three types of covering-based rough sets. IEEE Trans. Knowl. Data Eng. **19**(8), 1131–1144 (2007)

Information Technology Applications

Problems of Authorship Identification of the National Language Electronic Discourse

Algimantas Venčkauskas[1], Robertas Damaševičius[2(✉)], Romas Marcinkevičius[2], and Arnas Karpavičius[1]

[1] Computer Science Department, Kaunas University of Technology,
Studentų 50, Kaunas, Lithuania
[2] Software Engineering Department, Kaunas University of Technology,
Studentų 50, Kaunas, Lithuania
robertas.damasevicius@ktu.lt

Abstract. The paper presents a comprehensive overview and analysis of the authorship identification methods in the national language electronic discourse. First, an overview and analysis of methods for English language is presented. Next, adaptations of general methods and well as language specific methods for national languages are considered. Challenges of authorship identification in electronic discourse is discussed. The requirements for developing authorship identification systems for forensics applications are discussed. Finally, the recommendations for developers of authorship identification methods and tools are presented.

Keywords: Authorship identification · Text analysis · Text mining · National languages · Forensic linguistics · Expert system

1 Introduction

The Internet provides a convenient platform for cyber criminals to anonymously conduct their illegitimate activities, such as phishing and spamming. As a result, in recent years, authorship analysis of anonymous texts in Internets (such as emails, forum comments, tweets, SMSs) has received some attention in the cyber forensic and data mining communities. Forensic linguistics provides consultation to lawyers through the analysis of language-based evidence (such as anonymous or questioned texts used for crimes) during the pre-trial investigation. The forensic analysis of online textual documents for addressing the anonymity problem is called authorship analysis. Authorship analysis is the study of linguistic and computational characteristics of the written documents written by known or unknown authors. It involves analysing the writing styles or stylometric features from the document content.

The aim of authorship analysis deals is the correct classification of texts into classes based on the stylistic choices of their authors. Beyond the author identification and author verification tasks where the style of individual authors is examined, author

© Springer International Publishing Switzerland 2015
G. Dregvaite and R. Damasevicius (Eds.): ICIST 2015, CCIS 538, pp. 415–432, 2015.
DOI: 10.1007/978-3-319-24770-0_36

profiling can also distinguish between classes of authors such as gender, age, native language, or personality type. Authorship verification checks whether a target document was written or not by a specific individual.

Writing style is an unconscious habit of a person, which varies from one author to another in the way uses words, grammar and other elements of a language to communicate. The patterns of vocabulary and dictionary usage (such as lexical richness) composition and writing, such as particular syntactic and structural layout traits, patterns of vocabulary usage, unusual language usage, stylistic and sub-stylistic features could be a reliable indicator of the authorship. The identification and learning of these stylistic characteristics with a sufficiently high accuracy are the main challenges in authorship identification.

2   Challenges of Authorship Identification in Electronic Discourse

2.1   Linguistic Properties of Electronic Communications

Short internet texts have several characteristics which make authorship categorization challenging compared with longer, formal text documents such as literary works as follows. (1) Internet texts are generally short in length indicating that certain language based metrics that depend upon the number of words in the text may not be appropriate. (2) Internet texts may have a larger number of grammatical errors (3) A specific language dialect may be used (such as SMS language or *textese* [1]) which may prohibit we use of formal dictionary and lexical analysis techniques. (4) The author's composition style can vary depending upon the intended recipient. (5) Similar vocabulary subsets (e.g., technology-based words) may be used within author communities.

There are even more issues when standard approaches are used with SMS messages as the text source in digital forensics. First, most standard approaches assume a large text to work with in order to extract features and perform classification. However, in cellular phone forensics, data for a message and the number of messages for a user may be very limited. Concurrently the probable author set may be large which makes classification difficult. Secondly, SMS messages do not conform to a fixed syntactical structure (as most languages do) and vary from user to user. This renders syntactical features ineffective and reduces the relevant feature set for classification. Finally, in forensic analysis of SMS there is a need for high processing speed. Forensic investigators are bound by time constraints when working on cases and they cannot allocate too much time for finding a suspect author.

Segerstad [2] enumerates the following linguistic properties of short text messages: omitting punctuation, unconventional punctuation, omitting blank space, spoken-like spelling, consonant writing, conventional abbreviations, unconventional abbreviations, either all capitals or all lower-case, exchange long words for shorter, emoticons, asterisks, symbol replacing word, punctuation.

Thurlow [3] lists the following: (1) shortenings (i.e. missing end letters), contractions (i.e. missing middle letters), and G-clippings and other clippings (i.e. dropping final letter), (2) acronyms and initialisms, (3) letter/number homophones, (4) "misspellings" and typos, (5) non-conventional spellings, (6) accent stylizations.

Maclead and Grant [4] present a list of features specific to SMS language, which includes misspellings (any word not found in an English dictionary), accent stylization (using phonetic spelling to convey a specific accent), prosodic emphasizers (conveying specific pronunciation through spelling), whole word letter homophone substitution (replacing entire words with a single letter), whole word number homophone substitution (replacing entire words with a number), replacing syllables within words with a number shortenings (common words shortened to a few initial letters), emoticons (series of characters used to represent faces), etc.

2.2 Recognition of Parts of Language

Part-of-speech (POS) tagging assigns a morphosyntactic class to every word in a text, based on that word characteristics and the context, where it appears. POS tagging can be also named as morphological, word class or lexical tagging as well [5]. Part-of-speech tagging methods can be classified differently; however the prevailing classification divides the methods into two categories [6]:

1. Statistical methods
2. Rule-based methods

In accordance with actual tagging process, POS tagging can be classified into these categories [6]:

1. Bold approach – all information, which the tagger uses, is put together and the best matching solution is chosen.
2. Cautious approach – firstly all words are tagged with all of their possible POS tags, and then unsuitable tags are removed by contextual constraints.
3. Whimsical approach – at first, one tag to each word is assigned, and then tags are changed by transformation rules based on contextual conditions.

POS tagging can be also classified into the following categories by the way on how the linguistic information is acquired [6]:

1. Machine learning – necessary information is acquired automatically. The majority of POS tagging methods use machine learning (e.g. memory-based tagging, probabilistic tagging, transformation-based tagging, neural network tagging). Learning can be divided as a supervised learning (using tagged data for learning) and unsupervised learning (using raw data for learning), however better results are usually achieved using supervised machine learning.
2. Hand-crafting – a hand-crafted constraints are used for POS tagging system.

A general architecture of POS tagging consists of the following stages [5]:

1. Tokenization – a text is split into required tokens (e.g. Words, punctuation marks, utterances)
2. Ambiguity look-up – lexicon and guesser are used for tokens, which are not in a lexicon (a lexicon can be a dictionary of word forms and their corresponding parts of speech, or finite-state models). A guesser analyses the remaining tokens, they use

information about a lexicon, e.g. what kind of data the lexicon contains or not – which can be used to select the particular types of actions for the guesser. Lexicon and guesser, used along with compiler or interpreter, form a morphological/lexical analyser, which assigns all suitable part-of-speech categories to each token. Also compound tags and lemmatas may be used as tagging categories.

3. Ambiguity resolution/disambiguation – uses the information about the words themselves (e.g. a particular word form is more often used as a one part-of-speech, than another (if that word form belongs to multiple parts-of-speech)). This stage also uses contextual information or information about the sequences of tokens and their tags (e.g. to give a priority for analysing one part-of-speech over an another, if a preceding token-tag is more often used with a token, that belongs to that part-of-speech).

2.3 Cross-Language Authorship Identification

Cross-language authorship attribution is an extension for general authorship attribution with the aim of solving multilingual problems in this domain [7]. The purpose of this task is to identify the author of a document written in one language, while given data, attributed to authors, in another language. Cross-language authorship attribution is an important task, because authors may write in different languages, thus making the general authorship attribution not effective in this situation. It is a novel task and has not been actively addressed so far. Apart the mentioned research, few studies [8–10], focusing on cross-language plagiarism detection, were done as well.

For cross-language authorship attribution, it is necessary to present features, which would be both language independent and distinguishing the writing style of an author. In the research [7], language-independent stylometric features, that remain even after machine translation, were used, which are classified into these categories:

– Sentiment features (positive /negative word frequencies),
– Emotional features (frequencies of general emotions – joy, anger, fear, sadness, disgust, surprise),
– POS (Parts Of Speech) tags (nouns, verbs, adjectives, adverbs frequencies),
– Perceptual features (frequencies of audial, visual and kinesthetic perception markers), and
– Average sentence length.

According to [7], people express sentiments and emotions independently on their native language, moreover, a research, done in [11], approved, that people express sentiments differently. Despite the fact that frequencies of POS tags are language dependent, they still retain stability after translation. Also the research [12] shows, that majority of people can be classified as audial, visual and kinesthetic learners. The learning style reveals in the writings of an author, thus providing valuable information for cross-language authorship attribution task.

2.4 Curse of Dimensionality

There are problems, which are very difficult to compute because of the number of features, which results in solutions often exceeding available computing resources. This phenomenon is called curse of dimensionality, and its original definition was published in [13]. In information retrieval subject it was first mentioned in [14]. In highly dimensional vector space, data is very sparse and in order to calculate any parameter, a lot of samples are needed to achieve accurate enough results [15]. This problem also applies to text classification domain [16]. To solve it, multiple dimensionality reduction techniques were developed, with many of them specifically for text documents.

2.5 Attacks Against Author Identification

Authorship deception is a specific type of authorship attribution task particularly relevant for cybercrime forensic investigations. Detecting authorship deception can be thought of as a specific type of authorship attribution task [17].

Brennan et al. [18] analyses three specific approaches and their resilience against two types of adversarial attacks. The first is as an obfuscation attack, when an author attempts to write a document in such a way that their personal writing style will not be recognized. The second is an imitation attack, is when an author attempts to write a document in the style such that the writing style will be recognized as that of another specific author. In case of obfuscation, a subject attempts to hide his/her identity. In imitation, a subject attempts to frame another subject by imitating his/her writing style, and in case of translation, original phrases are obfuscated with machine translation services. These techniques can significantly reduce the effectiveness of traditional author identification methods.

3 Authorship Identification Methods in English Language

3.1 Feature Selection

The following features are used for authorship identification: character features, lexical features, syntactic features, semantic features and application-specific features. None of them are accepted to be significantly leading as comparing to each other.

Character features consider text as a sequence of characters and various measures are defined such as characters frequencies, digit frequencies, uppercase and lowercase character frequencies, punctuation marks frequencies, etc. [19].

Lexical features are characterized by dividing the text into a sequence of tokens (words), which are grouped into sentences, and features are defined as the length of words, word/character frequencies, word/character n-grams, the length of sentences and vocabulary richness [20]. Lexical features are language independent and can be used for different languages [21]. Word lengths are usually represented by a number of characters [3] and sentence lengths respectively by a number of words and/or characters. The vocabulary richness features estimate the vocabulary diversity of a text. Another variation is the number of words, appearing only once in the text (hapaxlegomena).

However word-based features like vocabulary richness is not very effective for short texts because of their length comparing to literary works and such features are usually dependent on context and can be deliberately manipulated by an author [22]. N-grams are a contiguous sequence of words, characters or bytes of a text. Byte-level n-grams represent text as sequences of bytes and include all printing and non-printing characters [23]. Word n-grams (or collocations) provide contextual information [24]. Character n-grams provide stylistic, lexical and some contextual information as well as reveal author's habits of capitalization and punctuation usage in a text. Character n-grams are tolerant to spelling variations and noise [25], because an error, made in a text, usually affects only a small number of character n-grams.

Syntactic features characterize the text by the presence and frequency of certain syntactic structures such as noun, verb and prepositional phrase frequencies, grammatical errors and informal styling (e.g., writing sentences in capital letters) [26]. Syntactic features describe how author organizes sentences along with a writing style of them. Syntactic features can be classified into frequency of function words, frequency of punctuations, frequencies of abbreviations, POS tags (part-of-speech statistics), chunking, and syntactical errors.

Despite the fact that some languages are stylistically similar, they often reveal different characteristics like word separation properties or function words [21]. Frequencies of specific punctuations can give information about sentence structure, especially syntactically classified punctuation (where punctuations are estimated by the type of boundary or edge, that they mark [29]), which is more effective comparing to traditional [30, 31] punctuation frequency measure.

Structural features provide information that defines how author organizes a layout of writing. Structural features are paragraph lengths, indentation statistics, quoted content statistics, signature features, separators between paragraphs usage, greeting / farewell statements usage. Structural features represent author's consistent writing patterns [22] and are very important for online messages identification task [19].

Content-specific features define author's interest in specific areas. These features are usually the frequencies of content specific keywords, phrases or characters. For example one author can write texts on relatively small number of topics and different authors can write texts on different topics. Martindale and McKenzie [32] have proved that these features are very important and can even outperform lexical features and increase the effectiveness of authorship identification task. The selection of such features depends on particular application areas.

Some feature types may belong to multiple categories, since they provide information, which can be used for different purposes of authorship analysis tasks (e.g. information of punctuation frequencies is useful for determination of the nuances of an author's punctuation usage (lexical category), as well as the structure of sentences (syntactical category)) [22].

3.2 Conversion of Text into Numerical Features

Conversion of text messages to numerical sequences is not a well-researched topic. Traditionally, documents are represented as feature vectors, which do not preserve the sequential information contained in text message. For example, common features such as the number of words in a message satisfying some linguistic property (e.g., ending in 'ing') will not change if an original sequence of words in a text is changed by a permutation. Therefore, important stylistic and sub-stylistic information is lost. Other documents features such as n-gram frequencies preserve only some local sequential information in the direct neighbourhood of n-gram location, but do not allow reconstruction of the original text from its n-gram frequencies.

Text fingerprinting using similarity preserving hash functions have been used for plagiarism detection. It involves generation of a unique numerical representation of a document or a text segment. Then, these representations are used in the comparisons against a corpus of documents to find a matching copy [33].

Yang and Lee [34] investigate if the mapping between text and time series data is feasible such that relevant data mining problems in text can find their counterparts in time series (and vice versa). The presented framework T3 utilizes different combinations of granularity (e.g., character or word level) and n-grams (e.g., unigram or bigram). To assign appropriate numeric values to each character, T3 adopts different space-filling curves (e.g., linear, Hilbert, Z orders) based on the keyboard layout.

3.3   Feature Reduction

There are 2 categories of dimensionality reduction methods [35]. Feature selection and feature extraction. In feature selection, a subset of original features is selected and remaining features are no more used in a computation process. In feature extraction, a reduction is performed in a new vector space (with special characteristics), that was transformed from the original one.

Principal Component Analysis (PCA) – the most popular method for computation of lower-dimensional multivariate data representations. This method iteratively computes the direction of highest variation that is followed by a projection onto vertical hyperplane, what gives few perpendicular directions, which account for the most of the variation in a data, resulting in reduced dimensional space [36].

3.4   Classification Based Authorship Attribution

Automated approaches of authorship attribution can be grouped as classification-based (machine learning) and similarity-based [26]. In classification based approach, a classifier, which is constructed by using texts of each known candidate author (a training set of distinct documents), is used to classify anonymous writings [4]. The most popular classification methods are as follows.

Support Vector Machines (SVM) – one of the most popular methods used in authorship attribution. In this classifier a non-linear mapping is used to transform training data to higher dimension. There it looks for the linear optimal separating hyperplane that separates two classes and is the reference for decisions.

Naïve Bayes classifier is a simple probabilistic classifier, which is based on Bayes theorem with strong assumptions of independence. Despite the fact that this method works on oversimplified assumptions, it usually yields good results. Naïve Bayes classifier works with a small amount of training data and is efficient in using the computing resources. In text classification domain, this classifier uses tokens (e.g. words) and the maximum a posteriori (MAP) decision rule to make classifications.

C4.5 is a decision tree based algorithm. It builds decision trees using training data. For each node in a tree, it selects one data attribute which most efficiently splits its set of the samples to subsets, complemented in one class or the other. The decisions are made upon the attributes with the highest normalized information gain.

3.5   Similarity Based Methods

Similarity based methods use various metrics for measuring the distance between two documents, and attributes a given document to an author, whose known texts collection (treated as a single document) is the most similar to it. These methods are better option when dealing with a large amount of candidate authors [37]. The most reasonable attribution is achieved when representing a document in a multidimensional space and attributing given document to an author using appropriate distance measure [38]. Similarity based methods also allow to verify that an author has written a given document, if the similarity between the known texts of an author and a given document exceeds specified threshold. The most prevalent methods are:

- Cosine similarity measure – one of the most popular measures for estimating the similarity between text documents. The correlation between term vectors of the documents represents the similarity. In cosine similarity, it is measured as a cosine of the angles between vectors [39].
- Euclidean distance is a standard geometrical metric. It measures the ordinary distance between two points. It is also widely used in text clustering [39].
- Jaccard coefficient compares the sum weight of terms that are present in both documents to the sum weight of terms, which are distinct in these documents and are not shared.
- Pearson correlation coefficient measures the extent to which feature vectors are related.

3.6   Compression Based Methods

The compression based methods are based on the theory of Kolmogorov Complexity that is estimated using data compression tools. The theory claims that similar data is compressed better than the dissimilar one.

In [67], text category models are constructed using the Prediction by Partial Matching (PPM) text compression using character-based contexts. Then the unknown text is categorized based on ranking by document cross entropy (average bits per coded symbol) with respect to a category model, and the document cross entropy difference between category and complement of category models.

In [68], the text of unknown authorship is appended to the texts of known authors and the expert looks for the text for which the difference between the lengths of the compressed original and appended texts is the smallest.

However, the compression-based methods require having a large collection of text for each author to achieve meaningful result.

3.7 Visualization-Based Authorship Attribution

A limited number of work has been done on visualisation based authorship attribution. In [40], a Principal Component Analysis (PCS) with cosine similarity measure were used for visualising writing patterns. In [41], a latent semantic indexing (LSI) was used to visualise authorship based on eigenvectors in multidimensional space. In [69], an authorship visualization method called Writeprints is proposed. The method is based on PCA and uses a feature-based sliding window algorithm. The visualization creates graphical patterns that can be compared and identified visually. However, due to the minimum length needs of the sliding window algorithm the method is not usable with shorter individual messages (i.e., messages less than 30–40 words).

3.8 Function Words

Function words, such as adverbs, prepositions, conjunctions, or interjections, are words that have little or no semantic content of their own, however, they determine how sentences are formed. Function words are good indicators of the author's style [27]. Function words usually indicate a grammatical relationship or a generic property. Due to the high frequency of the function words and their significant roles in the grammar, the author usually has no conscious control over their usage in a particular text. Since the introduction of function words as stylometric fingerprints many methods have been introduced to analyse the frequency of these words in texts written by different authors. Attention has also been given to analysing features other than appearances of high-frequency words. Examples of these are the use of vocabulary richness, word stability – the extent to which a word can be replaced by an equivalent –, or syntactical markers like POS taggers.

Typical collection of English function words, used for authorship analysis tasks, is usually consisted of few hundred words. Because of frequent use in a language and high grammatization, function words are less likely to be deliberately controlled by an author, while their use significantly differs between authors thus making that a good criterion for authorship analysis tasks [28].

The most notable method of using the most frequent words has been proposed by Burrows [42] under the name 'Delta'. Delta works as follows. First, the method calculates the z distributions of a set of function words (originally, the 150 most frequent words we used). Then, for each text, the deviation of each word frequency from the norm is calculated in terms of z-score, roughly indicating whether it is used more (positive z-score) or less (negative z-score) times than the average. Finally, the Delta measure is the mean of the absolute differences between the z-scores for the entire function word set in a set of training texts written by the same author and the corresponding z-scores of an unknown text, indicating the difference between the training texts and the unknown text. The smaller Delta measures the greater stylistic similarity between the unknown text and the candidate author.

Also Mosteller and Wallace [43] proved that the frequency of function words (such as "and", "any", "ever", "or", "until" and "with") can be employed to quantify the style of authors.

3.9 Misspellings

Misspellings (or syntactic errors) are common in electronic discourse. Such errors may reflect the background, nationality, gender and profile of the author. Examples of misspellings are excess repeated letter, missing repeated letter, letter inversion, excess letter, missing letter, modified letter, and word collision. When analysed, misspellings are usually corrected using a string edit distance algorithm (such as Levenshtein's) while the frequencies of error categories (such as letter inversion) as well as the total number of corrections are used as features [65].

3.10 Modelling Texts as Networks

Antiqueira *et al.* [44] demonstrate that texts can be modelled as networks of words and also introduced some network measures to be used in authorship characterization. The evaluation shows that it is possible to cluster some using pairwise combinations of three measures (clustering coefficient, outdegree, and degree correlation).

Segarra *et al.* [45] present an authorship attribution method based on modelling texts as normalized word adjacency networks. These networks are interpreted as Markov chains and can be compared using entropy measures. The authors focus on function words but instead of using their frequency distribution as an author signature they propose the use of the adjacency of function words. In order to classify the authorship of a text we compute an asymmetric network of function word adjacencies capturing how likely it is to find a particular function word within the next few words conditional on the occurrence of another given word. The resulting matrices can be interpreted as transition probabilities of a Markov chain. The similarity of different texts is estimated by the relative entropy of these transition probabilities.

Word collocation networks [46] are networks of words found in a document or a document collection, where each node corresponds to a unique word type, and edges correspond to word collocations. In the simplest case, each edge corresponds to a unique bigram in the original document. For example, if words A and B appeared together in a document as a bigram AB, then the word collocation network will have an edge A → B. Edges can be weighted (with frequency of the bigram) or unweighted global network properties like diameter, global clustering coefficient, shrinkage exponent [47], and smallworldliness [48] can be used for authorship identification.

Prominence networks [49] encode how often a word preceded the other words in the sentence separated by any number of words. To normalize these frequency counts, they were divided by the frequency that the two words occurred in together in the same utterance in any order.

Network motifs are connected and directed subgraphs occurring in complex networks at numbers that are significantly higher than those in randomized networks. Rizvic *et al.* [50] use network motifs to detect structural similarities between directed networks of different texts represented as directed co-occurrence networks. Such similarities could be used to classify texts based on their authorship.

3.11 Computational Topology of Text

Mining a higher dimensional topological structure within a set of text documents can give an important insight into the data [51]. In particular, a more desirable model would account for some functional form of spatial dependence between words, such as "attraction and repulsion" [52]. In linguistic models, the effects of attraction and repulsion of words is an ever present phenomenon [53]. In particular, it is possible to identify the authorship of books using intermittency of specific words.

4   Authorship Identification Methods in National Language

Our analysis is constrained to the languages which use Latin alphabets. The review is presented based on the most populous language families.

4.1   Romance Languages

In the research [54], n-gram features were used for authorship attribution of Italian corpus, treating that texts are only the sequences of symbols, ignoring grammar and content of a text (considering that letters, punctuations and spaces are only abstract symbols). The experiment concluded very successful results.

For classification of French texts, World lengths, Sentence lengths, Frequencies of nouns, adverbs, adjectives, verbs, simple/complex noun phrases were used in the study [55].

Varela *et al.* [56] proposed using pronouns and most used verbs of the Brazilian Portuguese language for authorship attribution for texts written in Portuguese.

Pavelec *et al.* [57] propose a stylometric feature set based on conjunctions and adverbs (77 conjunctions and 94 adverbs) of the Portuguese language to address the problem of author identification.

4.2   Germanic Languages

German language has a rich morphology, therefore such kind of features may give a valuable information about the text. In the research, done in [58], beside many general features, a derivational suffixes for German (ant, arium, ast, at, ator, atur, ei, er, ent, enz, eur, heit, ist, ion, ismus, ität, keit, ling, nis, shaft, tum, ung, ur, werk, wesen) were used to estimate the derivative nouns to nouns ratio.

Beside the general features, used for authorship attribution: word and sentence lengths, vocabulary richness /diversity, content-free function words, syntactic class of words, hapaxlegomena, etc., the counts of lower case word forms were applied as the support vector machine (SVM) classifier inputs, in the experiment, performed with German texts [59].

4.3 Slavic Languages

For Russian language, many general features were effectively applied, including the length of sentences (average number of words per sentence), the length of words (average number of syllables per word), the overall frequency of function words, frequency of nouns, frequency of verbs, frequency of adjectives, the number of function words in sentences (average number of conjunctions, prepositions and particles).

In research, done in [60], the following features were suggested:

1. Sequences of letter pairs, i.e., in words with spaces between them
2. Sequences of letter pairs in the lemmatized forms of words. For Russian language, this reduction is much more notable, because Russian words have a lot of various forms.
3. Sequences of pairs of the most generalized grammatical classes of words and parts of speech (POS) in sentences. For Russian language, 14 parts of speech are assigned.
4. Pairs of less generalized grammatical classes for words.

Reicher *et al.* [27] show that the authorship attribution problem, when applied to morphologically complex languages, such as the Croatian language, can be successfully solved using a combination of some relatively simple features such as function words, punctuation marks, words length, and sentence length frequencies.

For Serbian language, Zecevic and Utvic [61] propose decomposing text into words and words into syllables. Then author profile can be constructed from the syllable-based features such as an average number of syllables per word, a word length frequency distribution in syllables (the number of monosyllabic words, the number of disyllabic words and so on) and the average distance between i-syllable words, and syllable frequency. To compare the profiles of different authors, the distance measure between feature vectors is used.

4.4 Baltic Languages

In Lithuanian electronic discourse (specifically e-mail), there is often found these units of language [62]: vulgarisms, loanwords, abbreviations, symbols, language excess, emoticons. For the recognition of idiolect, the widest possible lexical analysis is necessary. The same research notes that lists of text unit frequencies are an important part for the research methods. A very important criteria for the authorship analysis, is an author's specific use of punctuations, especially a set of prevailing punctuation marks and the mark, for which a preference is given. The research notes that the use of punctuations significantly differs between authors.

The complex linguistic structure of the Lithuanian language introduces several challenges: inflection, diacritics, rich morphology and vocabulary, etc. Lithuanian language is a highly inflected language in which the relationships between parts of speech and their roles in a sentence are expressed by different inflections. Inflection increases the number of words, which can cause difficulties when extracting some lexical features. Lithuanian language is very richness in suffixes. As a result of rich vocabulary, using bag-of-words approaches results in an extremely sparse feature space, which complicates the construction of a classification model. Lithuanian alphabet has 9 letters with diacritics: ą, č, ę, ė, į, š, ų, ū, ž. However, in electronic discourse these are often are often replaced with matching Latin letters (e.g., ę → e) or pairs of letters matching the same sounds as in English (e.g., š [ʃ] → sh) [71].

5 Requirements for Forensic Authorship Identification Systems

After survey and analysis of authorship identification methods used in electronic discourse and, specifically, in national electronic discourse, we present the following general recommendations for developers of forensic authorship identification methods and tools.

The authorship identification systems for forensic applications must satisfy general requirements of expert systems, and forensic systems, and specific requirements of authorship identification systems.

The authorship identification system as a particular case of an expert system should work faster than its human counterparts providing an answer in a reasonable time interval, should be error-tolerant and function with uncertain data, and should provide a user-friendly and usable interface to its users [63].

As a forensic application, the authorship identification system must be able to capture the crime scene and formulate the potential hypotheses of the crime using structured arguments. Each hypothesis is a claim that is related to a set of facts necessary to prove or refute it. The facts represent the evidence to be collected from the evidence sources available at the crime scene.

Finally, the specific requirements of authorship identification systems must be satisfied. They should be capable of making efficient distinctions on which evidentiary properties are satisfied and be resistant against attacks against author identification.

According to Grant [64], successful presentation of authorship identification results as evidence requires a demonstration of combination of consistency and distinctiveness: Within-Author Consistency requires that authors have consistent values of features extracted from texts of known authorship for each possible author that make good comparison documents in terms of genre and other linguistic variables; and Between-Author Distinctiveness which requires that values of features selected for authorship identification would be statistically different for all pairs of authors.

A number of requirements for an "ideal tool" for forensic linguistics has been formulated in [66] as follows: flexibility in constructing own set of prominent features that would be able to discriminate the writing style of an individual, ability to perform automatic search for style markers at all linguistic levels (phonological, morpho-syntactical, lexico-semantical), assistance in marking up prominent features in the text(s), quantification of the data and their distribution across sets of texts, statistical testing for the significance of variables (e.g., standard error of difference, t-Test, analysis of variance) without having use other statistical packages, provide a measure of authorship discrimination (such as intra-author vs. inter-author variation).

6 Conclusions

This paper has presented an overview of an authorship identification domain, including main challenges, data and methods used. Specific challenges for discourse in electronic space were identifies, including shortenings, clipping, jargonisms, and the use of emoticons. Specific applications for Latin alphabet based national languages were analysed. Authorship identification methods can be categorized into topology-aware methods, which consider the position of lexical elements, and topology-free methods, which ignore information about position. For authorship identification in English, the spatial position information is usually ignored, however for some national languages spatial information can reveal important characteristics of personal authors' style. In case of a national discourse, two approaches are prevalent: one approach ignores the specifics of a national alphabet by transliterating national alphabet letters to English alphabet letters. Another approach leaves national letters in feature space for further analysis. Typically, similar sets of features are used and consequently the use of national-specific letters does not lead to significant improvement of author identification results. New national language specific features are required to capture the specificities of use of national language. There is a significant amount of research still to be done in formulating and studying national language specific features on all levels (syntactical, semantic, prosodic, etc.) such as frequency of national letters, frequency of n-grams with national letters, forbidden n-grams, etc. Novel methods such as holomorphic Chebyshev projectors of text features [71] should be explored, too.

Acknowledgement. The authors acknowledge the contribution of the project "Lithuanian Cybercrime Centre of Excellence for Training, Research and Education", Grant Agreement No. HOME/2013/ISEC/AG/INT/4000005176, co-funded by the Prevention of and Fight against Crime Programme of the European Union.

References

1. Sánchez-Moya, A., Cruz-Moya, O.: Whatsapp, textese, and moral panics: discourse features and habits across two generations. Procedia – Soc. Behav. Sci. **173**, 300–306 (2015)
2. Segerstad, Y.H.: Use and adaptation of written language to the conditions of Computer-Mediated Communication. PhD dissertation, Göteborg University (2002)
3. Thurlow, C.: Generation txt? The sociolinguistics of young people's text-messaging. Discourse Anal. Online **1**(1), 30 (2003)
4. MacLeod, N., Grant, T.: Whose tweet?: authorship analysis of micro-blogs and other short form messages. In: Proceedings of the International Association of Forensic Linguists' 10th Biennial Conference (2011)
5. Voutilainen, A.: Part-of-speech tagging. In: Mitkov, R. (ed.) The Oxford Handbook of Computational Linguistics, pp. 219–232. University Press, Oxford (2003)
6. Nivre, J.: Logic programming tools for probabilistic part-of-speech tagging. Master's thesis, Växjö University (2000)
7. Bogdanova, D., Lazaridou, A.: Cross-language authorship attribution. In: The International Conference on Language Resources and Evaluation, pp. 2015–2020 (2014)

8. Potthast, M., Barron-Cedeno, A., Stein, B., Rosso, P.: Cross-language plagiarism detection, language resources and evaluation (LRE). Spec. Issue Plagiarism Authorship Anal. **45**(1), 1–18 (2011)
9. Salvador, M.F., Gupta, P., Rosso, P.: Cross-language plagiarism detection using a multilingual semantic network. In: Proceedings of the 35th European conference on Advances in Information Retrieval, ECIR 2013, pp. 710–713 (2013)
10. Navigli, R., Ponzetto, S.P.: BabelNet: building a very large multilingual semantic network. In: Proceedings of the 48th Annual Meeting of the Association for Computational Linguistics, ACL 2010, pp. 216–225 (2010)
11. Panicheva, P., Cardiff, J., Rosso, P.: Personal sense and idiolect: combining authorship attribution and opinion analysis. In Proceedings of the 4th International Conference on Language Resources and Evaluation, LREC 2010 (2010)
12. Dunn, R., Beaudry, J., Klavas, A.: Survey of research on learning styles. Educ. Leadersh. **46**(6), 50–58 (1989)
13. Bellman, R.: Adaptive Control Processes: a Guided Tour. Princeton University Press, Princeton (1961)
14. Koller, D., Sahami, M.: Hierarchically classifying documents using very few words. In: Proceedings of International Conference on Machine Learning, pp. 170–178 (1997)
15. Fuka, K., Hanka, R.: Feature set reduction for document classification problems. In: Proceedings of IJCAI-01 Workshop: Text Learning: Beyond Supervision, Seattle (2001)
16. Zervas, G., Rüger, S.M.: The curse of dimensionality and document clustering. In: Proceedings of the IEEE Searching for Information: AI and IR Approaches (1999)
17. Pearl, L., Steyvers, M.: Detecting authorship deception: a supervised machine learning approach using author writeprints. LLC **27**(2), 183–196 (2012)
18. Brennan, M., Afroz, S., Greenstadt, R.: Adversarial stylometry: circumventing authorship recognition to preserve privacy and anonymity. ACM Trans. Inf. Syst. Secur. (TISSEC), **15**(3), Article 12, 22 p. (2012)
19. De Vel O.: Mining e-mail authorship. In: ACM International Conference on Knowledge Discovery and Data Mining, KDD 2000, Workshop on Text Mining (2000)
20. Holmes, D.: Authorship attribution. Comput. Humanit. **28**(2), 87–106 (1994)
21. Stamatatos, E.: A survey of modern authorship attribution methods. J. Am. Soc. Inf. Sci. Technol. **60**(3), 538–556 (2009)
22. Zheng, R., Li, J., Chen, H., Huang, Z.: A framework for authorship identification of online messages: writing-style features and classification techniques. JASIST (JASIS) **57**(3), 378–393 (2006)
23. Graovac, J.: A variant of n-gram based language-independent text categorization. Intell. Data Anal. **18**(4) (2014)
24. Coyotl-Morales, R.M., Villaseñor-Pineda, L., Montes-y-Gómez, M., Rosso, P.: Authorship attribution using word sequences. In: Martínez-Trinidad, J.F., Carrasco Ochoa, J.A., Kittler, J. (eds.) CIARP 2006. LNCS, vol. 4225, pp. 844–853. Springer, Heidelberg (2006)
25. Stamatatos, E.: On the robustness of authorship attribution based on character n-gram features. J. Law Policy **21**(2), 421 (2013)
26. Koppel, M., Schler, J., Argamon, S.: Authorship attribution in the wild. Lang. Resour. Eval. **45**, 83–94 (2011)
27. Reicher, T., Krišto, I., Belša, I., Šilić, A.: Automatic authorship attribution for texts in croatian language using combinations of features. In: Setchi, R., Jordanov, I., Howlett, R.J., Jain, L.C. (eds.) KES 2010, Part II. LNCS, vol. 6277, pp. 21–30. Springer, Heidelberg (2010)

28. Argamon, S., Levitan S.: Measuring the usefulness of function words for authorship attribution. In: Proceedings of the Association for Literary and Linguistic Computing/ Association Computer Humanities Conference (2005)
29. Chaski, C.E.: Who's at the keyboard? Authorship attribution in digital evidence investigations. Int. J. Digit. Evid. 4(1), 1–13 (2005)
30. Hilton, O.: Scientific Examination of Questioned Documents. CRC Press, Boca Raton (1993)
31. McMenamin, G.R.: Forensic Linguistics: Advances in Forensic Stylistics. CRC Press, Boca Raton (2003)
32. Martindale, C., McKenzie, D.: On the utility of content analysis in author attribution: the Federalist. Comput. Humanit. 29, 259–270 (1995)
33. Palkovskii, Y., Belov, A., Muzika I.: Exploring Fingerprinting as External Plagiarism Detection Method - Lab Report for PAN at CLEF 2010. CLEF (Notebook Papers/LABs/ Workshops) (2010)
34. Yang, T., Lee, D.: T3: On mapping text to time series. In: Proceedings of the 3rd Alberto Mendelzon International Workshop on Foundations of Data Management. CEUR Workshop Proceedings 450 (2009)
35. Fukunaga, K.: Introduction to Statistical Pattern Recognition. Academic Press, New York (1972)
36. Qu, Y., Ostrouchov, G., Samatovaz, N., Geist, A.: Principal component analysis for dimension reduction in massive distributed data sets. In: Proceedings of IEEE International Conference on Data Mining (ICDM) (2002)
37. Koppel, M., Schler, J., Argamon, S., Messeri, E.: Authorship attribution with thousands of candidate authors. In: Proceedings of the 29th ACM SIGIR Conference on Research and Development on Information Retrieval Seattle, Washington, pp. 659–660 (2006)
38. Koppel, M., Schler, J., Argamon, S., Winter, Y.: The "fundamental problem" of authorship attribution. Engl. Stud. 93(3), 284–291 (2012)
39. Huang, A.: Similarity measures for text document clustering. In: Proceedings of the 6th New Zealand Computer Science Research Student Conference NZCSRSC2008, pp. 49–56 (2008)
40. Kjell, B., Woods, W.A., Frieder, O.: Discrimination of authorship using visualization. Inf. Process. Manage. 30(1), 141–150 (1994)
41. Shaw, C.D., Kukla, J.M., Soboroff, I., Ebert, D.S., Nicholas, C.K., Zwa, A., Miller, E.L., Roberts, D.A.: Interactive volumetric information visualization for document corpus management. Int. J. Digit. Libr. 2, 144–156 (1999)
42. Burrows, J.F.: Delta: a measure of stylistic difference and a guide to likely authorship. Literary Linguist. Comput. 17, 267–287 (2002)
43. Mosteller, F., Wallace, D.L.: Inference and Disputed Authorship: the Federalist. Addison-Wesley, Reading, MA (1964)
44. Antiqueira, L., Pardo, T.A.S., das Gracas Volpe Nunes, M., de Oliveira Jr., O.N., da Fontoura Costa, L.: Some issues on complex networks for author characterization. Revista Iberoamericana de Inteligencia Artificial 11(36), 51–58 (2006)
45. Segarra, S., Eisen, M., Ribeiro, A.: Authorship attribution using function words adjacency networks. In: IEEE International Conference on Acoustics, Speech and Signal Processing, ICASSP 2013, pp. 5563–5567 (2013)
46. Ke, J., Yao, Y.: Analysing language development from a network, approach. J. Quant. Linguist. 15(1), 70–99 (2008)
47. Leskovec, J., Kleinberg J., Faloutsos, C.: Graph evolution: densification and shrinking diameters. ACM Trans. Knowl. Discov. Data, 1(1), Article 2 (2007)

48. Matsuo, Y., Ohsawa, Y., Ishizuka, M.: A document as a small world. In: Terano, T., Nishida, T., Namatame, A., Tsumoto, S., Ohsawa, Y., Washio, T. (eds.) JSAI-WS 2001. LNCS (LNAI), vol. 2253, pp. 444–448. Springer, Heidelberg (2001)
49. Chang, F., Lieven, E., Tomasello, M.: Automatic evaluation of syntactic learners in typologically-different languages. Cogn. Syst. Res. **9**(3), 198–213 (2008)
50. Rizvic, H., Martincic-Ipsic, S., Mestrovic, A.: Network Motifs Analysis of Croatian Literature. CoRR abs/1411.4960 (2014)
51. Wagner, H., Dłotko, P., Mrozek, M.: Computational topology in text mining. In: Ferri, M., Frosini, P., Landi, C., Cerri, A., Di Fabio, B. (eds.) CTIC 2012. LNCS, vol. 7309, pp. 68–78. Springer, Heidelberg (2012)
52. Beeferman, D., Berger, A., Lafferty, J.: A model of lexical attraction and repulsion. In: 35th Annual Meeting of the Association for Computational Linguistics (1997)
53. Amancio, D.R.: Authorship recognition via fluctuation analysis of network topology and word intermittency. J. Stat. Mech. P03005 (2015)
54. Basile, C., Benedetto, D., Caglioti, E., Degli Esposti, M.: An example of mathematical authorship attribution. J. Math. Phys. **49**, 125211–125230 (2008)
55. Todirascu, A., Pado, S., Krisch, J., Kisselew, M., Heid, U.: French and German corpora for audience–based text type classification. LREC **2012**, 1591–1597 (2012)
56. Varela, P., Justino, E., Oliveira, L.S.: Verbs and pronouns for authorship attribution. In: 17th International Conference on Systems, Signals and Image Processing (IWSSIP 2010), pp. 89–92 (2010)
57. Pavelec, D., Oliveira, L.S., Justino, E., Batista, L.V.: Using conjunctions and adverbs for author verification. J. Univ. Comput. Sci. **14**(18), 2967–2981 (2008)
58. Hancke, J., Meurers, D., Vajjala, S.: Readability classification for German using lexical, syntactic, and morphological features. In: Proceedings of the 24th International Conference on Computational Linguistics (COLING), pp. 1063–1080 (2012)
59. Diederich, J., Kindermann, J., Leopold, E., Paass, G.: Authorship attribution with support vector machines. Appl. Intell. **19**(1), 109–123 (2003)
60. Kukushkina, O.V., Polikarpov, A.A., Khmelev, D.V.: Using literal and grammatical statistics for authorship attribution. Probl. Inf. Transm. **37**(2), 172–184 (2001)
61. Zecevic, A., Utvic, M.: An authorship attribution for Serbian. In: BCI (Local), pp. 109–112 (2012)
62. Žalkauskaitė, G.: Idiolect signs in the e-mail. PhD dissertation, Vilnius University (2012)
63. Barragán, J.: Why some hard cases remain unsolved. Legal knowledge based systems. In: JURIX 1993 (1993)
64. Grant, T.: TXT 4N6 method, consistency, and distinctiveness in the analysis of SMS text messages. J. Law Policy **21**(2), 467–494 (2013)
65. Mohtasseb, H., Ahmed, A.: Two-layered blogger identification model integrating profile and instance-based methods. Knowl. Inf. Syst. **31**(1), 1–21 (2012)
66. Guillén-Nieto, V., Vargas-Sierra, C., Pardiño-Juan, M., Martínez-Barco, P., Suárez-Cueto, A.: Exploring state-of-the art software for forensic authorship identification. Int. J. Engl. Stud. **8**(1), 1–28 (2008)
67. Teahan, W.J., Harper, D.J.: Using compression-based language models for text categorization. In: Croft, W.B., Lafferty, J. (eds.) Language modeling for information retrieval, pp. 141–165. Springer, Dordrecht (2003)
68. Benedetto, D., Caglioti, E., Loreto, V.: Language trees and zipping. Phys. Rev. Lett. **88**(4), 048702 (2002)
69. Abbasi, A., Chen, H.: Applying authorship analysis to extremist-group web forum messages. IEEE Intell. Syst. **20**(5), 67–75 (2005)

70. Kapociute-Dzikiene, J., Vaassen, F., Daelemans, W., Krupavicius, A.: Improving topic classification for highly inflective languages. In: 24th International Conference on Computational Linguistics, COLING 2012, pp. 1393–1410 (2012)
71. Napoli, C., Tramontana, E., Lo Sciuto, G., Wozniak, M., Damasevicius, R., Borowik, G.: Authorship semantical identification using holomorphic Chebyshev projectors. In: Proceedings of 3rd Asia-Pacific Conference on Computer Aided System Engineering (APCASE) (2015)

Authorship Attribution of Internet Comments with Thousand Candidate Authors

Jurgita Kapočiūtė-Dzikienė[1]([✉]), Andrius Utka[1], and Ligita Šarkutė[2]

[1] Vytautas Magnus University, K. Donelaičio 58, 44248 Kaunas, Lithuania
jurgita.k.dz@gmail.com, a.utka@hmf.vdu.lt
[2] Kaunas University of Technology, K. Donelaičio 73, 44029 Kaunas, Lithuania
ligita.sarkute@ktu.lt

Abstract. In this paper we report the first authorship attribution results for the Lithuanian language using Internet comments with a thousand of candidate authors. The task is complicated due to the following reasons: large number of candidate authors, extremely short non-normative texts, and problems associated with morphologically and vocabulary rich language.

The effectiveness of the proposed similarity-based method was investigated using lexical, morphological, and character features; as well as several dimensionality reduction techniques. Marginally the best results were obtained with the word-level character tetra-grams and entire feature set. However, the technique based on the randomized feature sets even using a few thousands of features achieved very similar performance levels, besides it outperformed method's implementations based on the sophisticated feature ranking.

The best obtained *f-score* and *accuracy* values exceeded random and majority baselines by more than 10.9 percentage points.

Keywords: Similarity-based paradigm · Randomized feature set · Internet comments · The Lithuanian language

1 Introduction

The internet is replete with electronic text documents (comments, forum posts, tweets, etc.); however, the vast majority of them are written anonymously or pseudonymously. The anonymity factor makes the internet the perfect environment for expressing opinions on various issues. The internet is also the perfect place for negative deeds, e.g. harassment or bullying, impersonation of another individual, disclosure of the confidential information, and similar cyber crimes. The simple measures taken by the service providers trying to stop perpetrators are not always effective enough: he/she may change pseudonyms; write from the different IP addresses; or not reveal the real IP address by accessing websites through the Proxy servers. Even in these complicated cases when solely the plain text becomes the only evidence of an authorship, the identification problem can be still tackled due to an existing "stylometric fingerprint": i.e. specific, individual, persistent, and uncontrolled habit of humans to express thoughts in the certain unique ways, of course, having in mind a scenario that author makes no efforts to modify

© Springer International Publishing Switzerland 2015
G. Dregvaite and R. Damasevicius (Eds.): ICIST 2015, CCIS 538, pp. 433–448, 2015.
DOI: 10.1007/978-3-319-24770-0_37

his/her writing style. Hence, some anonymous writer may be prone to the specific expressions, vocabulary, emoticons, sentence structures, spelling errors or to have other recognizable idiosyncrasies. Van Halteren even named this phenomenon a "human stylome" [43] in deliberate analogy to the DNA "genome". Despite strict implications not always seem to be absolutely correct, because "genome" is stable, but human writing style tends to evolve over time [11], "stylome" can still be added to human biometrics, next to voice, gait, keystroke dynamics, handwriting, etc.

The authorship analysis involves several main research directions: author verification, when deciding if a given text is written by a certain author or not (e.g. [20]); author profiling, when extracting information about the traits of an author: typically covering the basic demographic information that includes age (e.g. [33]), gender (e.g. [15]) or psychometric characteristics (e.g. [3]); plagiarism detection, when finding similarities between the texts (e.g. [40]); etc. However, in this paper we focus on the Authorship Attribution (AA) – a task of identifying whom, from a set of the candidate authors, is an actual author of a given anonymous text document. AA is one of the oldest Computational Linguistic problems, dating back to 1887 [24] which for a long time in the past was mainly restricted to the literary texts only. With the beginning of the internet era AA became highly topical and more focused on the wide range of practical problems, e.g. identification of offenders in anonymous harassment and threatening cases [42], tracking authors of malicious source code [2], etc. Therefore literary texts were replaced with e-mails [1, 44], web forum messages [37], online chats [5, 9], internet blogs [16] or tweets [34, 38], which, in turn, contributed to the development of Computational Linguistic methods able to cope effectively with these types of non-normative texts. Not only application domain is changing, a number of candidate authors is gradually increasing as well. If the first AA analysis attempts were able to cope with only a few or dozens of authors, recently it is applied on thousands candidate authors (e.g. 10,000 [16] and even 100,000 [27]) and limited training data, thus AA problem has become a so-called "needle-in-a-haystack" problem.

In this paper the AA problem is restricted to one thousand Lithuanian authors, using a corpus composed of the internet comments. However, our problem is complicated due to a number of reasons. Firstly, the used texts contain just a few words, but cover a wide range of topics. It is known that the shorter the text, the more difficult it is to determine its authorship; moreover, the writing style of an author may differ a bit depending on the topic he/she is discussing (especially in terms of vocabulary and expressions). Secondly, we have to deal with the Lithuanian language, which is rich in vocabulary and morphology, highly inflective, has a complex word derivation system, relatively free word-order in a sentence, and missing diacritics in non-normative texts. Thus, AA methods achieving a high accuracy for English do not necessary have to be the best for Lithuanian. Thirdly, the AA problem for Lithuanian has never been tackled using such a large number of candidate authors, therefore it is difficult to say in advance, if the methods solving AA problem for a few [12] or hundred candidate authors [14] can be still effective in this case.

2 Related Works

If excluding archaic rule-based approaches (attributing texts to authors depending on the rules, constructed by linguist-experts), automatic AA methods can be divided in two main paradigms: machine learning and similarity-based (for review see [39]). In the machine-learning paradigm, the texts of known authorship (training texts) are used to construct a classifier that can then be used to classify anonymous documents. In the similarity-based paradigm, an anonymous text is attributed to the particular author whose text is the most similar according to the calculated similarity measure. Broadly-speaking, the AA research is mainly focused on the choice of feature types for document representation, on the methods for a dimensionality reduction of feature space, and on either the choice of learning algorithms for the machine learning or the choice of similarity measures or distance metrics for the similarity-based approaches.

Since the first modern pioneering work (where Mosteller and Wallace [26] demonstrated promising AA results on The Federalist papers using Bayesian methods applied on the frequencies of a small set of function words) until 1990s AA was based on quantitative features (so-called "style markers") such as a sentence or word length, syllables per word, type-token ratio, vocabulary richness functions, lexical repetition, etc. (the review of the early style markers can be found in [7]). However, these stylometric features are considered to be suitable only for the homogenous long texts (>1,000 words) and for the datasets having small number of candidate authors.

In the contemporary research the most widespread approach is to represent text documents as vectors of frequencies, which elements cover specific layers of linguistic information (e.g. lexical, syntactic, semantic, character, etc.). Lexical features are the most commonly used feature type, which require only tokenization, moreover, they can be easy interpretable to humans. Lexical features can be divided into two types: function words (articles, conjunctions, prepositions, pronouns, etc., carrying no semantic information) and content words (sometimes used in a longer n-gram patterns) (relating author's stylistic choices and providing topic information). When dealing with the multi-topic data the function words, which by consensus are considered as topic-neutral, are more often recommended [4] compared to the content words; however, function words still have to be used with caution, because some researchers proved them to correlate with the topic as much as with the authorship [25]. The effectiveness of syntactic and semantic features usually depend on the accuracy of applied linguistic tools (e.g. part-of-speech taggers, parsers) or exhaustiveness of external data resources (e.g. thesauruses, databases, ontologies). Although used alone syntactic or semantic features can hardly outperform lexical, but often show improvements when applied in combination [6]. However, character features are considered to be the most important document representation type for author's style detection: they are language-independent, able to capture style through lexical and contextual information, are tolerant to grammatical or typing errors, and able to handle limited data (the robustness of character n-grams was proved by many researchers, e.g. in [21, 41]).

After extracting the features, the most popular attempt to increase AA accuracy is based on the assumption that irrelevant and noisy features should be omitted. It is usually done by applying wrapper (performing a search over all possible subsets of features) or filtering (scoring the features first and then omitting the least informative ones) features selection methods on the primary feature set before the attribution process (the review about feature selection methods is in [8]).

AA task is the most often solved using machine learning methods (for the review see [35]). In the contemporary computational research, Support Vector Machines (SVMs) (considered as the most accurate thus the most suitable technique for text classification) are the most popular choice for AA tasks; however, other methods are explored as well. Some comparative experiments with Decision Trees (DTs), Back Propagation Neural Networks (BPNNs) and SVMs revealed that SVMs and BPNNs achieve significantly better performance compared to DTs [46]. However, comparative experiments prove that similarity-based methods often outperform machine learning techniques: e.g. Memory-Based Learning (MBL) produces better results compared to Naïve Bayes (NB) and DTs [45]; the Delta method can surpass the performance levels achieved by the popular SVMs [10]. Different proposed improvements for the similarity-based approaches contribute to their effectiveness even more. Thus, novel classification scheme based on the specific vocabulary outperforms Principal Component Analysis (PCA) and Delta [31]; Latent Dirichlet Allocation (LDA)-based classification scheme surpasses two classical AA approaches based on the Delta rule and chi-squared distance [32].

Virtually all previously discussed research works have focused on the problems with a small number of candidate authors and only recently larger datasets (in terms of a number of those authors) have been considered. Despite all advantages of the machine learning techniques, similarity-based approaches are considered to be more suitable for the problems with more candidate authors and limited training data (e.g. MBL method applied on 145 authors outperformed SVMs [22]; MBL method applied on 100,000 authors outperformed NB, SVM and Regularized Least Squares Classification (RLSC) [27]). However, some researchers argue that weaknesses of machine learning approaches are due to the difficulties when configuring complex models with many parameters having only a small number of training instances and, in particular, offer to use normalization which can make the huge impact: e.g. after normalization RLSC performs equally well as MBL [27]. Besides the same researchers experimenting with a blog corpus of 100,000 candidate authors developed a novel technique to estimate a confidence of the classifier outputs (by measuring a difference between the best and second-best matching classes, running two different classifiers and outputting the result only if they agree, and combining the results by the meta-learning) which resulted in increased overall precision. In [34] researchers experiment with the Twitter corpus (containing very short texts, limited to 140 characters) of at most 1,000 candidate authors, use SVMs machine learning classifier and demonstrate that introduced AA feature type (so-called "flexible patterns", capturing the context in which function words are used) is achieving significant improvement over baselines based on the character or word n-grams. Some researchers [36] argue that AA problem dealing with a blog corpus of over 19,000 candidate authors can be effectively solved with the similarity-based LDA (in particular, generative probabilistic model, where each text document is generated according to the distribution of topics and each word in the document – according per-topic word distribution) by calculating the distance between the LDA-based representations in the training documents of known authorship and anonymous text document. The researchers claim that LDA approach applied on the author profiles (created from concatenated training text documents) yields state-of-the-art performance in terms of accuracy with enough training data. The hybrid method dealing with three text representations types (tf-idf restricted to content words; binary idf restricted to content words; tf-idf on different stylistic features) and combining similarity-based with machine learning approaches, described in [18], effectively copes with 10,000 blog authors. Firstly, researchers rank authors by cosine similarity using all three text representation techniques, if at least one of them gives the top-rank, the pair (constructed of an anonymous text and the author ranked most similar for that text) is tested on the meta-learning SVM classifier: in case of success the anonymous text is attributed to that author, otherwise the method outputs an answer "don't know". The similarity-based approach using cosine measure applied on the blog dataset containing 10,000 candidate authors and character tetra-grams along with the multiple randomized feature sets can achieve high precision [16, 17, 19]. The researchers also adjusted the method to cope with the open-class cases: if calculated score value (aggregating several attribution decisions) is below some determined threshold the anonymous text is considered to belong none of the candidate authors. Nevertheless, the methods dealing with a huge number of the candidate authors are rather slow. In [28] researchers experiment with the corpus containing Japanese microblogs written by 10,000 candidate authors and test similarity-based methods using cosine measure and character n-grams (where n is 1, 2, and 3). The proposed novel weighting scheme (which strengthens the weight of n-gram depending on its n) applied on the morphemes converted to the part-of-speech-tags significantly shortens attribution execution time.

Considering all previously surveyed methods and given recommendations, we may conclude that similarity-based paradigm should be better choice for our task. However, the feature representation type and the feature selection method can be chosen only after experimental investigation.

3 Methodology

3.1 The Corpus

We composed our corpus of the internet comments harvested in January 2015 from the Lithuanian news portal www.delfi.lt. These comments were posted by anonymous users expressing their opinions about articles in two subjects "In Lithuania" and "Abroad". All text fragments containing non-Lithuanian alphabet letters (except punctuation marks and digits) were eliminated; all the replies and meta-information were filtered out as well leaving just the plain texts. Besides, the texts shorter than 30 symbols (excluding white-space characters) were not included into the corpus.

The composed corpus contains 1,000 authors. We made an assumption that identity of author can be revealed, if his/her texts are written under the same unique IP address and the same unique pseudonym (taking both together as a single unit). Although some exceptions (when a few authors write under the same pseudonym using the same IP address) may occur, these noisy cases are rather rare to make a significant influence on the overall AA results. However, in the real world applications ideal conditions are hardly possible; but on the other hand, the real environment is exactly what is needed to compose a bold and undistorted testbed for AA task: internet comments cover wide range of topics, are single units (not only the extracted snippets of long texts as it is done in e.g. [16] or [30]), do not necessary refer to each other; moreover, authors, hiding behind the anonymity curtain have no reasons to pretend "better" and therefore do not make any efforts to refine their writing style. As the result of it, the texts are full of out-of-vocabulary words, including diminutives and words with missing diacritics (where Lithuanian letters are replaced with appropriate Latin letters, e.g. $ė \rightarrow e$, $š \rightarrow s$, $ū \rightarrow u$, etc.).

The useful statistics about the composed corpus is given in Table 1. Random $\sum_j P^2(c_j)$ and majority $\max\left(P(c_j)\right)$ baselines (where $P(c_j)$ is the probability of some author c_j: texts written by particular c_j are divided by all texts in the corpus) show the lowest accuracy threshold which must be exceeded to claim that applied method is effective and reasonable enough for our AA task. Although on average one author gets ~35 texts, the distribution is not balanced. The smallest number of texts per author is 12, the largest – 425. Almost half of the authors (in particular, 554) have produced less than 25 texts and only 45 authors more than 100 texts.

Table 1. Statistics about the composed internet comments' corpus

Number of authors	1,000
Number of texts	34,946
Number of tokens (words/digits)	940,022
Avg. text length in tokens	26.899
Random baseline	0.002
Majority baseline	0.012

3.2 Formal Description of the Task

In essence, the AA task which we are solving in this paper can be formally described as follows:

The corpus D contains text documents d_i attributed to a closed-set of candidate authors (defined as classes) $C = \{c_j\}$. Any author's c_j profile Pr_j can be created by concatenating all d_i attributed to c_j into a single text document.

According to the determined sequence of features F_k (distinct text elements, e.g., tokens, lemmas, etc.) each d_i or Pr_j can be transformed into appropriate vectors $\vec{v}_i = \langle v_{ni} \rangle$ or $\vec{v}_j = \langle v_{nj} \rangle$, respectively, with elements representing absolute counts of these features found in the documents.

Function φ determines the mapping, relating text documents d_i with their authors c_j, i.e. $\varphi: D \rightarrow C$. Our goal is to offer a method, which could find as close approximation of φ as possible.

3.3 Similarity-Based Method

A decision to use the similarity-based paradigm for our solving task was already taken after the comprehensive analysis of related works (see Sect. 2); and a concept of the randomized feature set for our AA method was borrowed from [16, 17, 19].

```
Repeat K times:
  Compose feature set F_k
  Create v̄ for d depending on F_k
  For each j^th author:
    Construct profile Pr_j by concatenating d_i ∈ D
    Create v̄_j for Pr_j depending on F_k
    Memorize calculated sim(v̄,v̄_j): SIM = SIM ∪ sim(v̄,v̄_j)
  If max(SIM) > σ_1:
    Memorize determined candidate author c_j: CA = CA ∪ c_j
For each unique c_j ∈ CA:
  Calculate a number of times c_j is in CA: times(c_j ∈ CA)
  Memorize proportion: SCORE = SCORE ∪ times(c_j ∈ CA) / K
If max(SCORE) > σ_2:
  Anonymous text d is attributed to the determined c_j
```

In our method we are calculating a similarity between anonymous text document d and all profiles of the authors Pr_j. Indeed, profile-based approaches have advantages over instance-based when the text documents are very concise (as it is in our case, where an average text length is only ~27 tokens, see Table 1), then concatenation helps to create sufficiently long document, which is already suitable for capturing the author's writing style.

For calculating the similarities between the vectors $\vec{v}$ and $\vec{v}_j$ we have chosen one of the most popular similarity measures – usual cosine similarity [29] (used by many researchers for their AA tasks even without any considerations), presented in Eq. 1.[1] Calculated cosine similarity values fall into an interval ranging from 0 to 1, where 0 indicates that the vectors are not similar, 1 – that they are equal.

$$sim(\vec{v},\vec{v}_j) = \frac{\sum_{n=1}^{N} v_n \times v_{nj}}{\sqrt{\sum_{n=1}^{N} (v_n)^2 \times \sum_{n=1}^{N} (v_{nj})^2}} \tag{1}$$

The feature types; the feature set F_k size N; the values of two thresholds σ_1 and σ_2 still have to be investigated experimentally.

---

[1] Any other measure can be selected instead; however its effectiveness should be investigated experimentally. For the comparison reasons we investigated Euclidean distance metric. Since obtained results gave no statistically significant improvements over cosine similarity, they are not presented in this paper.

3.4 Main Research Directions

Our main focus is on the following research directions, which should fill the gaps in the AA method, described in Sect. 3.3:

1. Feature type for the text documents representation. We explored the impact of the most popular feature types, covering lexical, morphological, and character levels (for the statistics see Table 2):

   - *lex* – tokens (words + digits). It is the most popular lexical feature type (in our case involving both content-specific information and function words). This feature type is one of the most popular types used in AA.

   - *lem* – lemmas, based on the word tokens. To obtain lemmas (canonical forms of words) the texts were processed with the Lithuanian morphological analyzer-lemmatizer "Lemuoklis" [47], which changes recognized words into their lemma, transforms common words into the lower case and replaces digits with the special tag. "Lemuoklis" is not adjusted to deal with the out-of-vocabulary words, therefore it could not recognize even ~19.16 % (or 180,139 words) of all words in the corpus, leaving them in the original untouched form. This feature type is especially recommended for the morphologically rich languages.

   - *fwd* – function words. The content-free lexical feature which includes prepositions, pronouns, conjunctions, particles, interjections, and onomatopoeias. The words of these part-of-speeches were recognized by "Lemuoklis", instead of using pre-established list of function words. This feature type by consensus is considered as topic-neutral and by many researchers was proved to be a relatively good identifier of the author's writing style.

   - *chr4* – word level character tetra-grams. This character feature type is based on successions of 4 characters within the token boundaries (a window is sliding one character at the time). E.g. *chr4* for phrase "authorship attribution" would produce the following word-level character n-grams: "auth", "utho", "thor", "hors", "orsh", "rshi", "ship", "attr", "ttri", "trib", "ribu", "ibut", "buti", "utio", and "tion". We selected tetra-grams, because this feature type was already proved to be the best choice on the Lithuanian texts for the topic classification among all other n-grams and even other feature types, based on more sophisticated lexical and morphological information [13].

   Besides, we also explored the impact of the diacritics-fee character tetra-grams. Since an optional usage of diacritics makes the data very sparse (which may result in the lower accuracy) and there are no effective tools able to restore all missing diacritics, we replaced Lithuanian letters with the appropriate Latin letters before applying tetra-gram tokenizer.

Table 2. Statistics about the features in the corpus

Feature type	Maximum number of features
lex	137,748
lem	83,228
fwd	1,750
chr4	65,746
diacritics-free chr4	52,286

2. The dimensionality reduction of the feature set, when all irrelevant and noisy features are eliminated, is considered one of the key factors helping to increase the accuracy. We explored the impact of the following dimensionality reduction techniques:
   - *No reduction*, i.e. all available features (see in Table 2).
   - *Ranking and selecting the best N features.* The features were ranked according to the calculated chi-squared values (the ranking was done with *ChiSquaredAttributeEval* function implemented in Weka 3.7 Machine Learning toolkit)[2], and only then the top N features were selected to form F_k. A number of N was varied in our experiments having 1,000; 5,000; 10,000; 20,000; 30,000; 40,000; and 50,000.
   - *Random selection of N features.* N features were randomly selected from the entire composed feature set. We explored the same N values as described in the previous item. This dimensionality reduction technique was used with the randomized feature sets only, where the final attribution decision was taken after aggregation and generalization of all decisions obtained in $K > 1$ iterations (see *Pseudo-code* in Sect. 3.3).
3. The influence of thresholds:
   - Threshold σ_1 indicates the lowest cosine similarity value necessary to determine that the compared vectors are similar enough. We investigated the values from 0 to 1 with the interval of 0.1.
   - Threshold σ_2 indicates the lowest score value necessary to attribute anonymous text document to the particular class. This threshold is used with the randomized feature sets only having $K > 1$. We investigated the values of σ_2 equal to 0.1, 0.2, 0.4, 0.6, 0.8 and 1.0.

The default values in the preliminary experiments for K, σ_1, and σ_2 are 1, 0, and 0.1, respectively.

---

[2] Downloaded from http://www.cs.waikato.ac.nz/ml/weka/.

4   Experiments and Results

Our experiments involved several research directions, presented in Sect. 3.4.

During a single experiment we performed 50 runs, testing 100 text documents in each run; hence, the method (presented in Sect. 3.3) was tested 5,000 times. During a single test text document d was randomly selected from D, making an assumption that it's class is not known in advance; besides selected document was automatically removed from the dataset D: $D = D\backslash d$. The class of d, attributed by the method had to be compared with its real class. Despite our corpus is not balanced, a randomization function (used for selecting "anonymous" d) was not biased towards the largest classes (having the most texts), because the author was randomly selected at first, but his/her text was selected only afterwards.

The evaluation metrics– in particular, $accuracy$ (presented in Eq. 2) and f-$score$ (presented in Eq. 3)– were calculated for each run (testing 100 attributed text documents) and averaged in 50 runs.

$$accuracy = \frac{tp + tn}{tp + tn + fp + fn} \tag{2}$$

where tp – true positives (c_j texts correctly attributed to c_j); tn – true negatives (any other c_j' correctly attributed to c_j'); fp – false positives (c_j' erroneously attributed to c_j), f_n – false negatives (c_j erroneously attributed to c_j').

$$f\text{-}score = 2 \times \frac{precision \times recall}{precision + recall} \tag{3}$$

where $precision$ and $recall$ are presented in Eqs. 4 and 5, respectively.

$$precision = \frac{tp}{tp + fp} \tag{4}$$

$$recall = \frac{tp}{tp + fn} \tag{5}$$

To make sure that the differences between the obtained results are statistically significant we performed McNemar test [23] at the significance level $\alpha = 0.05$, meaning that the differences are considered statistically significant if calculated probability density function $P < \alpha$.

During a preliminary experiment we experimentally investigated the influence of the feature representation type, using no dimensionality reduction (see Fig. 1). The differences in accuracies between the best determined feature type $chr4$ and all the rest types lex, lem, fwd are statistically significant with P values equal to 0.006, 0.016, 0.000, respectively. We also ran control experiment using $diacritics$-$free$ $chr4$ and obtained averaged f-$score$ and $accuracy$ values equal to 0.105 and 0.119, respectively. Despite these values are a bit lower compared to $chr4$, the difference in accuracy is not statistically significant, because $P = 0.386 \gg alpha$.

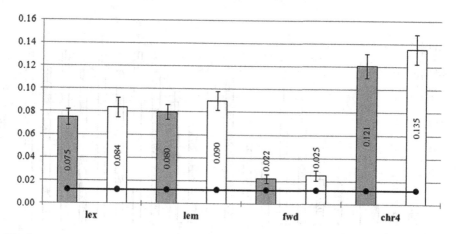

Fig. 1. The influence of the feature type on the results. The averaged values are given in columns (gray and white for *f-score* and *accuracy*, respectively) with the confidence intervals above; the black curve indicates the higher of random or majority baselines.

Using the best determined feature type *chr4* and no dimensionality reduction we ran another control experiment testing the influence of σ_1 value on the results. Starting from 0 we gradually increased σ_1 by 0.1 until it reached 1. The average *f-score/accuracy* values were gradually deteriorating and approaching to 0: 0.121/0.135, 0.106/0.117, 0.035/0.037, 0.009/0.009, 0.003/0.003, 0.000/0.000.

Using the best feature type *chr4* and $\sigma_1 = 0$ we explored the influence of the dimensionality reduction in terms of N; feature ranking; and the effect of the randomized feature set with $K = 20$ (see Fig. 2). Since the results obtained with $N = 30,000$ and $N = 50,000$ show almost the same trend as $N = 40,000$, we do not present them in Fig. 2 not to overload the reader with too much information. The differences in accuracies between the best obtained results (with all the features) and randomized feature set when N is 5,000, 10,000, 20,000, 30,000, 40,000, 50,000 are not statistically significant with P values equal to 0.039, 0.676, 0.940, 0.764, 0.949, 0.974, respectively; but significant when $N = 1,000$ with $P = 0.000$. The differences between the randomized feature set and appropriate top-ranked feature set are statistically significant when N is 1,000, 5,000, 10,000, and 20,000 with P values equal to 0.672, 0.001, 0.000, 0.037, respectively; and not statistically significant when N is 30,000, 40,000, 50,000 with P values equal to 0.983, 0.966, 0.966, respectively.

Using *chr4* and $\sigma_1 = 0$ we ran another control experiment to test the influence of σ_2 value on the results. The best results were achieved with the default 0.1 and any increase gave a drop in *f-score* and *accuracy*. However, a decline with the higher N values was much steeper compared with the lower, e.g. with $N = 50,000$ and σ_2 equal 0.1, 0.2, 0.4, 0.6, 0.8, and 0.9 we obtained *f-score/accuracy* values equal to 0.120/0.135, 0.120/0.135, 0.118/0.131, 0.106/0.116, 0.088/0.096, 0.061/0.066, respectively.

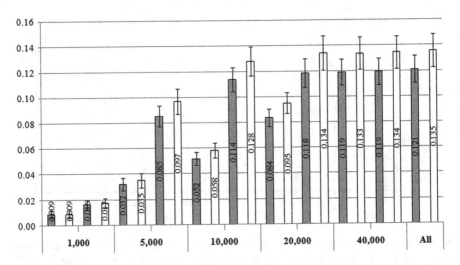

Fig. 2. The influence of N on the evaluation metrics. The first two columns next to each N represent the results with the top-rank feature set, the second two – with the randomized feature sets and $K = 20$. For the other notations see the caption of Fig. 1.

5   Discussion

All experimentally obtained results presented in Figs. 1 and 2 are reasonable and effective enough, because exceed random and majority baselines.

   The best determined feature type for the text documents representation is word-level character tetra-grams (giving the maximum *f-score* and *accuracy* of 0.121 and 0.135, respectively, with all available features). Neither tokens, nor token lemmas could outperform character tetra-grams. This probably happened due to the larger vocabulary, where all different inflective word forms have to be considered as the different features (making feature set very sparse), thus it is rather hard to find their matches between the anonymous text and profiles of the authors. Since we were dealing with the internet comments, lemmatizer could not recognize out-of-vocabulary words, therefore token lemmas, which are considered to be the most accurate type for the morphologically rich languages appeared only in the second best place. If tokens and token lemmas are too sparse to find their matches, function words are too rare to find consistent patterns between anonymous text and the profiles. It is likely that function words would produce better performance in the instance-based attribution scenario.

   If compared character tetra-grams with diacritics-free character tetra-grams, simple tetra-grams are marginally better. It seems that the author's choice to use or not to use diacritics in the texts is rather important constituent of his/her writing style.

   Since attributed texts are very short (average length is only ~27 tokens), even a poor similarity (in terms of σ_1 values) detected between it and the author's profile already makes positive impact on the results.

   Marginally the best results were achieved with the entire feature set; however, randomized feature sets containing only 5,000 features reached very similar AA performance levels (due to the statistical significance between the differences of the obtained results). The technique based on the top-ranked N features is not as effective as randomized feature sets: it could reach the same performance level only with $N \geq 30,000$. Thus, the power of aggregated decision is much stronger compared to the single one, despite that one is based on the top-ranked features.

Of all tested σ_2 values the best AA results were obtained with 0.1, which means if at least in 2 of 20 iterations some anonymous text is attributed to the same class it is already enough to make a final attribution decision. Thus, dealing with such sparse data and such short texts even disputed decision already seems to be better choice than no decision at all.

Unfortunately obtained results cannot be directly compared with the results for the other languages due to the very different experimental conditions: number of candidate authors, language types, text length, dataset sizes, etc.

6   Conclusions and Future Work

In this paper we were solving authorship attribution problem for one thousand candidate authors using Lithuanian internet comments. To tackle this problem we experimentally investigated the proposed similarity-based approach, the effects of the feature representation types (lexical, morphological, character), and several dimensionality reduction techniques (no reduction, top-ranked feature selection, randomized feature sets) on the attribution results.

Since the texts are too complicated to be effectively processed with the external morphological tools, the best results were obtained using word-level character tetragrams: the baselines were exceeded by more than ~10.9 % achieving 12.1 %/13.5 % of *f-score/accuracy*.

Marginally the best results were achieved with no feature reduction, however randomized feature sets with only a few thousands of features reached very similar performance levels. The technique based on the randomized feature sets outperformed the implementations based on the feature ranking.

In the future research we are planning to perform exhaustive linguistic error analysis, which could give us ideas on how to improve the method further; to investigate different similarity measures, and to test the method on the expanded number of the candidate authors up to tens of thousands.

Acknowledgments. Research was funded by a grant (No. LIT-8-69) from the Research Council of Lithuania.

References

1. Abbasi, A., Chen, H.: writeprints: a stylometric approach to identity-level identification and similarity detection in cyberspace. ACM Trans. Inf. Syst. **26**(2), 1–29 (2008)
2. Alrabaee, S., Saleem, N., Preda, S., Wang, L., Debbabi, M.: OBA2: an onion approach to binary code authorship attribution. Digit. Invest. **11**(1), S94–S103 (2014)

3. Argamon, S., Dawhle, S., Koppel, M., Pennebaker, J.W.: Lexical predictors of personality type. In: Proceedings of the Joint Annual Meeting of the Interface and the Classification Society of North America, pp. 1–16 (2005)
4. Argamon, S., Levitan, S.: Measuring the usefulness of function words for authorship attribution. In: Proceedings of the 2005 Joint Conference of the Association for Literary and Linguistic Computing and the Association for Computers and the Humanities, pp. 1–3 (2005)
5. Cristani, M., Roffo, G., Segalin, C., Bazzani, L., Vinciarelli, A., Murino, V.: Conversationally-inspired stylometric features for authorship attribution in instant messaging. In: Proceedings of the 20th ACM International Conference on Multimedia, pp. 1121–1124 (2012)
6. Gamon, M.: Linguistic correlates of style: authorship classification with deep linguistic analysis features. In: Proceedings of the 20th International Conference on Computational Linguistics, pp. 611–617 (2004)
7. Holmes, D.I.: The evolution of stylometry in humanities scholarship. Literary Linguist. Comput. 13(3), 111–117 (1998)
8. Ikonomakis, M., Kotsiantis, S.B., Tampakas, V.: Text classification using machine learning techniques. WSEAS Trans. Comput. 8(4), 966–974 (2005)
9. Inches, G., Harvey, M., Crestani, F.: Finding participants in a chat: authorship attribution for conversational documents. In: International Conference on Social Computing, pp. 272–279 (2013)
10. Jockers, M.L., Witten, D.M.: A comparative study of machine learning methods for authorship attribution. Literary Linguist. Comput. 25, 215–223 (2010)
11. Juola, P.: Future trends in authorship attribution. In: Advances in Digital Forensics III - IFIP International Conference on Digital Forensics, vol. 242, pp. 119–132 (2007)
12. Kapočiūtė-Dzikienė, J., Utka, A., Šarkutė, L.: Feature exploration for authorship attribution of lithuanian parliamentary speeches. In: 17th International Conference on Text, Speech, and Dialogue, pp. 93–100 (2014)
13. Kapočiūtė-Dzikienė, J., Vaassen, F., Daelemans, W., Krupavičius, A.: Improving topic classification for highly inflective languages. In: Proceedings of 24th International Conference on Computational Linguistics, pp. 1393–1410 (2012)
14. Kapočiūtė-Dzikienė, J., Šarkutė, L., Utka, A.: The effect of author set size in authorship attribution for lithuanian. In: NODALIDA: 20th Nordic Conference of Computational Linguistics, pp. 87–96 (2015)
15. Koppel, M., Argamon, S., Shimoni, A.R.: Automatically categorizing written texts by author gender. Literary Linguist. Comput. 17(4), 401–412 (2002)
16. Koppel, M., Schler, J., Argamon, S.: Authorship attribution in the wild. Lang. Resour. Eval. 45(1), 83–94 (2011)
17. Koppel, M., Schler, J., Argamon, S.: Authorship attribution: what's easy and what's hard? J. Law Policy 21, 317–331 (2013)
18. Koppel, M., Schler, J., Argamon, S., Messeri, E.: Authorship attribution with thousands of candidate authors. In: Proceedings of the 29th Annual International ACM SIGIR Conference on Research and Development in Information Retrieval, pp. 659–660 (2006)
19. Koppel, M., Schler, J., Argamon, S., Winter, Y.: The "fundamental problem" of authorship attribution. Engl. Stud. 93(3), 284–291 (2012)
20. Koppel, M., Schler, J., Bonchek-Dokow, E.: Measuring differentiability: unmasking pseudonymous authors. J. Mach. Learn. Res. 8, 1261–1276 (2007)
21. Luyckx, K.: Scalability Issues in Authorship Attribution. Ph.D. thesis, University of Antwerp, Belgium (2010)

22. Luyckx, K., Daelemans, W.: Authorship attribution and verification with many authors and limited data. In: Proceedings of the 22nd International Conference on Computational Linguistics, vol. 1, pp. 513–520 (2008)

23. McNemar, Q.M.: Note on the sampling error of the difference between correlated proportions or percentages. Psychometrika **12**(2), 153–157 (1947)

24. Mendenhall, T.C.: The characteristic curves of composition. Science **9**(214), 237–246 (1887)

25. Mikros, G.K., Argiri, E.K.: Investigating topic influence in authorship attribution. In: Proceedings of the 30th SIGIR, Workshop on Plagiarism Analysis, Authorship Identification, and Near-Duplicate Detection, pp. 29–35 (2007)

26. Mosteller, F., Wallace, D.L.: Inference in an authorship problem. J. Am. Stat. Assoc. **58**(302), 275–309 (1963)

27. Narayanan, A., Paskov, H., Gong, N.Z., Bethencourt, J., Stefanov, E., Shin, E.C.R., Song, D.: On the feasibility of internet-scale author identification. In: Proceedings of the 2012 IEEE Symposium on Security and Privacy, pp. 300–314 (2012)

28. Okuno, S., Asai, H., Yamana, H.: A challenge of authorship identification for ten-thousand-scale microblog users. In: IEEE International Conference on Big Data, pp. 52–54 (2014)

29. Salton, G., Buckley, C.: Term-weighting approaches in automatic text retrieval. Inf. Process. Manage. **24**(5), 513–523 (1988)

30. Sanderson, C., Guenter, S.: Short text authorship attribution via sequence kernels, Markov chains and author unmasking: an investigation. In: Proceedings of the 2006 Conference on Empirical Methods in Natural Language Processing, pp. 482–491 (2006)

31. Savoy, J.: Authorship attribution: a comparative study of three text corpora and three languages. J. Quant. Linguist. **19**(2), 132–161 (2012)

32. Savoy, J.: Authorship attribution based on a probabilistic topic model. Inf. Process. Manage. **49**(1), 341–354 (2013)

33. Schler, J., Koppel, M., Argamon, S., Pennebaker, J.W.: Effects of age and gender on blogging. In: Proceedings of AAAI Spring Symposium on Computational Approaches for Analyzing Weblogs, pp. 199–205 (2006)

34. Schwartz, R., Tsur, O., Rappoport, A., Koppel, M.: Authorship attribution of micro-messages. In: Empirical Methods in Natural Langauge Processing, pp. 1880–1891 (2013)

35. Sebastiani, F.: Machine learning in automated text categorization. ACM Comput. Surv. **34**, 1–47 (2002)

36. Seroussi, Y., Zukerman, I., Bohnert, F.: Authorship attribution with latent Dirichlet allocation. In: Proceedings of the Fifteenth Conference on Computational Natural Language Learning, pp. 181–189 (2011)

37. Solorio, T., Pillay, S., Raghavan, S., Montes-y Gómez, M.: Modality specific meta feature for authorship attribution in web forum posts. In: The 5th International Joint Conference on Natural Language Processing, pp. 156–164 (2011)

38. Sousa Silva, R., Laboreiro, G., Sarmento, L., Grant, T., Oliveira, E., Maia, B.: `twazn me!!!; ('automatic authorship analysis of micro-blogging messages. In: Muñoz, R., Montoyo, A., Métais, E. (eds.) NLDB 2011. LNCS, vol. 6716, pp. 161–168. Springer, Heidelberg (2011)

39. Stamatatos, E.: A survey of modern authorship attribution methods. J. Assoc. Inf. Sci. Technol. **60**(3), 538–556 (2009)

40. Stamatatos, E.: Plagiarism detection using stopword n-grams. J. Am. Soc. Inf. Sci. Technol. **62**(12), 2512–2527 (2011)

41. Stamatatos, E.: On the robustness of authorship attribution based on character n-gram features. J. Law Policy **21**(2), 421–439 (2013)

42. Tan, E., Guo, L., Chen, S., Zhang, X., Zhao, Y.: UNIK: unsupervised social network spam detection. In: Proceedings of the 22nd ACM International Conference on Conference on Information and Knowledge Management, pp. 479–488 (2013)
43. Van Halteren, H., Baayen, R.H., Tweedie, F., Haverkort, M., Neijt, A.: New machine learning methods demonstrate the existence of a human stylome. J. Quant. Linguist. **12**, 65–77 (2005)
44. de Vel, O., Anderson, A.M., Corney, M.W., Mohay, G.M.: Mining e-mail content for author identification forensics. SIGMOD Rec. **30**(4), 55–64 (2001)
45. Zhao, Y., Zobel, J.: Effective and scalable authorship attribution using function words. In: Lee, G.G., Yamada, A., Meng, H., Myaeng, S.-H. (eds.) AIRS 2005. LNCS, vol. 3689, pp. 174–189. Springer, Heidelberg (2005)
46. Zheng, R., Li, J., Chen, H., Huang, Z.: A framework for authorship identification of online messages: writing-style features and classification techniques. J. Am. Soc. Inf. Sci. Technol. **57**(3), 378–393 (2006)
47. Zinkevičius, V.: Lemuoklis – morfologinei analizei [Morphological Analysis with Lemuoklis] (in Lithuanian). Darbai ir dienos **24**, 246–273 (2000)

Lithuanian Digits Recognition by Using Hybrid Approach by Combining Lithuanian Google Recognizer and Some Foreign Language Recognizers

Tomas Rasymas[✉] and Vytautas Rudžionis

Kaunas Faculty, Vilnius University, 8 Muitinės st., Kaunas, Lithuania
{tomas.rasymas,vytautas.rudzionis}@khf.vu.lt

Abstract. In this paper we are presenting our results obtained by experimenting with different classification methods which are suitable for creating hybrid speech recognizer. We tried to create Lithuanian digits recognizer which is capable of producing more than 95 % accuracy. Classification methods that were used are: k-Nearest neighbors (5, 11, 15, and 21), Linear Discriminant Analysis, Quadratic Discriminant Analysis, Logistic Regression, Naïve Bayes, Support Vectors classifier. Experiments were taken using five foreign recognizers: English, Russian, two German and Google recognizer for Lithuanian language. Best results were received when Naïve Bayes classifier was used – 97.51 %. Average accuracy of single recognizers: English – 84.9 %, Russian – 80.6 %, German I – 63 %, German II – 81.4 % and Google recognizer – 82.6 %. By using hybrid approach accuracy was increased by 12.61 % compared with best single recognizer result.

Keywords: Hybrid speech recognition · Lithuanian digits recognition · Foreign language adaptation

1 Introduction

It is well known fact that speech recognition based interfaces could be a great value in many applications. Particular benefits could be achieved by disabled people or people working in areas where huge degree of freedom for control and input is needed. Digits recognition is a common task many applications, for example person ID code recognition, phone number recognition, catalog numbers recognition and etc. This is typical task for digits recognition.

The development of any speech recognition systems requires enormous resources: both material and human. It is difficult to gather such resources in a countries were relatively not widely spoken languages are used as a primary tool for communication. One of the solutions to solve that problem is to take other languages speech recognizers and adapt them for our needs. In other words, we need to create a hybrid recognizer which is based on several adapted recognizers. The main point of hybrid recognition is a parallel use of several different recognizers expecting at least one of the recognizers will produce correct result [3, 4, 6]. Hybrid approach is one of the ways to achieve

G. Dregvaite and R. Damasevicius (Eds.): ICIST 2015, CCIS 538, pp. 449–459, 2015.
DOI: 10.1007/978-3-319-24770-0_38

higher recognition accuracy of speech processing system. This implies combination of hypotheses provided by different recognition systems in order to get higher recognition accuracy. Currently hybrid speech recognition systems most often are using several methods to combine the results: if-then rules, maximum likelihood selection as well as discriminant analysis [3, 4, 6].

The idea of creating hybrid speech recognizer and adapting other languages acoustic models is not new. These kinds of researches are especially important for all under resourced languages. There were successful attempts to estimate acoustic models for new target language using speech data from varied source languages, but only limited data from the target language [9]. Also, Google researchers show very promising results in transformation of English to other languages such as Lithuanian, French and so on. What is more, researchers are experimenting with different acoustic models adaptation methods in order to maximize the recognition performance with small amount of non-native data available [10]. Statistical algorithms for combining different acoustic models are used quite often and produces promising results [3, 4, 6, 11, 12]. These researches shows, that in many cases it is possible to achieve high enough recognition accuracy by using hybrid systems with adapted acoustic models.

This paper presents our activities to create hybrid speech recognizer, which is capable of recognizing Lithuanian digits from 0 to 9 with more than 95 %. For creating hybrid speech recognition system we used four foreign languages recognizers: Russian (RU), English (EN), German I (DE_I) and German II (DE_II) and one recent Google recognizer for Lithuanian language (GO). By creating hybrid speech recognizer we also evaluated recent Google recognizer for Lithuanian language. In order to combine results of different speech recognizers, we used most popular classifiers: k-Nearest neighbors (5, 11, 15, and 21), Linear Discriminant Analysis, Quadratic Discriminant Analysis, Logistic Regression, Naïve Bayes, Support Vectors classifier.

2 Architecture of Hybrid Speech Recognition System

Proposed hybrid system architecture consists of four parts: recording the speech, passing speech to all recognizers in parallel, recognizing the speech, gathering results from recognizers and passing results to trained classifier. Block diagram of that system is displayed in Fig. 1.

Speech signal from microphone is recorded and then passed to all hybrid systems recognizers in parallel. Only best hypothesis from every recognizer was used. When best hypothesis from all recognizers are received, they are passed to trained classifier which makes the final prediction.

To develop speech recognizers, PocketSphinx toolkit was used. PocketSphinx is a lightweight speech recognition engine, specifically tuned for handheld and mobile devices, though it works equally well on the desktop computers and notebooks. It is distributed under the same permissive license as Sphinx toolkit itself. Algorithmically this is hidden Markov model based speech recognition framework which provides simple way for creating custom speech recognition systems. For the quicker classification methods realization we used scikit-learn library [7]. Scikit-learn is an open source machine learning library for the Python programming language. It realizes

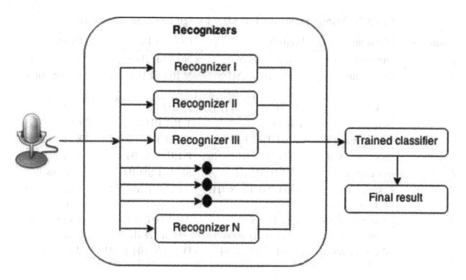

Fig. 1. Block diagram of hybrid speech recognition system

various classification, regression and clustering algorithms, including support vector machines, logistic regression, naïve Bayes, random forests, gradient boosting, k-means and is designed to interoperate with the Python numerical and scientific libraries NumPy and SciPy [8].

3   Foreign Language Speech Recognizers

In order to use foreign language acoustic models we must adapt them to recognize Lithuanian language. Adaptation is done by transcribing Lithuanian commands by using foreign language phonemes [1, 2, 5]. As mentioned earlier, in order to create hybrid speech recognition system, we will be using four foreign language acoustic models: Russian[1], English[2], German I[3] and German II[4]. Commands transcriptions, used to adapt selected foreign language recognizers, are displayed in Table 1.

These transcriptions where obtained experimentally, by checking which of the foreign language phoneme best fits Lithuanian ones. All transcribing rules are listed in Table 2.

As we can see, almost all letters in Lithuanian language has matching phonemes in foreign languages, except letters 'c', 'č', 'ė', 'j' which phonemes were selected by

---

[1] Downloaded from: http://sourceforge.net/projects/cmusphinx/files/Acoustic%20and%20Language%20Models/Russian%20Voxforge/.

[2] Downloaded from: http://sourceforge.net/projects/cmusphinx/files/Acoustic%20and%20Language%20Models/English%20Voxforge/.

[3] Downloaded from: http://goofy.zamia.org/voxforge/de/.

[4] Downloaded from: https://www.lt.informatik.tu-darmstadt.de/de/data/open-acoustic-models/.

Table 1. Transcriptions used to adapt foreign language recognizers

Command	Russian	English	German I	German II
0	nn uu ll ii ss	N UH L IH S	N UU L IH S	nn uu l ii s
1	v i ae nn a ss	V IY AE N AH S	V IIH EEH N AH S	v ii ee: nn a s
2	d uu	D UH	D UU	d uu
3	t rr yy ss	T R IY S	T RR IIH S	t r i: s
4	kk e t uu rr ii	K EH T UH R IH	K EH T UU RR IH	k ee t uu r ii
5	pp e nn kk ii	P EH N K IH	P EH N K IH	p ee nn k ii
6	sh e sh ii	SH EH SH IH	SH EH SH IH	ss ee ss ii
7	ss e pp t yy nn ii	S EH P T IY N IH	S EH P T IIH N IH	s ee p t i: nn ii
8	a sh t uu oo nn ii	AH SH T UW AO N IH	AH SH T Y OOH N IH	a ss t uu oo nn ii
9	d e v yy nn ii	D EH V IY N IH	D EH V IIH N IH	d ee v i: nn ii

similarity to other phonemes. There are only two diphthongs 'ie' and 'uo' in command set so only for those diphthongs transcribing rules were generated.

4   Google Recognizer for Lithuanian Language

We want to except Google recognizer for Lithuanian language and analyze it a little bit deeper. This year Google announced about speech recognizer for Lithuanian language. As we know, Google uses speech recognition in almost all it's products: Android OS, Chrome browser, search engine, etc. so languages such as English, Japanese, Russian, German and few other are recognized very well, because these languages has a huge market potential and Google is putting a lot of resources to make it better. For under resourced languages creating a good speech recognizer has no market potential. So create recognizer from scratch is not useful. Better way is to adapt already trained acoustic models. As we guessed, Google recorded some training data and retrained one of foreign language recognizer.

For our Lithuanian digits recognition experiments we recorded 1790 recordings and tested all recognizers. Top 3 Google recognizer incorrect recognized commands are displayed in Table 3.

As we can see, some English commands were recognized: 'fishki', 'ryanas', 'video', so we can make prediction, that English acoustic model was retrained for Lithuanian language recognition. Quantities of correct recognized commands are displayed in Table 4.

Number 8 was recognized very poorly. We think, that one of the reasons why Google recognizer produces incorrect results may be that recognition text is influenced by search results. For example, when command "8" is recognized, Google searches the web for that command and in our case produces very popular game site "www.y8.com".

Table 2. Transcribing rules used for foreign language recognizers adaptation

Lithuanian sound	Russian phoneme	English phoneme	German I phoneme	German II phoneme
a	a	AH	AH	a
ą	aa	AA	AAH	aa:
b	b	B	B	b
c	s	S	S	cc
č	ch	CH	X	cc
d	d	D	D	d
e	e	EH	EH	ee
ė	ae	EY	EEH	ee:
ę	ee	EY	EEH	ee:
f	f	F	F	f
g	gg, g	G	G	g
h	hh	HH	HH, CH	h
i	ii	IH	IH	ii
į	yy	IY	IIH	i:
y	yy	IY	IIH	i:
k	kk	K	K	k
l	ll	L	L	l
j	j	Y	Y	j
m	mm	M	M	m
n	nn	N	N	nn
o	oo	OW, OY	OO, OOOH	oo, o:
p	pp	P	P	p
r	rr	R	RR	r
s	ss	S	S	s
š	sh	SH	SH	ss
t	t	T	T	t
u	uu	UH	UU	uu
ų	ur	UW	UUH	uu:
ū	ur	UW	UUH	uu:
v	v	V	V	v
z	z	Z	Z	s
ž	zh	ZH	ZH	z
ie	i ae	IY AE	IIH EEH	ii ee:
uo	uu oo	UW AO	Y OOH	uu oo

5 Hybrid Speech Recognition System Experimental Evaluation

Proposed hybrid speech recognition systems accuracy was evaluated by using Windows 7 based laptop computer (Core i5 CPU, 4 Gb of RAM). Main speech corpus containing 10 digits names were used. Purposed corpus was gathered by recording

Table 3. Google recognizer for Lithuanian language recognition errors

Command	Quantity of miss recognized commands	Recognized text
0	38	dalis
0	10	noriu
0	7	žolės
1	34	diana
1	7	viena
1	5	ryanas
2	3	dujos
2	1	tele2
2	1	s2
3	1	tai
3	1	zvejys
3	1	try
4	2	turi
5	3	lenkija
5	3	iki
5	3	5a
6	8	sesija
6	7	6a
6	4	fishki
7	9	7a
7	3	septynis
7	1	video
8	1730	y8
8	6	8a
8	1	aštuonis
9	1010	(no results produced)
9	10	99
9	6	9a

Table 4. Quantity of correct recognized commands

Command	0	1	2	3	4	5	6	7	8	9
Quantity	1430	1665	1262	1705	1769	1756	1744	1751	48	1750

speech of random people. Every digit name was pronounced for 1790 times. 1000 recordings were used for classifiers training, 790 recordings were used for testing. Not all recordings were recognized by any recognizer. Detailed information on numbers of recordings used for testing and training are displayed in Table 5. Columns "Testing not recognized" and "Training not recognized" are listing number of recordings that were not recognized by any recognizer and were omitted in further training and testing.

First of all single recognizers were evaluated. Results are displayed in Fig. 2.

Table 5. Numbers of recordings used for training and testing classifiers

Command	Testing not recognized	Training not recognized	Total for testing	Total for training
0	1	3	789	997
1	7	4	783	996
2	3	8	787	992
3	1	1	789	999
4	1	1	789	999
5	0	3	790	997
6	1	5	789	995
7	0	0	790	1000
8	1	1	789	999
9	0	0	790	1000

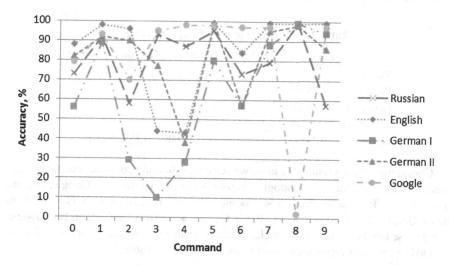

Fig. 2. Single command accuracy of single recognizers

As results show, obtained results are correlated. Few recognizers show very low accuracy in certain command recognition: German I recognizing "2", "3", "4" and Google recognizing "8". Average accuracy of single recognizer is displayed in Table 6.

As we can see, adapted English recognizer shows best result – almost 85 %. Google recognizer shows good result too – almost 83 %. We think these two recognizers achieved best results because of Lithuanian language specific and number of data used for acoustic models training. Before the experiments, we thought that Russian recognizer will be one of the best, because Russian language and Lithuanian language have a lot similar sounds, but as results shows, our guess failed. Worst results obtained by using German I – 63 %. This recognizer was outperformed by all the rest recognizers mainly because of small number of training data used for acoustic model training.

Table 6. Average acuracy of single recognizers

Recognizer	Average accuracy, %
Russian	80.6
English	84.9
German I	63
German II	81.4
Google	82.6

In order to create a hybrid speech recognizer, we need to find the best combinations of speech recognizers that produces highest results. For that purpose, correlation between all single speech recognizers results were calculated. Correlation indicates the strength and direction of a linear relationship between two variables. Correlation results are presented in Table 7. Recognizers which have biggest correlation difference will be tested with proposed method.

Table 7. Correlation results of single recognizers

	Russian	English	German I	German II	Google
Russian	1				
English	−0.257687	1			
German I	0.096511	0.796267	1		
German II	0.076148	0.754907	0.578372	1	
Google	−0.258597	−0.280868	−0.279548	−0.35579	1

Considering the correlation results, we selected following combinations for testing: Russian + English, Russian + Google, English + Google, German I + Google, German II + Google, Russian + English + Google, English + German II + Google, Russian + German II + Google and Russian + English + German I + German II + Google. Using these combinations different classification methods were trained and tested using selected corpus and recordings. Results are displayed in Table 8.

Table 8. Combined recognizers evaluation

	k-Nearest neighbors (5)	k-Nearest neighbors (11)	k-Nearest neighbors (15)	k-Nearest neighbors (21)	LDA	QDA	Logistic Regression	Naïve Bayes	SVC
RU + EN	92.66	93.81	94.11	94.17	94.37	94.75	93.43	94.49	94.21
RU + GO	93.25	93.83	94.33	94.70	96.83	95.17	95.24	95.28	94.91
EN + GO	94.75	95.28	95.48	95.53	94.42	96.36	96.28	96.45	95.49
DE_I + GO	94.42	95.17	95.25	95.36	95.00	95.35	95.46	95.40	95.34
DE_II + GO	93.03	94.30	94.40	94.75	95.95	96.12	95.22	96.18	94.85
RU + EN + GO	95.67	96.08	96.21	96.21	97.30	96.81	96.85	96.57	95.96
EN + DE_II + GO	95.13	95.63	95.57	95.81	94.05	96.32	95.24	96.57	95.74
RU + DE_II + GO	94.16	94.52	94.66	94.96	95.95	95.93	95.25	96.16	95.03
RU + EN + DE_II + GO	95.81	96.15	96.21	96.32	96.09	96.70	95.95	96.61	95.72
EN + DE_I + DE_II + GO	96.09	96.61	96.50	96.43	93.87	96.93	95.96	96.88	96.00
RU + DE_I + DE_II + GO	95.65	95.98	96.05	96.04	96.06	95.93	95.18	95.64	95.46
RU + EN + DE_I + DE_II	94.30	94.63	94.86	95.13	93.21	95.29	92.55	95.27	94.11
RU + EN + DE_I + DE_II + GO	96.73	96.74	96.83	96.90	96.00	96.98	96.28	97.51	96.18

Best result of 97.51 % was acquired when all foreign language recognizers and Naïve Bayes classifier was used. By using Russian, English and Google recognizers we achieved 97.30 % accuracy. We increased recognition accuracy by 12.61 % compared by best single recognizer. It is very interesting, that such a simple classifier as Naïve Bayes generated the best results. We think that it is because of data used to evaluate selected classification methods. As we know Naïve Bayes classifier requires a small amount of training data to estimate the necessary parameters. We are planning to increase number of data used for classification methods evaluation and repeat experiments to see if our guess is right.

Average accuracy of every hybrid system is displayed in Fig. 3.

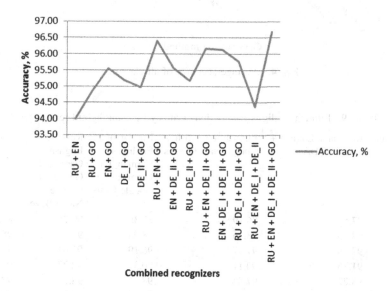

Fig. 3. Average accuracy of combined recognizers

Comparing different combinations of speech recognizers, best average accuracy was acquired by using all five recognizers – 96.69 % and Russian + English + Google recognizers – 96.41 %. As results shows, almost all recognizers achieved accuracy greater than 95 %.

Average accuracy of all classifiers is displayed in Fig. 4.

As comparing average accuracy of classifiers, best results were acquired when Naïve Bayes classifier was used – 96.08 %. When QDA was used we achieved 96.05 % accuracy.

Finally, best two classifiers and best two foreign language combinations were selected and analyzed deeper. Highest classification results were obtained by using QDA and Naïve Bayes classifiers and highest recognition accuracy was obtained by using English + Russian + German I + German II + Google and Russian + English + Google hybrid recognizers. Analyzes results are displayed in Table 9.

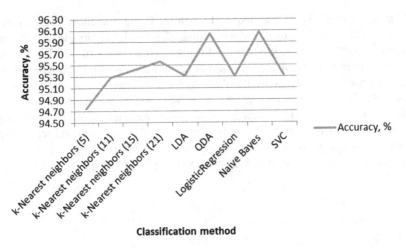

Classification method

Fig. 4. Average accuracy of all classifiers.

Table 9. Lithuanian digits recognition accuracy by using hybrid recognizers

Command	Russian + English + Google QDA	Russian + English + Google Naïve Bayes	Russian + English + German_I + German_II + Google QDA	Russian + English + German_I + German_II + Google Naïve Bayes	Avg.
0	87.58	86.19	89.35	90.75	**88.47**
1	98.46	98.46	98.98	98.98	**98.72**
2	97.08	97.97	96.19	97.84	**97.27**
3	91.76	90.11	90.37	92.27	**91.13**
4	98.22	97.84	98.86	98.98	**98.48**
5	99.87	99.62	99.75	99.87	**99.78**
6	97.20	97.58	97.32	97.58	**97.42**
7	99.36	99.49	99.87	99.74	**99.62**
8	99.37	99.11	99.62	99.62	**99.43**
9	99.24	99.37	99.49	99.49	**99.40**

As results shows, commands "0" and "3" were recognized with accuracy under 95 %. These results can depend on few factors: quality of transcriptions used for recognizers adaptation and Lithuanian language specifics. In the future, we are planning to experiment more on search of better transcriptions for foreign language adaptation. We think with correct transcriptions it is possible to increase these two commands recognition accuracy. All other commands are recognized with more than 97 %.

6 Conclusions

The results of our experiments showed that it is quite reasonable to use hybrid speech recognizer by combining different speech recognizers. We achieved 97.51 % accuracy in Lithuanian digits recognition. Comparing best single recognizer and best hybrid recognizer average error was decreased by 12.61 %. These experiments also demonstrated that it is possible to adapt foreign language acoustic models for Lithuanian language recognition using transcriptions. Best recognition accuracy was obtained by using hybrid recognizers with combined Russian + English + Google and Russian + English + German I + German II + Google and using QDA and Naïve Bayes classifiers.

References

1. Maskeliūnas, R., Rudžionis, A., Ratkevičius, K., Rudžionis, V.: Investigation of foreign languages models for lithuanian speech recognition. Electron. Electr. Eng. 3(91), 15–20 (2009)
2. Rudžionis, V., Raškinis, G., Rudžionis, A., Ratkevičius, K.: Comparative analysis of adapted foreign language and native Lithuanian speech recognizers for voice user interface. Electron. Electr. Eng. 19(7), 90–93 (2013)
3. Rudžionis, V., Raškinis, G., Rudžionis, A., Ratkevičius, K., Bartišiūtė, G.: Web services based hybrid recognizer of Lithuanian voice commands. Electron. Electr. Eng. 20(9), 50–53 (2014)
4. Rasymas, T., Rudžionis, V.: Combining multiple foreign language speech recognizers by using neural networks. In: Human Language Technologies – The Baltic Perspective, pp. 33–39. IOS Press, Amsterdam (2014). doi:10.3233/978-1-61499-442-8-33
5. Kasparaitis, P.: Lithuanian speech recognition using the English recognizer. Informatica 19(4), 505–516 (2008)
6. Rudžionis, V., Ratkevičius, K., Rudžionis, A., Raškinis, G., Maskeliunas, R.: Recognition of voice commands using hybrid approach. In: Skersys, T., Butleris, R., Butkiene, R. (eds.) ICIST 2013. CCIS, vol. 403, pp. 249–260. Springer, Heidelberg (2013)
7. Huggins-Daines, D., Kumar, M., Chan, A., Block, A.W., Ravishankar, M., Rudnicky, A.I.: Pocketsphinx: a free, real-time continuous speech recognition system for hand-held devices. In: IEEE ICASSP 2006 Proceedings, vol. 1, pp. 185–188 (2006)
8. Pedregosa, F., Varoquaux, G., Gramfort, A., Michel, V., Thirion, B., Grisel, O., Blondel, M., Prettenhofer, P., Weiss, R., Dubourg, V., Vanderplas, J., Passos, A., Cournapeau, D., Brucher, M., Perrot, M., Duchesnay, E.: Scikit-learn: machine learning in python. J. Mach. Learn. Res. 12, 2825–2830 (2011)
9. Schultz, T., Waibel, A.: Language-independent and language-adaptive acoustic modeling for speech recognition. Speech Commun. 35(1), 31–52 (2001)
10. Wang, Z., Schultz, T., Waibel, A.: Comparison of acoustic model adaptation techniques on non-native speech. In: IEEE International Conference on Acoustics, Speech, and Signal Processing (ICASSP), pp. 540–543 (2003)
11. Meneido, H., Neto, J.: Combination of acoustic models in continuous speech recognition hybdrid systems. Proc. Int. Conf. Spoken Lang. Process. 9, 1000–1029 (2000)
12. Bahi, H., Sellami, M.: A hybrid approach for Arabic speech recognition. In: ACS/IEEE International Conference on Computer Systems and Applications (2003)

Text Predictor for Lithuanian Language

Julius Gelšvartas[1(✉)], Rimvydas Simutis[1], and Rytis Maskeliūnas[2]

[1] Automation Department, Faculty of Electrical and Electronics Engineering,
Kaunas University of Technology, Kaunas, Lithuania
`julius.gelsvartas@ktu.edu`
[2] Department of Multimedia Engineering, Faculty of Informatics,
Kaunas University of Technology, Kaunas, Lithuania

Abstract. This paper describes the architecture of the open source text prediction package Presage. We trained the n-gram model used in the text predictor for Lithuanian language. The predictor was trained and evaluated using sixteen Lithuanian literature books. Each book was split into training and test sets containing 30 % and 70 % of words. The trained text predictor was integrated into a multifunctional user interface for disabled people to improve the text input speed.

Keywords: Text prediction · Word prediction · User interface

1 Introduction

People with disabilities usually have difficulty communicating. Assistive technologies that enable disabled people to communicate can greatly improve their quality of life. Most of the assistive technologies have specialized software packages that help the patients to communicate. Text predictor is a very important component of such software package because it can greatly enhance the text input rate [1]. Text predictor is a system that predicts the next block of characters (letters, syllables, words, sentences, etc.) that the user wants to enter. These software packages are however usually only available in English or other widely used languages. We used the open source package Presage [2] to create a Lithuanian text prediction component. This component was integrated into a multifunctional user interface for disabled people [3].

To make a useful prediction an accurate language model is necessary. There are a lot of different strategies that can be used to represent, train and use the language model. An in depth review of different prediction techniques and their evaluation can be found in [4]. Historically word predictors used word frequencies model to calculate the predictions [5]. Such predictor calculates the most probable word given the characters that the user has already entered. These systems were used because they were easy to implement and train. Word frequency model however assumes that each word is typed independently.

The assumption made by the word frequency model is of course not true. Each word in a sentence is closely related to the words that precede it. This relationship can be modeled using the N-gram language models [2]. N-gram model records not only the probabilities of single words but also the relationships between two or more words. Such model is still relatively easy to implement and train. The cardinality N of the model

G. Dregvaite and R. Damasevicius (Eds.): ICIST 2015, CCIS 538, pp. 460–468, 2015.
DOI: 10.1007/978-3-319-24770-0_39

determines the maximal number of words that are used to calculate the new prediction. For example, when a model with $N = 3$ cardinality is used two previously entered words are taken into account when predicting the current word. Note that a model with $N = 1$ cardinality is identical to word frequency model.

The N-gram model however has several limitations. The predictor completely ignores words that are outside the model cardinality. For example, when model cardinality is three and the user has already entered four words the prediction of the new word is calculated only taking two last words into account. Another limitation is that the model cannot differentiate similar phrases when the word order is changed. For example, phrases 'a beautiful girl' and 'girl is beautiful' are considered different although they are semantically very similar.

More advanced text predictors can be created using syntactic and semantic language models. Some of these methods use N-gram models but add some additional processing steps [6]. Latent Semantic analysis methods have been shown to have improved performance over N-gram model [7]. More complex text predictors use classification methods [8] or continuous space language models [9]. These methods usually produce better predictions but are more difficult to implement and require more computational resources. Moreover constructing such models is difficult and requires manually labeled data whereas N-gram model can be trained from a regular text samples.

An important property of any text prediction package is its ability to learn. Each user has a unique writing style. Text predictor has to collect the statistics of the text that the user has already entered to adapt to each individual user. This statistics adds the learning capabilities to the system. Such system can learn new words that were not present in the initial language model. Learning makes it possible to improve even an imperfect model by using and updating it over time. Updating a complex model online is however difficult or even impossible.

In this paper we describe the text predictor that was trained to predict Lithuanian language. Section 2 provides the overview of the text predictor system. The software architecture of the text predictor is described in Sect. 3. Section 4 describes text predictor integration with multifunctional user interface. The training data used for the predictor is described in Sect. 5. The text predictor training results are provided in Sect. 5 and conclusions in Sect. 6.

2   Text Predictor System

We chose Presage intelligent text prediction system for training the Lithuanian text predictor. The main advantage of Presage is its open source nature, multilingual support and portability. Presage is free software licensed under the GPL. It is developed in C++ and uses cross-platform libraries to ensure portability. The predictor system supports multiple languages but there is no Lithuanian language support in the system. New languages can be added to existing predictors by providing suitable training data. New predictor plug-in can also easily be implemented to account for a language specific semantics.

The input for the Presage predictor is a sequence of characters (context) that the user has already entered in the graphical user interface. The predictor output is a list of predicted words (suggestions). Suggestions are updated each time when the user enters new characters or selects one of the predicted words. When a suggestion is selected it is added to the current context replacing any characters that have already been entered for last word. In this case suggestions will be the words that are most likely to follow the last entered word.

Presage is designed to be easily integrated into any system. The system has a simple and well defined interface. Presage hides the complexity of the prediction mechanisms from the system integrator. This enables the client application to request a prediction by simply invoking a function that returns a list of predictions. Only characters entered by the user are required to make the predictions.

Another advantage of Presage is the modular architecture of the system. All the modules in the system have a high degree of decoupling. Modules are only dependant on the interfaces of other modules. The internal structure of each module can therefore be easily changed without changing other modules.

Plug-in architecture of the system allows having multiple predictors running simultaneously. Each predictor is implemented as a plug-in. There are plug-ins that implement the statistical predictions, semantic predictions, abbreviation expansions, repeating predictions suppression, etc. This architecture makes it easy to add new plug-ins. Plug-ins can contain new prediction mechanisms or add language specific predictors. The activated plug-in also determines the behavior of the system. The system could be configured to only be a simple abbreviation expansion predictor or a complete system of probabilistic-syntactic-semantic predictors. Plug-ins can even be inserted and removed at runtime, to change the behavior of the system on the fly. Adding a new plug-in does not require the recompilation of the whole system. Each active plug-in is executed concurrently in a separate thread. This reduces the time required to produce predictions and increase responsiveness of the system.

Presage is able to operate in a multi-user environment. User management is integrated into the system and not delegated to the operating system. The system creates a profile for each user of the system. The history of predictions used for training the system is stored in this profile. Every aspect of system is configurable to meet the needs of each user. Configurable properties are stored in XML format for easier management and portability.

3   Presage Architecture

The internal mechanisms of the Presage predictor are exposed to the outside by the main predictor class. Each time a user enters a new character the prediction method is called with the sequence of already entered characters and the predictor returns the list of suggestions. Calls to predict method also update the internal state of the system. All other modules discussed above are part of the main predictor. The class diagram of the Presage system can be seen in Fig. 1.

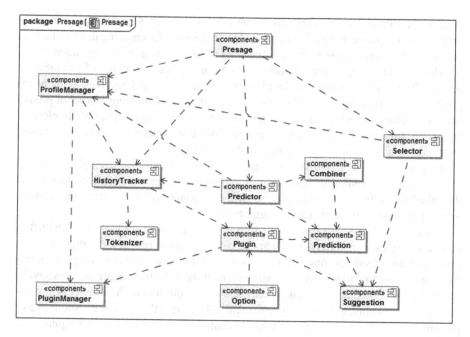

Fig. 1. Class diagram of the Presage system.

The core objects that are used within the Presage module are the suggestions and the predictions. Suggestion is any word that is returned by one of prediction plug-ins plus the probability of this word being the one that the user desired. Suggestion objects are the fundamental building blocks of the system. Most system components manipulate Suggestion objects. The other fundamental objects of the system are Prediction objects. Prediction is a collection object storing multiple suggestions. The suggestion objects of each prediction are sorted by their probability from most likely to least likely. Other objects of the system are history tracker, predictor, combiner, plug-in, selector, profile manager and plug-in manager.

The history tracker module provides two important services, namely is responsible for keeping track of the user interactions and provides essential services for the other system components. In the field of word prediction, the term history indicates the content that the user has previously entered. The history is essential to make an informed prediction. The History tracker module stores the text in two text buffers, namely the pastBuffer and the futureBuffer. pastBuffer contains all characters entered by the user that come before the insertion point of the current text, while futureBuffer contains previously entered characters that follow the current insertion point. The futureBuffer is necessary because the user is not constrained to compose text linearly. This is mainly used when the user wants to append words within already entered text.

Predictor is the component that exposes the Presage interface. It supervises the concurrent execution of prediction plug-ins and combines the returned predictions (using Combiner) and passes the resulting predictions to the Selector object. The number of predictor plug-ins is not known in advance and is configurable by the user. When the system starts Predictor initializes all the plug-ins and makes sure that each plug-in is executed in a separate thread. Predictor is also responsible for ensuring that during each prediction iteration plug-in runtime is bounded to some configurable time interval.

The Combiner object is responsible for combining the information from different sources (Plug-ins). Combiner is invoked by the Predictor and receives as input the predictions returned by all the Plug-ins. The output of the Combiner is a set of predictions. Combiner provides a common interface and the system has multiple implementations of this interface, namely linear interpolation, backoff, maximum entropy. Detailed explanation of these methods can be found in [2].

Plug-ins are the modules that perform suggestion calculations. Each plug-in implements a different prediction mechanism. Plug-ins use the language models to perform the calculations. In other words, plug-ins use the services offered by the other components of the system to calculate the suggestions.

Selector module selects suggestions from the prediction set that are provided as output to the user of the system. This step is necessary because the prediction set containing all the suggestions might be much larger than the number of suggestions that the user is expecting to receive. The parameters of the Selector module are managed by Profile manager module. The main parameters of the selector are the number of suggestions that this module should return and a flag indicating if the same suggestions can be proposed again. The former feature is implemented in selector module by keeping track of all the suggestions that already have been provided to the user.

The Profile manager module manages user profiles. Each user of the system can have one or more profiles. This makes it possible to use the system for multiple languages or easily enable and disable system features. The user can choose a particular plug-in at system startup or later during the program execution. All the information about a profile is stored in an XML format file.

The last module of the system is the Plug-in manager. This module has the following responsibilities: detecting available plug-ins in the system, dynamically loading plug-in libraries, instantiation and initialization of a plug-in, registering active plug-ins in the Predictor, unregistering and deallocation of the plug-in and unloading dynamic libraries. The available plug-ins are detected by scanning the dedicated plug-in directory. New plug-ins are added by copying the dynamic library containing the plug-in into this folder.

4   Multifunctional User Interface Integration

The presage predictor was integrated into the text input screen of the graphical user interface (GUI) software package for disabled people. The system integrates several input devices, namely the brain computer interface device, speech recognition device, sip/puff device and eye tracking device. The devices are chosen for each person individually based on their physical ability. The system can be configured to use a particular input device or even several devices simultaneously. The GUI is controlled using two input signals, namely selecting the current item and moving to the next item. Text input screen uses these signals to select the current letter in the GUI or move to the next letter. Sometimes users with severe disabilities can only generate a single input signal. In these situations the user input signal is mapped to the item selection signal and the moving to next item signal is changed to the timer signal that executes the moving action periodically. The text input GUI system diagram is provided in Fig. 2.

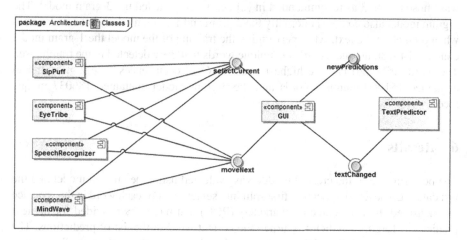

Fig. 2. The text input GUI system diagram.

The GUI contains the already entered text area, the current word predictions area and the keyboard layout area. We currently have two keyboard layouts, the standard QWERTY keyboard and the T9 keyboard. When using QWERTY keyboard the user has to perform more 'select next' actions and T9 keyboard requires more 'select current' actions. The predictions area is provided above the keyboard list. Predictions area is accessed after going through all of the keyboard keys and vice versa.

The text area shows the text that the user has already entered. Each time a user enters a new character the text area is updated and the text predictor is invoked with the currently entered text. The calculated suggestions are sent back to the GUI and the predictions list is updated accordingly. If user chooses one of the predictions the remaining letters of the current word are added to the text area and the text predictor is called again to suggest new words.

5 Model Training

The training data consisted of 16 Lithuanian literature books. The full dataset contains around 606000 words. The dataset was split into the training set containing 30 % or 202000 words (18363 sentences) and the test set containing 70 % or 404000 words (44642 sentences). Each author has a unique writing style. We took this into account when constructing the training and the test data sets. Each book was individually split into the training set and the test set. The full data sets were constructed by concatenating the data sets obtained from each book. This technique allowed creating a dataset that contains the writing styles of all the 16 book authors. The size of the book was however not taken into account.

The training data set was used to create the N-gram text predictor model. The N-gram models can be created automatically from the training data by recording the number of occurrences of unique data records. The cardinality parameter of the model was chosen to be 3 as recommended in [2] i.e. we constructed the 3-gram model. The 3-gram model also contains internally the 2-gram and 1-gram models that are also used when predicting the text. After performing the training of the model the 1-gram model contained 40736 unique records i.e. unique words that were detected in the training set. The word "ir" (and) had the highest count of 6872 occurrences. The 2-gram model contained 151060 unique records and the 3-gram model contained 186037 unique records.

6   Results

The performance of the created model was evaluated using the created model and the test data set. The test data set was first split into sentences. For each word in the sentence we measured the percentage of characters (POC) that had to be provided for the text predictor before the predictor returned the correct word in the list of predictions. The online learning capability of the system was disabled during the evaluation. The parameter controlling the suggestion repetition was set to true i.e. same suggestions can be offered in subsequent predictions. For each evaluated word the predictor was given up to two words preceding the predicted word. This was done to make sure that the predictor can use the model with cardinality of 3 when calculating new word predictions.

For example, we have a test sentence "Peter is my friend". When calculating the POC of word "Peter" the letters of this word are given one by one to the text predictor until the predictor returns the currently evaluated word or all letters of the word are provided to the predictor. If the predictor returns "Peter" after receiving "Pet" as an input the POC of this word is 60 %. When POC of the word "my" is calculated the predictor is first provided with the following input: "Peter is". In this case the predictor might return word "my" in a first prediction and the POC would be set to 0 %. Note that lower POC is better. Lastly when predicting the word "friend" the predictor will only receive "is my" as an input for the first prediction iteration. In this case there is no way for the 3-gram model to take word "Peter" into account when calculating the prediction of the word "friend".

After calculating the POC of each word in the test data set we calculated the total percent of characters (TPOC) for the Lithuanian text predictor using the (1).

$$TPOC = \frac{\sum_{i=1}^{n} POC_i \times nch_i}{\sum_{i=1}^{n} nch_i} \tag{1}$$

Here nch_i is the number of characters of the i-th word in the test data set and n is number of words in the test data set. We weighted the POC of each word according the number of characters of that word. This is done to show that POC of 50 % for a 6 character word is a lot better than the POC of 50 % for a 2 character word. In the former case the user could avoid typing 3 characters whereas in the later case the user only avoids typing 1 character.

We evaluated the TPOC of the text predictor for different number of suggestions (NOS) per prediction. The NOS parameter was varied from one to seven. The TPOC chart can be seen in Fig. 3.

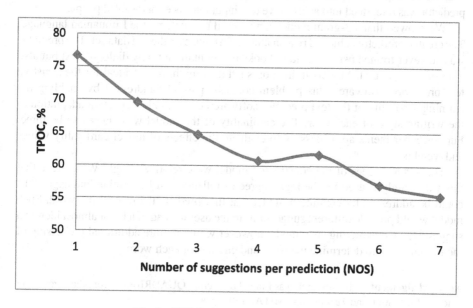

Fig. 3. TPOC of Lithuanian text predictor.

We can see that the TPOC of the predictor is directly related to NOS parameter. Increasing NOS parameter also increases the probability that at least one of the suggestions is going to match the word that we are currently trying. High NOS values however increase the computation time of the system and the user has to perform more actions to select the desired prediction from the list.

Experiments to evaluate the impact of the model cardinality were also performed. We trained two additional models, namely 2-gram and 4-gram. These models were tested with NOS parameter set to 6 suggestions. The TPOC of both models was very close to the TPOC of the 3-gram model. This could be explained by the fact that we only changed the cardinality of the model but did not find optimal weights for each cardinality class of the model.

The relatively high TPOC of the predictor could be explained by the high level of inflection in Lithuanian language. Lithuanian nouns have 7 singular cases and 7 plural cases. Each case usually has identical word root part and different word endings. For example word "namas" (house) would be "name" (in the house) in the different case. To predict this word correctly the user has to enter the majority of the letters. Verb inflictions add additional complexity for the predictor.

7 Conclusions

This paper describes the architecture of the text prediction package Presage. We created the Lithuanian language 3-gram model that can be used by the text predictor. The text predictor was integrated into an assistive text input interface for disabled people.

We showed that a 3-gram model can be used to represent the Lithuanian language. The created predictor achieved reasonable performance on the test data set. The predictor was however trained using literature books that contain not only dialogue text but also a lot of narrator text. Models trained on such data might not be ideal for the assistive text prediction software. This problem could be partially addressed by enabling the learning capability of the text predictor software i.e. the models constant adaptation to the writing style of each user. The cardinality of the model was chosen to be three. Further experiments are necessary to evaluate the effects of model cardinality values and weights.

The TPOC values of the constructed model were relatively high. We believe that this was mainly caused by the high degree of inflection in Lithuanian language. This could be addressed by creating a model that first predicts the root of the word. Such model would provide different suggestions to the user instead of a lot of almost identical suggestions. Constructing such model however would require additional processing of the training data to determine the roots and endings of each word.

Acknowledgement. This research was funded by a grant QUADRIBOT, from the Agency for Science, Innovation and Technology (MITA), Lithuania.

References

1. Anson, D., Moist, P., Przywara, M., Wells, H., Saylor, H., Maxime, H.: The effects of word completion and word prediction on typing rates using on-screen keyboards. Assistive Technol. **18**(2), 146–154 (2006)
2. Vescovi, M.: Soothsayer: un Sistema Multi-sorgente per la Predizione del Testo (Soothsayer: multi-source text prediction system), Milan (2004)
3. Gelšvartas, J., Simutis, R., Maskeliūnas, R.: Multifunctional user interface to control robotic arm for paralyzed people. In: Electrical and Control Technologies, p. 22 (2014)
4. Garay, N., Abascal, J.: Text prediction systems: a survey. Univ. Access Inf. Soc. **4**(3), 188–203 (2006)
5. Venkatagiri, H.: Efficiency of lexical prediction as a communication acceleration technique. Augmentative Altern. Commun. **9**(3), 161–167 (1993)
6. Trost, H., Matiasek, J., Baroni, M.: The language component of the FASTY text prediction system. Appl. Artif. Intell. **19**(8), 743–781 (2005)
7. Wandmacher, T., Antoine, J.Y.: Methods to integrate a language model with semantic information for a word prediction component (2008). arXiv:0801.4716
8. Van Den Bosch, A.: Scalable classification-based word prediction and confusible correction. Traitement Automatique des Langues **46**(2), 39–63 (2006)
9. Mikolov, T., Yih, W.T., Zweig, G.: Linguistic regularities in continuous space word representations. In: HLT-NAACL, pp. 746–751 (2013)

Towards a Formal Model of Language Networks

Tajana Ban Kirigin[1]([✉]), Ana Meštrović[2], and Sanda Martinčić-Ipšić[2]

[1] Department of Mathematics, University of Rijeka,
Radmile Matejčić 2, 51000 Rijeka, Croatia
bank@uniri.hr
[2] Department of Informatics, University of Rijeka,
Radmile Matejčić 2, 51000 Rijeka, Croatia
{amestrovic,smarti}@uniri.hr

Abstract. Multilayer networks and related concepts have been used for description and analysis of complex systems in many fields, such as for example biological, physical, social and information systems. In this paper we present the first steps towards defining a formal model for language networks representation - Multilayer Language Network (MLN) which is based on multilayer network formalism and which is suitable for representation, analysis and comparison of languages both in their entirety as well as in their various characteristics and complexity. The goal of this research is to define a universal formal model for languages, capturing various language levels (subsystems) and various language characteristics. As a starting point we apply standard network diagnostics on an MLN model for an English and Croatian text, considering word, syllable and grapheme language subsystems and various construction principles, and present obtained results.

1 Introduction

The complex networks theory has been recognized as a particularly powerful framework for studying phenomena from gene/protein or social interactions, to technological and infrastructure systems [9,23]. This generated a swift development of various fields and opened new research avenues [23]. One of them is network linguistics [8,11,19,24], which contributed significant results, ranging from new models of language evolution [11,24], to quantitative analysis of written novels [19].

The complexity of language as a natural evolving system is mirrored by the structural complexity of the corresponding network model. Various aspects of natural language can be represented as complex networks [23], whose nodes depict linguistic units (e.g. words), while edges model their morphosyntactic, semantic and/or pragmatic interactions [8,24]. This refers to language analysis through varying linguistic levels (syntactic, semantic, phonetic [8,24]), examination of language evolution, or modeling of language acquisition [1]. It has been shown that language networks share various non-trivial topological properties and may be characterized as small-world networks and scale-free networks which are well-known and studied classes of complex networks [11,19,24].

G. Dregvaite and R. Damasevicius (Eds.): ICIST 2015, CCIS 538, pp. 469–479, 2015.
DOI: 10.1007/978-3-319-24770-0_40

In the era of "big data", beside of the explosive growth of data, we are also witnessing the swift advances in the theoretical models of multilayer networks, suitable to consistently model different data sources in the same framework. However, the field of complex networks has shifted from the analysis of isolated network (capturing and modelling one aspect of the examined system) toward the analysis of the family of complex networks simultaneously modelling different phenomena (aspects) of examined system, or simultaneously modelling interactions and relationships among different subsystems. This pursuit opened a variety of different theoretical models: multilayer networks [10,16], multidimensional networks [4], multiplex networks [7,20], interdependent networks [13] and networks of networks [14]. A thorough discussion that compares, contrasts and translates between theoretical notions of multilayer, multiplex, interdependent networks and networks of networks is given in [15].

Multilayer network approach has been addressed in study of the international trade analysis [3], social interactions in the massive on-line game [25], web-search queries [4], in transport and infrastructure [7,16] and for examining the brain function [6]. However, although multilayer networks fit the language levels in a natural way, there have been no reports on multilayer language networks. So far there have only been efforts to model isolated phenomena of various language subsystems (e.g. co-occurrence [19]) and examine their unique function through complex networks, failing to explain mechanism of their mutual interaction or interplay. This paper presents the first steps towards a universal formal model suitable for representation, analysis and comparison of languages both in their entirety as well as in their various characteristics and complexity. Such a model would be more general and expressive then existing approaches [1,24].

Inspired by [15], we base our approach on multilayer networks and propose a formal model called Multilayer Language Network (MLN). MLN can informally be considered as a graph with some additional structure which is imposed through various perspectives forming subgraphs i.e. layers. Each layer reflects a possible combination of perspectives denoting a particular view on the examined language system. At the same time interlayer edges reflect relations and interactions among these subsystems.

The paper is organized as follows. Section 2 introduces the formal multilayer network model for languages. In Sect. 3 we focus on some diagnostics of the model and present some initial experiments and results. We conclude in Sect. 4 by pointing to future work.

2   Formal Model

This paper introduces a formal model for languages based on graphs or networks (for simplicity, we often interchange the terminology of a graph and a network). We aim to design a model that is universal in the sense that is suitable for the representation of all languages, for both written and spoken forms, as well as for the comparison of various languages, and likewise suitable for the linguistic analysis of any given language features.

Kivelä et al. in [15] review and unify the terminology of existing concepts for multilayer network structure and similar network structures from the literature. In order to relate to existing research, methodology and diagnostics we design our model as close as possible to the general framework and notions given therein. On the other hand, given the specifics of what is modelled by the formalism, i.e. languages in several of their features, we have adapted that framework and terminology. We introduce a definition of a Multilayer Language Network (MLN) as follows.

A **Multilayer Language Network** M is a quintuple $M = (V_M, E_M, V, L, C)$ where

- V is a non-empty set whose elements are called **nodes**;
- C is a nonempty set of **perspective elements**;
- L is a set of **perspects** L_i, where $\{L_0, L_1, L_2\}$ is a partition of C. Perspect L_0 is the **language perspect**, L_1 is the **hierarchy perspect** and L_2 is the **construction perspect**;
- For perspect $L_1 = \{g_1, \ldots, g_k\}$ sequence of its elements $g_1, \ldots, g_k$ is the subsequence of the following sequence:

$$discourse, sentence, phrase, syntagm, word, morphem, \\ syllable, phoneme, grapheme \quad (1)$$

Sequence (1) is called **hierarchy**, and is denoted by $h_1, \ldots, h_9$ in short;
- An element of the set $L_0 \times L_1 \times L_2$ is called a **layer**;
- $V_M \subseteq V \times L_0 \times L_1 \times L_2$ is the set whose elements are called **MLN-nodes**;
- $E_M \subseteq V_M \times V_M$ is the set of **edges**.

An example of a multilayer language network model is given in Fig. 1.

As custom in the graph theory, *edges* in an MLN may be directed or undirected, weighted or unweighted. Consequently, we differentiate between **directed** MLNs, **undirected** MLNs, **weighted** MLNs, and **unweighted** MLNs. For example, the MLN model presented in Fig. 1 is directed and unweighted.

The set of *nodes* contains all the elements under consideration, that is all linguistic units such as sentences, words, syllables, etc. that appear in the text that is modelled by the given MLN.

Language perspect denotes particular languages under consideration, e.g. English and Croatian. *Construction perspect* reflects approaches to the analysis of language structure, such as analysis of the syntax of a given text, and the analysis of the same text but with randomized word order. From the linguistic point of view *hierarchy perspect* is the most essential of all perspects. It represents levels of language subsystems denoted by the hierarchy sequence (1). Different MLN-s may focus on some of the language levels while other levels may be out of the scope. This is reflected in the *perspective elements* of the *hierarchy* that the *hierarchy perspect* contains.

A *layer* is specified by a single *perspective element* from each of the *perspects*. Moreover, *perspects* are studied in all combinations. This means that *layers* specify all possible perspectives or views on a language. Some

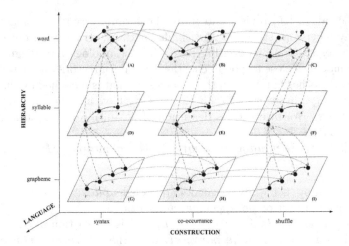

Fig. 1. Example of a directed unweighted MLN model. The model consists of perspects $L_0 = \{croatian\}$, $L_1 = \{word, syllable, grapheme\}$ and $L_2 = \{syntax, co\text{-}occurrence, shuffle\}$. There are 9 *layers* denoted by $(A) - (I)$. *Intralayer edges* are represented by solid arrows, while the *interlayer edges* are dotted.

of the *layers* in the model shown in Fig. 1 are $(croatian, word, syntax)$ and $(croatian, syllable, shuffle)$.

$MLN\text{-}nodes$ are copies of *nodes* placed on different *layers*. For an $MLN\text{-}node$ (a, l), where $a \in V$, $l \in L_0 \times L_1 \times L_2$, we say that the *node* a appears on *layer* l. Notice that by above definition, depending on the set V_M, some *layers* may be empty, with no $MLN\text{-}nodes$ on them.

Informally, we may think of an MLN model as a graph or a network with some additional structure. Then $MLN\text{-}nodes$ are "nodes" of that graph and E_M is the set of its "edges". For simplicity, we will sometimes say *node* for an $MLN\text{-}node$ when the meaning is clear from the context.

Edges in an MLN may be defined between any of the $MLN\text{-}nodes$. The set of *edges* in an MLN can, therefore, be partitioned into **intralayer edges** and **interlayer edges**. An *intralayer edge* connects two $MLN\text{-}nodes$ from the same *layer*, while an *interlayer edge* is an *edge* between two $MLN\text{-}nodes$ belonging to different *layers*.

In case that a language analysis does not require some *perspect*, that *perspect* may be omitted from the model. Submodels may for example be used in the analysis of a single language, as in the example model depicted in Fig. 1. In such cases the submodel would only contain the remaining two *perspects*, *hierarchy* and *construction perspect*.

Kivelä et al. in [15] review and classify multilayer networks based on the types of constraints imposed on the network. We, however, put no constraints on the model, both with respect to *nodes* as well as *edges*. More precisely, we allow *edges* between arbitrary $MLN\text{-}nodes$ but do not impose *edges* between some $MLN\text{-}nodes$ either. Also, a *node* does not need to appear on every *layer*.

This is different from the multiplex structure [7,15,20] where traditionally all nodes appear on every layer, i.e. all nodes are shared between all layers.

Additionally, in a multiplex there are edges between each node and its counterparts in different layers, that is, adjacency of a node with itself across multiple layers is explicit. At the same time, in a multiplex there is no adjacency of a node with remaining nodes from different layers. This is usually called diagonal coupling and categorical coupling in the literature [15].

One of the characteristics of the *MLN* model is that *hierarchy* imposes order of linguistic levels. The structure of language subsystems is preserved and modelled through *hierarchy perspect*. This is similar to ordinal couplings [15,22], in which layers are ordered and nodes are adjacent only to their counterparts in consecutive ("adjacent") layers. Another difference to the model presented in [15] is that we allow self-edges, that is an *MLN-node* being adjacent to itself. These *edges* would for example represent neighbouring words such as "bla bla bla" or *edges* between syllables in the same word, e.g. in "banana". Although our model can represent structures such as multiplex, in principle, we do not impose nor disallow adjacency. This approach allows wide and universal modelling and analysis of different linguistic phenomena.

2.1   Interpretation of *MLN*

MLN model has several features. It allows representation of languages, their analysis in a unified framework, as well as comparison of various language phenomena. For example, an *MLN* can model a particular Croatian novel and its linguistic units at chosen levels, e.g. all of the words, syllables and graphemes that appear in the novel. Besides original text of the novel, one could consider the same text but, for instance, with randomised word order on the sentence level, or consider the syntax dependencies of words in a sentence. The suitable model would have *perspects* $L_0 = \{croatian\}$, $L_1 = \{word, syllable, grapheme\}$ and $L_2 = \{syntax, co\text{-}occurrence, shuffle\}$.

The set of *intralayer edges* is typically defined in the following way. On the *layer* with *co-occurrence perspective element*, *intralayer edges* connect neighbouring sentences, neighbouring words in a sentence and neighbouring syllables in a word. Similarly, for the *shuffle layers*, *intralayer edges* are defined for linguistic units that are neighbouring in the randomized text. On the *layers* with the *syntax perspective element*, *edges* connect neighbouring sentences, neighbouring syllables in words and on the word level *edges* are defined between words adjacent in the syntax dependency tree of each sentence. For an example of the syntax dependency tree on a sentence in English see Fig. 2.

Co-occurrence as the network construction principle is sometimes extended to cover neighbouring for a wider window, for more details see e.g. [17]. There are many other candidates for *construction perspect* e.g. *clique*, where one would connect all words in a sentence as a clique, and likewise for other language levels. In another construction principle one could connect words that differ only in the last syllable [2].

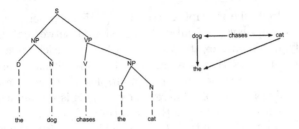

Fig. 2. An example of the syntax dependencies parsed in a tree for the sentence *"The dog chases the cat."* (as per [27]) is presented to the left. Corresponding directed graph is given to the right, where the syntax categories sentence (S), noun phrase (NP), verb phrase (VP), noun (N), verb (V), determiner (D) are omitted.

Through *language perspect* various languages could be compared, but also dialects of the same language as well as development and changes of a particular language over time.

Interlayer edges betwen *layers* that differ in the *hierarchy perspect* are typically defined on containment bases, connecting a word with syllables it contains, connecting a syllable with graphemes that it contains and so on, as in the *MLN* depicted in Fig. 1. Similarly, in some cases edges could be defined between linguistic units that are not necessarily on consequent levels, connecting for example a word with all of the graphemes it contains. *Interlayer edges* are defined to reflect the analysis and comparison of different subsystems of an *MLN* model, reflecting different perspectives one takes when considering one or several languages.

3   Diagnostics in *MLN* Model

So far diagnostic for language networks has been reported for isolated subsystems. *MLN* model has the potential to extent from isolated to integral diagnostics, enabling better insights in mutual interactions of language subsystems. Here we discuss initial steps in this direction.

Various graph and network diagnostics could be applied to individual *layers* of an *MLN*. For the linguistic analysis one can compare networks and perform relevant diagnostics for the chosen *layers*.

For example, Croatian is generally considered as a mostly free word-order language. In order to support this classification of Croatian language, some conclusions on the importance of word order in Croatian could be drawn e.g. from comparing layers (*croatian, word, syntax*) and (*croatian, word, shuffle*) of the *MLN* model shown in Fig. 1. These *layers* differ only in one *perspect*, that is *syntax* v.s. *shuffle*. Comparing *layers* that differ in more than one *perspect* can also be of interest. Since word-order is more strict in English than in Croatian, one could, for example, compare Croatian text with its English translation, but randomized on the sentence level. An *MLN* model suitable for such comparison could be obtained by considering the *MLN* given in Fig. 1 but with additional perspective element *english*, i.e. with *language perspect* $L_0 = \{croatian, english\}$.

One can visualize this model as two copies of the model from Fig. 1, one in Croatian, other in English, with additional interlayer edges as needed. Such MLN model would have 18 layers and, in particular, *layers* $(croatian, word, syntax)$ and $(english, word, shuffle)$ would be of interest for the analysis described above.

Moreover, MLN model can capture more language characteristics than just through its individual layers. Consider for example the graph given in Fig. 2. From that graph one cannot reconstruct the corresponding sentence in a unique way. This could however be done in an MLN e.g. through interlayer edges between (entire) sentences and words occuring in each sentence.

Kivela et al. [15] review attempts to generalize single-layer-network diagnostics to multilayer networks. This includes e.g. methods of multiway-data-analysis and tensor-decomposition. The later method is based on representing a multilayer network as adjacency tensor.

For the MLN model $M = (V_M, E_M, V, L, C)$ adjacency tensor

$$\mathcal{A} \in \{0,1\}^{|V| \times |V| \times |L_0| \times |L_0| \times |L_1| \times |L_1| \times |L_2| \times |L_2|}$$

is such that its tensor element has value 1 if and only if there is the corresponding edge in M, and has value 0 otherwise. Tensor representation enables one to directly apply methods from the tensor-analysis literature to multilayer networks. Kivela et al. [15] show how the rank of such a tensor can be reduced. This process of tensor "flattening" leads to the so-called supra-adjacency matrices enabling one to apply known tools and methodology that is used for matrices.

3.1 The Network Structure Analysis

We now review some of the standard network measures [23] that can be applied as network diagnostic to an individual *layer*. A network or graph $G = (V, E)$ is a pair of a set of nodes V and a set of edges E, where N is the number of nodes and K is the number of edges. A network is directed if the edges have a direction associated with them. A network is weighted if there is a weight function w that assigns value (real number) to each edge.

The degree of a node i, k_i is the number of edges incident to the node. Average degree, $< k >$ is the sum of the degree over all nodes divided by the number of nodes.

A path in a network is a sequence of edges which connect a sequence of nodes that are all distinct from one another. A shortest path between two nodes i and j is a path with the shortest length and it is called distance between i and j and is denoted as d_{ij}. The average path length, L, of a directed network is given by equation: $L = \sum\limits_{i,j} \dfrac{d_{ij}}{N(N-1)}$.

The clustering coefficient of a node measures the density of edges among the immediate neighbors of a node. For weighted networks the clustering coefficient of a node i is denoted by c_i and defined as the geometric average of the subgraph edges weights: $c_i = \dfrac{1}{k_i(k_i-1)} \sum\limits_{j,k} (\hat{w}_{ij}\hat{w}_{ik}\hat{w}_{jk})^{1/3}$, where k_i is the degree of the node i, and the edges weights $\hat{w}_{ij}$ are normalized by the maximum weight in the network $\hat{w}_{ij} = w_{ij}/\max(w)$. If $k_i < 2$, then the value of c_i is 0.

The average clustering of a network, C, is defined as the average value of the clustering coefficients of all nodes in an undirected network: $C = \dfrac{1}{N}\sum_i c_i$.

The network connected component is a subgraph in which any two nodes are connected to each other by paths. The number of connected components is denoted by ω. If $\omega > 1$, L is computed for the largest component - giant connected component (GCC).

Reciprocity of a network, ρ, is defined as $\rho = \dfrac{\sum_{i \neq j}(a_{ij} - \bar{a})(a_{ji} - \bar{a})}{\sum_{i \neq j}(a_{ij} - \bar{a})^2}$, where $a_{ij} = 1$ if a edge from node i to j is there, and $a_{ij} = 0$ if not, and the average value $\bar{a} = \frac{\sum_{i \neq j} a_{ij}}{N(N-1)}$. Reciprocity quantifies the tendency of vertex pairs to form edges in both directions between each other. According to the reciprocity, the networks can be classified as reciprocal networks ($\rho > 0$) or antireciprocal networks ($\rho < 0$).

3.2   Experiments and Results

We now present some results of the standard network diagnostics on an MLN. MLN model in this example allows analysis of five different realizations of the very same text. Namely, it contains three layers on the word-level for syntax, co-occurrence and shuffle and two layers on the sub-word level for syllables and graphemes, both for Croatian and for English.

Variations of the text described above, naturally fit the MLN model with the following perspects: $L_0 = \{croatian, english\}$, $L_1 = \{word, syllable, grapheme\}$ and $L_2 = \{syntax,\ co\text{-}occurrence,\ shuffle\}$. Such MLN model has 18 layers, but in this experiment is reduced to 10 non-empty layers, since for the syllabic and graphemic *layer* we only consider the co-occurrence construction principle. In each layer we establish edges between linguistic units according to their linguistic relation (e.g. syntax dependency, co-occurrence). Edges are directed and weighted, where weights reflect the frequency of relation among units. Interlayer edges across word-level layers are forming multiplex (the same words across layers are linked). Between word and subword layers we establish multiple interlayer edges: for instance word *chases* is linked with syllables *cha, ses*, and syllable *cha* is also linked to the word *charity*. The same principle is applied across syllable-grapheme layers.

The Croatian data for multilayer network is derived from Croatian Dependency Treebank HOBS corpus [26]. The corpus size is currently 3,465 sentences (88,045 tokens). Dataset from the Penn Treebank corpus [28] is used for the English layers construction. The dataset contains 3,829 sentences (94,084 tokens). Syntax Dependency Tree is a tree parsed from original sentence according to the syntax relationships among words. For this work we use the text of original sentences for the construction of co-occurrence [17] and shuffled layers [18], and syntax relationships from treebank corpora for the syntax layer. The shuffled

Table 1. Network measures for 10 layers (N no. of nodes, K no. of edges, $< k >$ average degree, L avg. path length, C clust. coeff., ω no. of components, N_{GCC} no. of nodes in GCC, ρ reciprocity) for co-occurrence (CO), syntax (SIN), shuffled (SHU), syllable (SYL) and grapheme (GR) network layers in Croatian (left) and English (right)

	CROATIAN layers					ENGLISH layers				
	CO	SIN	SHU	SYL	GR	CO	SIN	SHU	SYL	GR
N	23359	23359	23359	2634	34	10930	10930	10930	2599	26
K	71860	70155	86214	18849	491	50299	52221	58920	6053	333
$< k >$	6.15	6.01	7.38	14.31	28.88	9.20	9.55	10.78	4.66	25.62
L	4.01	1.81	3.74	1.86	1.58	3.47	1.96	0.45	1.88	1.51
C	0.167	0.120	0.182	0.255	0.636	0.286	0.153	0.295	0.057	0.838
ω	2	2	2	17	1	3	3	1	54	1
N_{GCC}	23357	23357	23357	2584	34	10926	10926	10930	2480	26
ρ	0.049	0.041	0.085	0.139	0.531	0.051	0.046	−0.0005	0.017	0.575

layer is constructed from randomized words in a sentence. Further, we decompose Croatian and English words to syllables and graphemes.

The standard network measures of all layers considered for Croatian and English are given in Table 1. The number of nodes (N) on the word-level layers is preserved in both languages (HR: 23359, EN: 10930). On subword-levels the inventory of linguistic units is smaller (around 2500 nodes in syllable layers and around 30 nodes in grapheme layers) which disables direct comparisons of network measures at word and subword-level. Average degree $< k >$ is higher for English than for Croatian on the word-level layers. On the subword-level layers average degree is lower for English due to the higher number of components (smaller GCC) and smaller number of nodes.

Still some additional remarks are worth noticing. The average path length (L) decreases from co-occurrence to syntax, as expected, but interestingly it is of the same range for the syntax and syllabic layer of both languages. The clustering coefficient (C) (obtained from the undirected versions of the same networks) increases on the syllabic sub-word level for Croatian and decreases for English. At the same time English layers are more clustered than the Croatian ones.

One of the explanations for this difference can be found in the number of connected components (ω) which is three times higher for English then for Croatian syllabic layer, see Table 1. Grapheme layers of both languages expectedly, exhibit the highest clustering coefficients. Moreover, the Croatian syllabic layer has higher reciprocity then the corresponding word layers for one order of magnitude. The graphemic layers of both languages exhibit peculiar features due to the small number of nodes or in other words due to the high density (0.88 - HR; 1.03 - EN). The reciprocity (ρ) is near to the zero for all layers except for grapheme layer which seems to be more reciprocal than others for both languages.

4   Conclusions and Future Work

Multilayer networks and related concepts have been used for the description and analysis of various complex systems in many fields, such as for example biological, physical, social and information systems, for an overview see [15]. This paper presents the first steps in the work on a multilayer network model for languages. MLN model is universal enough to allow extensions with additional perspects as needed. Indeed, in the future we plan to extend the model with as many perspects as is linguistically required to quantitatively study the structure of language in a unified framework of MLN.

From the point of view of diagnostics, MLN model allows various approaches. The most obvious approach is through the field of graph theory and network analysis by comparison of different *layers*. Moreover, MLN model allows deeper and more complete analysis by considering both intralayer and interlayer edges. In the future research plans we will consider tensors for better MLN diagnostics based on inter layer relationships, and expand the model according to linguistic theory of language subsystems (semantics, pragmatics etc).

Proposed MLN model can be of high relevance for computer science as well, especially for applications which process natural language or retrieve information, like in text summarization, text quality assessment, keyword extraction, etc. For instance in keyword extraction the most representative parts of the text are ranked according to different measures obtained from the structure of network. Considering all layers simultaneously can yield better extraction of representative candidates since different linguistic phenomena are reflected in different layers.

Acknowledgments. This work has been supported in part by the University of Rijeka under the LangNet project (13.13.2.2.07).

References

1. Antiqueira, L., Oliveira Jr, O.N., Costa, L.F., Nunes, V.: A complex network approach to text summarization. Inf. Sci. **179**(5), 584–599 (2009)
2. Ban, K., Ivakić, I., Meštrović, A.: A preliminary study of croatian language syllable networks. In: IEEE MIPRO Proceedings, pp. 1296–1300 (2013)
3. Barigozzi, M., Fagiolo, G., Garlaschelli, D.: Multinetwork of international trade: a commodity-specific analysis. Phys. Rev. E **81**(4), 046104 (2010)
4. Berlingerio, M., Coscia, M., Giannotti, F., Monreale, A., Pedreschi, D.: Foundations of multidimensional network analysis. In: IEEE Advances in Social Networks Analysis and Mining (ASONAM), pp. 485–489 (2011)
5. Bianconi, G. Dorogovtsev, S.N., Mendes, J.F.F.: Mutually connected component of network of networks. arXiv preprint arXiv:1402.0215 (2014)
6. Bullmore, E., Sporns, O.: Complex brain networks: graph theoretical analysis of structural and functional systems. Nature Rev. **10**(3), 186–198 (2009)
7. Cardillo, A., Gómez-Gardeñes, J., Zanin, M., Romance, M., Papo, D., del Pozo, F., Boccaletti, S.: Emergence of network features from multiplexity. Sci. Rep. **3**, 1344 (2013)

8. Cong, J., Liu, H.: Approaching human language with complex networks. Phys. Life Rev. **11**, 598–618 (2014)
9. Costa, L.F., Oliveira Jr, O.N., Travieso, G., Rodrigues, F.A., Villas Boas, P.R., Antiqueira, L., Viana, M.P., Correa Rocha, L.E.: Analyzing and modeling real-world phenomena with complex networks: a survey of applications. Adv. Phys. **60**(3), 329–412 (2011)
10. De Domenico, M., Solé-Ribalta, A., Cozzo, E., Kivelä, M., Moreno, Y., Porter, M.A., Gómez, S., Arenas, A.: Mathematical formulation of multilayer networks. Phys. Rev. X **3**(4), 041022 (2013)
11. Dorogovtsev, S.N., Mendes, J.F.F.: Language as an evolving word web. Proc. R. Soc. Lond. B Biol. Sci. **268**(1485), 2603–2606 (2001)
12. Estrada, E., Gómez-Gardeñes, J.: Communicability reveals a transition to coordinated behavior in multiplex networks. Phys. Rev. E **89**(4), 042819 (2014)
13. Gao, J., Buldyrev, S.V., Stanley, E.H., Havlin, S.: Networks formed from interdependent networks. Nature Phys. **8**(1), 40–48 (2012)
14. Gao, J., Li, D., Havlin, S.: From a single network to a network of networks. Nat. Sci. Rev. **1**(3), 346–356 (2014)
15. Kivelä, M., Arenas, A., Barthelemy, M., Gleeson, J.P., Moreno, Y., Porter, M.A.: Multilayer networks. J. Complex Netw. **2**(3), 203–271 (2014)
16. Kurant, M., Thiran, P.: Layered complex networks. PRL **96**(13), 138701 (2006)
17. Margan, D., Martinčić-Ipšić, S., Meštrović, A.: Preliminary report on the structure of croatian linguistic co-occurrence networks. In: 5th ITIS Proceedings, pp. 89–96 (2013)
18. Margan, D., Martinčić-Ipšić, S., Meštrović, A.: Network differences between normal and shuffled texts: case of croatian. In: Contucci, P., Menezes, R., Omicini, A., Poncela-Casasnovas, J. (eds.) Complex Networks V. SCI, vol. 549, pp. 275–283. Springer, Heidelberg (2014)
19. Masucci, A.P., Rodgers, G.J.: Network properties of written human language. Phys. Rev. E **74**(2), 026102 (2006)
20. Menichetti, G., Remondini, D., Panzarasa, P., Mondragón, R.J., Bianconi, G.: Weighted multiplex networks. PloS One **9**(6), e97857 (2014)
21. Morris, R.G., Barthelemy, M.: Transport on coupled spatial networks. Phys. Rev. Lett. **109**(12), 128703 (2012)
22. Mucha, P.J., Richardson, T., Macon, K., Porter, M.A., Onnela, J.: Community structure in time-dependent, multiscale, and multiplex networks. Science **328**(5980), 876–878 (2010)
23. Newman, M.: Networks: An Introduction. Oxford University Press, Oxford (2010)
24. Solé, R.V., Corominas-Murtra, B., Valverde, S., Steels, L.: Language networks: their structure, function, and evolution. Complexity **15**(6), 20–26 (2010)
25. Szell, M., Lambiotte, R., Thurner, S.: Multirelational organization of large-scale social networks in an online world. Proc. Natl. Acad. Sci. **107**(31), 13636–13641 (2010)
26. Tadić,   M.:   HOBS   1.0.   http://linghub.lider-project.eu/metashare/21e34dc6703d11e28a985ef2e4e6c59e1f1629e7806b4d5a8824e8ca19b113ba
27. Tadić, M.: Building the croatian dependency treebank: the initial stages. Suvremena Lingvistika **63**(1), 85–92 (2007)
28. Marcus, M.P., Marcinkiewicz, M.A., Santorini, B.: Building a large annotated corpus of English: the Penn treebank. Comput. Linguistics **19**(2), 313–330 (1993)
29. Wang, P., Robins, G., Pattison, P., Lazega, E.: Exponential random graph models for multilevel networks. Soc. Netw. **35**(1), 96–115 (2013)

First Steps in Automatic Anaphora Resolution in Lithuanian Language Based on Morphological Annotations and Named Entity Recognition

Voldemaras Žitkus and Lina Nemuraitė[✉]

Department of Information Systems,
Kaunas University of Technology, Kaunas, Lithuania
{voldemaras.zitkus,lina.nemuraite}@ktu.lt

Abstract. Anaphora resolution is an important part of natural language processing used in machine translation, semantic search and various other information retrieval and understanding systems. Anaphora resolution algorithms usually require linguistic pre-processing tools and various expensive resources for automatically identifying anaphoric expressions. Many smaller languages, like Lithuanian, lack such resources and tools. In this paper, an algorithm is proposed that requires only morphological annotations and recognized named entities. The paper presents experimental results showing the relevance of the solution for specific domains, and considers the further immediate ways towards dealing with the overall anaphora resolution problem for Lithuanian language.

Keywords: Anaphora resolution · Natural language processing · Named entity recognition · NER · Lithuanian language · References

1 Introduction

In Natural Language Processing (NLP), the anaphora is an expression the interpretation of which depends upon another word or phrase present in context (its antecedent or postcedent [1]. Anaphora resolution is important in semantic annotations for corpora and, consequently, in various systems, like semantic search, that use semantic annotations.

For example, "Tom skipped the school today. He was sick." Here words "Tom" and "He" form an anaphora, where "Tom" is an antecedent and "He" is an anaphoric object. Without anaphoric relationships, we would not be able to determine, why Tom skipped the school nor who was sick. In such cases, we would lose semantic information, amount of which mostly depends on the type of the text – for example, technical manuals less often tend to use anaphoric expressions than newspaper articles.

The relation between anaphoric object and its antecedent is intransitive, irreflexive and asymmetric. The interpretation of an anaphoric object requires another object (antecedent) that it refers to [2]. The order of an anaphoric object and the word that the anaphoric object refers to is important. If the anaphoric object follows the word that it refers to then that word is called "antecedent". If the word follows the anaphoric object

© Springer International Publishing Switzerland 2015
G. Dregvaite and R. Damasevicius (Eds.): ICIST 2015, CCIS 538, pp. 480–490, 2015.
DOI: 10.1007/978-3-319-24770-0_41

then that word is called "postcedent", and such type of reference is called "cataphora". Due to their similarity, and anaphora being more widely used, the distinction is usually not made. In this paper, we also do not distinguish between anaphoric and cataphoric expressions since the proposed algorithm applies to both types of references.

Anaphora resolution approaches fall into two broad categories: knowledge-rich and knowledge-poor ones [3]. While both approaches have different focus they require expensive resources like syntactic annotations and semantic information, or pre-annotated (often by hand) corpora. Smaller languages like Lithuanian language lack such resources. Therefore, an alternative that depends on existing Lithuanian language processing tools as morphological annotations and Named Entity Recognition (NER) is useful. It allows producing results while other, more expensive resources are still being created, and serves as a starting point from which anaphora resolution algorithms for Lithuanian language can progress further.

The rest of the paper is structured as follows. Sections 2 and 3 overview the application context, for which the anaphora resolution algorithm was developed, and related works. Section 4 explains a taxonomy of Lithuanian anaphoric expressions. Sections 5 and 6 present the anaphora resolution algorithm and its experimental evaluation results. Section 7 draws conclusions and presents future works.

2 Semantic Search Framework for Lithuanian Internet Corpus

The needs for automatic anaphora resolution in Lithuanian language had arisen in relation with creation of Semantic Analysis and Search Framework [4] for Lithuanian Internet corpus extracted from public portals (Fig. 1). Our semantic search framework is oriented towards answering questions, presented in Structured Lithuanian (SL) language. The framework transforms these questions into SPARQL queries and executes them in ontology populated by individuals discovered by semantic annotation tool from Internet corpus.

The Structured Lithuanian language is based on Semantics of Business Vocabulary and Business Rules (SBVR) [5]; this language was created as the result of the continuing research and currently is under further development [6–10]. SBVR SL allows specifying concepts, propositions and questions for domain under consideration in the form similar to the natural language. This language is understandable for human and interpretable by computers as it is based on the formal logics of SBVR. The Semantic Search Framework is domain-specific, capable to analyse specific domains (currently, it is directed towards analysing Politics, Business and Economy, and Public Administration domains). For example, it is possible to ask "Kokie įvykiai susiję su D. Grybauskaite?" ("What events are related with D. Grybauskaite?") during specified time intervals. For politics domain, events mean meetings, pronouncements, agreements, etc.

The semantic search by giving questions in SBVR SL is different from keywords-based search as the Semantic Search Framework uses SBVR vocabularies for describing the chosen domain, and ontologies, obtained from (or synchronized with) these vocabularies. SBVR SL questions, transformed into SPARQL, are capable

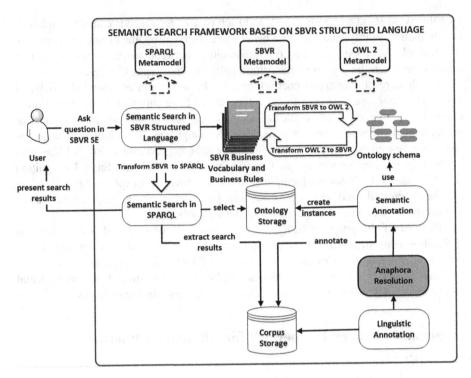

Fig. 1. Semantic search framework for Lithuanian Internet corpus [4]

to give precise results in the form of ontology individuals and their property assertions. Of course, if we want to analyse Internet contents, we have to deal with unstructured information, which must be processed by linguistic and semantic annotation tools. Semantic annotations relate recognized text fragments with individuals and their relations in ontologies; so these text fragments can be used for answering questions. The dependency on precision of linguistic and semantic annotation tools prevents from reaching full accuracy of answers; nevertheless, we have reached some encouraging results.

The anaphora resolution (Fig. 1) is just one component of this framework but it can significantly enrich the ontology population by identifying additional occurrences and links of entities, already identified after linguistic processing. To our knowledge, automated anaphora resolution tools are not available for Lithuanian language. Therefore, creation of such tools is important for further improvement of semantic search in Lithuanian language.

3   Anaphora Resolution Approaches in Other Languages

While no work has been done to solve anaphoric expressions in Lithuanian language, there are many approaches available for other languages, mostly for English. We provide the short overview of the most often cited approaches and compare their precision (Table 1). It is important to note that the presented evaluations were performed against different corpora. Therefore, the evaluation results are not directly comparable, but they give a general understanding about the achievable results.

Table 1. Comparison of anaphora resolution approaches

Method	Foundation	Types of anaphoric expressions resolved	Precision
Hobbs	Syntactic	Main pronouns: he, she, they, it	81.8–91.7 % (depends on type of text)
BFP	Centring Theory	Pronouns (their types are not specified)	49–90 % (depends on type of text)
Left-Right Centering	Modified Centring Theory	Pronouns (their types are not specified)	72.1–81 % (depends on type of text)
RAP	Salience factors	Third person pronouns, reflexive and reciprocal anaphors	85–86 %; reaches 89 % with inclusion of statistical algorithms
Statistical approach	Probabilistic model	He, she, it and their various forms	82.9–84.2 %
Machine learning	Machine learning	Noun phrases (including pronouns)	65.5–67.3 %
UNL based approach	Universal Networking Language	Pronouns	67 %
SE-DSNL	Pattern based approach	Pronouns, but can be used for other anaphora types	81.3 %

- Hobbs algorithm is one of the earliest anaphora resolution approaches [11]. It assumes the existence of fully parsed syntactic tree with labelled nodes. The algorithm finds first pronoun that has not been analysed yet and navigates syntactic tree searching for suitable noun. When the noun is found algorithm checks if pronoun and noun agree in number and gender.
- Centring Theory based approaches (e.g., BFP [12], Left-Right Centering [13]). This theory assumes that a centre (or the focus) of the previous sentence is most likely to be pronominalized in the following sentence.
- Similar to the Centring Theory approaches, there are approaches based on salience factors (e.g., RAP [14]). Like in the Centring Theory, assumption is made that the most prominent word is likely to be an antecedent for the pronoun. Prominence is based on a number of salience factors, e.g., sentence's recency, subject's emphasis, existential emphasis, accusative emphasis, etc.
- The statistical approach [15] builds a probabilistic model that takes into account the distance between a pronoun and the candidate antecedent; the placement in the syntax tree; gender; animation; an interaction between the head constituent of the pronoun and the antecedent, and the mention count of candidate antecedents (more often mentioned antecedents are preferable).

- Machine learning approaches [16] are usually end-to-end systems that perform various NLP tasks, not only anaphora resolution. Shortcomings of other constituents of the NLP system negatively affect the anaphora resolution.
- Approach based on Universal Networking Language (UNL) [17] focuses on relationships between pronouns and their possible antecedents in previous sentences; these relationships are built on the base of semantic meaning and types of pronouns.
- SE-DSNL [18] approach attempts to determine semantic compatibility between anaphoric objects and their possible antecedents on the base of real world knowledge. For example, whether a candidate antecedent can perform the same actions as the anaphoric object.

The main difference between these methods and our proposed approach is that our algorithm is rule-based, it requires only morphological and NER annotations, and was developed for Lithuanian language.

4   Taxonomy of Anaphoric Expressions in Lithuanian Language

In our earlier work [10], we presented a taxonomy of anaphoric objects (Fig. 2) that categorizes anaphoric objects on three different levels: morphological, lexical semantics and domain semantics. The goal behind such classification was better represent actual situation where the same anaphoric expression may include the anaphoric object

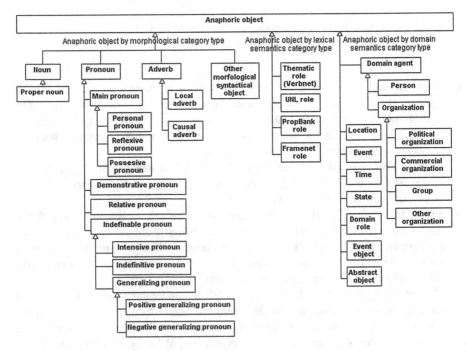

Fig. 2. Taxonomy of anaphoric expressions (adapted from [10])

that would be classified as a pronoun (morphological type), agent (lexical semantics type) and person (domain semantics type).

Some part of anaphoric relations may be detected using morphological annotations; additional relations can be found from results of lexical semantics analysis, and yet another part can be discovered from the domain semantics represented in ontology.

The generic domain semantics categories, characteristic for various domains, are adapted from [8] by extending them with state, domain role and abstract object, which are important for anaphora resolution. The "abstract object" represents such words or phrases as "person", "enterprise", "young man", etc., that can have anaphoric references. Similarly, domain roles as "president", "teacher", "politician", etc., can help discovering anaphoric relations. The morphological classification is language specific, but the lexical semantics based classification and domain semantics based classification are appropriate for other languages too.

5 Anaphora Resolution Algorithm Based on Morphological Annotations and Named Entity Recognition

In this section, we detail our proposed anaphora resolution algorithm, which was created for our Semantic Search Framework for Lithuanian Language. The algorithm was designed to provide annotations in such a way that other parts of the system can interpret its results. The algorithm was investigated on a corpus that collects articles from various Lithuanian Internet news sites focusing on political and economic matters.

Our proposed resolution method (Fig. 3) focuses on the cases where anaphoric objects are personal pronouns (subtypes of main pronouns who in turn are subtypes of pronouns in morphological categorization) and used to express persons (subtypes of domain agents in domain semantics categorization). This classification is based on our created taxonomy of anaphoric expressions as presented in Fig. 2.

The algorithm consists of the following steps:

1. Algorithm searches for the next pronoun for which anaphora resolution was not performed yet. If no new pronouns are found then we move to the ninth step.
2. Once a pronoun is found algorithm checks it against the pre-set list of invalid pronouns that usually are either pleonastic or tend not to refer to persons.
3. If the pronoun is valid, we go backwards from its position until we find a noun that is recognized as a person by Named Entity Recognition; or we reach a boundary of the sentence. If the pronoun is invalid, we return to the first step.
4. If a suitable noun is not found in the current sentence, we move backwards to the next sentence and perform the same search. This cycle continues until we either find a suitable noun, or until we pass X sentences backwards from the pronoun.
5. If we reach limit X then we move Y sentences forward from the pronoun searching for a suitable noun.
6. If we pass Y sentences forward without finding a suitable noun then the algorithm cannot determine a suitable antecedent and we return to the first step.

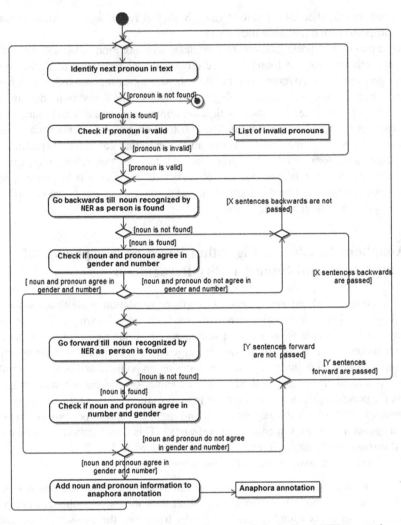

Fig. 3. Anaphora resolution method based on morphological and NER annotations

7. If during the fourth or fifth step we find a suitable noun then we determine if it agrees in number and gender with the pronoun. If it does not agree then we return to the fourth or fifth step.
8. If noun and pronoun agree in number and gender then their pair is added to anaphora annotations and we return to the first step.
9. If there is no remaining pronouns in the text, the algorithm finishes its work.

As can be seen from the detailed steps, the algorithm can be considered naive since it takes the first suitable noun that agrees in a number and gender as an antecedent, and the alternatives are not considered.

The list of invalid pronouns includes the following pronouns: kitas, tas, koks, visas, kuris, šis, joks. It has been observed that our algorithm usually is unable to find any suitable candidates for these pronouns; therefore, they are skipped in order to increase processing speed, which is relevant when working with large corpora. In addition, the omission of invalid pronouns makes the minimal impact on recall and precision. The algorithm can resolve the remaining pronouns, though it also depends on the domain under consideration. In other domains, the uses of pronouns and nouns representing persons might differ.

In our experiments, we have determined that three sentences backwards (i.e., $X = 3$) and one sentence forward ($Y = 1$) have produced the best results. These evaluations might wary for different languages and different types of texts. In total, we cover 4 sentences around anaphoric objects; the priority is given to antecedents since more steps backward is reasonable, and moving backwards is more effective.

In the following, we provide some examples on how algorithm operates on the corpus of Politics and Economy domains, annotated by morphological and NER annotation tools.

- Dalia Grybauskaitė nuvyko į Vilnių. Ji pasveikino vilniečius su šventėmis.

First, we identify pronoun "Ji". Since it is at the start of the sentence, we do not analyse remaining parts of the sentence and move one sentence backwards. At the next sentence, we start from the right and move left towards its beginning. First named entity we encounter is "Vilnių", but since it is recognized by NER as a location and not as a person we discard it, and move further to the left. Next named entity that we encounter is "Dalia Grybauskaitė", which is recognized by NER as a person. In this case, we determine the grammatical compatibility between the noun phrase (which consists of two nouns) and the pronoun. Both are singular and of female gender, therefore algorithm pairs them as the anaphoric object and its antecedent, and does not search for further candidates.

Another example:

- Kiek mažiau nei tikėtasi mokesčių mokėtojai papildė biudžetą ambicingai LR Finansų ministerijos suplanuotomis pajamomis iš akcizų (2 proc. mažiau), PVM (4 proc. mažiau), prabangaus nekilnojamojo turto mokesčio (71 proc. mažiau). Pastebėtina, kad prabangaus nekilnojamojo turto mokesčio surinkimo planas 2013 metams buvo 17 mln. litų, nepaisant to, kad 2012 m. šio mokesčio sumokėta mažiau nei 4 mln. litų (2013 m. surinkta beveik 5 mln. litų). GPM surinkimą labiausiai lėmė minimalaus mėnesinio atlyginimo (MMA) padidinimas: "Kiek man teko analizuoti, padidinus MMA tik nedidelė dalis Lietuvos įmonių sumažino etatą ar atleido darbuotojus, o tai lėmė nemažą papildomą indėlį į valstybės biudžetą" teigė Ž. Mauricas.

In this case, we first identify the pronoun "man" (the literal English translation "for me") and repeat the same steps as in the previous example. In the third sentence from the identified pronoun (the first one in the example) we find "LR finansų ministerijos" entity, which was recognized by NER as an organization and not as a person. We do not find any more entities moving backwards; therefore, we move back to our pronoun and proceed forward. The first entity we find is "Lietuvos", which is a location. We continue moving right until we locate "Ž. Mauricas" entity, which is recognized as a person. Since the pronoun "man" is ambiguous in gender (it can refer to both female and male persons), we compare the pronoun and the noun phrase only in a number. Both are singular; therefore, we pick "Ž. Mauricas" as a postcedent of anaphoric object "man".

If any person entity would not be present in the last analysed sentence then we would not look further for a possible postcedent and pronoun "man" would be left unresolved.

Most of the named entities that are recognized by NER as persons are singular, but sometimes families are mentioned, e.g., Paulauskai, Zuokai. Due to such cases, it is important to check for agreement in number between nouns (noun phrases) and pronouns.

6 Experimental Evaluation of the Anaphora Resolution Algorithm

The purpose of the experiment was to evaluate our proposed algorithm against the corpus of Politics and Economy domains collected from Lithuanian Internet news sites in the environment of the Semantic Search framework. The evaluation was made by analysing five hundred articles that were randomly selected from around 400 thousands of collected articles.

Precision and recall are most widely used criteria for evaluation of anaphora resolution approaches. Recall R determines the percentage of anaphoric expressions F correctly resolved by the algorithm from the total number T of anaphoric expressions presented in the text (1). Precision P determines the percentage of correctly resolved anaphoric expressions C from the number of resolved anaphoric expressions F (2):

$$R = C/T \tag{1}$$

$$P = C/F \tag{2}$$

Results of the experiment are presented in Table 2.

Table 2. Results of experimental investigation of anaphora resolution algorithm performed against the subset of Politics and Economy corpus

Number of articles	T (Actual number of anaphoric expressions)	F (Number of anaphoric expressions resolved by algorithm)	P (Number of anaphoric expressions correctly resolved by algorithm)	R (Recall)	P (Precision)
500	2352	1954	1446	61 %	74 %

Considering limitations of tools and resources that we have used for pre-processing texts and implementing the algorithm, we think that results are encouraging, but the following threats to validity must be taken into account:

- Anaphoric objects that refer to named entities that NER recognizes as persons are just one small subset of possible anaphoric expressions.
- Most of the articles in the investigated corpora are taken from news portals that focus on politics and economics. The most of articles of this type could be described as collections of quotations from various politics, economists or business participants. Such texts have many named entities that can be identified as persons. In other types of texts, named entities are less often used and the algorithm would be less effective.
- Mistakes that were made due to errors in morphological or NER annotations, e.g., incorrectly identified genders of persons, were fixed by hand. Without these adjustments, the recall decreases by approximately 9 % and precision by around 4 %.
- Some articles did not have any anaphoric expressions at all or did not have pronouns referring to named entities recognized as persons. Such articles were removed from the sample set and new ones were randomly picked to replace them.
- Analysing all collected Politics and Economy corpus, we have noticed that the algorithm has not identified any anaphoric expressions in approximately 30 % of the articles. We believe that the majority of them have no pronouns referring to named entities that our algorithm could identify. The reason may be the specifics of articles, or imperfection of NER or morphological annotation tools. However, at this time we lack resources and means to validate this assumption.

7 Conclusions and Future Works

In this paper, the anaphora resolution approach was proposed for Lithuanian Internet corpus collected from news sites focusing on political and economic matters. The algorithm depends only on morphological annotations and named entity recognition, and is the only possible way towards the overall anaphora resolution problem for small languages until they have no more sophisticated linguistic pre-processing tools and resources required for this purpose.

While the algorithm provides the precision, comparable to other analysed resolution approaches, it has numerous shortcomings and limitations: it is domain specific, capable resolve just a small subset of anaphora types and was experimentally investigated for the relatively small subset of articles. The future work is directed towards investigating possibilities to adapt the similar solutions for other relevant domains and creating more sophisticated anaphora resolution algorithms using emerging tools and resources for Lithuanian language that currently are under development and will appear at the nearest future. The Semantic Search Framework for Lithuanian Internet corpora provides the favourable environment for creation and perfection of such tools, which would allow dealing with abundant information amounts in our virtual space using our native Lithuanian language.

References

1. Mitkov, R.: Anaphora Resolution. Longman, London (2002)
2. Elango, P.: Coreference resolution: a survey. Technical report, University of Wisconsin-Madison, USA (2005)
3. Mitkov, R., Lappin, S., Boguraev, B.: Introduction to the special issue on computational anaphora resolution. Comput. Linguist. **27**(4), 473–477 (2001)
4. SemantikaLT: Syntactic-semantic analysis and search system for lithuanian internet, corpus and public sector applications (2012–2014), no VP2-3.1-IVPK-12-K (2014)
5. OMG: Semantics of Business Vocabulary and Business Rules (SBVR). SBVR 1.2, version 1.2, OMG Document Number: formal/2013-11-04, pp. 1–292 (2012)
6. Sukys, A., Nemuraite, L., Sinkevicius, E., Paradauskas, B.: Querying ontologies on the base of semantics of business vocabularies and business rules. In: Information Technologies' 2011: Proceedings of the 17th International Conference on Information and Software Technologies, IT 2011, pp. 247–254, Kaunas, Lithuania, 27–29 April 2011
7. Sukys, A., Nemuraite, L., Paradauskas, B.: Representing and transforming SBVR question patterns into SPARQL. In: Skersys, T., Butleris, R., Butkiene, R. (eds.) ICIST 2012. CCIS, vol. 319, pp. 436–451. Springer, Heidelberg (2012)
8. Bernotaityte, G., Nemuraite, L., Butkiene, R., Paradauskas, B.: Developing SBVR vocabularies and business rules from OWL2 ontologies. In: Skersys, T., Butleris, R., Butkiene, R. (eds.) ICIST 2013. CCIS, vol. 403, pp. 134–145. Springer, Heidelberg (2013)
9. Karpovic, J., Krisciuniene, G., Ablonskis, L., Nemuraite, L.: The comprehensive mapping of semantics of business vocabulary and business rules (SBVR) to OWL 2 ontologies. Inf. Technol. Contr. **43**(3), 289–302 (2014)
10. Zitkus, V., Nemuraite, L.: Taxonomy of anaphoric expressions as a starting point for anaphora resolution in Lithuanian corpus. In: IVUS 2014, pp. 177–182, Lithuania (2014)
11. Hobbs, J.R.: Resolving pronoun references. In: Grosz, B., Sparck-Jones, K., Webber, B. (eds.) Reading in Natural Language Processing, vol. 99, pp. 339–352. Morgan Kaufmann Publishers Inc., San Francisco (1986)
12. Tetrault, J.R.: A corpus-based evaluation of centering and pronoun resolution. Comput. Linguis. **27**(4), 507–520 (2001)
13. Byron, D. K.: Resolving pronominal references to abstract entities. In: Proceedings of the 40th Annual Meeting of the Association for Computational Linguistics (ACL), pp. 80–87, Philadelphia, USA (2002)
14. Lappin, S., Leass, H.J.: An algorithm for pronominal anaphora resolution. Comput. Linguis. **20**(4), 535–561 (1994)
15. Ge, N., Hale, J., Charniak, E.: A statistical approach to anaphora resolution. In: Proceedings of the Sixth Workshop of Very Large Corpora, pp. 161–170 (1998)
16. Soon, W.M., Ng, H.T., Lim, D.C.Y.: A machine learning approach to coreference resolution of noun phrases. Comput. Linguis. **27**(4), 521–544 (2001)
17. Balaji, J., Geetha, T.V., Parthasarathi, R., Karky, M.: Anaphora resolution in Tamil using universal networking language. In: Proceedings of the Indian International Conference on Artificial Intelligence, IICAI-2011, Karnataka, India (2011)
18. Fischer, W.: Linguistically motivated ontology-based information retrieval. Doctoral dissertation, University of Augsburg, GER (2013)

LDA and LSI as a Dimensionality Reduction Method in Arabic Document Classification

Rami Ayadi[1(✉)], Mohsen Maraoui[2], and Mounir Zrigui[3]

[1] LaTICE Laboratory, University of Sfax, Sfax, Tunisia
ayadi.rami@planet.tn
[2] Computational Mathematics Laboratory,
University of Monastir, Monastir, Tunisia
maraoui.mohsen@gmail.com
[3] LaTICE Laboratory, Faculty of Science of Monastir, Monastir, Tunisia
mounir.zrigui@fsm.rnu.tn

Abstract. In this work, we made an experimental study for compare two approaches of reduction dimensionality and verify their effectiveness in Arabic document classification. Firstly, we apply latent Dirichlet allocation (LDA) and latent semantic indexing (LSI) for modeling our document sets OATC (open Arabic Tunisian corpus) contained 20.000 documents collected from Tunisian newspapers. We generate two matrices LDA (documents/topics) and LSI (documents/topics). Then, we use the SVM algorithm for document classification, which is known as an efficient method for text mining. Classification results are evaluated by precision, recall and F-measure. The evaluation of classification results was performed on OATC corpus (70 % training set and 30 % testing set). Our experiment shows that the results of dimensionality reduction via LDA outperform LSI in Arabic topic classification.

Keywords: LDA · LSI · Topics model · Comparing · OATC · Arabic TC

1 Introduction

The text classification is a classic problem of text mining. In recent years, classification is proved to be effective in summarizing a search result or in distinguishing different topics latent in search results. In this work, we use and compare LDA and LSI for dimensionality reduction of feature vectors in Arabic document classification and verify if LDA can substitute LSI for the task. The original feature vectors have occurrences of terms as their entries and thus are of dimension equal to the number of vocabularies. The tow approaches LDA and LSI reduce the dimension of document vectors to the number of topics, which is far less than the number of vocabularies. We can regard each entry of the vectors of reduced dimension as a topic frequency, i.e., the number of words relating to each topic. We inspect the effectiveness of dimensionality reduction by conducting a classification on feature vectors of reduced dimension.

The rest of the paper is organized as follows. Section 2 gives the previous work concerning modeling document for the task of classification. Section 3 includes a short description of LDA. We omit the details about LSI from this paper and refer to the

© Springer International Publishing Switzerland 2015
G. Dregvaite and R. Damasevicius (Eds.): ICIST 2015, CCIS 538, pp. 491–502, 2015.
DOI: 10.1007/978-3-319-24770-0_42

original paper [1]. The results of the evaluation experiment are presented in Sect. 4. Section 5 draws conclusions and gives future work.

2 Related Work

In automatic text classification, it has been proved that the term is the best unit for text representation and classification [2]. Though a text document expresses a vast range of information, unfortunately, it lacks the imposed structure of traditional databases. Therefore, unstructured data, particularly free running text data has to be transformed into a structured data. To do this, many preprocessing techniques are proposed in literature [3, 4]. After converting an unstructured data into a structured data, we need to have an effective document representation model to build an efficient classification system. Bag of Word (BoW) is one of the basic methods of representing a document. The BoW is used to form a vector representing a document using the frequency count of each term in the document. This method of document representation is called as a Vector Space Model (VSM) [5]. Unfortunately, BoW/VSM representation scheme has its own limitations. Some of them are: high dimensionality of the representation, loss of correlation with adjacent words and loss of semantic relationship that exist among the terms in a document [6, 7]. To overcome these problems, term weighting methods are used to assign appropriate weights to the term to improve the performance of text classification [8, 9]. Li et al. in [10] used binary representation for a given document.

The major drawback of this model is that it results in a huge sparse matrix, which raises a problem of high dimensionality. Hotho et al., in [11] proposed an ontology representation of a document to keep the semantic relationship between the terms in a document. This ontology model preserves the domain knowledge of a term present in a document. However, automatic ontology construction is a difficult task due to the lack of structured knowledge base.

Cavana, in [12] used a sequence of symbols (byte, a character or a word) called N-Grams, that are extracted from a long string in a document. In an N-Gram scheme, it is very difficult to decide the number of grams to be considered for effective document representation. Another approach in [13] uses multi-word terms as vector components to represent a document. But this method requires a sophisticated automatic term extraction algorithm to extract the terms automatically from a document. Wei et al., in [14] proposed an approach called Latent Semantic Indexing (LSI) which preserves the representative features of a document. The LSI preserves the most representative features rather than discriminating features.

Statistical topic models have been successfully applied in many tasks, including classification, information Retrieval and data extraction, etc. [15, 16] These models may capture the correlation word in the corpus with a low-dimensional set of multinomial distribution, called "topics" and provide a short description for documents.

Latent Dirichlet Allocation (LDA) [16] is a widely used generative topic model. In LDA, a document is viewed as a distribution over topics, while a topic is a distribution over words. To generate a document, LDA firstly samples a document-specific multinomial distribution over topics from a Dirichlet distribution; then repeatedly samples the words in the document from the corresponding multinomial distribution.

The topics discovered by LDA can capture the correlations between words, but LDA cannot capture the correlations between topics for the independence assumption underlying Dirichlet distribution. However, topic correlations are common in real-world data, and ignoring these correlations limits the LDA's abilities to express the large-scale data and to predict the new data.

The most important aspect in the text representation is the reduction of the dimension of the space features. There are two goals for the reduction of dimension

- Reducing feature dimension to the computable degree makes the classification task feasible and executable
- Feature set selected should ensure the validity of classification.

There are two classes of dimension reduction techniques, feature selection (FS), and feature extraction (FE). Feature selection selects a representative subset of the input feature set, based on some criterion. An estimate function is used to rank original features according to the calculated score value for each feature. This value represents the quality or importance of a word in the collection. The features then ordered in descending or ascending order for the values, and then select a suitable number of words of the higher orders.

Feature selection algorithms are widely used in the area of text processing due to their efficiency.

Duwairi in [17] compared three dimensionality reduction techniques; stemming, light stemming, and word cluster. Duwairi used KNN to perform the comparison. Performance metrics are: time, accuracy, and the size of the vector. She showed that light stemming is the best in term classification accuracy.

Fouzi in [18] compares five reduction techniques; root based and, light stemming, document frequency DF, TF-IDF, and latent semantic indexing LSI. Then it shows that DF, TFIDF, and LSI methods were superior to the other techniques in term of classification problem.

Thabtahin in [19] investigates different variations of VSM and term weighting approaches using the KNN algorithm. Her experimental results showed that Dice distance function with tf-idf achieved the highest average score.

Said in [20] provided an evaluation study of several morphological tools for Arabic Text Categorization using SVMs. Their study includes using the raw text, the stemmed text, and the root text. The stemmed and root text is obtained using two different preprocessing tools. The results revealed that using light stemmer combined with a good performing feature selection method such as mutual information or information gain enhances the performance of Arabic Text Classification.

In [21] a semantic approach is presented using synonym merge to preserve features semantic and prevent important terms from being excluded. The resulting feature space was then processed with five feature selection methods, ID, TF-IDF, CHI, IG and MI. Experiment shows that classification performance is increased after merging terms and yielding better performance for CHI and IG selection method.

Forman and Yang compare different selection methods based on various aspects, including efficiency, discriminatory ability to obtain optimal performance, etc. In the view of results, statistical indicators such as CHI -2 and the information gain (IG) show their superiority. Different classifiers tend to accept different reduction strategy [22, 23]

Many applications of LDA to real-world problems are proposed, however, these researchers do not compare LDA with other probabilistic model for task of Text Classication. In [24], Mikio conduct intensive experiments comparing LDA with pLSI and Dirichlet mixture. While we can learn important things about the applicability of LDA and other document models, their work compares these document models not from a practical viewpoint, but from a theoretical one.

Tomonari in [25] compare latent Dirichlet allocation (LDA) with probabilistic latent semantic indexing (pLSI) as a dimensionality reduction method and investigate their effectiveness in document clustering by using Japanese and Korean Web articles. For clustering of documents, Tomonari use a method based on multinomial mixture. The experiment shows that the dimensionality reduction via LDA and pLSI results in document clusters of almost the same quality as those obtained by using original feature vectors. Therefore, the vector dimension is reduced without degrading cluster quality. This result suggests that LDA does not replace pLSI at least for dimensionality reduction in document clustering for Japanese and Korean language.

In [26], authors perform a series of experiments using LSA, PLSA and LDA for document comparisons in AEA (Automatic Essay Assessor) and compare the applicability of LSA, PLSA, and LDA to essay grading with empirical data. The results show that the use of learning materials as training data for the grading model outperforms the k-NN-based grading methods.

In this work, we check the effectiveness of LDA as a dimensionality reduction method in Arabic text classification and the effectiveness of quality of classified documents from testing set is checked to evaluate its effectiveness. Although Blei in [15] use LDA for dimensionality reduction, the authors compare LDA with no other methods. Further, their evaluation task is a binary classification of the Reuters-21578 corpus, a slightly artificial task. In this paper, we use LDA as a dimensionality reduction approach to make clear its effectiveness to the classification task for text written in Arabic by comparing it with LSI. Further, we compare LDA and LSI to know if LDA can provide better results than LSI.

3   Latent Dirichlet Allocation

Formally, we define the following terms [15]:

- A word is the basic unit of discrete data, defined to be an item from a vocabulary indexed by $\{1, \ldots, V\}$. We represent words using unit-basis vectors that have a single component equal to one and all other components equal to zero. Thus, using superscripts to denote components, the vth word in the vocabulary is represented by a V-vector w such that $wv = 1$ and $wu = 0$ for $u \neq v$.
- A document is a sequence of N words denoted by $w = (w_1, w_2, \ldots, w_N)$, where w_n is the nth word in the sequence.
- A corpus is a collection of M documents denoted by $D = \{w_1, w_2, \ldots, w_M\}$.

LDA is a generative probabilistic model of a corpus. The basic idea is that documents are represented as random mixtures over latent topics, where each topic is characterized by a distribution over words.

LDA assumes the following generative process for each document **w** in a corpus D:

   i. Choose $N \sim$ Poisson(ξ).
   ii. Choose $\theta \sim$ Dir(α).
   iii. For each of the N words w_n:
      a. Choose a topic $Z_n \sim$ Multinomial (θ).
      b. Choose a word w_n from $(w_n \mid Z_n)$ a multinomial probability conditioned on the topic Z_n.

Several simplifying assumptions are made in this basic model, some of which we remove in subsequent sections. First, the dimensionality k of the Dirichlet distribution (and thus the dimensionality of the topic variable z) is assumed known and fixed. Second, the word probabilities are parameterized by a $k \times V$ matrix β where $\beta_{ij} = (w_j = 1 \mid z_i = 1)$, which for now we treat as a fixed quantity that is to be estimated. Finally, the Poisson assumption is not critical to anything that follows and more realistic document length distributions can be used as needed. Furthermore, note that N is independent of all the other data generating variables (θ and z). It is thus an ancillary variable and we will generally ignore its randomness in the subsequent development.

A k-dimensional Dirichlet random variable θ can take values in the $(k - 1)$-simplex (a k-vector θ lies in the $(k - 1)$-simplex if $\theta_i \geq 0,$), and has the following probability density on this simplex:

$$p(\theta / \alpha) = \frac{\Gamma(\sum\limits_{i=1}^{k} \alpha_i)}{\prod_{i=1}^{k} \Gamma(\alpha)} \theta_1^{\alpha_1 - 1} \ldots \theta_k^{\alpha_k - 1} \tag{1}$$

Where, the parameter α is a k-vector with components $\alpha_i > 0$, and where $\Gamma(x)$ is the Gamma function. The Dirichlet is a convenient distribution on the simplex—it is in the exponential family, has finite dimensional sufficient statistics, and is conjugate to the multinomial distribution.

Given the parameters α and β, the joint distribution of a topic mixture θ, a set of N topics z, and a set of N words w is given by:

$$p(\theta, z, w / \alpha, \beta) = p(\theta / \alpha) \prod_{n=1}^{N} p(z_n / \theta) p(w_n / z_n, \beta) \tag{2}$$

Where is simply i for the unique i such that. Integrating over and summing over z, we obtain the marginal distribution of a document:

$$p(W / \alpha, \beta) = \int p(\theta / \alpha) \left(\prod_{n=1}^{N} \sum_{2z} p(z_n / \theta) p(w_n / z_n, \beta) \right) d\theta \tag{3}$$

Finally, taking the product of the marginal probabilities of single documents, we obtain:

$$p(D/\alpha, \beta) = \prod_{d=1}^{M} \int p(\theta_d/\alpha) \left(\prod_{n=1}^{N_d} \sum_{z_{dn}} p(z_{dn}/\theta_d) p(w_{dn}/z_{dn}, \beta) \right) d\theta_d \qquad (4)$$

The parameters α and β are corpus level parameters, assumed to be sampled once in the process of generating a corpus. The variables θ_d are document-level variables, sampled once per document. Finally, the variables and are word-level variables and are sampled once for each word in each document.

The LDA model starts with a set of topics. Each of these topics has probabilities of generating various words. Words without special relevance, like articles and prepositions, will have roughly even probability between classes (or can be placed in a separate category). A document is generated by picking a Dirichlet distribution over topics and given this distribution, picking the topic of each specific word. Then, words are generated given their topics. The parameters of Dirichlet distribution are estimated by the variation of the EM algorithm.

4 Evaluation of LDA and LSI as a Dimensionality Reduction Method

4.1 Pre-processing Step

For the validation of our study, firstly, the pre-processing step is performed for normalizing each document d in the corpus.

Second, each document is stemmed using a stemmer describe in [27, 28]. Third latent topics are learned with LDA for topic numbers K = 50. Then a supervised classification is performed on the reduced document distribution over topics. We apply the SVM algorithm for document classification.

Let D be a corpus, he has been split into a training set and testing set. Input is training set and testing set and output is the class of documents in testing set.

The process of validation follows these steps: first, we apply a preprocessing stage for all documents in the corpus by performing some linguistic choices in order to reduce the noise in the document as well as to improve the indexation efficiency. Some of the most popular choices are:

1. Each article in the Arabic dataset is processed to remove digits and punctuation marks{., :,/, !,§,&,',[,(,_,-,|,-,^,),],},}=,+,$,*,...
2. Remove all vowels except " " (الشدة).
3. Duplicate all the letters containing the symbols " " (الشدة).
4. Convert letters "ء" (hamza), "آ" (aleph mad), "أ" (aleph with hamza on top), "ؤ" (hamza on w), "إ" (alef with hamza on the bottom), and "ئ" (hamza on ya) to "ا" (alef).
5. Convert the letter "ى" to "ي" and the letter "ة" to "ه". The reason behind this normalization is that there is not a single convention for spelling "ى" or "ي"and "ة" or "ه" when they appears at the end of a word.
6. All the non Arabic words were filtered.
7. Arabic function words were removed.

8. Applied stemming Algorithm for each article in Arabic data set to obtain a stemmed text.

In the next step, after preprocess documents in the training set, we learn the parameters of LDA and get θ (matrix of "document*topic") and φ (matrix of "topic*word"). Then, we model documents in the testing set according to the parameter got from the first step, that is, transform documents in testing set into the form of matrix "document*topic", after this, we perform classification on corpus using SVM classifier, that is, input the matrix "document*topic" of training set and testing set into SVM classifier and finally evaluate on classification results by using various metrics.

In the Table 1, we can show the 20 most likely words for 2 topics (9 and 5).

Table 1. Most likely words for 2 topics

Topic 9th:			Topic 5th:		
English	Arabic word		English	Arabic word	
Higher	العالي	0.015508	Political party	النهضه	0.014895
Education	التعليم	0.010981	Movement	حركه	0.012978
University	الجامعيه	0.008299	Government	حكومه	0.012955
Certificate	شهاده	0.007566	Tunisia	تونس	0.012724
Search	البحث	0.007035	party	حزب	0.011570
Scientific	العلمي	0.006857	Political	السياسيه	0.009654
Students	الطلبه	0.006857	Politician	السياسي	0.009584
Baccalaureate	الباكالوريا	0.005492	party	الحزب	0.008384
Institute	المعهد	0.005365	Front	جبهة	0.008107
Respect	النسبه	0.004986	Coming	الاحزاب	0.007437
Year	السنه	0.004960	Revolution	الثوره	0.007368
Of Education	التربيه	0.004859	president	رايس	0.006929
Tunis	تونس	0.004859	Political party	ندا	0.006837
Visited	زاره	0.004581	National	الوطني	0.006167
Institute	المعهد	0.004530	Motion	الحركه	0.005659
Science	راضيه	0.004277	People	الشعب	0.005405
Section	اجل	0.004252	Coming	القادمه	0.005290
Satisfied	العلوم	0.004176	Parties	الاطراف	0.004874
First	الاولي	0.004126	Dialogue	الحوار	0.004782
Number	عدد	0.004126	Government	جمعه	0.004782

In addition, the evaluation is completed by applying SVM [29, 30] classification with LSI reduction. Sparse matrix is generated for each word to represent the corpus, with each column being the vector representation of documents in the original space. The detail about the coding method can be referred in [1]. Then the SVD toolkit [31] is used for Singular Value Decomposition. Each word in the vocabulary is represented as a 100-dimension vector in S-space.

4.2   Document Sets

In the evaluation experiment, we use a document set of Tunisian Web news articles. We start by building our data set. The OATC (Open Arabic Tunisian Corpus) contains 20.000 documents that vary in length and writing styles. These documents fall into 10 categories that equal in the number of documents. In this Arabic dataset, each document was saved in a separate file within the directory for the corresponding category, i.e., the documents in this data set are single-labeled. Tables 2 and 3 show more specified details about the collection.

Table 2. Number of documents in each category

OATC	NB of text	Average number of words per text	Number of words per category	Category Size (Mo)
Sport	2 000	141.261	282 522	2.99
regional	2 000	125.723	251 447	2.71
Culture	2 000	168.485	336 971	3.62
World	2 000	105.701	211 402	2.26
National	2 000	136.739	273 479	2.97
Political	2 000	164.356	328 712	3.53
Economic	2 000	148.922	297 845	3.27
Student	2 000	203.485	406 971	4.50
Investigation	2 000	253.602	507 205	5.43
Judicial	2 000	126.93	253 860	2.70

Table 3. Specified details about OATC

NB of text in the corpus	20.000
NB of words in the corpus	2 .523 .022
Size of corpus (Mb)	34.0 Mb
NB of category	10

The corpus is collected from online Arabic Tunisian newspapers, including attounissia, alchourouk, assabahnews and jomhouria, the Table 4 summarizes the percentage split between different sources. As we can show, for example, the "sport" category is composed of 25 % from Attounissia[1], 25 % from Alchourouk[2], 25 % from Assabahnews[3], 25 % from Jomhouria[4].

We adopt the open source of LDA [32] to model our corpus and we set topic number as K = 50 in LDA model.

---

[1] http://www.attounissia.com.tn/.

[2] http://www.alchourouk.com/.

[3] http://www.assabahnews.tn/.

[4] http://jomhouria.com/.

Table 4. Percentage split between different sources

Sources	Attou-nissia	Alchou-rouk	Assabah-news	Jom-houria
Sport	25 %	25 %	25 %	25 %
Regional	–	50 %	50 %	–
Culture	25 %	25 %	25 %	25 %
Word	25 %	25 %	25 %	25 %
National	25 %	25 %	25 %	25 %
Political	–	100 %	–	–
Economic	50 %	–	–	50 %
Student	100 %	–	–	–
Investigation	100 %	–	–	–
Judicial incidents	25 %	25 %	25 %	25 %

TC effectiveness is measured in terms of Precision, Recall, and the F1 measure [27]. Denote the precision, recall and F1 measures for a class Ci by Pi, Ri and Fi, respectively. We have:

$$P_i = \frac{TP_i}{TP_i + FP_i} \tag{5}$$

$$R_i = \frac{TP_i}{TP_i + FN_i} \tag{6}$$

$$F_i = \frac{2P_iR_i}{R_i + P_i} = \frac{2TP}{FP_i + FN_i + 2TP_i} \tag{7}$$

Where: TPi: (true-positive): number of documents correctly assigned.
FPi: (false positives): number of documents falsely accepted.
FNi: (false-negative): number of documents falsely rejected.

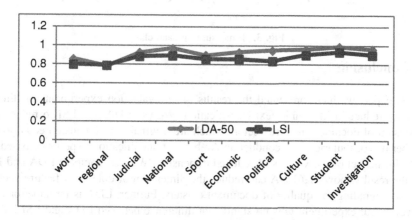

Fig. 1. Precision on each class

The results in Figs. 1, 2, 3 shows that the classification performances in terms of precision, recall and f-measure, in the reduced topics space (LDA-50) outperform those when using LSI reduction.

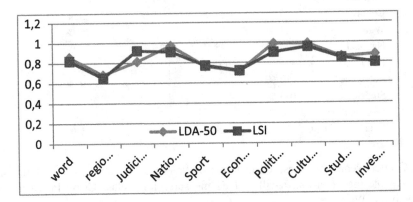

Fig. 2. Recall on each class

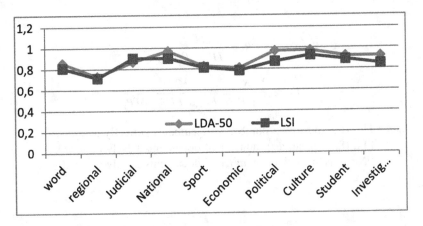

Fig. 3. F-measure on each class

5 Conclusion

In this paper, we have presented the results of an evaluation experiment for dimensionality reduction in Arabic text classification. We use LDA and LSI to reduce the dimension of document feature vectors which are originally of dimension equal to the number of vocabularies. We conduct an Arabic text classification experience based on SVM for the set of the vectors of reduced dimension. We also compare LDA and LSI and the results show that LDA can reduce the dimension of document feature vectors without degrading the quality of document clusters. Further, LDA is far superior LSI. However, our experiment tells no significant difference between LDA and LSI for the class with a small number of words.

References

1. Berry, M.W.: Large-scale sparse singular value computations. Int. J. Supercomputer Appl. **6** (1), 13–49 (1992)
2. Song, F., Liu, S., Yang, J.: A comparative study on text representation schemes in text categorization. Pattern Anal. Appl. **8**(1–2), 199–209 (2005)
3. Porter, M.F.: An algorithm for suffix stripping. Program **14**(3), 130–137 (1980)
4. Hotho, A., Nürnberger, A., Paaß, G.: A brief survey of text mining. In: Ldv Forum, pp. 19–62 (2005)
5. Salton, G., Wong, A., Yang, C.-S.: A vector space model for automatic indexing. Commun. ACM **18**(11), 613–620 (1975)
6. Bernotas, M., Karklius, K., Laurutis, R., et al.: The peculiarities of the text document representation, using ontology and tagging-based clustering technique. Inf. Technol. Control **36**(2), 117–220 (2015)
7. Ayadi, R., Maraoui, M., Zrigui, M.: Intertextual distance for Arabic texts classification. In: International Conference for Internet Technology and Secured Transactions, ICITST 2009, pp. 1–6. IEEE (2009)
8. Lan, M., Tan, C.L., Su, J., et al.: Supervised and traditional term weighting methods for automatic text categorization. IEEE Trans. Pattern Anal. Mach. Intell. **31**(4), 721–735 (2009)
9. Altinçay, H., Erenel, Z.: Analytical evaluation of term weighting schemes for text categorization. Pattern Recogn. Lett. **31**(11), 1310–1323 (2010)
10. Li, Y.H., Jain, A.K.: Classification of text documents. Comput. J. **41**(8), 537–546 (1998)
11. Hotho, A., Maedche, A., Staab, S.: Ontology-based text document clustering. KI **16**(4), 48–54 (2002)
12. Cavnar, W.: Using an n-gram-based document representation with a vector processing retrieval model. NIST Special Publication SP, pp. 269–269 (1995)
13. Milios, E., Zhang, Y., He, B., et al. Automatic term extraction and document similarity in special text corpora. In: Proceedings of the Sixth Conference of the Pacific Association for Computational Linguistics, pp. 275–284 (2003)
14. Wei, C.-P., Yang, C.C., Lin, C.-M.: A latent semantic indexing-based approach to multilingual document clustering. Decis. Support Syst. **45**(3), 606–620 (2008)
15. Blei, D., Lafferty, J.: Correlated topic models. Adv. Neural Inf. Process. Syst. **18**, 147 (2006)
16. Blei, D.M., Ng, A.Y., Jordan, M.I.: Latent dirichlet allocation. J. Mach. Learn. Res. **3**, 993–1022 (2003)
17. Duwairi, R., Al-Refai, M.N., Khasawneh, N.: Feature reduction techniques for Arabic text categorization. J. Am. Soc. Inform. Sci. Technol. **60**(11), 2347–2352 (2009)
18. Harrag, F., El-Qawasmah, E., Al-Salman, A.M.S.: Comparing dimension reduction techniques for Arabic text classification using BPNN algorithm. In: 2010 First International Conference on Integrated Intelligent Computing (ICIIC), pp. 6–11. IEEE (2010)
19. Thabtah, F., et al.: VSMs with K-Nearest Neighbour to categorise Arabic text data (2008)
20. Said, D., Wanas, N., Darwish, N., et al.: A study of Arabic text preprocessing methods for text categorization. In: The 2nd International Conference on Arabic Language Resources and Tools, Cairo, Egypt (2009)
21. Saad, E.M., Awadalla, M.H., Alajmi, A.F. Dewy index based Arabic document classification with synonyms merge feature reduction. In: IJCSI (2011)
22. Forman, G.: An extensive empirical study of feature selection metrics for text classification. J. Mach. Learn. Res. **3**, 1289–1305 (2003)

23. Rogati, M., Yang, Y.: High-performing feature selection for text classification. In: Proceedings of the Eleventh International Conference on Information and Knowledge Management. In: ACM, pp. 659–661 (2002)
24. Yamamoto, M., Sadamitsu, K.: Dirichlet mixtures in text modeling. University of Tsukuba, CS Technical report CS-TR-05-1 (2005)
25. Masada, T., Kiyasu, S., Miyahara, S.: Comparing LDA with pLSI as a dimensionality reduction method in document clustering. In: Tokunaga, T., Ortega, A. (eds.) LKR 2008. LNCS (LNAI), vol. 4938, pp. 13–26. Springer, Heidelberg (2008)
26. Kakkonen, T., Myller, N., Sutinen, E., et al.: Comparison of dimension reduction methods for automated essay grading. J. Educ. Technol. Soc. **11**(3), 275–288 (2008)
27. Zrigui, M., Ayadi, R., Mars, M., et al.: Arabic text classification framework based on latent dirichlet allocation. CIT. J. Comput. Inf. Technol. **20**(2), 125–140 (2012)
28. Ayadi, R., Maraoui, M., Zrigui, M.: SCAT: a system of classification for Arabic texts. Int. J. Internet Technol. Secured Trans. **3**(1), 63–80 (2011)
29. Joachims, T.: Making large scale SVM learning practical. Universität Dortmund (1999)
30. Joachims, T.: Text Categorization with Support Vector Machines: Learning with Many Relevant Features. Springer, Berlin, Heidelberg (1998)
31. Berry, M., Do, T., O'Brien, G., et al.: SVDPACKC (Version 1.0) User's Guide1 (1993)
32. Phan, X.-H., Nguyen, C.-T.: GibbsLDA++: AC/C++ implementation of latent Dirichlet allocation (LDA) (2007)

Identifying Road Artefacts with Mobile Devices

Marcin Badurowicz[✉] and Jerzy Montusiewicz

Institute of Computer Science, Lublin University of Technology,
Nadbystrzycka St. 38D, 20-618 Lublin, Poland
{m.badurowicz,j.montusiewicz}@pollub.pl
http://cs.pollub.pl

Abstract. In this paper, the concept of monitoring the state of roads by means of standard mobile devices (smartphones) is discussed. Using motion data from the device's sensors - accelerometer, gyroscope, compass - and in coordination with the current location from the Global Positioning System devices, it is possible to track and log any abnormal motion which may signal possible road infrastructure problems. The authors describe the software solution created to gather motion data, as well as the results of an experiment with a real-life car and real roads in different conditions. A pilot study carried out allows to test a developed application which provides precise localization of the artefacts occurring on the road.

Keywords: Road pavement · Potholes · Vertical acceleration · Accelerometer · GPS

1 Introduction

The problem of road quality is a broadly discussed issue concerning road transport security, technical problems of correct surface management and, last not least, user comfort. Studies in the field of road construction describe specialized devices used to estimate the state of the surface of the road and the specific parameters of the tarmac in particular. Relatively little space has so far been devoted to the determination of the quality of roads from the point of view of the driver and the passengers.

The authors apply a commonly used device of the smartphone equipped with a self-developed application able to register the amplitude of vibrations inside the car while negotiating problematic road artefacts such as potholes, speed bumps, etc. The objective was to find positions of such artefacts to provide in the future a possibility to include them into the overall state of the road in the navigation software, allowing users to omit low quality roads during route planning. In this paper the authors describe experiments showing if the chosen software solution was appropriate.

To recognize a road artefact a simple approach of detecting acceleration in the vertical axis above a threshold was used, and the proposed solution was able

© Springer International Publishing Switzerland 2015
G. Dregvaite and R. Damasevicius (Eds.): ICIST 2015, CCIS 538, pp. 503–514, 2015.
DOI: 10.1007/978-3-319-24770-0_43

to correctly identify a series of speed bumps. Similar research was performed earlier, however our solution is a little simplified - there is only one device where its positioning in space is known from the readings of integrated sensors, for example there is no need for external accelerometers or satellite navigation receivers. Instead of checking against video or audio recordings to prove the correctness of artefact recognition, human interaction was employed whereby a passenger manually ticked off the places noticed as road artefacts. Those results were compared with data samples on artefacts recognized by the software.

The paper is part of a broader research programme of identifying road quality issues in relation to driver and passenger comfort. The authors are currently working on preparing an effective software for collecting data on road surface anomalies encountered during a continuous car ride. The study is aimed at the creation of numerical assessment of road quality from the user's point of view.

2   Monitoring Road Artefacts

In recent years, the subject area has been studied by only a few researchers. In Nericell system [9], three different devices: a GPS receiver, a smartphone and a standalone accelerometer were used. A subsequent study [10], applying the devices mentioned, focused on traffic monitoring. Nowadays, it is possible to use only one smartphone equipped with the required sensors, as the concept presented in this paper.

In study [1], the mobile anomaly-sensing systems are discussed, with an emphasis on the problem of fuel consumption and the wear of car elements. Using the Android platform, data from mobile agents were processed on a central server, and the acceleration of vertical pulse was measured, and the vertical axis was determined using Euler angles. But, in the solution presented here a real world vertical axis is calculated by using the translation from the local to the global coordinate system by means of the rotation matrix generated by the operating system's APIs (Application Programming Interfaces).

The authors of [11] collected accelerometer readings with the frequency of 38 Hz along with GPS location and the noises were nullified by using the Kalman filter. For final post-processing, Fast Fourier Transform (FFT) was used, and the data were verified in comparison to a video camera. In our solution, however, the data automatically detected by the software are compared with human manual records.

In study [4], teledetection with smartphones with a 3-axis accelerometer and GPS receiver during 60 s segments and without turning the system off was also discussed, with correct identification of road artefacts in 45 % and 75 % of cases. Better results were obtained using an analysis of three elements of the acceleration vector in the SWAS system [6] with correct identification of 90 % for cars and 70 % for motorbikes. In our approach, however, acceleration in only one – vertical – axis is used, with still a high level of correct artefact recognition.

A very interesting technique is also presented by researchers from Massachusetts Institute of Technology with the "Pothole Patrol" system [5], where a

Symbian-based mobile device was used to record acceleration and location in Boston taxis in order to place potholes on the map. Unfortunately, Symbian-based devices were not equipped with gyroscopes, which limits the possibility of rotation matrix calculation. These studies also cannot be continued because the Symbian operating system is no longer available in currently produced devices. The presented solution is based on currently available smartphones and newer software.

A previous attempt of event detection using standard deviation of Z-axis acceleration over a defined threshold was proposed in [13], where the lowest false positive rate for this method was noted and pothole detection was proposed, in comparison to previous audio thresholding. Again, in our approach, comparison with human detection is used during road tests.

Finally, a similar approach is the Wolverine system [2], where to identify irregularities the standard deviation of acceleration was used. The Wolverine is using similar rotation matrix technique to achieve independence from the device's actual orientation. It is based on machine learning algorithms, but the emphasis in the system was on recording the use of car brakes, which was described as an important parameter in traffic smoothness. In this research, the authors are concentrating on detecting road artefacts as they are linked to passenger comfort, and not on the quality of driving, traffic jams and similar traffic issues.

In the light of the analysis carried out the authors are of the opinion that the topic of mobile monitoring of road quality from the point of view of driver and passenger comfort is not yet fully researched. Some existing solutions are obsolete at the moment of writing this paper, using unsupported application platforms. There is no integrated software solution comparing automated software recognition to the points marked by users, without the need for using additional devices like video camera or microphone. In the present work, only one device – the smartphone is used, lowering the cost of implementation. Using the rotation matrix, based a translation to the global coordinate system was made. Our solution is also independent from the device's physical location in a car, which allows for a greater versatility.

The results presented here are part of a broader series of research using GPS and mobile devices uploading data to a cloud computing system and performing data mining [3] to find low quality roads or possible road hazards. With this kind of information it will be possible to prepare mobile planning routes with existing navigation software or create a new solution [7] including the possibility of omitting low quality roads. Such transport optimisation may be used in a specialised way, for example in medical transport [8], but also in general navigation software to increase overall user comfort during rides.

3   The Software Solution

To acquire data in a post-processible way, a software solution had to be created. The prepared application is to be tested in densely built-up city centers with frequent speed limits of 30–40 km/h. The average vehicle velocity in such areas stays within 35 km/h. The authors have chosen the following functionalities to be included in the software:

- The software should allow recording data from accelerometer in a global coordinate system,
- The data acquired must be stamped with current location from the GPS receiver and with current time,
- On the assumption that our data will be collected from road fragments every 100 cm, at the average car speed of 35 km/h, the sampling frequency will be about 10 Hz,
- The user should have the possibility to press a button to record a noticed road anomaly,
- The application has to record data without a problem for up to 10 min of continuous recording.

There were also some additional requirements made, such as choosing the file format in which the data will be saved or allowing interoperation with the current software built for similar purposes. This means the software has to save data in CSV (Comma Separated Value) format, where values of acceleration are saved in all the axes in local and global coordinate system, with time and current location (latitude and longitude). The second CSV file should represent location (latitude and longitude) of user-noticed road artefacts. The application allows to save these files on the device itself, as well as to upload them to the REST (Representational State Transfer) service. Acceleration is measured in multiplicities of Earth's gravitational acceleration, marked g, which is equal to $9.81 \frac{m}{s^2}$. The g as a base data unit was chosen because it is the unit provided by operating system APIs. Sampling frequency of 10 Hz from accelerometer was chosen a priori by the authors, there is however a possibility to increase this value up to 62.5 Hz (a data sample every 16 ms) on used software platform. This limit is a result of API limitations, but such greater frequency will allow to cover most typical car solutions.

For the software solution, the Windows Phone platform was used and the application was created in the C# language.

3.1   User Interface

The application is showing current data in real time. Two large "start" and "stop" buttons allow to start and stop recording. These two functions are available at the fingertips without an extended interaction of the user and the device. This was necessary for the experiment to work properly, along with a "bump!" button, which records the position of a road artefact. A screenshot of the application's user interface for use during the recording is shown in Fig. 1.

There are also diagnostic messages about the accelerometer state, GPS (Global Positioning System) receiver state and NTP (Network Time Protocol) client state available at the bottom, showing the offset between current device time and the time from the NTP server. There is also a menu minimised by default with different software options, which do not require fast access such as data upload.

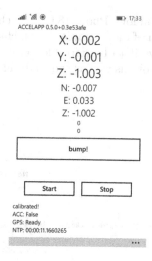

Fig. 1. Screenshot of the application's interface

The NTP (Network Time Protocol) time server allows to get current time and calculate an offset between current time and "true time", so every sample is now saved in true time synchronised with the NTP server pool. It was introduced because GPS data from API devices are unfortunately calibrated as a device time, not a GPS time. The Windows Phone platform has an internal NTP client, but the authors found it did not work properly.

There is also access to calibration, because recorded accelerations may be different not only due to different models of devices but even altogether different devices. Calibration is based on registering a set of first results from the accelerometer where the devices are lying on the ground flat, calculating average values for every axis separately. Because each record should consist of 0, 0, −1 (X, Y, Z), the calculated average is saved as a vector of three elements and is being subtracted for every record since calibration. Since calibration was set to get 10 records, it usually takes 1 s. The device is calibrated once after mounting in a car. The calibration is used only to smoothen the registered data – because when even not in motion, the accelerometer tends to read accelerations, so the authors believe this is a sufficient solution. In previous works, calibration was performed after every press of the "start" button. However, the authors discovered there were no significant issues when calibration was done only once. Because of calibration, baseline (idle) readings of the Z value will be very close to −1 g.

3.2   Data Acquisition

All the data recorded are being saved in AccelVal class, whose implementation INotifyPropertyChanged allows to notify the observing object if the data were modified, making it possible to use this class as a model for application written in C# and Silverlight for Windows Phone (8.0). To achieve future-proof interoperability, this representation of data samples was included into a PCL (Portable Class Library), which allows it to be portable between Windows Phone, Windows and using 3rd party tools, as well as the Android and iOS software systems (Fig. 2).

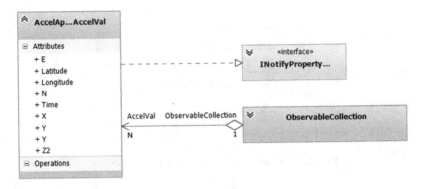

Fig. 2. Class diagram of the main application classes

All results are saved in an ObservableCollection instance in memory and saved to file only when the "stop" button is tapped, to nullify the effects of small storage card performance during recording. In previous versions of the software all results were displayed on its main screen, but this behaviour was scrapped because of information noise. All results are automatically saved when the "stop" button is tapped and a new text file is created in so called Isolated Storage. Isolated Storage in Windows Phone operating system is a specific file system region where applications can save all the data, but no other application can access it. Typically, even the user cannot access Isolated Storage content – it is not exposed to any APIs or to the computer. However, the authors used here two important elements of Windows Phone platform – the Isolated Storage Explorer (ISE) tool and an application deployment tool. Because the application was put on the device using Application Deployment on developer-unlocked application, access to Isolated Storage is allowed by ISE for this particular application. However, the application allows user to upload data to web services, but just copying files with ISE is a bit faster and can be performed offline.

One of the most important elements of the software is a global coordinate system used in samples. By default, all accelerometer data are vectors with data for the X, Y and Z axes, which are axes for the device itself. However, every time the device is not staying flat on its back, samples may not fully reflect motion data, as the Z value will change from $-1\,$g. The global coordinate system is shown in Fig. 3, and the Y axis is the Earth's north, the X axis is to the east and the Z one is directed up from the Earth's surface.

To calculate the coordinates from local to global system a rotation matrix is used. It is a matrix of scalar products of versors of all the following axes

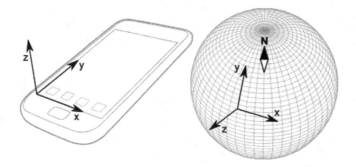

Fig. 3. Global and local coordinate systems [12]

of both systems. If the coordinates in a local system are given, it is possible to calculate the global coordinates by multiplying every directional vector by rotation matrix, which is the 3×3 matrix available from the OrientationSensor class as a property of the result of the GetCurrentReading() method [12]. Using the global coordinate system there is no need for the device to be placed in a specific position, because the Z axis, which is the base for the experiment, is always directed upwards so that the accelerations recorded are still valid with every position of the device.

4 Road Artefacts Study of the Calibration Experiment

To verify a solution a pilot study was prepared in two stages. The first was to compare results between the users' response to the road artefacts using the "bump" button discussed before. This allowed to work on data post-processing and finding a proper detection algorithm. The experiment was performed using a Nokia Lumia 820 device, which is a middle-class device launched in 2012. The device was immovable inside a car, held in a mobile phone holder which was mounted in the car's middle tunnel.

The first part of the experiment was to record the position of speed bumps on a small suburban road of a good overall quality. The existing 8 speed bumps, all with different heights and lengths (usually about two meters in length and about 15 cm in height, gradually rising and falling), were crossed at a speed slightly lower (about 20 km/h) than the assumed 35 km/h, which is under the speed limit on this road. Every time the user, in this case passenger, was driven across the speed bump, he touched the "bump" button on the device.

The data acquired in the first phase of the experiment were saved on a computer and analysed.

The Fig. 4 presented above is a representation of acceleration on the Z axis in time while traversing a stone speed bump during one of the experiments. In the beginning, the value of acceleration is between -0.8 g and -1 g. Between the 3rd and 5th second there is a sudden jump of acceleration up to the value of -0.4 g and a drop down to -1.4 g 400 ms later. These values are recognised as

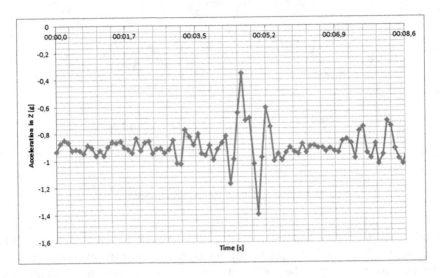

Fig. 4. Acceleration on the Z axis in a global coordinate system while traversing a speed bump

an anomaly by the software. They represent, respectively, the car going up (and the acceleration declining) and down the appropriate slopes of a speed bump.

Table 1. Standard deviation and number of anomalies detected

Standard deviation	Samples over threshold
3.7	24
3.9	21
4.1	20
4.3	16

There were 1167 data samples acquired. First, the average value of Z acceleration (in global coordinate system) from the whole population was calculated, which was equal to -0.9489. The maximum and minimum values were -0.5896 and -1.3858, respectively. Then, the standard deviation from the whole population was calculated, with the result of $\sigma = 0.06559$. The authors used map visualisation, plotting on a map all the points where the user clicked the "bump" button and all the points with an absolute difference of value from the average value greater than the tested one, in multiplications of sigma value.

After experimentation, the result was that with an interval from 3.7σ to 4.3σ all the user points were covered, and different numbers of samples are identified as anomalies, which is presented in the Table 1. With a 3.7σ, the results show 24 data points over a threshold, and with 4.5σ which is over the interval, there are 12 samples over this threshold, but not every speed bump was identified.

As the results show, there are more samples than tested speed bumps, which is to do with the fact that the user pressed "bump" only once on each speed bump, however acceleration on the Z axis was rising when the car was entering and exiting appropriate slopes.

The results with the threshold of 4.2σ are shown in Fig. 5. The diamonds are positions of speed bumps as registered by user pressing the "bump" button, and pushpins are positions of anomalies determined by the software. It proves that one of the speed bumps was not high enough to be registered as a road artefact. With a value of 4.2σ all speed bumps were registered, there were 17 data samples, and as the figure shows, 75 % of the speed bumps were registered with two data samples, for entering and exiting a bump.

Fig. 5. Speed bumps as located by the user and determined by the software with a 4.2σ threshold

5   Road Artefacts Study - The Experiment

The second experiment was performed with the same car, same mobile device and same software solution on a real road, without user interaction, only to check if the post-processing analysis for establishing a threshold would hold against different road conditions. The monitored track was in the length of about 1.46 km.

The proposed experiment track was placed near the Technological University, and started from the Muzyczna Street, through Szczerbowskiego Street, Dolna

Panny Marii, Środkowa, Wschodnia, Narutowicza and back through Środkowa to Dolna Panny Marii. The experiment was performed in the late afternoon when the traffic was low.

Fig. 6. The second part of the experiment with a marked track and positions of anomalies

The proposed track started with a steep hillock with an inclination of about 11 % with an asphalt surface degraded into a state similar to a washboard. The second interesting part was a fragment of uphill Środkowa street with a very steep inclination of 20 % and a large road artefact in a form of traverse ramp preceded by a ditch. These two locations were chosen by experts as potential very dangerous and impactful road artefacts.

During the experiment, there were about 1359 data samples acquired which were downloaded on a notebook PC after going back to the university's campus for post-processing. This time the average value was -1.00157, maximum was equal to -0.6509, and minimum was -1.4504. The calculated standard deviation was 0.063216. Using again a threshold of 4.2σ, a total of 18 data samples were visualized on a map, which is presented in a Fig. 6.

The identified artefacts were compared to locations chosen by experts as potentially problematic locations mentioned earlier, and both groups were correctly recognised. Additionally, during the second drive with the expert as a passenger, he correctly identified the artefacts previously found by the software.

6   Summary and Future Work

An important element of the proposed solution is the fact that it is based only on measuring the Z axis in the global coordinate system. Such an approach simplifies the post-processing used to finding only the values where upwards acceleration is above a defined threshold.

Despite using such a basic solution, the software designed was able to correctly confirm the existing artefacts in the shape of road artefacts like speed bumps, potholes or "washboard" and place them on the GPS map.

As mentioned before, in this paper the sampling frequency was selected to find road artefacts at every 100 cm, with the speed of about 35 km/h. However, to achieve more accurate results, it may be useful to change the sampling frequency together with altering the vehicle's velocity, in order to achieve a constant artefact length of 100 cm. Based on the APIs operating system, it is possible to increase the sampling frequency up to 62.5 Hz. Future work has to indicate automatic data upload and processing in the first place. The authors discuss two potential ways for a new study: the first one is to automatically upload and process data in the cloud computing system. These data may be used to create a system of automatic warning to users about potential road artefacts, similar to existing systems warning about accidents or speed control [14]. The second proposed advancement is to prepare a software with more self-adaptive solutions.

Acknowledgments. Marcin Badurowicz is a participant of the project: "Qualifications for the labour market - employer friendly university", cofinanced by European Union from European Social Fund.

References

1. Astartita, V., Vaiana, R., Iuele, T., Caruso, M.V., Giofre, V., De Masi, F.: Automated sensing system for monitoring of road surface quality by mobile devices. Procedia Soc. Behav. Sci. **111**, 242–251 (2014)
2. Bhoraskar, R., Vankadhara, N., Raman, B., Kulkarni, P.: Wolverine: traffic and road condition estimation using smartphone sensors. In: Fourth International Conference on Communication Systems and Networks (COMSNETS) (2012)
3. Czerwinski, D.: Influence of the VM manager on private cluster data mining system. In: Kwiecień, A., Gaj, P., Stera, P. (eds.) CN 2014. CCIS, vol. 431, pp. 47–56. Springer, Heidelberg (2014)
4. Das, T., Mohan, P., Padmanabhan, V.N., Ramjee, R., Sharma, A.: PRISM: platform for remote sensing using smartphones. In: MobiSys 2010, San Francisco, California, USA, 15–18 June 2010
5. Eriksson, J., Girod, L., Hull, B., Newton, R., Madden, S., Balakrishnan, H.: The pothole patrol: using a mobile sensor network for road surface monitoring. In: MobiSys 2008: Proceeding of the 6th International Conference on Mobile Systems. Applications, and Services, pp. 29–39. ACM, New York (2008)
6. Jain, M., Singh, A.P., Bali, S., Kaul, S.: Speed-breaker earlywarning system. In: NSDR 2012, 6th USENIX Conference, Boston (2012)

7. Łukasik, E., Skublewska-Paszkowska, M.: IOS mobile to route determining. Logistyka 3/2014, 5763–5770 (2014)
8. Miłosz, M., Badurowicz, M., Złomaniec, P.: Modele matematyczne optymalizacji tras w transporcie medycznym. Logistyka 6/2014, 7524–7533 (2014)
9. Mohan, P., Padmanabhan, V.N., Ramjee, R.: Nericell: using mobile smartphones for rich monitoring of road and traffic conditions. In: Proceedings of the 6th ACM Conference on Embedded Network Sensor Systems, SenSys 2008, pp. 357–358. ACM, New York, NY, USA (2008). http://doi.acm.org/10.1145/1460412.1460450
10. Mohan, P., Padmanabhan, V.N., Ramjee, R.: TrafficSense: rich monitoring of road and traffic conditions using mobile devices. Microsoft Research Technical Report MSR-RT-2008-59 (2008)
11. Perttunen, M., et al.: Distributed road surface condition monitoring using mobile phones. In: Hsu, C.-H., Yang, L.T., Ma, J., Zhu, C. (eds.) UIC 2011. LNCS, vol. 6905, pp. 64–78. Springer, Heidelberg (2012)
12. Skublewska-Paszkowska, M., Smołka, J., Łukasik, E., Badurowicz, M.: Pomiar przyspieszenia w globalnym układzie współrzędnych z użyciem urządzeń mobilnych. Logistyka 6/2014, 9646–9655 (2014)
13. Strazdins, G., Mednis, A., Kanonirs, G., Zviedris, R., Selavo, L.: Towards vehicular sensor networks with android smartphones for road surface monitoring. In: CONET 2011, CPSWeek 2011 (2011)
14. Antyradar i darmowa nawigacja - Yanosik.pl. http://www.yanosik.pl. Accessed 21 March 2015

The Use of Steganography to Control Multimedia Players

Grzegorz Koziel[✉] and Marek Milosz

Institute of Computer Science, Department of Electrical Engineering and Computer Science,
Lublin University of Technology, Nadbystrzycka 38A, 20-618 Lublin, Poland
{g.koziel,m.milosz}@pollub.pl

Abstract. Addition of automatic control to a multimedia player is desirable. It allows a user to save his/her preferences inside the multimedia content. It also gives the possibility of reducing the media size or delete a chosen part of the recording. Moreover, this solution allows to steer multimedia players during stream transmission. This kind of control is achievable with the use of steganography. Transparent markers are added to an audio track. Each marker can code a group of orders. Orders are used to control the multimedia content flow and its parameters. Markers have a certain structure allowing to keep multiple orders together with their parameters. Each marker is precisely set in time and has enough capacity to keep 256 various orders or their groups. The least significant bit method was used to insert markers.

Keywords: Steganography · Multimedia · Control · Steering

1 Introduction

A typical multimedia player is usually controlled by a user. He/she controls the multimedia stream according to his/her own preferences. The most common operations are to adjust a sound volume, its timbre, or saturation. Sometimes users want to omit some fragments of the multimedia stream. If a user wants to play the same multimedia with all these operations, he/she has to repeat all the activities previously performed. They are not saved. This would not be necessary if all the operations were stored inside the multimedia content. Adding additional data directly to the multimedia without introducing interference is possible only with steganography.

Audio steganography relies on attaching additional data directly to the sound data. It is used in various applications: watermarking [10], creating hidden file systems [9] or realising secret communication [11, 14]. Such applications do not exhaust all the possibilities.

The authors propose a new approach to control multimedia playback. Each user can save his preferences directly inside the multimedia data. This solution allows for introducing previously made settings in the subsequent re-playing. Saving preferences is done by adding special markers directly to the signal. This addition is done by steganographic techniques. To add markers to the signal and use them during later replays, a special multimedia player with additional functionality has been created. Moreover, this solution allows for steering the multimedia player during stream transmission. The

© Springer International Publishing Switzerland 2015
G. Dregvaite and R. Damasevicius (Eds.): ICIST 2015, CCIS 538, pp. 515–525, 2015.
DOI: 10.1007/978-3-319-24770-0_44

prepared signal is sent to users. All multimedia players adjust their settings automatically to obtain the desired effect.

The subject of multimedia stream control was presented previously in the SPCv0 method, described in [7]. The solution presented in this article is the improvement of the latter. The method created will be called Steganographic Player Control version 1 (SPCv1). The foundations of the steganographic marker concept were designed from scratch to obtain a more flexible and efficient solution.

2 Control Data Attachment

To make it possible to automatically control multimedia play it is necessary to attach control data to the multimedia data. It is possible to do it in two ways:

- attach them to the end of the multimedia data,
- place them directly within the multimedia stream, hiding control markers inside the container data.

The first solution requires addition of a time stamp attached to each command. Otherwise, the multimedia player will not know when to apply each action. Thus, it is necessary to reserve some spare place for the time data. What is more, this solution is not possible when using a continuous transmission. The next disadvantage is the necessity of adding data to the multimedia file behind the original data. This can cause some problems because control data exist beyond the end of the multimedia data marked in the file header.

The second solution is more flexible. It is possible to attach control data directly to the multimedia signal. This causes no data size increase. Control data is placed directly inside the multimedia stream with steganographic techniques. Commands to the player are placed directly where they should be applied. This allows for using this technique in multimedia streaming.

One more advantage of the proposed technique is the possibility of replaying the processed signal with the common multimedia player. Control data will not be recognized. It will be treated as sound data.

A technique used to attach markers has to offer significant informational capacity and transparency. If the method has to work in real time, the steganographic technique must be time-efficient. Various techniques were presented in the literature [2, 15]. Methods that work in the transform domain offer great robustness to hidden data removal [1, 3–5, 7, 13]. Unfortunately their informational capacity is low [6]. Similar parameters can be obtained with echo techniques [12]. Greater capacity and reduced complexity is offered by Least Significant Bit (LSB) methods [2, 8]. That was the reason for choosing the LSB method in the SPCv0 and SPCv1 methods.

As the next step, it is necessary to find which signal will be used to carry control markers. A multimedia stream can contain audio or video data. Both of them contain at least one audio track. An audio track may contain a varying number of channels. To design a universal solution, the number of channels is examined and they are all used to attach the control data.

In the SPCv0 method the assumption was to obtain the highest possible precision of control order application. Markers containing orders to multimedia player were set in the place where the orders should be applied. If there was no possibility to place a marker in the required place, tit was attached earlier in the signal. Each marker in the SPCv0 method is equipped with the time stamp, which defines the delay of order application. This allows for order application exactly at the time that the user set.

This solution was abandoned in the SPCv1 method. To save the time stamp it was necessary to put additional 16 bits in each marker, which increased the marker size and its complexity. As the experiments show, great precision in time is not necessary. Users are not able to mark precisely the moment in time where the order should be applied. The inaccuracy varies up to 0,5 s. Because of that, in the SPCv1 method time stamps were removed from markers. Markers are attached just in the place where the user ordered and executed them at the same time. If there is no possibility of marker attachment at the required time, the closest possible location of marker is used. This can mean an inaccuracy, but marker size reduction allows to put a lot of markers in each second of recording. The possibility of marker collision is negligible.

3   Marker Detection

The position of marker is unknown to multimedia player. Multimedia player must be able to determine where the marker is put in the signal. This problem was solved in the SPCv0 method by adding a starter and terminator sequences to the marker. These sequences will be recognised by the player as a marker beginning and end. To reduce the complexity, the sequence was established as a series of identical bit values. The length of the starting sequence was determined in the way that reduces any introduced interference and marker size. A shorter sequence needs less space and causes less interference in the container signal. If the sequence is too short, it is possible that it exists in many locations in the original signal. In that case it is necessary to change some bit values in such a sequence to avoid false marker detection. This operation, of course, introduces unnecessary interference. The optimal starting sequence length was adjusted on the basis of an analysis of existing sequences in the original signals. The results of the experiment are presented in Fig. 1.

Because of silent fragments in the audio track, the number of long zero sequences is greater than that of sequences of ones. This fact was the reason for choosing the ones series as a starting sequence. The length of this sequence has been set to 16 bits.

After the starting sequence, the control orders are inserted. Each time the necessity for using multiple commands can occur. Multiple commands are placed after the starting sequence. Each command contains an order code and its parameter value. The order code defines an operation as done. It is encoded on an eight-bit sequence.

After the order code, the parameter value is encoded. All parameter values are given as absolute values, not as a change value – it is possible for multimedia player to start in a random position in a signal.

Inside the marker the time stamp was added to define the time of performing the operation. Time was encoded as the time from the beginning of the control marker. This means that all orders placed in the marker are executed at the same time.

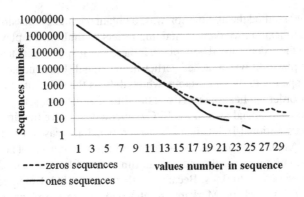

Fig. 1. Number of various length sequences having the same bit values [7].

To inform the multimedia player where the end of the control order sequence was placed, the terminator is used. This is a defined sequence of bits. It is a sequence of eight ones.

The minimum length of a control marker in the SPCv0 method was 32 bits. Such lengths had markers containing only one order code without a parameter. The maximum length of the marker was not defined. It depends on the order number included in the marker and its parameter size.

In the SPCv1 method the emphasis was put on the marker size reduction and its simplification. Because of this, the length of the starting sequence was shortened to 12 bits. The sequences of ones having more than 11 bits have only 0.05 % share in the common original signal. It is enough to change any bit in this sequence in order to avoid false marker recognition. The impact of the changed bits on the audio interference is negligible. The impact of changing one bit in one of 20,000 samples is shown in Table 1.

Table 1. Interference introduced during false marker removal.

Measure	Value
Signal noise ratio (SNR)	98 dB
Mean difference (MD)	6E-10
Mean square error (MSE)	7.3E-13
Normalised MSE	1.5 E-10

The length of this starting sequence allows for a marker length reduction of 4 bits in comparison to the SPCv0 method. This effect is important when a big number of markers is put inside the signal.

What is more, the structure of the marker in the SPCv1 method is precisely defined. This makes it possible to determine each marker size. Because of this, no terminator is necessary. It allows for an additional marker size reduction of about 8 bits in comparison to the SPCv0 method.

4   Marker Construction in the SPCv1 Method

To place orders in the multimedia stream a special structure is necessary. This structure will be called a marker. As described in [7], the beginning of this structure has to be marked. We decided to modify the previously invented markers structure. After the 12 bit-long beginning sequence, the order code is put. After that the parameters values are placed. Each order has a defined length of its parameter data. This makes it possible to calculate a marker's length and allows to abandon the terminator sequence. Because of a limited number of operation types, the orders were coded as an 8-bit(-long) sequence. To determine which orders are coded, a dictionary of orders and their combinations was - created. Each order or order combination is assigned to a unique number (code) ranging from 0 to 255. A selection of this dictionary is presented in Table 2.

Table 2. Part of the order dictionary.

Code	Order
0	Volume
1	Equaliser
2	Volume + equaliser
3	Go to
4	Brightness
5	Saturation
6	Brightness + saturation
7	Volume + equaliser + brightness + saturation
8	Insert a fragment

Apart from the orders list, the dictionary contains the specification of their arguments. Almost all orders require additional data to set the controlled parameter value. All values are given as absolute ones. No relative values are used. The reason is the necessity to ensure that the method is working during stream transmission.

In the case when the player begins its work after some time after the start of the transmission, markers inserted in the former part of the signal cannot be accessed.

The algorithm of marker placement was also changed in comparison to the SPCv0 method. We do not limit ourselves to one sound channel usage. All the available channels are used. To operate independently of the channels number we use the sound frame structure. The sound frame contains samples coming from all channels. The least significant bits of all samples from the frame are used to attach the subsequent bits of the marker. The used bits placement was marked grey in Fig. 2.

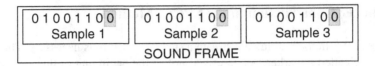

Fig. 2. Placement of bits used to attach markers data.

Because the number of channels can be easily determined by sound format analysis, the proposed method is reliable and easy to use. Moreover, it makes it possible to attach N times more data than the SPCv0 method, where N is the number of audio channels. This allows for the placement of a bigger number of markers and for increasing and reducing N times the possibility of marker collision.

The player has to start working properly even if there is no possibility of reading the earlier markers. Using orders containing relative values (for example: reduce volume twice) can result in improper action, because the previous parameter values are unknown.

The problem can be avoided while absolute parameter values are used. Each parameter has a defined number of bits to store its value. The most simple example is volume. Eight bits are designed to store the volume level. This gives 256 various levels of loudness. Value "0" means no sound. Value 256 means the maximum level of loudness. To use the natural character of this parameter, the logarithmic scale was used in this parameter. Even if the player does not know the previous value of this parameter, it can set the required value after it reaches the marker containing the volume order.

As was proven, using absolute values in the markers allows to employ the present method in the stream transmission as well. Of course, if the player starts playing the multimedia stream during its transmission, some problems can be found at the beginning. The player has no information about the signal, so it has to start with default settings. In some cases it can lead to finding some artifact. For example, two subsequent orders can be placed in the stream. The first one to make the signal very quiet (volume level = 30). After a while the second marker can contain an order having volume level equal to 60. The goal was to make the replay a bit louder to highlight a sound fragment. A multimedia player that starts working at the time between the above two markers will start from the default volume level of 128. After reaching the second marker it will adjust the sound, reducing its volume to level 60.

To avoid the above problem, it is necessary to read the current value of all the parameters while starting the multimedia player. This would take an additional communication channel to send this data, or periodically introduce into the signal additional markers containing all the parameter values. The second solution demands that the player wait with the start of the replay till the marker is obtained. Neither of these solutions were implemented in the algorithm, because it is out of range of the present work.

As previously said, almost all orders need a value to define the operation's parameters. Each of the orders has a defined parameter length. To make the marker as small as possible, the list of orders to be implemented is coded in eight bits. The subsequent bits carry parameter values. To find out which value should be applied to a particular operation, an analysis is performed. Parameter values are added into the sequence which results from the orders' sequence in the dictionary. According to the table containing parameter sizes, the sequence of bits is divided into fragments containing particular parameter values. A part of the table is presented in Table 3.

Table 3. Definition of the size of order parameters.

Order	Size [bit]
Volume	8
Equaliser	40
Go to	18
Brightness	8
Saturation	8
Insert a fragment	36

With Table 3 it is possible to precisely determine a marker's length. For example, the marker for the order having code 7 has the length of 84 bits. It contains a starting sequence having 12 bits. Order code of 8 bits and parameters to orders coded in the marker are stored at 64 bits.

The present method uses different marker structure than the SPCv0 method. It allows to omit a terminator at the end of the marker. In the SPCv0 method it was not possible to calculate where the end of the marker was.

Moreover, there is no necessity to use time stamps in the present method. All operations coded in the marker are applied 882/N samples after the marker beginning, where N is the number of audio channels. This is also the maximum size of the marker.

The algorithm of marker insertion is as follows:

1. wait for user command to insert a marker, take the list of orders and their parameters from user,
2. build a marker:
   (a) put the starting sequence;
   (b) put the code of chosen orders,
   (c) put the parameter values according to the defined sequence,
   (d) calculate the created marker's length (L),
3. check if there is any marker beginning in the last 882/N samples,
   (a) if it exists, check if the marker finishes before the sample selected by the user,
      (i) if not, move the projected marker beginning to the first sample after the existing marker,
   (b) check if the next marker exists in the next L/N sound frames,
      (i) if so, move the projected marker beginning to the first sample after the found marker and go to point 3b of this algorithm.
4. insert a new marker in the sound signal.

In comparison to the SPCv0 method, the average length of the marker was reduced by 53 %. The reduction of marker length resulted in a significant reduction of the interference introduced. Both the methods compared were used to introduce some set of orders. A comparison of the interference introduced into a signal by these methods is presented in Table 4.

Table 4. Interference level introduced by the methods compared.

	SPCv0 method	SPCv1 method
Signal noise ratio (SNR)	81.2	84.8
Mean difference (MD)	1.31E-07	5.77E-08
Mean square error (MSE)	1.58E-11	6.98E-12
Normalised MSE	7.52E-09	3.32E-09

5   Multimedia Player Control

A multimedia player, apart from playing the signal, has to read and write hidden markers. At the beginning, it is necessary to determine the mode in order to determine the player's behaviour. If the processed file is used for the first time, it is necessary to find all the starting sequences and remove them to avoid further false marker detection. A removal is done by changing single bits' values. This operation can be done during the usual multimedia replay. Additionally, an insertion of a marker can be done.

During the replay of the previously processed signal, the whole signal is analysed in order to find starting sequences. When found, the time of implementing commands coded in the marker is calculated and the marker content is read. A multimedia player implements changes when the calculated time comes. It is worth to notice, that in the presented method no time marker exists. Commands are implemented just in the place where they were inserted into the signal. It is possible thanks to marker length reduction and its simplification. Short markers allow for precision equal to 1/20 of a second. The algorithm of multimedia player control is as follows:

1. start from sample 1,
2. set the "ones" counter to zero,
3. read the least significant bit of the current sample; if its value is "one", increase the counter by one; if not, set the counter value to zero,
4. check if the counter value equals 8; if so, the marker was found; go to point 5; if not, go to the next sample and go to point 3,
5. read the orders code and determine the marker's structure and length,
6. read all the parameter values,
7. apply the orders, set the counter to "zero" and go to point 3.

Different commands are "go to" and "insert a fragment". They are not used for changing signal character. Their goal is to make it possible to change the sequence of the replayed signal. The "go to" command allows to jump to another place inside the signal. The length of this parameter's value is 18 bits. The jump operation allows to obtain the precision of 1/10 of a second. With this precision it is possible to code the jump up to 218 min on both sides, forward and backward. It is a big enough range for common recordings. In the stream transmission jumps forward cannot be applied, because of the lack of the signal data. Jumps backward can be done only if the signal is stored and available locally.

In both cases, local multimedia file and stream transmission, it is necessary to check if a point exists in the signal when the multimedia player should jump. If there is no such point in the signal, the command is ignored.

The next operation changing the sequence of playback is the "insert a fragment" one. It causes inserting another fragment in place of the command application. This command requires two parameters: the start time of the inserted fragment and its finish time. The time definition is the same as in the "go to" command. The "insert a fragment" command uses two time markers. Each of them gives relative time, defined as a shift to the command application time. The range and precision offered is the same as in the "go to" command.

Various users can attach their markers to the signal, or various versions of the same content can be prepared. It is possible because one of the order codes defines the user. It is not obligatory to define the user, but if various groups of markers need to be created, this is the only possibility. The algorithm allows for defining up to 16 various users or tracks. If multiple users or tracks are to be applied, each marker size is increased by 4 bits. These bits are used to code the user or track identifier.

The user definition, combined with "go to" and "insert a fragment" commands allow for preparing various versions of the same content. Each user can be served various fragments of the signal. For example, a version for children can be prepared by removal of some violent fragments or their replacement with the spare fragments that do not exist in the common version. This solution also allows for signal size reduction, because the repeated fragment can simply be inserted instead of multiple writing.

6 Multimedia Signal Processing

In common applications the signal is prepared to work with the present solution by removing false start sequences. When it is done, the marker attachment is possible. This operation can cause some problems, because one marker can overwrite the other. To properly process the signal it is necessary to check if there is enough available space to put a marker into the signal. If not, it is necessary to move the marker to the first free spot. The whole process was presented in Fig. 3.

In some cases, the user can trim the signal. If the beginning of the signal is removed, the present settings of the multimedia player are saved at the beginning of the signal. An additional marker, containing all the applied settings is created. The signal is trimmed a bit earlier than the user ordered. A spare signal fragment is used to attach the additional marker, without disturbing the part of the signal requested by the user. This solution is especially useful when a large number of markers exists in the signal and there is a problem with an additional marker attachment.

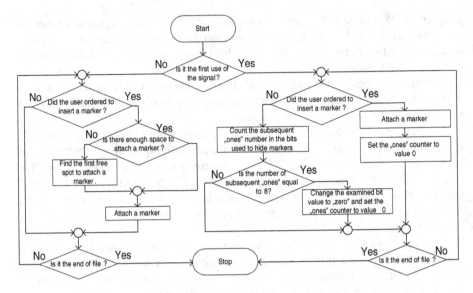

Fig. 3. Marker insertion process.

7 Conclusion

The paper presents a new algorithm of multimedia signal playback control. Various aspects of the solution were discussed. It was proven that it is possible to save user preferences in the signal with steganographic techniques. It is also possible to prepare various versions of the content on the basis of the same multimedia signal by controlling playback parameters and free signal fragments insertion or removal.

The present work introduces a big number of changes in comparison to the SPCv0 method. The most important is the marker size reduction by time stamps removal. It allows for a significant size reduction which results in smaller interference introduced into the signal and the latter's greater capacity.

The proposed solution can be used not only to control the multimedia playback. The next possibility is to use it to control devices. A special marker put in the signal can be used to change a device's state.

References

1. Badura, S., Rymaszewski, S.: Transform domain steganography in DVD video and audio content. In: 2007 IEEE International Workshop on Imaging Systems and Techniques Book Series: IEEE International Workshop on Imaging Systems and Techniques, pp. 195–199 (2007)
2. Cvejic, N.: Algorithms for Audio Watermarking and Steganography. Oulu University Press, Oulu (2004)
3. Djebbar, F., Ayad, B., Meraim, K.: Comparative study of digital audio steganography techniques. Eurasip J. Audio Speech Music Process. **2012**, 1–16 (2012) (Article Number: 25)

4. Gomez-Coronel, S., Escalante-Ramirez, B., Acevedo-Mosqueda, M., et al.: Steganography in audio files by hermite transform. Appl. Math. Inf. Sci. **8**(3), 959–966 (2014)
5. Koziel, G.: Fourier transform based methods in sound steganography. Actual Probl. Econ. **120**(6), 321–328 (2011). ISSN 1993-6788
6. Koziel, G.: Increasing steganographic capacity of the MF method. Actual Probl. Econ. **6**(132), 367–373 (2012). ISSN 1993-6788
7. Koziel, G.: Steganography usage to control multimedia stream. Adv. Sci. Technol. **8**(21), 5–8 (2014). doi:10.12913/22998624.1091870
8. Kumar, H., Anuradha: Enhanced LSB technique for audio steganography. In: 2012 Third International Conference on Computing Communication and Networking Technologies (ICCCNT), Book Series: International Conference on Computing Communication and Network Technologies (2012)
9. Lach, J.:. SBFS – steganography based file system. In: Proceedings of the 2008 1st International Conference on Information Technology, pp. 171–174 (2008)
10. Lipinski, P.: Watermarking software in practical applications. Bull. Pol. Acad. Sci. Tech. Sci. **59**(1), 21–25 (2011)
11. Mazurczyk, W., Szczypiorski, K.: Steganography of VoIP streams. In: Meersman, R., Tari, Z. (eds.) OTM 2008, Part II. LNCS, vol. 5332, pp. 1001–1018. Springer, Heidelberg (2008)
12. Shine, K.P., Krishna Kumar, S.: Extended bipolar echo kernel for audio watermarking. In: International Conference on Advances in Recent Technologies in Communication and Computing, IEEE Computer Society 2009, pp. 487–489 (2009)
13. Shirali-Shahreza, S., Sharif, M.: Adaptive wavelet domain audio steganography with high capacity and low error rate. In: Information and Emerging Technologies, ICIET 2007 (2007). doi:10.1109/ICIET.2007.4381305
14. Srivastava, M., Rafiq, M.: Novel approach to secure communication using audio steganography. In: Mems, Nano and Smart Systems, PTS 1-6, Book Series: Advanced Materials Research, vol. 403–408, pp. 963-969 (2012)
15. Zielinska, E., Mazurczyk, W., Szczypiorski, K.: Trends in steganography. Commun. ACM **57**(3), 86–95 (2014)

AeroFX - Native Themes for JavaFX

Matthias Meidinger[1]([✉]), Hendrik Ebbers[2], and Christian Reimann[1]

[1] University of Applied Sciences and Arts, Dortmund, Germany
`mamei003@stud.fh-dortmund.de, christian.reimann@fh-dortmund.de`
[2] Canoo Engineering AG, Basel, Switzerland
`hendrik.ebbers@canoo.com`

Abstract. The authors present an Open Source JavaFX skin, AeroFX, which is similar to the look and feel of Microsoft Windows 7.

Oracle announced to change the standard technology for graphical development of user interfaces away from Swing, which raised a strong response in the developer community. JavaFX is the announced successor of Swing, but it lacks the capability of developing user interfaces with a different look and feel than Modena, the default JavaFX skin. This look and feel can be customized with so called "skins", which Oracle announced not to develop themselves.

Keywords: JavaFX · Windows 7 · Usability · UX design · Native skin

1 Introduction

JavaFX has been placed as the successor of the still popular, yet outdated, Swing-Toolkit. Both technologies are used to build Graphical User Interfaces (GUI) for Java-based applications. JavaFX and Swing both support "skinning", which is the process of changing the visual appearance of a GUI by applying a skin. Because of its age, there are many skins for Swing, giving it the ability to mimic the native look and feel of Windows- or OSX-applications.

As JavaFX is an emerging technology recently introduced with the JRE 8, there are few skins available at the moment. Projects aiming for the development of JavaFX-skins are rare and differ in quality, despite the fact that Oracle announced that they will only develop a single platform independent skin, called "Modena". The development of such a skin is time-consuming and requires knowledge of Java and CSS, a quite exotic combination of skills, as these two languages origin from very different domains of computer sciences. However, the support of native look and feels for different Operating Systems (OS) is an important requirement for developers who face the challenge of building competitive GUIs. Because of the intelligent and modern design of JavaFX, there is a high probability that it will keep spreading across the Java developer community. To support this divulgement, this work shows the state of skin projects with native Windows 7 look and feel and introduces AeroFX, a JavaFX skin with aforementioned look and feel.

G. Dregvaite and R. Damasevicius (Eds.): ICIST 2015, CCIS 538, pp. 526–536, 2015.
DOI: 10.1007/978-3-319-24770-0_45

The remainder of this paper is organized as follows: Sect. 2 presents the problems of using non-native GUI skins from the usability view. Section 3 deals with related work that exists at the time of writing. Section 4 provides background information on the used technologies and design decisions, followed by a practical example of usage (Sect. 5), finally followed by Sect. 6, which outlines some conclusions and future work.

2 Problem Statement

The field of User Experience (UX) Design is gathering more and more interest lately, as it has been integrated in the development process of new software. Therefore, the term "UX Guidelines" was created. These guidelines define, how control elements and indicators for GUIs look like and when they are to be used. UX Guidelines also cover two different aspects, which have to be described independently: The look and the layout.

The look of native applications is defined by the OS. Parameters like the used colour scheme, size, and behaviour of buttons, right-click behaviour, etc. fall under this aspect. Transferred to JavaFX, this task falls under the liability of skins: They change the visual feedback of elements.

The layout is the second aspect of GUI design. Platform specific differences in layouts are not to be ignored. For example, the differences are obvious, if dialogues are examined. Windows dialogues are designed to show the "Accept" or "OK" button left of the "Abort" button. However, Linux takes a different approach and encourages designers to place "OK" right of "Abort". Such differences of the layout cannot be compensated by a skin, but have to be taken in respect by the UX designer.

But there is a third component that needs the attention in UX Design: The user. Every user has made positive and negative experiences and has expectations that influence his interaction with a system. As Windows is well distributed, many users internalised Microsoft's design principles and the Windows-specific look and feel. If an application succeeds in fulfilling the users' anticipations, the user is more likely to use said application again. Especially in the domain of User Experience there are parallels to human interaction: The first impression counts. If an application is easy to learn and easy to begin with, new users are motivated by their progress and are more likely to accept and learn the characteristics of said application. The concept of habits [1] should be considered, which also means paying attention to inner consistency:

> "The internal consistency of a product should disguise a lack of consistency in the functions it's handling. If the product is interacting with a dozen different 'backend' systems, the user shouldn't have any clue that's the case - everything should all feel like the same experience" [1].

Besides this inner consistency there is also an outer consistency, which has to be taken into account. It is the consistency against the surrounding OS. By designing the GUI consistent to the surrounding OS and changing its appearance through skins to match native applications, the attention of a user can be shifted away from handling the application to the goals the user wants to achieve by using the application.

If these findings are transferred to the most widespread OS family, namely Windows, a distinct and recognisable design can be found. Because of its distribution, it can be assumed that a significant part of users internalised the visual and operational concepts of Windows in such a way, that confronting them with different look or behaviour could raise problems.

As a representative of the Windows family, Windows 7 was chosen because of its distribution amongst the private sector as well as its ongoing roll-out in the commercial sector. Looking at JavaFX, one might see that it only ships a single skin, Modena, which truly is platform independent. It differs from native Windows 7 design in such a way, that it can easily be identified amongst native applications. Caused by this circumstance, the usage of JavaFX-based GUI applications under Windows is possible but not advisable, because of the strict visual separation of a given JavaFX application and its surrounding OS. If a developer wants to design a JavaFX-based application for Windows 7, he is confronted with the violation of all aforementioned design and usability principles. Thus, another problem raises: the violation of these principles is often accompanied by a loss of confidence in the application[1], which can be critical, especially in an enterprise domain. Under these circumstances, the use of skins with native Windows look and feel is not only useful but recommendable.

This situation is not likely to be changed by Oracle itself, as they clarified in a statement [12]: the development of native skins will be left to the community. Out of this situation, the need for native skins can be derived, which we will cover later in detail.

3   Related Work

Since there is a manageable amount of skin projects, we decided to present the most sophisticated ones. We consider projects as sophisticated if they show a recognisable effort and well-conceived design. But before we introduce these projects in detail, we will take a look at the state of research.

3.1   State of Research

UX Design is a topic that gained in importance recently, as various kinds of display devices are used to interact with digital systems. It is for this reason that the research focus shifted away from classic PC applications towards web- and mobile-first-technologies. Various research work which focuses on this can be found, including research on how business value can be created with mobile UX [2]

---

[1] "The very same issues that break engagement also have a tendency to injure the trustworthiness of the product(...)" [1].

or the detailed UI design for social media [3]. Also, the question if cultural background influences the way a user perceives a website, has been researched [4], as well as the integration options of UX design into agile development methods [5].

However, none of the related work takes the outer consistency of these applications with the surrounding OS into consideration, which this work focuses on.

3.2   JavaFX-Native-Themes

JavaFX-Native-Themes is a project aimed at creating both, a Windows- and an OS X-skin. The source code is completely available via BitBucket [9] but consists mainly of demo applications, screenshots and CSS files. The state of the skins can be described as exemplary and should be considered undone.

The skins can be enabled by including the chosen CSS file in the GUI code manually. Combined with its heavy dependence on the main CSS of Modena, this bears the risk of instability and incompatibility, if something changes either in the skins' or Modenas CSS. Finally, there is an unclear licensing situation, as there is neither a LICENSE file enclosed, nor is a copyright notice placed in the source code. This unclear situation in conjunction with the state of the project, a productive use is not advisable at the moment.

3.3   JMetro

JMetro is a project of a freelance software engineer, who aims to recreate the look and feel of Windows 8, as the name suggests. Updates and new versions can be found in his blog [10]. The term "recreate" has been chosen, since even the author speaks of getting inspired by "Metro UI", the default Windows 8 look and feel. Apart from the difference in the target platform, the project bears another risk: As there is neither a Version Control Management (VCS) nor a VCS service, as Git, Github or BitBucket, involved, updates are distributed through his personal Dropbox share. Besides the distribution channel, this project bears the same unclear licensing situation as the aforementioned JavaFX-Native-Themes. Also, the differing target platform disqualifies this project from the pool of candidates.

3.4   AquaFX

AquaFX is an Open Source project developed by a software engineer as her final project. The aim of AquaFX is the development of a skin with native OS X look and feel [8]. It is licensed under a BSD license, which allows commercial use and modifications of the codebase. The project consists of a facade class that hides the implementation details of the remaining components. The source code is versioned through a VCS and prepackaged distributions are available as a Maven dependency. Because of its well-designed architecture, some design decisions of AeroFX are inspired by AquaFX. However, this project also aims at developing a skin for a different target platform, thus it cannot be considered as an alternative.

4 Background

To ensure high code quality and good usability of our proposed solution, some specific design decisions have been made with regard to the architecture of AeroFX. But before explaining these in detail, we first provide some background information on the used technologies.

4.1 JavaFX

JavaFX has been positioned as the successor of Swing by Oracle. It is a completely rewritten framework for the development of Rich Client Applications with focus on graphical programming (User Interfaces). The architecture of JavaFX can be considered as sophisticated and forward-looking since it has been built with robustness and flexibility in mind.

This, amongst other things, is depicted by the fact that Oracle separated the styling of components from their logic. The layout of GUIs can be defined in a declarative XML document, whereas the appearance of elements can be changed through CSS.

Delimitation of Swing. Swing has been the default technology for building user interfaces until the release of JRE8. Until now, Swing has been unrivalled, for there has been no other toolkits with comparable functions that is recommended by Oracle itself. Both toolkits, JavaFX and Swing, are platform independent and completely written in Java. They are based on the same concept, being a "Lightweight UI", which means, that the OS only provides an empty window, in which the toolkit draws the needed components. Thus, a button showed in the UI is not represented by an OS-specific button, but a pure Java object.

Moreover, changing elements in JavaFX is considerably less complicated compared to Swing. To change an element in Swing, the element in question has to be subclassed and multiple functions have to be overridden and/or implemented. To achieve the same outcome in JavaFX, only the element in question has to be edited in the CSS file. If full control over the element is needed, subclassing still is possible, which enables the developer to change elementary properties of the element itself, as well as full control over the behaviour. Finally, to ease the migration effort for developers coming from Swing, JavaFX even ships a "Swing" node.

Native Skins in Swing. On all supported platforms there are two base skins, "Motif" and "Metal" are available, accompanied by a platform specific skin for Linux, Mac OS and Windows, respectively, which renders Java GUIs indistinguishable from their native representation. Swing is pixel- and not vector based, as a consequence all graphics are created pixel based. The drawing of a Combobox shall serve as an example for this process. If a Combobox shall be drawn in Swing, it passes an empty canvas object bundled with some parameters, i.e. its size, to the OS. On this canvas the OS draws a fitting Combobox as a pixel based graphic. JavaFX, on the other hand, is completely vector based, which renders this process obsolete.

4.2 The Design of AeroFX

Through the planning phase of our skin some specific decisions regarding the design were made, which we illustrate in this section. As mentioned earlier, Oracle laid a focus on the strict separation of form and function of skins in JavaFX. The form, or look, of elements can be changed through CSS. If the CSS options should be insufficient, the corresponding *SkinBase* classes can be subclassed and adapted for custom shapes or logic.

Figure 1 shows a potential layout of themes in JavaFX, which is also followed by AeroFX. The left side of Fig. 1 depicts the public JavaFX API, which contains the elements (i.e. *Button*) and their corresponding *SkinBase* classes (i.e. *ButtonSkin*). The right side of the figure shows the adaptions made by a skin. The private API of a skin contains the main CSS file with all optical changes, accompanied by subclasses, if any are needed.

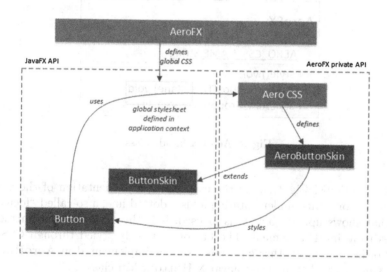

Fig. 1. Skin design

Besides the general layout we decided to hide the functionality and all used classes behind a facade pattern. This ensures an easy to use and consistent API, amongst good maintainability of the underlying codebase, without requiring developers to update their applications afterwards.

To minimize the effort of integrating and therefore using our skin in an application, it is not only distributed as source code through GitHub but also available as prepackaged Maven dependencies.

5   Case Study

To illustrate the technical background given in Sect. 4 and prove its viability, we implemented the architecture in a project called "AeroFX". The project itself is organised as a Maven project for easy dependency management and prepackaged deployment.

It mainly consists of aforementioned facade class *AeroFX*, whose layout is illustrated by Fig. 2. This class provides a consistent API and hides the implementation details behind few, easy to use functions.

It also contains the reference to the main CSS file and exposes the relevant function, *AeroFX.style()* for styling an application. This CSS file is, in contrast to many other skin projects, not based on Modena. This means that elements, which are not defined in the skins' CSS will not show up in an application, as JavaFX is missing the required information. On the other hand this renders the CSS of AeroFX more stable against changes in Modena, as these changes cannot influence any elements because of its independence.

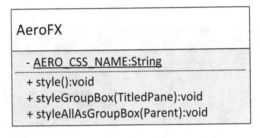

Fig. 2. AeroFX facade class

Aforementioned Fig. 1 shows the exemplary implementation of the custom AeroFX button. This implementation adds a dotted line, a so-called "focus border", that shows up, if a button is focused. It is the example for sophisticated changes to a JavaFX element. The button is mostly styled through CSS, the focus border, amongst other customisations, is implemented in **AeroButtonSkin**, which extends the native JavaFX **ButtonSkin** class.

Figure 3 shows a visual comparison between a native Windows 7 dialogue of the left and a JavaFX application styled with JavaFX. To emphasise the need of such a skin, Fig. 4 shows the same JavaFX application without applying AeroFX, thus showing the default JavaFX skin, Modena.

Building native interfaces for platform specific operating systems in a platform independent language also bears multiple problems and has limitations. First of all, though choosing the same font as Windows 7, Segoe UI, the Java font rendering differs from the OS' one. If compared on a pixel basis, small differences can be found. Amongst line- and horizontal spacing, hinting and subpixel rendering, also called font smoothing, is not available at the moment. Besides

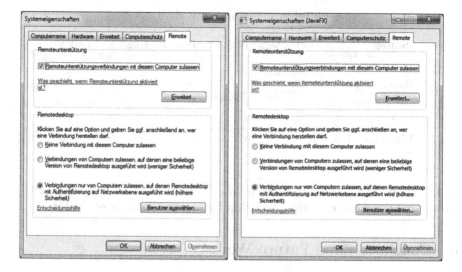

Fig. 3. Visual comparsion of Windows 7 and AeroFX

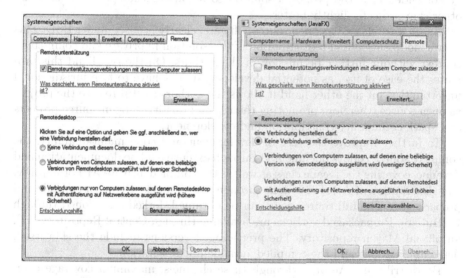

Fig. 4. Visual comparision of Windows 7 and Modena

the font rendering, we also identified a problem regarding the window decoration[2] of a JavaFX window, as JavaFX does not cover all possible combinations of Windows-specific decorations. Last but not least, we discovered an unexpected behaviour of one of the internal algorithms, more precisely the algorithm that selects the next target that gets the focus while shifting through the elements

---

[2] Window decorations include, amongst other things, the title bar with controls for minimizing, maximizing and closing a window.

Table 1. Feature comparison

Project	Modena	JFX-NT	JMetro	AquaFX	AeroFX
Licensing	+	-	-	+	+
Documentation	o	-	-	+	+
Architecture	+	o	o	+	+
Updates	+	o	-	+	+
Windows 7 L and F	-	o	-	-	+

by keyboard. This has been solved by overriding the default behaviour with a custom implementation of this algorithm for specific elements of the skin.

6   Conclusion and Future Works

Despite the problems we encountered through the development of AeroFX it can be concluded that the proposed solution solves approaches problems of many other skin projects slightly better.

AeroFX is released as open source software, clearly licensed under BSD. This allows modification and redistribution of this solution in private and commercial context without further permission of the authors. On the one hand this promotes the ease of use, as potential developers do not have to face jurisdictional uncertainties, on the other hand it allows the authors to still release the project as open source, therefore promoting the use and quality of open source projects and spark community contribution and development.

To further improve the ease of development and code maintainability, the complete source code is documented through extensive inline documentation and Javadoc, covering the facade class as well as the complete private API of AeroFX. The distribution of AeroFX is done through two channels: Plain source code and prepackaged. The full source code can be obtained, forked and cloned through GitHub [6]. Prepackaged versions are available through Central Repository [11], an official Maven repository. The prepackaged versions include the skin itself, demo applications and the compiled Javadoc documentation.

By distributing AeroFX through these channels, maximum coverage combined with effective update and dependency management is achieved. New versions of AeroFX only require a small change in the main configuration file of Maven projects using the proposed skin.

As a facade class hides the implementation details, any part of the implementation can be changed between releases without breaking the projects using AeroFX. Finally, as shown in Sect. 5, the Windows 7 look and feel is recreated satisfactory if evaluated under the criteria of not breaking immersion and keeping outer consistency. Table 1 visualises the aforementioned textual description and compares it to Modena, the JavaFX default skin, and the projects introduced in Sect. 3.

Modena is licensed under the same conditions as Java itself, therefore providing a clear situation. Developed by Oracle as a part of JavaFX, the architecture and update mechanism are both well designed. However, the documentation is not completely done at the time of writing, as the architecture could change in parts over the next versions of JavaFX. Because Modena is a platform independent skin, the design of Windows 7 is obviously not met.

JavaFX-Native-Themes tries to recreate the look and feel of Windows 7 but has to be considered both, unfinished and inactive[3]. Combined with the unclear licensing situation and missing documentation, the use of this project is not advisable.

JMetro faces the same licensing and documentation problems as JavaFX-Native-Themes, complemented by its unstable distribution strategy through Dropbox and the different design focus inspired by Windows 8.

AquaFX does not share any of these problems with the other projects. It is licensed enterprise-friendly, well documented and possesses a well engineered architecture, which inspired AeroFX.

With AeroFX we provide a state of the art Windows 7 look and feel skin for JavaFX that is unequalled in terms of architecture, availability, ease of use and licensing. To increase community contribution, a project homepage [7] has been created and several blog and news posts have been written to announce the development of the proposed solution. Community support is an important factor to be taken in account for the development of open source projects. This has also been recognised by Oracle for JavaFX.

To improve the acceptance and frequency of use, native themes, as AeroFX, are important. They are viable options for reducing inhibitions and ease the first use of non-native software on the respective target operating systems.

The state of AeroFX cannot be described as production ready, as there are still some elements missing. The implementation concentrated on implementing the most common control elements of dialogues. But there has been already good feedback to the development process, as multiple companies expressed their interest in the further development of AeroFX. Furthermore, since contact to the original developer of AquaFX can be established, it is to be discussed, if AquaFX and AeroFX could be merged into one larger skin project, therefore optimizing development efforts.

References

1. Anderson, J., McRee, J., Wilson, R.: Effective UI, pp. 12, 25, 30. O'Reilly, Sebastopol (2010)
2. Djamasbi, S., et al.: Designing for success: creating business value with mobile user experience. DigitalCommons@WPI (2014)
3. Hayes, J.R.: User interface design for online social media. B.Sc. thesis, California Polytechnic State University - San Luis Obispo (2014)

---

[3] Last commit to the VCS has been made in 02/2013.

4. Nawaz, A.: Website user experience. A cross-cultural study of the relation between users' cognitive style, context of use, and information architecture of local websites. Dissertation, Copenhagen Business School (2014)
5. da Silva, T.S., et al.: User experience design and agile development: from theory to practice. J. Softw. Eng. Appl. **5**, 743–751 (2012)
6. AeroFX GitHub Project. https://github.com/s1gpwr/aerofx
7. AeroFX Project Homepage. http://www.aerofx.org
8. AquaFX Project Homepage. http://aquafx-project.com
9. JavaFX-Native-Themes BitBucket Project. https://bitbucket.org/software4java/javafx-native-themes
10. JMetro Project Blog. http://pixelduke.wordpress.com
11. Maven Central Repository. https://search.maven.org
12. Oracle Bugtracker: [#RT-20299] Native Look and Feels. https://javafx-jira.kenai.com/browse/RT-20299

Haar Wavelet-Based Approach to Locating Defects in Texture Images

Gintarė Vaidelienė[✉] and Jonas Valantinas

Department of Applied Mathematics,
Kaunas University of Technology, Kaunas, Lithuania
{gintare.vaideliene, jonas.valantinas}@ktu.lt

Abstract. In this paper, a novel Haar wavelet-based approach to extracting and locating surface defects in grey-level texture images is proposed. This new approach explores space localization properties of the discrete Haar wavelet transform (HT), performs task-oriented statistical analysis of well-defined non-intersecting subsets of HT spectral coefficients, and generates parameterized defect detection criteria with an installed additional capability to locate surface defects in defective texture images. The preliminary experimental analysis results demonstrating the use of the developed approach to the automated visual inspection of ceramic tiles, obtained from the real factory environment, are also presented.

Keywords: Texture images · Defect detection · Discrete wavelet transforms · Automated visual inspection

1 Introduction

Visual inspection plays a vital role in assuring quality of industrial products. For many decades, industrial defects have been detected by human inspectors. However the human visual inspection, because of eye fatigue, is not efficient. Some studies indicate that human inspectors typically detect somewhere (60–75) % of significant industrial defects [1]. So, there is a great need of online visual-based systems capable to enhance not only the quality control but also the marketing of the products.

Detection of defects in texture surfaces, such as steel plates, glass sheets, weldment, ceramic tiles, fabric, etc., is an important area of automated industrial inspection systems. Numerous methods and approaches have been proposed for performing this task, i.e. for detecting surface defects like cracks, stains, broken points and so on [1–6]. With reference to many sources, the texture surface (image) analysis techniques, used for visual defect inspection, can be grouped as follows: statistical approach, filter-based approach, model-based approach and structural approach.

The statistical approach concentrates on the spatial distribution values. Various statistical texture features are explored, namely: histogram statistics, co-occurrence matrices, autocorrelation, local binary patterns, etc. [7–12]. The statistical approach is characterized, mainly, by low cost. Among the shortcomings of the approach one can mention the great number of grey levels in the texture image and irregular arrangement of textural elements.

© Springer International Publishing Switzerland 2015
G. Dregvaite and R. Damasevicius (Eds.): ICIST 2015, CCIS 538, pp. 537–547, 2015.
DOI: 10.1007/978-3-319-24770-0_46

In filter-based (Gabor, Gaussian, Sobel, Canny, Laplacian, etc.) approach, the main idea leans upon applying filter banks to texture images and computing the energy of filter responses. If no suitable kernel can be found in a spatial domain, filtering of the texture image is performed in a frequency domain (Fourier and Gabor transforms, wavelet transforms, etc.). The main vulnerability of the above techniques is their high dependence on the regular nature of texture images [13–19].

In model-based image processing, a model with desired parameters (autoregressive model, Markov random fields, fractal models, etc.) is selected to analyse the texture image. Despite the novelty and originality of the approach, implementation and application of many ideas is limited. The more detailed information on the matter can be found in [20–22].

In structural approach, the texture is characterized by texture elements (primitives) and the spatial arrangement of these primitives. Morphological operators and various edge detection techniques are explored. Among shortcomings of this approach, requirements for regular texture and time-consuming computational operations [23–25]. Lately, some hybrid defect detection methods that combine various ideas mentioned above have appeared [26–29].

In this paper, a new Haar wavelet-based parameterized defect detection system for grey-level texture images, distinguishing itself with an attached possibility to locate surface defects in the defective texture images and capability to be explored in real-time applications, is presented.

2   A New Parameterized Defect Detection System for Texture Images

The new parameterized defect detection system for grey-level texture images $X = [X(m_1, m_2)]$ $(m_1, m_2 \in \{0, 1, \ldots, N-1\}$, $N = 2^n$, $n \in \mathbb{N})$ has been developed and implemented in the Haar wavelet domain. The system explores specific properties of the discrete Haar wavelet (HT) spectrum $Y = [Y(k_1, k_2)]$ $(k_1, k_2 \in \{0, 1, \ldots, N-1\})$ of the image X and is based, mainly, on the following two factors [30]:

1. The numerical value of the Haar wavelet coefficient $Y(k_1, k_2)$ $(k_1, k_2 \in \{1, 2, \ldots, N-1\}$; $k_s = 2^{n-i_s} + j_s$, $i_s \in \{1, 2, \ldots, n\}$, $j_s \in \{0, 1, \ldots, 2^{n-i_s} - 1\}$, $i_s = 1, 2)$ is uniquely specified by the image block $X^{(k_1, k_2)}$ of size $2^{i_1} \times 2^{i_2}$, with $X^{(k_1, k_2)}(0, 0) = X(2^{i_1} \cdot j_1, 2^{i_2} \cdot j_2)$;

2. The discrete HT spectrum Y of X can be partitioned into a finite number of non-intersecting subsets (regions) $\Re(0, 0)$, $\Re(i_1, 0)$, $\Re(0, i_2)$ and $\Re(i_1, i_2)$ $(i_1, i_2 = 1, 2, \ldots, n)$, containing 1, 2^{n-i_1}, 2^{n-i_2} and $2^{2n-i_1-i_2}$ Haar wavelet coefficients, respectively, (Fig. 1). Numerical values of Haar wavelet coefficients, falling into a particular region $\Re(i_1, i_2)$ $(i_1, i_2 \in \{0, 1, \ldots, n\})$, are specified by non-overlapping image blocks covering the whole image X.

Let us denote the training set of defect-free texture images and the corresponding set of their discrete HT spectra by $S_X = \{X_j | j = 1, 2, \ldots, r\}$ and $S_Y = \{Y_j | j = 1, 2, \ldots, r\}$, respectively. Also, let Y_{test} be the HT spectrum of the test texture image X_{test}.

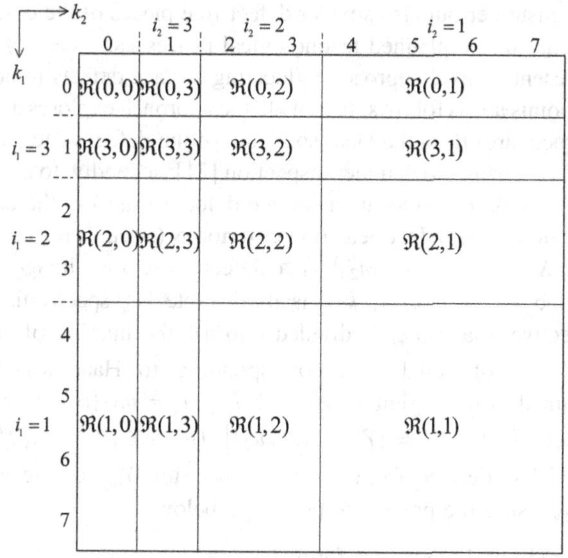

Fig. 1. The partitioning of the discrete Haar wavelet spectrum Y into a finite number of non-overlapping regions ($N = 8$)

Using the training set $S_X = \{X_j | j = 1, 2, \ldots, r\}$, the parameterized defect detection criterion $\aleph$ is generated for each region $\Re(i_1, i_2)$ (i_1, $i_2 = 0, 1, \ldots, n$). The criterion $\aleph$ represents a collection of open intervals, i.e. $\aleph = \{I_p(i_1, i_2) | i_1, i_2 = 0, 1, \ldots, n\}$, where $I_p = I_p(i_1, i_2) = (\Theta'_p(i_1, i_2), \Theta''_p(i_1, i_2))$; the endpoints $\Theta'_p(i_1, i_2)$ and $\Theta''_p(i_1, i_2)$ of the interval $I_p(i_1, i_2)$ are chosen in such a way that the mean value (designated as $\bar{Y}(i_1, i_2)$) of all Haar wavelet coefficients, contained in $\{\Re_j(i_1, i_2) | j = 1, 2, \ldots, r\}$ (here $\Re_j(i_1, i_2)$ is the region associated with Y_j in S_Y), fall into $I_p(i_1, i_2)$ with a priori prescribed probability (parameter) p ($p \in \{0.70, 0.71, \ldots, 0.99\}$). The intervals $I_p = I_p(i_1, i_2)$ (i_1, $i_2 \in \{0, 1, \ldots, n\}$) themselves are found using statistical analysis of the whole set of regions $\Re_j(i_1, i_2)$ (i_1, $i_2 \in \{0, 1, \ldots, n\}$, $j = 1, 2, \ldots, r$) in S_Y [32].

Now, the test texture image X_{test} is assumed to be defect-free if and only if the number of regions $\Re_{test}(i_1, i_2)$ (i_1, $i_2 \in \{0, 1, \ldots, n\}$) for which the condition $\bar{Y}_{test}(i_1, i_2) \in I_p(i_1, i_2)$ is fulfilled is not less than $p(n + 1)^2$. Otherwise, the test image X_{test} is assumed to be defective.

3 Locating Surface Defects in Texture Images

Another problem, closely related to the detection of defects in texture images (surfaces), turns out to be localization of defects on the defective surface. The problem is worth attention not only theoretically but also practically, purely for industrial needs. For instance, in the glass (card-board, plastic, ceramic, etc.) industry, it often happens that not only large defect-free sheets of the production are manufactured, processed and dispatched to the customer but also smaller defect-free pieces of the defective sheet are processed repeatedly in the planned technological processes.

Below, we present a novel approach to locating surface defects in defective texture images. The key points are as follows: first of all, the approach explores a newly proposed fast transition (procedure) from the Haar spectrum of the defective texture image to the Haar spectrum of the image block under inspection [31]; secondly, to estimate quality of a particular image block, i.e. to locate a surface defect (if any) in the defective texture image, the earlier described defect detection criterion ℵ (Sect. 2) is employed.

Suppose that $X_{def} = [X_{def}(m_1, m_2)]$ is a defective texture image of size $N \times N$ ($N = 2^n$, $n \in \mathbb{N}$) and $Y_{def} = [Y_{def}(k_1, k_2)]$ is its discrete HT spectrum. To answer the purpose, the defective image X_{def} is divided into a finite number of non-overlapping image blocks $X^{(k_1, k_2)}$ of equal size, corresponding to Haar wavelet coefficients $Y_{def}(k_1, k_2)$ contained in the region $\Re_{def}(i_1, i_2)$, $i_1 = i_2 = m \in \{n - 1, n - 2, \ldots\}$. The discrete HT spectrum $Y^{(k_1, k_2)} = [Y^{(k_1, k_2)}(u_1, u_2)]$ ($u_1, u_2 \in \{0, 1, \ldots, 2^m - 1\}$) of the image block $X^{(k_1, k_2)}$ is derived from the Haar spectrum Y_{def} of the whole defective texture image X_{def} using the procedure presented below:

1. The four ordered number sets are formed:

$$S_V = \{\alpha_0, \alpha_1, \ldots, \alpha_{n-m}\}, \ \alpha_0 = k_1, \ \alpha_s = [\alpha_{s-1}/2], \ s = 1, 2, \ldots, n - m; \quad (1)$$

$$S_H = \{\beta_0, \beta_1, \ldots, \beta_{n-m}\}, \ \beta_0 = k_2, \ \beta_t = [\beta_{t-1}/2], \ t = 1, 2, \ldots, n - m; \quad (2)$$

$$\Im_1 = \{k_1\} \cup \left\{ \bigcup_{q=1}^{m-1} \Im_1(q) \right\}, \ \Im_1(q) = \{2^q \cdot k_1, 2^q \cdot k_1 + 1, \ldots, 2^q \cdot (k_1 + 1) - 1\}; \quad (3)$$

$$\Im_2 = \{k_2\} \cup \left\{ \bigcup_{q=1}^{m-1} \Im_2(q) \right\}, \ \Im_2(q) = \{2^q \cdot k_2, 2^q \cdot k_2 + 1, \ldots, 2^q \cdot (k_2 + 1) - 1\}. \quad (4)$$

2. The Haar wavelet coefficients $Y^{(k_1, k_2)}(0, 0)$, $Y^{(k_1, k_2)}(u_1, 0)$ and $Y^{(k_1, k_2)}(0, u_2)$ ($u_1, u_2 = 1, 2, \ldots, 2^m - 1$) of the image block $X^{(k_1, k_2)}$ are found in accordance with the formulae given below, namely:

$$Y^{(k_1, k_2)}(0, 0) = \frac{1}{2^{n-m}} Y_{def}(0, 0) + \frac{1}{\sqrt{2^{n-m}}} \sum_{s=1}^{n-m} \frac{(-1)^{\alpha_{s-1}}}{\sqrt{2^s}} \cdot Y_{def}(\alpha_s, 0)$$

$$+ \frac{1}{\sqrt{2^{n-m}}} \sum_{t=1}^{n-m} \frac{(-1)^{\beta_{t-1}}}{\sqrt{2^t}} \cdot Y_{def}(0, \beta_t)$$

$$+ \sum_{s, t=1}^{n-m} \frac{(-1)^{\alpha_{s-1} + \beta_{t-1}}}{\sqrt{2^{s+t}}} \cdot Y_{def}(\alpha_s, \beta_t) ; \quad (5)$$

$$Y^{(k_1,k_2)}(u_1,0) = \frac{1}{\sqrt{2^{n-m}}} Y_{def}(k_1^*,0) + \sum_{t=1}^{n-m} \frac{(-1)^{\beta_{t-1}}}{\sqrt{2^t}} \cdot Y_{def}(k_1^*,\beta_t); \qquad (6)$$

$$Y^{(k_1,k_2)}(0,u_2) = \frac{1}{\sqrt{2^{n-m}}} Y_{def}(0,k_2^*) + \sum_{s=1}^{n-m} \frac{(-1)^{\alpha_{s-1}}}{\sqrt{2^s}} \cdot Y_{def}(\alpha_s,k_2^*); \qquad (7)$$

for all $u_1, u_2 = 1, 2, \ldots, 2^m - 1$; k_1^* and k_2^* are the u_1-th and the u_2-th elements of the sets $\Im_1$ and $\Im_2$, respectively (numbering of elements in $\Im_1$ and $\Im_2$ starts with one);
3. The remaining spectral coefficients are derived directly from the HT spectrum Y_{def} of the texture image X_{def}, i.e. $Y^{(k_1,k_2)}(u_1,u_2) = Y_{def}(k_1^*,k_2^*)$, for all $u_1, u_2 = 1, 2, \ldots, 2^m - 1$; k_1^* and k_2^*, as before, are the u_2-th and the u_2-th elements of the sets $\Im_1$ and $\Im_2$, respectively (numbering of elements in $\Im_1$ and $\Im_2$ starts with one).

To locate defects on the defective surface (image) X_{def}, the HT spectra of all image blocks $X^{(k_1,k_2)}$ of size $2^m \times 2^m$ ($m \in \{n-1, n-2, \ldots\}$) are analysed successively. To find out whether the block under inspection $X^{(k_1,k_2)}$ is defective or defect-free, its discrete spectrum $Y^{(k_1,k_2)}$ ($k_1, k_2 \in \{2^{n-m}, 2^{n-m}+1, \ldots, 2^{n-m+1} - 1\}$), obtained using the above procedure, is partitioned into the non-intersecting regions $\Re^{(k_1,k_2)}(0,0)$, $\Re^{(k_1,k_2)}(i_1,0)$, $\Re^{(k_1,k_2)}(0,i_2)$ and $\Re^{(k_1,k_2)}(i_1,i_2)$ ($i_1, i_2 \in \{1,2,\ldots,m\}$).

Now, for a fixed value of the parameter p, the image block $X^{(k_1,k_2)}$ is assumed to be defect-free if and only if in at least $p(m+1)^2$ cases (out of $(m+1)^2$ cases possible) the following is true (Fig. 2): (1) the Haar wavelet coefficient $Y^{(k_1,k_2)}(0,0)$ from the region $\Re^{(k_1,k_2)}(0,0)$, multiplied by 2^{n-m}, falls into the interval $I_p = I_p(0,0)$ (Criterion $\aleph$; Sect. 2); (2) the mean values $\bar{Y}^{(k_1,k_2)}(i_1,0)$ and $\bar{Y}^{(k_1,k_2)}(0,i_2)$ ($i_1, i_2 \in \{1,2,\ldots,m\}$) of Haar wavelet coefficients, contained in $\Re^{(k_1,k_2)}(i_1,0)$ and $\Re^{(k_1,k_2)}(0,i_2)$, respectively, and multiplied by the scalar $(\sqrt{2})^{n-m}$, fall into the intervals $I_p(i_1,0)$ and $I_p(0,i_2)$; (3) the mean value $\bar{Y}^{(k_1,k_2)}(i_1,i_2)$ of Haar wavelet coefficients, contained in $\Re^{(k_1,k_2)}(i_1,i_2)$ ($i_1, i_2 \in \{1,2,\ldots,m\}$) fall into the interval $I_p = I_p(i_1,i_2)$.

Exploration of the same defect detection criterion $\aleph$ (Sect. 2) for locating surface defects in the defective texture image, undoubtedly, is an indisputable advantage of the proposed defect detection and localization system.

4   Experimental Analysis Results

To motivate the developed parameterized defect detection and localization system for texture images, the system has been applied to processing of the set of defect-free ceramic tile images of size 256×256 (100 training samples) and the set of defective tile images of size 256×256 (100 samples), obtained from the real factory environment. Some typical samples are presented in Fig. 3.

For the experiment, 50 defect-free ceramic tile images and 50 defective tile images were selected randomly. The experimental analysis results (Table 1) showed that the

$I_p(0,0)$	$I_p(0,n)$	$I_p(0,n-1)$	...	$I_p(0,m)$	...	$I_p(0,2)$	$I_p(0,1)$
$I_p(n,0)$	$I_p(n,n)$	$I_p(n,n-1)$	...	$I_p(n,m)$	...	$I_p(n,2)$	$I_p(n,1)$
$I_p(n-1,0)$	$I_p(n-1,n)$	$I_p(n-1,n-1)$	...	$I_p(n-1,m)$	...	$I_p(n-1,2)$	$I_p(n-1,1)$
$\vdots$	$\vdots$	$\vdots$	$\ddots$	$\vdots$	$\vdots$	$\vdots$	$\vdots$
$I_p(m,0)$	$I_p(m,n)$	$I_p(m,n-1)$	...	$I_p(m,m)$	...	$I_p(m,2)$	$I_p(m,1)$
$\vdots$	$\vdots$	$\vdots$	$\vdots$	$\vdots$	$\ddots$	$\vdots$	$\vdots$
$I_p(2,0)$	$I_p(2,n)$	$I_p(2,n-1)$	...	$I_p(2,m)$	...	$I_p(2,2)$	$I_p(2,1)$
$I_p(1,0)$	$I_p(1,n)$	$I_p(1,n-1)$	...	$I_p(1,m)$	...	$I_p(1,2)$	$I_p(1,1)$

Fig. 2. The defect detection criterion $\aleph$ for texture images of size $2^n \times 2^n$; for the quality analysis of image blocks of size $2^m \times 2^m$, only the white part of the criterion $\aleph$ is explored

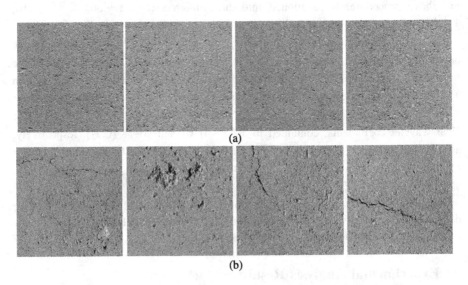

(a)

(b)

Fig. 3. Sample ceramic tile images: (a) defect-free tiles; (b) defective tiles

defect detection success rate (TP + TN)/(TP + FN + TN + FP) (here: TP – true positives, i.e. the percentage of actually defective images detected as defective; FP – false positives, i.e. the percentage of actually defect-free images detected as defective; TN – true negatives, i.e. the percentage of actually defect-free images detected as defect-free; FN – false negatives, i.e. the percentage of actually defective images detected as defect–free) of the system was very high (in comparison with other

Table 1. Ceramic tiles classification results

The probability, p		The serial number of an experiment				
		1	2	3	4	5
0.99	TP	94 %	96 %	100 %	96 %	100 %
	FP	4 %	6 %	4 %	2 %	6 %
	TN	96 %	94 %	96 %	98 %	94 %
	FN	6 %	4 %	0 %	4 %	0 %
0.95	TP	96 %	94 %	100 %	96 %	98 %
	FP	4 %	8 %	6 %	4 %	8 %
	TN	96 %	92 %	94 %	96 %	92 %
	FN	4 %	6 %	0 %	4 %	2 %
0.80	TP	94 %	94 %	98 %	94 %	96 %
	FP	12 %	10 %	6 %	8 %	8 %
	TN	88 %	90 %	94 %	92 %	92 %
	FN	6 %	6 %	2 %	6 %	4 %

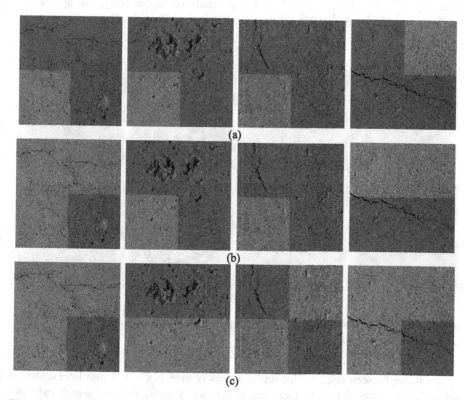

Fig. 4. Localization of surface defects in defective ceramic tile images ($m = 7$): (a) $p = 0.99$; (b) $p = 0.95$; (c) $p = 0.8$

approaches in the area [28, 29]), namely: 0.964, for $p = 0.99$; 0.954, for $p = 0.95$; 0.938, for $p = 0.80$. We here note that, for the above values of the parameter (probability) p, the four actually defective texture images (Fig. 3b) were detected as defective.

For the localization of surface defects in the defective ceramic tile images, two approaches (A and B) have been explored, namely:

Approach A. The defective texture image X_{def} of size $2^n \times 2^n$ is partitioned into four image blocks of size $2^{n-1} \times 2^{n-1}$. Then, if a particular image block of size $2^{n-1} \times 2^{n-1}$, i.e. the block $X^{(k_1,k_2)}$ $(k_1, k_2 \in \{2,3\})$ appears to be defective, it is partitioned into smaller blocks of size $2^{n-2} \times 2^{n-2}$, i.e. into blocks $X^{(k_1,k_2)}$ $(k_1, k_2 \in \{4,5,6,7,8\})$, and so on. The quality inspection is stopped when a priori prescribed minimal size $2^m \times 2^m$ $(m \in \{n-1, n-2, \ldots\})$ of the image block (answering some industrial needs) is reached.

Approach B. The defective texture image X_{def} of size $2^n \times 2^n$ is partitioned into a finite number of image blocks of a priori prescribed minimal size $2^m \times 2^m$ $(m \in \{n-1, n-2, \ldots\})$. The latter image blocks, i.e. the blocks $X^{(k_1,k_2)}$ $(k_1, k_2 \in \{2^{n-m}, 2^{n-m}+1, \ldots, 2^{n-m+1}-1\})$ are analysed successively, one by one.

Some experimental analysis results are presented in Figs. 4 and 5.

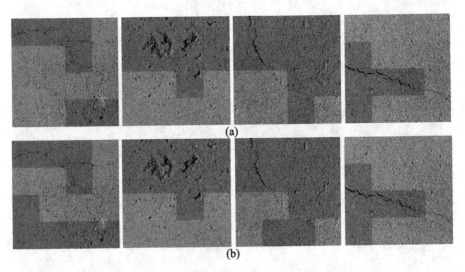

Fig. 5. Localization of surface defects in defective ceramic tile images ($m = 6$) with $p = 0.99$: (a) Approach A; (b) Approach B

As it can be seen (Fig. 4), for image blocks of size 128×128 (the lowest localization level), some lesser texture defects (cracks, bumps, pits, etc.) turn indistinguishable, if the value of the parameter (probability) p is decreased. The same tendency is observed for smaller sizes of image blocks, i.e. at higher localization levels. So, higher values of the probability p are more preferable to locating surface defects in the defective texture images. We here observe that, for image blocks of size 128 × 128, both approaches (A and B) are identical, i.e. lead to the same results.

The usage of image blocks of smaller sizes (Fig. 5), in the defect localization process (the higher level of localization), showed that many parts of the defective texture image were treated, quite properly, as defect-free zones, in contrast to the earlier case (Fig. 4). On the other hand, experimental analysis made it clear that the Approach B was more sensitive to texture defects, in comparison with the Approach A, because more parts of the defective texture image were picked out as defective zones.

5 Conclusion

In the paper, a novel Haar wavelet-based approach to detecting and locating defects in texture surfaces (images) is proposed. This new approach (system) explores space localization properties of the discrete Haar wavelet transform (HT) and makes use of highly efficient procedures for computing HT spectra for the selected image blocks. The level of localization of defects in the defective texture image is specified by the size of the selected blocks.

An indisputable advantage of the proposed defect detection and localization system manifests itself in applying simultaneously a unique parameterized criterion to detecting surface defects in texture images and locating them in the defective ones.

Numerous experimental analysis results confirm comparatively high performance of the developed system and stimulate implementation of the system in organizing the on-line texture image quality inspection processes in real industrial environment.

In the future, similar research concerning possibility to employ discrete wavelet transforms of higher orders (Le Gall, Daubechies, etc.) is supposed.

References

1. Lebrun, V.: Quality Control of Ceramic Tiles by Machine Vision. Flaw Master 3000, Surface Inspection Ltd. (2001)
2. Kumar, A.: Neural network based detection of local textile defects. Pattern Recogn. 36, 1645–1659 (2003)
3. Xie, X.: A review of recent advances in surface defect detection using texture analysis techniques. Electron. Lett. Comput. Vis. Image Anal. 7(3), 122 (2008)
4. Rebhi, A., Abid, S., Fnaeich, F.: Texture defect detection using local homogeneity and discrete cosine transform. World Appl. Sci. J. 31(9), 1677–1683 (2014)
5. Mishra, R., Shukla, D.: A survey on various defect detection. Int. J. Eng. Trends Technol. 10 (13), 642–648 (2014)
6. Haralick, R.M., Shanmugan, K., Dinstein, I.H.: Textural features for image classification. IEEE Trans. Syst. Man Cybern. SMC 3, 610–621 (1973)
7. Latif-Amet, A., Ertüzün, A., Erçil, A.: An efficient method for texture defect detection: sub-band domain co-occurrence matrices. Image Vis. Comput. 18, 543–553 (2000)
8. Huang, Y., Chan, K.: Texture decomposition by harmonics extraction from higher order statistics. IEEE Trans. Image Process. 13(1), 1–14 (2004)

9. Gururajan, A., Sari-Sarraf, H., Hequet, E.F.: Statistical approach to unsupervised defect detection and multiscale localization in two texture images. Optical Eng. **47**(2), 027202 (2008)
10. Ghazini, M., Monadjemi, A., Jamshidi, K.: Defect detection of tiles using 2D wavelet transform and statistical features. World Acad. Sci. Eng. Technol. **3**(1), 773–776 (2009)
11. Chen, J., Jain, A.K.: A structural approach to identify defects in textural images. In: IEEE International Conference on Systems, Man and Cybernetics, vol. 1, pp. 29–32. Beijing (1988)
12. Wen, W., Xia, A.: Verifying edges for visual inspection purposes. Pattern Recogn. Lett. **20**, 315–328 (1999)
13. Mallick-Goswami, B., Datta, A.: Detecting defects in fabric with laser-based morphological image processing. Text. Res. J. **70**, 758–762 (2000)
14. Kumar, A., Pang, G.: Defect detection in textured materials using optimized filters. IEEE Trans. Syst. Man Cybern. B Cybern. **32**(5), 553–570 (2002)
15. Habib, H., Yousaf, M., Mohibullah, M.: Modified laws energy descriptor for inspection of ceramic tiles. In: National Conference on Emerging Technologies, pp. 137–140 (2004)
16. Chan, C., Pang, G.: Fabric defect detection by fourier analysis. IEEE Trans. Ind. Appl. **36**(5), 1267–1276 (2000)
17. Tsai, D., Huang, T.: Automated surface inspection for statistical textures. Image Vis. Comput. **21**, 307–323 (2003)
18. Kumar, A., Pang, G.: Defect detection in textured materials using Gabor filters. IEEE Trans. Ind. Appl. **38**(2), 425–440 (2002)
19. Tsai, D., Lin, C., Huang, K.: Defect detection in coloured texture surfaces using Gabor filters. Imag. Sci. J. **53**(1), 27–37 (2005)
20. Conci, A., Proenca, C.: A system for real-time fabric inspection and industrial decision. In: 14th International Conference on Software Engineering and Knowledge Engineering, pp. 707–714. New York, USA (2002)
21. Li, S.: Markov Random Filed Modeling in Image Analysis. Springer, Berlin (2001)
22. Xie, X., Mirmehdi, M.: Localising surface defects in random colour textures using multiscale texem analysis in image eigenchannels. In: 12th IEEE International Conference on Image Processing, pp. 1124–1127 (2005)
23. Xie, X., Mirmehdi, M.: TEXEM: texture exemplars for defect detection on random textured surfaces. IEEE Trans. Pattern Anal. Mach. Intell. **29**(8), 1454–1464 (2007)
24. Fathi, A., Monadjemi, A.H., Mahmoudi, F.: Defect detection of tiles with combined undecimated wavelet transform & GLCM features. Int. J. Soft Comput. Eng. **2**(2), 2231–2307 (2012)
25. Shahrood, I.: A novel approach for detecting defects of random textured tiles using gabour wavelet. World Appl. Sci. J. **7**(9), 1114–1119 (2009)
26. Najafabadi, F.S., Pourghassem, H.: Corner defect detection based on dot product in ceramic tile images. In: 7th IEEE International Colloquium on Signal Processing and its Application, pp. 293–297 (2011)
27. Sharma, M., Kaur, G.: Integrated approach for defect detection in ceramic tiles. Int. J. Comput. Technol. **3**(2), 259–262 (2012)
28. Meena, Y., Mittal, A.: Blobs and crack detection on plain ceramic tile surface. Int. J. Adv. Res. Comput. Sci. Softw. Eng. **3**(7), 647–653 (2013)
29. Sivabalan, K.N., Gnanadurai, D.: Detection of defects in digital texture images using segmentation. Int. J. Eng. Sci. Technol. (IJEST) **2**(1), 5187–5191 (2010)
30. Sivabalan, K.N., Gnanadurai, D.: Efficient defect detection algorithm for grey level digital images using Gabor wavelet filter and Gaussian filter. Int. J. Eng. Sci. Technol. **3**(4), 3195–3202 (2011)

31. Valantinas, J., Kančelkis, D., Valantinas, R., Viščiūtė, G.: Improving space localization properties of the discrete wavelet transform. Informatica **24**(4), 657–674 (2013)
32. Vaidelienė, G., Valantinas, J., Ražanskas, P.: On the use of discrete wavelets in implementing controllable defect detection system for texture images. Information Technology and Control (2015, to appear)

From UML Statecharts to LOTOS Expressions Using Graph Transformation

Salim Djaaboub[1,3(✉)], Elhillali Kerkouche[2,3], and Allaoua Chaoui[3]

[1] Department of Mathematics and Computer Sciences, Centre Universitaire de Mila, Mila,
Algeria
[2] Département of Computer Sciences, Université de Jijel, Jijel, Algeria
[3] MISC Laboratory, Université de Constantine 2, Constantine, Algeria
{dja_salim,elhillalik}@yahoo.fr, a_chaoui2001@yahoo.com

Abstract. The use of UML Statecharts for modeling dynamic behaviors of systems
is very widespread. UML Statechart diagrams support developers by means of
graphical notation, but the lack of formal semantics for this diagram makes the
detection of errors and behavioral inconsistencies difficult. On the other hand, the
specification language LOTOS has been proved to be an essential technique for
specifying and verifying distributed and communicating systems. However, the
strong and obscure textual algebraic notation of LOTOS makes its utilization in
software development an onerous and complex task. In the order to combine UML
Statecharts with LOTOS for the formal specification and verification of system
behaviors, we propose in this paper an approach and a tool environment to automatically generate behavioral LOTOS expressions from UML Statechart diagrams. The
approach uses the meta-modeling tool AToM³.

Keywords: UML · Statechart diagram · LOTOS · Formal methods · Graph
transformation · Atom³

1 Introduction

It is now recognized that UML (Unified Modeling Language) [14] is considered nowadays as a standard software modelling language. UML consists of many diagrams. Some
diagrams are used to model the structure of a system while others, such Statechart
diagram, are used to model the behavior of a system. The use of UML Statecharts for
modeling the dynamic behaviors of systems is very widespread. Such diagrams provide
an effective graphical notation for the specification and design of system behaviors.
However, the lacks of a precise formal semantics of Statechart diagrams hinders the
formal analysis and verification of system design.

In the other hand, the specification language LOTOS (Language Of Temporal
Ordering Specification) [3] has been proved to be an essential technique for specifying
distributed and communicating systems. It is based on a rigorous mathematical model
and provides many verification tools that allow the early detection of errors in a specification before its implementation. However, the obscure and textual algebraic notation

© Springer International Publishing Switzerland 2015
G. Dregvaite and R. Damasevicius (Eds.): ICIST 2015, CCIS 538, pp. 548–559, 2015.
DOI: 10.1007/978-3-319-24770-0_47

of LOTOS makes its utilization in software development an onerous task, which limits its widespread adoption in industry and confines most of the research activity to academia [2, 15].

So, combining UML Statecharts with LOTOS is a promising approach for modelling and verification of dynamic system behaviors. We can benefit from the conceptual visuality by UML Statechart to model systems behavior and from the formal notation of LOTOS for early detection of errors in specifications before their implementation.

In this paper, we propose an approach to automatically generate LOTOS processes from UML Statechart diagrams. This approach is based on the combined use of Meta-Modelling and Graph Transformation grammars which are supported by the Metamodeling tool AToM3. Our approach will allow developers to model system behaviors using a set of UML Statechart diagrams and automatically convert them into their equivalent LOTOS processes. Then, these processes can be composed to form the global specification of the system using a set of predefined LOTOS operators.

The rest of this paper is organized as follows. Section 2 outlines the major related work. Section 3 gives a brief description of the UML Statechart, LOTOS, graph grammars and AToM3. Section 4 discusses the transformation rules used in our approach. Section 5 is the main section which presents the proposed approach. An ATM machine example and its transformation into LOTOS are presented in Sect. 6. Section 7 concludes the paper and gives some perspectives.

2 Related Work

Several works have focused on the UML models transformation towards formal methods such as Petri nets [16–18], Collared Petri nets [10], Maude [7], Object-Z [1], B method [11] and LOTOS. In this paper we have chosen the specification language LOTOS as one of the predominant and standard formal methods. It can be used in different application domains and provides a great modularity to structure and to analyze complex specifications. LOTOS specifications are precise, unambiguous and can be rigorously analyzed, verified and validated using several tools and methods based on theorem-proving, equivalence test or model-checking. The verification tools existing around LOTOS, such as CADP [20], provide much functionality such as model-checking, equivalence test (bisimulation, trace equivalence, observational equivalence … etc.), counter example visualization and code generation.

No much research has been done about the transformation of UML Statechart LOTOS. In [5], the authors present a model transformation of UML Statechart to LOTOS applied in the automotive industries. LOTOS is used in [13] to give a semantic model for compositional UML Statecharts. In [8], a transformation approach from a subset of UML Statechart to LOTOS behavior expressions is presented. In [15], the authors present how one can use LOTOS operators to gradually transform a particle form of UML State Machines into verifiable LOTOS specifications, in spite of not proposing precise transformation rules. However, the complexity of these approaches is high due to their manual, rigid and complex transformation rules. In the other hand, these approaches require the familiarity with LOTOS and the transformation process.

From the practical point of view, we believe that developers cannot use these approaches to convert Statechart diagrams to LOTOS.

In this paper, we propose a graph transformation based approach to automatically generate LOTOS expressions from UML Statechart diagram. The approach which is based on graph transformation is implemented as a tool environment using the meta-modeling tool AToM3. This approach will allow developers to model the system behaviors using UML Statechart diagrams and then automatically convert them into LOTOS for the verification purposes.

3   Background

3.1   UML Statechart

The Unified Modelling Language (UML) is a language for specifying, constructing, visualizing, and documenting the artifacts of a software development process [4]. It consists of a large number of diagrams. Some diagrams are used to model the structure of a system while others, such as Statechart diagram, are used to model the behavior of system.

A Statechart diagram [14] is a graph that models the lifetime of an object in response to events. Statechart diagrams describe state machines by emphasizing the potential states and transitions between them. A state can be considered as a situation during which some invariant condition holds. States can be either simple, composite or concurrent that can have several orthogonal regions. A transition is a relationship between two states indicating that an object in the transition source state may leave it and after that enters to the state target by the transition. Graphically, states and transition are represented as state boxes and transition arrows.

3.2   Lotos

LOTOS (Language Of Temporal Ordering Specification) is a standard formal description technique developed within ISO for specifying, among others, distributed concurrent information processing systems [2, 3]. This language adopts most of its concepts from Hoare's CSP [9] and Milner's CCS [13]. LOTOS is based on process algebraic methods for the description of process behaviors and interactions. For the description of data structures, it is based on the abstract data type language ACT ONE [6]. In this paper, we focus on the control aspect of the system, which is also called Basic LOTOS, and we leave the abstract data type description for future research.

In Basic LOTOS, a distributed concurrent system is seen as a process, possibly consisting of several subprocesses. A sub-process is a process in itself, so that in general a LOTOS specification describes a system via a hierarchy of process definitions [3]. A process is an entity able to perform internal, unobservable actions, and to interact with other processes, which form its environment. The typical structure of a basic LOTOS process definition is as presented in Fig. 1.

The essential component of a process definition is its behavior expression, which describes its behavior and its interaction with the environment through a number of small

```
process <proc_name> [gate list]:functionality:=
behaviour
     Behavior expression
where
     Process definitions
endproc
```

Fig. 1. Structure of basic LOTOS process

atomic actions denoted as gates. Behavior expressions are built from actions and other behavior expressions by using a predefined set of operators.

3.3 Graph Grammar and AToM³

AToM³ [21] is a visual tool for multi-formalism modeling and meta-modeling. By means of meta-modeling, we can describe or model the different kinds of formalisms needed in the specification and design of systems. The AToM³ meta-layer allows a high-level description of models using UML Class Diagram formalism or Entity Relation-ship (ER) formalism extended with the ability to express constraints. Based on these descriptions, AToM³ can automatically generate tools to manipulate models in the formalisms of interest [22].

AToM³ also supports graph rewriting, which is based on Graph Grammars to visually guide the procedure of model transformation. Model transformation refers to the process of translating, converting or modifying a model of a given formalism into another model that might or might not be in the same formalism. Graph Grammars [22] are a generalization of Chomsky grammars for graphs. It is a formalism in which the transformation of graph structures can be modeled and studied. The main idea of graph transformation is the rule-based modification of graphs as shown in Fig. 2.

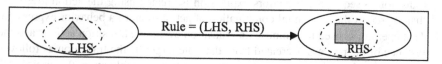

Fig. 2. Rule-based modification of graphs

4 Overview of the Transformation Rules

In LOTOS, behaviors of systems are usually specified as a set of processes, each of them specifies the behavior of an entity of the system. The global specification of the system is formed by composition of these processes using a set of predefined operators [2, 3]. For this reason, we assume in this work that the behavior of the system is specified as a set of Statechart diagrams, each of them models the behavior of an entity or an object of the system. These diagrams are translated into a set of processes in LOTOS. Then, these processes are composed to form the global specification using the fallowing process composition operators: parallel operators (Interleaving, Partial synchronization, full synchronization), enable and disable operators.

Converting Statechart diagrams directly into LOTOS is a very complex process. This is due to the complexity of the transformation rules, which makes its automation a very complex task. For this reason, we have chosen to flatten the hierarchical and concurrent structure of composite states in the Statechart diagram before its conversion into LOTOS process. Thus, Statechart diagrams are first converted to Flat State Machine (FSM) models which contain just simple states and arcs. Then, these FSM are converted into LOTOS processes.

Several algorithms and tools have been proposed to flatten Statechart diagrams [19]. In this work, we will use the graph transformation rules proposed in [10]. These rules are presented in Sect. 5. In the following, we will present only the mapping rules to convert an FSM diagram into a LOTOS process.

1. *Events to actions.* Events and actions in the FSM diagram are specified as actions in the equivalent LOTOS process.
2. *FSM states to LOTOS processes.* For each state in the FSM diagram, a LOTOS process is created as that presented in Fig. 3. The name of this process is the name of the state and its gate list ([gatelist]) is the list of events and actions in the transitions outgoing from the state.

```
process <proc_name> [gate list]:functionality:=
behavior
      Behavior expression
endproc
```

Fig. 3. The LOTOS process created for a state

3. *State Transitions to the behavior expression of the equivalent process.* For each transition, a sequential behaviors expression is created using the action prefix ";" that expresses the sequential combination of actions before a behavior expression. This operator is used to compose the transition event, the transition actions and the instance of the process is created from the state target by the transition as follows. In the case where there are several transitions from a single state, the choice "[]" operator is used to compose the behavior expressions corresponding to these transitions.
4. *Final state to stop process.* Final state is translated to "stop" process. "stop"is a predefined basic behavior used to express the process that finishes its execution or to represent deadlock situation.
5. *The FSM diagram to a LOTOS process.* The format of the LOTOS process generated for an FSM is presented in Fig. 4. The name of this process (proc_name) is the name of the class of objects modelled by the Statechart diagram. Its gate list ([gate list]) is the list of events and actions in the FSM diagrams. The behavior expression of this process is the instantiation of the process generated from the state target by the initial transition. Processes created from states are inserted as sub-processes of this process.

```
process <proc_name>[gate list]:functionality:=
behavior
     state1_name [gatelist1]
where
     process <state1_name> [gatelist1]:functionality:=...
     process <state2_name> [gatelist2]:functionality:=...
     . . .
endproc
```

Fig. 4. The structure of LOTOS specification created for an FSM.

5   The Proposed Approach

In this section, we describe our automated approach that transforms UML Statechart diagrams into their equivalent LOTOS processes. The approach performs the transformation as follows: first, flattening Statechart diagrams into Flat State Machines (FSM). Then, converting FSM models results into LOTOS processes.

For automating our approach using the meta-modeling tool AToM3, we have performed two following steps as follows (see Fig. 5): The first step consists of Meta-Modeling of UML Statechart and FSM formalism. The second step is the definition of graph transformation grammars used to perform the transformation. So, we have defined two Graph Grammars: the first Graph Grammar (1st GG): converts the Statechart diagrams to FSM models. The second Graph Grammar (2nd GG): generates LOTOS processes from the obtained FSM models.

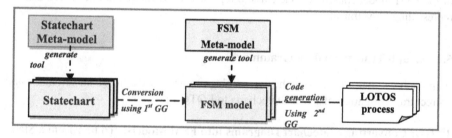

Fig. 5. The proposed approach

5.1   Meta-Modeling of UML Statechart and FSM Model

Since the visual tool AToM^3 has a meta-modeling layer that allows us to graphically model the different formalisms (Fig. 6), we have created two meta-models, Statechart diagrams meta-model and FSM meta-model. Then, we have used AToM^3 to generate a visual modeling tool for each of them according to their proposed Meta-Models.

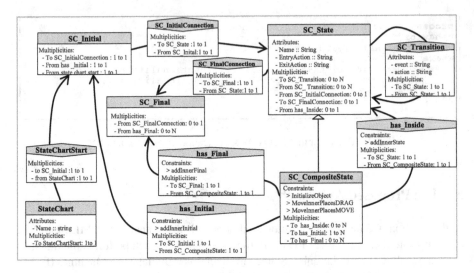

Fig. 6. UML Statechart meta-model

In this paper, we deal with a subset of UML Statechart which consists of states (simple and composite), transitions, events, actions that generate events, and initial and final states. The created meta-model for UML Statechart diagram is composed of five classes linked by seven associations as shown in Fig. 6.

A FSM is a State Machine without composite states. States in FSM are represented by rounded boxes, while transitions between them are represented with arcs. The meta- model of the FSM model consists of one class to represent FSM states and one association for representing FSM transitions.

5.2   Graph Transformation Grammars

In this sub-section, we describe the two graph grammars used to reach an automatic and correct transformation of UML Statecharts to LOTOS process.

1ˢᵗ GG: Converting Statechart Diagrams into FSM Models. To transform a State-chart into its equivalent FSM model, we have used the graph transformation grammar proposed in [10]. This graph grammar is named Statechart2FSM and containing twenty three rules which will be applied in ascending order. Only some representative rules are of this graph grammar shown here (see Fig. 7).

The idea of the transformation in Statechart2FSM grammar can be summarized by the following main steps: The first step is to select a Statechart and convert its initial state to FSM state using rule 22. The second step is to traverse the Statechart from its initial state (which is processed in the first step). Each exit transition of a processed Statechart state is converted into the corresponding FSM transition and the destination Statechart state is also converted if it has not previously processed (see rule 6). For each composite state in the statechart, the graph grammar uses a flag attribute indicating that this composite state is traversed but not processed (see rule 7). In third step, all composite states in the Statechart

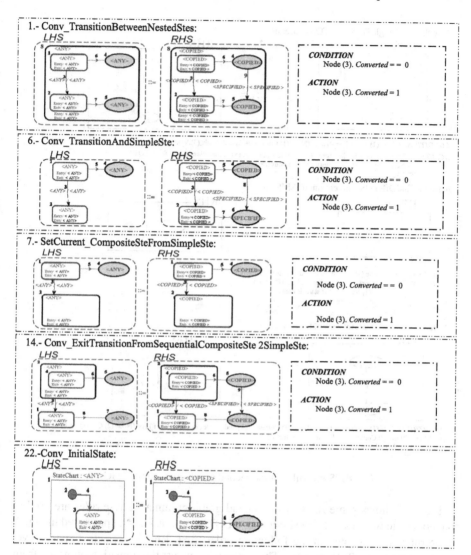

Fig. 7. Some rules of the first graph grammar (1^{St} GG)

(if any) will be converted. The process of the conversion is the same for Statechart diagrams (see rule1). The last step is to relate the equivalent FSM segment of composite state to FSM model of the Statechart (see rule 14).

2nd GG: Generating LOTOS Processes from FSM Models. In this grammar, we have concerned by the automatic generation of the LOTOS code. We have named this second graph grammar FSM2LOTOS which is composed of 14 rules. Applying this grammar, after the first grammar, leads to the generation of a file ".LOT" containing the corresponding LOTOS processes.

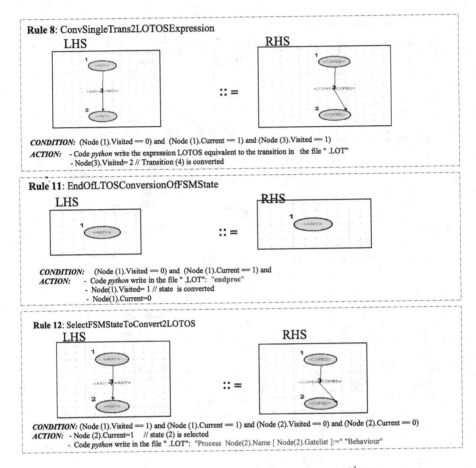

Fig. 8. Some rules of the second graph grammar (2nd GG)

Figure 8 shows some rules of the second graph grammar. These rules are used to convert a state with a single transition into a LOTOS process as that presented in Fig. 3. These rules are executed in the following order: first, Rule 12 selects a state no yet converted into a LOTOS process. Then, Rules 8 convert the transition outgoing from the state into the behavior expression of the process equivalent. At last, the Rule 11 finishes the conversion and actualises the flag attributes.

6   Example

We consider an example of an ATM machine, dispensing cash to a user. The system is composed of two objects ATMmachine and User. The Statechart diagrams model the behaviors of these objects are shown in Fig. 9.

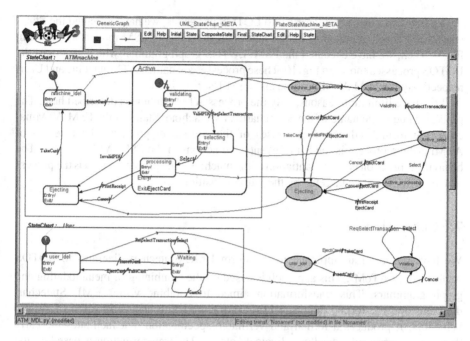

Fig. 9. Statecharts ATMmachine and user with their equivalent FSM models.

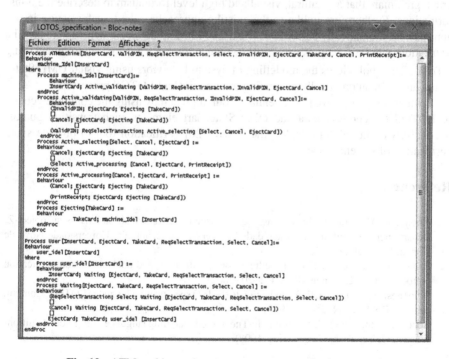

Fig. 10. ATMmachine and user processes generated using our tool

To transform these Statecharts into LOTOS processes, we have executed the State-chart2FSM graph grammar to flatten Statechart diagrams to FSM models as shown in Fig. 9. Then, we have executed the FSM2LOTOS graph grammar which generates the LOTOS processes shown in Fig. 10. These processes are named ATMmachine and User, respectively for FSM ATMmachine and FSM User.

For space limitation reasons, only the process ATMmachine is described here. The process name is the name of the Statechart ATMmachine. States in the FSM ATMmachine are formalized as sub-processes of the equivalent process. The gate list of ATMmachine process is the list of events and actions in the FSM ATMmachine. The behavior expression is the instantiation of the machine_Idle process, which is the process generated for the state targeted by the initial transition.

7   Conclusion

We have proposed an approach to transform UML Statechart diagrams to LOTOS performed by AToM^3. This approach is based on the combining of metamodeling and graph grammars. This transformation aimed to combine visual UML Statechart diagrams and the formal language LOTOS for modeling and verification of system behaviors. It produces a formal and verifiable specification that facilitates the early detection of errors like deadlock, livelock, etc..... The transformation is based on the graph grammars that are natural, visual and high level formalism to describe the trans-formations. Furthermore unlike to the existing approaches, the transformation in our approach is automatically performed. The use of FSM model in our approach makes the translation rules less complex which allows their automation as a tool environment using AToM^3. This tool allows the modelling of system behaviors using visual UML State-charts and then automatically generating their equivalent LOTOS processes.

In the future works, we plan to enhance our approach by using the complete version of LOTOS to represent data and other Statechart elements such transition guards. Secondly, we plan also to exploit the CADP [20] verification tool to provide some verification of system properties.

References

1. Araujo, J., Moreira, A.: Specifying the behavior of UML collaborations using object-Z. Departamento de Infomatica, Faculdade de Ciências e Tecnologia, Universidade Nova de Lisboa, Portugal (2000)
2. Babich, F., Deotto, L.: Formal methods for specification and analysis of communication protocols. IEEE Commun. Surv. **4**, 2–20 (2002)
3. Bolognesi, T., Brinksma, E.: Introduction to the ISO specification language LOTOS. Comput. Netw. ISDN Syst. **14**, 25–59 (1987)
4. Booch, G., Rumbaugh, J., Jacobson, I.: The unified modeling language user guide. Addition-Wesley, Object Technology Series (1998)

5. Chimisliu, V., Schwarzl, C., Peischl, B.: From UML statecharts to LOTOS: a semantics preserving model transformation. In: Ninth International Conference on Quality Software (2009)
6. Ehrig, H., Fey, W., Hansen, H.: Act one an algebraic specification language with two levels of semantics (1983)
7. Gagnon, P., Mokhati, F., Badri M.: Applying model checking to concurrent UML models. J. Object Technol. 7(1), 59–84 (2008). http://www.jot.fm/issues/issue_2008_01/article1/
8. Hnatkowska, B., Huzar, Z.: Transformation of dynamic aspects of uml models into lotos behaviour expressions. Int. J. Appl. Math. Comput. Sci. 11(2), 537–556 (2001)
9. Hoare, C.A.R.: Communicating Sequential Processes. Prentice Hall International Series in Computer Science. Prentice Hall, New Jersey (1985)
10. Kerkouche, E., Chaoui, A., Bourennane, E., Labbani, O.: A UML and colored petri nets integrated modeling and analysis approach using graph transformation. J. Object Technol. 9(4), 25–43 (2010)
11. Ledang, H., Souquières, J.: Formalizing UML behavioral diagrams with B. In: Tenth OOPSLA Workshop on Behavioral Semantics: Back to Basics, Tampa Bay, Florida, USA (2001)
12. Milner, R.: Formal a calculus of communication systems. LNCS, vol. 92. Springer, Heidelberg (1980)
13. Mrowka, R., Szmuc, T.: UML statecharts compositional semantics in LOTOS. In: ISPDC 2008, pp. 459–463 (2008)
14. OMG, Object Modeling Group: Unified Modeling Language Specification, version 2.0 (July 2005)
15. Babaee, R., Babamir, S.M.: From UML state machines to verifiable lotos specifications. In: Pichappan, P., Ahmadi, H., Ariwa, Ezendu (eds.) INCT 2011. CCIS, vol. 241, pp. 121–129. Springer, Heidelberg (2011)
16. Saldhana, J.A., Shatz, M., Hu, Z.: Formalisation of object behavior and interaction from UML models. Int. J. Softw. Eng. Knowl. Eng. 11(6), 643–673 (2001)
17. Xinhong, H., Lining, C., Weigang, M., Jinli G., Guo, X.: Automatic transformation from UML statechart to petri nets for safety analysis and verification. In: ICQR2MSE 2011, Conference Publications, pp. 948–951 (2011). ISBN 978-1-4577-1229-6
18. Wang, M., Lu, L.: A transformation method from UML statechart to petri nets. In: IEEE International Conference on Computer Science and Automation Engineering (CSAE) 2012, vol. 2, pp. 89–92, 25–27 May 2012
19. Devroey, X., Perrouin, G., Cordy, M., Legay, A., Schobbens, P.Y., Heymans, P.: State machine flattening: mapping study and assessment. CoRR abs/1403.5398 (2014)
20. CADP: Construction and analysis of distributed processes. http://cadp.inria.fr/
21. AToM3 Home page. http://atom3.cs.mcgill.ca/
22. Lara, J.D., Vangheluwe, H., Alfonseca, M.: Meta-modelling and graph grammars for multi-paradigm modelling in AToM^3. In: Software and Systems Modelling, vol. 3, pp. 194–209. Springer, Heidelberg (2004) (Special Section on Graph Transformations and Visual Modeling Techniques)

The Testing Method Based on Image Analysis for Automated Detection of UI Defects Intended for Mobile Applications

Šarūnas Packevičius[✉], Andrej Ušaniov, Šarūnas Stanskis,
and Eduardas Bareiša

Department of Software Engineering,
Kaunas University of Technology, Kaunas, Lithuania
{sarunas.packevicius,andrej.usaniov,
eduardas.bareisa}@ktu.lt,sarunas.stanskis@stud.ktu.lt

Abstract. Large amounts of defects found in applications are classified as user interface defects. As more and more applications are provided for smart phones, it is reasonable to test those applications on various possible configurations of mobile devices such as screen resolution, OS version and custom layer. However, the set of mobile devices configurations is quite large. Developers are limited to testing their applications on all possible configurations.

In this paper, we present an idea of the testing method for automated detection of UI defects intended for mobile applications. The testing method is based on static testing approach. It allows (1) to extract navigation model by code analysis of the application under test, (2) to execute application on a large set of mobile devices with different configurations (mobile cluster), (3) to capture images of application windows on each devices, (4) and to perform detection of defects by analyzing each image and comparing with predefined list of possible user interface defects.

Keywords: Software testing · Mobile devices · User interface testing · Static testing

1 Introduction

Testing mobile application not only relates to executing unit tests. There are large amounts of different device configurations with various screen resolutions, OS versions and custom layers, and their combinations in the market. A variety of configurations requires additional consideration from developers when they have to ensure correct behavior of application they are developing. Recently appeared mobile device clusters provide services allowing simultaneous execution of application on many different physical or virtual mobile devices.

Robinson and Brooks have performed the analysis on user submitted bug reports and found that majority (65 %) of customers-reported graphical user interface (GUI) defects had major impact on their day-to-day operations and that at least 60 % of

© Springer International Publishing Switzerland 2015
G. Dregvaite and R. Damasevicius (Eds.): ICIST 2015, CCIS 538, pp. 560–576, 2015.
DOI: 10.1007/978-3-319-24770-0_48

all reported defects were GUI based [1]. While Issa et al. [2] conducted a study of defects found in open source systems and found that visual defects represents between 16 % and 33 % of all bug reports, thus proposed a method for fault classification for visual testing of GUI based systems.

2 Mobile Software Testing Challenges

Many various concepts related to software testing are well understood, analyzed and practiced for decades [3], but developing mobile applications faces its own challenges [4], due to differences from usual desktop applications in various ways: (1) they use touch-screen interface, (2) they are responding to various sensors, (3) they are run with very limited resources, and (4) there are many different mobile platforms and their configurations [5].

Wasserman [6] and Kirubakaran et al. [7] indicated these mobile development and testing issues: (1) Interaction with other applications; (2) Sensor related issues; (3) Type of mobile application (Native or hybrid); (4) Different configurations of devices; (5) Security; (6) User interfaces issues; (7) Complexity; (8) Power consumption; (9) test selection and the test execution to the challenges list.

3 Related Work

The market of mobile applications is still growing. There are even attempts to develop mobile device clusters that allow splitting of the job that the application is requested to perform and offload it to other mobile devices nearby [8]. Such approach may have possible uses in certain cases, but therefore it alleviates the necessity to test the same application on many different mobile devices as it could be impossible to know where given application or task may be executed.

There are many different approaches in assaulting those problems. Reeder and Maxion [9] proposed to test user interface usability by tracking user hesitation and how long it takes to perform a certain task. This way they can indicate problematic GUI parts and point out GUI design parts that developers should check and improve. Hu and Neamtiu explored the possibility to utilize random testing of mobile applications [10].

Also, there are numerous attempts to automatically test Android applications with symbolic execution. For instance, Mirzaei et al. [11] suggested to modify Android classes and in this way make those applications run on Java Virtual Machine thus developing a new approach for symbolic execution of Android applications by adapting those used for java programs. Similarly, Anand et al. suggested a possible approach of exercising Android applications by leverage of concolic testing [12]. Authors have proposed a way to modify a Java byte code of the application under test alongside any third party library that the application uses by adding additional fields that store symbolic values for that particular field. They also suggested to inject new assignment calls that manipulate those symbolic variables before original fields are altered and in such a way to generate the graph of application execution paths.

Liang et al. [13, 14] presented a cloud based testing service that uses real world device definitions to provide a large set of realistic mobile contextual parameters for developer usage in emulators. Also, authors analyzed 147 mobile applications and grouped them by similar resource usage as well as attempted to develop a service for testing those applications on the cloud made of both real and virtual mobile devices. Gao et al. [15] analyzed various approaches for providing testing as a service and concluded that adapted for mobile testing it provides following advantages: (1) the ability to test mobile applications on demand; (2) cost reduction due to sharing of mobile resources and (3) support for scalable and agile testing process. Candea et al. [16], Gao et al. [17] and Haller [18] described a possibility to provide software testing as a service on the cloud systems. However, Huang and Gong [19] proposed slightly different approach by providing remote access to mobile device enabling testers to test applications on various devices they do not poses.

Another challenge is testing of GUI. Takala et al. [20] proposed the model based Android application testing method. Authors suggested using an emulator and GUI model to exercise the application under test. Xun and Memon [21] and Memon et al. [22] suggested extending application model by using feedback generated at program run time. Also Amalfitano et al. [23] proposed to extend model generation algorithm by including context events such as device movements, phone calls and other mobile device related triggers. While Yang et al. [24] presented the way of extracting model from a mobile application by static analysis and dynamic execution. A program code is statically analyzed and all GUI events are extracted, then they exercise analyzed application GUI and invoke previously collected events in this way creating the application model. Azim and Neamtiu [25] suggested to exercise an application by analyzing its internal dataflow and in this way to extract application GUI model without statically analyzing its source code.

Yeh et al. [26] suggested using image recognition for searching and automation of the application GUI testing. Similarly, Chang et al. [27] suggested using this approach by extending application test scenarios by allowing to write use cases by defining visual elements that can be searched in GUI and interacted.

As there are many various attempts to automate different aspects of mobile application testing, only few of them are focusing on actual GUI testing. Even those involve manually written scripts that check for existence of predefined elements in indicated location. Thus there is room for automated GUI testing tool that would attempt to determine if there are any visible interface defects like missing or overlapping controls. Moreover, such an approach could be used as an extension to already proposed Testing as a Service concept.

4   User Interface Visual Defects

Mobile applications user interfaces do not differ from usual desktop applications in many aspects. Here we present a possible checklist of user interfaces defects. The defects are grouped into several categories.

Layout problems:
- Invisible control – the control can be obscured by other control or can be rendered outside of the screen, in case when a device has a smaller screen than the application was designed on.
- Clipped control – the control can be partially obscured by other control, or rendered near the screen edge and as a result a part of it goes out of screen bounds.
- Too small control – the control is rendered on a low resolution device with a small screen size, the control could be too small to see or touch.
- Misaligned controls –text boxes are usually placed alongside labels. The label can be improperly aligned to the text box on devices with smaller screen resolution than the one the application was originally designed with.

Text problems:
- Too small text – text can be too small to read on some devices (with small physical screens and low resolutions).
- Partial text – text, similarly as a control, can be obscured by other controls or screen edges. One of common problems is that application is designed in one user language and later in the phase of development developers provide resources translation texts for other languages. In other languages than the application was developed (for example, English), text messages could be longer in character length, and not always properly fit into the text placeholders.

Image problems:
- Bad scaling – the image aspect ratio can be lost when the image control is rendered on a device with different screen aspect ratio.
- Bad resolution – the image could be of a lower resolution than the screen (for example, a 100dpi image on a 400 dpi screen). The image could look blocky or blurry on devices like that.

Color problems:
- Hidden control – colors can be selected for controls in a way that controls vanish between other controls (for instance, using white text on light grey background).
- Not matching colors – controls colors can be selected incorrectly, for example, white text on yellow background is not easy to read.
- Poor color choice – the colors that were selected for the application might look good on testing device, but can look poorly when low screen brightness is used or when the device is not under ideal environment light conditions. Also color choice could be inappropriate for some target user audiences [28].

Application menu problems:
- Menu does not fit to a screen/toolbar – the menu could be of a right size for a large screen device, but on a small screen a part of it could be obscured, thus preventing user from invoking some application functions.
- Missing icons – as devices have various screens with different resolutions and screen sizes, the developer has to add menu icons for many device configurations, in the result the developer can miss some required icons.

Navigation problems:
- Stuck at screen – due to faulty implementation the application cannot leave some window – thus cannot function properly.

- Wrong window – the application can show an unexpected window.
- App crash – the application can just crash due to memory, network, limited hardware features, or implementation error.
- Timing problems – the application can be not responsive enough – the time interval between showing windows could be too long, which annoys users or discourages them from a further application usage.

5   User Interface Defects Detection Method

Proposed automated method is based on a static analysis of User Interface (UI) representations captured on certain devices under test. During analysis pictures of UI controls are extracted and compared against defined checklist of UI defects. Methods algorithm is presented in Fig. 1.

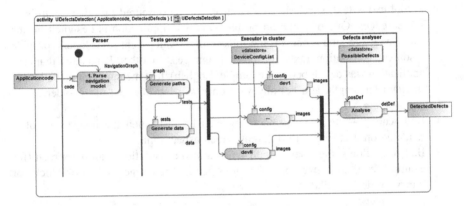

Fig. 1. UI defects detection method in UML activity diagram.

The complete testing procedure is composed of those steps:

1. Parsing of a navigation model – a user interface navigation model is extracted from an application code.
2. Path generation –generation of paths in a navigation model.
3. Data generation –generation of test data that will drive an application through all navigation paths.
4. Application execution with generated test data on provided mobile device configurations with screenshots capture at each step.
5. The analysis of captured images against defined checklist of user interfaces defects.

5.1   Model Extraction

The starting data for detection of defects is the application user interface navigation model. We propose to extract the model directly from the application source code. The main model elements that are of interest are:

- Application windows and dialogs (later referred to as windows, as they mainly are the main containers for user interface elements);
- Control events that cause transitions between windows;
- Transition constraints that define what values have to be entered in input fields to cause transition from one window to another;
- Controls, their initials sizes and positions.

The user interface model is represented as a directed graph. The application windows are presented as graph nodes and control events that cause transitions between windows are presented as directed edges in the constructed graph.

Model extraction algorithm consists of these steps:

```
1. Read source code location and get all source code files
2. for each source code file
3.  extract all classes
4.  for each class
5.   if class contains displayable content then
6.    if the class node is not added to the graph then
7.     add found class as graph node
8.    end if
9.    extract all inner components
10.     add node metadata about existing GUI components with information
        about their location and sizes
11.     for each component
12.      if component is a button or a link then extract its event
         handler method
13.       parse located event handler and search for navigation
          activities
14.       if navigation activity is found then
15.        locate navigation destination window
16.        if destination window is not already defined in the
           graph then
17.         add new node header
18.        end if
19.        add a link between the two nodes
20.        if there is any constraints involved in transition then
21.         add metadata information that constraint solving will be
            required
22.        end if
23.       end if
24.      end if
25.     next
26.    end if
27.   next
28. next
```

5.2   Navigation Paths Extraction

The navigation model of the application is created from the source code in the first step, and it is used to generate all possible navigation paths. At this step it is necessary to find all possible or at least as much as possible application navigation paths that would allow showing all application windows.

This translates to the already solved problem of visiting all nodes in the graph. For this several methods can be used – for example, finding all elementary circuits [29] or depth search algorithms [30].

5.3   Test Data Generation

Input actions that force transition from one window to another are generated. In most cases, input actions are simple events and there is no need to enter any parameter values (enter value in the text field, or select list item). Usually only one event is required to trigger transition. The event consists of control such as button or menu and its action (such as a click). In situations, when transition is not possible due to constraints (that were discovered in the first step) and actual parameter values are required. Existing test data generation methods should be used: such as PathFinder [31], constraints solving [32, 33], feedback-based random generation [34].

5.4   Tests Execution on Each Device

When testing the application for user interface defects, the application has to be executed on all possible device configurations. Testing devices should be connected into mobile devices cluster [8]. This allows for test execution on devices with various configurations that could be physical [35] or emulated [14] and should have:

- Various screen resolutions of a device.
- Various screen sizes of a device.
- Various screen color depths of a device.
- Various screen orientations of a device.
- Various memory sizes of a device.
- Various CPU speeds of a device.
- Various versions of device operating systems.

The application under test is executed on each device. The tests executor drives the application by feeding test data and forcing application to follow the navigation path defined by the test.

The screenshots are taken at each test step for each device in the cluster and for each taken screenshot the following meta-data are assigned:

- Expected application state (Window name, ID).
- The device ID, the screenshot was taken on.
- Device Operating system version.
- Screen resolution of a device.

- Screen size of a device.
- Screen color depth of a device.
- Time taken to reach this window from previous window.

5.5 Defects Analysis from Captured Screenshots

When all screenshots are captured the analysis of each image is performed. This analysis is similar to the static analysis [36] approach. Each image is analyzed and checked against a defined defect list. For each defect there is a rule how to check it:

Layout problems:
- Invisible control – as we know on which window screenshot was taken, the analysis tool knows what controls are declared on that window and should be available. The control usually has square shape and has 4 edges. Image recognition algorithms might be used to detect button presence, for instance, edge detection algorithm [37]. If no edges are detected, the control could be invisible.
- Clipped control – similarly to an invisible control, if not all controls edges are detected, the control can be partially clipped.
- Too small control – the actual control size can be calculated by measuring control size on the image and using device resolution and screen size, to calculate how large the control is on screen in actual measurements in mm. If the control is smaller than predefined size it could be too small for the user to see or interact.
- Misaligned controls – the controls are usually aligned with each other. For example, the text label is aligned to the text input box. If the tool detects several controls nearby, it can check if they are at the same horizontal or vertical coordinates on the image and to determine if they are aligned (if coordinates matches) or misaligned (if there is a difference between coordinates).

Text problems:
- Too small text –text recognition from the images algorithm can be used in order to find the text on the image [38]. If the tool does not manage to find the text or part of it, it can be too small to read. If the text is found, its size on the screen can be calculated similarly as it can be calculated for a control. If the text size in actual mm is smaller than some predefined value, the text might be considered as unreadable by the user.
- Partial text – the text could be clipped by the screen edge or covered by the other control. Usually developers develop an application interface and provide a text in one language and then provide translations in other languages assuming that the text will be nicely replaced. However, not all texts in the other languages are of the same length. When the translated text does not fit the control bounds, an operating system could render just "…" in its place. If the tool detects those dots in the image, it can flag it as possibly clipped text.

Image problems:
- Bad scaling – the original image size can be known by analyzing initial application, the tool can measure the rendered image size on the screenshot and

compare it to the original one. The aspect ratio can be calculated from the initial image and if this ratio is different than that of the rendered image, the defect might be suspected.

- Low resolution – the image that has poor resolution, or the image of improper resolution selected for display is rendered poorly on the screen. If the image is too small or too big, the application/operating system scales it, thus making it blurry. The blurry image detection algorithm used in analyzing photo graphics [39] can be used. If the blur level is too high then predefined level, the defect could be suspected.

Color problems:

- Hidden control – the control can use the same or similar color as the surrounding controls, thus making it invisible. The tool can calculate control's average color and compare it with the color of its surrounding controls and check if the difference of colors is too small. If the difference is a small one, the defect can be suspected.
- Not matching colors – sometimes developers are bad at choosing colors for the application. For example, black text on yellow background is really difficult to read and is distracting. The tool can calculate components and texts colors and compare them using color harmonization method [40]. The colors of components are placed on the color wheel and the distance between them is calculated, if the colors are too far away or does not match criteria of harmonious colors defined in the paper [40], the defect can be suspected.
- Poor colors choice – the developers can choose poor color scheme that does not suit the intended audience or are bad for a user segment (for example, using red text on green background could make such a text invisible for users with certain disabilities). By using some predefined criteria about color choices [28] the tool can calculate color values of the components and check if they match the colors defined in [28]. If they do not match, defects can be suspected.

Application menu problems:

- Menu does not fit the screen/toolbar – from the application model it is possible to determine menu structure and discover menu text labels. The tool analyses images and discovers menu texts; if some of menu texts are not discovered, the partial menu defect can be suspected.
- Missing icons – using the tool the application user interface model can determine if a menu item has an associated icon. The tool can analyze the image and find the menu text, then check if there is an image nearby (by predefined distance in pixels) that matches the image from the application model using image comparison algorithm [41]. If the image is not found, the defect can be suspected.

Navigation problems:

- Stuck at screen – the test tool can check, if screenshots before window transition and after transition are the same. If the window is the same, the navigation event has failed, the navigation defect can be suspected.
- Wrong window – the application model allows us to determine what window should be shown after some transition event occurrence. The tool can analyze the image and its meta-data after the event to check if a corresponding window is

shown. If the window does not match the expected one from the model, navigation defect can be suspected.

- Application crash – if the application testing has unsuspectedly terminated after invoking transition event, the application crash defect can be suspected.
- Timing problems – during the tests execution transitioning time is measured. The difference between time when event was invoked and the new window is displayed can show if the user interface is responsive. If the response time is smaller than the defined value [42], the usability defect can be suspected. Liepinaitis et al. propose a method for detecting defects for Windows phone applications by analyzing application screen and driving the application through predefined execution path [43].

As it is with static analysis, the detected defects may not necessary be the software faults. The tool/method could only identify suspicious situations and flag them for the tester to review. The tool/method should provide the fault image, device configuration and other information related to the suspected fault for the tester to review.

6 Proposed Solution Testing Execution Framework

The proposed testing method relies on the tool. Here we present a brief overview of the tool architecture. The tool should be composed on two main parts:

Devices Cluster. It is the virtual or physical environment composed of mobile devices and network connectivity. Each device should have a testing service installed. This service should be responsible for:

- Receiving the application under test from the devices coordinator and installing it.
- Receiving test from the devices coordinator and executing them.
- Capturing application under test screenshots and returning them to the devices coordinator.

Testing Framework. It relates to system components that are responsible for generating tests, executing them on devices, gathering testing results and interpreting testing results. Its main parts are:

- Tests generator – responsible for analyzing code of software under test and extracting navigation graph, preparing test data.
- Devices coordinator – responsible for getting generated tests and executing tests on each device in the devices cloud. The coordinator takes tests one by one and sends tests to each device using the testing services interface. The testing service performs actual test execution and gathers results. Later the device coordinator extracts captured images from each device using the testing service.
- Images analyzer – analyses all captured images and produces a list of possible application defects.

The testing tool design principle is presented in the Fig. 2.

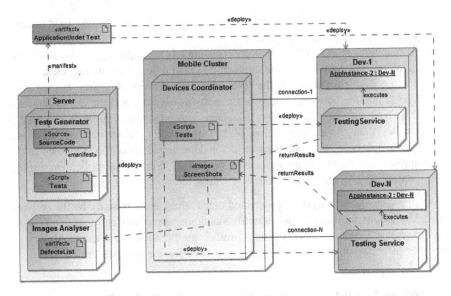

Fig. 2. Testing tool architecture.

7 Example

In order to illustrate the expected results we will demonstrate the proposed defect detection method, by analyzing how it will perform on a sample Android application. The application performs one simple function – converts item price into time indicating how long the user has to work to earn enough money to afford some item. The application consists of three windows:

- The main window that performs conversion.
- Settings window that allows entering user income data.
- The saved items history window, which contains previously performed conversions.

The first testing step is to analyze application and to build application graph. This application graph is presented in Fig. 3.

The application windows are presented as "Main", "History", and "Settings" nodes. Transitions between windows are presented as directed edges "history menu click", "settings menu click", and "back click". The tool also analyses application windows and discovers that they are composed of:

- Main window: 3 text boxes and 3 labels.
- Settings window: 3 text boxes, 4 labels and 1 combo box.
- History window: one list box.

The second step is to build navigation paths of the application which would force application to display all windows. There are two generated paths:

- Main → History (invoked by the "history menu click" event")
- Main → Settings (invoked by the "settings menu click" event).

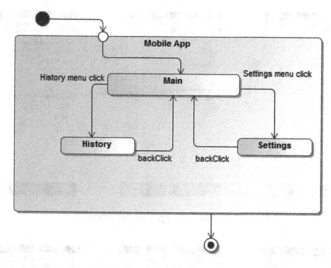

Fig. 3. Application under test navigation graph.

The back events are ignored as they would bring the application to already visited window, and it is assumed that it would be just unnecessary step.

The third step is to select test data that will drive application through selected navigation paths. As there are no entry fields that constraint transitions between windows, it is only needed to raise application events. For selected two navigation parts the corresponding test data are:

- Invoke "history menu click" event" on the main window.
- Invoke "settings menu click" event on the main window.

The fourth step is the actual test execution. In order to execute this step we have to rely on the big amount of devices with various hardware and software configurations. For this example, we selected a pair of devices that represent two extreme situations – powerful, high end device, and very simple device. The main configuration aspects of the devices are:

- Device1: Android 4.0, 1 GB RAM, 5″ screen, 1280 × 768 resolution screen.
- Device2: Android 4.3, 128 MB RAM, 2.5″ 320 × 240 resolution screen.

The testing tool executes application on each device and takes screenshots at each step (step 5). Captured images are presented in Figs. 4 and 5.

The last step relates to the analysis of captured images. The testing tool has to go through all captured images and check if there are defects listed in the possible errors checklist.

On device 1 there are no discovered issues, as it is a device on which the developer created the application and checked its user interface. The developer assumed that the application will look good on all other devices. The developer's assumption has been correct for the main and history windows – they look good. But there are layout problems on the settings window when the application is executed on device 2.

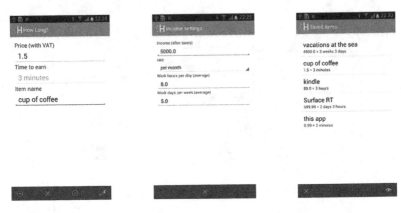

Fig. 4. Captured images on the device 1.

Fig. 5. Captured images on the device 2.

The tool can now detect several possible faults on the settings window image on device 2:

- Clipped control: the input boxes are clipped on the right edge of the screen.
- Clipped text: text labels are clipped on the right edge of the screen. This problem has been detected by analyzing text labels declared in application code and text labels recognized from the image. In this case, text labels do not match the ones declared in the application code.

Image 3 also contains one problem – the lists are missing the second item. Nonetheless, as the tool has discovered that this application window contains only a list box control, and verified that it is present and not clipped by screen edges, no fault is detected. The application functionality problem instead of user interface problem could be the missing list item.

8   Conclusions and Future Work

We have presented an idea of the automated user interfaces defects analysis method for mobile devices. The proposed method executes application under test in a mobile cluster - a large set of mobile devices with various hardware and software configurations. When test execution takes place, screenshots are captured at each test step on each device. Then those screenshots are analyzed against defined checklist of user interfaces defects.

Various already existing image recognition, text recognition and image comparison algorithms are suggested for identifying user interface elements on the captured images to determine user interface element presence (or not presence at all), position and size. Based on the detected graphical element properties, those properties can be compared with the properties of the application model elements to determine if elements are presented correctly. The possible defects are discovered by checking images against predefined defects list similarly as the static analysis is performed on source code. Similarly to static analysis the discovered defects are just possible defects that the tester has to manually review later.

The proposed approach is fits best for testing applications that consist of form type windows with standard data entry fields. It would be difficult or even impossible to test more interactive applications such as computer games because it would be difficult to recognize more artistic graphic components such as images used as a buttons or animated controls. Besides, more interactive applications such as game might pose additional problems by using such actions as scaling, rotating by few degrees and various animations and complicating control recognition.

As the proposed method is still in early stages, the future work refers to investigating what actual defects can be detected, what actual image analysis methods could be effectively used for extracting information from application screenshots and evaluation of the performance metrics and accuracy metrics.

References

1. Robinson, B., Brooks, P.: An initial study of customer-reported GUI defects. In: International Conference on Software Testing, Verification and Validation Workshops, ICSTW 2009, pp. 267–274 (2009)
2. Issa, A., Sillito, J., Garousi, V.: Visual testing of graphical user interfaces: an exploratory study towards systematic definitions and approaches. In: 2012 14th IEEE International Symposium on Web Systems Evolution (WSE), pp. 11–15 (2012)
3. Bertolino, A.: Software testing research: achievements, challenges, dreams. In: 2007 Future of Software Engineering, pp. 85–103. IEEE Computer Society (2007)
4. Holl, K., Elberzhager, F.: A mobile-specific failure classification and its usage to focus quality assurance. In: 2014 40th EUROMICRO Conference on Software Engineering and Advanced Applications (SEAA), pp. 385–388 (2014)
5. Muccini, H., Di Francesco, A., Esposito, P.: Software testing of mobile applications: Challenges and future research directions. In: 2012 7th International Workshop on Automation of Software Test (AST), pp. 29–35 (2012)
6. Wasserman, A.I.: Software engineering issues for mobile application development. In: Proceedings of the FSE/SDP Workshop on Future of Software Engineering Research, pp. 397–400. ACM, Santa Fe, New Mexico, USA (2010)

7. Kirubakaran, B., Karthikeyani, V.: Mobile application testing - challenges and solution approach through automation. In: 2013 International Conference on Pattern Recognition, Informatics and Mobile Engineering (PRIME), pp. 79–84 (2013)

8. Huerta-Canepa, G., Lee, D.: A virtual cloud computing provider for mobile devices. In: Proceedings of the 1st ACM Workshop on Mobile Cloud Computing and Services: Social Networks and Beyond, pp. 1–5. ACM, San Francisco, California (2010)

9. Reeder, R.W., Maxion, R.A.: User interface defect detection by hesitation analysis. In: International Conference on Dependable Systems and Networks, DSN 2006, pp. 61–72. (2006)

10. Hu, C., Neamtiu, I.: Automating GUI testing for android applications. In: Proceedings of the 6th International Workshop on Automation of Software Test, pp. 77–83. ACM, Waikiki, Honolulu, HI, USA (2011)

11. Mirzaei, N., Malek, S., Păsăreanu, C.S., Esfahani, N., Mahmood, R.: Testing android apps through symbolic execution. SIGSOFT Softw. Eng. Notes 37, 1–5 (2012)

12. Anand, S., Naik, M., Harrold, M.J., Yang, H.: Automated concolic testing of smartphone apps. In: Proceedings of the ACM SIGSOFT 20th International Symposium on the Foundations of Software Engineering, pp. 1–11. ACM, Cary, North Carolina (2012)

13. Liang, C.-J.M., Lane, N., Brouwers, N., Zhang, L., Karlsson, B., Chandra, R., Zhao, F.: Contextual fuzzing: automated mobile app testing under dynamic device and environment conditions. Microsoft. Microsoft, nd Web (2013)

14. Liang, C.-J.M., Lane, N.D., Brouwers, N., Zhang, L., Karlsson, B.F., Liu, H., Liu, Y., Tang, J., Shan, X., Chandra, R., Zhao, F.: Caiipa: automated large-scale mobile app testing through contextual fuzzing. In: Proceedings of the 20th Annual International Conference on Mobile Computing and Networking, pp. 519–530. ACM, Maui, Hawaii, USA (2014)

15. Gao, J., Tsai, W.-T., Paul, R., Bai, X., Uehara, T.: Mobile testing-as-a-service (MTaaS) – infrastructures, issues, solutions and needs. In: Proceedings of the 2014 IEEE 15th International Symposium on High-Assurance Systems Engineering, pp. 158–167. IEEE Computer Society (2014)

16. Candea, G., Bucur, S., Zamfir, C.: Automated software testing as a service. In: Proceedings of the 1st ACM Symposium on Cloud Computing, pp. 155–160. ACM, Indianapolis, Indiana, USA (2010)

17. Gao, J., Xiaoying, B., Wei-Tek, T., Uehara, T.: Testing as a service (TaaS) on clouds. In: 2013 IEEE 7th International Symposium on Service Oriented System Engineering (SOSE), pp. 212–223 (2013)

18. Haller, K.: Mobile testing. SIGSOFT Softw. Eng. Notes 38, 1–8 (2013)

19. Huang, J.F., Gong, Y.Z.: Remote mobile test system: a mobile phone cloud for application testing. In: 2012 IEEE 4th International Conference on Cloud Computing Technology and Science (CloudCom), pp. 1–4 (2012)

20. Takala, T., Katara, M., Harty, J.: Experiences of system-level model-based GUI testing of an android application. In: 2011 IEEE Fourth International Conference on Software Testing, Verification and Validation (ICST), pp. 377–386 (2011)

21. Xun, Y., Memon, A.M.: Generating event sequence-based test cases using GUI runtime state feedback. IEEE Trans. Softw. Eng. 36, 81–95 (2010)

22. Memon, A., Banerjee, I., Nagarajan, A.: GUI ripping: reverse engineering of graphical user interfaces for testing. In: 2013 20th Working Conference on Reverse Engineering (WCRE), pp. 260–260. IEEE Computer Society (2003)

23. Amalfitano, D., Fasolino, A.R., Tramontana, P., Amatucci, N.: Considering context events in event-based testing of mobile applications. In: 2013 IEEE Sixth International Conference on Software Testing, Verification and Validation Workshops (ICSTW), pp. 126–133 (2013)

24. Yang, W., Prasad, M.R., Xie, T.: A grey-box approach for automated GUI-model generation of mobile applications. In: Cortellessa, V., Varró, D. (eds.) FASE 2013 (ETAPS 2013). LNCS, vol. 7793, pp. 250–265. Springer, Heidelberg (2013)

25. Azim, T., Neamtiu, I.: Targeted and depth-first exploration for systematic testing of android apps. SIGPLAN Not. **48**, 641–660 (2013)

26. Yeh, T., Chang, T.-H., Miller, R.C.: Sikuli: using GUI screenshots for search and automation. In: Proceedings of the 22nd Annual ACM Symposium on User Interface Software and Technology, pp. 183–192. ACM, Victoria, BC, Canada (2009)

27. Chang, T.-H., Yeh, T., Miller, R.C.: GUI testing using computer vision. In: Proceedings of the SIGCHI Conference on Human Factors in Computing Systems, pp. 1535–1544. ACM, Atlanta, Georgia, USA (2010)

28. Reinecke, K., Bernstein, A.: Knowing what a user likes: a design science approach to interfaces that automatically adapt to culture. MIS Q. **37**, 427–453 (2013)

29. Johnson, D.B.: Finding all the elementary circuits of a directed graph. SIAM J. Comput. **4**, 77–84 (1975)

30. Cormen, T.H., Leiserson, C.E., Rivest, R.L., Stein, C.: Depth-first search. In: Introduction to Algorithms, pp. 540–549. MIT Press, Cambridge and McGraw-Hill, New York (2001)

31. Visser, W., Pasareanu, C.S., Khurshid, S.: Test input generation with java PathFinder. In: Proceedings of the 2004 ACM SIGSOFT International Symposium on Software Testing and Analysis. ACM Press, Boston, Massachusetts, USA (2004)

32. Arnaud, G., Bernard, B., Michel, R.: Automatic test data generation using constraint solving techniques. In: Proceedings of the 1998 ACM SIGSOFT International Symposium on Software Testing and Analysis. ACM Press, Clearwater Beach, Florida, United States (1998)

33. Packevicius, S., Krivickaite, G., Barisas, D., Jasaitis, R., Blazauskas, T., Guogis, E.: Test data generation for complex data types using imprecise model constraints and constraint solving techniques. Inf. Technol. Control **42**, 191–204 (2013)

34. Pacheco, C., Lahiri, S.K., Ernst, M.D., Ball, T.: Feedback-directed random test generation. In: Proceedings of the 29th International Conference on Software Engineering. IEEE Computer Society (2007)

35. Baride, S., Dutta, K.: A cloud based software testing paradigm for mobile applications. SIGSOFT Softw. Eng. Notes **36**, 1–4 (2011)

36. Ernst, M.: Static and dynamic analysis: synergy and duality. In: ICSE 2003 International Conference on Software Engineering, pp. 25–29 (2003)

37. Ganesan, L., Bhattacharyya, P.: Edge detection in untextured and textured images-a common computational framework. IEEE Trans. Syst. Man Cybern. B Cybern. **27**, 823–834 (1997)

38. Mishra, A., Alahari, K., Jawahar, C.V.: Top-down and bottom-up cues for scene text recognition. In: 2012 IEEE Conference on Computer Vision and Pattern Recognition (CVPR), pp. 2687–2694 (2012)

39. Tsomko, E., Hyoung Joong, K.: Efficient method of detecting globally blurry or sharp images. In: Ninth International Workshop on Image Analysis for Multimedia Interactive Services, WIAMIS 2008, pp. 171–174 (2008)

40. Cohen-Or, D., Sorkine, O., Gal, R., Leyvand, T., Xu, Y.-Q.: Color harmonization. ACM Trans. Graph. **25**, 624–630 (2006)

41. Guoshen, Y., Morel, J.M.: A fully affine invariant image comparison method. In: IEEE International Conference on Acoustics, Speech and Signal Processing, ICASSP 2009, pp. 1597–1600 (2009)

42. Waloszek, G., Kreichgauer, U.: User-centered evaluation of the responsiveness of applications. In: Gross, T., Gulliksen, J., Kotzé, P., Oestreicher, L., Palanque, P., Prates, R.O., Winckler, M. (eds.) INTERACT 2009. LNCS, vol. 5726, pp. 239–242. Springer, Heidelberg (2009)
43. Liepinaitis, D., Motiejūnas, G., Kuckis, T.: The errors search method for mobile devices software using timing characteristics. In: Information Society and University Studies, pp. 55–59 (2014)

Predicting Defect Prone Modules in Web Applications

Mehmet Serdar Biçer$^{(\boxtimes)}$ and Banu Diri

Computer Engineering Department, Yıldız Technical University,
Istanbul, Turkey
mehmet.serdar.bicer@std.yildiz.edu.tr, banu@ce.yildiz.edu.tr

Abstract. Predicting defect proneness of software products has been an active research area in software engineering domain in recent years. Researchers have been using static code metrics, code churn metrics, developer networks, and module networks as inputs to their proposed models until now. However, domain specific characteristics of software has not been taken into account. In this research, we propose to include a new set of metrics to improve defect prediction performance for web applications by utilizing their characteristics. To validate our hypotheses we used datasets from 3 open source web applications to conduct our experiments. Defect prediction is then performed using different machine learning algorithms. The results of experiments revealed that overall performance of defect predictors are improved compared to only using existing static code metrics. Therefore we recommend practitioners to utilise domain-specific characteristics in defect prediction as they can be informative.

Keywords: Software metrics · Software quality · Web sites

1 Introduction

According to 2014 statistics, 87 % of North America, 70 % of Europe uses the Internet [34]. Annual total of worldwide Internet-based transactions is valued with trillions of dollars [31]. Besides e-commerce, millions of users use different web pages like search engines (e.g. Google), social sharing platforms (e.g. Facebook, Twitter), information sharing (e.g. Wikipedia) every day. Considering such a big Internet usage, being accessible has become a big necessity for companies. Latest browser wars and in parallel improvements in technology and performance has allowed developers to create better applications with freedom. New requirements (e.g. small screen support) has been added to web applications with increasing usage of mobile devices.

The key element that affects the success of a software project is its quality [30]. It's closely related to testing activities in software development, which also affects conformity with time and budget constraints. Simplest approach in software testing is exhaustive testing, i.e. testing all possibilities in a given

© Springer International Publishing Switzerland 2015
G. Dregvaite and R. Damasevicius (Eds.): ICIST 2015, CCIS 538, pp. 577–591, 2015.
DOI: 10.1007/978-3-319-24770-0_49

code piece. However, that is impossible due to time and budget limitations. For this reason, software managers often use learning based oracles to predict defect proneness of their products.

Researchers have been using static code metrics, code churn metrics, developer networks, and module networks as inputs to their proposed models until now. In recent years researchers discovered that these metric sets have already hit a performance ceiling [20]. We have two options to eliminate this ceiling effect:

– Using new data mining techniques with existing metric sets.
– Changing training data to use with existing data mining techniques.

There are some specific studies on web applications. Although they are focused on different aspects of applications, they had helped us to see there are some characteristic differences. To the best of our knowledge, attributes of web applications have not been analysed in defect prediction until today. Because of these reasons, we propose to take a data centric approach where we introduce new set of metrics for web applications.

In this study, we have two research questions to investigate value of extracting a new set of metrics for predicting defect proneness of web applications:

– **How can we utilize web application characteristics to introduce a new set of metrics?**
– **What is the benefit of using web metrics to predict defects?**

In order to be able to answer our research questions, we used data from 3 web applications and applied 3 different machine learning algorithms to construct our defect prediction models.

The rest of the paper is organized as follows. In Sect. 2 we briefly discuss the related work. In Sect. 3 we explain our reasoning and proposed metric set. In Sect. 4 we explain dataset, data extraction process and experimental set up in detail. In Sect. 5 we present our results and conclude the paper with discussion on the threats to validity and future work.

2   Related Work

Predicting defect proneness of software products has been done since 1970s, and researches in this area has been more active since 2005 [7]. Static code metrics are the most famous type of software metrics that is used extensively by many researchers [13,14,16,19,20,30,36]. They give indications about the size and the complexity of the implemented code and can be extracted from source code automatically. These metrics are widely used in defect prediction studies today. But in these studies, metrics are extracted from desktop or embedded applications and none of them used datasets from web applications in their experiments.

Another type of software metrics is code churn metrics. This metric set is derived from version control systems such as SVN and GIT. Code churn was first introduced by Munson et al. [22]. This research also showed that code churn metrics are highly correlated with problem reports than static code metrics. This metric set includes features like added/deleted lines of code, age of code, status of code, number of changes made on the code, number of developers worked on the code, etc.

In addition to these, social network metrics are also used in software error estimate [6,18,26,38,39] as a relatively new type of metric. This type of metrics are independent from programming language or code itself, social networks are constructed of developers or files. Researchers in this field constructed social networks by connecting interdependent files or developers who are contributed to the same files and extracted features from these networks by using social network analysis techniques.

There are some studies on web applications in similar areas. Some of them [21,23] focused on identifying quality attributes of applications. But most of the research is focused on improving or automatizing test cases [3,5,8,15,27,28]. There are also some researches in taxonomy of faults in web applications [4,10, 15,24,35]. These studies helped us to identify diversities in characteristics of web applications.

In a study researchers investigated defect-proneness of web applications compared to desktop applications, and they found that presentation layer of web applications is more defect-prone compared to desktop applications [32].

Although there are some static code metric sets [17,29,37] special to web applications, they are used to be protected against attacks like SQL injection and XSS.

3   Web Metrics

In this section, we will explain what types of metrics can be extracted from web applications. For this purpose common fault[1] types in web applications will be introduced first. Then proposed metrics and their value will be investigated.

3.1   Web Applications

Errors in web applications cost millions of dollars to companies. Unlike desktop applications, web applications are required to have high availability. Even the smallest problems have high costs. For example, problems in Amazon's website costed half million dollars in twenty minutes in thanksgiving of 2001 [2]. But the invisible costs of errors is bigger. Every error deteriorates user loyalty and reduces number of customers [24].

What makes web applications so special? What could be the reason behind increasing usage in web?

---

[1] Fault is used interchangeably in this study with the terms 'defect', 'bug' or 'error' to mean a fault in software code.

- Web applications can be accessed from everywhere,
- Changes are reflected to end users easily and quickly,
- Richer and more interactive user interfaces can be created with ease,
- Ability to access and use resources from other web applications (e.g. social platform integration, video embed, etc.).
- Ability to combine and utilize different technologies in one place. A web page can have different components such as markup, CSS files, scripts, server-side code, database access [9].

These features are exciting for users and developers but they also bring difficulties in development and test. Although the same application development lifecycles that are used in other type of applications can also be used for web applications, there are some technical points they diverge:

- For starters different programming languages, design features, external components are used for development. Examples of these are traditional programming languages, scripting languages, HTML pages, XML-based template files, databases, images and CSS code. Components of applications can be physically distributed to different devices in production and development and they have to run in a harmony.
- Web applications depend on browsers to run. The same piece of code can work in a different way or do not work in different browsers. Coding must be done to ensure cross-browser compatibility and tested in different browsers.
- There are more security vulnerabilities. First of all, it's easier to access and view client-side scripts. Furthermore since these kind of applications can be accessed by a wider audience through Internet, they are exposed to more threats.
- They are much more vulnerable to changes in the outside world. If slowing down or loss of Internet connection is not accounted during development, there is a good chance of encountering undesirable situations.

All of these factors increase complexity in web applications [23].

3.2   Faults in Web Applications

In order to be able to answer our first research question, we need to inspect characteristics of web applications first. For this purpose we need to analyze faults in web applications. Without doing that we can't address special metrics. There are several studies on faults in web applications [10,15,24,35]. Although there are small differences in these studies, their results are approximately the same. Marchetto's study [15] provides the most comprehensive taxonomy of web application faults. Marchetto's taxonomy is given in Table 1. We made use of the taxonomy by identifying our candidate metrics to be extracted from web applications.

Table 1. Web application fault taxonomy [15]

Characteristics	Classes of faults
Multi-tier architecture	Faults realted to browser incompatibility
	Faults related to back button
	Faults related to the needed plugins
	Faults in the construction of dynamically built client-side pages
	Faults related to inputs of server-side pages
	Faults during file-system access
	Faults related to server environment
	Faults related character encoding of the input data
	Faults during form construction
	Faults during database interactions or management
	Faults on the information search process
	Wrong storage of information in cache
GUI	Faults related to HTML interpretation by the browser
	Faults while manipulating DOM objects
	Faults on frame synchronization
	Faults on frame loading
	Faults related to character encoding
	Unintended jump among languages
Session-based	Faults in session synchronization
	Faults in persistence of session objects
	Faults while manipulating cookies
Hyperlinked structure	Faults related to the Web pages integrations
	Faults while build dynamic URL
	Faults due to the unreached resources
	Faults due to the not available resources
Protocols-based	Faults related to the use of encrypted communication
	Proxies do not support a given used protocols
Authentication	Fault during user authentication
	Faults in account management
	Faults in accessing/using resources without permission
	Faults in role of management

3.3 Proposed Metrics

We shall use automated tools to extract metrics for defect prediction studies. Otherwise it would take precious time of project members' and doesn't comply with its purpose which is saving resources. For some fault types it's hard or not possible to address them to software metrics. For example a fault during user authentication can be identified by a human but it's not possible for an automated tool to identify such a high level scenario. Such an automated analysis tool can only understand that some parameters are sent to the server and session

Table 2. Mapping of proposed metrics to fault classes

Metrics	Classes of faults
Header Access	Faults related to inputs of server-side pages
Has Request Parameters	Faults related character encoding of the input data
Request Parameter Reads	Faults during form construction
Database Queries	Faults during database interactions or management
Has Database Query	Faults on the information search process
Context Switches	Unintended jump among languages
Has Session Parameters	Faults in session synchronization
Session Reads	Faults in persistence of session objects
Session Writes	Faults in account management
	Faults in role of management
	Fault during user authentication
Cookie Access	Faults while manipulating cookies

access and may be some database operations are made. But most of them can be derived from source code and a custom metric set can be built. We are proposing following metrics to address fault characteristics of web applications. For now, we have been able to extract 10 metrics by only inspecting server-side code:

- Has Session Parameters: If a session parameter is read or written in file or not.
- Session Reads: Number of reads from session parameters in file.
- Session Writes: Number of writes to session parameters in file.
- Cookie Access: Number of reads from or writes to cookies in file.
- Header Access: Number of reads from or writes to request headers in file.
- Has Request Parameters: If a request parameter is used in file or not.
- Request Parameter Reads: Number of reads from request parameters in file.
- Context Switches: Number of switches between server-sided and client-sided code in file.
- Database Queries: Number of select queries in file.
- Has Database Query: If a database query is executed in file or not.

These metrics are chosen by inspecting taxonomy given in Table 1. Fault types given in the taxonomy are mostly related with characteristics of web applications. This gave us a starting point to identify candidate metrics to include in our research. Table 2 shows the mapping of our metrics to fault classes related with characters of web applications. The table should be interpreted as metrics showing in left column are considered to be related with fault classes in right column which are in same section. Ordering of metrics and/or faults is not important.

12 out of 31 fault classes are mapped by 10 metrics. Remaining fault types are ignored because either they cannot be mapped properly by automated metric extraction or they are related with client-side. In both cases they are out of scope for this research.

4   Methodology

This section explains proposed metrics and techniques we used to answer research questions.

4.1   Dataset

We used data of 3 PHP based open source projects in our experiments. All of the code bases are located in GitHub. Some statistics about selected projects can be seen from Table 3. Statistics include entire code base for specified versions. These projects include different type of files such as HTML, CSS, JavaScript, etc. We ignored files that is not a PHP file because: (a) Static code metrics are only available for traditional programming languages, (b) Scope of this work is limited with server-side part of web applications.

Table 3. Application statistics

Name	Category	Version	Developers	LOC	Files	Commits
phpPgAdmin	DB management	5.0	26	149136	496	1957
Wordpress	CMS	3.0	53	382600	1246	25712
Joomla	CMS	3.1	239	581606	5573	15726

4.2   Data Extraction

First of all snapshots were downloaded from Github pages for versions in Table 3. We have taken downloaded modules as snapshot and bug fixes were identified within 1 year of snapshot for labeling modules as defective or not. In order to be able to label a commit as bug fix we looked for some keywords like (bug, error, fix, fail) in commit messages. Then static code metrics are calculated separately for each file. Since this type of metrics is only available for programming languages, only PHP files were added in data sets. Finally, affected files are labeled as defective. Result of this step is a dataset, which has static code metrics as attributes. Source files were analyzed using Understand [33] and php-ast [25] tools and custom scripts written in Python language.

4.3   Defect Prediction Model

Machine learning algorithms have been used to generate models of program properties that are known to cause errors. Defect prediction models have been prepared by using learning based models. We designed a learning based system to predict the defectiveness of software modules. We chose Naive Bayes, Bayes Net, Random Forest data mining algorithms as they are commonly used and well-performing algorithms for defect prediction. Source code of projects and code commit history are taken as input to the model. The system is trained with datasets using three machine learning algorithms and tested with 10×10-fold cross validation to eliminate a bias would be caused from ordering effect in dataset. After the training-testing process, prediction results are obtained. The output represents which files are predicted as defective and which files are predicted as defect-free. Finally performance of the system is evaluated using pd, pf, balance measures.

We have also applied CFS attribute selection filter to evaluate correlation of proposed metrics with defectiveness. CFS is based on the hypothesis that a good feature subset is highly correlated with class [11]. After feature selection is applied to entire dataset, remaining features will be the ones that are more relevant with defectiveness. CFS is applied to the datasets separately. The same prediction model is applied to filtered and non-filtered datasets. We used Weka Software to implement the algorithms and the experiments [12].

4.4 Performance Measures

We evaluated the performance of our proposed metrics in terms of probability of detection (pd) and probability of false alarms (pf) as they have been the widely used performance measures in defect prediction studies [14,19]. Pd, which is also defined as recall, indicates how successful the predictor is in finding actual defective modules, while pf indicates the false alarms of the predictor, classifying defect-free modules as defective. These values are extracted from ROC curves.

We seek predictors which maximize pd and minimize pf at the same time. Thus, we need to achieve a prediction performance which is as near to ideal point (1, 0) in terms of (pd, pf) rates as possible. The ideal case is very rare in practice [1]. Even state of the art predictors are far away from reaching that point [20]. Engineers have to trade-off between pd and pf. We use a third performance measure called balance to choose the optimal (pd, pf) pairs. Balance is defined as the normalized Euclidean distance from the desired point (1, 0) to (pd, pf) in a ROC curve [19]. These parameters are calculated with (1)–(3) measures. It makes possible to see how close our estimates to the ideal case. Higher balances are better because their points (pd, pf) are closer to the ideal point (1, 0). Predictors with different (pd, pf) values can have the same balance value. This does not mean that all predictors with the same balance value have the same practical usage. Domain specific requirements leads us to choose between predictor with different (pd, pf) values. For safety-critical systems having high pf rate would not cause a problem because cost of unnecessary inspection is lower than failures in production. But for rest of the projects, especially with tight budgets, having very low-low pf rate is more desirable.

We conducted Mann-Whitney U Test with 0.05 significance level to show statistical significance of the results. Mann-Whitney U test (a.k.a. Mann-Whitney-Wilcoxon) is a nonparametric test which is used to test if two independent samples of observations belong to the same distribution or not. It's used as an alternative to t-test. In t-test data is assumed to be in normal distribution.

But we can't make this assumption in defect prediction datasets. Using nonparametric tests is more appropriate in these cases. Mann-Whitney U Test is a nonparametric test which can be used for discretized or continuous numeric tests which makes it a good candidate for our study. Multiple comparisons problem in statistical testing does not apply this case because even though we have three performance metrics, overall performance is measured with a single metric, which is balance.

$$pd = \frac{TP}{TP + FN} \tag{1}$$

$$pf = \frac{FP}{FP + TN} \tag{2}$$

$$balance = 1 - \frac{\sqrt{pf^2 + (1 - pd)^2}}{\sqrt{2}} \tag{3}$$

5 Results

For each project, we have used 4 different datasets.

- **Full:** Both existing static code metrics and proposed metrics have been used together. If we think this setup as a controlled experiment, this dataset has the role of experiment group.
- **Old:** Only existing static code metrics are used. This is the control group in our controlled experiment.
- **Full-Filtered:** We have applied Correlation-Based Feature Selection (CFS) algorithm to our entire dataset (which consists both of old and new metrics) and only take attributes which could pass from filter.
- **Old-Filtered:** Same logic with Full-Filtered was also applied here, but only to existing static code metrics.

Results of attribute selection filter are different for each dataset. Selected attributes from entire dataset are shown in Table 4 for every project. Metrics were explained in Sect. 3.3.

Table 4 shows signs of something promising about our first research question. First of all we can see that at least 1 metric has passed attribute filter for all projects. Metrics in bold are from our proposed metric set. Ratio of proposed metrics to existing code metrics vary between projects. We have proposed 10 metrics and in total 5 of them are able to pass CFS attribute filter. We can't say that remaining metrics are totally irrelevant, but they have lower correlation with defectiveness. Most selected metric type is number of DB queries and its boolean representation. This shows us that this metric type may be useful in defect prediction. Access to request parameters is ranked at second place by 2 out of 3 projects. This is somewhat consistent as these parameters are directly related with fault classes "inputs of server-side pages" and "database interactions or management" caused from multi-tier architecture given in Sect. 3.2. DB related metrics are also related with "faults on the information search process" class. The other chosen metrics are "Context Switches" and "Session Reads".

We have to evaluate defect prediction performance for our second research question. We have 4 different feature vectors for 3 projects, which makes 12 datasets in total. Each of them was evaluated using 3 different machine learning algorithms. Results of pd, pf, and balance measures in our experiments can be seen from Tables 5, 6 and 7. Results are compared to each other in pairs. That means we have compared Full vs Old and Full-Filtered vs Old-Filtered. Values marked with * means shows the marked value is statistically significantly higher than its pair. Significance of difference is checked using Mann-Whitney U Test.

For every metric type we have made 18 comparisons. For pd rates 7 out of 18 ($\approx$39 %) comparisons show significant difference. 86 % of the differences are positive, that means pd rate is increased significantly in general. In pf rate values there are 11 significant differences in 18 comparisons ($\approx$61 %). 10 out of 11 ($\approx$91 %) of them are negative, that means pf rates are generally decreased using our proposed metrics. That's a good thing because we already want to decrease pf rates in defect prediction studies.

These differences in pd and pf values also effected balance values in result. Higher balance values indicates better predictors. In our experiment 14 out of 18 results ($\approx$78 %) are found to be significant according to Mann-Whitney U Test. Moreover 13 of 14 significant results, which makes 93 %, are increasing compared to previously used metric set. From this aspect we can say that our proposed metric set affects performance of defect prediction studies by increasing performance of prediction algorithms.

Overall gain in balance ranges from 1 % to 12 % depending on dataset. Despite the changes are small in value, they show us they provide some info to predictors and information content of datasets can further be enriched.

From practical point of view, our proposed metrics has some beneficial outcomes:

– Our proposed metrics either considerably decreases high false alarm rates or increases low prediction rates. In both cases this results in increase of overall prediction performance. Increase has been observed in a significant portion ($13/18 \approx 72$ %) of the balance values compared to existing static

Table 4. Filtered attributes from all metrics

WordPress	Joomla	phpPgAdmin
AvgLineCode	CountLine	AvgLine
CountLine	CountLineCode	AvgLineBlank
Cyclomatic	RatioCommentToCode	CountLineBlank
MaxCyclomatic	**DB Query**	CyclomaticModified
Req. Param Reads	**Has DB Query**	MaxCyclomaticModified
Context Switches		**Session Reads**
DB Query		**Req. Param Reads**
Has DB Query		

Table 5. pd rate

Dataset	Algorithm	Full	Old	Full-Filtered	Old-Filtered
WordPress	NaiveBayes	**0.44***	0.36	**0.43***	0.25
	RandomForest	0.72	0.74	0.71	0.72
	BayesNet	**0.55***	0.52	0.55	0.54
Joomla	NaiveBayes	0.88	0.88	0.85	0.85
	RandomForest	0.81	0.81	0.74	**0.79***
	BayesNet	0.70	0.69	0.74	0.74
phpPgAdmin	NaiveBayes	**0.67***	0.63	**0.60***	0.43
	RandomForest	**0.76***	0.72	0.73	0.73
	BayesNet	0.96	0.96	0.86	0.87

Table 6. pf rate

Dataset	Algorithm	Full	Old	Full-Filtered	Old-Filtered
WordPress	NaiveBayes	0.15	**0.18***	**0.12***	0.10
	RandomForest	0.48	**0.51***	0.44	**0.49***
	BayesNet	0.25	**0.28***	0.18	**0.25***
Joomla	NaiveBayes	0.78	**0.81***	0.70	**0.77***
	RandomForest	0.37	**0.39***	0.39	0.40
	BayesNet	0.34	**0.35***	0.35	**0.37***
phpPgAdmin	NaiveBayes	0.13	0.13	0.10	0.10
	RandomForest	0.09	0.10	0.09	0.09
	BayesNet	0.20	0.20	0.14	0.12

Table 7. Balance

Dataset	Algorithm	Full	Old	Full-Filtered	Old-Filtered
WordPress	NaiveBayes	**0.59***	0.53	**0.59***	0.47
	RandomForest	0.61	0.60	**0.63***	0.60
	BayesNet	**0.63***	0.61	**0.66***	0.63
Joomla	NaiveBayes	**0.44***	0.42	**0.49***	0.45
	RandomForest	0.70	0.69	0.67	**0.68***
	BayesNet	**0.68***	0.67	**0.69***	0.68
phpPgAdmin	NaiveBayes	**0.75***	0.73	**0.71***	0.59
	RandomForest	**0.82***	0.79	0.80	0.80
	BayesNet	0.85	0.85	0.86	0.87

code metrics. This indicates improvement of overall prediction performance by using additional metric set. Thus we recommend practitioners to collect domain-specific metrics in defect prediction.

– Results also show that proposed metric set helps to reduce false alarm rates more than increasing probability of detection. Web applications are in tight-budget project domain where having low pf rate is more important. In this aspect proposed metric set is also appropriate for domain-specific needs of prediction model.

– To the best of our knowledge, this is the first time usage of web-domain-specific metrics in defect prediction. Although the observed gain is low, we can interpret this result as domain specific features of applications can be utilized in defect prediction. Extra research can be performed to fully explore and exploit these features.

6   Threats to Validity

One possible threat to validity would be restricting dataset to projects with single programming language. There are many programming languages which can be used in web applications but we only inspected PHP based projects. None of our proposed metrics is specific to language used in applications. Although this reduces severity of the threat, these metrics still need to be validated by using additional datasets with other programming languages.

7   Conclusion

In this study, we attempted to answer two research questions. First of them was: **How can we utilize web application characteristics to introduce a new set of metrics?**

To answer this research question, we examined web applications and mapped fault types to software metrics. We consider this is the most efficient way of addressing diversity of web applications because we can directly gather metrics from errors. In this study, only server-sided codes of web applications were examined. 10 metrics are defined for this purpose. We prepared datasets from repository data of 3 PHP based open source projects to evaluate value of these metrics by feature selection algorithms. To evaluate relevance of proposed metric set we applied CFS filter to entire dataset. 50 % of proposed metrics were able to pass the filter in total. In result, from Table 4, we can see that database related metrics are the most frequently selected ones.

The second question was: **What is the benefit of using web metrics to predict defects?**

For this research question we used datasets, which were used to answer previous research question, in our prediction model. A learning based defect prediction model is constructed to predict defect proneness of web applications. We compared our findings with performance of existing metrics to assess effectiveness of our proposed metrics. Performance of classifiers was assessed using pd, pf, and balance metrics after 10×10-fold cross validation. In result we achieved small but statistically significant differences in performance. Values marked with * in Table 5, 6 and 7 shows marked value is statistically significantly higher than its pair. Among these significant differences, pd rates are mostly increased, pf rates are mostly decreased and in result most of the balance values are increased. Increase in overall prediction performance ranges from 1 % to 12 % depending on dataset. This result leads us to our proposed metrics can be useful in defect predictors and this value might increase if they are further supported by additional metrics.

In future we plan to analyze client-side part of web applications (such as HTML and CSS) and extract additional metrics to use in defect prediction.

References

1. Alpaydın, E.: Introduction to Machine Learning, 2nd edn. The MIT Press, Cambridge (2010)
2. California power outages suspended-for now. http://news.cnet.com/2100-1017-251167.html. Accessed 12 April 2014
3. Andrews, A.A., Offutt, J., Alexander, R.T.: Testing web applications by modeling with FSMs. Softw. Syst. Model. **4**, 326–345 (2005)
4. Arshad, F.A.: Failure characterization and error detection in distributed web applications. Ph.D. thesis, Purdue University (2014)
5. Artzi, S., Kiezun, A., Dolby, J., Tip, F., Dig, D., Paradkar, A., Ernst, M.D.: Finding bugs in dynamic web applications. In: Proceedings of the 2008 International Symposium on Software Testing and Analysis. ISSTA 2008, pp. 261–272. ACM, New York (2008). http://doi.acm.org/10.1145/1390630.1390662
6. Biçer, S., Bener, A.B., Çağlayan, B.: Defect prediction using social network analysis on issue repositories. In: Proceedings of the 2011 International Conference on Software and Systems Process. ICSSP 2011, pp. 63–71. ACM, New York (2011). http://doi.acm.org/10.1145/1987875.1987888
7. Çatal, C., Diri, B.: Review: a systematic review of software fault prediction studies. Expert Syst. Appl. **36**(4), 7346–7354 (2009). doi:10.1016/j.eswa.2008.10.027
8. van Deursen, A., Mesbah, A.: Research issues in the automated testing of Ajax applications. In: van Leeuwen, J., Muscholl, A., Peleg, D., Pokorný, J., Rumpe, B. (eds.) SOFSEM 2010. LNCS, vol. 5901, pp. 16–28. Springer, Heidelberg (2010)
9. Dholakia, U., Rego, L.L.: What makes commercial web pages popular? An empirical investigation of web page effectiveness. Eur. J. Mark. **32**(7), 724–736 (1998)
10. Guo, Y., Sampath, S.: Web application fault classification - an exploratory study. In: Proceedings of the Second ACM-IEEE International Symposium on Empirical Software Engineering and Measurement. ESEM 2008, pp. 303–305. ACM, New York (2008). http://doi.acm.org/10.1145/1414004.1414060
11. Hall, M.: Correlation-based feature selection for machine learning. Ph.D. thesis, University of Waikato (1999)
12. Hall, M., Frank, E., Holmes, G., Pfahringer, B., Reutemann, P., Witten, I.H.: The weka data mining software: an update. SIGKDD Explor. Newsl. **11**(1), 10–18 (2009). doi:10.1145/1656274.1656278
13. Halstead, M.H.: Elements of Software Science. Operating and Programming Systems. Elsevier Science Inc., New York (1977)

14. Lessmann, S., Baesens, B., Mues, C., Pietsch, S.: Benchmarking classification models for software defect prediction: a proposed framework and novel findings. IEEE Trans. Softw. Eng. **34**(4), 485–496 (2008). doi:10.1109/TSE.2008.35
15. Marchetto, A., Ricca, F., Tonella, P.: Empirical validation of a web fault taxonomy and its usage for fault seeding. In: Huang, S., Penta, M.D. (eds.) WSE 2007, pp. 31–38. IEEE Computer Society (2007)
16. McCabe, T.: A complexity measure. IEEE Trans. Soft. Eng. **SE–2**(4), 308–320 (1976)
17. Medeiros, I., Neves, N.F., Correia, M.: Automatic detection and correction of web application vulnerabilities using data mining to predict false positives. In: Proceedings of the 23rd International Conference on World Wide Web. WWW 2014, pp. 63–74. ACM, New York (2014). http://doi.acm.org/10.1145/2566486.2568024
18. Meneely, A., Williams, L., Snipes, W., Osborne, J.: Predicting failures with developer networks and social network analysis. In: Proceedings of the 16th ACM SIGSOFT International Symposium on Foundations of Software Engineering. SIGSOFT 2008/FSE-16, pp. 13–23. ACM, New York (2008). http://doi.acm.org/10.1145/1453101.1453106
19. Menzies, T., Greenwald, J., Frank, A.: Data mining static code attributes to learn defect predictors. IEEE Trans. Softw. Eng. **33**(1), 2–13 (2007)
20. Menzies, T., Milton, Z., Turhan, B., Cukic, B., Jiang, Y., Bener, A.: Defect prediction from static code features: current results, limitations, new approaches. Autom. Softw. Eng. **17**(4), 375–407 (2010)
21. Misra, S., Cafer, F.: Estimating quality of javascript. Int. Arab J. Inf. Technol. **9**(6), 535–543 (2012). http://dblp.uni-trier.de/db/journals/iajit/iajit9.html#MisraC12
22. Munson, J.C., Elbaum, S.G.: Code churn: a measure for estimating the impact of code change. In: Proceedings of the International Conference on Software Maintenance. ICSM 1998, p. 24. IEEE Computer Society, Washington (1998). http://dl.acm.org/citation.cfm?id=850947.853326
23. Offutt, J.: Quality attributes of web software applications. IEEE Softw. **19**(2), 25–32 (2002). doi:10.1109/52.991329
24. Pertet, S., Narasimhan, P.: Causes of failure in web applications. Technical report CMU-PDL-05-109, Parallel Data Laboratory, Carnegie Mellon University (2005)
25. php-ast. https://github.com/nikic/php-ast. Accessed 14 December 2014
26. Pinzger, M., Nagappan, N., Murphy, B.: Can developer-module networks predict failures? In: Proceedings of the 16th ACM SIGSOFT International Symposium on Foundations of Software Engineering. SIGSOFT 2008/FSE-16, pp. 2–12. ACM, New York (2008). http://doi.acm.org/10.1145/1453101.1453105
27. Praphamontripong, U., Offutt, J.: Applying mutation testing to web applications. In: 2010 Third International Conference on Software Testing, Verification, and Validation Workshops (ICSTW), pp. 132–141, April 2010
28. Ricca, F., Tonella, P.: Anomaly detection in web applications: a review of already conducted case studies. In: Ninth European Conference on Software Maintenance and Reengineering. CSMR 2005, pp. 385–394, March 2005
29. Shar, L.K., Tan, H.B.K.: Mining input sanitization patterns for predicting sql injection and cross site scripting vulnerabilities. In: 2012 34th International Conference on Software Engineering (ICSE), pp. 1293–1296, June 2012
30. Shull, F., Basili, V., Boehm, B., Brown, A.W., Costa, P., Lindvall, M., Port, D., Rus, I., Tesoriero, R., Zelkowitz, M.: What we have learned about fighting defects. In: Proceedings of the 8th International Symposium on Software Metrics. METRICS 2002, p. 249. IEEE Computer Society, Washington (2002). http://dl.acm.org/citation.cfm?id=823457.824031

31. Sprenkle, S.E.: Strategies for automatically exposing faults in web applications. Ph.D. thesis, University of Delaware, Newark, DE, USA (2007)
32. Torchiano, M., Ricca, F., Marchetto, A.: Are web applications more defect-prone than desktop applications? Int. J. Softw. Tools Technol. Transfer **13**(2), 151–166 (2011). doi:10.1007/s10009-010-0182-6
33. Understand - source code analysis & metrics. http://scitools.com. Accessed 3 May 2014
34. World internet users statistics usage and population stats. http://www.internetworldstats.com/stats.htm. Accessed 20 October 2014
35. Vijayaraghavan, G.V.: A taxonomy of e-commerce risks and failures. Ph.D. thesis, Florida Institute of Technology (2003)
36. Wang, H., Khoshgoftaar, T.M., Seliya, N.: How many software metrics should be selected for defect prediction? In: Murray, R.C., McCarthy, P.M. (eds.) FLAIRS Conference. AAAI Press (2011)
37. Wassermann, G., Su, Z.: Static detection of cross-site scripting vulnerabilities. In: Proceedings of the 30th International Conference on Software Engineering. ICSE 2008, pp. 171–180. ACM, New York (2008). http://doi.acm.org/10.1145/1368088.1368112
38. Wolf, T., Schroter, A., Damian, D., Nguyen, T.: Predicting build failures using social network analysis on developer communication. In: Proceedings of the 31st International Conference on Software Engineering. ICSE 2009, pp. 1–11. IEEE Computer Society, Washington (2009). http://dx.doi.org/10.1109/ICSE.2009.5070503
39. Zimmermann, T., Nagappan, N.: Predicting defects using network analysis on dependency graphs. In: Proceedings of the 30th International Conference on Software Engineering. ICSE 2008, pp. 531–540. ACM, New York (2008). http://doi.acm.org/10.1145/1368088.1368161

Dynamic Analysis of 4-Node Degenerated Shell Element with Updated Thickness

Dalia Calneryte[(⊠)] and Rimantas Barauskas

Faculty of Informatics, Department of Applied Informatics,
Kaunas University of Technology, Studentu, 50-407 Kaunas, Lithuania
{dalia.calneryte,rimantas.barauskas}@ktu.lt

Abstract. There is a variety of approaches available to model the large strain behavior of shells in dynamic analysis. This article examines the significance of the iterative shell thickness update for the 4-node degenerated shell element with Reissner-Mindlin assumptions. The updated Lagrangian formulation in explicit and implicit dynamic integration schemes is described. The rigid link correction is employed to reduce the warp of the element. Numerical examples including dynamic analysis of fixed beam and pinched cylinder are presented. The results show that significance of the thickness update occur for the large strains.

Keywords: Updated Lagrangian formulation · 4-node degenerated shell element · Bathe integration scheme · Nonlinear dynamic analysis

1 Introduction

Dynamic finite element analysis is widely used to investigate the response of the structure under the desirable load and boundary conditions. If the dimensions of the structure are significantly small in one direction compared with others, the shell elements are convenient in finite element model simulation. Shell elements are classified into three main groups: the curved shell elements based on classical shell theories, degenerated shell elements and flat shell elements combining properties of membrane and bending plate [6]. The 4-node degenerated shell element is considered in this paper.

If large strain behavior is simulated, the change in shell thickness should be considered. Three different approaches applied to model the large strain behavior of shells are discussed in [9]. The simplest and the most cost-efficient approach is to update the thickness iteratively. The element thickness is updated to ensure the incompressible behavior for the thin basic shell triangles in [7] using this approach. The same update scheme is applied for the thick 4-node shell element in this paper. Other approaches presented in [4] consist of using solid elements or three dimensional higher order shell elements with at least 7 parameters. However, evaluation of additional parameters increase computational cost of the model.

The aim of this paper is to examine the significance of the iterative shell thickness update in dynamic behavior. Damping effects are not considered in the research. Firstly, the 4-node degenerated shell element with the rigid link correction and transformation from global to local system in case of the warped element is described. Secondly, the updated Lagrangian formulation with explicit and implicit integration

© Springer International Publishing Switzerland 2015
G. Dregvaite and R. Damasevicius (Eds.): ICIST 2015, CCIS 538, pp. 592–603, 2015.
DOI: 10.1007/978-3-319-24770-0_50

schemes is presented. Finally, the numerical examples including beam with fixed ends and pinched cylinder with rigid diaphragms at the ends are proposed to illustrate the effects of thickness update.

2   4-Node Degenerated Shell Element

Degenerated shell element was derived from the solid element by defining all displacements (translational and rotational) with respect to the mid-surface [8]. Any shell element is defined by material properties, mid-surface normals at each node, geometry and thickness of the element [12]. Shear strains γ_{yz}, γ_{zx} are considered to be not equal to zero for the thick shell with Reissner-Mindlin assumptions. Reissner-Mindlin theory states that a straight line normal to the undeformed middle surface remains straight but not necessarily orthogonal to the middle plane after deformation [8]. Shear correction factor $\kappa = 5/6$ is employed to compensate the error due to the assumption of constant shear strains within plate thickness although the shear stresses σ_{yz}, σ_{zx} are quadratic functions of thickness coordinate [11].

A 2×2 Gauss integration rule is employed to obtain stiffness matrix and internal force vector for the 4 node element in plane. Reduced through-thickness integration is used to avoid shear locking.

2.1   Transformation to Local Coordinates

Local coordinate system is calculated with respect to the mean plane of the element. Means plane passes through all mid-side points of the element (12, 23, 34, 41 in Fig. 1) [6] and is defined by a normal vector and a point through which it passes [13]. If all nodes of the elements are located in one plane, the mean plane coincides with the element. Vectors $\mathbf{V}_{12,34}$ connecting mid-side points 12 and 34 and $\mathbf{V}_{41,23}$ connecting mid-side points 41 and 23 are defined to calculate vector $\mathbf{V}_3$ normal to the mean plane:

$$\mathbf{V}_3 = \mathbf{V}_{41,23} \times \mathbf{V}_{12,34}. \tag{1}$$

$\mathbf{V}_1$ is perpendicular to $\mathbf{V}_3$ and parallel to $\mathbf{V}_{41,23}$. The third vector $\mathbf{V}_2$ employed to define local coordinate system is calculated as follows:

$$\mathbf{V}_2 = \mathbf{V}_3 \times \mathbf{V}_1. \tag{2}$$

Local axes $\mathbf{x}$, $\mathbf{y}$, $\mathbf{z}$ in the global system correspond to normalized orthogonal vectors $\mathbf{V}_1$, $\mathbf{V}_2$, $\mathbf{V}_3$ at the center of the mean plane of element [13] and are used to transform variables between local and global axes [12].

2.2   Shell Formulation

Any point of shell element can be defined by nodal coordinates, shell thickness h and a normalized vector $\mathbf{v}_{3k}$ connecting upper and lower surfaces at the kth node:

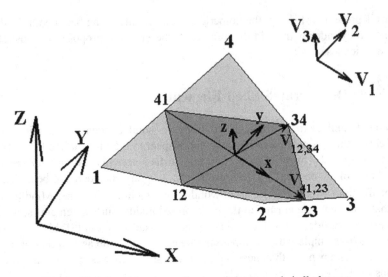

Fig. 1. Global and local coordinates of the warped shell element.

$$\left\{ \begin{array}{c} x \\ y \\ z \end{array} \right\} = \sum N_k(\xi, \eta) \cdot \left(\left\{ \begin{array}{c} x_k \\ y_k \\ z_k \end{array} \right\} + \frac{1}{2} \zeta \, h \, \mathbf{v}_{3k} \right), \tag{3}$$

where the shape function $N_k(\xi, \eta)$ is a bi-linear Lagrangian polynomial of the kth node and ζ is a linear coordinate in the thickness direction.

The displacements at each node of shell are uniquely defined by three translational displacements u, v, w and two rotations θ_x, θ_y about the vectors $\mathbf{v}_{1k}$ and $\mathbf{v}_{2k}$ orthogonal to vector $\mathbf{v}_{3k}$. The drilling degree of freedom θ_z (rotation about the $\mathbf{z}$ axis) is added to apply a unified procedure for the transformation of translational and rotational displacements from local to global coordinate system [12]. This degree of freedom constrained in the global system. Displacements at any point of the element are calculated according the formula:

$$\left\{ \begin{array}{c} u \\ v \\ w \end{array} \right\} = \sum N_k(\xi, \eta) \cdot \left\{ \begin{array}{c} u_k \\ v_k \\ w_k \end{array} \right\} + \zeta \sum N_k(\xi, \eta) \cdot \left[\mathbf{g}_{1k} \quad \mathbf{g}_{2k} \right] \left\{ \begin{array}{c} \theta_{xk} \\ \theta_{yk} \end{array} \right\}, \tag{4}$$

where $\mathbf{g}_{1k} = -\frac{h}{2} \mathbf{v}_{2k}$, $\mathbf{g}_{2k} = \frac{h}{2} \mathbf{v}_{1k}$ [1].

2.3   Rigid Link Correction for the Warped Shell Element

The initial mesh of the analyzed structure consists of flat 4-node shell elements. The stiffness matrix **K** is calculated with the assumption that all four nodes of the element are in the same plane. However, if the initial structure assembled of elements is curved, the initial geometry of element is often warped. Moreover, if out-of-plane loads of the different magnitude are applied on the nodes of the element during the simulation, the element warps and the flat element assumption is not satisfied in later calculations. The rigid link correction is applied to the stiffness matrix of the warped element before the transformation to the global coordinate system [6]:

$$\mathbf{K}_{local} = \mathbf{W}\mathbf{K}_{flat}\mathbf{W}^T, \tag{5}$$

where $\mathbf{W}$ is a projection matrix to the mid-plane of the element consisting four diagonally located blocks $\mathbf{W}_k$, $k = \overline{1,4}$:

$$\mathbf{W}_k = \begin{bmatrix} 1 & 0 & 0 & 0 & 0 & 0 \\ 0 & 1 & 0 & 0 & 0 & 0 \\ 0 & 0 & 1 & 0 & 0 & 0 \\ d_k & 0 & 0 & 1 & 0 & 0 \\ 0 & d_k & 0 & 0 & 1 & 0 \\ 0 & 0 & 0 & 0 & 0 & 1 \end{bmatrix} \tag{6}$$

and d_k is the offset of the kth node with respect to the mid-plane.

3 Updated Lagrangian Formulation in FEM Dynamic Analysis

Updated Lagrangian formulation relates 2nd Piola-Kirchhoff stress to Green-Lagrange strain referred to the configuration at time t [1]. Explicit and implicit integration techniques can be employed to get the response of structure at time t. The central difference scheme employed in explicit analysis has a low computational cost but is only conditionally stable and requires a small time step in nonlinear analysis when large deformations are considered. On the contrary, a composite implicit two-substep time integration scheme proposed in [2, 3] is stable in both linear and nonlinear analysis.

A superscript on the left of the variable indicates the configuration the quantity occurs and the subscript on the left indicates the reference configuration [1]. It is assumed that all variables are known at time t and the variables at time $t + \Delta t$ are computed. All variables but mass matrix are evaluated at the last known configuration at time t [2, 3]. The diagonal mass matrix $\mathbf{M}$ is calculated once with respect to the initial configuration. Mass matrix for the 4-node shell element consists of 4 diagonally located blocks $\mathbf{M}_k$, $k = \overline{1,4}$ [10]:

$$\mathbf{M}_k = \begin{bmatrix} m_u\mathbf{I}_{3\times3} & 0 \\ 0 & m_\theta\mathbf{I}_{3\times3} \end{bmatrix}, \quad m_u = \frac{\rho A h}{4}, \quad m_\theta = \frac{h^2}{12}m_u, \tag{7}$$

where $\mathbf{I}_{3\times3}$ is a 3×3 identity matrix, ρ is the density of the material, A is the area of the element, h is the thickness of the element.

The shell thickness $^{t+\Delta t}h$ is updated at each iteration for the implicit dynamic analysis and each time step for the explicit analysis [7]:

$$^{t+\Delta t}h = \frac{^tA^th}{^{t+\Delta t}A},$$ (8)

where A is the area of the element.

3.1   Explicit Analysis

The equations of the motion solved in explicit analysis at time $t + \Delta t$ in the matrix form are:

$$\mathbf{M} \cdot {}^{t+\Delta t}\ddot{\mathbf{U}} = {}^{t+\Delta t}\mathbf{R} - {}^{t+\Delta t}\mathbf{F},$$ (9)

where $\mathbf{M}$ - mass matrix at the initial configuration, $^{t+\Delta t}\ddot{\mathbf{U}}$ - vector of accelerations, $^{t+\Delta t}\mathbf{R}$ - vector of external forces, $^{t+\Delta t}\mathbf{F}$ - vector of internal forces. The vector of internal forces $^{t+\Delta t}_{t+\Delta t}\mathbf{F}$ is evaluated using the formula:

$$^{t+\Delta t}_{t+\Delta t}\mathbf{F} = \int\limits_{t+\Delta t_V} {}^{t+\Delta t}_{t+\Delta t}\mathbf{B}_L^T \cdot {}^{t+\Delta t}\mathbf{S}^{t+\Delta t}dV,$$ (10)

where $\mathbf{B}_L$ is strain – displacement matrix, such that $\boldsymbol{\varepsilon} = \mathbf{B}_L\mathbf{U}$ where $\boldsymbol{\varepsilon}$ is Green-Lagrange strain vector, $\mathbf{S}^T = \begin{bmatrix} \tau_{xx} & \tau_{yy} & \tau_{zz} & \tau_{xy} & \tau_{yz} & \tau_{zx} \end{bmatrix}$ is a 2nd Piola-Kirchhoff stress vector at time $t + \Delta t$ [1]. Displacements at the time $t + \Delta t$ are explicitly computed using central difference formula with constant time step Δt [5]:

$$^{t+\Delta t}\mathbf{U} = \Delta t^2 \cdot \mathbf{M}^{-1} \cdot ({}^{t+\Delta t}\mathbf{R} - {}^{t+\Delta t}\mathbf{F}) + 2 \cdot {}^t\mathbf{U} - {}^{t-\Delta t}\mathbf{U}.$$ (11)

3.2   Implicit Integration Scheme

The equation of the motion solved in implicit integration scheme for the Updated Lagrangian formulation is:

$$^t_t\mathbf{K}^{(i-1)} \cdot \Delta\mathbf{U}^{(i)} = {}^{t+\Delta t}\mathbf{R} - {}^{t+\Delta t}_{t+\Delta t}\mathbf{F}^{(i-1)} - \mathbf{M} \cdot {}^{t+\Delta t}\ddot{\mathbf{U}}^{(i)},$$ (12)

where $\mathbf{M}$ - mass matrix at the initial configuration, $^{t+\Delta t}\ddot{\mathbf{U}}$ - vector of acceleration, $^{t+\Delta t}\mathbf{R}$ - vector of external forces, $^{t+\Delta t}\mathbf{F}$ - vector of internal forces. Superscript on the right indicates the iteration the variable was obtained.

Stiffness matrix $\mathbf{K}$ is a sum of linear and nonlinear matrices [1]:

$$
{}_t^t\mathbf{K}_L = \int\limits_{{}^tV} {}_t^t\mathbf{B}_L^T\mathbf{D}_t^t\mathbf{B}_L{}^t dV, \quad {}_t^t\mathbf{K}_{NL} = \int\limits_{{}^tV} {}_t^t\mathbf{B}_{NL}^T {}^t\mathbf{S}_t^t\mathbf{B}_{NL}{}^t dV, \tag{13}
$$

where $\mathbf{D}$ is elasticity tensor for isotropic material, $\mathbf{S} = \begin{bmatrix} \tau_{xx}I_3 & \tau_{xy}I_3 & \tau_{xz}I_3 \\ \tau_{xy}I_3 & \tau_{yy}I_3 & \tau_{yz}I_3 \\ \tau_{xz}I_3 & \tau_{yz}I_3 & \tau_{zz}I_3 \end{bmatrix}$,

τ_{rs} are the components of a 2nd Piola-Kirchhoff stress, I_3 is 3×3 identity matrix, $\mathbf{B}_{NL}$ part for the kth node has the form:

$$
\mathbf{B}_{NLk} = \begin{bmatrix} N'_{kx}I_3 & g_{1k}(\varsigma \cdot N'_{kx} + \varsigma'_x \cdot N_k) & g_{2k}(\varsigma \cdot N'_{kx} + \varsigma'_x \cdot N_k) \\ N'_{ky}I_3 & g_{1k}(\varsigma \cdot N'_{ky} + \varsigma'_y \cdot N_k) & g_{2k}(\varsigma \cdot N'_{ky} + \varsigma'_y \cdot N_k) \\ N'_{kz}I_3 & g_{1k}(\varsigma \cdot N'_{kz} + \varsigma'_z \cdot N_k) & g_{2k}(\varsigma \cdot N'_{kz} + \varsigma'_z \cdot N_k) \end{bmatrix}. \tag{14}
$$

The time step is divided to two equal substeps and the Newton-Raphson iterative scheme is employed to correct the solutions at each substep until the convergence is reached. Stiffness matrix $\mathbf{K}$ and internal force vector $\mathbf{F}$ are calculated at each iteration with respect to the corrected displacements. The trapezoidal rule is used to compute the solution in the 1st substep [3]:

$$
\left(\frac{16}{\Delta t^2}\mathbf{M} + {}^{t+\Delta t/2}\mathbf{K}^{(i-1)}\right)\Delta\mathbf{U}^{(i)} =
$$

$$
{}^{t+\Delta t/2}\mathbf{R} - {}^{t+\Delta t/2}\mathbf{F}^{(i-1)} - \mathbf{M}\left(\frac{16}{\Delta t^2}\left({}^{t+\Delta t/2}\mathbf{U}^{(i-1)} - {}^t\mathbf{U}\right) - \frac{8}{\Delta t}{}^t\dot{\mathbf{U}} - {}^t\ddot{\mathbf{U}}\right), \tag{15}
$$

where $\Delta\mathbf{U}^{(i)}$ is the correction of displacements in the ith Newton-Raphson iteration of the 1st substep:

$$
{}^{t+\Delta t/2}\mathbf{U}^{(i)} = {}^{t+\Delta t/2}\mathbf{U}^{(i-1)} + \Delta\mathbf{U}^{(i)}. \tag{16}
$$

The velocities and accelerations at the time $t + \Delta t/2$ are computed according the formulas [2]:

$$
{}^{t+\Delta t/2}\dot{\mathbf{U}} = \left({}^{t+\Delta t/2}\mathbf{U} - {}^t\mathbf{U}\right)\frac{4}{\Delta t} - {}^t\dot{\mathbf{U}}, \tag{17}
$$

$$
{}^{t+\Delta t/2}\ddot{\mathbf{U}} = \left({}^{t+\Delta t/2}\mathbf{U} - {}^t\mathbf{U} - \frac{\Delta t}{2}{}^t\dot{\mathbf{U}}\right)\frac{16}{\Delta t^2} - {}^t\ddot{\mathbf{U}}. \tag{18}
$$

The three-point Euler backward method is employed in the 2nd substep with governing equations [3]:

$$\left(\frac{9}{\Delta t^2}\mathbf{M} + {}^{t+\Delta t}\mathbf{K}^{(i-1)}\right)\Delta \mathbf{U}^{(i)} = {}^{t+\Delta t}\mathbf{R} - {}^{t+\Delta t}\mathbf{F}^{(i-1)}$$
$$- \mathbf{M}\left(\frac{9}{\Delta t^2}{}^{t+\Delta t}\mathbf{U}^{(i-1)} - \frac{12}{\Delta t^2}{}^{t+\Delta t/2}\mathbf{U}^{(i-1)} + \frac{3}{\Delta t^2}{}^{t}\mathbf{U} - \frac{4}{\Delta t}{}^{t+\Delta t/2}\dot{\mathbf{U}} + \frac{1}{\Delta t}{}^{t}\dot{\mathbf{U}}\right), \tag{19}$$

where $\Delta \mathbf{U}^{(i)}$ is the correction of displacements in the ith Newton-Raphson iteration of the 2nd substep:

$$^{t}\mathbf{U}^{(i)} = {}^{t}\mathbf{U}^{(i-1)} + \Delta \mathbf{U}^{(i)}. \tag{20}$$

The velocities and accelerations at the time $t + \Delta t$ are updated using formulas [3]:

$$^{t+\Delta t}\dot{\mathbf{U}} = \frac{1}{\Delta t}{}^{t}\mathbf{U} - \frac{4}{\Delta t}{}^{t+\Delta t/2}\mathbf{U} + \frac{3}{\Delta t}{}^{t+\Delta t}\mathbf{U}, \tag{21}$$

$$^{t+\Delta t}\ddot{\mathbf{U}} = \frac{1}{\Delta t}{}^{t}\dot{\mathbf{U}} - \frac{4}{\Delta t}{}^{t+\Delta t/2}\dot{\mathbf{U}} + \frac{3}{\Delta t}{}^{t+\Delta t}\dot{\mathbf{U}}. \tag{22}$$

4   Numerical Examples

The linearly increasing force with increment $\Delta \mathbf{P}$ in time step Δt is applied for three structures with different geometry and boundary conditions. Central difference and Bathe integration schemes are employed for all examples to get a dynamic response on the applied loads. An isotropic material with parameters in Table 1 is used in calculations. The initial thickness of the shell element $h = 0.1$ m in all examples.

Conditional parameter uTH determines whether the thickness is updated during the calculations.

Table 1. Material parameters.

Young's modulus, N/m^2	$75 \cdot 10^9$
Poisson's ratio	0.32
Mass density, kg/m^3	2700

4.1   Tensioned Beam

A beam is loaded at the ends with linearly increasing force $\mathbf{P}$ (Fig. 2). The highlighted part of the beam in Fig. 2(a) is simulated using finite element method with the symmetry conditions applied for the thick lines in Fig. 2(b). The geometry of the beam: $a = 0.2$ m, $L = 1$ m.

As the in-plane load is applied, all elements become thinner in the deformed configuration during dynamic analysis (Fig. 3). The thickness of the elements near the end is reduced earlier than the thickness of the elements in the center due to the load type.

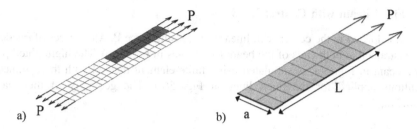

Fig. 2. (a) Initial geometry and loads. (b) Finite element mesh for 1/4 of the beam.

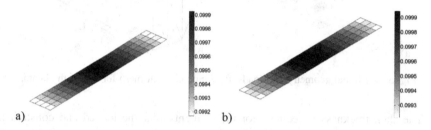

Fig. 3. Shell thickness at time $t = 2 \cdot 10^{-4}$ s: (a) central difference scheme ($\Delta t = 10^{-5}$ s, $\Delta P = 10^{6}$ N), (b) Bathe scheme ($\Delta t = 2 \cdot 10^{-5}$ s, $\Delta P = 2 \cdot 10^{6}$ N).

If the thickness update is applied, the x displacements at the end of the beam reach higher values compared with the displacements computed otherwise (Fig. 4). This is caused by the fact that the deformed beam becomes thinner and weaker than the beam with constant thickness.

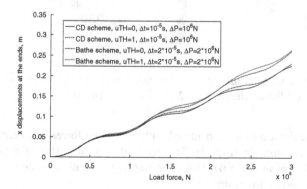

Fig. 4. x displacement at the end of the beam. Parameter $uTH = 0$ if shell thickness is not updated and $uTH = 1$ if shell thickness is updated, CD – central difference scheme.

4.2   Fixed Beam with Central Load

A beam is loaded in the center with linearly increasing force **P**. All degrees of freedom are constrained at both ends of the beam (dash lines in Fig. 5(a)). The highlighted part of the beam in Fig. 5(a) is simulated using finite element method with the symmetry conditions applied for the thick lines in Fig. 5(b). The geometry of the beam: $a = 0.2\,\text{m}$, $L = 1\,\text{m}$.

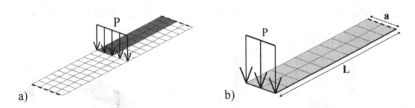

Fig. 5. (a) Initial geometry and loads. (b) Finite element mesh for 1/4 of the beam.

The shell thickness is reduced for the elements near the loaded and constrained nodes (Fig. 6). Under this type of load the behavior of the structure is mainly governed by the rotational displacements without significantly affecting the area of element. The vertical displacements computed with the updated thickness have minor differences compared with the displacements computed otherwise (Fig. 7).

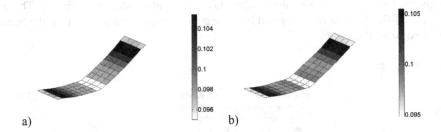

Fig. 6. Shell thickness at time $t = 10^{-3}\,\text{s}$: (a) central difference scheme ($\Delta t = 10^{-5}\,\text{s}$, $\Delta P = 5 \cdot 10^5\,\text{N}$), (b) Bathe scheme ($\Delta t = 2 \cdot 10^{-5}\,\text{s}$, $\Delta P = 10^6\,\text{N}$).

If long-time durations are considered with increasing forces, the central difference scheme becomes unstable (Fig. 7). The reduced time step should be employed to maintain stability of the scheme. However, the reduction of time step increases computational cost and is not desirable.

4.3   Pinched Cylinder with End Diaphragms

A cylindrical shell is pinched by two opposite forces applied at the middle section. The cylinder is closed at both ends by rigid diaphragms which constrain translations in **X**

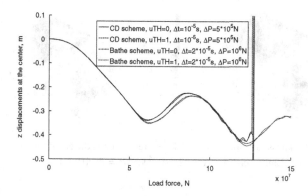

Fig. 7. z displacement at the center of the beam. Parameter $uTH = 0$ if shell thickness is not updated and $uTH = 1$ if shell thickness is updated, CD – central difference scheme.

and **Y** directions and rotations about the **X** axis at the edges. This test involves inextensional bending and complex membrane states of stress [13]. For example, the elements near the pinched node undergo warping effects. As the symmetric load is applied, only the highlighted part of the cylinder (Fig. 8(a)) is simulated using finite element method with linearly increasing force **P** and appropriate symmetry conditions applied for the thick lines in Fig. 8(b). The geometry of the cylinder: $r = 1$ m, $L = 1$ m.

The shell thickness is thinner than the initial thickness for the elements near the pinched node and thickens farther from the pinched zone (Fig. 9). The thickness at the sides of the cylinder are not affected significantly. The shell thickness computed using Bathe implicit integration scheme varies in a wider range compared to the thickness computed using central difference scheme under the same load and boundary conditions.

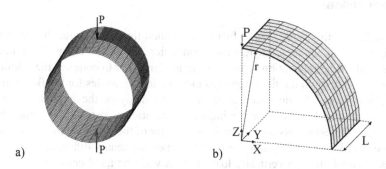

Fig. 8. (a) Initial geometry and loads. (b) Finite element mesh for 1/8 of the cylinder.

If the thickness update is applied, the deflections at the pinched node are smaller compared with the deflections computed otherwise (Fig. 10). However, these differences are not significant as there are no evident boundaries between the displacement curves computed with constant and updated thickness assumptions in the analyzed period under the considered boundary and load conditions.

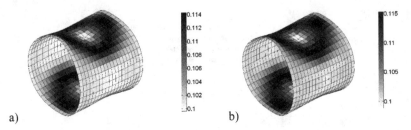

a)   b)

Fig. 9. Shell thickness at time $t = 2 \cdot 10^{-3}$ s: (a) central difference scheme ($\Delta t = 10^{-5}$ s, $\Delta P = 2 \cdot 10^5$ N), (b) Bathe scheme ($\Delta t = 2 \cdot 10^{-5}$ s, $\Delta P = 4 \cdot 10^5$ N).

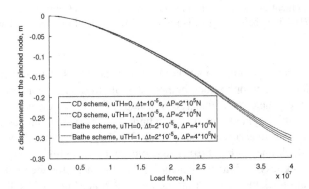

Fig. 10. z displacement at the pinched node. Parameter $uTH = 0$ if shell thickness is not updated and $uTH = 1$ if shell thickness is updated, CD – central difference scheme.

5   Conclusions

The objective of this paper was to focus on the shell thickness update in the dynamic analysis with the updated Lagrangian formulation. Explicit central difference and implicit Bathe time integration schemes were implemented to compare the response of the structure. Although the time step used in numerical examples for the Bathe implicit analysis was twice the time step used in explicit analysis, the implicit Bathe time integration scheme has considerably higher computational cost. This is caused by the fact that the stiffness matrix and internal force vector of the structure are reassembled at each iteration. However, this scheme is stable when the central difference scheme fails as in the example for the vertically loaded beam with the fixed ends.

If the thickness of the element is updated, the changes in geometry of the structure are taken into consideration. For the examples with out-of-plane loads, the behavior is governed by rotational displacements and the changes in element area and therefore thickness are minor. If element undergoes large deformations, the stiffness of the element is updated by reducing its thickness and the displacements reach higher values.

References

1. Bathe, K.J.: Finite Element Procedures. Prentice Hall, Englewood Cliffs (1996)
2. Bathe, K.J., Baig, M.M.I.: On a composite implicit time integration procedure for nonlinear dynamics. Comput. Struct. **83**, 2513–2524 (2005)
3. Bathe, K.J.: Conserving energy and momentum in nonlinear dynamics: a simple implicit time integration scheme. Comput. Struct. **85**, 437–445 (2007)
4. Echter, R., Oesterle, B., Bischoff, M.: A hierarchic family of isogeometric shell finite elements. Comput. Methods Appl. Mech. Eng. **254**, 170–180 (2013)
5. Miller, K., Joldes, G., Lance, D., Wittek, A.: Total Lagrangian explicit dynamics finite element algorithm for computing soft tissue deformation. Commun. Numer. Meth. Eng. **23**, 121–134 (2007)
6. Nguyen-Van, H., Mai-Duy, N., Tran-Cong, T.: An improved quadrilateral flat element with drilling degrees of freedom for shell structural analysis. CMES-Comp. Model. Eng. **49**(2), 81–110 (2009)
7. Oñate, E., Cendoya, P., Miquel, J.: Non-linear explicit dynamic analysis of shells using the BST rotation free triangle. Eng. Comput. **19**, 662–706 (2002)
8. Oñate, E.: Structural Analysis with the Finite Element Method. Linear Statics. Volume 2. Beams, Plates and Shells. Lecture Notes on Numerical Methods in Engineering and Sciences. Springer, Berlin (2013)
9. Sussman, T., Bathe, K.J.: 3D-shell elements for structures in large strains. Comput. Struct. **122**, 2–12 (2013)
10. Tabiei, A., Tanov, R.: Sandwich shell finite element for dynamic explicit analysis. Int. J. Numer. Meth. Eng. **54**, 763–787 (2002)
11. Voyiadjis, G.Z., Woelke, P.: Elasto-Plastic and Damage Analysis of Plates and Shells. Springer, Berlin (2008)
12. Zienkiewicz, O.C., Taylor, R.L.: The Finite Element Method for Solid and Structural Mechanics. Elsevier, Amsterdam (2005)
13. Wisniewski, K.: Finite Rotation Shells. Basic Equations and Finite Elements for Reissner Kinematics. Lecture Notes on Numerical Methods in Engineering and Sciences. Springer, Berlin (2010)

Obtaining Dispersion Curves of Damped Waves by Employing Semi Analytical Finite Element Formulation

Audrius Neciunas[(⊠)], Rimantas Barauskas, and Vitalija Kersiene

Faculty of Informatics, Kaunas University of Technology,
Studentu 50-407, Kaunas, Lithuania
audrius.neciunas@ktu.lt

Abstract. Semi-analytical finite element (SAFE) method is used for modelling propagation of elastic waves in waveguides of cross-sections uniform along the propagation direction. Dispersion curves, which express the relation between the circular frequency and the wavenumber of propagating wave were obtained. Linear proportional damping of propagating waves is taken into account. The results of simulation have been compared with theoretical and experimental data available in the literature.

Keywords: Semi-analytical FEM · Dispersion curve · Elastic wave · Complex wavenumber

1 Introduction

Applications of guided waves have already a long history and variety of fields of usage especially for non-destructive-testing and ultrasonic measurement. Finite element methods are widely used for modelling and simulation of wave propagation. Finite element structures based on 3D elastic elements are well-suited for modelling waves in bodies of complex geometry. The waves in infinite uniform structures such as rails, bars, beams, pipes, etc., can be efficiently treated by applying the semi analytical finite element (SAFE) method. In these conditions properties of waves along the length of the uniform waveguide can be well predicted [2].

The goal of this paper is to extend the SAFE technique for obtaining dispersion relations in a damped waveguide. Dispersion curve shows the change of velocity of the wave with the change of circular frequency. SAFE methodology was first introduced by Lagasse [5] and Aalami [1]. Gavric assumed that displacement along the direction of a propagating wave is shifted by a phase of $\pi/2$ in relation with two dimensional displacement field in cross-section of the waveguide [4]. Viola et al. [7, 8] developed this technique further introducing complex stiffness member into the model allowing modeling wave propagation in damped media. This paper explores the possibility to use a damping term in the wave equation in order to represent the wave damping phenomena.

The SAFE technique combines the analytical solution of propagating wave along the length of the uniform waveguide with the numerical solution of 3D displacement field

© Springer International Publishing Switzerland 2015
G. Dregvaite and R. Damasevicius (Eds.): ICIST 2015, CCIS 538, pp. 604–613, 2015.
DOI: 10.1007/978-3-319-24770-0_51

over the cross-section of the waveguide. SAFE has an advantage compared with conventional 3D FEM approach as it offers solutions at lower computational costs. Simultaneously it enables the modeling of very short waves, since the polynomial approximation of the displacement field along the length of the waveguide is avoided [8]. Any geometrical shape of the cross section is allowed as long as the shape remains constant along the length of the waveguide. On the contrary, pure analytical solutions are feasible just for specific geometrically simple shapes of the cross-section.

2 Derivation the Governing Equation

Consider the elastic wave in isotropic homogenous media. We say elastic in the sense that Hooke's law for strain-stress relationship holds. The SAFE structural dynamic equation for the propagating wave reads as

$$[M]\{\ddot{U}\} + [C]\{\dot{U}\} + [K]\{U\} = 0, \tag{1}$$

where $[M]$, $[U]$, $[K]$ are the mass, damping and stiffness matrices correspondingly. $\{U\}$ is the nodal complex displacement vector of a harmonic wave as:

$$\{U\} = \{\hat{U}\}e^{i(kz-\omega t)}, \tag{2}$$

where $\{\hat{U}\}$ is the real vector of amplitudes, k is the wave number (a spatial wave characteristic having a measure unit of rad/m), ω is the angular frequency (a temporal wave characteristic, having a measure unit of rad/s), t represents time, $i-$ imaginary unit, and z is the coordinate along the direction propagation the wave. The first and the second time derivatives of displacements R:

$$\{\dot{U}\} = \{\hat{U}\}(-i\omega)e^{i(kz-\omega t)}, \quad \{\ddot{U}\} = \{\hat{U}\}(-\omega^2)e^{i(kz-\omega t)} \tag{3}$$

Equation (1) now can be rewritten as

$$\left([M](-\omega^2) + [C](-i\omega) + [K]\right)\{\hat{U}\}e^{i(kz-\omega t)} = 0. \tag{4}$$

At any point of the waveguide displacements $\{U\}$, strains $\{\varepsilon\}$ and stresses $\{\sigma\}$ and the relations between them can be expressed in Cartesian coordinates as:

$$\{U\} = \left\{\begin{array}{c} u \\ v \\ w \end{array}\right\}, \{\varepsilon\} = \left\{\begin{array}{c} \varepsilon_{xx} \\ \varepsilon_{yy} \\ \varepsilon_{zz} \\ \varepsilon_{xy} \\ \varepsilon_{xz} \\ \varepsilon_{yz} \end{array}\right\} = \left\{\begin{array}{c} \partial u/\partial x \\ \partial v/\partial y \\ \partial w/\partial z \\ \partial u/\partial y + \partial v/\partial x \\ \partial u/\partial z + \partial w/\partial x \\ \partial v/\partial z + \partial w/\partial y \end{array}\right\}, \{\sigma\} = [D]\{\varepsilon\}, \tag{5}$$

$$\text{where } [D] = E/(1+v) \begin{bmatrix} \frac{1-v}{1-2v} & \frac{v}{1-2v} & \frac{v}{1-2v} & 0 & 0 & 0 \\ \frac{v}{1-2v} & \frac{1-v}{1-2v} & \frac{v}{1-2v} & 0 & 0 & 0 \\ \frac{v}{1-2v} & \frac{v}{1-2v} & \frac{1-v}{1-2v} & 0 & 0 & 0 \\ 0 & 0 & 0 & 1/2 & 0 & 0 \\ 0 & 0 & 0 & 0 & 1/2 & 0 \\ 0 & 0 & 0 & 0 & 0 & 1/2 \end{bmatrix}$$

with E being Young's modulus and v Poisson's ratio. Expression for strains can be presented as:

$$\{\varepsilon\} = \left[[L_x]\frac{\partial}{\partial x} + [L_y]\frac{\partial}{\partial y} + [L_z]\frac{\partial}{\partial z} \right]\{U\} \tag{6}$$

where

$$[L_x] = \begin{bmatrix} 1 & 0 & 0 \\ 0 & 0 & 0 \\ 0 & 0 & 0 \\ 0 & 0 & 0 \\ 0 & 0 & 1 \\ 0 & 1 & 0 \end{bmatrix} \quad [L_y] = \begin{bmatrix} 0 & 0 & 0 \\ 0 & 1 & 0 \\ 0 & 0 & 0 \\ 0 & 0 & 1 \\ 0 & 0 & 0 \\ 1 & 0 & 0 \end{bmatrix} \quad [L_z] = \begin{bmatrix} 0 & 0 & 0 \\ 0 & 0 & 0 \\ 0 & 0 & 1 \\ 0 & 1 & 0 \\ 1 & 0 & 0 \\ 0 & 0 & 0 \end{bmatrix}. \tag{7}$$

In SAFE the finite element discretization is carried out only over the cross-section of the waveguide, therefore element shape functions of two variables $a(x,y)$, $b(x,y)$ and $c(x,y)$ describing the distribution of the amplitudes over the cross-section are introduced, [8].

The scheme of the finite element discretization of the rectangular cross-section of the waveguide is shown in Fig. 1. We employ four-node first order Serendipity element, the nodal displacements of which are presented as:

$$\{\hat{U}\}_e = \begin{Bmatrix} \sum_{k=1}^{4} N_k(x,y)a_k \\ \sum_{k=1}^{4} N_k(x,y)b_k \\ \sum_{k=1}^{4} N_k(x,y)c_k \end{Bmatrix}_e e^{i(kz-\omega t)} = [N(x,y)]\{d_e\}e^{i(kz-\omega t)} \tag{8}$$

where (a_k, b_k, c_k) are the displacements of k-th node along Ox, Oy and Oz directions and $N_k(x,y)$ is the shape function of k-th node, $\{d_e\} = \{ a_1 \quad b_1 \quad c_1 \quad \ldots \quad a_4 \quad b_4 \quad c_4 \}^T$ presents all displacements of all nodes of the element and matrix $[N(x,y)]$ contains all shape functions:

$$[N(x,y)] = [[NN_1(x,y)][NN_2(x,y)][NN_3(x,y)][NN_4(x,y)]] \tag{9}$$

where $[NN_j(x,y)] = \begin{bmatrix} N_j(x,y) & 0 & 0 \\ 0 & N_j(x,y) & 0 \\ 0 & 0 & N_j(x,y) \end{bmatrix}$ with $j = \overline{1,4}$.

The exponential term in Eq. (4) represents the harmonic wave displacement in time and along the propagation axis. The solution is obtained by calculating all nodal displacement a, b, c amplitudes over the cross-section and one unknown for choice, ω

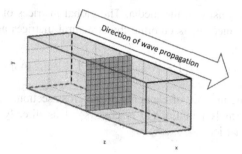

Fig. 1. Finite element representing the cross –section of the waveguide

or k. If wavenumber k is chosen as a free argument, then ω as a function $\omega(k)$ is obtained. If angular frequency ω is chosen freely, the function $k(\omega)$ is to be found. The exponential term is the analytical part of the solution while amplitude vector $\{\hat{U}\}$ is found via finite element (FE) model. Combining the two terms together into one solution is the basic idea of SAFE method. $\{\hat{U}\}$ is considered as a vector of amplitudes of all finite elements in the cross-section of a waveguide.

Now the strain in the element can be expressed as

$$
\begin{aligned}
\{\varepsilon_e\} &= \left[[L_x]\frac{\partial}{\partial x} + [L_y]\frac{\partial}{\partial y} + [L_z]\frac{\partial}{\partial z} \right] [N(x,y)]\{d_e\}e^{i(kz-\omega t)} \\
&= \left[[L_x][N(x,y)'_x] + [L_y][N(x,y)'_y] + ik[L_z][N(x,y)] \right] \{d_e\}e^{i(kz-\omega t)}.
\end{aligned}
\tag{10}
$$

By introducing matrices $[B_1] = [L_x][N(x,y)'_x] + [L_y][N(x,y)'_y]$ and $[B_2] = [L_z][N(x,y)]$, relation (10) is rewritten as

$$
\{\varepsilon_e\} = [[B_1] + ik[B_2]]\{d_e\}e^{i(kz-\omega t)}.
\tag{11}
$$

By using Hamilton's principle it can be shown [8] that the terms in Eq. (4) for a FE can be expressed as

$$
[m]_e = \int_x \int_y [N(x,y)]^T \rho [N(x,y)]dxdy,
\tag{12}
$$

$$
[k_1]_e = \int_x \int_y [B_1]^T [D][B_1]dxdy,
\tag{13}
$$

$$
[k_2]_e = \int_x \int_y [[B_1]^T [D][B_2] - [B_2]^T [D][B_1]]dxdy,
\tag{14}
$$

$$
[k_3]_e = \int_x \int_y [B_2]^T [D][B_2]dxdy,
\tag{15}
$$

where ρ is the mass density of the media. The global matrices of the elements of the cross-section are obtained by assembling the structural matrices as

$$[M] = \bigcup_{j=1}^{Nel} [m]_e, \; [K_1] = \bigcup_{j=1}^{Nel} [k_1]_e, \; [K_2] = \bigcup_{j=1}^{Nel} [k_2]_e, \; [K_3] = \bigcup_{j=1}^{Nel} [k_3]_e \quad (16)$$

where Nel defines the number of elements of the cross-section.

The damping term $[C]$ in Eq. (1) is considered as directly proportional to the stiffness and mass matrices as:

$$[C] = \alpha[M] + \beta[K], \quad (17)$$

where α and β are the proportionality coefficients. For the sake of simplicity assume that damping is proportional to the mass only and can be expressed as

$$[c]_e = \int_x \int_y [N(x,y)]^T \mu [N(x,y)] dx dy \quad (18)$$

where μ is the damping coefficient of the material. Then global damping matrix is obtained:

$$[C] = \bigcup_{j=1}^{Nel} [c]_e = \alpha[M]. \quad (19)$$

The final form of Eq. (4) reads as

$$[-[M](\omega^2) + [C](-i\omega) + [K_1] + [K_2]ik + [K_3]k^2]\{\hat{U}\}e^{i(kz-\omega t)} = 0. \quad (20)$$

Finding a non-zero solution to this equation leads to corresponds to the generalized eigenvalue problem as

$$\det\left(-[M](\omega^2) + [C](-i\omega) + [K_1] + [K_2]ik + [K_3]k^2\right) = 0. \quad (21)$$

It is required to solve the eigenvalue problem of dimensionality equal to total number degrees of freedom of the cross-section of the waveguide. The eigenvalue problem is solved either with a given ω, or with a given k. In case the wavenumber k is chosen freely, the eigenvalue problem is simplified as:

$$[-[M](\omega^2) + [C](-i\omega) + [K(k)]]\{\hat{U}\} = 0 \quad (22)$$

where $K(k)$ matrix contains complex numbers and its value depends on wavenumber k.

As complex value eigen problem is to be solved, its dimension doubles in order to encompass the real and the complex parts. By using notation:

$$[A]_1 = \begin{bmatrix} 0 & [K] \\ [K] & [C](-i) \end{bmatrix}, \; [B]_1 = \begin{bmatrix} [K] & 0 \\ 0 & [M] \end{bmatrix}, \; \{Q\} = \begin{bmatrix} \{\hat{U}\}/\omega \\ \{\hat{U}\} \end{bmatrix}, \quad (23)$$

Equation (23) can be rewritten as:

$$[[A]_1 - [B]_1 \omega]\{Q\} = 0. \tag{24}$$

In case the angular frequency ω is chosen freely, the eigen problem is simplified using $[A]_2$ and $[B]_2$ matrices and vector $\{Q\}$ to another form as:

$$[[A]_2 - [B]_2 k]\{Q\} = 0 \tag{25}$$

$$[A]_2 = \begin{bmatrix} 0 & [K_1] - [M]\omega^2 - [C](i\omega) \\ [K_1] - [M]\omega^2 - [C](i\omega) & [K_2] \end{bmatrix},$$

$$[B]_2 = \begin{bmatrix} [K_1] - [M]\omega^2 - [C](i\omega) & 0 \\ 0 & -[K_3] \end{bmatrix}, \{Q\} = \begin{bmatrix} \{\hat{U}\} \\ \{\hat{U}\}k \end{bmatrix}. \tag{26}$$

3 Results

Consider a waveguide of rectangular cross-section 0.01×0.01 m. The material is aluminum with density $\rho = 2700$ kg/m^3, Young's modulus $E = 6.9 \times 10^9$ Pa and Poisson's ratio $v = 0.32$. We investigate the convergence of angular frequency value as

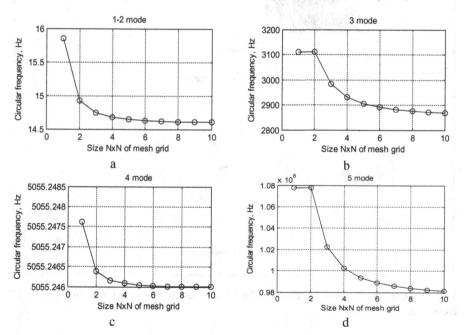

Fig. 2. ω convergence of the wave angular frequencies values as mesh refinement is increased at wavenumber $k = 1$ rad/m (a) first and second modes (b) third mode (c) fourth mode (d) fifth mode.

the mesh refinement over the cross-section is increased at selected constant wave number of 1 rad/m. The results for first five modes are shown below (Fig. 2).

Consider the same waveguide, the cross-section mesh 10×10 in the undamped case ([C] = 0 in Eq. (22)). In ω versus k scenario eigen problem (22) becomes

$$\left[-[M](\omega^2) + [K] \right] \{\hat{U}\} = 0. \tag{27}$$

There are $tdof = 11 \cdot 11 \cdot 3 = 363$ solutions for ω, which are real numbers. Dispersion curves are obtained as in Fig. 3a. For a comparison a dispersion curve extracted from the single_cross-section element model of the same waveguide (1×1 mesh) having $tdof = 2 \cdot 2 \cdot 3 = 12$ is presented in Fig. 3b. $F0$, $F1$ indicate first and second flexular modes, $T0$- first torsional mode, $L0$- first longitudinal mode.

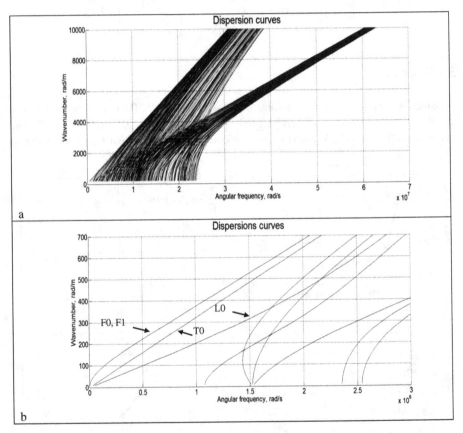

Fig. 3. Dispersion curves at cross-section discretization 10×10 (a) and single FE cross-section 1×1(b)

Consider the same waveguide, where the SAFE model of which formulated as (26). This means that the wave numbers are treated as unknowns while the values of circular frequencies are selected freely. Here we investigate the impact of damping on the obtained dispersion curves. In eigen problem (26) 2 × *tdof* complex solutions for wavenumbers are obtained. We are interested only in solutions expressed as $k = \pm(a + bi)$, while the solutions of the form $k = \pm(a - bi)$ are discarded for they are meaningless because the solutions of this form would mean increasing amplitudes of propagating wave (here a and b are scalars of the same signs). The imaginary part of the wavenumber describes the spatial attenuation of the wave envelope. The results with 1 × 1 single FE model grid in cross-section of a waveguide are shown in (Fig. 4) as different values of the coefficient α in the damping term $[C] = \alpha[M]$ are used. The results are presented as angular frequency against the real part of the wavenumber. It can be seen that coefficient α has to take rather large values in order to exhibit a tangible effect on the dispersion curve.

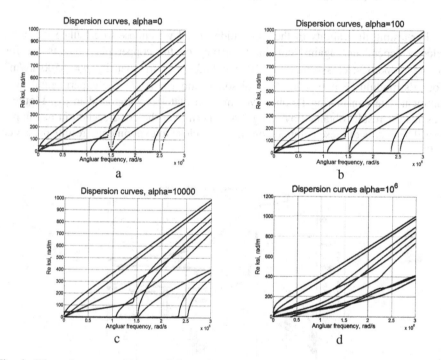

Fig. 4. Dispersion curves in case of damped waveguide: (a) $\alpha = 0$, (b) $\alpha = 100$, (c) $\alpha = 10^4$, (d) $\alpha = 10^6$

Solving (26) eigen problem provides more physically feasible solutions when compared to Eq. (25). Figure 5 displays the results obtained by using *3 × 3* mesh cross-section in the waveguide. Dependency $\omega(k)$ provides less solutions than $k(\omega)$. In the undamped case solutions only for propagating modes are extracted from (25) eigen problem while (26) eigen problem Therefore a deeper investigation on angular frequency versus complex wavenumbers k is required. It would be appropriate to plot ω, $\text{Re}(k)$ and $\text{Im}(k)$ of the solutions in 3D space. Hao Liu suggest sorting of wavenumber in three-dimensional space by curvature of dispersion curves [6]. Further research on this subject is planned in near future.

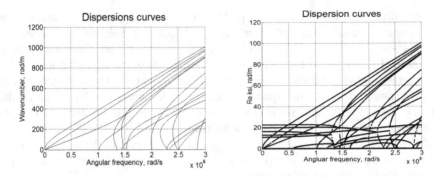

Fig. 5. Dispersion curves acquired on different dependencies: $\omega(k)$ and $k(\omega)$

For testing the validity of the waveguide model we choose to calculate the phase velocity dependence against circular frequency on the copper plate having the following properties: cross-section $2 \cdot 10^{-2} \times 2.83 \cdot 10^{-5}$ m^2, density $\rho = 8500$ kg/m^3, Young's modulus $E = 99 \cdot 10^9$ Pa, Poisson's ratio $v = 0.37$. The experimental measurement data considering Lamb waves in such plate were reported in [3]. Figure 6 presents the results obtained by using 2×4 mesh over the cross-section in undamped case. The results of these computations are very close to experimental results presented in [3].

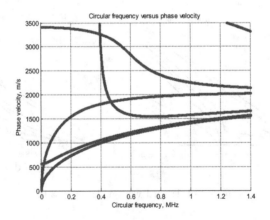

Fig. 6. Angular frequency versus phase velocity in copper plate

4   Conclusions

The SAFE method offers an efficient approach for modeling and simulation of wave propagation along uniform cross-section waveguides. The cross-section may be composed of different materials or layers, isotropic or anisotropic. Here the SAFE method was successfully used to obtain dispersion curves in undamped, as well as, proportionally damped structures, the convergence of the model and adequacy of the obtained results were demonstrated. However, deeper insight into proper sorting for wave-numbers obtained in the solution and automatic grouping of the obtained modes into proper categories is needed. The assumption that angular frequency is taken as a selected real number is similar to the analysis of forced wave propagation, discussion on which is not included in this paper. This topic is to be covered in near future. It is worth reminding that in this research we considered a very simple approach to damping, the term of which is proportional to mass matrix only.

References

1. Aalami, B.: Waves in prismatic guides of arbitrary cross section. J. Appl. Mech. **40**, 1067–1072 (1973)
2. Drozdz, M.B.: Efficient finite element modelling of ultrasound waves in elastic media. Ph.D. thesis, University of London (2008)
3. Gao, W., Glorieux, Ch., Thoen, J.: Laser ultrasonic study of lamb waves: determination of the thickness and velocities of a thin plate. Int. J. Eng. Sci. **41**, 219–228 (2003)
4. Gavrić, L.: Computation of propagative waves in free rail using a finite element technique. J. Sound Vibr. **185**, 531–543 (1995)
5. Lagasse, P.E.: Higher-order finite element analysis of topographic guides supporting elastic surface waves. J. Acoust. Soc. Am. **53**, 1116–1122 (1973)
6. Liu, H.: Wave modelling techniques for medium and high frequency vibroacoustic analysis including porous materials. Ph.D. thesis, KTH Royal Institute of Technology (2014)
7. Viola, E., Marzani, A., Bartoli, I.: Modeling wave propagation in damped waveguides of arbitrary cross-section. J. Sound Vibr. **295**, 685–707 (2006)
8. Viola, E., Marzani, A., Bartoli, I.: Semi analytical formulation for guided wave propagation. In: Elishakoff, I. (ed.) Mechanical Vibration: Where do We Stand?, vol. 488, pp. 105–121. Springer, Vienna (2007)

Author Index